The Global Prehistory
of Human Migration

The Global Prehistory of Human Migration

Edited by

Peter Bellwood

Originally published as Volume I of *The Encyclopedia of Global Human Migration*
edited by Immanuel Ness.

WILEY Blackwell

This paperback edition first published 2015
© 2013 John Wiley & Sons, Ltd.

Edition history: Blackwell Publishing Ltd (hardback, 2013)
Originally published as Volume I of *The Encyclopedia of Global Human Migration* edited by Immanuel
Ness.

Registered Office
John Wiley & Sons Ltd, The Atrium, Southern Gate, Chichester, West Sussex, PO19 8SQ, UK

Editorial Offices
350 Main Street, Malden, MA 02148-5020, USA
9600 Garsington Road, Oxford, OX4 2DQ, UK
The Atrium, Southern Gate, Chichester, West Sussex, PO19 8SQ, UK

For details of our global editorial offices, for customer services, and for information about how to apply
for permission to reuse the copyright material in this book please see our website at www.wiley.com/
wiley-blackwell.

The right of Peter Bellwood to be identified as the author of the editorial material in this work has been
asserted in accordance with the UK Copyright, Designs and Patents Act 1988.

Library of Congress Cataloging-in-Publication data is available for this book.

ISBN 9781118970591 (paperback)

A catalogue record for this book is available from the British Library.

Cover image: detail of Bronze Age rock carvings, Tanum, Sweden © The Art Archive

Set in 10/12 pt Minion by Toppan Best-set Premedia Limited

Printed in Singapore by C.O.S. Printers Pte Ltd

1   2015

Contents

Notes on Contributors

Alexandra Y. Aikhenvald is Distinguished Professor and Research Leader (People and Societies of the Tropics) in the Cairns Institute of James Cook University. She has worked on descriptive and historical aspects of Berber languages, and has published a grammar of Modern Hebrew and several grammars of Arawak languages from Brazil, including Bare (1995) and Warekena (1998), in addition to grammars for Tariana from Northwest Amazonia (2003), and Manambu from East Sepik, Papua New Guinea (2008).

Bryant Allen retired from the Australian National University in 2009 and is now a Visiting Fellow in the State Society and Governance in Melanesia Project, College of Asia and the Pacific, the Australian National University, Canberra. His main interests are in the sustainability of agricultural systems and rural development. With Mike Bourke and Robin Hide, he has defined, mapped, and described all Papua New Guinea agricultural systems.

Atholl Anderson is an Emeritus Professor of the Australian National University. He specializes in the archaeology, palaeoecology, and traditional history of islands, and in maritime migration and seafaring. He has undertaken research across the Pacific and Indian Oceans and in Scandinavia. He is the author of *Prodigious Birds* (1989) and *The Welcome of Strangers* (1998), coauthor of *Tangata Whenua: an Illustrated History* (2014) and coeditor of *The Global Origins and Development of Seafaring* (2010). His current research is in the Indian Ocean, New Zealand and Ecuador.

Peter Bellwood is an Emeritus Professor (Archaeology) at The Australian National University in Canberra, Australia. He is author of *First Farmers* (2005), *Prehistory of the Indo-Malaysian Archipelago* (2007), and *First Migrants* (2013), as well as editor of the prehistory volume in the Wiley-Blackwell *Encyclopedia of Global Human Migration*. He is currently involved in archaeological fieldwork in Vietnam, Indonesia, and the Philippines.

David Beresford-Jones is a fellow of the McDonald Institute for Archaeological Research, Cambridge University. He uses archaeobotany and geoarchaeology to study prehistoric human ecology, particularly in the Andes and the European Upper

Palaeolithic. He also has interests in the synthesis of archaeology and historical linguistics. He is the author of *The Lost Woodlands of Ancient Nasca* (2011) and the co-editor of *Archaeology and Language in the Andes* (2012).

Václav Blažek is a professor of comparative Indo-European linguistics at Masaryk University in Brno, Czech Republic. He concentrates on Indo-European, Afroasiatic and Uralic linguistics, but some of his studies have also been devoted to Nilo-Saharan, Kartvelian, North Caucasian, Elamite, Dravidian, Altaic, 'Palaeo-Siberian', Ainu, Austric, and Australian languages. In addition to many contributions to linguistics journals and edited volumes, he is the author of *Numerals: Comparative-etymological Analyses of Numeral Systems and Their Implications* (1999), and *Indo-European 'Smith' and his Divine Colleagues* (2010).

Robert Blust is a historical linguist with special interest in the Austronesian language family. He is the author of *The Austronesian Languages* (2009), and over 200 other publications on Austronesian linguistics and culture history, as well as several other topics, including the origin of the worldwide belief in dragons. His largest project, the *Austronesian Comparative Dictionary*, is still ongoing.

Angela Bruch is a paleobotanist at the ROCEEH research center funded by the Heidelberg Academy of Sciences and Humanities at Senckenberg Research Institute in Frankfurt am Main, Germany. Her research focuses on the understanding of spatial and temporal differences in the reaction of terrestrial ecosystems to Pleistocene global climatic changes, with particular emphasis on the quantitative reconstruction of terrestrial paleoenvironments, including climate quantification based on plant fossils. During the last decade she contributed to the reconstruction of Neogene environments in Eurasia.

Joachim Burger is Professor of Anthropology at Johannes Gutenberg University, Mainz, Germany. His research is on the population genetics of interaction between early Neolithic farmers and late hunter-gatherers in Europe. He draws inferences from ancient and modern DNA data using next-generation sequencing technology and biostatistical methods. In addition, he works on the domestication process and the early population history of domestic animals.

Mike T. Carson investigates natural-cultural histories, landscape ecology and evolution, and human-environmental relations throughout the Asia-Pacific region. His most recent work includes the book *First Settlement of Remote Oceania* published by Springer in 2014 and co-editorship of the journal *Asian Perspectives*.

Lounes Chikhi is a senior researcher at the National Center for Scientific Research (CNRS) in Toulouse and head of the Population and Conservation Genetics group at the Gulbenkian de Ciência Institute in Lisbon. He has worked on the recent evolutionary history of humans, especially on the Neolithic transition in Europe through data analysis and computer simulations.

Murray P. Cox is an associate professor at Massey University, New Zealand. He uses genetic information and advanced statistical inference to reconstruct human prehistory, particularly for populations in the Indo-Pacific region. He has published widely on human genetics in the journals *Current Anthropology*, *Proceedings of the National Academy of Sciences USA*, and *Nature Genetics*.

Christopher Ehret is Distinguished Professor of African history at the University of California at Los Angeles. He has undertaken extensive linguistic, anthropological, and historical fieldwork in Africa and written extensively on the interfaces between archaeological and linguistic reconstructions of the past. His recent books include *History and the Testimony of Language* (2011) and *The Civilizations of Africa: A History to 1800*, 2nd edition (2015).

Michael Fortescue is Emeritus Professor of General Linguistics at the University of Copenhagen. He has carried out extensive field work in the Arctic and sub-Arctic, principally in Greenland but also in Canada, Alaska, and Siberia, and is the author of a number of books concerning the Eskimo-Aleut and Chukotko-Kamchatkan languages, including the synthetic *Language Relations across Bering Strait* (1998).

T. Max Friesen is Professor of Archaeology in the Department of Anthropology, University of Toronto. During over 20 field seasons in the Canadian Arctic, he has studied every era of human settlement from early Palaeoeskimo to historic Inuit, focusing on social organization, intersocietal interaction, and economic change. He is the author of *When Worlds Collide: Hunter-Gatherer World-System Change in the 19ᵗʰ Century Canadian Arctic* (2012).

Dorian Q. Fuller is Professor of Archaeobotany at the Institute of Archaeology, University College London. His doctoral thesis at Cambridge University was on the origins of agriculture in South India. He has carried out archaeological work in several parts of India, Pakistan, and Sri Lanka, and worked on archaeobotany and plant domestication studies in China, Sudan, West Africa, and the Near East. He is coauthor (with Eleni Asouti) of *Trees and Woodlands of South India: Archaeological Perspectives* (2008).

Gregory P. Gilbert is an adjunct associate professor in the School of Humanities and Social Sciences at the University of New South Wales in Canberra. He has broad research interests including the archaeology of warfare, Egyptology and the Ancient Near East. He has excavated prehistoric sites at Sais, Koptos, Helwan and Hierakonpolis in Egypt. His publications include *Weapons, Warriors and Warfare in Early Egypt* (2004) and *Ancient Egyptian Sea Power and the Origin of Maritime Forces* (2008).

Colin Groves is a mammalian taxonomist, with special interest in primates. His *Primate Taxonomy* (2001) is regarded as the definitive textbook in that field, and he has revisited the field with *Ungulate Taxonomy* (with the late Peter Grubb, 2011). He has also applied his expertise to palaeoanthropology in *Bones, Stones and Molecules* (with David Cameron, 2004).

Katerina Harvati is head of paleoanthropology in the Department of Early Prehistory and Quaternary Ecology, Senckenberg Center for Human Evolution and Paleoecology, Eberhard Kars University, Tübingen. Her research centers on Neanderthal evolution and paleobiology, modern human origins, and the relationship of skeletal morphology to population history and the environment, with a methodological focus on geometric morphometrics and virtual anthropology.

Michael Heckenberger is an associate professor in anthropology at the University of Florida and has conducted fieldwork in Brazil, Guyana, Tobago, and Suriname. His work focuses on the origin and nature of early settled and monumental sites, beginning around 5,000 years ago, and, particularly, late pre-Columbian and historical complex societies and their built environment, or "garden cities," in tropical South America. He is the author of *The Ecology of Power* (2005), coeditor (with Bruna Franchetto) of *Os Povos do Alto Xingu* (2001) and (with Carlos Fausto) *Time and Memory in Indigenous Amazonia* (2007), and author of numerous articles.

Paul Heggarty is a researcher in the linguistics department of the Max Planck Institute for Evolutionary Anthropology in Leipzig. He focuses on how our languages can open up a 'window on our past', and on explaining how that perspective is relevant and valuable outside linguistics too. He co-operates closely with archaeologists, geneticists, anthropologists and historians, to work towards a vision of human (pre)history that is more holistic and coherent across those different disciplines. His interests range worldwide, although he has specialised particularly in the languages of Europe and the Andes.

Christine Hertler is paleobiologist at the ROCEEH research center funded by the Heidelberg Academy of Sciences and Humanities at Senckenberg Research Institute in Frankfurt am Main, Germany. Here she develops methods for quantitative evaluation of large mammal assemblages in conjunction with hominin paleoecology and dispersal. She focuses in her work on hominin-bearing faunas in Indonesia, Tanzania, and South Africa and contributes to the reconstruction of hominin distribution patterns in the Quaternary.

Evelyne Heyer is full professor in the department "Hommes, Natures, Sociétés" of the National Museum of Natural History in Paris. She is team leader for anthropological genetics. Her research interests include the study of evolutionary forces that shape human genetic diversity, including natural selection, past demography, and social behaviors. Her two main geographical areas of research are Central Africa and Central Asia where hunter-gatherers coexist with farmers.

Charles F. W. Higham is research professor in the Department of Anthropology, University of Otago, honorary fellow of St. Catharine's College, Cambridge, and a fellow of the British Academy and the Royal Society of New Zealand. He has excavated in Thailand for the past 40 years. His publications include many site reports and summaries of the prehistoric period in Southeast Asia, and *Encylopaedia of Ancient Asian Civilizations* (2004). He has brought the early cultures of China and Southeast Asia to a wide audience through several television documentary programmes.

Jane H. Hill is Regents' Professor of Anthropology and Linguistics (Emerita) at the University of Arizona. She is a specialist on Native American languages, focusing on the Uto-Aztecan family, with fieldwork on Cupeño, Tohono O'odham, and Nahuatl. She published *A Grammar of Cupeño* in 2005. Her current work focuses on the prehistory of the Uto-Aztecan family, including especially the U-A presence in Mesoamerica, the Southwest, and California.

Peter Hiscock is Tom Austen Brown Professor of Australian Archaeology in the Department of Archaeology at the University of Sydney. He is a fellow of the Society of Antiquaries and of the Australian Academy of Humanities. His book *Archaeology of Ancient Australia* (2008) won the John Mulvaney Book Award.

Mark J. Hudson is a professor in the Faculty of Rehabilitation Sciences, University of West Kyushu, Japan, where he teaches anthropology and environmental humanities. He is also a founding member of the History Working Group of the Center for Ainu and Indigenous Studies, Hokkaido University. His publications include *Ruins of Identity: Ethnogenesis in the Japanese Islands* (1999) and, as coeditor, *Multicultural Japan: Palaeolithic to Postmodern* (1996) and *Beyond Ainu Studies: Changing Academic and Public Perspectives* (2013). His current research focuses on resilience and environmental change in the Japanese Islands.

Hung Hsiao-chun is a senior research fellow in the Department of Archaeology and Natural History, Australian National University, Canberra. Her research interests are in Neolithic transitions and ancient trading networks in East Asia, Southeast Asia, and western Micronesia. Her publications in English include several papers with Zhang Chi in *Antiquity* and *Asian Perspectives*, as well as with Mike Carson on aspects of Southeast Asian and Micronesian archaeology.

William Keegan is Curator of Caribbean Archaeology at the Florida Museum of Natural History, and Professor of Anthropology and Latin American Studies at the University of Florida, Gainesville. Over the past thirty years he has conducted research throughout the Caribbean and published many books and articles, including *Bahamian Archaeology: Life in the Bahamas and Turks and Caicos Before Columbus* (1997), *Taíno Indian Myth and Practice* (2007), *The Oxford Handbook of Caribbean Archaeology* (edited with C. L. Hofman and R. Rodríguez Ramos, 2013), and *Through the Kaleidoscope: Diversity and Complexity in Caribbean Archaeology* (with C. L. Hofman, forthcoming).

Toomas Kivisild is a lecturer in human evolutionary genetics at the University of Cambridge. His past research has been on genetic diversity and population structure of human populations across the world with a particular focus on South Asian populations, including mutation rates and the effect of selection on human mitochondrial DNA diversity. His current research focuses on the understanding of the genetic basis of human environmental adaptations and their evolution.

Yaroslav V. Kuzmin is Senior Researcher, Institute of Geology and Mineralogy, Siberian Branch of the Russian Academy of Sciences, Novosibirsk, Russia. His major publications include (with A. Ono et al.) *Methodological Issues for Characterisation and Provenance Studies of Obsidian in Northeast Asia* (2014); (with M. D. Glascock) *Crossing the Straits: Prehistoric Obsidian Exploitation in the North Pacific Rim* (2010), and (with S. M. Nelson et al.) *Archaeology of the Russian Far East: Essays in Stone Age Prehistory* (2006).

Randy J. LaPolla is Professor of Linguistics and Head of the Division of Linguistics and Multilingual Studies at Nanyang Technological University, Singapore. His research focuses on the history and typology of Sino-Tibetan and Austronesian languages and issues related to the nature and development of communicative behaviour.

Steven A. LeBlanc is an archaeologist at Harvard's Peabody Museum. Recent work includes *Painted by a Distant Hand: Mimbres Pottery from the American Southwest* (2005) and (with Lucia Henderson) *Symbols in Clay: Seeking Artists' Identities in Hopi Yellow Ware Bowls* (2011). He also has an interest in warfare in the past, resulting in *Prehistoric Warfare in the American Southwest* (1999) and *Constant Battles* (2003).

Martin P. R. Magne is Director of the Cultural Sciences Branch for Parks Canada, overseeing archaeological and historical staff in Calgary, Winnipeg, Cornwall, Ottawa, Quebec City, and Halifax. He is also adjunct associate professor in the Department of Anthropology at the University of Toronto and the Department of Archaeology at the University of Calgary. His principal archaeological interests are Athapaskans, early period archaeology of North America, lithic technology, and rock art.

Michael Märker is a geographer at the ROCEEH research center at the Institute for Geography, University of Tübingen. His special focus lies on the detection and identification of erosion and mass movement processes and their quantification.

R. G. Matson is Professor of Archaeology (Emeritus), University of British Columbia. He has worked in the US Southwest, the Northwest coast and in the interior of British Columbia, where he and Martin Magne have been working together on Athapaskan issues for more than 30 years and producing *Athapaskan Migrations; The Archaeology of Eagle Lake, British Columbia* (2007). He was awarded the Smith-Wintemberg Award in 2005 for his contributions to Canadian archaeology by the Canadian Archaeological Association.

Hirofumi Matsumura is Professor of School of Health Science, Sapporo Medical University in Japan. His extensive research on prehistoric human skeletal remains has led to many publications examining the population history of Northeast and Southeast Asia, especially Japan, China, and Mainland Southeast Asia.

David W. McAlpin is a former member of the Department of South Asian Studies at the University of Pennsylvania. His research publications include *Proto-Elamo-Dravidian: The Evidence and its Implications* (1981). He has also contributed to the online *Dictionary of South Asia*. He is currently working on Elamite and its relationship to Brahui.

Patrick McConvell is a research fellow at the Australian National University. He is a linguist/anthropologist who has worked mainly in the Northern Territory and the north of Western Australia. He has a long-term interest in interdisciplinary prehistory, especially the nexus between archaeology and linguistics about which he organized two international conferences, and edited (with Nicholas Evans) *Archaeology and Linguistics: Aboriginal Australia in Global Perspective* (1997).

David J. Meltzer is an archaeologist and the Henderson-Morrison Professor of Prehistory, Southern Methodist University, Texas. His research focus is on the origins, antiquity, and adaptations of the first Americans (Paleoindians). Among his many published works are *Folsom: New Archaeological Investigations of a Classic Paleoindian Bison Kill* (2006) and *First Peoples in a New World: Colonizing Ice Age America* (2009). He is a member of the US National Academy of Sciences.

Marc Oxenham is a Reader in Archaeology and Bbiological anthropology (and Australian Research Council Future Fellow) at the Australian National University. His main research has concentrated on aspects of human paleohealth, paleopathology and behaviour through analysis of hunter-gatherer–Neolithic interface human skeletal and dental material in Southeast Asia, with the majority of his work in Vietnam and more recently the Philippines (with Peter Bellwood). Recent publications include *Man Bac: The Excavation of a Neolithic Site in Northern Vietnam, the Biology* (with Hirofumi Matsumura & K. T. Nguyen, 2011) and *Bioarchaeology of East Asia: Movement, Contact, Health* (with Kate Pechenkina).

Mehmet Özdoğan Mehmet Özdoğan is Professor Emeritus at Istanbul University and a member of numerous academic institutions, including the National Academy of Sciences of the USA. His main focus of interest is the emergence and expansion of early village farming economies. He has conducted several archaeological field projects, including at the Neolithic sites of Çayönü, Mezraa-Teleilat, Yarımburgaz, Hoca Çeşme and Aşağı Pınar. He has published 14 books and over 272 articles, mainly on the Turkish Neolithic, heritage and politics in Turkish archaeology.

Ron Pinhasi is an Associate Professor in prehistoric archaeology and physical anthropology, University College Dublin, Ireland. He is the author of various publications on the spread of farming in Europe and the bioarchaeology of past populations, and director of a European Research Council project on the evolution and spread of modern humans in Europe and the transition to agriculture, using ancient DNA together with anthropological and archaeological methods. He is engaged in several fieldwork projects on the Middle–Upper Palaeolithic transition in the Caucasus.

Peter Robertshaw is Chair of the Department of Anthropology at California State University, San Bernardino. He has carried out archaeological fieldwork in a number of African countries and has written or edited several books on African archaeology and later prehistory, as well as over 70 articles and book chapters. He is particularly interested in the development of social complexity in the African Great Lakes region and in the chemical analysis of glass beads as a means of reconstructing changing patterns of trade between Africa and the rest of the world.

Jorge Rocha is Associate Professor in the Department of Biology, University of Porto, Portugal, and Senior Researcher at the Research Center In Biodiversity and Genetic Resources (CIBIO) from the same university. His research interests include the study of genetic variation in African insular populations related to the slave trade, such as São Tomé and Cape Verde, as well as continental areas affected by the Bantu dispersals, such as Angola and Mozambique.

Anne-Marie Sémah is a senior researcher in the French Research Institute for Development (IRD), specializing in the paleoenvironmental study of the South Pacific and Southeast Asian Quaternary through pollen analysis. She currently focuses on Late Pleistocene and Holocene sedimentary records in Indonesia, the Philippines, New Caledonia, and Vanuatu.

François Sémah is an engineer in applied geology, originally specializing in Quaternary geology. He is currently professor at the National Museum of Natural History, Paris. His PhD thesis addressed the chronology of hominid-bearing sites in Java, where he has undertaken excavations since 1987. He was awarded the CNRS silver medal in 1994.

Paul Sidwell is Australian Research Council Future Fellow in Linguistics in the College of Asia and the Pacific at the Australian National University. From 2007 to 2011 he was director of the Mon-Khmer Language Project for the Center for Research in Computational Linguistics, Bangkok. He also serves as managing editor for Pacific Linguistics Publishing and the *Journal of the Southeast Asian Linguistic Society*. As a comparative-historical linguist his research focuses on the Austroasiatic languages of mainland Southeast Asia.

Dean R. Snow has held professorial appointments at the University of Maine, the University at Albany, SUNY, and Pennsylvania State University, where he served as department head from 1995 to 2005. He subsequently served as President of the Society for American Archaeology. His latest book is entitled *The Archaeology of Native North America* (2010).

Simon G. Southerton is a principal research scientist in the CSIRO Division of Plant Industry, Canberra. His research focuses on the study of genetic variation in forest trees and he has coauthored about 40 research papers in the field of plant molecular genetics. He is the author of *Losing a Lost Tribe* (2004) which explores widely held Mormon beliefs regarding the origins of Native Americans in light of recent genetics research.

Franklin C. Southworth taught linguistics and South Asian languages in the Department of South Asia Regional Studies, University of Pennsylvania, from 1959 to 2001. He is the author of *Linguistic Archaeology of South Asia* (2005) and numerous articles on South Asian linguistics, and is a co-Compiler of SARVA (the South Asian residual vocabulary assemblage).

Matthew Spriggs is Professor of Archaeology in the School of Archaeology and Anthropology at the Australian National University. He has conducted field research in Pacific and island Southeast Asian archaeology for the last 36 years, most recently concentrating on the archaeology of Vanuatu and the Lapita cemetery site of Teouma. His many publications include *The Island Melanesians* (1997).

Mark Stoneking leads the Human Population History group in the Department of Evolutionary Genetics at the Max Planck Institute for Evolutionary Anthropology in Leipzig, Germany, and is also Honorary Professor of Biological Anthropology at the

University of Leipzig. His research interests focus on the origins, relationships, and migrations of human populations, as well as the impact of recent positive selection on human genetic diversity.

Mark G. Thomas is Professor of Evolutionary Genetics at University College London. He has used genetic data, including ancient DNA, to understand how humans have evolved and migrated around the world. In recent years he has worked on modelling cultural evolution to understand the origins of modern human behaviour, on modelling archaeological material culture and radiocarbon data to infer past demography, on testing genetic signatures of natural selection, and on gene-culture co-evolution, particularly the origins of lactase persistence and dairying in Europe and Africa.

Alexander Vovin is Directeur d'études at the Ecole des hautes études en sciences sociales (Centre de recherche sur les langues de l'Asie Orientale). As a historical linguist and philologist his main interests are in the early history of Japanese, Korean, Ainu, and Inner Asian languages as well as in the early ethnolinguistic history, textology, and literature (especially poetry) of these regions. He is author of ten books and about 100 articles.

Seonbok Yi is Professor of Archaeology and Director of the Seoul National University Museum. He has excavated in Korea, Vietnam, Mongolia, and Azerbaijan. He was commissioned in 2008 by the Society of Korean Archaeology to edit the synthetic volume *Lectures in Korean Archaeology* and oversaw its revision in 2010.

Zhang Chi is Professor and also currently the Vice-Dean of the School of Archaeology and Museology, Peking University, Beijing, China. His major research is on the Chinese Neolithic. He has been involved in several national and international archaeological projects and has excavated important sites in China, such as Baligang (Henan), Shijiahe (Hubei), and Xianrendong (Jiangxi: a joint project with Harvard University). His publications in English include several papers with Hung Hsiao-chun in *Antiquity* and *Asian Perspectives*.

1

Prehistoric migration and the rise of humanity

Peter Bellwood

The focus in this first volume of the *Encyclopedia of Global Human Migration* is on the founding, through migration, of the human world as we can reconstruct it at the dawn of written history. Using information from human biology, archaeology, and comparative linguistics (the latter discipline only available for societies within the past 10,000 years), the authors travel in time and space from the initial migrations of the incipient genus *Homo*, around two million years ago, to the relatively recent but still prehistoric migrations of populations such as the Eastern Polynesians and Thule Inuit. They introduce to us an enormous array of past human groups, both hunter-gatherer and agriculturalist. The prehistoric migrations of many of these populations were essential foundations for the ethnic and linguistic patterning that spanned the globe before 1500 CE, and indeed still does in many regions today.

In global terms, when was "prehistory," and when was "history"? In fact, there was no universal chronological divide. History began in many diverse times and places across the world as a result of the development of coherent historical recording, via the use of writing. This was a development of profound significance for humanity, but one that only occurred after 1500 CE in most regions. However, there were small pockets of more ancient scribal enterprise. Pictographic writing had commenced by 3000 BCE in the Middle East, including Mesopotamia, Egypt, and Pakistan, by 1500 BCE in China, and by 100 BCE amongst the Mayas of Mesoamerica. Coherent recording of history in a narrative sense usually followed long after the first appearance of any given ancient script, but occasionally the converse happened, as when putative historical events recorded in the Rigveda (Pakistan and northern India) or by Homer (Greece) were only recorded in writing long after they were created as recited epics. Even so, historical records were mostly confined to western Eurasia and China until around the birth of Christ, after which they became much more widespread across other regions of Eurasia and northern Africa, from Britain at one extreme to Indonesia at the other. But vast areas of Africa, northern Eurasia, Australasia, Oceania, and the Americas remained essentially prehistoric until European explorers intruded after 1492 CE.

The Global Prehistory of Human Migration: The Encyclopedia of Global Human Migration Volume 1,
First Edition. Edited by Peter Bellwood.
© 2013 John Wiley & Sons, Ltd. Published 2015 by John Wiley & Sons, Ltd.

For this volume, the rather loose rule of thumb is that human migrations are included if their verifiable existence *does not* depend on historical records to any significant degree. Hence, migrant Eurasian populations such as the many Germanic and Turkic-speaking groups who invaded the declining Roman empire in the early Middle Ages are considered in the later historical volumes of the *Encyclopedia*. But we do consider Bantu speakers in Africa, the Thule Eskimos in the Canadian Arctic, Apache and Navajo speakers in the US Southwest, and the Eastern Polynesians, all of whom were still migrating when Gothic architects in Europe were busily designing their cathedrals and contemplating the development of the Renaissance. Indeed, many chapters in this volume refer on occasion to history from written records because there was, of course, no massive change in the evolution of human affairs just because something was written down.

In terms of the definition used for this volume, "migration" should be regarded as permanent translocation, rather than the kind of cyclical or seasonal movement engaged in by some groups of hunters, pastoralists, or shifting agriculturalists. Ancient migrants entered new territory and stayed there, or moved on further. In doing so, they found that new territories were either already inhabited, or devoid of other humans. It takes little imagination to understand that the consequences of migration would have been different in each of these cases. Previous inhabitants naturally demanded some kind of accommodation from incoming migrants, even if some situations were rather one-sided, whereas previously empty landscapes would have allowed a much freer rein for expansion where environments were suitable.

Migration in human prehistory

In terms of the overall course of human migration through time, the very first bipedal hominin (proto-human) migrants from Africa began to colonize tropical and temperate latitudes of Eurasia, as far as Indonesia and China, soon after two million years ago. *Homo sapiens* did the same from its African origins much later, within the past 100,000 years, and also traveled much further than its archaic forebears, across oceans and into very cold latitudes. Since 50 kya (see below for abbreviations), the Native Australians, Pacific Islanders, and Native Americans have been the most significant populations whose ancestors colonized uninhabited lands, only completing the process around 1300 CE in the case of the Eastern Polynesians. Most importantly, many of the tropical and temperate regions of the world have also witnessed extensive expansions and migrations of agricultural populations during the past 10,000 years, initially in many cases through landscapes already peopled much earlier by hunter-gatherers. These early farmer expansions were deeply involved in the initial dissemination of many of the world's largest language families, especially in Africa, Eurasia, and Oceania.

The great enemy for the prehistorian of ancient migration is time – the more of it, the less information that survives, and the greater become the chances of other migrations and expansions erasing the traces of the first-comers. We would have few coherent data on the origins and dispersals of the Indo-European-speaking peoples if archaeologists had not discovered the lost writings of the ancient Anatolians of Turkey and the

Tocharians of Xinjiang in western China. The immense historical migrations of Chinese southwards from the Yellow and Yangzi basins since 100 BCE erased many layers of linguistic history in southern China, especially those related to the remote ancestry and initial migrations of the modern Austronesian, Austroasiatic, and Tai-speaking peoples. But here again, historical and comparative linguistic records come to the rescue. Further back in time there were no such records, and sadly, not all episodes of past human migration will have left evidence behind. Luck has always been a major factor in the survival of evidence, but broad and multidisciplinary perspectives can sometimes winkle out remarkable, if almost erased, colonizing achievements from deep in time.

Differing perspectives and sources of data on prehistoric migration

This volume brings together essays by human biologists, archaeologists, and linguists, but it also keeps them separate from each other. The human past is best understood if authors are encouraged to present data and interpretations, in the first instance, from within their own disciplines. When this has been done, all can discuss how to compare the perspectives from each discipline in order to draw the most convincing inferences about the unfolding of the human past. This is how knowledge grows, with constant debate – and often dispute – between specialists, both within and between disciplines. Because the major disciplines operate independently of each other and with independent data sets, we can try to avoid the confusion that derives from circular reasoning if we keep their conclusions separate.

Some of the major reasons for disagreement within and between disciplines stem from the fact that most migrants in prehistory, except for the very first ones in each region, had to negotiate with, interbreed with, and/or fight with indigenous inhabitants. Because of this, we often find that the conclusions drawn from different disciplines do not always match each other very well, owing to the complications caused by such population mixing. For instance, humans can sometimes change their primary language without moving, in such a way that a language can migrate without a distinct human population in train. However, language shift of this type has generally been rather localized in recorded history, and it is more likely that humans moved together with their languages when the dispersals were on the scales of the major language families, whether associated with hunter-gatherers or farmers. In addition, with any coherent colonizing movement of a new population into a new territory, especially one that was previously uninhabited, we can expect that the pertinent records from biology, linguistics, and archaeology will match quite well. The situation obviously becomes more complex if dense indigenous populations were already in place.

Indeed, there is no guarantee that all the authors in this collection agree precisely on every point of past migration. Human prehistory offers very few significant situations in which one perspective is obviously the final one. Readers must make their own decisions about who is right or wrong, although there are very few cases of open opposition, mostly just faint glancing blows. Some of the chapters overlap a little in time and place content, but not extensively; this is also healthy since it can allow slightly different perspectives on a single situation to be presented.

Can we ever "understand" an ancient migration in anything but the vaguest terms? What really happened when humans crossed the Bering Strait land bridge from Siberia in freezing temperatures, about 15 thousand years ago, to face the enormous glaciers that still blocked much of the way into the Americas? How did they hunt and kill mammoths and other large mammals? Did they use boats to travel down the western coastline, eventually to reach South America? How did they survive under trying circumstances, not just the most able men and women, but also the geriatric and the very young? How did early Micronesians and Polynesians survive Pacific crossings of thousands of kilometers in small boats with no compasses or GPS technology? Alas, none of them carried notebooks or video cameras. None wrote history. In the chapters that follow, the individual or family migration "events" that must once have occurred in day-to-day prehistoric reality tend to be submerged within more generalized narratives, since the surviving data on ancient migrations are, by their very nature, more easily related to the activities of large populations through broad time spans than to those of single individuals on single journeys.

One way we can understand ancient migrations, at least to a comparative degree, is to examine the records of migrations by pre-urban populations in both the historical and the ethnographic records. The Greek historian Herodotus referred to the migration of the Scythians from their probable homeland in Iran, before 500 BCE, across the Araxes River and through the Caucasus Mountains into the northern littoral of the Black Sea. The Roman general Julius Caesar recorded in great detail the failed migration of the whole population of the Helvetii, with an immense baggage train, from Lake Geneva into the Rhone Valley of Celtic Gaul in 58 BCE (they failed because the Romans attacked them and turned them back). The Vandals, Goths, and Mongols were quintessential conquerors and would-be migrants, but let us not forget that the kind of far-flung conquest that these groups favored led to very little actual settlement on a permanent basis, and precious little linguistic or genetic replacement. Genghis Khan is reputed to have sired many children, but modern Eurasian populations throughout the regions that his armies conquered do not speak Mongolian, or even carry significant genetic influence from his 13th-century conquests. Migration, if it is to have serious consequences, must be backed up by substantial demographic growth by the immigrant population in the newly settled areas. In addition, it also helps if the numbers of migrants are greatly in excess of the numbers of natives and (unfortunately) if they can bring in diseases that will reduce those natives to small numbers, as happened so tragically in the New World after 1492 CE. In many medieval migrations in Africa and Eurasia, significant demographic superiority on the part of the conquerors simply did not develop, so absorption rather than domination was their ultimate linguistic and genetic fate. The Iberians and British after 1500 CE had things a little easier, because they were able to find in Australia and the Americas whole continents in which populations were often only lightly settled (especially in Australia), with indigenous populations who had very little resistance to Old World diseases.

The ethnographic and early colonial historical records also detail some quite significant examples of migration by tribal peoples. The rice-cultivating Iban of Sarawak and Brunei spread over 850 km through equatorial Borneo during the 19th century, opening up new rice fields along rivers and incorporating weaker indigenous groups as they did so. The Nuer of Sudan spread across 75,000 sq km of territory in the upper Nile basin during the 19th century in the search for more cattle pasture, in the process invading and incorporating many of their Dinka neighbors, especially women and children. Bantu-speaking populations were also undertaking major expansion into South Africa just before the arrival of European colonists. Such expansions usually involved warfare and capture, so that conquered populations became incorporated genetically into the conquering groups on a large scale. After all, superiority in population numbers would always have mattered to any population that was trying to expand into new territory, and numbers could either be increased from within or captured from without. In the premodern world, many women and children captured from defeated groups may perhaps have preferred life in relative servitude amongst the conquerors than life in permanent refuge, for ever in fear of fresh attack.

Important definitions and abbreviations used in this volume

In all following chapters, the abbreviations *mya* and *kya* are used for millions and thousands of years ago, respectively, until the past few thousand years, when we switch to the use of BCE (before Common Era, replacing BC meaning "before Christ") and CE (Common Era, replacing *anno domini*, or AD in Latin – in the year of the lord). Chronology is always "calibrated," in the sense that the radiocarbon dates that form the backbone of the archaeological chronology for the past 40,000 years are calibrated against real solar time by the dating of annual growth rings counted backwards from the present in overlapping series of ancient trees. Other dating methods, such as palaeomagnetism, optical luminescence, potassium-argon, electron spin resonance and uranium series are significant mainly for the Pleistocene, before 12 kya, and technical descriptions should be sought in archaeological textbooks.

The Pleistocene epoch of geological time, within which all major human biological evolution described in this *Encyclopaedia* took place, has three biostratigraphic divisions of unequal length:

1   Early or Lower Pleistocene (2.58–0.8 mya);
2   Middle Pleistocene (0.8 mya–125 kya, marine isotope stages 20 to 6 in Figure 2.2);
3   Late or Upper Pleistocene (125–12 kya, marine isotope stages 5 to 2).

The Pleistocene is followed by the Holocene (marine isotope stage 1 in Figure 2.2), that commenced about 11,650 years ago (c. 9500 BCE) with dramatic warming after the Younger Dryas mini-glaciation that marked the end of the Pleistocene. The Holocene is essentially the period marked by the world climatic pattern that still exists today.

The Middle and Late Pleistocene witnessed the most severe of the Ice Ages, swinging through 100-millennium cycles from extreme glacial drought and cold into warm wet interglacial conditions like those of the Holocene, then back into glaciation again. The Pleistocene glaciations were periods of low sea level across the world, down to as much as 130 m below the present level at glacial maxima, giving rise to land bridges across exposed continental shelves. Climatic slides into glacials were fairly gradual, although bumpy, but ameliorations into interglacials were extremely rapid. Hence the incredible growth in the rate of cultural complexity since the world swung back dramatically from the last glacial maximum, at 24-18 kya, into the present Holocene interglacial, with temperatures slightly warmer than today attained in some regions by about 10 kya. Unfortunately, many scientists believe we are now extending the Holocene interglacial beyond its current time span of 11,500 years by uncontrolled global warming. In the future, as deserts expand, as permafrost and glaciers melt, and as sea levels rise further, we can perhaps look forward to lots more human migration.

Part I

The Peopling of the World during the Pleistocene

2

The earliest stages of hominin dispersal in Africa and Eurasia

Christine Hertler, Angela Bruch, and Michael Märker

This chapter describes the earliest potential movements of hominins (proto-humans) within Africa, starting from almost 7 mya, and focusing on the genesis of Australopithecus *and* Homo *and the dispersal of the latter into Eurasia soon after 2 mya. The emphasis here is on the fossil record.*

Miocene origins and Pliocene dispersals

The oldest hominin specimens known at present date to the Miocene epoch of geological time (7.0 to 5.3 mya) and have been discovered in Sub-Saharan Africa, in Chad (Toros-Menalla, *Sahelanthropus tchadensis*), Kenya (Tugen Hills, *Orrorin tugenensis*), and Ethiopia (the Middle Awash region, *Ardipithecus kadabba*) – see Figure 2.1 for site locations. Although these specimens are assigned by biologists to a variety of species, they may well represent geographical variants of a single taxon. Skulls and postcranial skeletons uniformly indicate an early development of bipedalism, this being a distinctively hominin gait that might have developed as a result of environmental adaptations in more open environments. Extended rainforest areas in equatorial Africa in the Early to Middle Miocene gave way in the Late Miocene to drier, more open, and more variable habitat types in eastern Africa (Cerling et al. 1997). The above-mentioned hominin find places represent such habitats on the boundaries of forested areas (Foley & Elton 1998).

During the Pliocene (5.3 to 2.6 mya), a new species named *Ardipithecus ramidus* has been described from a wide region in eastern Africa, including the middle Awash Basin in Ethiopia as well as Lothagam and the Baringo Basin in Kenya. After 4.4 mya this species gave way to a variety of australopithecine species (*Australopithecus anamensis, A. afarensis, A. bahrelghazali*). Until 3.5 mya, these species are only known from Ethiopia, Kenya, Tanzania, and Chad, but after that time they dispersed successfully into higher latitudes and reached South Africa. The oldest hominins from South Africa

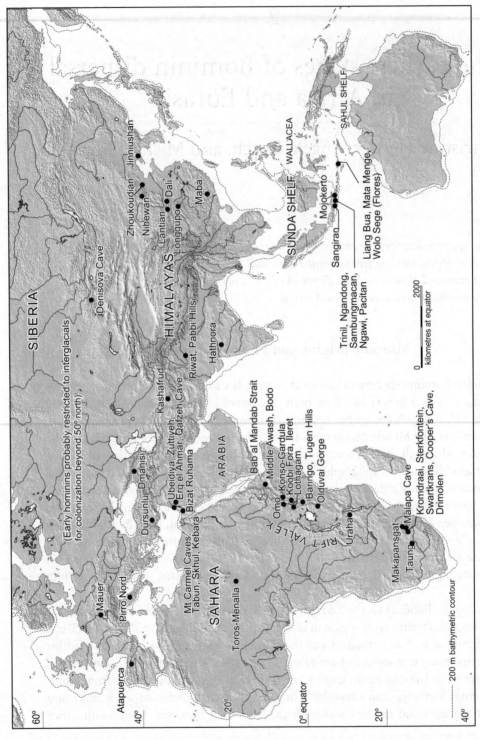

Figure 2.1 Important Pleistocene hominin sites in Africa and Eurasia prior to the dispersal of *Homo sapiens*. Continental shelves are delineated to −200 m. Base mapping by Education and Multimedia Services, College of Asia and the Pacific, The Australian National University.

come from cave breccias at Sterkfontein, Makapansgat and Taung, with ages between 3.5 and 2.6 mya. The gracile australopithecines from South Africa are attributed to *Australopithecus africanus*.[1] The expansion process into southern Africa was paralleled by a global warming trend between 4.5 and 3 mya (Ravelo et al. 2004). Such an enormous expansion in the distribution area of the gracile australopithecines might imply an increased level of ecological flexibility within this genus, but the ecological orientations of these groups are not yet well established and evidence for a major adaptational shift is so far lacking. However, as a result of the warmer climate conditions, the habitats to which East African australopithecines became adapted may have shifted ever further away from the equator. Although paleobotanical evidence for vegetation conditions is largely absent in the Pliocene (Jacobs et al. 2010), it can be assumed that the southern part of the East African Rift Valley might have served as a prime corridor linking eastern and southern Africa.

Paranthropus and early *Homo* in the Plio-Pleistocene

Between 3 and 2 mya, global climatic trends went into reverse, leading to lower temperatures (see Figure 2.2 for chronology and climatic cycles). Australopithecines in eastern and southern Africa were subjected to unique habitat changes. Rapid, short-term climatic shifts and increased seasonality (Trauth et al. 2005) led to the appearance of larger-toothed species that were capable of dealing with tougher food items in drier environments. This applied not only to hominins, but to other mammal taxa as well (Turner & Wood 1993). These climatic changes may have led to further hominin speciation, in that two consecutive and highly robust *Paranthropus* species (*P. aethiopicus* and *P. boisei*), along with early representatives of the genus *Homo*, appeared in East Africa. *Paranthropus* specimens dated between 2.7 and 1.4 mya occur in Ethiopia, Kenya, Tanzania, and Malawi. Molars of enormous size equipped with thick enamel provide evidence for a dietary change in *Paranthropus*, whereas early representatives of the genus *Homo* are believed to have responded to the same changes by developing methods of food preparation using stone artifacts, a more flexible strategy over the long term.

Paranthropus represents an ecologically restricted and ecologically specialized side branch in the hominin lineage (Sponheimer et al. 2007; but for an opposing view see Wood & Strait 2004). In South Africa, paranthropine hominins appeared between 2.0 and 1.0 mya at Kromdraai, Drimolen, Coopers cave, and Swartkrans. Evidence for the presence of early *Homo* in South Africa is disputed by Kuman and Clarke (2000), although a case has more recently been made for an endemic species of *Homo* in South Africa at this time (Curnoe 2010). Following the global climate cooling between 3 and 2 mya, the gracile australopithecines in South Africa would have found their preferred habitats shifting northwards towards the equator.

There is perhaps no other segment of the hominin lineage over which there is such taxonomic debate as that which incorporates the origin of the genus *Homo*. Historically, the taxon was first described from Olduvai Gorge in Tanzania, and termed *Homo habilis* in terms of morphology and the presence of stone artifacts. Coeval hominins

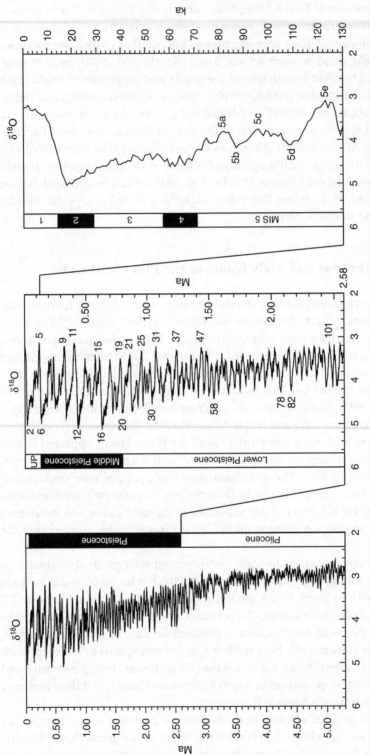

Figure 2.2 $\delta^{18}O$ isotope records at increasing resolutions for the last 5.3 myr (left), the Pleistocene and Holocene (130–0 kyr, right). The ratios between the oxygen isotopes $\delta^{18}O$ and $\delta^{16}O$ in marine cores reflect trends in the global temperature record. Higher temperatures are shown as excursions to the right, lower temperatures to the left. The oscillations are used to divide the record in the two right hand diagrams into marine isotope stages (MIS). Interglacials are identified by uneven MIS numbers (the Holocene is MIS 1), glacials by even numbers.

Data source: Lisiecki & Raymo 2005.

with more robust dentitions and less primitive postcranial skeletons have since been discovered in Kenya (Koobi Fora), Ethiopia (Omo), and Malawi (Uraha), and a new taxon has been suggested for these, namely *Homo rudolfensis* (Wood 1992). If both species are valid, one of them should represent an extinct evolutionary side branch. The other will have given rise to all subsequent *Homo* species.

One way around this problem is to suggest that *Homo habilis* in East Africa was the successor of *Australopithecus africanus* that migrated northwards from South Africa around 2 mya, whereas *H. rudolfensis* was a separate lineage, restricted to eastern Africa, that slightly antedated *habilis* and persisted there until 1.9 mya. At Uraha in Malawi, *H. rudolfensis* was associated with an essentially East African fauna (Bromage et al. 1995), demonstrating that this specimen was not part of the northward expansion from southern Africa that gave rise to the evolution of *habilis*. It will be possible to test this scenario by providing comparative ecological preferences for *Australopithecus africanus* and both of the *Homo* species. *A. africanus* and *H. habilis* should possess comparatively wide ecological adaptations because they occur in a wide corridor between eastern and southern Africa, from the equator into higher latitudes. In contrast, *H. rudolfensis* appears to have been restricted to equatorial and tropical environments.

Early Pleistocene corridors between Africa and Eurasia

After 2 mya, representatives of an Early Pleistocene *Homo* species (attributed either to *Homo erectus* or *H. ergaster*, the latter being an East African geographical variant of *H. erectus*) evolved from early *Homo* ancestors. Unlike their predecessors, these hominin species were extremely mobile. The oldest fossil evidence for them, with an age of 1.9 mya, comes from Kenya (Koobi Fora). Within the next 100 millennia, *H. ergaster/ erectus* spread across a huge area incorporating Tanzania (Olduvai), South Africa (Swartkrans), and beyond the African continent to Georgia (Dmanisi). *H. ergaster/ erectus* had a comparatively large cranial capacity of more than 800 cubic cm and essentially modern body proportions, with comparatively long legs. This species apparently overcame many of the ecological barriers that were still operative for *Paranthropus* and *H. habilis* (Antón 2003).

In Africa, the period between 3 and 2 mya witnessed considerable taxonomic diversification, whereas in the following million years this taxonomic diversity gradually vanished to leave only the genus *Homo* in Africa by 1 mya. The global cooling trend continued, and there is some evidence that continental climates in eastern and southern Africa were characterized by increasing aridity (Feaking & de Menocal 2010), as well as by increasing seasonality and rapid shifts in humidity (Trauth et al. 2005). By 1 mya, extinctions had eliminated all hominin species in Africa apart from the descendants of *Homo ergaster/erectus*. In eastern Africa, *Homo habilis* and *Paranthropus boisei* became extinct by 1.4 mya, the youngest specimens being described from Ileret in the East Turkana region of Kenya and from Konso-Gardula in Ethiopia. In southern Africa, *H. habilis* survived until 1.5 mya at Sterkfontein, *P. robustus* possibly until 1 mya at Swartkrans. Climatic change, in conjunction with competition with an ecologically more flexible *Homo* taxon, certainly influenced extinction rates amongst Early Pleistocene hominins.

The oldest direct evidence for hominin fossils in Eurasia comes from Dmanisi in Georgia, dated to 1.77 mya (Lordkipanidze et al. 2007). Over 50 hominin specimens have been discovered here, representing at least seven individuals. The spectrum of finds also includes fauna and artifacts. Initially described as small-brained *Homo ergaster*, the hominins were later attributed to a new species, *H. georgicus*. Artifacts associated with the Dmanisi hominins represent an Oldowan pebble-tool and flake industry. With respect to anatomy, the Dmanisi hominin sample is not sufficiently homogenous to fit a single taxonomic designation, and a large-scale dispersal of an early *Homo* taxon preceding *H. ergaster/erectus* is possible.

A West Asian corridor through the Levant links eastern Africa and the Caucasus. Several studies have recently examined the question of whether a hominin dispersal through here between 2.0 and 1.8 mya is reflected by other large mammal dispersals along the same corridor. However, the large mammal fauna described from Dmanisi has an essentially Eurasian character and lacks elements of clear African provenance. Although African large mammals occasionally entered Eurasia, no particular dispersal events can be recognized at this time. The Dmanisi hominins apparently arrived on their own without fellow travelers (O'Regan et al. 2011).

Dispersals into eastern Asia

The earliest direct evidence for a hominin presence in eastern Asia comes from central Java, where Lower Pleistocene hominins from Sangiran, with an age of more than 1.5 mya, have been assigned to *Homo erectus* (see chapter 6). The first hominins in Java are comparatively robust. The *Homo erectus* type specimen from Trinil represents a more evolved stage and could possess an age of more than 1 mya (Larick et al. 2001). *H. erectus* persisted and evolved in Java until the Upper Pleistocene. Immigrations into Java were limited by the alternating drowning and exposure of the Sunda Shelf, linking the Southeast Asian mainland with the Greater Sunda islands. Hominin occurrences are linked to the emergence and consolidation of an Early to Middle Pleistocene fauna characterized by the occurrence of the proboscidean genus *Stegodon*. This fauna indicates habitats which were more open and less forested than at present.

For the wide area between East Africa, the Caucasus, and Java, fossil evidence for the earliest hominins is absent. Relations between the Dmanisi and Javan hominins are not straightforward, given the small size of the Dmanisi individuals – those from Java are particularly large and robust. The hominins from Java may thus result from an independent dispersal out of Africa, perhaps across the mouth of the Red Sea and through the Arabian peninsula. With his "Savannahstan" hypothesis, Robin Dennell (2010) provides a model for hominin dispersal out of Africa and into Asia that reflects patterns of climate change and corresponding environmental shifts. Dennell postulates a uniform type of grassland environment that stretched from northern Africa to central Asia around two million years ago, and this could have supported hominin dispersals out of Africa. However, both the uniformity of the environment and the suggested close link between hominins and grasslands are contentious.

In China, hominins were present from 1.2 mya onwards, with the oldest so far identified coming from Gongwangling and Chenjiawo in Lantian district, Shaanxi province. The specimens have been attributed to *Homo erectus*. Previously discussed potential hominin specimens from Longgupo with an age of 1.9 mya have now been reassigned to a fossil ape species. It has recently been suggested that the spread of *Homo erectus* to China was associated with the high-latitude northern Chinese *Mammuthus/ Coelodonta* fauna (Ciochon 2010), rather than the subtropical *Stegodon/Ailuropoda* fauna. The boundary region between both of these faunas lay in central China and shifted north and south with climatic change (Tong 2007).

Dispersals into Europe

Earliest evidence for the presence of hominins in Europe comes from Atapuerca in northern Spain, where the oldest specimen (a hominin mandible) comes from Sima del Elefante, with an age of 1.2 to 1.1 mya. Larger samples come from Gran Dolina, dated to 780 kya, and Sima de los Huesos, with an age of 600 kya. The older hominins have been attributed to *Homo antecessor*, the younger to *Homo heidelbergensis*. Prior to 1 mya, the hominin presence in Europe was restricted to the Mediterranean region, in accordance with contemporary archaeological evidence from Algeria, Morocco, France, Italy, and Israel. It is still not clear whether *Homo antecessor* arrived in Spain separately from *H. heidelbergensis*. However, Leroy and her colleagues (2011) assume that ancient hominins could only have survived in Europe during transitions from glacial to interglacial periods, with full glacials being too cold for them and the interglacial to glacial transitions too heavily forested. Faunal data presented by Kahlke and his colleagues (2011) confirm mild temperatures and a low degree of seasonality at early hominin sites in Europe, but the region north of the Alps was not colonized by *Homo heidelbergensis* until 800 kya (Parfitt et al. 2010), and evidence from here prior to 150 kya is limited to warm interglacial periods.

Conclusions

The undisputed evidence for early hominin dispersals prior to the emergence of *Homo sapiens* can be summarized in three brief statements. The hominin lineage originated from the African continent. Early representatives of the genus *Homo* left the African continent and colonized Eurasia. According to current evidence from fossil discoveries and stone artifacts, this first "out of Africa" dispersal happened around 1.8 mya. These brief statements set the stage for many regional expansions and retreats, which depended to some extent on the multiple ways in which hominins related to their respective habitats. For instance, detailed reconstructions of African habitats have revealed previously unrecognized dispersals of early hominins within that continent.

Links, corridors, and barriers between environments in eastern and southern Africa are beginning to emerge, and provide exciting perspectives for further research. The initial out-of-Africa event around 1.8 mya represents an enormous expansion over the prior hominin distribution, involving migrations that somehow circumvented sea straits and mountain chains and reached latitudes up to 45°N in Asia. This latitudinal barrier was only overcome much later by *Homo sapiens*.

SEE ALSO: 3 Hominin migrations before *Homo sapiens*: Out of Africa – how many times?; 6 Pleistocene migrations in the Southeast Asian archipelagos

Note

1   To which should be added the recently announced *A. sediba* from Malapa cave near Sterk-fontein, dated to just under 2 mya (Pickering et al. 2011). (Ed.)

References and further reading

Antón, S. C. (2003) Natural history of *Homo erectus*. *Yearbook of Physical Anthropology* 122 Suppl. 37, 126–170.

Bromage, T. G., Schrenk, F., & Zonnefeld, F. W. (1995) Paleoanthropology of the Malawi Rift: an early hominid mandible from the Chiwondo Beds, northern Malawi. *Journal of Human Evolution* 28, 37–57.

Cerling, T. E., Harris, J. M., MacFadden, B. J., et al. (1997) Global vegetation change through the Miocene/Pliocene boundary. *Nature* 389, 153–158.

Ciochon, R. L. (2010) Divorcing hominins from the *Stegodon-Ailuropoda* fauna: new views on the antiquity of hominins in Asia. In Fleagle, Shea, Grine, et al. (2010), pp. 111–126.

Curnoe, D. (2010) A review of early *Homo* in southern Africa focusing on cranial, mandibular and dental remains, with the description of a new species (*Homo gautengensis*). *Homo* 61, 151–177.

Dennell, R. W. (2010) The colonization of "Savannahstan": issues of timing(s) and patterns of dispersal across Asia in the Late Pliocene and Early Pleistocene. In Fleagle, Shea, Grine, et al. (2010), pp. 7–30.

Feaking, S. J. & de Menocal, P. (2010) Global and African regional climate during the Cenozoic. In Werdelin & Sanders (2010), pp. 45–55.

Fleagle, J. G., Shea, J. J., Grine, F. E., et al. (2010) (eds.) *Out of Africa I*. Dordrecht: Springer.

Foley, R. A. & Elton, S. (1998) Time and energy: the ecological context for the evolution of bipedalism. In E. Strasser, J. Fleagle, A. Rosenberger, & H. McHenry (eds.), *Primate Loco-motion: Recent Advances*. New York: Plenum, pp. 419–433.

Jacobs, B. F., Pan, A. D., & Scotese, C. R. (2010) A review of the Cenozoic vegetation history of Africa. In Werdelin & Sanders (2010), pp. 57–72.

Kahlke, R.-D., García, N., Kostopoulos, D. S., et al. (2011) Western Palaearctic palaeoenviron-mental conditions during the Early and early Middle Pleistocene inferred from large mammal communities, and implications for hominin dispersal in Europe. *Quaternary Science Reviews* 30, 1368–1395.

Kuman, K. & Clarke, R. J. (2000) Stratigraphy, artefact industries and hominid associations for Sterkfontein, Member 5. *Journal of Human Evolution* 38, 827–847.

Larick, R., Ciochon, R. L., Zaim, Y., et al. (2001) Early Pleistocene ^{40}Ar/^{39}Ar ages for Bapang Formation hominins, Central Jawa, Indonesia. *Proceedings of the National Academy of Sciences* 98, 4866–4871.

Leroy, S. A. G., Arpe, K., & Mikolajewicz, U. (2011) Vegetation context and climatic limits of the Early Pleistocene hominin dispersal in Europe. *Quaternary Science Reviews* 30, 1448–1463.

Lisiecki, L. E. & Raymo, M. E. (2005) A Plio-Pleistocene stack of 57 globally distributed benthic δ^{18}O records. *Paleoceanography* 20: PA1003 (online doi: 10.1029/2005PA001164).

Lordkipanidze, D., Jashashvili, T., Vekua, A., et al. (2007). Postcranial evidence from early Homo from Dmanisi, Georgia. *Nature* 449, 305–310.

O'Regan, H. J., Turner, A., Bishop, L. C., et al. (2011) Hominins without fellow travelers? First appearances and inferred dispersals of Afro-Eurasian large mammals in the Plio-Pleistocene. *Quaternary Science Reviews* 30, 1343–1352.

Parfitt, S. A., Ashton, N. M., Lewis, S. G., et al. (2010) Early Pleistocene human occupation at the edge of the boreal zone in northwest Europe. *Nature* 466, 229–233.

Pickering, R., Dirks, P., Jinnah, Z., et al. (2011) *Australopithecus sediba* at 1.977 mya and implications for the origins of the genus *Homo*. *Science* 333, 1421–1423.

Ravelo, A. D., Andreasen, D., Lyle, M., et al. (2004) Regional climate shifts caused by gradual global cooling in the Pliocene epoch. *Nature* 429, 263–267.

Sponheimer, M., Lee-Thorp, J., & de Ruiter, D. (2007) Icarus, isotopes and Australopith diets. In P. S. Ungar (ed.), *Evolution of the Human Diet*. Oxford: Oxford University Press, pp. 132–149.

Tong, H. W. (2007) Occurrences of warm-adapted mammals in north China over the Quaternary Period and their paleoenvironmental significance. *Science in China Series D: Earth Sciences* 50(9), 1327–1340.

Trauth, M. H., Maslin, M. A., Deino, A., & Strecker, M. R. (2005) Late Cenozoic moisture history of East Africa. *Nature* 309, 2051–2053.

Turner, A. & Wood, B. (1993) Taxonomic and geographic diversity in robust australopithecines and other African Plio-Pleistocene mammals. *Journal of Human Evolution* 24, 147–168.

Werdelin, L. & Sanders, W. J. (2010) (eds.) *Cenozoic Mammals of Africa*. Berkeley: University of California Press.

Wood, B. (1992) Origin and evolution of the genus *Homo*. *Nature* 355, 783–790.

Wood, B. & Strait, D. (2004) Patterns of resource use in early *Homo* and *Paranthropus*. *Journal of Human Evolution* 46(2), 119–162.

3

Hominin migrations before *Homo sapiens*: Out of Africa – how many times?

Colin Groves

This chapter discusses both the fossil and the archaeological records for early Homo *dispersal, especially beyond Africa to eastern Asia. The author also offers a simplified classification of hominin genera by subsuming most into* Homo.

The phrase "Out of Africa" is associated in the public mind with *Homo sapiens*, dispersing at around 70 kya (see chapter 4) into Eurasia from their place of origin in sub-Saharan Africa. But there were several other "Out of Africa" events prior to the spread of *Homo sapiens*. To explain, I commence with a baseline discussion of the concepts of genus and species, focused on the genus *Homo*.

Genera are groupings of related species which have a certain time-depth. I suggest (Groves 2012) that any extant mammal genus should have a time-depth back to at least 4 mya to secure separate taxonomic recognition. From this perspective, which I follow in this chapter, the genus *Homo* should include species until now included by other authorities in other hominin genera, such as *Australopithecus*, *Paranthropus*, and *Kenyanthropus*, and could even include the earlier species *Ardipithecus ramidus* (see chapter 2, where these genera are kept separate).

Species are diagnosable biological entities, that is to say they are populations or metapopulations (groups of populations) that have fixed heritable differences from each other. This is the Phylogenetic Species Concept (Groves 2012), the only concept that is applicable to the fossil record. The alternative Biological Species Concept, still all too frequently employed in biology, demands reproductive isolation. Evidence for this is difficult or impossible to obtain even among living organisms, let alone fossils.

Here, I use appropriate species names for geographically and chronologically circumscribed samples that are plausibly regarded as metapopulations, and are on present evidence diagnosable as required under the Phylogenetic Species Concept. It may be that the discovery of future specimens will close the gaps between some of the species

The Global Prehistory of Human Migration: The Encyclopedia of Global Human Migration Volume 1, First Edition. Edited by Peter Bellwood.

listed here, but an a priori lumping approach (for instance, a lumping of the species *Homo ergaster, H. georgicus, H. pekinensis*, and perhaps others as subspecies of *Homo erectus*) will tend to pre-empt phylogenetic, biogeographic, and other conclusions, rather than test them.

The suggestion made here is that a number of different species of *Homo* lived in Africa in the Gelasian chronostratigraphic stage (earliest Pleistocene, 2.6–1.8 mya). *Homo africanus* inhabited southern Africa, and *Homo garhi, Homo walkeri, Homo rudolfensis,* and *Homo habilis* inhabited eastern Africa. In the succeeding Calabrian chronostratigraphic stage (the later part of the Early Pleistocene, 1.8–0.8 mya), one of these species, *Homo habilis*, was still present. The others were replaced by *Homo robustus* (formerly termed *Paranthropus* or "robust australopithecines"), *Homo gautengensis* and *Homo sediba* in southern Africa, and *Homo boisei* (also a "robust australopithecine"), *Homo ergaster*, and *Homo louisleakeyi* (if this latter is a valid species) in eastern Africa.

Although the vagaries of discovery may change present perceptions, I presume that the eastern rather than southern African species were the prime candidates for ancestors of the first hominins outside Africa. (See Chapter 2 for further discussion of this [Ed.].) These ancestors presumably carried an Oldowan stone tool industry based on flaked pebble tools (named after Olduvai Gorge in Tanzania).

The oldest hominin records in Eurasia – Out of Africa 1

Of the earliest hominin archaeological sites outside Africa with Oldowan stone tool industries (see Figure 2.1 for site locations), a group of three sites in Israel (primarily based on Dennell 2009) are well substantiated: Erq al-Ahmar at 1.95–1.77 mya, Bizat Ruhama at 1.96–0.78 mya (Zaidner et al. 2010), and Ubeidiya at c.1.4 mya. These three sites contain fauna with Afrotropical affinities (typical for sub-Saharan Africa), and so could represent temporary northeasterly extensions of the Afrotropical region into the Levant. The presences of these East African faunal elements in Israel do not in themselves imply that hominins necessarily migrated further into Eurasia.

However, the following sites beyond the Levant also contain Oldowan tools without hominin fossils so far, but their faunas are not Afrotropical and so they could represent early *Homo* outside their original comfort zone. These sites are Pirro Nord in Italy at 1.6–1.3 mya (Arzarello et al. 2007); Dursunlu in Turkey, Kashafrud in Iran, and Riwat and Pabbi Hills in Pakistan, all before 1 mya.

Eurasian sites that contain hominin fossils of Early Pleistocene date are far fewer than those with stone tools alone and are so far confined to Georgia, Spain, Indonesia, and China. They include Dmanisi in Georgia at 1.8 mya (Gabunia et al. 2001), which has yielded fossil hominins classified as *Homo georgicus*. This species most closely resembles *Homo ergaster* of eastern Africa, having the same long legs and arched foot, but a primitive shoulder joint. However, the Dmanisi cranial capacities are smaller than those of *ergaster*, and there was apparently considerable sexual dimorphism in size if the large mandible D2600, the type of *Homo georgicus*, belongs to the same population.

In Spain, Sima del Elefante (1.2 mya) and Gran Dolina (0.78 mya), both at Atapuerca, Burgos, represent genuine range extensions for early *Homo*. The tools of Gran Dolina are described as simple Oldowan (Carbonell et al. 1999). A sub-adult specimen from Gran Dolina has been made the type for *Homo antecessor*, and the Sima del Elefante specimens have also been referred to this species. The Sima del Elefante mandible has symphyseal structures resembling an incipient chin, and the juvenile from Gran Dolina has a canine fossa (a vertical depression lateral to the canine alveolus); both of these features anticipate those of *Homo sapiens*. We do not at present know whether *Homo antecessor* represents another dispersal out of Africa, or whether it descended from an ancestral form that had already been in Eurasia for some time – *Homo georgicus*, perhaps?

In Java, Mojokerto at an uncertain 1.81 mya and Sangiran beginning at 1.66 mya (see also chapter 6), contain the oldest hominin remains. The only specimen from Mojokerto is the calvaria of an infant. As far as the fossil-rich region of Sangiran is concerned, Kaifu and his colleagues (2005a, 2005b) have pointed to similarities in the dentitions of the oldest hominin specimens with the two African species *Homo habilis* and *Homo ergaster*. Most authors have included the oldest Javan specimens in *Homo erectus*, but Walters (1996) suggested that the mandibular specimens previously designated *Meganthropus palaeojavanicus* may warrant re-examination, and in my opinion the type specimen, Sangiran 6, and another remarkably robust mandibular fragment, Ardjuna 9, are indeed dramatically different from all contemporary Sangiran fossils. If this is so, then two hominin species may have coexisted in Java during the Calabrian (1.8-0.8 mya).

During the Middle Pleistocene in Java, Trinil is the type site for *Homo erectus*, and fossils from the Middle Pleistocene Bapang Formation at Sangiran are also universally attributed to *Homo erectus*. The maximum ages of these sites are in question, but could be over 1 mya. Are the fossils from the Middle Pleistocene Bapang Formation in Sangiran different from those from the Early Pleistocene Sangiran Formation? Kaifu and his colleagues (2005a, 2005b) have argued that there are striking differences between them in teeth and jaws, and that two dispersal events from Africa may have been involved (see chapter 6). As far as crania are concerned, there are too few specimens from the Sangiran formation (and those are too incomplete) to form a good basis for comparison. However, the cheek teeth of S17 from the Bapang Formation are considerably smaller than those of the two available specimens (S27 and S4) from the preceding Sangiran Formation, and are comparable to those of *Homo pekinensis* (Indriati & Antón 2008: 222, Table 1).

In China, the sites in the Nihewan Basin in Shanxi (1.66 mya) have stone tools of Oldowan type. A calvaria from Gongwangling in Shaanxi (before 1.15 mya according to Martinón-Torres et al. 2011) is too eroded to permit a definite assessment of its affinities, except to say that it does not resemble the younger (Middle Pleistocene) *Homo pekinensis*, and has a low cranial capacity, supposedly about 780 cc, which would be within the range of *Homo georgicus*. Its apparently arched brow ridges most resemble those of *Homo georgicus* and *Homo ergaster*. Later in time, Zhoukoudian near Beijing (going back to 0.77 ± 0.08 ma according to Shen et al. 2009) is the type site for *Homo pekinensis*. Specimens from other Middle Pleistocene sites in China, such as Chenjiawo in Shaanxi (0.65 mya), and the later sites of Hexian (Anhui) and Nanjing

(Jiangsu), are also commonly placed in *Homo pekinensis*. Stone tools associated with these Chinese sites are still of Oldowan affinity.

Homo pekinensis has not usually been distinguished from Javan *Homo erectus*, except at subspecies level. Nonetheless, the two taxa remain 100 percent distinguishable on available material, as first shown more than half a century ago by Weidenreich (1943), and more recently emphasized by Antón (2002), though it is not denied that they possess important shared features. In neither case does the range of variation incorporate any of the Early Pleistocene African specimens. Indications are that not only the skulls but also the postcranial skeletons may be distinguishable (Kennedy 1983; Grimaud-Hervé et al. 1994).

The enigma of late *Homo erectus* in Java

The fossils from Ngandong, Sambungmacan, and Ngawi in Java are much later in time than those from Sangiran and Trinil, but resemble them closely. They have been alternatively classed as *Homo erectus* or *Homo soloensis*. A separate species status (*soloensis*) seems to be indicated, although it is likely that they descended in Java from earlier *Homo erectus*. Antón (2002) has recently proposed long periods of isolation in Java punctuated by only intermittent land bridge connections to the Southeast Asian mainland.

These late specimens are claimed to date to as recently as 50 kya, but this is very controversial. Two of the specimens from Ngandong have been directly dated to between about 40 and 60–70 kya (Yokoyama et al. 2008; Huffman et al. 2010). Strikingly, this dating makes them approximately contemporary with the earliest presumed Southeast Asian specimens of *Homo sapiens*, dated to about 52 kya in the West Mouth of the Niah Caves in Sarawak (Hunt et al. 2007).

Were these direct descendants of *Homo erectus* still in Java when *Homo sapiens* arrived in Southeast Asia? If so, was there interbreeding? The question is still open. Given the evidence cited in chapter 5, that some ancestral modern humans did incorporate a small percentage of their genes from the peoples across whose territory they spread, it is perfectly possible.

The enigma of Flores

Homo floresiensis, known from Liang Bua on Flores Island between perhaps 95 and 12 kya, has become needlessly controversial. It has been suggested that the remains are actually those of modern humans affected by microcephaly, dwarfism, non-specific growth deficiency, Laron Syndrome, cretinism, or some combination of these medical conditions. Most authorities, however, have no compunction about treating it as a perfectly valid distinct species.

But *Homo floresiensis* does raise questions about Out of Africa movements of early hominins. Its anatomy most closely recalls Early Pleistocene species such as *Homo garhi*, *Homo habilis*, *Homo ergaster*, and *Homo georgicus*. Was there, perhaps, a dispersal episode prior to the Out of Africa 1 at about 1.8 mya delineated above? And, if so, does *floresiensis* have an unrecognized ancestor in the earliest levels in Java? I have already drawn attention to the existence of hyper-robust specimens in the Early Pleistocene Sangiran Formation at Sangiran, possibly distinct from contemporaneous *Homo erectus*, and these should be closely examined in the light of *Homo floresiensis* (Argue et al. 2009). However, others have suggested that insular dwarfing might have played a role in the evolution of *Homo floresiensis*, although we know little about the long bones and stature of *Homo habilis*, and hence whether dwarfing would even have been required to produce *floresiensis*.

Out of Africa 2

After 0.6 mya, a series of fossils evidently representing quite a different form of proto-human became widespread through Africa and Europe. Because there is a fair degree of homogeneity among them, they are generally referred to as a single species for which the prior available name is *Homo heidelbergensis*, based on a mandible from Mauer, Germany. Included in this species are fossils from both Europe and Africa, dating from as early as 0.6 mya. Where there are associations with stone artifacts, they are typically bifacial Acheulian, with hand axes. However, a claim for Acheulian tools in India at well over 1 mya has very recently been published (Pappu et al. 2011), raising questions about where the non-African Acheulian makers, and perhaps *Homo heidelbergensis* itself, might have come from – Africa, or Eurasia?

Although it is possible that *Homo heidelbergensis* was descended from Eurasian *Homo antecessor*, so far known only from Atapuerca in northern Spain, the fact that the earliest occurrence of *heidelbergensis* is (as far as we know) in Bodo, Ethiopia does suggest that Africa was the place of origin, and supports the idea that here we have an Out of Africa 2 migration. By approximately 300 kya, *Homo heidelbergensis* had reached Hathnora in the Narmada Valley of India (Cameron & Groves 2004), and by 200 kya the species had reached Dali and Jinniushan in central and northern China. According to the Javan fossil record it appears not to have reached Indonesia.

Out of Africa 3?

Between about 300 and 120 kya, modern humans (*Homo sapiens*) and Neanderthals (*Homo neanderthalensis*) diverged from *Homo heidelbergensis*, their common ancestor. The intermediate stages in both lineages are becoming increasingly well-known. Modern humans developed during this time span in Africa as the Afrotropical species, with one specimen also known from Israel, at Zuttiyeh in the Galilee. Neanderthals, meanwhile, developed separately in Europe, as the temperate-zone species, associated with a Palaearctic fauna, but this should not be taken to mean that Neanderthals were particularly cold-adapted (Rae et al. 2011).

For most of the time between 500 and 125 kya, a desert belt prevented serious interchange between Africa and the Middle East (Dennell 2009; Martinón-Torres et al. 2011), but during the last interglacial after 125 kya the Levant became a crossroads between Africa and Eurasia, as indeed it is today. The Afrotropical fauna spread north into the Levant during such warm interglacial phases, and the Palaearctic fauna moved south during glacial periods, both with their associated human species (Tchernov 1992). Thus, in northern Israel, we have a Neanderthal skeleton in Tabun Cave dating to 120–150 kya, followed by modern humans in Skhul and Qafzeh caves around 100–120 kya (last interglacial), and Neanderthals again in Kebara Cave at 62 kya and in Amud Cave around 50–70 kya.

There were additional movements across Eurasia of other pre-*sapiens* hominins, as highlighted recently by a mass of publicity surrounding the discovery of a human finger bone from Denisova Cave, in the Altai Mountains of southern Siberia (48–30 kya). DNA extracted from this specimen indicated that the taxon it represents was different from both *H. sapiens* and *H. neanderthalensis*, but somewhat closer to the latter (Reich et al. 2010). I also draw attention to the calvaria from Maba in southern China (129–135 kya), for which tentative Neanderthal affinities were noted by the describers, Woo and Peng (1959), and elaborated by Howells (1977). Whether or not Maba is relevant to the Denisova mystery, a separate Out of Africa movement to explain it is neither required (Martinón-Torres et al. 2011), nor plausible in my opinion.

Overall, it seems likely that the appearance of *Homo sapiens* in Israel around the Middle–Late Pleistocene boundary (Skhul, Qafzeh) marked no more than a brief range extension out of Africa, along with a limited expansion of Afrotropical fauna. The definitive Out of Africa excursion of *Homo sapiens* did not occur until well into the Late Pleistocene, perhaps 60–70 kya (for detailed reviews see chapters 4 and 5). *Homo sapiens* was in island Southeast Asia before 50 ka (Hunt et al. 2007) and in Australia shortly thereafter, but not in Europe until about 10,000 years later. There was a slight amount of interbreeding between non-African moderns and Neanderthals (Green et al. 2010), corresponding to what is known as the "Weak Out of Africa" hypothesis, in which the spread of modern humans was not watertight with respect to antecedent species. For that matter, Reich and his colleagues (2010) have demonstrated a small amount of genetic transmission from the Denisova Cave population into some modern Australian and Melanesian populations, this being further evidence that there were small amounts of interbreeding between expanding *Homo sapiens* populations and the species that they replaced in different parts of the world.

SEE ALSO: 2 The earliest stages of hominin dispersal in Africa and Eurasia; 4 Early Old World migrations of *Homo sapiens*: human biology; 5 Early Old World migrations of *Homo sapiens*: archaeology; 6 Pleistocene migrations in the Southeast Asian archipelagoes

References and further reading

Antón, S. C. (2002) Evolutionary significance of cranial variation in Asian *Homo erectus*. *American Journal of Physical Anthropology* 118, 301–323.

Argue D., Morwood, M. J., Sutikna, T., et al. (2009) *Homo floresiensis*: a cladistic analysis. *Journal of Human Evolution* 57, 623–39.

Arzarello, M., Marcolini, F., Pavia, G., et al. (2007) Evidence of earliest human occurrence in Europe: the site of Pirro Nord (Southern Italy). *Naturwissenschaften* 94, 107–112.

Cameron, D. W. & Groves, C. P. (2004) *Bones, Stones and Molecules*. London: Elsevier.

Carbonell, E., García-Antón, M. D., Mallol, C., et al. (1999) The TD6 level lithic industry from Gran Dolina, Atapuerca (Burgos, Spain): production and use. *Journal of Human Evolution* 37, 653–693.

Dennell, R. (2009) *The Paleolithic settlement of Asia*. Cambridge: Cambridge University Press.

Gabunia, L., Antón, S. C., Lordkipanidze, D., et al. (2001) Dmanisi and dispersal. *Evolutionary Anthropology* 10, 158–170.

Green, R. E., Krause, J., Briggs, A. W., et al. (2010) A draft sequence of the Neandertal genome. *Science* 328, 710–722.

Grimaud-Hervé, D., Valentin, F., Sémah, F., et al. (1994) Le fémur humain Kresna 11 comparé à ceux de Trinil [The human femur Kresna 11 compared to those of Trini]. *Comptes Rendus de l'Académie des Sciences, Paris, Sciences II* 318, 1139–1144.

Groves, C. P. (2012) Speciation in hominin evolution. In Reynolds, S. C. and A. Gallagher (eds.), *African Genesis: Perspectives on Hominin Evolution*, pp. 45–62. Cambridge: Cambridge University Press.

Howells, W. W. (1977) Hominid fossils. In W. W. Howells & P. Jones Tsuchitani (eds.), *Palaeoanthropology in the People's Republic of China*. Washington, DC: National Academy of Sciences, pp. 66–78.

Huffman, O. F., de Vos, J., Berkhout, A. W., & Aziz, F. (2010) Provenience reassessment of the 1931–1933 Ngandong *Homo erectus* (Java): confirmation of the bone-bed origin reported by the discoverers. *PaleoAnthropology* 2010, 1–60.

Hunt, C. O., Gilbertson D. D., & Rushworth G. (2007) Modern humans in Sarawak, Malaysian Borneo, during Oxygen Isotope Stage 3: palaeoenvironmental evidence from the Great Cave of Niah. *Journal of Archaeological Science* 34, 1953–1969.

Indriati, E. & Antón S. (2008) Earliest Indonesian facial and dental remains from Sangiran, Java: a description of Sangiran 27. *Anthropological Science* 116, 219–229.

Kaifu, Y., Aziz, F., & Baba H. (2005a) Hominid mandibular remains from Sangiran: 1952–1986 collection. *American Journal of Physical Anthropology* 128, 497–519.

Kaifu, Y., Baba, H., Aziz, F., et al. (2005b) Taxonomic affinities and evolutionary history of the Early Pleistocene hominids of Java: dentognathic evidence. *American Journal of Physical Anthropology* 128, 709–726.

Kennedy, G. E. (1983) Some aspects of femoral morphology in *Homo erectus*. *Journal of Human Evolution* 12, 587–616.

Martinón-Torres, M., Dennell, R., & Bermúdez de Castro, J. M. (2011) The Denisova hominin need not be an out of Africa story. *Journal of Human Evolution* 60, 251–255.

Pappu, S., Gunnell, Y., Akhilesh, K., et al. (2011) Early Pleistocene presence of Acheulian hominins in South India. *Science* 331, 1596–1599.

Rae, T. C., Koppe, T., & Stringer, C. B. (2011) The Neandertal face is not cold adapted. *Journal of Human Evolution* 60, 234–239.

Reich, D., Green, R. E., Kircher, M., et al. (2010) Genetic history of an archaic hominin group from Denisova Cave in Siberia. *Nature* 468, 1053–1060.

Shen, G., Gao, X., Gao, B. et al. (2009) Age of Zhoukoudian *Homo erectus* determined with $^{26}Al/^{10}Be$ burial dating. *Nature* 458, 198–200.

Tchernov, E. (1992) Biochronology, paleoecology and dispersal events of hominids in the southern Levant. In T. Akazawa, K. Aoki, & T. Kimura (eds.), *The Evolution and Dispersal of Modern Humans in Asia*. London: Academic Press, pp 149–188.

Walters, I. (1996) *Meganthropus* and the hominid taxa of Java. *Bulletin of the Indo-Pacific Prehistory Association* 15, 229–234.

Weidenreich, F. (1943) The skull of *Sinanthropus pekinensis*: a comparative study on a primitive hominid skull. *Paleontologica Sinica*, n.s., 10, 1–484.

Woo, Ju-kang & Peng, Ru-ce (1959) Fossil human skull of early Paleoanthropic stage found at Mapa, Shaoquan, Kwangtung Province. *Vertebrata Palasiatica* 3, 176–182.

Yokoyama, Y., Falgueres, C., Sémah, F., et al. (2008) Gamma-ray spectrometric dating of late *Homo erectus* skulls from Ngandong and Sambungmacan, Central Java, Indonesia. *Journal of Human Evolution* 55, 274–277.

Zaidner, Y., Yeshurun, R., & Mallol, C. (2010) Early Pleistocene hominins outside of Africa: recent excavations at Bizat Ruhama, Israel. *PaleoAnthropology* 2010, 162–195.

4

Early Old World migrations of *Homo sapiens*: human biology

Mark Stoneking and Katerina Harvati

This chapter presents the genetic and fossil evidence concerning the origins and earliest dispersals of Homo sapiens *across the Old World. The authors begin by reviewing the evidence for an African origin of* Homo sapiens, *and then consider the following questions: how many major dispersals of modern humans were there out of Africa, when did they occur, and by what routes?*

African origin of *Homo sapiens*: genetic evidence

The genetic evidence for an African origin of *Homo sapiens* is overwhelming. Initial studies of mitochondrial DNA (mtDNA) variation found the highest levels of diversity in Africa, and showed that mtDNA diversity outside Africa was a subset of the African diversity (reviewed in Pakendorf & Stoneking 2005). Moreover, phylogenetic trees relating human mtDNA types indicated an African origin for the human mtDNA ancestor, and a molecular clock approach suggested that all existing human mtDNA variation was generated over a period of roughly 200,000 years. The mtDNA evidence was thus interpreted as indicating a recent African origin of contemporary human mtDNA variation, with no indications of genetic contributions from Neanderthals or other non-African archaic humans. This interpretation received strong support from mtDNA sequences retrieved from Neanderthals, which fall well outside the range of contemporary human mtDNA variation. All subsequent mtDNA work has continued to support a recent African origin of human mtDNA (Pakendorf & Stoneking 2005).

MtDNA studies of human maternal history were soon followed by studies of human paternal history, based on variation in the non-recombining regions of the Y chromosome (NRY). These studies (Underhill et al. 2000) also found that most NRY diversity exists in African populations and that NRY diversity outside Africa is a subset of the diversity within Africa. Again, phylogenetic analyses indicated a recent African origin

The Global Prehistory of Human Migration: The Encyclopedia of Global Human Migration Volume 1, First Edition. Edited by Peter Bellwood.
© 2013 John Wiley & Sons, Ltd. Published 2015 by John Wiley & Sons, Ltd.

for the human NRY ancestor. Thus, like mtDNA, NRY variation supported a recent African origin of *Homo sapiens*.

Analyses of the remainder of the human genome, autosomal DNA, are more complicated due to uncertainties introduced by recombination as well as ascertainment biases in the choices of the polymorphisms analyzed. Ascertainment bias occurs because many polymorphisms were first determined to be variable in populations of European ancestry, and hence overestimate European genetic diversity relative to non-European genetic diversity. Nonetheless, studies of genome-wide diversity that correct for such ascertainment bias, as well as the growing body of genome sequence data, also point to an African origin of *Homo sapiens* (Li et al. 2008). Perhaps the strongest evidence for an African origin coming from autosomal DNA studies is the demonstration that there is an astonishingly high negative correlation between the genetic diversity of a population and its migration distance (calculated by considering the most likely ways in which humans would have moved on foot) from East Africa, the presumed homeland for the dispersal of *Homo sapiens*. The most likely explanation for this pattern is an African origin followed by serial bottlenecks as modern humans dispersed from Africa (Prugnolle et al. 2005).

Another source of inference about the origins and dispersal of *Homo sapiens* comes from our parasites. Obligate parasites of humans travel with their hosts and genetic analyses of one such obligate parasite, the stomach bacterium *Helicobacter pylori*, strongly suggest an African origin for its genetic diversity (Linz et al. 2007). In sum, the genetic evidence for a recent African origin of *Homo sapiens* is compelling.

African origin of *Homo sapiens*: fossil evidence

During the Middle Pleistocene we have evidence for archaic humans throughout the Old World. These fossils show similarities to the earlier *Homo erectus*, but are also in several ways intermediate between *Homo erectus* and modern humans, *Homo sapiens*. Specifically, they show larger brains than earlier hominins, with a cranial capacity that extends into the lower part of the modern human range of variation in normal brain size. These Middle Pleistocene fossil humans from Africa, Europe, and possibly Asia are very similar to each other and are often grouped together into a single species, *Homo heidelbergensis*, thought to be broadly ancestral to later hominins. To trace the ancestry of modern humans we should therefore look for a series of intermediate forms, progressively increasingly modern, from such a Middle Pleistocene archaic ancestor.

Such a series of fossil specimens can be demonstrated only in Africa, strongly indicating an African origin for modern humans in agreement with conclusions drawn from genetic data. Earlier fossil representatives such as those from Bodo in Ethiopia (dated to c.600 kya), Ndutu and Lake Eyasi in Tanzania, and Broken Hill (Kabwe) in Zambia (thought to date to approximately 300 kya), closely resemble their Eurasian contemporaries (e.g. Stringer 2002; Harvati et al. 2010). Later specimens dating broadly to the late Middle and early Late Pleistocene, such as the Laetoli Hominid 18 (Tanzania), Eliye Springs (Kenya), and Jebel Irhoudh (Morocco), are highly variable but generally show morphology intermediate between archaic and modern humans (e.g.

Stringer 2002; Harvati et al. 2010). Finally, the material from Omo and Herto, Ethiopia, dated to c.190 and 150 kya respectively (McDougal et al. 2005; White et al. 2003), is well-preserved and convincing evidence for early *H. sapiens* in East Africa at this time. Several early modern humans dating from subsequent periods have been recovered from East and Southern Africa, as well as from North Africa. To the genetic and fossil human evidence can be added the archaeological evidence, which points to an early appearance of modern human behavior in Africa. Such modern behavior is reflected in the use of more sophisticated technology and personal ornamentation, appearing earlier in Africa than elsewhere in the world, though some of these behaviors also occur early in the Near East (e.g. Henshilwood et al. 2009; and see chapter 5).

How many dispersals from Africa?

The serial bottleneck model used to explain human genetic diversity outside Africa (Prugnolle et al. 2005) strongly suggests that there was a single major dispersal of *Homo sapiens* from Africa. MtDNA evidence also supports this view, as there are just two major groups of mtDNA types outside of Africa, called M and N, which in turn branch from just one of the four major groups of mtDNA types found within Africa (Pakendorf & Stoneking 2005). The thinking is that given all of the genetic diversity observed within Africa, multiple migrations from Africa would have brought more genetic diversity outside Africa than is currently observed. Thus, the limited genetic diversity outside Africa suggests one major dispersal.

However, as discussed in more detail below, a separate, early dispersal of modern humans from Africa that went along a southern route to Sahul, the combined New Guinea and Australian landmass, has been proposed (see review in Mellars 2006). According to this view, modern humans left East Africa about 60 kya, traveled along the coast of India and eventually reached Sahul by about 50 kya. Subsequent dispersals would then have erased most of the genetic legacy of this early migration, except in certain populations such as Andamanese, Australians, and New Guineans, and/or "Negrito" groups. The genetic data claimed to support this early southern route model consist largely of a rapid radiation of basal mtDNA lineages that diverged about 50–60 kya (Mellars 2006). However, only recently have the predictions of a multiple-dispersal versus single-dispersal model been directly tested (Wollstein et al. 2010); using simulations and genome-wide data from an African, a European, an East Asian and a highland Papua New Guinean population, this study found strongest support for a single dispersal of *Homo sapiens* from Africa.

Perhaps the strongest evidence for a single major dispersal from Africa comes from the Neanderthal genome sequence (Green et al. 2010). Various analyses of this sequence indicate that all non-Africans tested (including not only Europeans but also Han Chinese and Papua New Guineans), but no Africans, carry in their genomes the signature of a small genetic contribution from Neanderthals, about 1–4%. This suggests that the Neanderthal admixture occurred in a single population ancestral to all non-Africans, and hence that all non-Africans are descended from a single major dispersal from Africa.

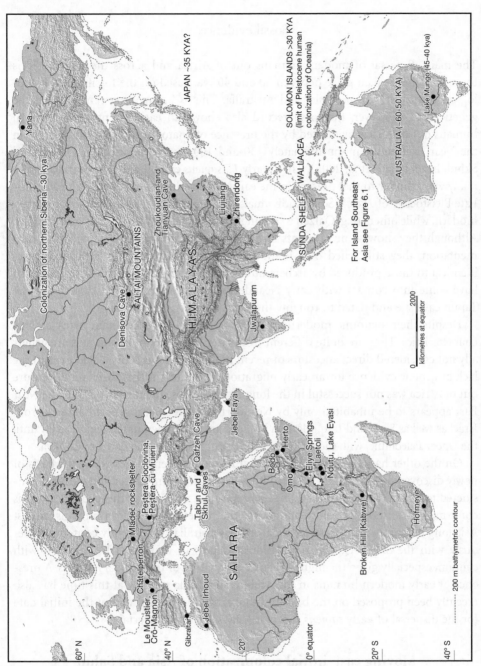

Figure 4.1 Important Upper Pleistocene sites in Africa and Eurasia relevant for the dispersal of *Homo sapiens*. Continental shelves are delineated to −200 m. Base mapping by Education and Multimedia Services, College of Asia and the Pacific, The Australian National University.

Fossil evidence

The main dispersal of modern humans out of Africa and across the Old World is thought to have taken place between 60 and 40 kya, based on the fossil and archaeological record of Europe, Asia, and Australia. This is again in agreement with the genetic data. However, the fossil record also shows an earlier venture of modern humans out of Africa, evidenced by the presence of anatomically modern humans in the Near East between approximately 130 and 100 kya, in the caves of Qafzeh and Skhul, Israel (Grün et al. 2005). These early *H. sapiens* exhibit a degree of variation in many ways similar to that present in the early modern humans from the late Middle– Late Pleistocene of Africa. Some individuals (e.g. Qafzeh 9) appear almost completely modern, while others (e.g. Qafzeh 6) retain many archaic features in their morphology. Although they show some elements of behavioral modernity, such as personal ornamentation, they still relied on Middle Paleolithic technology (i.e. lithic industries identical to those produced by archaic humans such as Neanderthals). They may also have come into contact with early Neanderthal populations, found close by in the Tabun cave site and dated to roughly the same time period.

Despite their anatomic modernity, the Qafzeh–Skhul people retain many archaic characteristics. They are quite different from later human populations and are generally not considered direct ancestors of recent modern humans. This would explain the lack of genetic evidence for an early migration. It is thought that their initial venture out of Africa was not successful in the long term. In subsequent time periods the Near East appears to be inhabited only by Neanderthals and several sites are known from Israel as well as Syria and Iraq. Modern humans are not known in the region again until the Upper Paleolithic, with the earliest Upper Paleolithic industries dated to c.40 kya.

On the other hand, an early dispersal into Asia has been suggested on the basis of newly discovered fragmentary modern human remains from Zhirendong, China, considered to be as old as, or older than, 100 kya (Liu et al. 2010). If this geological age is confirmed, this finding could demonstrate the presence of modern humans in East Asia long before their dispersal into Europe or Australia, and roughly contemporaneously with the Skhul–Qafzeh populations. At present they must be regarded with caution, especially given the highly fragmentary nature of the skeletal remains. A presence of early modern humans in the Arabian peninsula roughly at this time has also recently been proposed on the basis of lithic artifacts (see below). But the initial date for the dispersal of early *sapiens* through Asia is still very uncertain.

Moving east: initial colonization of Asia and Sahul

As described above, recent genetic evidence does not support the popular version of the "southern route" model of a separate migration from Africa leading to the initial colonization of Asia and Sahul. However, genetic evidence does support a modified version of the southern route hypothesis, in which a single dispersal from Africa was followed by Neanderthal admixture with a population ancestral to all non-African *Homo sapiens* (Green et al. 2010). This was followed in turn by an early dispersal from this ancestral non-African population to Sahul, and a later dispersal to East Asia. This scenario is supported by genome-wide data indicating that highland Papuans diverged from a common Asian–European ancestral population, followed by divergence of Asians from Europeans (Wollstein et al. 2010). Analysis of an Australian genome sequence obtained from a 100-year-old lock of hair also indicates separate waves of dispersal in the ancestry of Australians versus East Asians (Rasmussen et al. 2011).

The recent genome sequence from a finger bone dated to c.40 kya from Denisova Cave in the Altai Mountains of central Asia also supports this scenario, as there is a signal of admixture with the Denisova genome sequence in modern-day Papua New Guineans, Australians, Philippine Negritos, and populations from eastern Indonesia (Reich et al. 2010, 2011), but not in any other populations examined, including populations from western Indonesia and mainland Southeast Asia. This admixture signal strongly indicates a separate history for the ancestors of the groups with Denisova admixture and suggests that the Denisova hominins were more widespread than just southern Siberia.

Finally, a separate migration to Sahul is also supported by analyses of the stomach bacterium *Helicobacter pylori*. A novel strain of this bacterium is shared by Australian and New Guinean populations, but (so far) not found elsewhere in the world (Moodley et al. 2009). In sum, two major dispersals to Asia are indicated by the genetic data, one leading to the colonization of Sahul, the other leading to the colonization of most of East Asia (see chapter 37).

Fossil evidence

Modern human dispersal out of Africa has been proposed to be a two-tiered process, with an earlier dispersal into Australia and Sahul following a southern migration route through Ethiopia and the Arabian peninsula; and a later (post-50 kya) migration following a northern route through North Africa and the Near East into Eurasia (see above). Modern humans are thought to have reached Australia at approximately 50 ± 5 kya (chapter 7). Early modern human skeletal remains from Lake Mungo are currently dated to 40 ± 2 kya (Bowler et al. 2003), an interval that places them close to the initial settlement of the continent. These and other early Australian remains were argued in the past to show continuity with earlier Indonesian *Homo erectus*. However, the archaic aspects of early Australian morphology more likely reflect ancestral retentions or functional adaptation. Recent work suggests that early Australian morphology is similar to that of other early *H. sapiens* (Schillaci 2008).

Despite this relatively early presence in Australia, evidence for an early modern human dispersal along the southern migration route is elusive. The early presence of modern humans at the Jwalapuram localities, southern India and Jebel Faya, United Arab Emirates (before 74 kya and c.100 kya respectively) has been inferred on the basis of archaeological remains (Petraglia et al. 2007; Armitage et al. 2011). Both these stone tool assemblages are described as Middle Paleolithic or Middle Stone Age. The conclusions must therefore be considered tentative until human remains are recovered which can confirm the identity of the toolmakers. A human third metatarsal discovered recently at Callao Cave, Philippines and directly dated to c.67 kya (U-series ablation), may be the best evidence for early modern human dispersal along this route (Mijares et al. 2010). The identification of this bone to taxon, however, is ambiguous, as its dimensions are consistent with both those of modern humans and those of the Flores small-bodied hominins (chapters 3 and 6). The oldest securely identified and dated modern human remains in Southeast Asia are the "Deep Skull" and associated post-cranial elements from Niah cave, Sarawak, Borneo. A direct U-series date on this specimen, together with associated U-series dates on faunal bones and ^{14}C dates on charcoal place this individual between 45 and 39 kya (Barker et al. 2007). This chronology makes the Niah cave skull one of the oldest modern humans known from Eurasia. The morphology of the cranium suggests affinities to recent populations of the Andaman Islands, Peninsular Malaysia, and the Philippines, as well as to Australian aborigines.

The East Asian record has produced several sites with modern human remains and/ or Late Paleolithic artifacts. Some have been proposed to date to before 100 kya, notably the skeleton from Liujiang and more recently the mandibular fragment from Zhiren-dong (Liu et al. 2010), but many questions remain over the integrity of these dates and the reliability of their association with the human remains. The partial skeleton from Tianyuan cave is the earliest currently known, securely dated modern human from East Asia. The remains were dated to 39–42 kya by direct AMS radiocarbon dating and have been described as showing a mixture of modern and archaic features. The three crania and partial skeletons from the Upper Cave at Zhoukoudian are the best pre-served Late Pleistocene human remains from East Asia and are thought to date to up to 33 kya. These crania are not similar to recent modern humans from East Asia, but instead resemble other fossil humans of similar age, such as the Upper Paleolithic sample from Europe (see Norton & Jin 2009).

Moving west: the colonization of Europe

Although Europe is perhaps the best-studied area of the world genetically, there is still much uncertainty concerning its genetic history. This is because there are at least three major dispersals that may have influenced contemporary European genetic diver-sity (Soares et al. 2010): initial colonization about 40 kya, most likely from the Near East; contraction during the Last Glacial Maximum (LGM) followed by expansions from various refugia about 15–18 kya; and the spread of farmers from the Near East beginning about 10 kya. Disentangling the relative contribution of these (and other) dispersals to the contemporary European gene pool remains a major challenge. There is also a history of over-interpretation of phylogeographic analyses of mtDNA and NRY variation, which rely heavily on estimating the ages of haplogroups. However, the most common method for estimating the age of a haplogroup may not be reliable (Cox 2008), and in any event ages of haplogroups do not equate to ages of populations, as a haplogroup that arose tens of thousands of years ago may have been contributed to a population quite recently. Ancient DNA analyses would be expected to help sort out the relative contributions of these various dispersals. However, because of preservation issues, ancient DNA analyses of European remains are so far limited to small samples of mtDNA sequences, which are moreover subject to conflicting interpretations (e.g., compare Haak et al. 2010 with Sampietro et al. 2007) and plagued by the possibility of modern DNA contamination.

It might be imagined that, given the various prehistoric dispersals to Europe, as well as the various major population movements within Europe during historical times, there would be little geographic structure evident within contemporary European genetic data. Surprisingly, this is not the case: genome-wide data show an amazingly close correlation between a genetic map based on principal components analysis and a geographic map of Europe (Novembre et al. 2008), for individuals whose four grandparents all come from the same location. Given that the genetic data from contemporary Europeans retain such a strong signal of geographic origin, there is reason to be optimistic that model-based approaches could be used to distinguish among competing hypotheses for the impact of various dispersals on European populations (e.g. as used for Oceanic populations by Wollstein et al. 2010).

Fossil evidence

Until recently, *H. sapiens* were thought to have arrived in Europe between 40 and 42 kya, when Neanderthals still lived in Eurasia, based on the archaeological appearance of Upper Paleolithic industries beginning with the Aurignacian. Commonly thought to be evidence of cultural modernity and produced by modern humans, the Aurignacian first appears at various sites around Europe around this time. However associated human remains from this early period are scarce and often unhelpful for the purposes of diagnosis. Two recent studies have pushed the appearance of modern humans to as early as 43–45 kya in Southern Europe and slightly later (41.5–44.2 kya) in north-western Europe (Benazzi et al. 2011; Higham et al. 2011). Both used high-resolution computer tomography to identify previously undiagnostic dental remains as belonging to modern humans. It therefore appears that *H. sapiens* coexisted in Europe for a significant period of time with *H. neanderthalensis*, who disappeared from the fossil record c.30 kya – although our understanding of this interval is restricted by the limitations of radiocarbon dating, on which we rely for the chronology of the majority of the relevant sites (see Conard & Bolus 2008).

Several "transitional" industries also appear at this time in various parts of Europe (e.g. the Châtelperronian in France, the Szeletian in Central Europe, Uluzzian in Italy and perhaps Greece), which combine Upper Paleolithic-like features with elements reminiscent of the Middle Paleolithic industries produced in Europe by Neanderthals. These transitional industries are sometimes thought to have been manufactured by late-surviving Neanderthal populations, perhaps in imitation of incoming modern human technology. The strongest case for acculturation has been made for the Châtelperronian industry which has been found associated with Neanderthal remains at two sites, although the stratigraphic interpretations of these localities have been questioned (see Higham et al. 2010). Recent analyses of the isolated dental remains associated with the Uluzzian and the single isolated molar associated with the Szeletian have shown that these specimens are modern human (Bailey et al. 2009; Benazzi et al. 2011), suggesting that these industries might have been produced by *H. sapiens*.

The earliest securely dated and relatively complete European modern human remains come from Romania and the Czech Republic. Well preserved human remains were found in three cave sites in Romania: Peştera cu Oase, dating to c.40.5 kya, and the later Peştera cu Muierii and Peştera Cioclovina, dating to between 35 and 32 kya. In the Czech Republic, the Mladeč remains represent the most extensive securely dated human skeletal sample known that is associated with the Aurignacian lithic industry. Two direct AMS radiocarbon dates from two individuals indicate an age of c.31 radiocarbon kya, making them roughly contemporaneous with the Romanian remains (Trinkaus 2007).

The overall anatomical character of these earliest modern Europeans is unquestionably and overwhelmingly modern, displaying a suite of derived *H. sapiens* features. Early Upper Paleolithic Europeans, however, are not similar to recent Europeans in their cranial morphology (e.g. Harvati et al. 2007). They show morphology indicative of recent tropical ancestry, including their nasal sill configuration and body proportions (see Holt & Formicola 2008). An African ancestry was recently supported by overall morphological similarities between Upper Paleolithic Europeans and the cranium from Hofmeyr, South Africa, dated to a similar time period (c.36 kya; Grine et al. 2007). Some of these individuals also exhibit features that have been interpreted as archaic or Neanderthal-like. Traits most frequently discussed in this respect include a moderate projection of the occipital bone in some specimens, termed an occipital "hemibun"; a depression above inion in the occipital bone, termed "suprainiac fossa"; and mandibular foramen bridging. Some authors have argued that these features are evidence of Neanderthal-modern human admixture in Europe (e.g. Trinkaus 2007) and possibly also of the assimilation of Neanderthals into the modern human gene pool (e.g. Smith et al. 2005). An alternative interpretation sees many of these features as retentions from archaic humans in Africa, who represent the ancestral populations of Upper Paleolithic modern Europeans (e.g. Harvati et al. 2007). The fossil evidence for interbreeding is therefore equivocal. This is perhaps not surprising given the very low levels of admixture suggested by the recent genetic studies (Green et al. 2010).

In agreement with inferences from genetic data, the fossil record suggests a break in Europe between pre- and post- LGM Upper Paleolithic populations. Skeletal remains from the latter time period differ from those from the former in several respects, including their cranial and dental dimensions, their stature and limb proportions, and their pathologies. These changes have been interpreted in part as the result of increased territoriality and regionalization imposed by harsh climatic conditions during the LGM. Post-LGM groups show smaller stature and cold-adapted body proportions when compared to pre-LGM groups, suggesting a degree of adaptation to local climatic conditions. Later populations also show smaller teeth and more gracile crania, perhaps as a response to increasing technological intensification (Holt & Formicola 2008).

Concluding thoughts

The fossil record agrees roughly with the genetic data, but in general it appears less straightforward and more difficult to interpret. This is to be expected, as it documents not only "successful" evolutionary events (i.e. those directly linked to the ancestry of recent human groups), but also "unsuccessful" ones (i.e. past dispersals and contractions, local extinctions, etc). The fossil and archaeological records therefore give us a more complex and wider image of the past events that shaped modern human origins. Moreover, ancient genome sequences from Neanderthal and Denisova hominins, as well as the rapidly increasing amount of genome-wide data from modern populations, are also pointing to a more complicated history involving a major dispersal event from Africa but also multiple admixture events, both between the ancestors of various modern human populations and different ancient hominins, as well as between the ancestors of different modern human populations. Dispersal and admixture, rather than long-term isolation, appear to be the key to understanding the evolution of early *Homo sapiens*.

SEE ALSO: 5 Early Old World migrations of *Homo sapiens*: archaeology; 6 Pleistocene migrations in the Southeast Asian archipelagos; 7 The human colonization of Australia; 37 Southeast Asian islands and Oceania: human genetics

References and further reading

Armitage, S. J., Jasim, S. A., Marks, A., et al. (2011) The southern route "out of Africa": evidence for an early expansion of modern humans into Arabia. *Science* 331, 453–456.

Bailey, S. E., Weaver, T. D., Hublin, J.-J. (2009) Who made the Aurignacian and other early Upper Paleolithic industries? *Journal of Human Evolution* 60, 281–298.

Barker, G., Barton, H., Bird, M. et al. (2007) "The human revolution" in lowland tropical Southeast Asia: the antiquity and behavior of anatomically modern humans at Niah Cave (Sarawak, Borneo). *Journal of Human Evolution* 52, 243–261.

Benazzi, S., Douka, K., Fornai, C. et al. (2011) Early dispersal of modern humans in Europe and implications for Neanderthal behavior. *Nature* 479, 525–528.

Bowler, J. M., Johnston, H., Olley, J. M., et al. (2003) New ages for human occupation and climatic change at Lake Mungo, Australia. *Nature* 421, 837–840.

Conard, N. J. & Bolus, M. (2008) Radiocarbon dating the late Middle Paleolithic and the Aurignacian of the Swabian Jura. *Journal of Human Evolution* 55, 886–897.

Cox, M. P. (2008) Accuracy of molecular dating with the rho statistic: deviations from coalescent expectations under a range of demographic models. *Human Biology* 80, 335–357.

Green, R. E., Krause, J., Briggs, A. W., et al. (2010) A draft sequence of the Neanderthal genome. *Science* 328, 710–722.

Grine, F. E., Bailey, R. M., Harvati, K., et al. (2007) Late Pleistocene human cranium from Hofmeyr, South Africa. *Science* 315, 226–229.

Grün, R., Stringer C., McDermott, F., et al. (2005) U-series and ESR analyses of bones and teeth relating to the human burials from Skhul. *Journal of Human Evolution* 49, 316–334.

Haak, W., Balanovsky, O., Sanchez, J. J., et al. (2010) Ancient DNA from European early Neolithic farmers reveals their near eastern affinities. *PLoS Biology* 8, e1000536.

Harvati, K., Gunz, P., & Grigorescu, D. (2007) Cioclovina (Romania): morphological affinities of an early modern European. *Journal of Human Evolution* 53, 732–746.

Harvati, K., Hublin, J.-J., & Gunz, P. (2010) Evolution of Middle-Late Pleistocene human craniofacial form: a 3-D approach. *Journal of Human Evolution* 59, 445–464.

Henshilwood, C. S., d'Errico, F., & Watts, I. (2009) Engraved ochres from the Middle Stone Age levels at Blombos Cave, South Africa. *Journal of Human Evolution* 41, 631–678.

Higham, T., Jacobi, R., Julien, M., et al. (2010) Chronology of the Grotte du Renne (France) and implications for the context of ornaments and human remains within the Châtelperronian. *Proceedings of the National Academy of Sciences USA* 107, 20234–20239.

Higham, T., Crompton, T., Stringer, C., et al. (2011) The earliest evidence for anatomically modern humans in northwestern Europe. *Nature* 479, 521–524.

Holt, B. M. & Formicola, V. (2008) Hunters of the Ice Age: the biology of Upper Paleolithic people. *American Journal of Physical Anthropology* 51, 70–99.

Li, J. Z., Absher, D. M., Tang, H., et al. (2008) Worldwide human relationships inferred from genome-wide patterns of variation. *Science* 319, 1100–1104.

Linz, B., Balloux, F., Moodley, Y., et al. (2007) An African origin for the intimate association between humans and Helicobacter pylori. *Nature* 445, 915–918.

Liu, W., Jin C.-Z., & Zhang, Y.-Q. (2010) Human remains from Zhirendong, South China, and modern human emergence in East Asia. *Proceedings of the National Academy of Sciences USA* 107, 19201–19206.

McDougal, I., Brown. F. H., & Fleagle, J. G. (2005) Stratigraphic placement and age of modern humans from Kibish, Ethiopia. *Nature* 433, 733–736.

Mellars, P. (2006) Going east: new genetic and archaeological perspectives on the modern human colonization of Eurasia. *Science* 313, 796–800.

Mijares, A. S., Detroit. F., Piper, P., et al. (2010) New evidence for a 67,000-year-old human presence at Callao Cave, Luzon, Philippines. *Journal of Human Evolution* 59, 123–132.

Moodley, Y., Linz, B., Yamaoka, Y., et al. (2009) The peopling of the Pacific from a bacterial perspective. *Science* 323, 527–530.

Norton C. J. & Jin, J. J. H. (2009) The evolution of modern human behavior in East Asia: current perspectives. *Evolutionary Anthropology* 18, 247–260.

Novembre, J., Johnson, T., Bryc, K., et al. (2008) Genes mirror geography within Europe. *Nature* 456, 98–101.

Pakendorf, B. & Stoneking, M. (2005) Mitochondrial DNA and human evolution. *Annual Review of Genomics and Human Genetics* 6, 165–183.

Petraglia, M., Korisettar, R., Boivin, M., et al. (2007) Middle Paleolithic assemblages from the Indian subcontinent before and after the Toba super-eruption. *Science* 317, 114–116.

Prugnolle, F., Manica, A., & Balloux, F. (2005) Geography predicts neutral genetic diversity of human populations. *Current Biology* 15, R159–R160.

Rasmussen, M., Guo, X., Wang, Y., et al. (2011) An aboriginal Australian genome reveals separate human dispersals into Asia. *Science* 334, 94–98.

Reich, D., Green, R. E., Kircher, M., et al. (2010) Genetic history of an archaic hominin group from Denisova Cave in Siberia. *Nature* 468, 1053–1060.

Reich, D., Patterson, N., Kircher, M., et al. (2011) Denisova admixture and the first modern human dispersals into southeast Asia and Oceania. *American Journal of Human Genetics* 89, 516–528.

Sampietro, M. L., Lao, O., Caramelli, D., et al. (2007) Palaeogenetic evidence supports a dual model of Neolithic spreading into Europe. *Proceedings of the Royal Society B* 274, 2161–2167.

Schillaci, M. A. (2008) Human cranial diversity and evidence for an ancient lineage of modern humans. *Journal of Human Evolution* 54, 814–826.

Smith, F. H., Jankovic, I., & Karavanic, I. (2005) The assimilation model, modern human origins in Europe, and the extinction of Neanderthals. *Quaternary International* 137, 7–19.

Soares, P., Achilli, A., Semino, O., et al. (2010) The archaeogenetics of Europe. *Current Biology* 20, R174–R183.

Stringer, C. (2002) New perspectives on the Neanderthals. *Evolutionary Anthropology* 11, 58–59.

Trinkaus, E. (2007) European early modern humans and the fate of the Neanderthals. *Proceedings of the National Academy of Sciences USA* 104, 7367–7372.

Underhill, P. A., Shen, P., Lin, A. A., et al. (2000) Y chromosome sequence variation and the history of human populations. *Nature Genetics* 26, 358–361.

White, T. D., Asfaw, B., DeGusta, D., et al. (2003) Pleistocene *Homo sapiens* from Middle Awash, Ethiopia. *Nature* 423, 742–747.

Wollstein, A., Lao, O., Becker, C., et al. (2010) Demographic history of Oceania inferred from genome-wide data. *Current Biology* 20, 1983–1992.

5

Early Old World migrations of *Homo sapiens*: archaeology

Peter Hiscock

This chapter complements chapter 4 by focusing on the cultural evidence for the origins and dispersal of early Homo sapiens. *It points out that the dispersal of modern humans across the Old World was not so clearly marked in the archaeological record as some earlier models suggested, especially those focused only on Africa, the Near East, and Europe.*

One of the great unanswered questions of archaeology is how the first modern humans (*Homo sapiens*) dispersed across the globe. The evidence from studies of modern and ancient genetics as well as preserved human skeletons makes it clear that they did disperse. *Homo sapiens* evolved in Africa, probably eastern/southern sub-Saharan Africa, at least 200 kya and migrated across the rest of the globe during the last 100,000 years (chapter 4; Campbell & Tishkoff 2010). This global dispersal is likely to have been at least the third major movement of hominids from Africa, and has been termed "Out of Africa 3" (Klein 2008). Questions that remain largely unanswered concern how these populations spread, when they reached each region, by what paths they moved, and the adaptive strategies they employed during their dispersion.

Maps of migratory routes in this dispersal of modern humans have been produced, typically hypothesizing pathways similar to those shown in Figure 5.1. Broadly similar maps are common in the literature (e.g. Pettitt 2009). Figure 5.1 reflects the proposition that modern humans originated in eastern Africa and expanded their geographic range mostly to the north, from where they spread westward across northern Africa and eastward out of Africa. It is presumed that they then moved either through the Sinai land bridge into the Middle East and/or across the narrow Bab al Mandab Strait at the mouth of the Red Sea into the southerly portion of the Arabian peninsula. From here it is presumed that human groups moved in several directions: into Europe across the Dardanelles and then along the Danube and/or the Mediterranean lowlands; into northern and northeastern Asia through the steppes north of the Black Sea; and

The Global Prehistory of Human Migration: The Encyclopedia of Global Human Migration Volume 1,
First Edition. Edited by Peter Bellwood.
© 2013 John Wiley & Sons, Ltd. Published 2015 by John Wiley & Sons, Ltd.

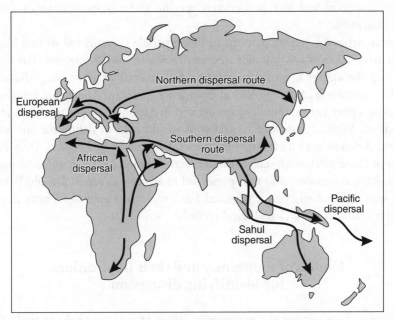

Figure 5.1 Suggested dispersal routes for the early migrations of Homo sapiens out of Africa. Map production by Education and Multimedia Services, College of Asia and the Pacific, The Australian National University.

into eastern and southeastern Asia through the lowlands encircling the Indian Ocean. From peninsula Southeast Asia it is commonly proposed that modern humans moved into Sahul, the glacial-period continent combining Australia and New Guinea, via a "Sahul route." People also moved into the Bismarck and Solomon Islands of Melanesia via the "Pacific route." Dispersal of people into the New World has been much debated but has often been seen as a movement from Siberia, continuing the northern dispersal (as described in chapter 8).

While these proposed migratory routes are plausible, they are founded largely on propositions about geography and are often based in the presumption that the shortest, flattest land pathways would have been employed. Even where specific routes shown in Figure 5.1 have some support in genetic or archaeological evidence, that support is limited and alternative pathways are also conceivable, as for instance suggestions of movement from North Africa into Europe across the Gibraltar Strait (e.g. Sharon 2011).

While genetic analyses have demonstrated the reality of the dispersal out of Africa (chapter 4), they have been of limited value in plotting routes and precise timings. Genetic analyses of biological divergence amongst modern humans have been used to frame discussions of global migration, but such calculations have large errors attached to them (Ho & Larson 2006). Once put at 45–60 kya, such estimates now need to be revised upwards to 50–100 kya in order to accommodate new and earlier dates for relevant human skeletons (e.g. Stoneking & Delfin 2010). This very wide age-range helps propel discussions of human movement, but it offers insufficient precision for confident linkage between specific archaeological changes and early *sapiens* migration.

Most importantly, genetic patterns in living people typically tell us that biological changes have taken place, but not necessarily where they originated. For example, identifying the age of a common ancestor for Australians does not indicate when Australia was colonized; the biological divergence of extant Aboriginal groups might have begun either before these groups arrived in Sahul, or even some time after the colonization. While a sequence of skeletons would help to define the spread, well-preserved skeletons are rare for the time period between 50 and 100 kya. Only material residues of ancient behavior, such as the artifacts and food debris found in archaeological deposits, are abundant and well-preserved in all regions across the Old World. For this reason, archaeologists have searched for a material signal to identify dispersing modern humans in the archaeological record.

Models of modernity and their implications for identifying dispersion

The notion that *sapiens* populations moving out of Africa might have carried a distinctive form of behavior is entwined with the theory that distinctively "modern behavior" emerged at a particular point in the last 100,000 years. This notion of behavioral modernity implies that there was a set of material objects (1) that were distinctive of the kinds of social and economic lives led by modern *H. sapiens*, and (2) that appeared before people left Africa but were carried with them throughout their global dispersion, thereby explaining the set of behaviors shared by all modern peoples. If both these conditions were true, then the model of modernity offers archaeologists working outside Africa a very useful signature. Much debate has been generated about this proposition, but less about its logic than about whether the two conditions were true. Different researchers have offered slightly different lists of traits as distinctive of behaviorally "modern" hominins (compare Mellars 1989; McBrearty & Brooks 2000; Klein 2008). However, such lists typically share material manifestations of symbols used for public signaling, such as jewelery or art, together with economic or social behaviors deemed to signify planning of resource use or campsite structure; as well as evidence for successful adaptations like colonizations of harsh environments or major sea crossings.

A recent example by Klein (2008) illustrates such a pattern, in that recent behaviorally modern *H. sapiens* are stated to have had, in comparison to earlier hominins, tools made from bone/ivory and shell, art and ornamentation, different campsite arrangements, economic systems that transported stone for knapping over tens or hundreds of kilometers, the ability to live in extremely cold climates, higher population densities, a greater range of standardized tools, and technologies that changed rapidly. But while these characteristics have frequently been claimed to be distinctive of *Homo sapiens*, recent archaeological discoveries cast doubt on each of them.

Initiation of working bone, ivory and shell. Bone, ivory, and shell shaped through carving, drilling, or abrading are not commonly reported outside Africa prior to 50 kya, but even after they do appear in the Eurasian record they were clearly not made in all times and at all places. They appear more commonly at higher latitudes and their production might therefore have been a technological strategy that suited some conditions more than others. Furthermore, if the ornaments found in the Châtelperronian cave assemblages of southern France were produced by Neanderthals, without enculturation by modern humans, then we have examples of other hominins working these kinds of materials (see d'Errico et al. 1998; Riel-Salvatore et al. 2008; Bar-Yosef & Bordes 2010).

Appearance of art and ornamentation. The use of coloration agents such as ocher extends back at least 300,000 years, preceding the evolution of *Homo sapiens* (Barham 1998; Hovers et al. 2003). Additionally, Châtelperronian Neanderthals were perhaps manufacturing ornaments. Hence art and ornamentation were common amongst early modern humans, but not diagnostic of modernity.

Spatial organization of campsites. In at least some well-described sites there was no significant difference in the spatial arrangement of campsite activities between modern and earlier hominins (Hovers 2009).

Transport of large quantities of desirable stone materials over tens or hundreds of kilometers.

In Western Europe there is evidence that Pleistocene *Homo sapiens* often had exchange systems that moved stone materials very long distances. But there are also examples of other hominins moving rock over such distances for purposes that were clearly planned (Turq 2000; Meignen et al. 2009; Hiscock et al. 2009). The transport distances probably related to local economic and social issues and are not a clear signal of modernity.

Initiation of ceremonies and rituals shown in evidence such as graves. Ritual behavior, such as burial, is found amongst hominins other than *sapiens* (e.g. Pettitt 2011). While there may have been different rituals employed by the latter, it is not true that the mere existence of rituals is distinctive of modern humans.

Human ability to live in cold climates in Europe and Asia. It has been suggested that the occupation of the northern sub-arctic landscapes of Eurasia was accomplished only by modern humans because of their technological advantage over other hominins in creating clothing. For instance, Gilligan (2007a, 2007b) has argued that a lack of sewn clothing was a limiting factor in the northward expansion of Neanderthals and a contributing factor in their extinction, while *Homo sapiens* had such clothing and were able to occupy extremely cold environments. However, these claims do not provide a signature of the arrival of anatomically modern humans (AMH) in more southerly, hence warmer, lands.

Increase in population densities to levels seen in the historic period for similar environments and economies. Estimates of prehistoric population sizes have proved difficult and they have often been based on site numbers. Recent modeling has shown that site numbers can largely be a reflection of greater destruction with increasing age (Surovell et al. 2009), limiting inferences about population size in the past. While genetic evidence clearly points to population increase during the global dispersal of modern humans, we do not have similar information for other hominins, nor is it a simple matter to compare size signals with those of historic non-agricultural people.

Diversification of economies to extract energy, such as fishing. Evidence is increasingly emerging of pre-*sapiens* economies that were more elaborate and diverse than had previously been thought. For example, in Gorham's and Vanguard Caves in Gibraltar, the faunal material indicates Neanderthal exploitation of marine mammals, mollusks, fish, and birds, as well as terrestrial fauna (Stringer et al. 2008). This kind of evidence means that economic diversity in itself is not a signal of a modern human presence.

Significant increase in tool diversity and standardization within each type. It is now clear that measurements of tool diversity are often arbitrary and correlated with assemblage size. Consequently, the calculated diversity of tool classes depends on the typological system employed by each individual archaeologist, as well as on the mobility of the ancient foragers themselves, given that the latter will influence the number of tools discarded in any one location. When studies in Western Europe have systematically examined these factors they have demonstrated that there was no difference in tool-type richness between assemblages created by Neanderthals and those created by modern humans (Grayson & Cole 1998). Detailed studies of the standardization of tool sizes also reveal no difference between those made by *Homo sapiens* and those made by earlier Neanderthals (Marks et al. 2001).

Increase in the rate of tool variation through time and space. Largely derived from the sequence of changes in Western Europe, this rate increase is not applicable to all regions to which modern humans spread. For instance, the rate of tool change in Pleistocene Australia has been described as lower than the rate observed in other regions (Hiscock 2008; Hiscock et al. 2009).

The problems described above create significant difficulties for any attempt to trace the dispersion of modern humans across Eurasia using the residues of their activities. With the exceptions of Australia, the Americas, the extreme north of Eurasia, and isolated islands such as Greenland, Iceland, and the Pacific islands, most of the globe's land surface had already been colonized by culture-bearing, tool-using hominins long before the arrival of *Homo sapiens*. Without distinctive objects or behaviors made or used *only* by the latter it is difficult or impossible in most regions to distinguish the debris created by dispersing modern humans from that created by the hominins who preceded them. This has been the challenge facing archaeologists seeking to employ cultural residues to map the global migration of *H. sapiens* after the species left Africa.

Despite the above problems, a number of attempts have been made to identify more specific technology-based archaeological signals of the spread. Three of the most prominent are discussed here.

The Middle to Upper Palaeolithic transition in Europe

It is from Europe that some of the strongest arguments have emerged for a distinct cultural signal for the arrival of *Homo sapiens,* or Crô-Magnon as they are known locally. This proposition developed in the 19th century because some of the earliest systematic archaeological excavations in the Dordogne region of France provided evidence for an association of Neanderthals with Middle Palaeolithic assemblages at sites such as Le Moustier, and of *H. sapiens* with Upper Palaeolithic assemblages at sites such as the Abri de Crô-Magnon itself (Lartet & Christy 1875). For the next century the idea of broad association between hominin taxa and archaeological assemblages was repeatedly encouraged by suggestions that the replacement of Neanderthals by *H. sapiens* in Western Europe occurred in the early Upper Palaeolithic. The evidence from skeletons suggested that the replacement occurred about 45–35 kya.

This model is only viable in Europe and adjoining regions and cannot be extrapolated to Africa, East Asia, Australasia, or the Americas since the division of archaeological sequences into Middle and Upper Palaeolithic is not appropriate in those locations. However, even in Europe the connection of these cultural changes with the dispersion of *Homo sapiens* is ambiguous. For instance, the Châtelperronian is the earliest archaeological phase in Europe with worked bone, ivory, teeth, and antler. As it represents a substantial behavioral change, it was once thought to mark the arrival of *sapiens*. Yet, many of the elements of the Châtelperronian lithic technology show continuity/similarity with the preceding Middle Palaeolithic industries that were definitely produced by Neanderthals. Recently, archaeologists have offered a variety of opinions about the identity of the hominins who made Châtelperronian objects: some have suggested that Neanderthals alone were responsible, others suggest that Crô-Magnons were present and that they influenced any Neanderthals who may also have been present, and some argue that the makers of the Châtelperronian still cannot be defined (e.g. Mellars et al. 2007; Bar-Yosef & Bordes 2010). This uncertainty is not restricted to the Châtelperronian but also extends to the Aurignacian, the succeeding Upper Palaeolithic cultural phase.

The Aurignacian is a geographically diverse set of industries, typically with an emphasis on the production of thin stone blades, and has often been discussed as the most likely archaeological indicator of the spread of *H. sapiens* from the Levant into Western Europe. The recent evidence cited in support of this model is an east to west trend in radiocarbon dates for the appearance of Aurignacian and related industries, consistent with the idea that migrating modern humans might have carried these technological behaviors with them (Mellars 2006a). This model predicts that the initiation of the Aurignacian should represent a sharp cultural break with preceding technological, economic, and social traditions in the path of this migration.

While Aurignacian assemblages appear in some places as a radical change to earlier industries, there are also a number of regions across Europe where they show links to local variants of Middle Palaeolithic industries (Kuhn et al. 2004). Furthermore, in eastern Europe, Crimea, and the Levant the appearance of the Aurignacian may not mark the point at which key behavioral changes occurred, since ornaments and bone tools were already in use. These complexities are compounded in the Levant, where the early modern human inhabitants of Skhul and Qafzeh caves in Israel produced distinctively Middle Palaeolithic assemblages, and across Europe by a scarcity of human remains dating to the critical period between 45 and 35 kya.

Such complexities raise the possibility that, even in Europe, archaeological industries such as the Châtelperronian and the Aurignacian do not map on to human biology in any simple way. Until these uncertainties are resolved it seems that the appearance of early Upper Palaeolithic industries in Europe is not a reliable marker of the dispersal of modern humans (Kuhn et al. 2004), even though the sequence of skeletons in Europe points to a window about 10–15,000 years long during which the dispersal probably took place.

The microlith dispersion model

Another model suggests that dispersing populations carried with them what archaeologists call "microliths," small flakes of stone with a blunted back which often have distinctive symmetrical shapes. Such tools are often very small, only a few centimeters long, and were probably hafted on to wooden or bone shafts to construct tools such as saws, knives, or projectiles with stone points/barbs (Lombard 2005; Lombard & Pargeter 2008; Robertson et al. 2009). While such tools may be explained as adaptations to changing environmental and economic conditions (Attenbrow et al. 2009), they have commonly been seen as stylistic markers, perhaps indicating a common technological and cultural tradition. This view forms the basis for the idea that they might also have been stylistically loaded tools carried by humans dispersing beyond Africa. Developed in its most recent form by Paul Mellars (2006b), this model is founded on the observation that not only do microliths occur in European deposits close in time to the appearance of anatomically modern humans, but similar microliths have also been observed in southern and eastern Africa at more than 60 kya. They also occur across large areas of South Asia, perhaps representing material signals of the dispersal of microlith-using modern humans through the arc of land surrounding the Indian Ocean, from Africa to Australia.

However, the proposition that lithic technologies based on blade production were carried by modern humans spreading from Africa does not work well, as Mellars (2006b) has recognized. In Africa, these tools and technologies were present prior to the appearance of modern humans, by at least 300 kya, and have oscillated in and out of use since that time (Barham 2002; Hiscock & O'Connor 2006). Hence, it appears that even within Africa there was not a simple relationship between these tools and early *Homo sapiens*.

Nor does the evidence from India conform to a microlithic-linked model of human dispersal. For instance, at sites in Andhra Pradesh there were no dramatic changes in technology in the period 50–80 kya, when modern human populations are predicted to have dispersed through the area (Haslam et al. 2010). Instead, microliths appeared in the region around 34 kya in response to climate change, and noticeably after modern humans arrived (Clarkson et al. 2009; Majumder 2010; Perera et al. 2011). In this context, the idea that the earliest dispersal across the lands around the Indian Ocean was linked to the use of microliths is implausible, especially if that dispersal also resulted before 50 kya in the colonization of Australia. If the appearance of microliths in India was a result of large-scale population dispersal then it probably reflected a secondary migration.

The earliest archaeological sites in Australia indicate that human occupation had commenced by about 50–55 kya (see chapter 7). For the first 30,000 years lithic technologies were diverse, based on many different forms of core reduction, and no microliths were made until about 20 kya, around the time of the last glacial maximum (LGM). This pattern is not what would be expected if the original colonists had employed microlithic tools. Mellars (2006b) recognized the problem that Australia posed for his microlith dispersion model and proposed as explanations local adaptations to low-quality raw materials, different functional needs for such tools, and a reduction of technological diversity through multiple founder effects as successive landscapes were colonized. While this could be the case, it is puzzling that such a model invokes adaptive processes only at the eastern end of human dispersion along the southern route, while implying that microliths were a traditional, invariant element in the toolkits of groups dispersing from Africa across the Middle East and South Asia. If dispersing Pleistocene foraging groups could, and did, choose not to make microliths for tools then the association of this kind of implement with the first wave of modern humans spreading out of Africa is weak. The evidence from India suggests that the earliest modern human migrants did not make microliths and that they were introduced by subsequent migrations.

The Mode 3 hypothesis

The apparent arrival of modern humans in south Asia and Australia well before microliths were introduced is an example of the reason why Lahr and Foley (1994; Foley & Lahr 1997, 2003) argued that the global spread of AMH must have been associated with an earlier suite of tools and cultural material. They hypothesized that the migrants carried what is called "Mode 3" technology, stoneworking using "prepared core" strategies such as Levallois. They argued that whereas earlier and later modes were geographically restricted, Mode 3 is found across much of the Old World and has a time depth that matches with the emergence of *Homo sapiens* in Africa. In one sense they must be correct, but this does not mean that Mode 3 industries are diagnostic of the dispersal of *H. sapiens*. Several contemporary hominin taxa, including *H. neandertalensis* and *H. floresiensis*, employed Mode 3 technologies and hence these artefacts cannot be used as diagnostic for a presence of modern humans (Moore et al. 2009). In any case, the use of Mode 3 as an indicator of any specific hominin taxon is complicated by its status as the least well-defined technological system in the Palaeolithic. Foley and Lahr may well be looking merely at generic core reduction processes that appear similar between regions only because distinctive elements are not present.

The dispersal of anatomically modern humans and the nature of cultural transitions in the archaeological record

The failure of these various attempts to identify a clear and direct archaeological signature of the initial global migration of modern humans is significant. This is best understood not as a failure of archaeologists to see the distinctive culture or technology of dispersing hominins, but as an indication that there was no simple connection between taxon and culture, between the biological and cultural phylogenies associated with population radiations. Instead of our species inflexibly carrying forth a particular set of behaviors or technologies which assisted their success, the evidence points us to a different image. Colonization of the diverse landscapes across the globe was facilitated by the capacity of early *Homo sapiens* to adapt its social, economic, and technological activities to the different contexts in which it existed. While the reorganization of the behavioral systems of migrating humans was no doubt contingent on tradition, those systems did not merely reproduce previously existing habits. The diversification of archaeological patterns and the lack of a coherent global signal created by modern humans in their spread beyond Africa reveal that the creation of behavioral diversity, either through maintenance of existing social and material culture systems or through repeated adjustment to those systems, may typify the adaptive process that under-pinned the migration of *Homo sapiens* across the Old World.

SEE ALSO: 4 Early Old World migrations of Homo sapiens: human biology; 7 The human colonization of Australia; 8 The human colonization of the Americas: archaeology

References

Attenbrow, V., Robertson, G., & Hiscock, P. (2009) The changing abundance of backed artefacts in south-eastern Australia: a response to Holocene climate change? *Journal of Archaeological Science* 36, 2765–70.

Barham, L. (1998) Possible early pigment use in South-Central Africa. *Current Anthropology* 39(5), 703–10.

Barham, L. (2002) Backed tools in Middle Pleistocene central Africa and their evolutionary significance. *Journal of Human Evolution* 43, 585–603.

Bar-Yosef, O. & Bordes, J.-G. (2010) Who were the makers of the Châtelperronian culture? *Journal of Human Evolution* 59, 586–593.

Campbell, M. & Tishkoff, S. (2010) The evolution of human genetic and phenotypic variation in Africa. *Current biology* 20(4), R166–R173.

Clarkson, C., Petraglia, M., Korisettar, R., et al. (2009) The oldest and longest enduring micro-lithic sequence in India: 35,000 years of modern human occupation and change at the Jwalapuram Locality 9 rockshelter. *Antiquity* 83, 326–348.

d'Errico, F., Zilhao, J., Julien, M., et al. (1998) Neanderthal acculturation in western Europe? A critical review of the evidence and its interpretation. *Current Anthropology* 39, S1–S44.

Foley, R. & Lahr, M. (1997) Mode 3 technologies and the evolution of modern humans. *Cambridge Archaeological Journal* 7, 3–36.

Foley, R. & Lahr, M. (2003) On stony ground: lithic technology, human evolution, and the emergence of culture. *Evolutionary Anthropology: Issues, News, and Reviews* 12, 109–122.

Gilligan, I. (2007a) Neanderthal extinction and modern human behavior: the role of climate change and clothing. *World Archaeology* 39(4), 499–514.

Gilligan, I. (2007b) The prehistoric development of clothing: archaeological implications of a thermal model. *Journal of Archaeological Method and Theory* 17(1), 15–80.

Grayson, D. & Cole, S. (1998) Stone tool assemblage richness during the Middle and Early Upper Palaeolithic in France. *Journal of Archaeological Science* 25, 927–938.

Haslam, M., Clarkson, C., Petraglia, M., et al. (2010) Indian lithic technology prior to the 74,000 BP Toba super-eruption: searching for an early modern human signature. In K. V. Boyle, C. Gamble, & O. Bar-Yosef (eds.),*The Upper Palaeolithic Revolution in global perspective.* Cambridge: McDonald Institute for Archaeological Research, pp. 73–84.

Hiscock, P. (2008) *Archaeology of Ancient Australia.* New York: Routledge.

Hiscock, P. & O'Connor, S. (2006) An Australian perspective on modern behavior and artefact assemblages. *Before Farming* 2006/2, article 4. At www.waspress.co.uk/journals/beforefarming/index/issue.php#20061, accessed Dec. 9, 2011.

Hiscock, P., Turq, A., Faivre, J.-P., et al. (2009) Quina procurement and tool production. In B. Adams & B. S. Blades (eds.), *Lithic Materials and Paleolithic Societies*. New York: Wiley-Blackwell, pp. 232–246.

Ho, S. & Larson, G. (2006) Molecular clocks: when times are a changin. *Trends in Genetics* 22, 79–83.

Hovers, E. (2009) *The Lithic Assemblages of Qafzeh Cave*. Oxford: Oxford University Press.

Hovers, E., Ilani, S., & Barâ-Yosef, O. (2003) An early case of color symbolism: ochre use by modern humans in Qafzeh Cave. *Current Anthropology* 44(4), 491–522.

Klein, R. (2008) Out of Africa and the evolution of human behavior. *Evolutionary Anthropology: Issues, News, and Reviews* 17(6), 267–281.

Kuhn, S. L., Brantingham, P. J., & Kerry, K. W. (2004) The Early Upper Paleolithic and the origins of modern human behavior. In P. J. Brantingham, S. L. Kuhn, & W. Kerry (eds.),*The Early Upper Paleolithic beyond Western Europe*. Berkeley: University of California Press, pp. 242–248.

Lahr, M. & Foley, R. (1994) Multiple dispersals and modern human origins. *Evolutionary Anthropology: Issues, News, and Reviews* 3(2), 48–60.

Lartet, E. & Christy, H. (1875) *Reliquiae Aquitanicae*. Edinburgh: Williams & Norgate.

Lombard, M. (2005) Evidence of hunting and hafting during the Middle Stone Age at Sibidu Cave, KwaZulu-Natal, South Africa: a multianalytical approach. *Journal of Human Evolution* 48(3), 279–300.

Lombard, M. & Pargeter, J. (2008) Hunting with Howiesons Poort segments: pilot experimental study and the functional interpretation of archaeological tools. *Journal of Archaeological Science* 35(9), 2523–2531.

Majumder, P. (2010) The human genetic history of South Asia. *Current Biology CB* 20(4), R184–R187.

Marks, A., Hietala, H. J., & Williams, J. K. (2001) Tool standardization in the Middle and Upper Palaeolithic: a closer look. *Cambridge Archaeological Journal* 11, 17–44.

McBrearty, S. & Brooks, A. (2000) The revolution that wasn't: a new interpretation of the origin of modern human behavior. *Journal of Human Evolution* 39, 453–563.

Meignen, L., Delagnes, A., & Bourguignon, L. (2009) Patterns of lithic material procurement and transformation during the Middle Paleolithic in Western Europe. In B. Adams & B. S. Blades (eds.), *Lithic Materials and Paleolithic Societies*. Oxford: Wiley-Blackwell, pp. 25–46.

Mellars, P. (1989) Major issues in the emergence of modern humans. *Current Anthropology* 30, 349–85.

Mellars, P. (2006a) Archeology and the dispersal of modern humans in Europe: deconstructing the "Aurignacian." *Evolutionary Anthropology: Issues, News, and Reviews* 15(5), 167–82.

Mellars, P. (2006b) Going East: new genetic and archaeological perspectives on the modern human colonization of Eurasia. *Science* 313(5788), 796–800.

Mellars, P., Gravina, B., & Ramsey, C. B. (2007) Confirmation of Neanderthal/modern human interstratification at the Chatelperronian type-site. *Proceedings of the National Academy of Sciences* 104, 3657–3662.

Moore, M. W., Sutikna, T., & Jatmiko (2009) Continuities in stone flaking technology at Liang Bua, Flores, Indonesia. *Journal of Human Evolution* 57(5), 503–526.

Perera, N., Kourampas, N., & Simpson, I. A. (2011) People of the ancient rainforest: Late Pleistocene foragers at the Batadomba-lena rockshelter, Sri Lanka. *Journal of Human Evolution* 61, 254–269.

Pettitt, P. (2009) The rise of modern humans. In C. Scarre (ed.), *The Human Past*. London: Thames & Hudson, pp. 124–173.

Pettitt, P. (2011) *The Palaeolithic Origins of Burial*. London: Routledge.

Riel-Salvatore, J., Miller, A. E., & Clark, G. A. (2008) An empirical evaluation of the case for a Chatelperronian-Aurignacian interstratification at Grotte des Fees de Chatelperron. *World Archaeology* 40, 480–492.

Robertson, G., Attenbrow, V., & Hiscock, P. (2009) Multiple uses for Australian backed artefacts. *Antiquity* 83(320), 296–308.

Sharon, G. (2011) Flakes crossing the straits? Entame flakes and northern Africa–Iberia contact during the Acheulean. *African Archaeological Review* 28, 125–140.

Stoneking, M. & Delfin, F. (2010) The human genetic history of East Asia: weaving a complex tapestry. *Current Biology* 20(4), R188–R193.

Stringer, C., Finlayson, J., & Barton, R. (2008) Neanderthal exploitation of marine mammals in Gibraltar. *Proceedings of the National Academy of Sciences* 105(38), 14319–14324.

Surovell, T. A., Byrd Finley, J., Smith, G. M., et al. (2009) Correcting temporal frequency distributions for taphonomic bias. *Journal of Archaeological Science* 36, 1715–1724.

Turq, A. (2000) Paléolithique inférieur et moyen entre Dordogne et Lot [Lower and Middle Paleolithic between the Dordogne and Lot]. *Paléo*, Supp. 2. Les Eyzies: SAMRA.

6

Pleistocene migrations in the Southeast Asian archipelagos

François Sémah and Anne-Marie Sémah

This chapter describes further the migrations of early hominins within Southeast Asia, especially to the sometime-island and sometime-peninsula formed by Java. The island of Flores was also reached at least one million years ago by crossing ocean passages between islands. Early modern human migrations beyond the Sunda Shelf are also discussed.

The islands of Southeast Asia encompass a large archipelagic area that runs for about 5,000 km from Sumatra in the west to New Guinea in the east, and from Luzon in the north to Timor in the south. During Pleistocene times, changing environmental conditions are likely to have played a major part in allowing hominin and other mammal dispersals into this region, especially over the periodic land bridges that formed during glacial periods of low sea level.

The Indonesian–Australian region can be divided, from the viewpoint of human and animal migration, into three major regions (see Figure 2.1 and Figure 6.1 below). In the west lies the Sunda continental shelf (Sumatra, Borneo, Java, and Bali). The Sahul continental shelf (Australia and New Guinea) occupies the east. A region of non-continental islands separated by deep seas, termed Wallacea by biogeographers, lies in between. Sundaland and Sahul saw periodic land bridges, respectively from mainland Asia through Java to Bali, and between New Guinea and Australia, as shallow sea beds emerged during periods of high latitude glaciation. The Wallacean Islands in between (Philippines, Sulawesi, Lesser Sundas, Moluccas) were always divided by ocean gaps owing to their steeply plunging coastlines.

At the end of the 19th century, the Dutch physician and anthropologist Eugène Dubois, supporter of the newly developing evolutionary perspective, discovered what he regarded as a "missing link" between humans and the rest of the animal world at Trinil, in the Solo Valley of eastern Java. He named it *Pithecanthropus erectus*. Modern dating methods now assign an age of c.1.6 mya to the oldest Javan hominin fossils,

The Global Prehistory of Human Migration: The Encyclopedia of Global Human Migration Volume 1, First Edition. Edited by Peter Bellwood.
© 2013 John Wiley & Sons, Ltd. Published 2015 by John Wiley & Sons, Ltd.

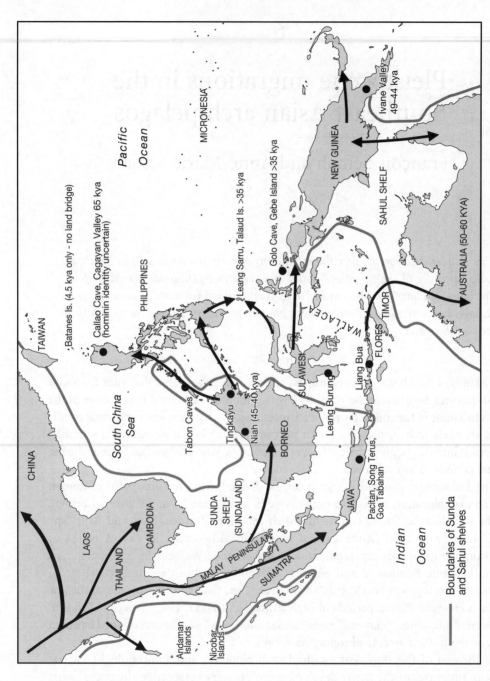

Figure 6.1 The settlement of island Southeast Asia and Sahul by early modern humans. For earlier hominins see Figure 2.1.

which have been found in the eroded core of the Sangiran uplifted dome in central Java (Swisher et al. 1994; A. M. Sémah et al. 2010). They postdate only slightly the oldest known hominin fossils outside Africa, those from Dmanisi in Georgia, dated to c.1.8 mya. The straight-line distance from East Africa to Java is more than 8,000 km, far more if following coastlines.

The remains of the oldest fossil specimens recovered from Java, though quite fragmentary, display very robust characteristics, so much so that there was a short-lived movement in the 1930s to classify some of them as a new genus, *Meganthropus*, now subsumed into *Homo erectus* (see further discussion of Javan *erectus* in chapters 2 and 3). These Javan hominins were the first beyond Africa to move off mainland Asia, through the equatorial rainforest zone into the southern hemisphere. Their anatomical features might have reflected biological adaption to the specific tropical island environments of Sundaland, with immense coastal mangrove swamps and inland rainforest. Alas, the archaeological record regarding these ancient islanders is still very fragmentary, owing to the geological and taphonomic context of the discoveries (mostly scattered in lacustrine clays), but they cohabited with a well-adapted fauna that included proboscideans – elephant-like animals that could swim across limited ocean straits. No definite discoveries of stone tools from this early period have yet been made in Java.

The rhythm and amplitude of the major climatic cycles intensified from around the Lower to Middle Pleistocene boundary (c.1–0.8 mya – see Figure 2.2), inducing more severe climatic contrasts and paleogeographical changes. New vertebrate taxa reached Java at this time (e.g. *Elephas*, hyenas), and the earlier robust/archaic population is no longer present in the Middle Pleistocene layers. Most of the hominin fossils that have been recovered on Java date back to this period, and are usually described in the literature as classic forms of *Homo erectus,* resembling the holotype from Trinil discovered by Dubois. Because the biostratigraphic record documents faunal immigration at this time, it is likely that a new wave of hominin colonization arrived. However, palaeoanthropological research is not yet conclusive on this question, and it is also possible that *in situ* evolution occurred from the former more robust *Homo erectus* population.

Archaeological assemblages in Java from contexts believed related to early Middle Pleistocene *Homo erectus* include elements related to the Acheulian tradition, such as cleavers made on large andesitic flakes and bolas (stone balls) (F. Sémah et al. 1992). Such tools were widespread at this time in Africa, Europe, and India. Some discoveries in river beds in South Sumatra and the Pacitan region, bordering the Indian Ocean coast of eastern Java, also include hand axes, but without good chronological contexts.

During the Middle Pleistocene, the emergent surfaces of Sundaland during glacial phases (the even-numbered marine isotope stages in Figure 2.2) experienced much drier conditions and increased climatic seasonality. Open forests or even savannah occupied regions between fragmented patches of tropical rainforest that was often restricted to galleries along rivers (Wurster et al. 2010). Low sea-level conditions might have allowed one group of hominins to take advantage of a narrowing of sea passages to reach the island of Flores, possibly from Sundaland or Sulawesi. Mata Menge and Wolo Sege in the Soa Basin of central Flores have yielded lithic assemblages dated back to the Early to Middle Pleistocene boundary (Brumm et al. 2010). Although no actual fossils date from this time period in the island, the significance of Flores is that hominins must have crossed sea passages to reach there, even if they were narrow and offered visibility to a volcano on the opposite shore.

Paradoxically, the later history of *Homo erectus* in Indonesia is only poorly recorded, even though remains have been recovered in large numbers from Pleistocene fluvial sediments in eastern Java, especially with the spectacular discovery during the 1930s of a dozen faceless and jawless crania from a terrace of the Solo River at Ngandong. Their age is still much debated in the literature, ranging from Middle to Upper Pleistocene (between 300 and 50 kya), which is not a very satisfactory situation. The Ngandong, Sambungmacan, and Ngawi remains display further evolution, especially in their larger cranial capacity, and can be attributed either to a derived form of *Homo erectus*, or to another specific paleontological taxon (*Homo soloensis*).

The conditions that led to the final demise of *Homo erectus* in the archipelagos represent a current challenge for scientific research, including issues such as the possible coexistence of the latest and most derived *erectus*-like forms with the earliest *Homo sapiens* immigrants. Such issues have become even more crucial with the amazing discovery of *Homo floresiensis* in Liang Bua cave (Wae Racang valley, western Flores), who existed from at least 75 kya until after the LGM (possibly 12 kya or later; Brown et al. 2004; Morwood et al. 2004), long after the spread of modern humans across most other regions of Eurasia. The status of this 1-meter-high hominin is still much debated. While its endemic biological status is acknowledged, it has been regarded by different groups of scholars as a member of either a *sapiens* or an *erectus* population, in the latter case perhaps descended from the makers of the Mata Menge and Wolo Sege artifacts at about 1 mya. Some scholars (see chapter 3) even point to a more ancient possible derivation, relating it to an Out of Africa hominin lineage older than *Homo erectus*.

Homo sapiens in Indonesia

We know that *Homo sapiens* reached Australia and New Guinea (joined by the Sahul Shelf – see Figure 6.1 for site locations) via Indonesia by at least 50 kya, but no certain *sapiens* skeletal remains are as yet dated older than this in island Southeast Asia. From a palaeoenvironmental point of view, there was a conspicuous warm and wet period during the last interglacial, between 130 and 83 kya, accompanied by quite high sea levels and, in Java, by an overwhelming development of a rainforest environment (Sémah et al. 2004). New rainforest fauna appeared in Java from mainland Asia at this time, including the orangutan and the Malay sun bear (*Helarctos*). Such non-swimming forest species could not have reached Java during periods when sea levels were at their highest, but more likely migrated during an early interglacial phase when climate had already become warmer and wetter, but before sea levels had attained their maxima and while a narrowing land bridge to Java from the Asian mainland was still open. A human molar recently described in old collections of the Upper Pleistocene Punung fauna, from caves near Pacitan in East Java, is claimed to represent the earliest evidence for *Homo sapiens* in the archipelago, but the exact taxonomic status of this tooth is uncertain (Storm et al. 2005). Current excavations in cave fillings in the same limestone area (Gunung Sewu) have yielded a stone artifact assemblage which dates back to

300 kya in the lower alluvial layers of Song Terus. Later horizons dated 120–85 kya reflect actual human occupation of the caves more clearly, but this assemblage shows no marked changes that allow discrimination of the arrival of *H. sapiens* as a new species separate from H. *erectus.*

Dated remains of *Homo sapiens* in island Southeast Asia include a very important skull dated to c.45–39 kya from the West Mouth of the Niah Caves in Sarawak (Borneo). Other cranial remains are dated to 35 kya from Tabon cave on Palawan Island in the southern Philippines. A recently discovered human metatarsal dated to about 65 kya comes from Callao Cave, on a tributary of the Cagayan in northeastern Luzon, but the taxonomic attribution of this specimen is still considered uncertain by the excavators (Mijares et al. 2010).

Archaeology suggests a richness and diversity of Upper Pleistocene material culture in the Indonesian archipelago, a large part of which still remains to be disclosed by further excavations. Both bone and shell implements, as well as stone tools, date between 60 and 20 kya at Song Terus and Goa Tabuhan caves in East Java (Sémah et al. 2000; Simanjuntak et al. 2002). In Wallacea, lithic industries are dated to between 30 and 20 kya at Leang Burung 2 cave in the karst of South Sulawesi and to 35 kya at Golo cave in the northern Moluccas (Bellwood et al. 1998; Szabo et al. 2007). Bifacial chert tools from Tingkayu in Sabah are possibly of Late Pleistocene age (Bellwood 1988), but this requires confirmation. The island Southeast Asian lithic industries are different from the well-known Hoabinhian industry (characterized among other forms by unifacially trimmed pebble tools called sumatraliths) on the Southeast Asian mainland and in Sumatra. The Hoabinhian extended across more than 20° of latitude during the late Upper Pleistocene (from c.30 kya onwards), but it does not seem to have reached the islands beyond Sumatra.

However, early populations of *Homo sapiens* in the islands were able to migrate over considerable sea gaps before the LGM, for instance over about 100 km of sea by at least 35 kya to reach the Talaud Islands in northeastern Indonesia (Ono et al. 2009), and similarly to Australia, settled perhaps from Timor or via New Guinea by 50 kya at the latest (see chapter 7). New Guinea also required a sea crossing from the Moluccas, made in the same time period, according to evidence from the Ivane Valley in the eastern part of the island (Summerhayes et al. 2011). These distances were considerable achievements over the distances reached by earlier hominins such as *Homo erectus*, who (as far as we know) did not cross Wallacea to reach the Moluccas or New Guinea, even though some clearly reached Flores.

SEE ALSO: 2 The earliest stages of hominin dispersal in Africa and Eurasia; 3 Hominin migrations before *Homo sapiens*: Out of Africa – how many times?; 4 Early Old World migrations of *Homo sapiens*: human biology; 7 The human colonization of Australia

References

Brumm, A., Jensen, G., van den Bergh, G., et al. (2010) Hominins on Flores, Indonesia, by one million years ago. *Nature* 464, 748–752.

Bellwood, P. (1988) *Archaeological Research in South-eastern Sabah*. Kota Kinabalu: Sabah Museum Monograph No.2.

Bellwood, P., Nitihaminoto, G., Irwin, G., et al. (1998) 35,000 years of prehistory in the Northern Moluccas. *Modern Quaternary Research in S-E Asia* 15, published as G. Bartstra (ed.), *Bird's Head Approaches*. Rotterdam: Balkema, pp. 233–275.

Brown, P., Sutikna, T., Morwood, M., et al. (2004) A new small-bodied hominin from the Late Pleistocene of Flores, Indonesia. *Nature* 431, 1055–1061.

Mijares, A. S., Détroit, F., Piper, P., et al. (2010) New evidence for a 67,000-year-old human presence at Callao Cave, Luzon, Philippines. *Journal of Human Evolution* 59, 123–132.

Morwood, M., Soejono, R., Roberts, R., et al. (2004) Archaeology and age of a new hominin from Flores in eastern Indonesia. *Nature* 431, 1087–1091.

Ono, R., Soegondho, S., & Yoneda, M. (2009) Changing marine exploitation during Late Pleistocene in northern Wallacea. *Asian Perspectives* 48, 318–41.

Sémah, A. M., Sémah, F., Moudrikah, R., et al. (2004) A late Pleistocene and Holocene sedimentary record in Central Java and its palaeoclimatic significance. *Modern Quaternary Research in S-E Asia, Balkema*, 19, 63–88.

Sémah, A. M., Sémah, F., Djubiantono, T., et al. (2010) Landscape and hominid environmental changes between the Lower and the early Middle Pleistocene in Java (Indonesia). *Quaternary International* 223–224, 451–454.

Sémah, F., Sémah, A. M., Djubiantono, T., et al. (1992) Did they also make stone tools? *Journal of Human Evolution* 23, 439–446.

Sémah, F., Saleki, H., Falguères, C., et al. (2000) Did Early Man reach Java during the Late Pleistocene? *Journal of Archaeological Science* 27, 763–769.

Simanjuntak, T. (2002) *Gunung Sewu in Prehistoric Times*. Yogyajarta, Indonesia: Gajah Mada University Press.

Storm, P., Aziz, F., de Vos, J., et al. (2005) Late Pleistocene *Homo sapiens* in a tropical rainforest fauna in East Java. *Journal of Human Evolution* 49, 536–545.

Summerhayes, G., Leavesley, M., Fairbairn, A., et al. (2011) Human adaptation and plant use in highland New Guinea 49,000 to 44,000 years ago. *Science* 330, 78–81.

Swisher III, C. C., Curtis, G. H., Jacob, T., et al. (1994) Age of the earliest known hominids in Java, Indonesia. *Science* 263, 1118–1121.

Szabo, K., Brumm, A., & Bellwood, P. (2007) Shell artefact production at 32,000 BP in Island Southeast Asia: thinking across media? *Current Anthropology* 48, 701–724.

Wurster, C., Bird, M. I., Bull, I. D., et al. (2010) Forest contraction in north equatorial Southeast Asia during the Last Glacial Period. *Proceedings of the National Academy of Sciences*, 107: 11508–11511.

7

The human colonization of Australia

Peter Hiscock

The colonization of Australia between 50 and 60 kya required a significant sea crossing in eastern Indonesia, and led to the development of one of the world's most remarkable hunter-gatherer cultural traditions.

The dispersal of modern humans along the northern edge of the Indian Ocean eventually led them to the islands bordering the Sunda shelf, in the area of modern-day Indonesia (see chapters 4 and 5, and Figure 6.1). From there, the colonization of Australia was a culmination of the arc of global dispersal of *H. sapiens* out of Africa. The general timing and pattern of human dispersal throughout the Ice Age continent of Sahul, comprising Australia and its continental neighbours of Tasmania, New Guinea, and the Aru Islands, is known from archaeological, environmental, and genetic evidence. While the impact of dispersing humans on the extinct Australian megafauna is still much debated, the history of human arrival and settlement of the continent can be sketched with confidence (Figure 7.1).

Homo sapiens probably landed on the continental shelf of Sahul between 50 and 60 kya. It is unclear whether regional biogeography at that time played a role in constraining the age for colonization. From 70 kya until about 13 kya, sea levels were substantially lower, more than 60 meters below their current level. Much of the continental shelf in the Arafura Sea was then exposed, creating Sahul by joining northern Australia with New Guinea. The exposed Sahul Shelf stretched hundreds of kilometers to the north of modern Australia, with dry land containing tropical savannas and woodlands in what is now the Gulf of Carpentaria, Arafura Sea, and Joseph Bonaparte Gulf. The lower sea level not only expanded the land mass of Sahul, it also reduced the ocean distances required to reach Australia from the exposed continental shelf of Southeast Asia, effectively making it a larger, closer target.

We have no specific knowledge of the maritime technology or seafaring knowledge of the colonizers, and hence cannot estimate how important the reduced ocean crossings

The Global Prehistory of Human Migration: The Encyclopedia of Global Human Migration Volume 1,
First Edition. Edited by Peter Bellwood.
© 2013 John Wiley & Sons, Ltd. Published 2015 by John Wiley & Sons, Ltd.

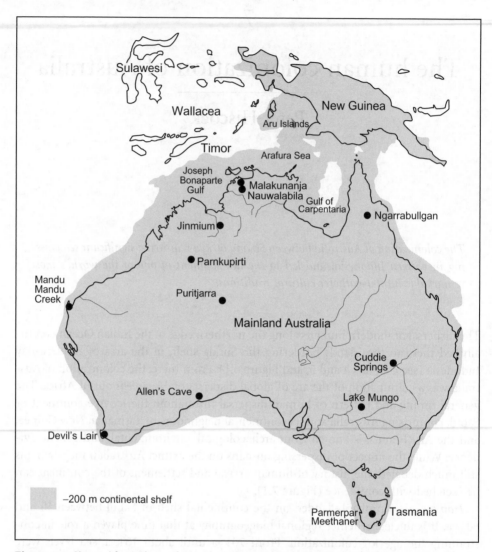

Figure 7.1 Sites with evidence for early human occupation in Australia. Base mapping by College of Asia and the Pacific, Australian National University.

were to their capacity to reach Sahul. Archaeologists initially presumed that only a small group of humans reached Sahul, with only a basic maritime technology, so that crossing the water barriers may have been difficult or even accidental. Speculation, most notably by Joseph Birdsell (1977), about the route taken by colonizing groups on their journey to Australia, was based on the presumption that poor maritime abilities forced people to select the shortest water crossings and perhaps wait until low sea levels occurred. However, such conjectures are not consistent with emerging evidence of the relatively large scale of initial migrations to Sahul. Mitochondrial DNA diversity amongst modern Aborigines suggested to Merriwether and colleagues (2005) that there was a large founding population of about a thousand people, including several hundred women. Such a large colonizing population indicates the use of sound watercraft, a capacity to adapt to different landscapes, and substantial population growth in the region from which they came, presumably Southeast Asia.

It has also been suggested that population growth following the explosion at c.72 kya of the Toba volcano in northern Sumatra caused groups to migrate away from the recovering region, towards Australia (Lahr 1996). However, colonization of Australia and New Guinea occurred long after this event, and Sahul was only one of many landscapes occupied at this time by expanding early modern human populations. It seems likely that the global migration of *Homo sapiens* did not need to be triggered by local environmental change, and that these groups colonized and were able to adapt quickly to new environments. The relatively rapid spread of humans from Africa to Southeast Asia, and subsequently throughout Sahul, is evidence of their colonizing abilities.

Archaeological evidence for the arrival of modern humans in Sahul indicates their presence in several parts of the continent at 50–60 kya. Although there have been claims for substantially earlier archaeological materials, such dates have been revealed to be either inaccurate or not properly associated with archaeological materials (Hiscock 2008). For instance, the inference of early occupation, more than 100 kya, at Jinmium rockshelter in the north was based on luminescence analysis of geologically old sand grains that retained a time signal unrelated to the artifacts buried in the sands. This site has now been redated to less than 20 kya. When claims such as this are excluded, there is a consistent pattern throughout the continent for the appearance of archaeological materials.

The appearance of humans in the landscape of northern Australia is documented in the rock shelters of western Arnhem Land. For example, at Malakunanja II the lowest artifacts were in sands estimated, by luminescence analysis of associated sand grains, to be 50–60,000 years old. At Nauwalabila, the lowest artifacts were estimated to be 53,500–67,000 years old (Roberts et al. 1993). Critiques of these associations, and suggestions that artifacts have moved vertically through the deposit (O'Connell & Allen 2004), overlook stratigraphic evidence in Malakunanja II for a small pit dug more than 40 kya, and this cannot have been vertically displaced. Humans were probably occupying these sites more than 45–50 kya.

In southern Australia, the archaeological evidence points to human occupation of the same antiquity. The best documented instance is on the Lake Mungo lunette in the inland southeast, where the stratigraphically lowest stone artifacts so far excavated are estimated to be 45–50,000 years old (Bowler et al. 2003). Here too, there have been concerns that disturbance makes these claims problematic (O'Connell & Allen 2004), but the arguments against these age estimates are not compelling (Hiscock 2008). Occupation of southeastern Australia at approximately 45 kya, or slightly earlier, is therefore documented by the materials in the Lake Mungo deposit.

A similar antiquity for initial occupation older than 45 kya is observed in many regions across Australia. For instance, the Parnkupirti site in north western Australia (Veth et al. 2009) and Devil's Lair in the southwest (Turney et al. 2001) have artifacts from this time period. Together with the sites from Arnhem Land and Lake Mungo, this evidence makes it clear that *H. sapiens* dispersed rapidly across the continent, within only a few millennia. This dispersal was accomplished through many different environments, so that early sites have been found in sandy deserts (Puritjarra), rocky deserts (Allen's Cave), semi-arid grasslands (Cuddie Springs), tropical savannah (Malakunanja), tropical woodland (Ngarrabullgan), tropical coasts (Mandu Mandu Creek), and southern alpine uplands (Parmerpar Meethaner). The widespread evidence for settlement in these different landscapes shortly after colonization refutes notions that colonizers were slow to adapt to different conditions, and were consequently restricted to the coastal margins of Sahul until much later in prehistory. Instead, the evidence shows the first occupants had flexible and adjustable economic systems, combined with expanding populations, creating the capacity to colonize not only Sahul but also the diversity of environments within the landmass.

Although ideas of multiple large-scale migrations to Australia from different source areas have occasionally been proposed, there is currently no evidence for this. Genetic patterns indicate colonization by one large group, with subsequent biological diversification. The mtDNA lineage of the oldest Australian skeleton, the 43-kya Willandra Lakes H3 from western New South Wales, is still found amongst living Aboriginal people. Furthermore, mtDNA lineages extracted from terminal Pleistocene skeletons reveal no systematic differences from modern populations; they indicate that all shared a common origin and were not descended from multiple populations (Adcock et al. 2001). This conclusion can be expected, because once the colonizing population expanded and occupied all parts of the continent, the new arrival of additional small groups would not have much impact on the gene pool as a whole (Pardoe 2006). The Sahul mtDNA evidence is consistent with a single colonization event followed by a long period of genetic isolation. There is evidence for population movements *within* Australia following colonization, including a dispersal of genetic patterns from New Guinea to northern Australia, but with the exception of localized coastal populations in the north there is no clear evidence for major subsequent migrations *to* Sahul (Hudjashov et al. 2007). The physical and cultural variation evident in the Australian archaeological, historical and biological records emerged essentially from adaptations to social and physical environments within the continent.

One question frequently discussed concerns the extent to which colonizers relied on the exploitation of large game, the so-called "megafauna," and the impact of any predation on the Australian ecosystem. A large number of studies have concluded that many species of megafauna went extinct shortly after the arrival of humans in the continent, and have interpreted this as evidence that human hunting, or perhaps human firing of the landscape, was responsible (see Hiscock 2008). The implication of "overkill" is that colonization of the unfamiliar environments within Sahul was facilitated by a strategy of large-game hunting that employed the same technologies irrespective of the nature of the landscape in which people were foraging. Tempting though such an image has been, there is little archaeological evidence to support it. The timing of most extinctions is poorly known, and many species may have become extinct long before or long after the arrival of humans (Wroe & Field 2006). The large-animal extinctions at the time of human colonization are thus part of a long-term trend. Additionally, small animals as well as large game disappeared, suggesting that climatic change rather than human predation was the driver of the extinctions (see Hiscock 2008). Furthermore, no megafaunal kill sites have ever been located, and the few early archaeological sites that have good preservation of animal bones indicate that foraging did not focus on large game.

The economic and social practices of the colonizers were apparently diverse. Archaeological excavations show that early foraging in the sub-arctic Tasmanian highlands was based on intensive wallaby harvesting, involving the extraction of marrow from long bones. In desert and temperate zones the economic focus was often more varied, although with an emphasis on stable or rich environments. Tools used in exploiting resources also varied across regions. Detailed descriptions of the earliest technologies are rare, but examples of regional variation, before 35–40 kya, include the manufacture of ground-edged and hafted stone axes in northern Australia, and a focus on small "end-scrapers" in the Tasmanian highlands (Hiscock 2008; Geneste et al. 2010). These stone artifacts were probably hafted, and functioned as versatile tools that facilitated resource exploitation. Archaeological excavations have also documented a range of symbolic activities prior to 40 kya, including formal burials in which the body was covered in ocher and provided with bone and shell beads. Ocher pellets were also used for creating art. These discoveries illustrate evidence for a rapid and dramatic colonization of Australia, and all its environments, by an anatomically and culturally modern population that had already dispersed successfully from Africa through much of Eurasia.

SEE ALSO: 4 Early Old World migrations of *Homo sapiens*: human biology; 5 Early Old World migrations of *Homo sapiens*: archaeology

References

Adcock, G., Dennis, E., Easteal, S., et al. (2001) Mitochondrial DNA sequences in ancient Australians: Implications for modern human origins. *Proceedings of the National Academy of Science* 98, 537–42.

Birdsell, J. (1977) The recalibration of a paradigm for the first peopling of Greater Australia. In J. Allen, J. Golson, & R. Jones (eds.), *Sunda and Sahul: prehistoric studies in Southeast Asia, Melanesia and Australia*. New York: Academic Press, pp. 113–67.

Bowler, J., Johnston, H., Olley, J., et al. (2003) New ages for human occupation and climatic change at Lake Mungo, Australia. *Nature* 421, 837–40.

Geneste, J-M., David, B., Plisson, H., et al. (2010) Earliest evidence for ground-edge axes: 35,400 ± 410 cal BP from Jawoyn country, Arnhem Land. *Australian Archaeology* 71, 66–69.

Hiscock, P. (2008) *Archaeology of Ancient Australia*. New York: Routledge.

Hudjashov, G., Kivisild, T., Underhill, P. A., et al. (2007) Revealing the prehistoric settlement of Australia by Y chromosome and mtDNA analysis. *Proceedings of the National Academy of Sciences* 104, 8726–8730.

Lahr, M. (1996) *The Evolution of Modern Human Diversity*. Cambridge: Cambridge University Press.

Merriwether, D., Hodgson, J., Friedlaender, F., et al. (2005) Ancient mitochondrial M haplogroups identified in the Southwest Pacific. *Proceedings of the National Academy of Sciences* 102, 13034–9.

O'Connell, J. & Allen, J. (2004) Dating the colonization of Sahul (Pleistocene Australia – New Guinea): a review of recent research. *Journal of Archaeological Science* 31, 835–53.

Pardoe, C. (2006) Becoming Australian: evolutionary processes and biological variation from ancient to modern times. *Before Farming,* 2006/1, article 4. At www.waspress.co.uk/journals/beforefarming/index/issue.php#200614, accessed Dec. 9, 2011.

Roberts, R., Jones, R., & Smith, M. (1993) Optical dating at Deaf Adder Gorge, Northern Territory, indicates human occupation between 53,000 and 60,000 years ago. *Australian Archaeology* 37, 58–9.

Turney, C., Bird, M., Fifield, L., et al. (2001) Early human occupation at Devil's Lair, southwestern Australia, 50,000 years ago. *Quaternary Research* 55, 3–13.

Veth, P., Smith, M., Bowler, J., et al. (2009) "Excavations at Parnkupirti, Lake Gregory, Great Sandy Desert: OSL Ages for Occupation before the Last Glacial Maximum," *Australian Archaeology* 69, 1–10.

Wroe, S. & Field, J. (2006) A review of the evidence for a human role in the extinction of Australian megafauna and an alternative interpretation. *Quaternary Science Reviews* 25, 2692–2703.

8

The human colonization of the Americas: archaeology

David J. Meltzer

The colonization of the Americas from Siberia after 16 kya was one of the most remarkable achievements of early modern humanity. This chapter outlines the archaeological evidence for this dramatic founding human migration into two new continents.

It was long assumed that the first Americans were Siberian hunters, lured by game across the Bering Land Bridge (Beringia). Beringia emerged during the Pleistocene as precipitation over high latitudes froze, forming glaciers instead of returning to the oceans, thereby drawing down global sea levels by up to 130 m during the coldest phases. Such low sea levels exposed the shallow continental shelf below the Bering Sea, making it possible to walk to America without noticing one was leaving Asia. Yet, once in Alaska, travel further south was blocked by two vast ice sheets – the Cordilleran, which covered present-day British Columbia and portions of the Yukon, and the Laurentide, which stretched from Newfoundland to Alberta, and from the high Arctic to the American Midwest. These buried much of northern North America for thousands of years before, during and after the Last Glacial Maximum (LGM) that peaked at about 21 kya (18 kya bp[1]) (Dyke 2004).

Until recently, the earliest sites known in the Americas were from the Clovis culture, which appeared around 13,340 years ago (11,500 bp), soon after the Cordilleran and Laurentide ice sheets retreated and an ice-free corridor opened between them. In less than a millennium, Clovis fluted projectile points (Figure 8.1) spread throughout North America, suggesting a rapid movement across the continent – and perhaps even the hemisphere. Although no precise examples of Clovis points are found south of Panama (Ranere 2006), many believe Clovis descendants made it to the tip of South America. How had they moved so far so fast? Since Clovis points were early on found with mammoth remains, it was inferred they were big-game hunters, who pursued

The Global Prehistory of Human Migration: The Encyclopedia of Global Human Migration Volume 1,
First Edition. Edited by Peter Bellwood.
© 2013 John Wiley & Sons, Ltd. Published 2015 by John Wiley & Sons, Ltd.

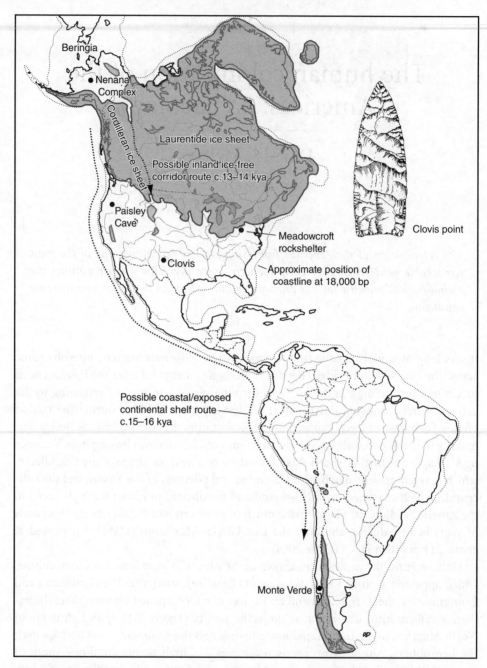

Figure 8.1 The initial settlement of the Americas, from archaeological and genetic perspectives.

their highly mobile prey across the continent. As many large mammals seemingly vanished from the landscape about the same time, it was even suspected they drove those animals to extinction (Martin 1973).

The idea that the first Americans were wide-ranging fast-moving hunters, whose arrival was tied to the rhythms of glaciation, made sense. For a time. But there were also persistent claims of pre-Clovis sites said to be twenty, fifty, or even several hundred thousand years old. Yet none withstood scientific scrutiny. In some instances, the estimated ages were shown to be spurious, in others the supposed artifacts proved to be made by natural processes that fractured stone or bone in ways that mimicked human tool-making. Archaeologists became highly skeptical of pre-Clovis claims (Dincauze 1984).

But then support for pre-Clovis got an unexpected boost. In the late 1980s, geneticists began to develop "molecular clocks" using uniparentally inherited mitochondrial DNA (passed from mother to child), and a decade later the non-recombining portion of the Y-chromosome (inherited from father to son). By gauging the genetic distances between modern Asians and Native Americans, and calculating the time elapsed since they were part of the same gene pool, these molecular-clock estimates seemingly confirmed that the first Americans left their Asian relations in pre-Clovis times.

Yet, genes cannot be directly dated in themselves (though bones or organic material yielding ancient DNA can be radiocarbon-dated, giving some measure of the antiquity of a particular genetic marker). To prove a pre-Clovis presence, a radiocarbon-dated pre-Clovis archaeological site was needed. That came with the excavations at Monte Verde, an extraordinary site in southern Chile where, soon after its occupants departed, the surface on which they had been living was covered by a water-logged peat. That stalled the usual decay processes and preserved a stunning array of organic remains, including wooden timbers, some with bits of adhering mastodon hide, "tent stakes" from huts, a wide range of plants, some charred and others apparently well chewed, and a range of wood, stone, bone, and ivory artifacts (Dillehay 1997). All were dated to 14,625 years ago (12,500 bp).

Although just one thousand years older than Clovis, Monte Verde's distance (about 16,000 km) from Beringia, and the decidedly non-Clovis look of its projectile points, raised questions about who were the first Americans, where they came from, when they arrived, how they traveled south from Alaska at a time when the ice-free corridor had yet to open, whether Monte Verde and Clovis were part of the same or separate colonizing pulses, and how these groups adapted to a landscape that was completely unknown, highly diverse, and changing.

Consider the who and from where questions. Although we assume the first Americans came from northeast Asia, finding their traces has been a challenge. The oldest site in the Siberian Arctic – Yana RHS, dating to 27 kya (Pitulko et al. 2004) – is still about 2,000 km west of the Chukotka Peninsula, the jumping-off point for America (see Figure 4.1 for its location). Currently, the earliest site in far northeastern Asia close to America is only slightly older than 13 kya (11 kya bp) (Goebel et al. 2010). That's too late to be ancestral to Clovis, let alone pre-Clovis. But then, the Siberian archaeological record is sparse and poorly known; earlier evidence may yet be discovered. Even so, on the more intensively surveyed eastern side of Beringia, the earliest Alaskan sites (belonging to the Nenana Complex) are scarcely more than 14,000 years old (12,200 bp) – likewise too young to represent ancestral Monte Verdeans. Nenana sites precede Clovis, but their artifacts don't look particularly Clovis-like.

Our inability to spot ancestral Americans in the Beringia region hardly disproves that they came from Asia. Sites produced by small, highly mobile populations were likely ephemeral, and difficult to find after time and erosion have taken their toll. Nonetheless, the scarcity of sites calls into question the "standstill model" from genetics, which hypothesizes that humans were isolated in Beringia for some 15,000 years before migration into the rest of North America began (Tamm et al. 2007). Such a prolonged occupation ought to have produced a more visible archaeological record than exists.

So *when* and *how* did the first colonists reach America? Colonizers could have walked across Beringia anytime after 33 kya until nearly 11.5 kya (28–10 kya bp) (Brigham-Grette et al. 2004). The landscape was flat, unglaciated, cold, dry, and covered in grassy steppe-tundra, across which people and animals could move east (or even west) with relative ease (which explains why, with a few exceptions, the Pleistocene fauna is virtually identical on both sides of the Bering Sea).

Travel to North America south of the ice sheets was not so easy. The Cordilleran ice sheet covered much of the Pacific coast. Intermittent ice-free areas would not have provided much food or fuel, and travel – whether on foot or by boat – would have been impeded by icebergs, sea ice, heavily crevassed and unstable ice fronts, and sediment draining the ice fields that would have choked tidal waters.

As the ice sheets melted two routes south opened, though not simultaneously. The coast was clear by around 16 kya (13.4 kya bp). The ice-free corridor opened from both ends, roughly along the eastern flank of the Rocky Mountains (Figure 8.1). Initially, this corridor was an impassable wasteland of mudflats, meltwater lakes, and glacial deposits, kept cold by nearby glaciers. It only became stocked with plants and animals, and thus a viable route for humans, around 13.8 kya (12 kya bp) (Dyke 2004).

If colonization took place *before* the LGM, groups could have come via the coast or interior. Although we lack secure evidence of pre-LGM groups in the Americas, we cannot preclude the possibility. On a continent this large, colonists were surely present long before their traces appear on our archaeological radar. But unless we find the very first site in the Americas, the oldest site we have provides only a minimum age for colonization. Correspondingly, genetics may provide a maximum age for colonization, in so far as it reveals when ancestral Asians and Native Americans were part of the same population. Molecular clocks currently put that common ancestry at c.15 kya (see Chapter 9), but this is at best a ballpark figure for several reasons, not least the imprecision of calibrating the ticking of those clocks – more properly, the rate by which mutations occur – against absolute years.

If colonization occurred after the LGM, then presumably colonizers came via the Pacific coast, since the interior corridor was impassable, and remained so until well after Monte Verde was abandoned. Although there are a few late Pleistocene sites along the coast, none are pre-Clovis in age. The effort to find older ones is hampered by postglacial sea-level rise, which drowned much of the Pleistocene coast. Nonetheless, there are regions of southeast Alaska where isostatic rebound (land rising after the heavy load of glaciers has been lifted) and/or tectonic uplift have outpaced sea-level rise, and so preserve the Pleistocene coastline by raising it above contemporary sea level. These areas have yet to receive much archaeological attention.

Although ancestral Monte Verdeans could not have traveled through the ice-free corridor because of their early date, the appearance of Clovis coincides neatly with the opening of that route. So, were Clovis and Monte Verde descendents of the same colonizing pulse? There are no obvious historical or technological links between their artifacts (Dillehay 2008) – but these are cultures widely separated in space and time, so links may be difficult to discern.

Even so, there are hints that Clovis was a separate migration which traversed North America in just a few centuries (Waters & Stafford 2007). That suggests they were crossing an empty landscape. If so, what became of any pre-Clovis colonizers who presumably passed through earlier? It's a good question, but one without a good answer. There are a few pre-Clovis contenders in North America, most notably Paisley Cave, Oregon, which has yielded 14,200-year-old (12,300 bp) human coprolites preserving ancient DNA (Gilbert et al. 2008). Why haven't more pre-Clovis sites been found? It may be that the search has not been in the right places or in the right ways.

The genetic record is equivocal on the question of whether there was more than one migration to the Americas. There are a limited number of mtDNA (only five in total) and Y chromosome (only two) lineages among modern Native American tribes, and it has seemed unlikely that completely separate migrations from Asia would have introduced so few founding lineages. Still, the sample of DNA is small and many groups are not well represented, and recent discoveries in ancient DNA are revealing previously unrecorded lineages, suggesting a more complex colonization history (Malhi et al. 2007).

Assuming Clovis was a separate, later migration into North America, the question of how fast it spread is perhaps not as interesting as *how* and *why* Clovis, and possibly related South American groups, moved so far, so fast, across such a vast, unknown, dynamic, and diverse landscape. The traditional explanation is that they were pursuing wide-ranging big-game, now-extinct Pleistocene mammals, which in North America included some 35 genera, plus another 52 in South America. Of the latter, nearly 70 percent were unique to that continent (Barnosky et al. 2004). Many were large mammals, including several proboscideans (mammoth, mastodon, gompothere), and multiple genera of giant ground sloths (especially in South America). Also headed toward extinction were camels, horses, tapirs, peccaries, and some highly unusual animals like the glyptodont, a mammal weighing upwards of one ton encased in a turtle-like carapace. Preying on these herbivores were carnivores such as the giant short-faced bear, lions and cheetahs, and the aptly named *Smilodon fatalis*, the sabertooth cat (Grayson 2007).

As noted, it has been claimed that Clovis and related South Americans hunted these mammals to extinction (Martin 1973), but there is reason to be skeptical. Despite a rich fossil record of many of these extinct animals, evidence of actual slaughter by hunters is extremely rare. Of the 76 North American archaeological sites said to testify to big-game hunting, only 14 provide unequivocal evidence that humans killed and dismembered the animals (Grayson & Meltzer 2002). And just two genera appear in those sites: mammoth and mastodon. There are no kill sites of the other 33 North American genera that went extinct. The record from South America is equally telling: kill sites of large mammals are extremely rare, limited to two genera (horse and ground sloth), and even these lack secure evidence of human involvement (Borrero 2009).

To be sure, early Americans could, and occasionally did, take big game, perhaps with four-footed help: they had brought their dogs, recently domesticated from wolves, along with them to the Americas (Snyder & Leonard 2006). Still, even with such help there was no strong incentive to tackle large prey. Hunter-gatherers aim to reduce risk, and there is considerable risk of coming home empty-handed or, worse, not coming home at all, when preying on large game (Meltzer 2004).

So what was behind the possibly rapid dispersal of colonists into the Americas? Colonization occurred at the end of the Pleistocene, when the plant and animal communities on which humans depended were changing. Yet, even during the Younger Dryas, a millennium span of northern-hemisphere cooling and biotic change starting 12.9 kya (11 kya bp), those changes proved to be variable across the hemisphere and occurred on a time scale of centuries (Meltzer & Holliday 2010). That was likely not fast enough to be detectable by hunter-gatherers who had to respond to daily, weekly, and seasonal conditions. Moreover, adapting to changing environments was nothing new to them: they'd been meeting the challenges of novel habitats since their ancestors left northeast Asia.

The environment is important in another way, however. As colonists moved south into an ever-more exotic New World, they carried with them a general knowledge of animals and plants, but were increasingly encountering species they had never seen and even some they could not see: colonists would have been exposed to a variety of novel pathogens when they entered the American tropics (Dillehay 2008). They would have faced the greatest risk of failure early on, when their numbers were low, and the landscape and its resources unknown and unpredictable. To reduce that risk, it was to their advantage to learn the landscape as quickly as possible (Meltzer 2004). They had to learn about the abundance and distribution of impermanent resources like animals and plants, as well as more permanent ones like stone or reliable freshwater, in order to know *how to move*. They needed to understand weather and climate, to anticipate better their effects on vital resources and thus to know *when* to move. Furthermore, they had to learn the geography of each unfamiliar place, in order to move across it without getting lost and, importantly, to find the way back, in order to know *where* to move.

Landscape learning must have involved more than their immediate surroundings: insurance for hunter-gatherers is not just knowing what resources are available locally, it's knowing where to go when local conditions deteriorate (Binford 1983). There would have been an incentive to range widely and rapidly across the new landscape to see what was over the next hill, so as to reduce uncertainty and risk.

But there are costs involved in moving too far too fast, since this almost certainly would have meant moving away from other people. Colonizers also had to maintain contact with other dispersing groups, to avoid inbreeding costs or extinction. This would have been more or less difficult depending on the group's size, growth rates, kin structure, age and sex composition, and how rapidly it was moving away from other groups (Moore 2001). Arguably, colonization involved a compromise between multiple demands: maintaining resource returns, maximizing mobility, minimizing group size to hedge the possibility of some environmental calamity, and maintaining contact between dispersed groups to sustain the gene pool (Meltzer 2004).

As one might expect of hunter-gatherers new to a landscape and unfamiliar with its resources, there was a range of items on the menu, including a variety of mammals from bison and caribou to rabbit and fox, as well as birds, fish, turtles, and occasionally (though the evidence is sparse) plants (Cannon & Meltzer 2004). There is tantalizing evidence that they brought one plant – the bottle gourd – to America, though perhaps for use as a container rather than food (Erickson et al. 2005). Likewise, South American colonists in inland areas exploited an extinct species of llama, deer, guanaco, and a variety of small mammals, and along the coast, seabirds, marine fish, and shellfish; in many areas plants such as tubers, pine and palm nuts, prickly pear, and wild potato were gathered (Borerro 2006; Dillehay 1997; Sandweiss 2008).

The toolkit Clovis groups used to exploit those resources is remarkably uniform across North America, though there were variations. It is primarily a biface-based technology, with distinctive tools and tool classes, for example blades, ivory tools, limaces (a slug-shaped unifacial tool), and adze-like forms, occurring in some areas but not others. The toolkit was generalized, adaptable to a variety of tasks and often made out of exotic high-quality stone, which had the virtue of being less prone to failure, longer lasting, and more readily resharpened and quickly refurbished into other forms, as the circumstances required (Ellis 2008).

In contrast, stone tools in early South American assemblages are more diverse, but can be grouped into several apparently contemporaneous traditions: a bifacial tradition, including diagnostic forms such as El Jobo, Fishtail, and Paijan, which is typically found in the Andean region from Columbia to the Southern Cone of Patagonia, and various unifacial, edge-trimmed tools found in forest and parkland areas of northern and central South America (Dillehay 2008). Unlike Clovis groups to the north, South American colonists were not as finicky about the quality of the stone they used to make their tools, which may in turn speak to differences in mobility and adaptation (Borrero 2006).

Sites of this time period throughout the Americas were relatively ephemeral. Evidence of structures, perhaps built of wood, reeds, or other materials that quickly degraded and disappeared are rare, though not absent (Sandweiss 2008). Curiously, caves and rockshelters were commonly used in South America, rarely so in North America. Groups appear not to have stayed long in any one spot, nor returned. Such is the advantage to colonists inhabiting a landscape with few other people, and ample resources.

On such a landscape, hostility toward strangers would have been decidedly disadvantageous; rather, colonists likely had social systems that were sufficiently open to help recognize even strangers as friends. Open social systems are difficult to detect archaeologically, but we may be seeing this in proxy form in their distinctive projectile points. These are stylistically similar within North America, and in broad swaths of South America, and perhaps helped groups recognize one another as descendents of a common people who had gone separate ways years or decades earlier.

But even if it was sometimes temporarily checked, that centrifugal process of dispersal never stopped, and over the centuries, as groups spread farther from one another, they began to settle into different areas and local populations began to expand (Meltzer 2009). As they did, the ties between different groups that had been so vital when there were few people on the landscape and they needed to keep in contact with one another began to break down. So too, the need to maintain common artifacts and cultural bonds. And so, by 12.5 kya (10.5 kya bp) across much of North and South America, the early, nearly pancontinental cultures were replaced by a variety of regionally distinctive groups. These were more restricted geographically, often had new adaptive strategies and new technologies, and more restricted mobility. By then, the initial colonization of the Americas was complete; the process of settling in had begun.

SEE ALSO: 9 The human colonization of the Americas: population genetics

Note

1   Radiocarbon years are provided in parentheses, followed by bp (before present). This is done because the time period under discussion falls partly within the Younger Dryas Chronozone, when amounts of atmospheric radiocarbon fluctuated significantly, leading to calibrations that often have multiple intercepts and thus are imprecise. Calibration curves have improved over the years, but as they are likely to change in the future including radiocarbon ages provides a measure of constancy, and they can be recalibrated with each new calibration iteration.

References

Barnosky, A. D., Koch, P. L., Feranec, R. S., et al. (2004) Assessing the causes of late Pleistocene extinctions on the continents. *Science* 306, 70–75.

Binford, L. R. (1983) Long term land use patterns: some implications for archaeology. In R. C. Dunnell and D. K. Grayson (eds.), *Lulu Linear Punctated: Essays in Honor of George Irving Quimby*. University of Michigan Anthropological Papers 72, pp. 27–53.

Borrero, L. A. (2006) Paleoindians without mammoths and archaeologists without projectile points? The archaeology of the first inhabitants of the Americas. In J. Morrow and C. Gnecco (eds.), *Paleoindian Archaeology: A Hemispheric Perspective*. Gainesville: University Press of Florida, pp. 9–20.

Borrero, L. A. (2009) The elusive evidence: the archaeological record of the South American extinct megafauna. In G. Haynes (ed.), *American Megafaunal Extinctions at the end of the Pleistocene*. New York: Springer, pp. 145–168.

Brigham-Grette, J., Lozhkin, A., Anderson, P. M. et al. (2004) Paleoenvironmental conditions in western Beringia before and during the Last Glacial Maximum. In D. Madsen (ed.), *Entering America: Northeast Asia and Beringia Before the Last Glacial Maximum*. Salt Lake City: University of Utah Press, pp. 29–61.

Cannon, M. D. and Meltzer, D. J. (2004) Early Paleoindian foraging: examining the faunal evidence for large mammal specialization and regional variability in prey choice. *Quaternary Science Reviews* 23 (18/19), 1955–1987.

Dillehay, T. D. (1997) *Monte Verde: A Late Pleistocene Settlement in Chile*, vol. 2: *The Archaeological Context and Interpretation*. Washington, DC: Smithsonian Institution Press.

Dillehay, T. D. (2008) Profiles in Pleistocene history. In H. Silverman and W. Isbell (eds.), *Handbook of South American Archaeology*. New York: Springer, pp. 29–43.

Dincauze, D. (1984) An archaeological evaluation of the case for pre-Clovis occupations. *Advances in World Archaeology* 3, 275–323.

Dyke, A. (2004) An outline of North American deglaciation with emphasis on central and northern Canada. In J. Ehlers and P. L. Gibbard (eds.), *Quaternary Glaciations-Extent and Chronology*, part II: *Developments in Quaternary Science*. Amsterdam: Elsevier, vol. 2b, pp. 373–424.

Ellis, C. (2008) The fluted point tradition and the Arctic small tool tradition: what's the connection? *Journal of Anthropological Archaeology* 27, 298–314.

Erickson, D., Smith, B., Clarke, A. et al. (2005) An Asian origin for a 10,000 year old domesticated plant in the Americas. *Proceedings of the National Academy of Sciences* 102, 18315–18320.

Gilbert, T., Jenkins, D., Götherstrom, A. et al. (2008) DNA from pre-Clovis human coprolites in Oregon, North America. *Science* 320, 786–789.

Goebel, T., Slobodin, S. and Waters, M. (2010) New dates from Ushki-1, Kamchatka, confirm 13,000 cal BP age for earliest Paleolithic occupation. *Journal of Archaeological Science* 37, 2640–2649.

Grayson, D. K. (2007) Deciphering North American Pleistocene extinctions. *Journal of Anthropological Research* 63, 185–213.

Grayson, D. K. and Meltzer, D. J. (2002) Clovis hunting and large mammal extinction: a critical review of the evidence. *Journal of World Prehistory* 16, 313–359

Malhi, R., Kemp, B., Eshelman, J., et al. (2007) Mitochondrial haplogroup M discovered in prehistoric Americans. *Journal of Archaeological Science* 34, 642–648.

Martin, P. S. (1973) The discovery of America. *Science* 179, 969–974

Meltzer, D. J. (2004) Modeling the initial colonization of the Americas: issues of scale, demography, and landscape learning. In C. M. Barton, G. A. Clark, D. R. Yesner and G. A. Pearson (eds.), *The Settlement of the American Continents: a Multidisciplinary Approach to Human Biogeography*. Tucson: University of Arizona Press, pp. 123–137.

Meltzer, D. J. (2009) *First Peoples in a New World: Colonizing Ice Age America*. Berkeley: University of California Press.

Meltzer, D. J. and Holliday, V. T. (2010) Would North American Paleoindians have noticed Younger Dryas age climate changes? *Journal of World Prehistory* 23, 1–41.

Moore, J. (2001) Evaluating five models of human colonization. *American Anthropologist* 103, 395–408.

Pitulko, V., Nikolsky, P., Girya, E. et al. (2004) The Yana RHS site: humans in the Arctic before the Last Glacial Maximum. *Science* 303, 52–56.

Ranere, A. (2006) The Clovis colonization of central America. In J. Morrow and C. Gnecco (Eds.), *Paleoindian Archaeology: a Hemispheric Perspective*. Gainesville: University Press of Florida, pp. 69–85.

Sandweiss, D. (2008) Early fishing societies in western South America. In H. Silverman and W. Isbell, (Eds.), *Handbook of South American Archaeology*. New York: Springer, pp. 145–156.

Snyder, L. M. and Leonard, J. (2006) Dog. *Handbook of North American Indians, Volume 3, Environment, Origins, and Population*. Washington, DC: Smithsonian Institution Press, pp. 452–462.

Tamm, E., Kivisild, T., Reidla, M. et al. (2007) Beringian standstill and spread of Native American founders. *PLoS One* 9, e8291–e8296.

Waters, M. R. and Stafford, T. W. Jr. (2007) Redefining the age of Clovis: Implications for the peopling of the New World. *Science* 315, 1122–1126.

9

The human colonization of the Americas: population genetics

Simon G. Southerton

This chapter documents the genetic evidence for the colonization of the Americas, a topic already introduced archaeologically in chapter 8. On this occasion, the two chronologies (archaeological and genetic) appear to be in relatively good agreement.

Important new insights into the nature of human migration into the Americas have emerged from the study of genetic variation in Native American and Siberian populations. The Asian origin of essentially all Native Americans was confirmed by the middle of the 20th century, using classical genetic markers such as blood group and enzyme polymorphisms (O'Rourke & Raff 2010). During the last two decades, much higher resolution molecular studies have shed considerable light on the Asian source populations of these ancestral groups, the timing of migrations into the Americas, the number of colonizing populations, and the routes these people took as they entered North and South America (Schurr 2004). Discoveries from these studies are contributing to significant revisions in our understanding of Native American prehistory.

As the ancestors of Native Americans separated from neighboring Asian populations they gradually became genetically distinct. The earliest ancestral groups carried a subset of the genetic variation contained in the surrounding Asian populations. Mutations unique to Native Americans have also arisen in their populations since separation. Most research to date has focused on uniparentally inherited mitochondrial DNA or the non-recombining portion of the Y chromosome (NRY). By analyzing molecular variation in these maternal and paternal lineages, molecular geneticists have been able to detect signals of the patterns and timing of past migrations. Rapid advances in genomics technology are also now making it feasible to study the vast stores of genetic variation present in the autosomes.

The Global Prehistory of Human Migration: The Encyclopedia of Global Human Migration Volume 1,
First Edition. Edited by Peter Bellwood.

Migration to Beringia

The earliest immigrants to the Americas brought with them a subset of the maternal and paternal DNA lineages present in their Asian source populations. Mitochondrial and Y-chromosome DNA variation in North, Central and South America indicate unambiguously that the ancestors of Native Americans originated in Asia. Virtually all modern Native Americans possess an mtDNA lineage that belongs to one of five founding haplogroups, which are all present among native populations of Siberia. These maternal lineages have been designated A, B, C, D, and X (Brown et al. 1998; Schurr et al. 1990). Of these haplogroups, only X is present in both central Asian and European populations; however, the X haplogroup is large and diverse, and the X lineage (X2a) found in Native American populations represents a distinct branch on the Eurasian X lineage tree (Reidla et al. 2003). A small proportion of mtDNA lineages found in indigenous peoples (<1%) are derived from recent non-native (European or African) admixture. Ancient mtDNA analysis has revealed the same founding haplogroups described in extant populations, thus confirming the genetic continuity between extinct and contemporary Native Americans (Stone & Stoneking 1998).

Much higher rates of male-mediated admixture into Native American populations (over 16%) since colonial times has made the analysis of Native American-specific Y chromosomes more complicated. The two most common founding NRY lineages within Native American populations are Q-M3 (also called Q1a3a) and C-3b (Karafet et al. 2008). In addition, recent studies of autosomal genetic variation have revealed a decline in genetic variation with distance from Bering Strait (Wang et al. 2007).

The paternal and maternal ancestors of Native Americans likely derived from central Asia, in the vicinity of southern Siberia and northern Mongolia. Asian populations that have the highest proportions of New World maternal and paternal lineages are generally located in the region immediately surrounding Lake Baikal, encompassing the Altai and Sayan Mountains (Karafet et al. 1999; Starikovskaya et al. 2005). Interestingly, these late Pleistocene migratory parties included domesticated dogs, as mtDNA sequences isolated from ancient dog remains from Latin America and Alaska are most closely related to the DNA lineages present in Old World dogs (Leonard et al. 2002).

Each of the maternal and paternal founding lineage groups found among Native Americans contains lineages with mutations that occurred after the original founders became separated from their Asian source population. Analysis of the degree of variation in each lineage has been used to calculate approximately when central Asian and American populations separated from each other. Recent estimates of coalescence times for each of the five founding New World mtDNA lineages are 25 to 20 kya, while estimates based on NRY variability suggest that divergence occurred after 22.5 kya, possibly as late as 20 to 15 kya (Goebel et al. 2008), thus after the LGM, which peaked at around 20 kya. The coalescence data have led some geneticists to conclude that all Native Americans descend from a single founding population that colonized northeast Asia, including Beringia, prior to the LGM (Fagundes et al. 2008), although archaeological evidence for the presence of humans in Beringia around the LGM is currently non-existent (see Goebel et al. 2010). The degree of mtDNA lineage diversity in contemporary Native Americans has also been used to estimate the size of the original founding population. Although imprecise, between 100 and 1,000 females may have been in the founding groups from which all Native Americans descend (Fagundes et al. 2008).

Migration into North and South America

Geographic patterns in the distribution of the five founding mtDNA lineages in the Americas have been used to shed light on the number of founder migrations and the possible routes these migratory groups took. Haplogroups A–D are observed in extant Amerindian populations from North, Central, and South America (Schurr 2004), which strongly suggests that all four of these mtDNA lineages were present in the original migration(s) to the New World. There are different trends within the three Native American linguistic groups (Amerind, Na-Dené, Eskimo-Aleut) proposed by Greenberg and his colleagues (1986). Na-Dené and Eskimo-Aleut speaking populations have predominantly haplogroup A and D mtDNAs, and their original founders may have lacked haplogroups B and C. Consequently, they are thought to have resulted from a later expansion into North America than that giving rise to the original Amerindians. It was recently shown that a subclade of D2 lineages present in Chukchi, Siberian Inuit, and Aleuts (D2b) has a coalescence date of 8 to 6 kya (Derenko et al. 2007). This implies that the ancestors of modern Eskimo-Aleuts spread from Siberia into the Americas in the middle-Holocene (see chapters 44 and 45), which is in harmony with earlier explanations based on dental evidence (Greenberg et al. 1986).

Analyses of mtDNA subclades within haplogroups has been particularly useful for exploring the nature of Native American migrations from Beringia into the remainder of the Americas. Three subclades of mtDNA subhaplogroup C1 are widely distributed among North, Central, and South American Indians but absent in Asian populations (Tamm et al. 2007). This suggests that these subclades evolved after the central Asian–Native American split, as the first Americans were dispersing from Beringia. The coalescence estimates for them is 16.6–11.2 kya, which suggests that the colonization of the Americas south of the continental ice sheets may have occurred after the LGM. A date of 16–17 kya, as suggested by the genetic evidence, is in agreement with recent archaeological discoveries (e.g. from Monte Verde in Chile and Meadowcroft in Pennsylvania) that predate Clovis lithic sites in North America.

Until recently, it was widely accepted that people belonging to the Clovis culture were the first to enter the Americas, around 13 kya and thus during the period of postglacial climatic amelioration. They were believed to have entered North America through Alaska via an interior ice-free corridor, and then rapidly expanded into the remainder of the Americas. However, the distribution of molecular genetic variation observed in contemporary Native American populations is not consistent with such a late entry or rapid dispersal of humans across the whole of the New World, as the Clovis-First model would require (Fagundes et al. 2008; Perego et al. 2009). A recent statistical analysis of nuclear DNA data was also most consistent with a pre-Clovis settlement model (Ray et al. 2010). Meanwhile, human coprolites recovered from Paisley Cave, Oregon, have been found to predate the Clovis complex by more than 1000 ^{14}C years (Gilbert et al 2008).

Revised migration models have recently been proposed to account for the accumulating molecular data. Schurr and Sherry (2004) proposed that there were two migrations from Siberia to South America around 20–15 kya. The first migration was along the Pacific coast, bringing lineages from haplogroups A, B, C, and D. This was followed by a second migration (containing haplogroup X) into North America after the ice-free corridor appeared. This model is supported by the geographic distribution of two rare mtDNA lineages: the D4h3 lineage which appears at highest frequency along the Pacific coast of North and South America, and the X2a lineage which is restricted to northeastern North America (Perego et al. 2009). O'Rourke and Raff (2010) recently proposed that pre-LGM coastal migration may have occurred via the northern Beringian coastline. Such a migration scenario along the northern and eastern seaboards of North America may have provided source populations for the development of the Clovis culture in the region where the earliest appearance and highest density of Clovis artifacts occurs. However, there is no archaeological support as yet for such an early entry, especially along the Arctic seaboard.

The initial colonization of South America appears to have taken place along the western coastline (Perego et al. 2009; Rothhammer & Dillehay 2009). Once south of the developing ice masses, coastal populations could have moved more rapidly than migratory groups located in the interior of the continents, reaching the southern regions of South America within a relatively short time period. The highest levels of genetic diversity are observed in western populations, and these are considerably lower in Brazilian populations. Wang et al (2007) also found high genetic similarity between Andean and Mesoamerican populations. This was interpreted as being consistent with an early coastal colonization along the west coast of South America, and a subsequent peopling of the eastern coastline.

Comparisons between molecular data from past and present Amerindian populations have revealed regional and temporal patterns of population settlement and movement within the Americas. In general, ancient DNA studies indicate that once Amerindian populations settled a particular region, they tended to become and remain genetically distinct over thousands of years (O'Rourke et al. 2000). Continuity has been observed between Anasazi and modern Puebloan groups, ancient Tainos and modern Puerto Ricans, and ancient and modern populations in southern Chile and Patagonia (reviewed by Schurr 2004). However, evidence of regional migration has also been detected. For example, clear differences in haplogroup frequencies between ancient and historical populations from the Great Basin are thought to be due to the arrival of Numic peoples in that area (Kaestle & Smith 2001). Ancient Hopewell and Adena remains from the Ohio Valley have genetic ties with contemporary Great Lakes populations (see Schurr 2004).

Controversial migration theories

Molecular genetics discoveries are contributing important new data to often heated debates surrounding less widely supported hypotheses of the settlement of the Americas. The restricted distribution of the X lineage in eastern North America was initially seen to support a "Solutrean hypothesis," that the ancestors of the Clovis people were derived from an Upper Paleolithic population that migrated from Iberia (Bradley & Stanford 2004). According to this model, Solutrean people migrated from Western Europe during the LGM across an ice sheet skirting the Atlantic Ocean until they reached North America, where their descendants developed the Clovis lithic technology. However, the sum of the molecular evidence lends little support to this hypothesis. The coalescence ages of all five founding maternal lineages are very similar, suggesting they were all present in the Beringian founding population from which the Americas were colonized between 20 and 15 kya (Fagundes et al. 2008; Perego et al. 2009). The failure to identify a closely related X lineage in Siberian populations is most likely due to the low frequency of this haplogroup in Asia.

There is currently little evidence that Native Americans migrated beyond the Americas into the Pacific or that Polynesians settled in large numbers in the Americas. A distinctive "Polynesian lineage" belonging to the mtDNA B haplogroup, which is shared by almost all extant Polynesians, has not been detected among Native American populations. There is currently no genetic evidence that peoples from Melanesia, Polynesia, Australia, Africa, Europe, China, or the Middle East contributed significantly to the pre-historic Native American gene pool. The molecular genetic data thus offer little support for settlement theories at the fringe of mainstream anthropology and archaeology. Interestingly, in response to molecular research, the Mormon Church (Church of Jesus Christ of Latter-day Saints) recently changed its belief that Israelites were the "principal ancestors" of Native Americans to a still overly hopeful qualification that they were "among the ancestors of the American Indians" (Moore 2007). However, the question of whether there could have been small admixtures from other parts of the world is frequently raised by journalists, maverick anthropologists, and revisionist historians.

Summary and outlook

Evidence from molecular research using mtDNA, NRY, and autosomal genetic systems suggests ancestral Native Americans entered the Americas after the LGM, between 20 and 15 kya. Their entry predated the opening of the ice-free corridor and the appearance of the Clovis culture, and colonization was most likely to have occurred via a coastal route during their initial migration. The data suggest the ancestors of modern circumarctic populations, such as the Inuit, Aleuts, and Na-Dené entered the Americas during the middle Holocene. Further refinements of migration scenarios during the colonization of the Americas are likely to emerge as modern archaeological and genetics tools are used to address common questions. Research in more widely dispersed ancient populations will increase the accuracy of coalescence estimates.

SEE ALSO: 8 The human colonization of the Americas: archaeology; 41 Polynesia, East and South, including transpacific migration; 44 North America: Eskimo-Aleut linguistic history; 45 North America: Paleoeskimo and Inuit archaeology

References

Bradley, B. & Stanford, D. (2004) The North Atlantic ice-edge corridor: a possible Palaeolithic route to the New World. *World Archaeology* 36, 459–478.

Brown, M. D., Hosseini, S. H., Torroni, A., et al. (1998) MtDNA haplogroup X: An ancient link between Europe western Asia and North America? *American Journal of Human Genetics* 63, 1852–1861.

Derenko, M., Malyarchuk, B., Grzybowski, T., et al. (2007) Phylogeographic analysis of mitochondrial DNA in Northern Asian Populations. *American Journal of Human Genetics* 81, 1025–1041.

Fagundes, N. J. R., Kanitz, R., Eckert, A., et al. (2008) Mitochondrial population genomics supports a single pre-Clovis origin with a coastal route for the peopling of the Americas. *American Journal of Human Genetics* 82, 583–592.

Gilbert, M. T. P., Jenkins, D. L., Götherstrom, A., et al. (2008) DNA from pre-Clovis human coprolites in Oregon, North America. *Science* 320, 786–789.

Goebel, T., Waters, M. R., & O'Rourke, D. H. (2008) The Late Pleistocene dispersal of modern humans in the Americas. *Science* 319, 1497–1502.

Goebel, T., Slobodin, S. B., & Waters, M. R. (2010) New dates from Ushki-1, Kamchatka, confirm 13,000calBP age for earliest Paleolithic occupation. *Journal of Archaeological Science* 37, 2640–2649.

Greenberg, J. H., Turner, C. G., & Zegura, S. L. (1986) The settlement of the Americas: a comparison of the linguistic, dental and genetic evidence. *Current Anthropology* 27, 477–497.

Kaestle, F. A. & Smith, D. G. (2001) Ancient mitochondrial DNA evidence for prehistoric population movement: the Numic expansion. *American Journal of Physical Anthropology* 115(1), 1–12.

Karafet, T. M., Zegura, S. L., Posukh, O., et al. (1999) Ancestral Asian source(s) of New World Y-chromosome founder haplotypes. *American Journal of Human Genetics* 64, 817–831.

Karafet, T. M., Zegura, S. L., & Hammer, M. F. (2008) Y Chromosomes. In D. Ubelaker (ed)., *Handbook of North American Indians*, vol. 3, *Environment, Origins, and Population.* Washington, DC: Smithsonian.

Leonard, J. A., Wayne, R. K., Wheeler, J., et al. (2002) Ancient DNA evidence for Old World origin of New World dogs. *Science* 298, 1613–1616.

Moore, C. A. (2007) Intro change in Book of Mormon spurs discussion. Deseret News, Salt Lake City. (http://www.deseretnews.com/article/695226049/Intro-change-in-Book-of-Mormon-spurs-discussion.html) accessed Jan 22, 2010.

O'Rourke, D. H. & Raff, J. A. (2010) The human genetic history of the Americas: the final frontier. *Current Biology* 20, R202–R207.

O'Rourke, D. H., Hayes, M. G., & Carlyle, S. W. (2000) Ancient DNA studies in physical anthropology. *Annual Review of Anthropology* 29, 217–242.

Perego, U. A., Achilli, A., Angerhofer, N., et al. (2009) Distinctive Paleo-Indian migration routes from Beringia marked by two rare mtDNA haplogroups. *Current Biology* 19, 1–8.

Ray, N., Wegmann, D., Fagundes, N. J. R., et al. (2010) A statistical evaluation of models for the initial settlement of the American continent emphasizes the importance of gene flow with Asia. *Molecular Biology and Evolution* 27, 337–345.

Reidla, M., Kivisild, T., Metspalu, E., et al. (2003) Origin and diffusion of mtDNA haplogroup X. *American Journal of Human Genetics* 73, 1178–1190.

Rothhammer, F. & Dillehay, T. D. (2009) The Late Pleistocene colonization of South America: an interdisciplinary perspective. *Annals of Human Genetics* 73, 540–549.

Schurr, T. G. (2004) The peopling of the New World: perspectives from molecular anthropology. *Annual Review of Anthropology* 33, 551–583.

Schurr, T. G., Ballinger, S. W., Gan, Y. Y., et al. (1990) Amerindian mitochondrial DNAs have rare Asian mutations at high frequencies, suggesting they are derived from 4 primary maternal lineages. *American Journal of Human Genetics* 46, 613–623.

Schurr, T. G. & Sherry, S. T. (2004) Mitochondrial DNA and Y chromosome diversity and the peopling of the Americas: evolutionary and demographic evidence. *American Journal of Human Biology* 16, 420–439.

Starikovskaya, E. B., Sukernik, R. I., Derbeneva, O. A., et al. (2005) Mitochondrial DNA diversity in indigenous populations of the southern extent of Siberia, and the origins of Native American haplogroups. *Annals of Human Genetics* 69, 67–89.

Stone, A. C. & Stoneking, M. (1998) MtDNA analysis of a prehistoric Oneota population: Implications for the peopling of the New World. *American Journal of Human Genetics* 62, 1153–1170.

Tamm, E., Kivisild, T., Reidla, M., et al. (2007) Beringian standstill and spread of Native American founders. *Public Library of Science (PLoS) ONE* 2(9); online e829. doi:10.1371/journal.pone.0000829.

Wang, S., Lewis, C. M., Jakobsson, M., et al. (2007) Genetic variation and population structure in Native Americans. *Public Library of Science (PLoS) Genetics* 3, 2049–2067.

Part II
Holocene migrations

10

Neolithic migrations: food production and population expansion

Peter Bellwood

This chapter introduces the development of food production amongst Holocene human societies and discusses the likely repercussions in terms of population growth and territorial expansion, as visible in the archaeological record. It leads into the following chapter, on the expansions of language families in prehistoric times.

The worldwide archaeological record offers many instances, dated with varying degrees of reliability, of the appearance of domesticated crops and animals and the beginnings of settled agricultural life. At present, this database indicates that agriculture emerged directly from a hunter-gatherer background, without external diffusion, in at least six regions of the world (see Figure 10.1). These were the Fertile Crescent of the Middle East (c.9500–8000 BCE), the middle and lower courses of the Yangzi and Yellow river basins of China (c.7000–5000 BCE), the New Guinea highlands (before 4500 BCE), central Mexico (c.3000–2000 BCE), the western slopes of the Peruvian Andes (c.3000–2000 BCE), and the Eastern Woodlands of the USA (c.2000–1000 BCE) (Barker 2007; Bellwood 2005; Kennett & Winterhalder 2006; Zeder et al. 2006). Other possible regions of early agriculture, of less certain date and significance, occur in the Amazon basin, India, and sub-Saharan Africa, in the latter case in Ethiopia, the Sahel parkland zone at about 15°N, and the northern rainforest fringes of West Africa. However, it is quite possible that native crops and animals were domesticated by people who entered some of these regions with an existing knowledge of cultivation and animal husbandry – current data are simply not always strong enough for firm statements to be made. All of the above-mentioned regions are discussed in the following chapters.

It is necessary to stress here that two separate issues are involved in all debates about where, when, and why agriculture developed. One issue concerns human agricultural behavior, expressed through systems of plant cultivation and animal husbandry. Such behavior was conscious, repetitive, seasonal, and carried landscape consequences in terms of the creation of fields, ditches, terraces, forest clearance, and so

The Global Prehistory of Human Migration: The Encyclopedia of Global Human Migration Volume 1,
First Edition. Edited by Peter Bellwood.
© 2013 John Wiley & Sons, Ltd. Published 2015 by John Wiley & Sons, Ltd.

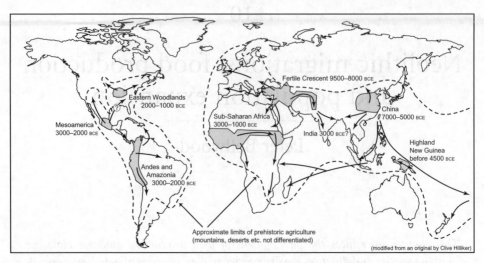

Figure 10.1 The many homelands of agriculture, with directions of dispersal and dates that refer to the transition periods from pre-domesticated and low-level food production to high levels of agricultural dependency.

forth. The other issue is domestication per se – visible in the genetic changes selected for by human interference in the breeding cycles of animals and plants. Cultivation/husbandry and domestication are not one and the same thing. In the Middle East, for instance, people were cultivating wild annual cereals for a millennium or more before the carbonized remains of those cereal species recovered from archaeological sites reveal the basic changes in stem, seed coat, and grain structure that botanists recognize as characteristic of "domesticated" plants. In the annual cereals such changes included loss of the ability to disperse seeds through shattering when ripe, loss of seasonal seed dormancy and the correlated sensitivity to day length, reduction in the thicknesses of the protective coats around seeds, increased ear or panicle size, and the development of synchronous ripening of seed heads. For animals they included reductions in body size, together with increases in docility in behavior, and in the yields of secondary products such as wool and milk. Selection for such features would have been enhanced when cultivators moved husbanded crops and animals outside their home ranges, away from the risk of back-crossing with wild populations.

Of the major regions of early agriculture, we look to the Middle East for the origins of wheat, barley, flax (for linen), certain legumes (pod-bearing plants like peas and lentils), sheep, goats, pigs, and cattle; to China for the origins of rice (*Oryza sativa japonica*), foxtail millet, soybean, pigs, and chickens; to Africa and India for cattle, legumes, rice (*Oryza glaberrima* and *Oryza sativa indica*, respectively), and several species of millet; and to various regions of the Americas for maize, manioc, beans, squashes, tomatoes, potatoes, and animals such as turkeys and llamas. These are only some of the major species – the minor ones would make a very lengthy list indeed. Some animals in Eurasia, such as pigs and cattle, and some plants, especially in the Americas, were domesticated more than once. However, as noted above, this need not mean that every domestication of a plant or animal species was necessarily associated with a totally independent transition to agriculture from a foraging background. Many of these multiple domestications occurred as farmers moved into new regions and naturally paid attention to local wild species and their usage by indigenous hunter-gatherers.

How and why did agriculture begin?

As the Middle East is one of the best understood regions of agricultural origin, there are reasonably detailed answers to this question for that region, in terms at least of context, but perhaps not of total causality. This is the region that witnessed by far the earliest and most significant transition to agriculture, in demographic terms, followed very closely by that in China. The transition to agriculture in Western Asia was based on local resources of wild annual cereals, legumes (peas and lentils), and wild rumi-nants such as sheep and goats. The original distributions of these species can be reconstructed in reasonable detail (Diamond 2002; Willcox 2005; Zeder 2008). The transition occurred between 9500 and 8000 BCE from a baseline of relatively sedentary "Natufian" (microlith-using) hunter-gatherer communities, during a time when cli-mates attained levels of warmth, reliable winter growing-season rainfall, and long-term stability much greater than during the immediately preceding Younger Dryas mini-glaciation, a correlation which probably was not coincidental for the rise of incipient agriculture (Richerson et al. 2001; see also chapter 1).

However, climate alone does not explain agriculture – if it did, then the whole world within agricultural latitudes would have undergone the transition in unison, and this manifestly did not happen. In the Middle East, the sheer concentration of domesticable annual plants and herd animals capable of high and reliable yields of food and other products undoubtedly helped. Many archaeologists believe that the transition in the Middle East reflected Younger Dryas (mini-glacial) risk management prior to the early Holocene period of climatic warmth and stability, and/or the existence of social competition via feasting as an inducement to increased food production in growing sedentary communities. Prior population growth amongst late Palaeolithic hunter-gatherers could have been another factor. In fact, we do not know exactly why farming began anywhere in the world, and it is unlikely that there was ever a single worldwide cause. It is also not absolutely clear whether it was connected with the production of more food for humans (and perhaps domesticated animals), with the need for fibers for clothing and cordage, or with both (Gilligan 2011).

As far as the Middle East is concerned, agriculture developed initially, and rapidly, in an overall region covering the lands at the eastern edge of the Mediterranean, extending into southeastern Turkey, northern Iraq, and western Iran (see chapters 16 and 17). The transition to agriculture here involved a shift from the harvesting and replanting of wild cereals, perhaps collected while still slightly unripe or green (a stage at which they will not shatter and lose their seeds on collection), to a harvesting of fully ripe grain. With continual replanting in new ground each autumn of stored seed from the previous harvest, the resulting selection pressures on the plant genotypes would eventually have produced the altered features which today we recognize as "domesticated." In western Asia, this development of fully domesticated features in cereals required perhaps two to three millennia, as it did in China (Willcox 2005; Fuller 2007; Fuller et al. 2010). As for the humans, they grew rapidly in numbers (Bocquet-Appel & Bar-Yosef 2008; Gignoux et al. 2011), as indeed did their domesticated plants and animals, and developed a remarkably fast-spreading propensity for sedentary village life and associated cultural habits.

In understanding the origins of agriculture in all of the six or more homeland regions, we need to stress that the key to success was the practice of cultivation with replanting, usually in a specially prepared plot which then had to be guarded against pests while the crop was ripening. As noted, morphological (genetic) domestication of plants and animals was a logical result of cultivation and husbandry, but, in most regions for which good evidence exists, this occurred later than the initial evidence for human production of cereal crops, often several millennia later. Indeed, it could have been an unintentional result of human action in many cases, although we are hardly in a position to pronounce strongly on this. The first cultivated crops were wild in a genetic sense, but as selection pressures increased with human manipulation, they began to change their visual appearances and growth habits. Some have even become totally dependent on human management for survival, for instance some modern cereals such as maize can no longer disperse their seeds by natural means when ripe. The relationship between humans and their domesticated food species is truly one of mutual dependence.

What happened in the interval between full foraging and full farming?

The above narrative will perhaps give the impression that the transition to agriculture was a fairly straightforward and relatively rapid progression, with few complications. However, some hunter-gatherers as observed ethnographically can be said to impose selective pressures on the species they exploit, and occasionally to indulge in activities akin to cultivation (replanting, protection, even casual irrigation, and the like). This means that hunters and farmers are not like chalk and cheese, ever separate in behavior. All agriculturalists hunt and gather if and when they can – we still go fishing in the wild today and some people in modern urban societies are still keen on recreational hunting practices. Hunters and gatherers can also exploit domesticated species that they acquire from adjacent farmers. Bruce Smith (2001) has coined the term "low-level food production" to refer to such combinations of hunting, gathering, and minor exploitation of domesticated crops and animals. If we apply such observations from the recent past to interpretations of deeper prehistory, they can give the impression that the development of successful food production was always a drawn-out and very gradual process, in which populations laboriously increased their dependence upon produced food, perhaps by a few percent per millennium.

I have doubts about such interpretations because there are important issues of historical contingency about low-level food production that must be considered. If we examine the ethnographic record of the past two centuries or so, we find that very few tribal populations existed in economies where hunting/gathering and farming were evenly mixed. Furthermore, some ethnographic hunter-gatherer groups who followed such practices, for instance in the Great Basin of North America, did so because their ancestors were formerly farmers in regions that became marginal for agriculture and so had to turn to hunting and gathering to survive (Hill 2002; Bellwood 2005). Low-level food production only existed in agriculturally marginal circumstances where more efficient food producers could not compete or where former food producers had switched to increased foraging in difficult environmental circumstances. The concept is undoubtedly significant, but it needs to be kept in perspective.

While early farmers clearly had to undergo some kind of low-level food production stage in the transition from foraging into farming, the successful groups did not remain in this "middle ground" for very long. "Very long," of course, is a relative concept, and it has already been noted that domesticated crops and animals perhaps required two or three millennia to develop fully from wild forebears. But 2000 years is not a long time in the total span of human evolution, even if we focus only on *Homo sapiens*. During these two millennia in the Middle East, China, and Mesoamerica, people progressed from the occasional cultivation of wild plants and the taming of wild animals to an eventual dependence on the most useful domesticated species of food and fiber-bearing plants, together with meat, milk, and wool-bearing animals. Similar transitions probably occurred in tropical regions where tubers and fruits were domesticated, such as New Guinea and Amazonia, but these regions never developed the high productivity associated with cereals such as maize and rice, at least not until these crops were introduced from outside sources (Harris 2002). Likewise, only the Middle East, China, and the Andes had important tameable and high meat-yielding native animal species available for domestication (Diamond 2002).

In human demographic terms, the massive significance of agriculture based on the major cereals and domesticated animals cannot be emphasized enough. Tropical regions with only domesticated fruits and tubers never generated the huge human populations of regions such as the Middle East and China, or, in later millennia, Mesoamerica and the Andes. How many people can be supported by an agricultural system as it develops in a fertile environment from origins to a full state of animal and plant domestication? I give here some examples from the Yellow and Yangzi river basins of China, which underwent these changes between 6500 and 2000 BCE, prior to the development of the historical Shang Dynasty and the Chinese Bronze Age (see chapter 26). For Shandong Province in the lower Yellow River basin, Liu (2004) records an increase in site numbers from 16 in the early Neolithic Beixin phase (6000 BCE) to 893 in the late Neolithic Longshan phase (2500 BCE). Beixin sites are small, but Longshan sites are up to 246 ha in size. The Zhengzhou and Luoyang regions of Henan (Yellow River) witnessed a growth trajectory from 68 settlements up to 6 hectares in maximum size, at 6500 BCE, to 516 settlements up to 1 sq km in maximum size, at 2500 BCE (Yang 2004: 126). Further south, in the Dongting Lake region of the middle Yangzi Basin, Zhang and Hung (2008) record an increase from 22 small sites in the Peng-toushan Phase (6000 BCE) to 200 sites, including some very large ones, in the Qujialing-Shijiahe Phase (3000 BCE).

In situations such as these, over the three-to-four-millennia time periods involved, we could clearly have factors of 50 to 100, or more, in multiplications of population in the survey regions concerned. By 3000 BCE, the Yellow and Yangzi basins probably had some of the densest populations in the world, at that time. Actual population numbers can be roughly estimated if one makes assumptions about individual or family requirements for floor space. For instance, based on settlement areas, Qiao (2007) estimates a 50-fold increase in population between the Peiligang Phase (6000 BCE) and the Erlitou Phase (2000 BCE) in the 219 sq km Yiluo region of Henan Province (Yellow River Valley), with total population estimates of 217 people for the Peiligang and over 10,000 for the Erlitou.

Similar figures to the above can be presented for other regions of agricultural origin and expansion, but China was perhaps pre-eminent in the demographic stakes because of the tremendous fertility of its riverine plains, its terraces of loess (wind-blown fertile silt of glacial origin), and its benign monsoonal and warm temperate climate. Other regions such as the Middle East and Mesoamerica had more fragile environments, although this certainly did not stop them from creating wonderful patterns of cultural complexity as agricultural societies evolved.

Once a lifestyle based on cultivation had developed, the momentum towards increasing dependence on cultivation would have grown rapidly. Richerson, Boyd, and Bettinger (2001: 395) have used the graphic term "competitive ratchet" to describe such situations. Once one group obtained a demographic advantage as a result of adopting systematic cultivation and planting, others would have followed rapidly, if only to maintain a *status quo*, a balancing of numbers. Eventually, a need for new space would have arrived, and so we see beginning the great expansions of early agricultural populations from their homeland regions into other parts of the world, hand in hand with their languages and genes, albeit involving complex patterns of admixture with preceding indigenous populations. (Languages and their constituent families are discussed in chapter 11, and the prehistories of both languages and genes are covered in considerable detail in many of the following chapters.)

Agriculture, with animal husbandry, was a relatively rare development in human prehistory, hence the comparatively few regions referred to above. Once it had developed it had remarkable abilities to expand, spreading into most regions of the world (Diamond & Bellwood 2003; Bellwood 2005, 2009). But this only occurred after systems of food production had developed that could provide the demographic impetus. The very first tentative farmers in the Fertile Crescent and Yellow River loess lands most probably did not spread very far. Several millennia later, their descendants had domesticated their plants and animals to the degree that they could be carried across environmental zones to faraway places (e.g. Bellwood 2011 for Chinese rice), something that was hard to do with wild plants when growing conditions and climates differed, and certainly difficult to do with wild animals (although translocation of wild animal species in pre-Neolithic times is well recorded for faunally impoverished small islands in the western Pacific). Once agriculture was well under development, the earlier limits to Pleistocene hunter-gatherer population growth were lifted. The results created the basic patterns of the human world prior to 1500 CE – even to the present day if one adds the post-1500 outcomes of what Alfred Crosby (1986) has rather dramatically termed "ecological imperialism."

SEE ALSO: 1 Prehistoric migration and the rise of humanity; 11 Human migrations and the histories of major language families; 26 Eastern Asia: archaeology

References

Barker, G. (2007) *The Agricultural Revolution in Prehistory*. Oxford: Oxford University Press.

Bellwood, P. & Renfrew, C. (eds.) (2002) *Examining the Farming/Language Dispersal Hypothesis.* Cambridge: McDonald Institute for Archaeological Research.

Bellwood, P. (2005) *First Farmers*. Oxford: Blackwell.

Bellwood, P. (2009) The dispersals of established food-producing populations. *Current Anthropology* 50, 621–626, 707–708.

Bellwood, P. (2011) The chequered prehistory of rice movement southwards as a domesticated cereal – from the Yangzi to the Equator. *Rice* 4, 93–103.

Bocquet-Appel, J.-P. & Bar-Yosef, O. (eds.) (2008) *The Neolithic Demographic Transition and its Consequences*. Dordrecht: Springer.

Crosby, A. W. (1986) *Ecological Imperialism*. Cambridge: Cambridge University Press.

Diamond, J. (2002) Evolution, consequences and future of plant and animal domestication. *Nature* 418, 700–707.

Diamond, J. & Bellwood, P. (2003) Farmers and their languages: the first expansions. *Science* 300, 597–603.

Fuller, D. (2007) Contrasting patterns in crop domestication and domestication rates. *Annals of Botany* 100, 903–924.

Fuller, D. Q., Sato, Y.-I., Castillo, C., et al. (2010) Consilience of genetics and archaeobotany in the entangled history of rice. *Archaeological and Anthropological Sciences* 2, 115–131.

Gignoux, C., Henn, B., & Mountain, J. (2011) Rapid, global demographic expansions after the origins of agriculture. *Proceedings of the National Academy of Sciences* 108, 6044–6049.

Gilligan, I. (2011) Agriculture in Aboriginal Australia: why not? *Bulletin of the Indo-Pacific Prehistory Association* 30, 145–156.

Harris, D. (2002) The expansion capacity of early agricultural systems. In Bellwood & Renfrew (2002), pp. 31–40.

Hill, J. (2002) Proto-Uto-Aztecan cultivation and the northern devolution. In Bellwood & Renfrew (2002), pp. 331–340.

Kennett, D. & Winterhalder, B. (eds.) (2006) *Behavioral Ecology and the Transition to Agriculture*. Berkeley: University of California Press.

Liu, L. (2004) *The Chinese Neolithic*. Cambridge: Cambridge University Press.

Qiao, Y. (2007) Complex societies in the Yiluo region: a GIS based population and agricultural area analysis. *Bulletin of the Indo-Pacific Prehistory Association* 27, 61–75.

Richerson, P., Boyd, R., & Bettinger, R. (2001) Was agriculture impossible during the Pleistocene but mandatory during the Holocene? *American Antiquity* 66, 387–411.

Smith, B. (2001) Low-level food production. *Journal of Archaeological Research* 9, 1–43.

Willcox, G. (2005) The distribution, natural habitats and availability of wild cereals in relation to their domestication in the Near East: multiple events, multiple centres. *Vegetation History and Archaeobotany* 14, 534–541.

Yang, X. (2004) Urban revolution in late prehistoric China. In X. Yang (ed.), *Chinese Archaeology*, Vol. 1, *Cultures and Civilizations Reconsidered*. New Haven: Yale University Press, pp, 98–143.

Zeder, M. (2008) Domestication and early agriculture in the Mediterranean basin: origins, diffusion and impact. *Proceedings of the National Academy of Sciences* 105, 11597–11604.

Zeder, M., Bradley, D., Emschwiller, E., & Smith, B. (eds.) (2006) *Documenting Domestication*. Berkeley: University of California Press.

Zhang, C. & Hung H.-C. (2008) The Neolithic cultures of southern China: origin, development and dispersal. *Asian Perspectives* 47, 299–330.

11

Human migrations and the histories of major language families

Peter Bellwood

This chapter continues the theme of chapter 10, in this case with respect to the expansions of major language families as a result of the demographic increases and dispersals of Holocene human populations, especially, but not entirely, with agricultural (food-producing) subsistence economies.

The origins of language families pose important questions for human migration since it is obvious that most people speak a language (sometimes more than one) that they inherit from their parents and peers, and that they normally do not change during their lifetimes. Of course, people and populations can change languages from time to time, and languages can become extinct. But the use of a language as a marker of ethnic identity is a property of all human groups recorded in ethnography and in our modern world. Language possession is a fairly stable feature of most normally functioning human societies, except in circumstances of major conflict, translocation (e.g. slavery) or depopulation. It follows that migrating humans are a major source of language spread, and likewise served as the major source throughout human prehistory.

This encyclopedia contains a number of chapters that deal with the histories of major and widespread families of related languages (see Figures 11.1, 11.2). In Africa, we deal with Niger–Congo, Nilo-Saharan and Afroasiatic. In Asia, we deal with Afroasiatic (again), Indo-European, Dravidian, Altaic, Sino-Tibetan, Austroasiatic, Austronesian and Tai. In Europe, we deal with Indo-European and Uralic. In Australia, we deal with Pama-Nyungan, and in the Americas with Quechua, Aymara, Arawak, Carib, Tucanoan, Athabaskan, Eskimo-Aleut, Algonquian, Siouan and Iroquoian. And these are only the largest and most widespread of the world's language families. Some of them were associated until colonial times mostly with hunter-gatherer or pastoralist populations (e.g. Altaic, Uralic, Athabaskan, Eskimo-Aleut and Pama-Nyungan), while the rest were associated mainly with agricultural peoples. Indeed, many of the language families of predominantly agriculturalist populations have large reconstructable

The Global Prehistory of Human Migration: The Encyclopedia of Global Human Migration Volume 1,
First Edition. Edited by Peter Bellwood.
© 2013 John Wiley & Sons, Ltd. Published 2015 by John Wiley & Sons, Ltd.

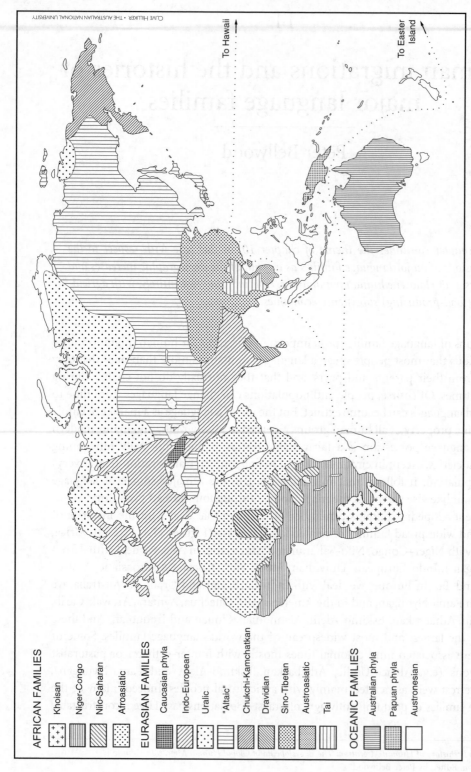

To Hawaii

To Easter Island

AFRICAN FAMILIES

Khoisan

Niger-Congo

Nilo-Saharan

Afroasiatic

EURASIAN FAMILIES

Caucasian phyla

Indo-European

Uralic

"Altaic"

Chukchi-Kamchatkan

Dravidian

Sino-Tibetan

Austroasiatic

Tai

OCEANIC FAMILIES

Australian phyla

Papuan phyla

Austronesian

Figure 11.1 Map of the major language families of the Old World prior to the spread of colonial era languages. The term "phyla" (singular "phylum") means that more than one language family is present in the grouping. After Ruhlen (1987), originally published as Figure 1.1 in Bellwood (2005). Original map rendering by Clive Hilliker, The Australian National University.

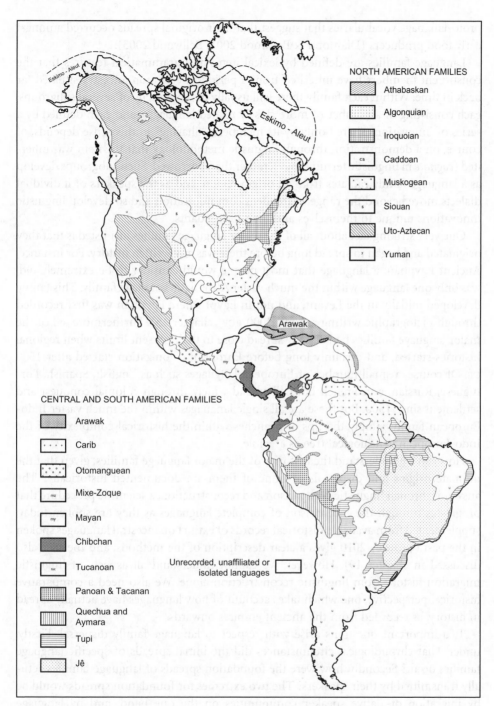

NORTH AMERICAN FAMILIES

- Athabaskan
- Algonquian
- Iroquoian
- ca Caddoan
- Muskogean
- s Siouan
- Uto-Aztecan
- y Yuman

Eskimo - Aleut

Eskimo - Aleut

Arawak

Mainly Arawak & Unaffiliated

CENTRAL AND SOUTH AMERICAN FAMILIES

- Arawak
- Carib
- Otomanguean
- mz Mixe-Zoque
- my Mayan
- Chibchan
- tuc Tucanoan
- Panoan & Tacanan
- Quechua and Aymara
- Tupi
- Jê

Unrecorded, unaffiliated or isolated languages · u

Figure 11.2 Map of the major language families of the New World prior to the spread of colonial era languages. After Ruhlen (1987), originally published as Figure 1.2 in Bellwood (2005). Original map rendering by Clive Hilliker, The Australian National University.

proto-language vocabularies that suggest that their original spreads occurred amongst early food producers (Diamond & Bellwood 2003; Bellwood 2005).

Language families are defined by lexical items and grammatical features that the constituent members have inherited from a period of common ancestry situated far back in time. Within each family there will usually be a hierarchy of several subgroups, each consisting of a number of more closely related languages, and each defined by a series of innovations shared only by its members. "Sharing" in this sense depends, of course, on a demonstration through linguistic methodology that the item was inherited (*cognate* in linguistic terminology), rather than borrowed. Such subgroups develop as a language family radiates from an origin region, and as the speakers of individual dialects move beyond the range of frequent communication and so develop linguistic innovations unique to themselves and their descendants.

One very striking fact about all of the major language families just listed is that they originated and began to spread long before there was any written history. For instance, Ancient Egyptian, a language that most people would consider to be extremely old, was only one language within the much vaster Afroasiatic language family. This family developed initially in the Levant, and not in Egypt where Egyptian was first recorded through pictographic writing around 3000 BCE (chapter 15). Furthermore, all of the major language families had already spread close to their present limits when regional histories started, and certainly long before European colonization started after 1500 CE. Of course, a small number of European languages such as English, Spanish, Portuguese, Russian, and French have all spread widely through colonial conquest and settlement since 1500. But these are all single languages within the much vaster Indo-European family, simply the tips of branches within the historical complexity of the Indo-European genealogical tree as a whole.

How can we understand the histories of the major language families, given that the ultimate origins and dispersals of none of them are documented historically? The answer is through linguistic comparison and reconstruction, a scientific procedure that progresses through the comparison of complete languages as they are spoken today, supplemented from available historical records of extinct or ancestral languages spoken in the past (Crowley 2010 gives a clear description of the methods, and they are also discussed in chapter 19). However, we cannot understand all aspects of linguistic migration history from linguistic reconstruction alone. We also need a comparative historical perspective, one which takes account of how languages have actually spread in history, as recorded from the ancient empires onwards.

Two important questions arise with respect to language-family dispersal. Firstly, under what chronological circumstances did the initial spreads of specific language families occur? Secondly, how were the foundation spreads of language families actually transmitted by their speakers? The two extremes for foundation spreads would be by migration of native speaker communities on the one hand, and by language shift through nodes in a chain with no speaker movement at all on the other. But extremes such as these rarely fit historical observations if just considered alone. Reality might generally have been something in-between, yet allowing for the allocation of different relative significances to the polarities of speaker movement versus language shift.

How language families might have spread: lessons from history

The historian Alfred W. Crosby (1986) has noted out how intensive European colonization in temperate locations with few indigenous inhabitants – Argentina, Uruguay, North America, New Zealand, Australia – led to the establishment of what he termed "Neo-Europes." Over 50 million European emigrants between 1820 and 1930 founded predominantly European populations speaking European languages (Spanish or English in most of the above cases). European-introduced epidemic diseases, domesticated crops and animals, tough weeds, and high levels of European population fecundity in new-found fertile lands led to a tragedy for the indigenous populations of absolutely unparalleled proportions. For instance, Denevan (1992) has estimated native population declines of between 74 and 99 percent (the latter in Hispaniola) across the moving frontier of European conquest after 1492 CE in the Americas (see also Fallon & Fehren-Schmitz 2011).

Crosby went on to compare the Neo-Europes with locations that clearly were *not* Neo-Europes, mostly Old World tropical-to-equatorial locations with their own diseases to which Europeans had no resistance, and all with dense populations living at high levels of social and political integration. The Middle East with North Africa, many regions of tropical Africa, and southern and eastern tropical Asia offer many examples. The tropical Americas do not because the linguistic outcome here was so heavily structured by the massive loss of native populations due to introduced diseases, and the lack of any major reverse disease impact on the Europeans. European nations were unable to colonize very successfully in the Old World tropics, and once their empires had decayed, their languages faded from memory. Try speaking Dutch in Indonesia, French in Vietnam, or even English in many parts of India today. As Crosby (1986: 63) rather amusingly commented on the attempts of the Crusaders to conquer the Holy Land: "the conquerors, taken collectively, were like a lump of sugar presiding in a hot cup of tea."

The conclusion to be drawn is that language spread on a permanent basis, at the vernacular and whole-population level, has generally required a successful demographic profile from the immigrants. A similar conclusion can be drawn from the many historical observations made by linguist Nicholas Ostler (2005), who surveys in considerable detail the histories of most of the major recorded languages during the past 5,000 years. He concludes that the languages of imperial administrations, and lingua francas of traders, did not survive for very long after the systems that nourished them went into decline, *unless* there were implantations of very large numbers of native-speaker colonists of the imported languages concerned, or only a low density of aboriginal populations.

Many examples can be given of the reluctance of major historical languages to spread successfully and permanently: Sumerian, Ancient Egyptian outside Egypt, Aramaic after its widespread use as a lingua franca in the Persian empire, Hellenistic Greek in Asia, Latin beyond the Romance-speaking areas (in which there was substantial colonization by Latin-speaking army veterans), Germanic languages across post-Roman continental Europe, Arabic after the 7th century conquests (only a minority of modern Moslems speak modern Arabic), Mongol (Genghis Khan spread lots of genes, but rather little linguistic heritage!), Norman French (only French loan words remain in English), and many more. Most of these examples show that, despite military conquest, actual language spread only occurred in rough proportion to the degree of permanent population movement into the conquered areas (Bellwood 2008, 2010).

Perhaps the history of Greek following the conquests of Alexander is one of the most striking examples of non-spread over the long term by a conqueror language. Greek colonies in central Asia incorporated core Greek-speaking populations, but always in a sea of others speaking Indo-Aryan and Semitic languages – Greek was definitely the lump of sugar, not the tea. In Bactria, Greek declined in usage rapidly after the Greek garrison towns were ultimately overrun by Parthians, Sakas, and Kushans, and by the early centuries of the Christian Era only survived as a script used for the writing of Prakrit documents (Liu 2004). In Anatolia it survived through the Byzantine empire, there to be replaced ultimately by Turkish after the fall of Byzantium in 1453. Why did Greek die so quickly? In central Asia, the reason is that there were never enough Greek speakers to push their language to the tipping point of success, compared to the much larger indigenous populations who surrounded them.

The moral to be drawn is that the long-distance spreads of the foundation languages that differentiated into the major existing language families of the world must have occurred with a continuous flow of native speakers, albeit with substrate linguistic incorporation, and not purely by processes of language shift. Language shift was important in prehistory, as when Papuan speakers began to adopt Austronesian languages in the Bismarck archipelago around 3,000 years ago (Pawley 2002: 267), or when the descendants of Julius Caesar's Gallic opponents eventually learnt Latin (or Proto-French!) (Bauer 1996). But language shift must be seen in perspective in terms of geographical scale. Although it occurs all around us today as the languages of nation-states aggrandize and spread, most on-the-ground cases of language shift are small in terms of extent.

Dates of spread and homelands of language families

As noted, all of the major food-producing language families (i.e. those for which a food-producing vocabulary can be reconstructed from an early stage) had attained their 1500 CE distributional limits long before written history and any conquest empires. The majority would appear also to have spread from homelands either within or very close to the archaeologically defined homelands of food production (Middle East, west and central Africa, central China, New Guinea Highlands, Mesoamerica, Andes and upper Amazonia, eastern United States – see Figures 10.1, 11.3), at least in terms of the majority homeland opinions of linguists (as summarized by Bellwood 2005, 2010). There may be argument, for instance, over whether early Indo-European languages spread from Anatolia (Renfrew 1987) or the steppes north of the Black Sea (Anthony 2007; chapter 19 in this volume), but both of these regions are far closer to the Middle Eastern region of agricultural origin than are the Irish Republic, Norway, or Bangladesh. Major language families that have sufficiently reconstructed tree-like and hierarchical genealogies to allow homeland suggestions with some confidence

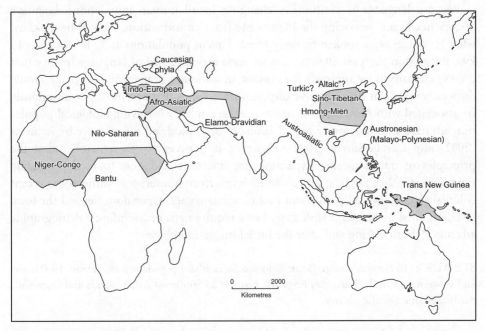

Figure 11.3 Suggested homelands for the major Old World language families whose populations are predominantly agriculturalists, derived from interpretations of the linguistic literature. The Levant with Anatolia, West Africa, central East Asia ("China") and the New Guinea highlands are all recognized homeland regions for food production (homelands transferred from Figure 10.1). Original map rendering by Clive Hilliker, The Australian National University.

include Indo-European, Bantu (in this case, within the broader Niger–Congo family), Dravidian, Tai, Austronesian, Uto-Aztecan, Arawak, and Tupian. Other families such as Afroasiatic, Austroasiatic and Sino-Tibetan do not have such clearly hierarchical genealogies, and their relatively rake-like subgrouping structures allow less certainty. All of these language families are discussed in more detail in many of the following chapters.

The two factors discussed above - relative age of spread before the appearance of historical records, and substantial extent of spread - allow us to suggest that the most significant point of change in world prehistory within the agricultural latitudes could well have been the "transition" from hunting and gathering into food production, as suggested by Renfrew (1991, 1996). This conclusion is strengthened by the observation that major language dispersal also required population movement and demographic growth. The development of food production was undeniably a major transition in the archaeological record, and perhaps the most significant fault line for language spread and replacement in human prehistory. But it is important to remember that population growth and expansion did not necessarily occur in the earliest periods of "low level" food production (chapter 10), but was much more likely to have occurred amongst populations which had begun to depend to a substantial degree on food production, especially with both crops and domestic animals (Harris 2002; Bellwood 2009).

Because language is continually changing in all human populations, language history has limits, removing the Pleistocene from consideration. We will never know what languages were spoken by early *Homo sapiens* populations at 30 kya or even 15 kya. But within the past 10,000 years we have a rich record of language history that grows in density as we approach the present. In summary, many major language-family dispersals represent demographic dispersal trajectories that can most parsimoniously be associated with movement of native speakers, mostly involving biological population admixture in previously settled landscapes, as modeled for instance by Renfrew (2002) and Cavalli-Sforza (2002). However, it is necessary to remember that the principles of native-speaker expansion are not restricted only to food-producing populations – they apply at all economic levels from hunters and gatherers to recent colonial settlers. But all permanent prehistoric language expansions beyond the local levels attained by language shift shared one requirement in common: a demographic advantage, both during and after the initial migration phase.

SEE ALSO: 10 Neolithic migrations: food production and population expansion; 19 Europe and western Asia: Indo-European linguistic history; 35 Southeast Asian islands and Oceania: Austronesian linguistic history

References

Anthony, D. (2007) *The Horse, the Wheel, and Language*. Princeton: Princeton University Press.

Bauer, B. (1996) Language loss in Gaul. *Southwestern Journal of Linguistics* 15, 23–44.

Bellwood, P. (2005) *First Farmers*. Oxford: Blackwell.

Bellwood, P. (2008) Archaeology and the origins of language families. In A. Bentley, H. Maschner, & C. Chippindale (eds.), *Handbook of Archaeological Theories*. Lanham: Altamira, pp. 225–243.

Bellwood, P. (2009) The dispersals of established food-producing populations. *Current Anthropology* 50, 621–626, 707–708.

Bellwood, P. (2010) Language families and the history of human migration. In J. Bowden, N. Himmelmann, & M. Ross (eds.), *A Journey through Austronesian and Papuan Linguistic and Cultural Space: Papers in Honour of Andrew K. Pawley*. Canberra: Pacific Linguistics, pp. 79–93.

Bellwood, P. & Renfrew, C. (eds.) (2002) *Examining the Farming/Language Dispersal Hypothesis*. Cambridge: McDonald Institute for Archaeological Research.

Cavalli-Sforza, L. L. (2002) Demic diffusion as the basic process of human expansions. In Bellwood & Renfrew (2002), pp. 79–88.

Crosby, A. W. (1986) *Ecological Imperialism*. Cambridge: Cambridge University Press.

Crowley, T. (2010) *An Introduction to Historical Linguistics*. Oxford: Oxford University Press.

Denevan, W. M. (1992) The pristine myth: the landscapes of the Americas in 1492. *Annals of the Association of American Geographers* 82, 369–385.

Diamond, J. & Bellwood, P. (2003) Farmers and their languages: the first expansions. *Science* 300, 597–603.

Fallon, B. & Fehren-Schmitz, L. (2011) Native Americans experienced a strong population bottleneck coincident with European contact. *Proceedings of the National Academy of Sciences* 108, 20444–20448.

Harris, D. (2002) The expansion capacity of early agricultural systems. In Bellwood & Renfrew (2002), pp. 31–40.

Liu, X. (2004) Hellenistic residue in central Asia under Islamic regimes. *Journal of Interdisciplinary Studies in History and Archaeology* 1(2), 79–86.

Ostler, N. (2005) *Empires of the Word*. London: Harper Perennial.

Pawley, A. (2002) The Austronesian dispersal: languages, technologies and people. In Bellwood & Renfrew (2002), pp. 251–274.

Renfrew, C. (1987) *Archaeology and Language*. London: Jonathan Cape.

Renfrew, C. (1991) Before Babel. *Cambridge Archaeological Journal* 1, 3–23.

Renfrew, C. (1996) Language families and the spread of farming. In D. Harris (ed.), *The Origins and Spread of Agriculture and Pastoralism in Asia*. London: UCL Press, pp. 70–92.

Renfrew, C. (2002) "The emerging synthesis": the archaeogenetics of language/farming dispersals and other spread zones. In Bellwood & Renfrew (2002), pp. 3–16.

12

Sub-Saharan Africa: linguistics

Christopher Ehret

This chapter deals with the developments and speaker migrations of the main language families of sub-Saharan Africa, offering a chronology derived from linguistic considerations.

From the end of the last Ice Age, at 11.5 kya, three histories of long-term language and population spread, each of vast extent, fundamentally shaped the long-term course of change across most of sub-Saharan Africa. Each history progressed episodically over several millennia. Peoples speaking languages of two African language families, Niger-Congo and Nilo-Saharan, along with the speakers of the Cushitic subfamily of Afrasian (Afroasiatic), carried these long histories of recurrent migration forward. The circumstances of a fourth African language family, Khoesan (or Khoisan), may accord with similar processes even earlier in time, following the Last Glacial Maximum that occurred between 24 and 18 kya. The distributions of these language families are shown in Figures 12.1 and 12.2.

The factors impelling the major early language-family spreads in Africa belong to a category of causation that frequently emphasizes the acquisition of agriculture as the engine of population growth and the dispersal of people with their languages (chapter 11). The paradigm gains greater explanatory reach, however, if re-couched as the acquisition of subsistence advantage in more general terms, whether in food production or in foraging. In Africa, the evidence of lexical reconstruction implies that the developments of food production often did come into play, especially during and after the Middle Holocene. But at the threshold of the Holocene, advantage accrued to those peoples who were the first to adopt new foraging strategies for taking advantage of the great environmental shifts of that time. If the new strategies they adopted served as pathways toward food production, so much the better for the prospects of the renewed expansions of their descendant peoples in subsequent eras.

The Global Prehistory of Human Migration: The Encyclopedia of Global Human Migration Volume 1,
First Edition. Edited by Peter Bellwood.
© 2013 John Wiley & Sons, Ltd. Published 2015 by John Wiley & Sons, Ltd.

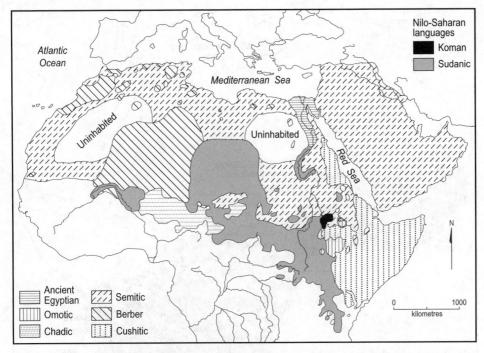

Figure 12.1 The distributions of the main subgroups of the Afroasiatic and Nilo-Saharan languages families. Map production by Education and Multimedia Services, College of Asia and the Pacific, The Australian National University.

Niger-Congo speakers and ancient migrations in Africa

The most far-reaching of these histories of language and population movement was the establishment, by stages, of the Niger-Congo-speaking communities over two-thirds of sub-Saharan Africa. The full phonological reconstruction of Proto-Niger-Congo (PNC) is a project still in progress (Stewart 2002), but the strength of the lexical and grammatical evidence across the family (Williamson & Blench 2000; Nurse et al. 2008) is such that scholars have no doubts about its validity.

A consensus subclassification of the family, with some differences in detail, has held the field since the 1980s (Bendor-Samuel 1989). This subclassification requires three major periods of extended divergence and expansion of the speakers of Niger-Congo languages. At the first stage, shown in Figure 12.3, Proto-Niger-Congo diverged into two daughter languages, each of which in turn became the proto-language of one of the two deepest branches of the family. These branches are Mande and Atlantic-Congo, the latter of which then divided into several sub-branches in relatively close order – giving rise first to a distinct Atlantic sub-branch and then, not long after, to the Dogon, Ijo, and Volta-Congo sub-branches of Ijo-Congo.

The linguistic geography of these primary divergences places the Proto-Niger-Congo society somewhere in an east–west span of savanna and steppe environments,

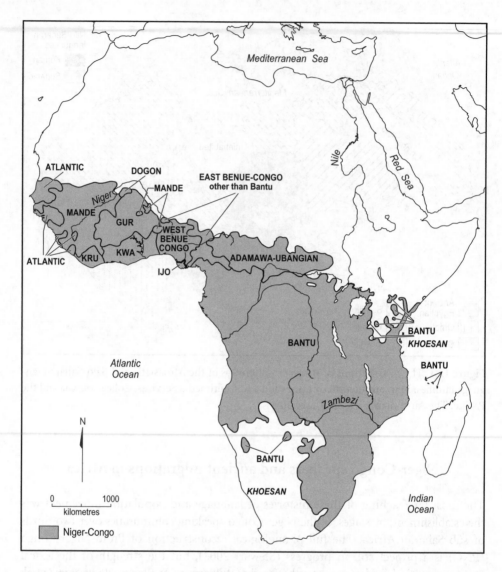

Figure 12.2 The major subgroups of the Niger-Congo language family. Map production by Education and Multimedia Services, College of Asia and the Pacific, The Australian National University.

between roughly 15°N and 20°N, centering on modern-day Mali. The languages of the first divergence, Mande, today occupy the heart of this belt. The Atlantic languages both anciently and recently have been the immediate western neighbors of Mande. Dogon forms an enclave adjacent to the central Mande areas, while the center of diversity within the Volta-Congo sub-branch lies east of the Dogon from modern Burkina Faso to western central Nigeria. Only a single outlier, the Ijoid sub-branch, is today found to the south, in the Niger Delta. The evidence strongly supports the conclusion that the earliest Niger-Congo migrations into new lands, from the Proto-Niger-Congo era down to the breakup of Proto-Volta-Congo, took place in the savanna and steppe between Senegal to the west and Burkina Faso to the east.

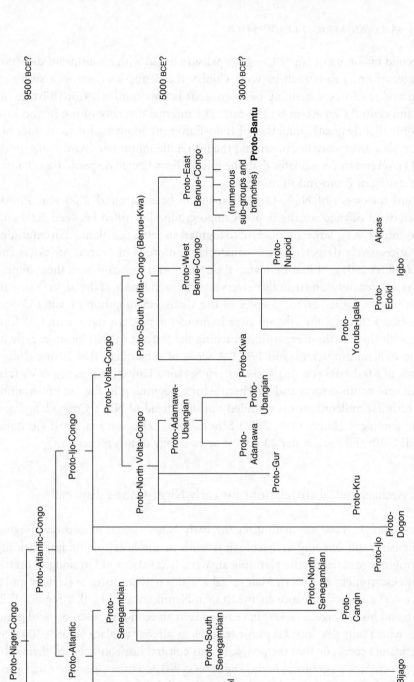

Figure 12.3 Classification of the Niger-Congo languages. The Niger-Congo languages are so numerous, and the complexity of their subclassification is so great, that only the major subdivisions of the family can be displayed here. It is often claimed that there are as many as 1,200 languages in the family, but the total number is closer to 800. The Atlantic branch of the family, for example, contains over forty languages. East Benue-Congo has perhaps as many as 600, with around 400 of these belonging to the vastly spread Bantu subgroup of East Benue-Congo. The suggested dates down the right-hand side of the tree identify the proposed archaeological correlations described in the chapter.

The second major era of Niger-Congo expansion began with a southward dispersal of languages of one sub-branch of Volta-Congo, the Benue-Kwa, across a swath of woodland and rainforest extending between what is now southern Côte d'Ivoire on the west and central Cameroon on the east. The internal diversity of the Benue-Kwa group is only slightly greater than that of Indo-European, implying for some linguists that Benue-Kwa divergence began around the fifth millennium BCE (Armstrong 1964; Ehret 2011), several millennia later than the initial Niger-Congo dispersal (see chapter 19 on the dating of Proto-Indo-European).

The third major era of Niger-Congo expansion began around 3000 BCE. Proto-Bantu society, an offshoot of the Benue-Congo group, diversified between 3000 and 1000 BCE into a very large number of daughter societies, as Bantu communities migrated successively deeper into the equatorial rainforests of central Africa (Heine et al. 1977; Ehret 2001). At first following the Sangha and Congo Rivers, these migrations then scattered out along tributary rivers into more and more of the basin (Klieman 2003). During the same period, peoples of the Ubangian subgroup of Volta-Congo spread eastward through the Ubangi river basin of the modern-day Central African Republic, with their farthest expansion reaching the far east of that basin as early as the second millennium BCE (Saxon 1982). A series of subsequent East Benue-Congo movements of Mashariki (Bantu) and Western Savanna Bantu peoples across eastern Africa and into south central and southern Africa, beginning in the 1st millennium BCE and early 1st millennium CE, rounded out the spread of Niger-Congo languages across the continent (Ehret 1998, 2001; Schoenbrun 1998; Vansina 2004; Gonzales 2009; Saidi 2010; and see chapter 13 for the archaeology of this movement).

Archaeological correlations for early Niger-Congo dispersal

What factors might have set in motion the early Niger-Congo expansions (Figure 13.1)? Intensive, still ongoing archaeological work in the heart of the linguistically inferred origin areas offers some plausible answers. Excavations at Ounjougou on the Bandiagara escarpment of eastern Mali reveal a major new subsistence strategy and a major pyrotechnological advance in the 10th millennium BCE. In this region, Erik Huysecom and his colleagues (2009) have uncovered an economy based on wild grain collection, with a fully developed ceramic technology already in place before 9400 BCE. The investigators conclude that the people of this cultural horizontal based their subsistence on such African grains as *fonio* (*Digitaria exilis*) and other species, which grow in extensive and often dense stands in these steppe and dry savanna grassland environments. They propose that communities of this time and place did not grind their grains into flour, but instead boiled them whole in their pots, and that the invention of ceramic technology was therefore integral to the emergence of this economy. Provisionally reconstructed lexicon indicates that in the next couple of thousand years the Niger-Congo peoples may have taken the initial steps toward protecting and eventually cultivating grains, but this proposal remains to be archaeologically tested.

A new stage in the evolution of West African agricultural practices began by no later than the 5th millennium BCE. The archeological signature of this development is indirect: the adding of ground (and polished) stone axes to the existing West African microlithic toolkit. This development took place initially across the woodland and rainforest regions from Ghana to Cameroon, in just the span of lands where the linguistic arguments place the expansions of the Benue-Kwa branch of the Niger-Congo peoples (e.g. Shaw & Daniels 1984). The linguistic evidence suggests the hypothesis that the breakthrough development was to bring under cultivation two new crops: Guinea yams and oil palms. Oil palms were valued not just for cooking oil but as a source of palm wine. Yams and oil palms, although both high-rainfall crops, required open sunlight. Stone axes would have made possible the necessary clearing of forest.

After 3000 BCE, cultures with pottery and stone axes, of the kinds associated with the Benue-Kwa peoples, spread southward from Cameroon into the equatorial rainforest regions of Africa, in keeping both chronologically and in location with the linguistically inferred early migrations of Bantu speakers. A considerable number of detailed linguistic and other studies have probed the multiple histories of the regional movements that spread Bantu languages across a third of Africa, and raised hypotheses about the archaeological reflections of these movements. The evidence strongly suggests that the initial penetration of Bantu speakers into the equatorial rainforest zone, between 3000 and 1000 BCE, followed river routes (Klieman 2003). Only subsequently did Bantu spread wider into rainforest areas away from the main rivers, with the last major agricultural expansion of Bantu, that of the Mongo, penetrating up several rivers into the heart of the Congo Basin between 400 and 1100 CE. Other studies have combined linguistics with the available archaeology, and sometimes with palynology and oral tradition, for constructing detailed regional histories of Bantu expansion into regions south and east of the rainforest since 1000 BCE (Ehret 1998; Schoenbrun 1998; Gonzales 2009; Saidi 2010; and see chapter 13, this volume).

Nilo-Saharans and the Holocene pastoral Sahara

A second, almost equally early succession of population spreads took place in the eastern Sahara and Sudan belt of Africa (Figure 12.4). Speakers of languages of the Nilo-Saharan family were the prime movers of this history. Again, subsistence innovations in response to climatic shift seem to have provided the driving force for vast population spreads. The locations of the Koman and Central Sudanic branches place the first Nilo-Saharan divergence in a restricted span of regions around and southwards from the confluence of the White and Blue Nile rivers. This first stage of Nilo-Saharan linguistic history may belong to the terminal Pleistocene interval of climatic amelioration termed the Bølling-Allerød interstadial, 12700–11800 BCE, but this possibility remains to be investigated archaeologically.

The major subsistence shifts and expansions among Nilo-Saharan peoples began later, however, with the shift northward of the tropical African rainfall belts after the end of the brief Younger Dryas glacial phase. In the eastern Sahara this shift took hold at around 8500 BCE (Kröpelin & Kuper 2006). Two major subsistence transformations followed. A vast resettlement of much of the southern Sahara took place, by people who established an intensive fishing and hippopotamus-hunting economy around the

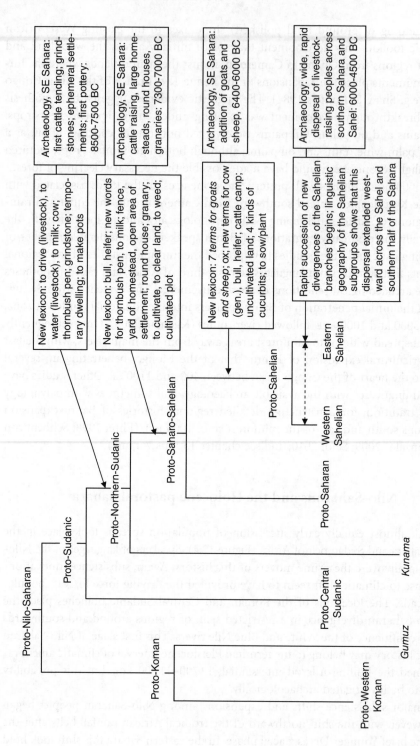

Figure 12.4 A Nilo-Saharan family tree: new developments in lexicon from Proto-Sudanic to Proto-Sahelian, with parallel archaeological sequences.

large lakes and perennial streams of the newly green former desert. Especially salient material features of this "Aquatic" civilization were pottery and finely made bone harpoons.

The pottery of the Aquatic peoples links them culturally and probably linguistically to a smaller contemporary group of communities living in the southeastern Sahara. These communities responded in a different manner to the changed environment. Living in more arid areas away from rivers, they embarked after 8500 BCE on developments leading toward food production. The earliest sites concerned, around Nabta Playa in the Western Desert of Egypt, contain evidence of incipient cattle raising, grindstones, and wild grain collection. By 7200 BCE, the communities of this tradition were building settlements with round houses and granaries. After 6500 BCE, they added ovicaprines to their existing cattle keeping (Wendorf & Schild 1998; Kröpelin & Kuper 2006). Finally, over the course of the 6th millennium BCE, societies with developed pastoral economies spread rapidly across the breadth of the southern Sahara and adjacent Sahel zones. In most areas, the Aquatic tradition disappeared in the face of this new expansion, although where permanent lakes and rivers persisted, such as along the Nile River and around the ancient Lake Megachad, the new expansions of the pastoralists led to the blending of livestock raising with aquatic pursuits.

The agents of this particular economic changeover and accompanying demographic expansions were surely speakers of the early languages of the Northern Sudanic branch of Nilo-Saharan. The succession of archaeological developments in the southeastern Sahara is matched, almost point-for-point, by the creation of new lexicon in the descendant languages of Proto-Northern Sudanic, and by the linguistically inferred histories of cultural expansion. Figure 12.4 summarizes these correlations, which have been published in detail elsewhere (Ehret 2011).

The lexical evidence suggests also that, by the late 8th millennium BCE, the descendant societies of Proto-Northern Sudanic were beginning to manage their wild food sources and to shift toward the cultivation of such indigenous crops as sorghum, melons, gourds, and cotton. Although current archaeobotanical knowledge is insufficient to test these implications, the presence of spindle whorls for spinning thread in 6th millennium BCE sites (Arkell 1949) implies cotton cultivation by this time. The early presence of domesticated African melons in Egypt and the probable spread of sorghum all the way to north China by the 3rd millennium BCE (Kimber 2000) also would be in keeping with placing the beginnings of cultivation during this period.

Cushites in the Horn of Africa

The Nilo-Saharans were not the only peoples to spread widely in northeastern Africa during the early Holocene. The linguistic findings imply that the early Cushites of the Afrasian (Afroasiatic) language family, similar to and as early as the Northern Sudanic peoples, made the transition to a food-producing economy and, with this economy in place, spread out widely through the Horn of Africa (see also chapter 15). Reconstructed lexicon shows that, before the Proto-Cushitic language diverged into daughter languages, its speakers knew of and probably herded cattle, kept sheep and goats, and collected wild grains, including sorghum. Other evidence places the Proto-Cushites most probably in the southern Red Sea hills (Ehret 2011). Direct archaeological knowledge of these areas is as yet almost nil, making this an urgent region for future archaeological investigation.

One particular linguistic link allows us to place the initial divergence of Proto-Cushitic into daughter languages before 6500 BCE. At least two words for the goat, an animal of southwest Asian origin which the Proto-Sahelian descendants of the Proto-Northern Sudanians began to herd after 6500 BCE, came into the Proto-Sahelian language specifically from the ancestral language of the Northern (Bedauye) branch of Cushitic. We know this because the reconstructed Proto-Sahelian pronunciations of these words preserved regular sound changes specific to Northern Cushitic (Ehret 2011). The breakup of Proto-Cushitic therefore had already happened before 6500 BCE.

Following the breakup of the Proto-Cushitic society, the speakers of Cushitic languages spread first to the lowland northern fringes of the Ethiopian highlands and then into the eastern highlands, particularly, it appears, following the Ethiopian Rift Valley south to northern Kenya. The latest possible date for the last stage in these expansions is provided by the establishment, around 3000 BCE in Kenya, south of the Ethiopian highlands, of the Savanna Pastoral Neolithic (Ambrose 1982; Barthelme 1985), associated with Southern Cushitic-speaking peoples (Ambrose 1982; also Ehret 1998). Reconstructed lexicon identifies the intervening period between 6500 and 3000 BCE as the time when Cushites began to cultivate crops, including the indigenous finger millet of the Ethiopian highlands. This period in the northern and eastern highlands and the Ethiopia Rift is as yet almost entirely unknown archaeologically (Barnett 1999), however, and so remains another important field for future investigation.

Khoesan peoples and the Eastern African Microlithic

A fourth African language family, Khoesan (also spelled Khoisan), has probable links to the Eastern African Microlithic complex (Munson 1986). The distributions of proposed Khoesan languages extend over the same broad areas as the Eastern African Microlithic and, after 7000 BCE, its southern African counterpart, Wilton. The validity of the Khoesan family has been contested, but the comparative data overall are difficult to explain on any other hypothesis than relationship. The substantive evidence linking the Southern African members of the family to the Sandawe language of Tanzania includes basic lexical items and grammatical features, while the evidence from Hadza of Tanzania includes, as well, numerous words of kinds highly unlikely to have been borrowed (Ehret 1986). In addition, notable loanword sets of apparent Khoesan origin occur in the Southern Cushitic languages, implying the former presence of related languages in several parts of Kenya before the Southern Cushites arrived five thousand years ago. (Chapter 14 also discusses the former distribution of Khoesan peoples from a genetic perspective.)

From the perspective of palaeoclimate, the known early East African dates and distributions of the Eastern African Microlithic tend to coincide with lands that would have been quite arid during the Last Glacial Maximum (LGM). The Eastern African

Microlithic, in other words, appears to have arisen as an adaptation to arid condi-tions. The speakers of the early Khoesan languages can be proposed to have spread this tradition over large areas of eastern Africa, and later into southern Africa, because they were the ones, after the onset of the LGM, who developed the most effective ways to exploit the foraging resources of the drier environments of those regions.

Migration did not recede as a factor in African history during the past three thou-sand years. The literature of African history since 1000 BCE abounds with population movements, far more numerous and diverse than could begin to be considered here – varying from the movements of whole communities into new areas, to the establish-ing of merchant groups in distant towns, to the urban colonization of formerly rural countryside, as in the case of the Yoruba in Nigeria between 700 and 1000 CE (Ogundiran 2003). The most widespread of these later migrations was that of the Bantu speakers, considered in the next chapter.

SEE ALSO: 11 Human migrations and the histories of major language families; 13 Sub-Saharan Africa: archaeology; 14 Sub-Saharan Africa: human genetics; 15 Levant and North Africa: Afroasiatic linguistic history

References

Ambrose, S. H. (1982) Archaeology and linguistic reconstructions of history in East Africa. In C. Ehret & M. Posnansky (eds.), *The Archaeological and Linguistic Reconstruction of African History*. Berkeley: University of California Press.

Arkell, A. J. (1949) *Early Khartoum*. London: Oxford University Press.

Armstrong, R. G. (1964) *The Study of African Languages*. Ibadan: Institute of African Studies.

Barnett, T. (1999) *The Emergence of Food Production in Ethiopia*. British Archaeological Record International Series 763. Oxford: Archaeopress.

Barthelme, J. (1985) *Fisher-Hunters and Neolithic Pastoralists in East Turkana*. British Archaeo-logical Record International Series 254. Oxford: Archaeopress.

Bendor-Samuel, J. (ed.) (1989) *The Niger-Congo Languages*. Lanham, MD: University Press of America.

Ehret, C. (1986) Proposals on Khoisan reconstruction. *Sprache und Geschichte in Afrika* 7(2), 105–130.

Ehret, C. (1998) *An African Classical Age*. Charlottesville: University of Virginia Press.

Ehret, C. (2001) Bantu expansions: re-envisioning a central problem of early African history; and Christopher Ehret responds. *International Journal of African Historical Studies* 34(1), 5–41 and 82–87.

Ehret, C. (2011) *History and the Testimony of Language*. Berkeley: University of California Press.

Gonzales, R. M. (2009) *Societies, Religion, and History: Central-East Tanzanians and the World They Created, c. 200 BCE to 1800 CE*. New York: Columbia University Press.

Heine, B., Hoff, H., & Vossen, R. (1977) Neuere Ergebnisse zur Territorialgeschichte der Ban-tusprachen [New findings in the territorial history of the Bantu languages]. In W. J. G. Möhlig, F. Rottland, & B. Heine (eds.), *Zur Sprachgeschichte und Ethnohistorie in Afrika* [Toward linguistic history and ethnohistory in Africa]. Berlin: Reimer.

Huysecom, E., Rasse, M., Lespez, L., et al. (2009) The emergence of pottery in Africa during the tenth millennium cal BC: new evidence from Ounjougou (Mali). *Antiquity* 83(322), 905–917.

Kimber, C. T. (2000) Origins of domesticated sorghum and its early diffusion to India and China. In C. W. Smith & R. A. Fredriksen (eds.), *Sorghum: Origin, History, Technology, and Production*. New York: John Wiley.

Klieman, K. (2003) *"The Pygmies were our compass": Bantu and Batwa in the History of West Central Africa*. Portsmouth, NH: Heinemann.

Kröpelin, S. & Kuper, R. (2006) Climate-controlled occupation in the Sahara: motor of Africa's evolution. *Science* 313(5788) (Aug. 11), 803–807.

Munson, P. (1986) Africa's prehistoric past. In P. Martin & P. O'Meara (eds.), *Africa*. 2nd edn., Bloomington: Indiana University Press.

Nurse, D., Hewson, J., Rose, S., et al. (2008) *Verbal Categories in Niger-Congo*. St. Johns: Memorial University of Newfoundland.

Ogundiran, A. (2003) Chronology, material culture, and pathways to the cultural history of the Yoruba-Edo region, 500 BC–AD 1800. In T. Falola & C. Jennings (eds.), *Sources and Methods in African History: Spoken, Written, Unearthed*. Rochester: University of Rochester Press.

Saidi, C. (2010) *Women's Authority and Society in Early East-Central Africa*. Rochester: Rochester University Press.

Saxon, D. E. (1982) Linguistic evidence for the eastward spread of Ubangian peoples. In C. Ehret & M. Posnansky (eds.), *The Archaeological and Linguistic Reconstruction of African History*. Berkeley, Los Angeles: University of California Press, pp. 66–77.

Schoenbrun, D. L. (1998) *A Green Place, a Good Place: Agrarian Change, Gender, and Social Identity in the Great Lakes Region to the 15th Century*. Portsmouth, NH: Heinemann.

Shaw, T. & Daniells, S. G. H. (1984) Excavations at Iwo-Eleru, Ondo State, Nigeria. *West African Journal of Archaeology* 14, 7–100.

Stewart, J. M. (2002) The potential of Proto-Potou-Akanic-Bantu as a pilot Proto-Niger-Congo, and the reconstructions updated. *Journal of African Languages and Linguistics* 23, 197–224.

Vansina, J. (2004) *How Societies Are Born: Governance in West-Central Africa before 1600*. Charlottesville: University of Virginia Press.

Wendorf, F. & Schild, R. (1998) Nabta Playa and its role in northeastern African history. *Anthropological Archaeology* 20, 97–123.

Williamson, K. & Blench, R. (2000) Niger-Congo. In B. Heine & D. Nurse, *African Languages*. Cambridge: Cambridge University Press, pp. 11–42.

13

Sub-Saharan Africa: archaeology

Peter Robertshaw

This chapter discusses human migrations south of the Sahara during the Holocene, focused mainly on pastoral populations in eastern Africa and the migrations of Bantu speakers during the past 3000 years. The dating provided by archaeology currently places these migrations more recently than that derived from linguistics.

For the peoples of Africa, migration has been a fact of life since early humans began to expand their range across the continent. Migrations continue today with the African diaspora to developed countries, as well as rural-to-urban migration within Africa. In the face of variable climates and the challenges and opportunities presented by political, economic, and social circumstances, Africans have frequently chosen the option of migration, linked often to flexibility of ethnic identity and an ability to speak several languages. Archaeologists thus face the challenge of discerning the larger-scale migrations of the past against this background of constant movement, as, for example, in the nomadic existence of pastoral peoples in semi-arid regions.

Perusal of a distribution map of African language families (see Figure 11.1) reveals their spread across much of the continent during the Holocene (chapter 12). While language spread cannot be simplistically equated to population migration, it is nevertheless probable that such language spreads frequently involved movements of people. Clearly, potential exists for the reconstruction of prehistoric migrations by combining data from linguistics, genetics, and archaeology. However, the history of research has demonstrated how easy it is for practitioners of one discipline to accept the results provided by another discipline as incontrovertible facts and then bend their own interpretations to suit these "facts," which often turn out to have been originally proposed as no more than plausible hypotheses. Therefore, I intend to stick closely to the archaeological evidence for Holocene migrations in sub-Saharan Africa; this does not always tally with the evidence for migrations proffered by other disciplines.

The Global Prehistory of Human Migration: The Encyclopedia of Global Human Migration Volume 1,
First Edition. Edited by Peter Bellwood.
© 2013 John Wiley & Sons, Ltd. Published 2015 by John Wiley & Sons, Ltd.

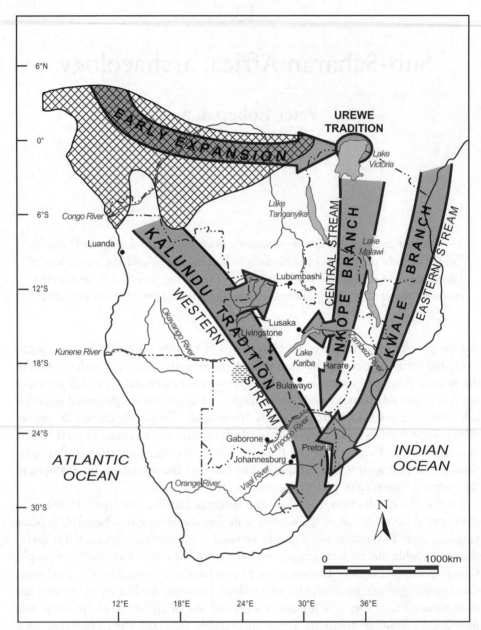

Figure 13.1 The spread of Bantu speakers according to the archaeological record (modified from Huffman 2007: 336). The central African rainforest region is hatched. With the permission of University of KwaZulu-Natal Press.

The recognition of migrations from archaeological data is a methodological challenge that has vexed archaeologists for decades. Migration has also fallen in and out of favor among archaeologists as an explanation of culture change. For the Holocene archaeology of sub-Saharan Africa, migration has been mostly identified from the examination of the distribution of particular styles of pottery decoration in combination with radiocarbon dating evidence. Critics of migration hypotheses have been quick to seize upon the problems inherent in an overreliance on studies of pottery decoration. They have argued that such decoration cannot be simply equated to ethnic identity but is something that was (and still is) actively employed by individuals, families, factions, and other social groups in the negotiation of political, economic, ritual, and social relationships as well as in the creation and manipulation of individual, group, and ethnic identity. Indeed, recent ethnographic research in Africa has demonstrated that it is the manner in which pots are made, rather than their decoration, that more closely reflects ethnic identity.

Nevertheless, while it may be difficult to identify migrations from archaeological data, this does not mean that migrations did not occur. Armed with these caveats, I investigate the archaeology of migrations in sub-Saharan Africa from the end of the last Ice Age to about the end of the first millennium CE.

The Green Sahara and its aftermath

Throughout prehistory, the Sahara Desert has acted as a pump, drawing people in during episodes of wetter climate and forcing them out as the desert expanded during drier periods (Kröpelin & Kuper 2006). Thus, it is with the Sahara that we must begin our account of migrations in the regions to the south. Following the end of the last Ice Age, the Sahara became relatively verdant. There developed a way of life characterized by lacustrine and riverine settlements with evidence for fishing, hunting, and the gathering of wild cereal grains. In time domestic livestock – primarily cattle, sheep, and goats – were added to the available resources. Not only is there evidence of these adaptations in the Sahara, but they are also found further south, prompting debate about whether they were spread by migrations and about where they originated.

Distinctive artifacts associated with the fishing-gathering-hunting adaptation that preceded animal domestication are bone harpoons and pottery with wavy-line and dotted wavy-line decoration. Harpoons are found all the way from the site of Ishango in the eastern Democratic Republic of Congo, northwards to Lake Turkana in Kenya, on the middle Nile in the Sudan, and westwards across the Sahara (Yellen 1998). The pottery is more or less confined to the middle Nile and the Sahara, though there are a few small sherds of possible dotted wavy-line pottery from sites in Kenya. While some archaeologists posit migration as an explanation for these artifact distributions, the fact that there exists considerable variation in the stone artifact tool kits found on the sites in question indicates diverse cultural traditions tied together by stimulus diffusion and/or independent invention of harpoons and pottery in different regions (Holl 2005). Furthermore, the dating evidence lacks any clear geographical trends and thus cannot be easily shoehorned into a migration scenario.

Migrations out of the Sahara by cattle-keeping pastoralists must have taken place as the Sahara became drier, albeit with wetter episodes, from the mid-Holocene. The expansion of herding peoples towards West Africa is evident archaeologically at sites in the Tilemsi Valley and the Chad Basin (Smith 1980; Breunig et al. 1996). Indeed, it was proposed many years ago that the migration of pastoralists into the Sahel and savannah regions and consequent population growth stimulated the development of African agriculture (Clark 1976). Further south, in present-day Ghana, the first adoption of farming, evident from sites of the Kintampo Complex (c. 2500–1400 BCE), has been explained as the result of either diffusion or migration (Stahl 1994; Watson 2005).

Pastoral peoples in East Africa and the Cape region of South Africa

Domestic livestock (cattle, sheep, and/or goats) made their first appearance in East Africa around the northern shores of Lake Turkana in the middle of the third millennium BCE (Barthelme 1985). The date of their arrival fits well with a model of a northwest to southeast spread from the Sahara via the middle Nile, though the paucity of archaeological research and thus evidence for early domestic animals across Ethiopia and the southern Sudan inhibits our understanding of the scale of any migration that might be associated with the spread of these animals. We have more archaeological evidence of early domestic animals and pastoral communities from East Africa itself. It now appears probable that domestic animals spread south through East Africa from the Lake Turkana region in advance of what may have been a series of migrations of stone-tool-using (and not iron-using) herding peoples. The earliest bones of domestic animals, found in the Lake Victoria basin and in the Rift Valley and adjacent regions of southern Kenya and northern Tanzania around the end of the third millennium BCE, occur in small numbers in what are otherwise hunter-gatherer occupation sites, whose pottery and stone tool traditions indicate that their inhabitants had been present in these regions long before they acquired domestic animals (Bower 1991).

Perhaps as much as a thousand or more years later, in the last millennium BCE, we find settlement sites in the Rift Valley and adjacent savannas of southern Kenya and northern Tanzania inhabited by peoples with large herds of cattle, sheep, and goats, as well as occasional donkeys. These sites contain distinctive stone artifact and pottery assemblages. Notable is a bewildering variety of pottery decoration styles, whose taxonomy and interpretation has vexed archaeologists for many years (Karega-Munene 2003). One interpretation, which has not gone unchallenged, is that there are several chronologically and/or geographically distinct ceramic traditions in the savanna regions of East Africa in the last millennium BCE and early centuries CE (Collett & Robertshaw 1983), which may be correlated with speakers of different languages from two of Africa's language families, Afroasiatic and Nilo-Saharan (Ambrose 1982). The historical linguistic evidence clearly shows that there were expansions southwards through East Africa during this period of peoples speaking Southern Cushitic (i.e. Afroasiatic) and Southern Nilotic (i.e. Nilo-Saharan) languages, who herded domestic animals (chapter 12). The most parsimonious interpretation would link this linguistic evidence for migration to these archaeological sites, often collectively called the "Pastoral Neolithic" or simply the "Neolithic" of East Africa. More precise correlations between linguistics and archaeology are hazardous; for example, one comparatively well-defined archaeological tradition is the Elmenteitan (Robertshaw 1988), which has been correlated with Southern Nilotic speakers. However, vocabulary-based reconstructions of the cultural traits of these people indicates that they never engaged in fishing and considered fish unsuitable for consumption (Ehret 1998: 181), yet Elmenteitan sites in the Lake Victoria region contain lots of fish bones (Lane et al. 2007). Similarly, both proto-Southern Nilotic and proto-Southern Cushitic speakers probably cultivated domestic cereals, but no direct evidence in the form of plant remains has yet been found at any of the relevant archaeological sites.

Setting aside these linguistic and archaeological conundrums, it seems clear that the archaeological evidence is indicative of one or more migrations into the savannas of East Africa by pastoral peoples. These migrations were likely propelled by the search for new grazing opportunities for the domestic herds, but also hampered by the challenges posed by encounters with new vectors of disease (Gifford-Gonzalez 2005). By late in the last millennium BCE, if not earlier, pastoral peoples and their livestock were well established as far south as the southern edge of the Serengeti ecosystem where further expansion was likely inhibited by the presence of tsetse fly, the vector of the livestock disease, trypanosomiasis.

However, by about 2000 years ago, and apparently in advance of the migrations of iron-using Bantu speakers (see below), sheep (but not cattle) and pottery had reached the southwestern corner of Africa (Sealy & Yates 1994). Debate rages as to whether the first arrival of sheep at the Cape was the result of diffusion without any significant human population movements, or a migration of the ancestors of the Khoekhoe, the people whom early Dutch travelers referred to as "Hottentots" (Fauvelle-Aymar & Sadr 2008). Similarities between early pottery at the Cape and the Elmenteitan pottery of East Africa have been cited in support of the migration hypothesis (Smith 2005: 175–179), which received a recent boost from genetic research (Henn et al. 2008). However, from an archaeological perspective there are huge geographical gaps in our knowledge along the probable tsetse-free corridor between Tanzania and the Cape. Nevertheless, if there was no Khoekhoe migration from northern Botswana to the Cape about 2000 years ago, then there was a later one, probably in the late first millennium CE (Sadr 1998).

Archaeology and the Bantu expansions

The remarkable similarity between numerous languages, grouped together as the Bantu branch of the Niger–Congo language family, distributed across a vast swath of Africa and now spoken by more than 250 million people, is best explained by invoking a complex series of migrations, population expansions, and language spreads. Bantu languages occur from their region of origin in eastern Cameroon to the southernmost limit of summer-rainfall agriculture in the eastern Cape of South Africa. They can be separated into one major branch, East Benue-Congo, including Bantu proper, and several smaller branches grouped together as Western Savanna Bantu (Ehret 2001; Figure 12.1).

When it comes to archaeological evidence for the Bantu expansions, a link is usually made to sites that provide evidence for the first appearance of iron-working, agriculture, and settled village life in southern Africa. These sites were often referred to as belonging to the Early Iron Age, a term that has fallen out of favor and mostly been replaced by "Chifumbaze Complex" (Phillipson 2005: 249–261), named after a site in Mozambique where the distinctive pottery was first excavated. Nowadays, the Chifumbaze Complex can be correlated with Savanna Bantu or more narrowly with Eastern Bantu. On the basis of pottery vessel shapes, decorative motifs and the layout of the decoration on the pots, two major traditions (Urewe and Kalundu) and branches thereof have been identified (Mitchell 2002: 262–271; Huffman 2007). When these are plotted on a map and considered together with the dates for the different sites, patterns of expansion can be discerned (Figure 13.1), with the earliest dates, from the middle of the last millennium BCE or earlier, found on Urewe tradition sites in the Great Lakes region of central Africa and the latest dates, around the 10th century CE, from the Eastern Cape of South Africa. The archaeological evidence for these Savanna Bantu expansions comprises not only the pots and the dates for the sites in which they are found, but also and more controversially indications of a shared worldview, expressed in the layout of the settlements as what has been called the "Central Cattle Pattern" (Huffman 2007).

A minority view among archaeologists (e.g. Robertson & Bradley 2000) is that the Bantu languages spread across Africa without any significant population movements, an argument that is entirely plausible in theory. However, this view is virtually untenable in this case in the light of both new genetic data (see Pakendorf et al. 2011; chapter 14) and the fact that agriculture, settled village life, iron-working, and perhaps herding arrived together over most of southern Africa, though not further north. Earlier researchers added the "Negroid physical type" to this trait list, but we now recognize both the inadequacy of pigeonholing human biological diversity into types such as "Negroid" and "Bushmanoid" and the fact that the human skeletons found on Chifumbaze Complex sites exhibit considerable physical variability. Similarly, readers should not equate the bold arrows on Figure 13.1 to mass migrations of populations streaming across Africa like army divisions on modern battlefields. These farmers probably "hopped" from one preferred region, with suitable arable soils, to the next, maintaining contacts with the people left behind and gradually filling in the intervening areas with villages. Political fissions, droughts, and other calamities may have fueled these movements as much as population growth. The expansion process also frequently involved the assimilation of indigenous hunter-gatherer peoples, as well as perhaps the wholesale adoption of agriculture and other traits of village life by erstwhile hunter-gatherer communities.

The makers of the Urewe tradition reached the Great Lakes region as a result of a process of gradual expansion of Bantu-speaking communities through the central African rainforest from their original homeland further to the northwest. A dearth of archaeological field research, particularly on the western side of the continent south of the equatorial forest, hampers our understanding. However, we know that farming settlements were established in the tropical forests during the last millennium BCE (Eggert 1997). Here, food came not from cereal crops and cattle, but from vegetatively propagated crops such as yams and perhaps bananas, the latter a crop introduced to Africa from across the Indian Ocean. Iron smelting, vital for the manufacture of tools needed in all likelihood to farm successfully within the forests, *may* also have been practiced as early as the third millennium BCE in parts of Cameroon and the Central African Republic (Zangato & Holl 2010).

Later migrations

The second millennium CE saw numerous migrations in many parts of the continent, indeed far more than can be mentioned, let alone discussed, in this chapter. These were motivated by a variety of causes, including climate changes, political upheavals, religion, economic opportunities, and slavery; and abetted by factors such as the arrival of the horse and chain mail in West Africa, which encouraged predatory expansion. Our knowledge of these migrations derives primarily from historical, rather than archaeological, sources. They include the diasporas of the Mande and Fulbe in West Africa; the migrations of Shuwa Arabs west from the Nile Valley; the expansion of various Nilotic- and Cushitic-speaking peoples, including the Luo, Maasai, Rendille, and Borana, southwards into East Africa; and the upheavals and migrations in southern Africa, known as the *Mfecane*, associated with the rise of the Zulu state in the 19th century. Finally, we should not forget the forced migrations of millions of Africans who were taken as slaves to North Africa, the Middle East, and the Americas, about which there is considerable archaeological evidence.

SEE ALSO: 12 Sub-Saharan Africa: linguistics; 14 Sub-Saharan Africa: human genetics

References

Ambrose, S. H. (1982) Archaeological and linguistic reconstructions of history in East Africa. In C. Ehret & M. Posnansky (eds.), *The Archaeological and Linguistic Reconstruction of African History*. Berkeley: University of California Press, pp. 104–157.

Barthelme, J. W. (1985) *Fisher-Hunters and Neolithic Pastoralists in East Turkana, Kenya*. BAR International Series 254. Oxford: British Archaeological Reports.

Bower, J. R. F. (1991) The Pastoral Neolithic of East Africa. *Journal of World Prehistory* 5(1), 49–82.

Breunig, P., Neumann, K., & van Neer, W. (1996) New research on the Holocene settlement and environment of the Chad Basin in Nigeria. *African Archaeological Review* 13, 111–145.

Clark, J. D. (1976) Prehistoric populations and pressures favoring plant domestication in Africa. In J. R. Harlan, M. J. de Wet, & A. B. L. Stemler (eds.), *Origins of African Plant Domestication*. The Hague: Mouton, pp. 67–105.

Collett, D. & Robertshaw, P. (1983) Pottery traditions of early pastoral communities in Kenya. *Azania*, 18, 107–125.

Eggert, M. K. H. (1997) Equatorial African Iron Age. In J. O. Vogel (ed.), *Encyclopedia of Precolonial Africa*. Walnut Creek: Altamira, pp. 429–435.

Ehret, C. (1998) *An African Classical Age: Eastern and Southern Africa in World History, 1000 B.C. to A.D. 400*. Charlottesville: University Press of Virginia.

Ehret, C. (2001) Bantu expansions: re-envisioning a central problem of early African history. *International Journal of African Historical Studies*, 34(1), 5–41.

Fauvelle-Aymar, F.-X. & Sadr, K. (eds.) (2008) Khoekhoe and the origins of herding in Southern Africa [special themed issue]. *Southern African Humanities* 20(1), 1–248.

Gifford-Gonzalez, D. (2005) Pastoralism and its consequences. In Stahl (2005), pp. 187–224.

Henn, B. M., Gignoux, C., Lin, A. A., et al. (2008) Y-chromosomal evidence of a pastoralist migration through Tanzania to southern Africa. *Proceedings of the National Academy of Sciences* 105(31), 10693–10698.

Holl, A. F. C. (2005) Holocene "aquatic" adaptations in north tropical Africa. In Stahl (2005), pp. 174–186.

Huffman, T. N. (2007) *Handbook to the Iron Age: The Archaeology of Pre-Colonial Farming Societies in Southern Africa*. Scottsville: University of KwaZulu-Natal Press.

Karega-Munene (2003) The East African Neolithic: a historical perspective. In C. M. Kusimba & S. B. Kusimba (eds.), *East African Archaeology: Foragers, Potters, Smiths, and Traders*. Philadelphia: University of Pennsylvania Museum Publications, pp. 17–32.

Kröpelin, S. & Kuper, R. (2006) Climate-controlled Holocene occupation in the Sahara: motor of Africa's evolution. *Science* 313, 803–807.

Lane, P., Ashley, C., Seitsonen, O., et al. (2007) The transition to farming in eastern Africa: new faunal and dating evidence from Wadh Lang'o and Usenge, Kenya. *Antiquity* 81, 62–81.

Mitchell, P. J. (2002) *The Archaeology of Southern Africa*. Cambridge: Cambridge University Press.

Pakendorf, B., Bostoen, K., & de Filippo, C. (2011) Molecular perspectives on the Bantu expansion: a synthesis. *Language Dynamics and Change* 1, 50–88.

Phillipson, D. W. (2005) *African Archaeology*, 3rd edn. Cambridge: Cambridge University Press.

Robertshaw, P. (1988) The Elmenteitan: an early food-producing culture in East Africa. *World Archaeology* 20, 57–69.

Robertson, J. H. & Bradley, R. (2000) A new paradigm: the African Early Iron Age without Bantu migrations. *History in Africa* 27, 287–323.

Sadr, K. (1998) The first herders at the Cape of Good Hope. *African Archaeological Review* 15, 101–132.

Sealy, J. & Yates, R. (1994) The chronology of the introduction of pastoralism to the Cape, South Africa. *Antiquity* 68, 58–67.

Smith, A. B. (1980) Domesticated cattle in the Sahara and their introduction into West Africa. In M. A. J. Williams & H. Faure (eds.), *The Sahara and the Nile*. Rotterdam: Balkema, pp. 489–501.

Smith, A. B. (2005) *African Herders: Emergence of Pastoral Traditions*. Walnut Creek: Altamira.

Stahl, A. B. (1994) Innovation, diffusion and culture contact: the Holocene archaeology of Ghana. *Journal of World Prehistory* 8, 51–112.

Stahl, A. B. (ed.) (2005) *African Archaeology: A Critical Introduction*. Malden, MA: Blackwell.

Watson, D. J. (2005) Under the rocks: reconsidering the origin of the Kintampo tradition and the development of food production in the savanna-forest/forest of West Africa. *Journal of African Archaeology* 3(1), 3–55.

Yellen, J. (1998) Barbed bone points: tradition and continuity in Saharan and Sub-Saharan Africa. *African Archaeological Review* 15, 173–198.

Zangato, É. & Holl, A. F. C. (2010) On the iron front: new evidence from north-central Africa. *Journal of African Archaeology* 8(1), 7–23.

14

Sub-Saharan Africa: human genetics

Evelyne Heyer and Jorge Rocha

This chapter uses newly derived autosomal genetic data on African populations to propose a population history based on the distributions of eight different ancestral configurations, classified in terms of the linguistic families discussed in chapters 12 and 13.

The fact that Africa is the continent of origin of our species has been formally demonstrated with genetic data using two complementary approaches. Based on uniparental mitochondrial data, Vigilant and colleagues (1991) showed that non-African individuals form only a susbset of the global phylogenetic tree of our species, and that the root of the tree can be found in Africa. This result has been further confirmed with Y-chomosome data (Thomson et al. 2000). More recent studies of multi-locus autosomal data confirm that African populations have a higher level of genetic diversity than populations elsewhere, and that this genetic diversity decreases with distance from Africa (Li et al. 2008; Jakobsson et al. 2008).

Most genetic studies show that the current patterns of biological and cultural variation in Africa are likely to have been strongly influenced by the superimposition during the Holocene of different migratory streams over an ancient population structure. According to Ehret (chapter 12, this volume), most Holocene population movements apart from those of the Khoisan are likely to have been driven by the emergence of three separate food-producing economies: (1) a tradition associated with peoples speaking early Cushitic (Afroasiatic) languages west of the Red Sea basin; (2) a tradition associated with early Nilo-Saharan-speaking peoples who originated near the confluence of the White and Blue Niles; and (3) a tradition developed among early Niger-Congo-speaking peoples in West Africa (the locations of these language families are shown in Figures 11.1 and 12.1). All these economies relied essentially on local plant domestication, and it is possible that cattle rearing was an early innovation

The Global Prehistory of Human Migration: The Encyclopedia of Global Human Migration Volume 1,
First Edition. Edited by Peter Bellwood.

associated with the Nilo-Saharan tradition before the arrival of other domesticated animals from the Middle East.

The summary of African population history given in this chapter is based on detailed phylogenetic studies of uniparental markers and, more recently, multi-locus autosomal data in living African populations. In particular, we explore the recent study of Tishkoff et al. (2009), which used a panel of 1,327 autosomal DNA polymorphisms to characterize genetic variation in 2,432 individuals from 113 populations. They found that African populations had different proportions of 14 basic genetic components that could represent major ancestral population clusters. In this chapter we follow Tishkoff's et al. (2009) nomenclature and term them Associated Ancestral Components (AACs). In order to illustrate how human migrations have affected different regions of Africa, we have used this multi-locus dataset to construct maps that display the geographical distributions and regional frequencies of eight of the more widespread ancestral components (Figure 14.1).

East Africa

Eastern Africa has produced the earliest fossil evidence for anatomical modern humans and is the most likely source for the modern human colonization of Eurasia (see chapters 3 and 4). Using classical genetic markers, Cavalli-Sforza et al. (1994) noted that genetic variation in Ethiopians (including Cushitic and Ethio-Semitic Afroasiatic-speaking groups) was a likely result of admixture between a sub-Saharan African substrate (around 60%) and a northern African or southwest Asian exogenous component (around 40%). Consistent with these findings, studies based on mitochondrial DNA (Kivisild et al. 2004; Olivieri et al. 2006) have shown that some lineages with Eurasian ancestry entered the area at different time periods. In addition, Y-chromosome analyses have shown evidence of Holocene gene flow from southern Arabia across the Bab-el-Mandab strait (Kivisild et al. 2004; Luis et al. 2004).

The multi-locus genetic pattern in eastern Africa is dominated by "Cushitic" and "Nilo-Saharan" AACs, representing, on average, about 60 percent of the genetic composition of populations sampled in the region (Figure 14.1 (a) and (b)). Genetic components associated with Niger–Congo speakers are also important in Kenya and Tanzania (28%, on average) and will be discussed in the context of the Bantu expansions. On a continental scale, high levels of heterogeneous ancestry are observed in this region.

The "Cushitic" AAC (Figure 14.1 (a)) predominates among Cushitic-speaking populations from Sudan, Ethiopia, Kenya, and Tanzania, but is also common in Nilo-Saharan and Niger-Congo-speaking populations in Kenya and Tanzania. These patterns are concordant with linguistic and archeological evidence which suggests that dispersal and admixture between neighboring Nilo-Saharan and Cushitic-speaking peoples with strong pastoralist habits were major events shaping current patterns of human diversity between 8000 BC and 500 BCE (Newman 1995; Blench 2006: 98–99; 158–160). Amongst other Afroasiatic-speaking populations, the "Cushitic" AAC is also common amongst the Ethiosemitic-speaking Beta Israel from Ethiopia and the Berber-speaking Mozabite from Algeria, but it remains rare among Chadic Afroasiatic speakers (Tishkoff et al. 2009). Thus, it is likely that this AAC reflects an ancestral genetic link between non-Chadic Afroasiatic-speaking peoples. This link is also illustrated by the distribution of the Y-chromosome haplotype carrying the M35 mutation (E-M35 or E3b1b1), which partially overlaps with that of the "Cushitic" AAC (Underhill et al. 2001; Cruciani et al. 2004; Ehret et al. 2004).

The "Nilo-Saharan" AAC (Figure 14.1 (b)) is predominant (39%) among sampled Nilo-Saharan populations from Sudan and Kenya, who speak Nilotic languages from the Eastern Sudanic branch of Nilo-Saharan. The present distribution of the A3b2 (A-M13) Y-chromosome haplotype provides further evidence for a close relationship between Nilo-Saharan and Afroasiatic-speaking populations (Semino et al. 2002; Wood et al. 2005; Tishkoff et al. 2007; Hassan et al. 2008).

Sahel

Based on analysis of mtDNA variation, Cerný et al. (2007) stress the importance of the Sahel region immediately south of the Sahara as a corridor connecting West and East Africa. In general, the mtDNA lineage composition of Chad Basin groups is relatively homogeneous and poorly differentiated from neighboring populations in West Africa, west central Africa, and East Africa (Cerný et al. 2007, 2009). However, two mtDNA haplogroups – L3e5 and L3f3 – are relatively frequent only in populations speaking the Chadic branch of Afroasiatic. Based on the phylogenetic relationship between L3f3 and L3f lineages from East Africa, Cerný and his colleagues (2009) conclude that L3f3 could have been carried into Lake Chad during the Holocene by proto-Chadic speakers originating from a Cushitic–Chadic motherland in East Africa, in accordance with a linguistic model for Chadic dispersals proposed by Blench (Blench 2006: 159–162; see also chapter 15, this volume).

Analysis of Y-chromosome variation provides even stronger evidence for a pronounced genetic peculiarity of Chadic-speakers. Cruciani et al. (2010) found that the NRY haplotype R1b1a (R-V88), with an estimated mutation age of 7000-5000 BCE, reaches frequencies as high as 90 percent in Chadic-speaking groups, while remaining rare in neighboring non-Chadic populations. According to phylogeographic considerations this haplogroup is likely to have originated outside Africa, although presently it is only rarely observed in Eurasia. Outside the Chad Basin, the only other region where R-V88 is found at moderate frequencies is North Africa, suggesting a genetic link between Chadic-speaking peoples from the Sahel and other Afroasiatic-speaking groups to the north. Cruciani et al. (2010) argue that, unlike the mtDNA L3f3-based evidence, this link favors an alternative linguistic model proposed by Ehret (2002), in which proto-Chadic arrived in lake Chad from the north rather than the east, across the central Sahara, as an offshoot of a North Erythraean group within Afroasiatic that also included Semitic, Berber, and Ancient Egyptian.

Multi-locus data have disclosed a "Chadic" AAC (Figure 14.1 (c)), that predominates among Chadic-speaking groups (around 47%) and partially overlaps the distribution of the Y-chromosome haplogroup R-V88. However, unlike R-V88, this AAC is not restricted to Chadic-speaking populations and is also significant in Nilo-Saharans,

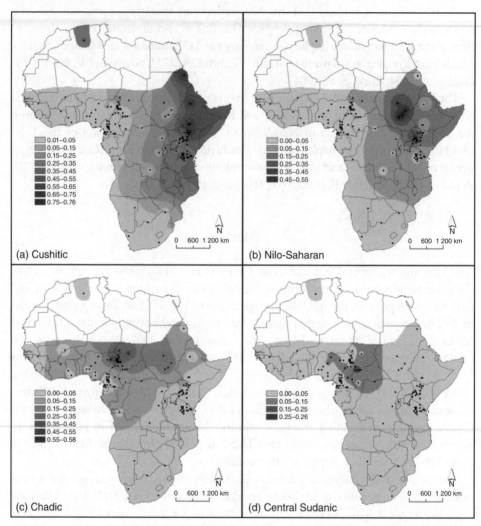

Figure 14.1 Maps displaying the geographical distributions and frequencies of major Associated Ancestral Components in Sub-Saharan Africa (after Tishkoff et al. 2009). The black dots represent sampled populations. (Note that Niger-Congo languages are designated "Niger-Kordofonian" in Tishkoff et al. 2009). The maps were generated with the ArcGIS 9.2 program (www.esri.com) using an Inverse Distance Weighted method to interpolate the data. The darker the tone, the higher the frequency of an Associated Ancestral Component.

including Central Sudanic and Saharan-speaking groups from Chad (around 24%), and even Nilotes from Sudan (around 24%). This distribution seems to suggest that Chadic speakers dispersed westwards into lake Chad from eastern Africa, leaving genetic footprints of their passage through admixture with local Nilo-Saharan speakers along the way.

An additional "Central Sudanic" AAC (Figure 14.1 (d)) is most frequent among Sahelian populations that speak languages belonging to the Central Sudanic branch of Nilo-Saharan (around 20%). This component is probably associated with westward

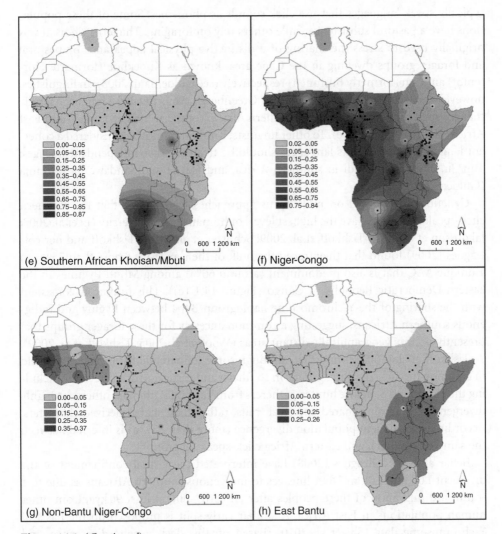

Figure 14.1 (*Continued*)

migration of Nilo-Saharan groups from northeast Africa into lake Chad (Tishkoff et al. 2009). However, some Nilo-Saharan groups from Chad have very low fractions of the "Central Sudanic" AAC, possibly as a consequence of language shift from Chadic to Nilo-Saharan, or genetic assimilation of Chadic groups by Nilo-Saharan-speaking populations. These examples show close cultural and/or genetic interaction between Central Sudanic and Chadic peoples that parallel, to some extent, that between Cushites and Nilotes further east.

Southern Africa

The peoples who inhabited southern Africa before the arrival of Bantu-speaking agriculturalists form a complex group of populations, generally designated *Khoisan*, who typically speak languages that use click sounds as phonemes. Some of these populations have a pastoral subsistence while others rely on foraging. The term Khoisan was originally used to stress the sharing of a distinctive physical appearance by pastoral and forager groups dwelling in the Cape area, known as Khoekhoe (formerly Hottentot) and San (formerly Bushmen) respectively (see Güldemann 2008). In linguistics, however, the term "Khoisan" was used by Greenberg (1963) to label a language family that grouped click-languages from southern Africa (southern Africa Khoisan) and East Africa (Hadza and Sandawe). To other linguists, Khoisan cannot be considered a coherent language group and its languages should be treated as five independent lineages: Tuu, Ju, and Khoe-Kwadi in southern Africa, and Hazda and Sandawe in Tanzania (Güldemann 2008).

Genetic studies based on multi-locus approaches have shown that the southern click-speaking groups have the highest levels of human genetic diversity (Li et al. 2008; Jakobsson et al. 2008; Tishkoff et al. 2009; Schuster et al. 2010). Tishkoff and her colleagues (2009) found that they traced the bulk of their ancestry (more than 75%) to a unique AAC that is also predominant (around 60%) among Mbuti Pygmies in the eastern Democratic Republic of Congo (Figure 14.1 (e)). This finding is consistent with the sharing of the Y-chromosome haplogroup B2b4 between Pygmy and indigenous southern Africans, suggesting a common ancestry for these forager groups that presently occupy geographically distant areas (Wood et al. 2005; Tishkoff et al. 2009).

Tishkoff et al. (2007) found that, although some uniparental haplogroups are held in common by click-speaking groups in southern and eastern Africa (the latter including the Hazda and Sandawe hunter-gatherers from Tanzania), they are otherwise highly divergent, representing shared ancestral traits, rather than shared derived characters. Accordingly, an ancient population divergence (more than 35 kya) is inferred between the sampled southern and eastern Africa click-speaking groups.

Behar and his colleagues (2008) have interpreted the virtual confinement of the divergent L0d and L0k mtDNA lineages to indigenous southern Africans as due to a southward migration of these peoples after an early split, at least 90 kya, from other human populations in East Africa. A similar early split is proposed on the basis of Y-chromosome data (Shi et al. 2010). Based on this deep genetic divergence, and assuming that phonemic use of clicks arose only once, it has been suggested that click languages were originally spoken in the early history of modern humans (Tishkoff et al. 2007).

A much more recent link between eastern and southern African populations has been recently proposed by Henn et al. (2008), based on the sharing of high frequencies of the Y-chromosome haplotype E-M293 (E-M293) between Nilotic and Cushitic groups from Tanzania and the Khoe-speaking Khwe (Kxoe) from the Angolan/Namibian border. By analyzing patterns of microsatellite diversity and lineage sharing across sampled populations, this study suggested that the E-M293 haplotype was carried to southern Africa by a pastoralist migration originating in East Africa about 2,000 years ago. In general accordance with this hypothesis, Güldemann (2008) has presented linguistic evidence that the spread of pastoralism into southern Africa could have been associated with intruding Khoe-Kwadi speakers originating in eastern Africa. Coelho and colleagues (2009) have additionally suggested that migrating Khoe pastoralists might have carried the C-14010 lactose tolerance mutation from East Africa into southern Angola.

West Africa, central Africa, and the Bantu expansions

Major population movements in West Africa are likely to have been associated with the independent development by Niger–Congo-speaking peoples of a local Holocene agricultural tradition based on yams and oil palm. As the climate shifted towards wetter regimes, the West African planting tradition began to spread from woodland savanna into expanding rainforest environments, extending from the west Atlantic coast to Cameroon. The progressive settlement of rainforest areas by West African agricultural communities eventually led to the arrival, between eastern Nigeria and Cameroon, of Niger–Congo peoples speaking proto-Bantu (see chapter 12). By 1000 BCE, Bantu-speaking communities had begun to disperse out of their west central African home-land into subequatorial Africa (see chapter 13).

Central Africa is currently peopled by numerous sedentary agricultural populations, as well as by the mobile hunting-and-gathering rainforest Pygmies. An autosomal study of the latter has revealed a high level of genetic diversity, whereas neighboring non-Pygmy populations show an extremely low level of genetic differentiation (Verdu et al. 2009). The expansion of these non-Pygmy agriculturalists after 1000 BCE led to a fragmentation of the Pygmy populations, after which admixture with the farmers enabled rapid and substantial genetic differentiation. Recent studies estimate a total time span of Pygmy genetic history extending back for at least 50,000 years (Verdu et al. 2009; Batini et al. 2011).

One of the striking results of all genetic analyses is the extremely low level of genetic differentiation among the so called "Bantu populations." The spread of Bantu-speaking agriculturalists out of west central Africa provides a remarkable illustration of human long-range migration, and has been considered one of the clearest examples of con-cordance between cultural, linguistic, and genetic variation (Diamond & Bellwood 2003).

Until recently, most genetic studies of the Bantu focused almost exclusively on uniparental markers. The E1b1a (E-M2) haplogroup is the predominant Y-chromosome lineage in most sampled Niger-Congo-speaking peoples (more than 60%), providing clear evidence for genetic continuity between all the inheritors of the West African planting tradition (Underhill et al. 2001; Rosa et al. 2007; Berniell-Lee et al. 2009; de Filippo et al. 2011). However, some E-M2 sublineages reach high frequencies only in Bantu-speaking populations, and are thus good markers for Bantu expansion. In con-trast, several mtDNA haplogroups (rather than just one) are associated with Bantu-speaking populations (Salas et al. 2002). This might reflect larger effective population sizes of females than males, and/or sex-biased patterns of gene flow with pre-existing indigenous populations (Underhill et al. 2001; Salas et al. 2002; Wood et al. 2005; Berniell-Lee et al. 2009, Coelho et al. 2009).

The lower male effective population sizes are probably related to Bantu polygyny, which accelerates male lineage extinction if some males fail to sire children (Destro-Bisol et al. 2004; see Ségurel et al. 2008 for an alternative hypothesis). Biased gene flow patterns are likely to be caused by sociocultural factors favoring assimilation by farmers of indigenous hunter-gatherer females, but not of males. For example, some Bantu in west central Africa have virtually no Pygmy Y-chromosome lineages but carry mtDNA haplogroups, like L1c1a, which have a likely Pygmy origin (Quintana-Murci et al. 2008, Batini et al. 2011). However, neighboring Pygmy hunter-gatherer populations have relatively high frequencies of the Bantu Y-chromosome haplogroup E-M2 (25–60%), but virtually no Bantu mtDNA lineages (Destro-Bisol et al. 2004; Wood et al. 2005; Quintana-Murci et al. 2008; Berniell-Lee et al. 2009).

Despite the diversification of mtDNA lineages caused by assimilation of females from indigenous groups, Bantu-speaking peoples are still found to be closely related on the basis of their mtDNA haplogroup frequency profiles, and even populations from peripheral areas like southwestern and southeastern Africa can trace the bulk of their maternal heritage to the original heartland of the Bantu expansions in west central Africa (Salas et al. 2002; Coelho et al. 2009).

In the multi-locus study of Tishkoff and her colleagues (2009), a single ancestral component was found to predominate (about 63%) across all sampled Niger-Congo-speaking groups, providing additional evidence for the genetic closeness of these populations (Figure 14.1 (f)). In addition to this AAC, two more localized components were found: (1) a Non-Bantu Niger-Congo AAC, which is most frequent (about 19%) among populations from West Africa, from Senegal to Nigeria (Figure 14.1 (g)); and (2) an "Eastern Bantu" AAC, which is almost completely confined to sampled Bantu-speaking groups from Kenya, Rwanda, and Tanzania, with an average proportion of approximately 22 percent (Figure 14.1 (h)).

The distribution of the Niger-Congo AAC provides additional evidence of the genetic impact of the Bantu expansions on pre-existing populations in different African regions. For example, in Central Africa, western Pygmy groups have relatively high average fractions of this AAC (around 27%), while in the Chad Basin this AAC may reach proportions close to 50 percent in some Chadic and Central Sudanic speakers. On other hand, high levels of gene flow from pre-existing groups into Bantu newcomers can also be found in southern Africa and in East Africa (Salas et al. 2002; Coelho et al. 2009; Tishkoff et al. 2009).

SEE ALSO: 5 Early Old World migrations of *Homo sapiens*: archaeology; 12 Sub-Saharan Africa: linguistics; 13 Sub-Saharan Africa: archaeology

References

Batini, C., Lopes, J., Behar, D. M., et al. (2011) Insights into the demographic history of African Pygmies from complete mitochondrial genomes. *Molecular Biology and Evolution* 28, 1099–1110.

Behar, D. M., Villems, R., Soodyall, H., et al. (2008) The dawn of human matrilineal diversity. *American Journal of Human Genetics* 82, 1130–1140.

Blench, R. (2006) *Archeology, Language and the African Past*. Lanham, MD: AltaMira.

Berniell-Lee, G., Calafell, F., Bosch, E., et al. (2009) Genetic and demographic implications of the Bantu expansion: insights from human paternal lineages. *Molecular Biology and Evolution* 26, 1581–1589.

Cavalli-Sforza, L. L., Menozzi, P. P., & Piazza, A. (1994) *The History and Geography of Human Genes*. Princeton: Princeton University Press, pp. 169–174.

Cerný, V., Salas, A., Hájek, M., et al. (2007) A bidirectional corridor in the Sahel–Sudan belt and the distinctive features of the Chad Basin populations: a history revealed by the mitochondrial DNA genome. *Annals of Human Genetics* 71, 433–452.

Cerný, V., Fernandes, V., Costa, M. D., et al. (2009) Migration of Chadic speaking pastoralists within Africa based on population structure of Chad Basin and phylogeography of mitochondrial L3f haplogroup. *BMC Evolutionary Biology* 9, 63.

Coelho, M., Sequeira, F., Luiselli, D., et al. (2009) On the edge of Bantu expansions: mtDNA, Y chromosome and lactase persistence genetic variation in southwestern Angola. *BMC Evolutionary Biology* 9(80).

Cruciani, F., La Fratta, R., Santolamazza, P., et al. (2004) Phylogeographic analysis of haplogroup E3b (E-M215) Y chromosomes reveals multiple migratory events within and out of Africa. *American Journal of Human Genetics* 74, 1014–1022.

Cruciani, F., Trombetta, B., Sellitto, D., et al. (2010) Human Y chromosome haplogroup R-V88: a paternal genetic record of early mid Holocene trans-Saharan connections and the spread of Chadic languages. *European Journal of Human Genetics* 18, 800–807.

Destro-Bisol, G., Donati, F., Coia, V., et al. (2004) Variation of female and male lineages in sub-Saharan populations: the importance of sociocultural factors. *Molecular Biology and Evolution* 21, 1673–1682.

Diamond J. & Bellwood P. (2003) Farmers and their languages: the first expansions. *Science* 300, 597–603.

Ehret, C. (2002) *The Civilizations of Africa: A History to 1800*. Charlottesville: University of Virginia Press, pp. 78–80.

Ehret, C., Keita, S. O., & Newman, P. (2004) The origins of Afroasiatic. *Science* 306, 1680.

Filippo, C. de, Barbieri, C., Whitten, M., et al. (2011) Y-chromosomal variation in Sub-Saharan Africa: insights into the history of Niger-Congo groups. *Molecular Biology and Evolution* 28, 1255–1269.

Greenberg, J. H. (1963) *The Languages of Africa*. Bloomington: Indiana University, pp. 66–82.

Güldemann, T. (2008) A linguist's view: Khoe-Kwadi speakers as the earliest food producers of southern Africa. *Southern African Humanities* 20, 93–132.

Hassan, H. Y., Underhill, P. A., Cavalli-Sforza, L. L., & Ibrahim, M. E. (2008) Y-chromosome variation among Sudanese: restricted gene flow, concordance with language, geography, and history. *American Journal of Physical Anthropology* 137, 316–323.

Henn, B. M., Gignoux, C., Lin, A. A., et al. (2008) Y-chromosomal evidence of a pastoralist migration through Tanzania to southern Africa. *Proceedings of the National Academy of Sciences USA* 105, 10693–10698.

Jakobsson, M., Scholz, S. W., Scheet, P., et al. (2008) Genotype, haplotype and copy-number variation in worldwide human populations. *Nature* 451, 998–1003.

Kivisild, T., Reidla, M., Metspalu, E., et al. (2004) Ethiopian mitochondrial DNA heritage: tracking gene flow across and around the gate of tears. *American Journal of Human Genetics* 75, 752–770.

Li, J. Z., Absher, D. M., Tang, H., et al. (2008) Worldwide human relationships inferred from genome-wide patterns of variation. *Science* 319, 1100–1104.

Luis, J. R., Rowold, D. J., Regueiro, M., et al. (2004) The Levant versus the Horn of Africa: evidence for bidirectional corridors of human migrations. *American Journal of Human Genetics* 74, 788.

Newman, J. L. (1995) *The Peopling of Africa: A Geographic Interpretation*. New Haven: Yale University Press, pp. 51–57; 89–103; 158–177.

Olivieri, A., Achilli, A., Pala, M., et al. (2006) The mtDNA legacy of the Levantine early Upper Palaeolithic in Africa. *Science* 314, 1767–1770.

Quintana-Murci, L., Quach, H., Harmant, C., et al. (2008) Maternal traces of deep common ancestry and asymmetric gene flow between Pygmy hunter-gatherers and Bantu-speaking farmers. *Proceedings of the National Academy of Sciences* 105, 1596–1601.

Rosa, A., Ornelas, C., Jobling, M. A., et al. (2007) Y-chromosomal diversity in the population of Guinea-Bissau: a multiethnic perspective. *BMC Evolutionary Biology* 7(124).

Salas, A., Richards, M., De la Fe, T., et al. (2002) The making of the African mtDNA landscape. *American Journal of Human Genetics* 71, 1082–1111.

Schuster, S. C., Miller, W., Ratan, A., et al. (2010) Complete Khoisan and Bantu genomes from southern Africa. *Nature* 463, 943–947.

Ségurel, L., Martínez-Cruz, B., Quintana-Murci, L., et al. (2008) Sex-specific genetic structure and social organization in Central Asia: insights from a multi-locus study. *PLoS Genetics* 4(9), e1000200.

Semino, O., Santachiara-Benerecetti, A. S., Falaschi, F., et al. (2002) Ethiopians and Khoisan share the deepest clades of the human Y-chromosome phylogeny. *American Journal of Human Genetics* 70, 265–268.

Shi, W., Ayub, Q., Vermeulen, M., et al. (2010) A worldwide survey of human male demographic history based on Y-SNP and Y-STR data from the HGDP-CEPH populations. *Molecular Biology and Evolution* 27, 385–393.

Thomson, R., Pritchard, J. K., Shen, P., et al. (2000) Recent common ancestry of human Y chromosomes: evidence from DNA sequence data. *Proceedings of the National Academy of Sciences USA* 97, 7360–7365.

Tishkoff, S. A., Gonder, M. K., Henn, B. M., et al. (2007) History of click-speaking populations of Africa inferred from mtDNA and Y chromosome genetic variation. *Molecular Biology and Evolution* 24, 2180–2195.

Tishkoff, S. A., Reed, F. A., Friedlaender, F. R., et al. (2009) The genetic structure and history of Africans and African Americans. *Science* 324, 1035–1044.

Underhill, P. A., Passarino, G., Lin, A. A., et al. (2001) The phylogeography of Y chromosome binary haplotypes and the origins of modern human populations. *Annals of Human Genetics* 65, 43–62.

Verdu, P., Austerlitz, F., Estoup, A., et al. (2009) Origins and genetic diversity of pygmy hunter-gatherers from Western Central Africa. *Current Biology* 19, 312–318.

Vigilant, L., Stoneking, M., Harpending, H., et al. (1991) African populations and the evolution of human mitochondrial DNA. *Science* 253, 1503–1057.

Wood, E. T., Stover, D. A., Ehret, C., et al. (2005) Contrasting patterns of Y chromosome and mtDNA variation in Africa: evidence for sex-biased demographic processes. *European Journal of Human Genetics* 13, 867–876.

15

Levant and North Africa: Afroasiatic linguistic history

Václav Blažek

This chapter examines the linguistic history of the Afroasiatic language family that spans much of the Near East and North Africa. It extends further the discussions of North African population history in chapters 12 and 14, and favors an Asian rather than African ultimate source for the whole Afroasiatic family.

Afroasiatic classification and homeland

The prehistoric Afroasiatic migrations (see Figure 12.1 for the distribution of this family) can be linguistically determined only indirectly, on the basis of ecological and cultural lexicon and mutual borrowings from and into substrata, adstrata, and superstrata. Very useful is a detailed genetic classification, ideally with an absolute chronology of sequential divergences. Without literary documents and absolute chronology of loans the only linguistic tool is the method called glottochronology. Although in its "classical" form, as formulated by Swadesh, it was discredited, its recalibrated modification developed by Sergei Starostin gives much more realistic estimations. For Afroasiatic, Starostin (2010) and Militarev (2005) have obtained almost the same shape of tree-diagram (Figure 15.1), although they operated with 50- and 100-word lists of basic vocabulary items respectively.

Rather problematic results for Omotic should be ascribed to extremely strong substratum influences. Various influences, especially Nilo-Saharan, are also apparent in Cushitic, plus Khoisan and Bantu in Dahalo and South Cushitic. Less apparent, but identifiable, is the Nilo-Saharan influence in Ancient Egyptian (Takács 1999: 38–46) and Berber (Militarev 1991: 248–65); stronger in Chadic are influences of Saharan from the east (Jungraithmayr 1989), Songhai from the west (Zima 1990), plus Niger-Congo from the south (Gerhardt 1983).

To map the early Afroasiatic migrations, it is necessary to localize the Afroasiatic homeland in space and time. The fact that five of the six branches of Afroasiatic are situated in Africa has been interpreted as an axiomatic argument against an Asiatic

The Global Prehistory of Human Migration: The Encyclopedia of Global Human Migration Volume 1,
First Edition. Edited by Peter Bellwood.
© 2013 John Wiley & Sons, Ltd. Published 2015 by John Wiley & Sons, Ltd.

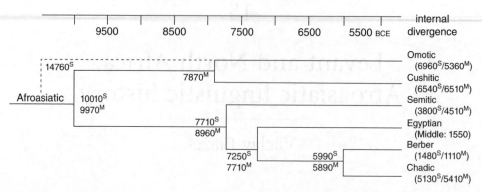

Figure 15.1 Classification of the six major subgroups of the Afroasiatic languages (S = Starostin 2010; M = Militarev 2005). Chronology is in calendar years BCE.

homeland (Fellman 1991–93:56). But it is possible to find many counter-examples of languages spreading from relatively small regions into distant and significantly larger areas: for example, English from England to North America and Oceania; Spanish from Spain to Latin America; Portuguese from Portugal to Brazil; Arabic from Central Arabia to the Near East and North Africa; Swahili from Zanzibar to Equatorial Africa. Among whole language families the most striking example is Austronesian, spreading initially from South China, through Taiwan, to innumerable islands from Madagascar to Easter Island (chapter 35).

A number of arguments speak for a Levantine location for Proto-Afroasiatic, as modeled in Figure 15.2. The family has distant relationships with Kartvelian, Dravidian, Indo-European, and other Eurasiatic language families within the framework of the Nostratic hypothesis (Illič-Svityč 1971–84; Blažek 2002; Dolgopolsky 2008; Bomhard 2008). There are lexical parallels connecting Afroasiatic with other Near Eastern languages which cannot be explained from Semitic; these include Sumerian-Afroasiatic lexical parallels indicating an Afroasiatic substratum in Sumerian (Militarev 1995). There are also Elamite-Afroasiatic lexical and grammatical cognates explainable as a common heritage (Blažek 1999), and North Caucasian-Afroasiatic parallels in cultural lexicon explainable by ancient geographical proximity (Militarev & Starostin 1984).

Regarding the tree-diagram in Figure 15.1, the hypothetical scenario of the disintegration of Proto-Afroasiatic should contain two non-synchronic migrations from the Levantine homeland. Firstly, Cushitic (and Omotic?) separated circa the 10th millennium BCE (during the late Natufian archaeological phase) and spread into the Arabian peninsula and ultimately across the Red Sea into Eritrea/Ethiopia (chapter 12). Secondly, Egyptian, Berber, and Chadic split from Semitic (the latter remaining in the Levant) around the 8th millennium BCE and dispersed into the Nile Delta and Valley.

The dispersal of the Cushitic languages

There is general agreement about the classification of Cushitic; only the positions of Yaaku and Dahalo are problematic, having been influenced by strong substrata and adstrata (Ehret et al. 1989). Having identified a Cushitic-like substratum in modern

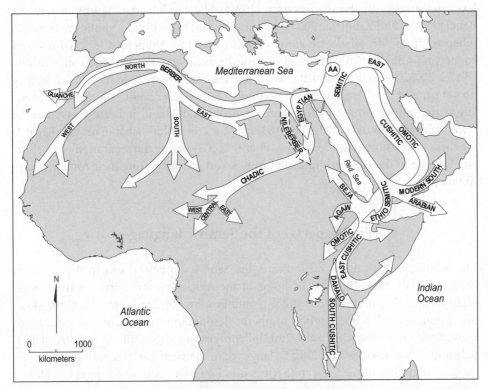

Figure 15.2 The Levant homeland (suggested as AA on the map) and likely routes of expansion of the subgroups within the Afroasiatic language family. Map production by Education and Multimedia Services, College of Asia and the Pacific, The Australian National University.

South Arabian, Militarev (1984: 18–19; cf. also Belova 2003) proposes that Cushites originally lived throughout the Arabian peninsula; thus they would have been the original southern neighbors of the Semites, who then assimilated those Cushites who did not move into Ethiopia. The spread of Cushites in Africa is connected with the Rift Valley. In the coastal area of Eritrea and Djibouti, where the Rift enters into the African mainland, three archaic representatives of the north, central (=Agaw) and eastern branches of Cushitic appear: Beja, Bilin, and Afar-Saho respectively. In this place the disintegration of Cushitic probably began. Ancestors of the Agaw spread in the north of Eritrea and Ethiopia, the Beja also in Sudan between the Nile and the Red Sea. Other East and South Cushitic languages moved southward along the Rift Valley through Ethiopia, Kenya, as far as Central Tanzania. Partial migrations from the Rift reached areas more distant, for example the Horn by Somaloid populations (Heine 1978: 65–70) or the lower basin of the Tana in Kenya by the Dahalo and recently by the South Oromo.

The dispersal of the Omotic languages

Both external and internal classification of Omotic are controversial. Separation of "West Cushitic" as Omotic, an independent branch of Afroasiatic, was based on the lexicostatistical estimations of Bender (1975). The careful grammatical analyses by Bender (2000) and Zaborski (2004) demonstrate that most of the Omotic grammemes inherited from Afroasiatic are common with Cushitic. Numerous lexical isoglosses connecting Omotic with other Afroasiatic branches, to the exclusion of Cushitic (Blažek 2008: 94–139), attest that Omotic and Cushitic are sister-branches, that is, they do not support the West Cushitic conception. On the other hand, Nilo-Saharan parallels to the unique pronominal systems of Aroid and Maoid indicate they could be "Omoticized" (Zaborski [2004: 180–183] proposes their Nilo-Saharan origin). Regarding these conclusions, the model by Militarev (2005) dating the separation of Cushitic and Omotic to the early 8th millennium BCE and reconstructing their route through Arabia seems valid.

The dispersal of the Semitic languages

The Semitic ecological lexicon indicates the Semitic homeland was in the northern Levant (Kogan 2009: 18–19). The home of the Akkadians was northern and central Mesopotamia. From the time of the Sargonid Empire (24–23rd centuries BCE), Akkadian began to push Sumerian into southern Mesopotamia. Akkadian also spread into Elam, Syria, and Anatolia. In the 2nd millennium BCE the southern Semitic dialect, Babylonian, was used as a diplomatic language in the Near East, including Egypt. The massive migration of the Canaanite tribes into Lower (northern) Egypt at c.1700 BCE has been connected with the campaigns of the Hyksos. A part of this multiethnic conglomeration could have been the Hebrews, whose return c.1200 BCE was described in the book of Exodus in the Old Testament. This mythic narration is supported by linguistic analysis of Egyptian toponyms from the Bible (Vycichl 1940).

The oldest Phoenician inscriptions are known from Byblos (11–10th centuries BCE), later also from Tyre, Sidon, and other Levantine ports. During the 1st millennium BCE, Phoenicians founded numerous bases in southern Anatolia, Cyprus, Malta, Sicily, Sardinia, Ibiza, and along the coasts of Libya, Tunisia, Algeria, Morocco, and Iberia, including several points along the Atlantic coast (modern Tangier, Cadiz). Although the strongest Phoenician state, Carthage, was destroyed by the Romans in 146 BCE, the Phoenician/Punic language survived in North Africa until the 5th century CE, and traces of Punic influence are identifiable in modern Berber languages (Vycichl 1952).

From the late 2nd millennium BCE, Arameans spread from northern Syria and Mesopotamia throughout the whole Fertile Crescent, and came into northern Mesopotamia as captives of the Assyrians from the end of the 9th to the mid-7th century BCE. By the time of the fall of Assyria (612 BCE), Aramaic was already a dominant language in northern Mesopotamia, and from the Babylonian captivity (586–539 BCE) it began to replace Hebrew in Palestine. Aramaic became a dominant Near Eastern language in the time of the Achaemenid empire (539–331 BCE), where it served as a language of administration from Egypt and northern Arabia to Central Asia and the borders of India, where the Aramaic script was adapted into local alphabetic scripts such as Kharoshthi and Brahmi. The dominant role of Aramaic in the Near East continued until the expansion of Arabic in the 7th century CE, but its presence there has never died.

Five hundred years before the rise of Islam, Arabs expanded from northern Arabia into the Levant and Mesopotamia. Two states dominated by Arabs controlled the commercial routes between the Mediterranean, the Red Sea, and the Persian Gulf: Palmyra, and the Nabatean kingdom centered on Petra, although for official documents Aramaic still served. With the spread of Islam an unprecedented expansion of Arabic began, and by the 8th century Arabic was used from Morocco and Iberia to central Asia. Although in some areas Arabic lost its position (Iberia, Sicily, Persia), elsewhere its role expanded. In Africa, Arabic extended to the southern border of the Sahara and along the East African coast. One of the pre-Islamic Semitic languages of Yemen crossed the Red Sea in the role of a trade lingua franca in the early 1st millennium BCE and became the founder of the Ethio-Semitic branch (Gragg 1997: 242). Separation of north and south Ethio-Semitic sub-branches can be dated to c.890 BCE (Militarev 2005: 399).

Egyptian

Ancient Egyptian was spoken in the Nile Valley from Lower Nubia to the Delta, probably also in oases of the Western Desert, and also in Sinai and Palestine in the times of Egyptian expansion during the New Kingdom. The unification of Upper and Lower Egypt, ca. 3226 BCE (Ignatjeva 1997: 20), probably stimulated a process of homogenization of local dialects (see also chapter 16).

The dispersal of the Berber languages

To the Berber branch belong not only modern Berber languages spoken in North Africa from Senegal and Mauritania to Egypt (Siwa Oasis), but also the language(s) of Libyco-Berber inscriptions attested from the Canary Islands to Libya and dated from the 7-6th centuries BCE to the 4th century CE, together with fragments of Canary Island languages recorded by Spanish and Italian chroniclers in the 14–16th centuries. The oldest archaeological traces of a human settlement in the Canary Islands are known from Tenerife at c.540 BCE, including an archaic inscription from Hierro (Pichler 2007: 57–59). Taking account of glottochronological dating of the disintegration of Proto-Berber to the 7th century BCE (Blažek 2010), it is possible to see here the impact of Phoenician influence spreading from the Mediterranean coast. The adaptation of the Phoenician script and borrowing of about 20 Canaanite cultural terms, with different reflexes in all Berber branches (i.e. adapted before the disintegration of Common Berber), support this reconstruction. From this perspective, it is probable that the ancestors of the Berbers originally spread along the North African coast. The model of classification of the Berber languages prepared by George Starostin (2010), with the disintegration of Zenaga dated to 1480 BCE and disintegration of north, east and south sub-branches dated to 1080 BCE, is not compatible with the distribution of Phoenician loans in all Berber sub-branches. Their spread is thinkable only in the 1st millennium BCE.

Militarev (1991: 154) localized the area where the South Berber (Tuareg) sub-branch formed in the triangle Ghudāmis-Ghāt-Sabhah in west Libya. The ancient city of Garama also lay in this area, inhabited by the Garamantes, who are frequently identi-fied with the ancestors of Tuaregs. More difficult is the reconstruction of the route of the West Berbers, represented by the Zenaga, living along the Senegal-Mauritanian border now, but in a large part of West Mauritania until the 17th century. The closest linguistic relative, Tetserret/Tameseghlalt, is spoken by a small, non-Tuareg, minority living among the Tuaregs of Niger (Souag 2010: 178). Other substratal traces of West Berber appear in the Arabic dialect Hassaniya, spoken in Mauritania, West Sahara, and Algeria, and in the North Songhai dialects Tadaksahak (East Mali, West Niger), Tagdal (West-Central Niger), and Kwarandzyey (West Algeria). Souag (2010: 186) favors a movement of Kwarandzyey from the basin of the Niger. In this case the migration of the West Berbers probably preceded the spread of the Tuaregs into the southwest.

In the 3rd and 2nd millennia BCE, before the formation of the historically attested Berber dialect continuum, linguistic traces of Berber related idioms appear in the Nile Valley. About 20 etymons occur in Nubian languages, all with good Berber etymologies (Blažek 2000). These Nubian lexemes are not limited to Nile Nubian, but are distrib-uted in all Nubian branches. This means they would have been adopted before the disintegration of Nubian, dated to the 11th century BCE (Starostin 2010). The contact zone was perhaps around the mouth of Wadi al-Milk in the Nile valley in North Sudan (Behrens 1984: map 7.5; Blažek 2000: 40).

The dispersal of the Chadic languages

Starostin's date of 5130 BCE for the disintegration of Proto-Chadic (Figure 15.1) agrees very well with the estimate of 5410 BCE by Militarev (2005: 399). The easternmost Chadic language is Kajakse, from the archaic group Mubi, spoken in the Waddai high-lands in southeast Chad. This area is accessible from the Nile Valley only in two ways: along the Wadi Howar north of Darfur (Blench 2006: 162) or along the Bahr al-Ghazal and its north tributary Bahr al-CArab to the south of Darfur. The northern route could have led along the Batha river, today flowing into Lake Fitri, forming in a wetter past a part of Lake Chad (400,000 sq km at 4000 BCE; 1,350 sq km today). The southern route could have continued along the Bahr Azoum/Salamat into the basin of the Chari, the biggest tributary of Lake Chad.

Summary

The present scenario for the origins and dispersal of the Afroasiatic language family has its analogy in the much later spread of Semitic languages into Africa. In both cases, the movements occurred via a northern route through Sinai (Egyptian, chapter 16; Chadic; Berber; Aramaic; and Arabic), and a southern route through Bab el-Mandeb (Cushitic, chapter 12; Omotic; and Ethio-Semitic).

SEE ALSO: 12 Sub-Saharan Africa: linguistics; 14 Sub-Saharan Africa: human genetics; 16 Levant and North Africa: archaeology

References and further reading

Behrens, P. (1984) "Wanderungsbewegungen und Sprache der frühen Saharanischen Viehzüchter ['Migrational dynamics and language of early Saharan pastoralists']". *Sprache und Geschichte in Afrika* 6, 135–216.

Belova, A. (2003) Isoglosses yéménites-couchitiques [Yemenite-Cushitic isoglosses]. *Orientalia* III. *Studia Semitica*, 219–229.

Bender, M. L. (1975) *Omotic: A New Afroasiatic Language Family*. Carbondale: University Museum Studies 3.

Bender, M. L. (2000) *Comparative Morphology of Omotic Languages*. München: Lincom Europa.

Blažek, V. (1999) Elam: a bridge between Ancient Near East and Dravidian India? In R. Blench & M. Spriggs (eds.), *Archaeology and Language* IV. *Language Change and Cultural Transformation*. London: Routledge, pp. 48–78.

Blažek, V. (2000) Toward the discussion of the Berber-Nubian lexical parallels. In S. Chaker (ed.), *Études berbères et chamito-sémitiques. Mélanges offerts à Karl-G. Prasse [Berber and Hamito-Semitic Studies. Miscellanea offered to Karl-G. Prasse]*. Paris: Louvain Peeters, pp. 31–42.

Blažek, V. (2002) Some new Dravidian–Afroasiatic parallels. *Mother Tongue* 7, 171–199.

Blažek, V. (2008) A lexicostatistical comparison of Omotic languages. In J. D. Bengtson (ed.), *In Hot Pursuit of Language in Prehistory. Essays in the Four Fields of Anthropology*. Amsterdam: Benjamins, pp. 57–148.

Blažek, V. (2010) On classification of Berber. Paper presented at the 40th Colloquium of African languages and Linguistics, August 23–25, Leiden.

Blench, R. (2006) *Archaeology, Language, and the African Past*. Oxford: AltaMira.

Bomhard, A. R. (2008) *Reconstructing Proto-Nostratic: Comparative Phonology, Morphology, and Vocabulary*, Vol. I–II. Leiden-Boston: Brill.

Dolgopolsky, A. (2008) *Nostratic Dictionary*. At www.dspace.cam.ac.uk/handle/1810/196512, accessed March 7, 2012.

Ehret, C. et al. (1989) Dahalo lexis and its sources. *Afrikanistische Arbeitspapiere* 18, 5–49.

Fellman, J. (1991–93) Linguistics as an instrument of pre-history: the home of proto Afro-Asiatic. *Orbis* 36, 56–58.

Gerhardt, L. (1983) Lexical interferences in the Chadic/Benue-Congo border area. In: E. Wolff & H. Meyer-Bahlburg (eds.), *Studies in Chadic and Afroasiatic linguistics*. Hamburg: Buske, pp. 301–310.

Gragg, G. (1997) *Geᶜez (Ethiopic)*. In R. Hetzron (ed.), *The Semitic Languages*. London: Routledge, pp. 242–260.

Heine, B. (1978) The Sam languages. A history of Rendille, Boni and Somali. *Afroasiatic Linguistics* 6(2), 23–115.

Ignatjeva, L. (1997) New data for early Egyptian chronology. *Discussions in Egyptology* 37, 11–22.

Illič-Svityč, V. M. (1971–84) *Opyt sravnenija nostratičeskix jazykov [An attempt at comparison of the Nostratic languages]*, Vol. I–III. Moscow: Nauka.

Jungraithmayr, H. (1989) Zur frühen Geschichte des Zentralsudan im Lichte neuerer Sprachforschung [To early history of Central Sudan in the light of new linguistic research]. *Paideuma* 35, 155–167.

Kogan, L. (2009) Semitskie jazyki [Semitic languages]. In *Semitskie jazyki* I, pp. 15–112. Moscow: Academia.

Militarev, A. (1984) Sovremennoe sravnitel'no-istoričeskoe afrazijskoe jazykoznanie: čto ono možet dat' istoričeskoj nauke? In I. F. Vardul' (ed.), *Lingvističeskaja rekonstrukcija i drevnejšaja istorija Vostoka 3: Jazykovaja situacija v Perednej Azii v X-IV tysjačiletijax do n.e.* [Present comparative-historical Afroasiatic linguistics: What it can offer to historical sciences? In I. F. Vardul' (ed.), *A linguistic reconstruction and earliest history of the Near East in the 10-4th mill. BCE*], pp. 3–26. Moscow: Nauka.

Militarev, A. (1991) Istoričeskaja fonetika i leksika livijsko-guančskix jazykov [Historical phonology and lexicon of the Libyan-Guanche languages]. In I. M. Djakonov (ed.), *Afrazijskie jazyki 2* [*Afrasian languages*], pp. 238–267. Moscow: Nauka.

Militarev, A. (1995) Šumery i afrazijcy [Sumerian and Afrasians]. *Vestnik drevnej istorii 2* [Bulletin of ancient history], 113–127.

Militarev, A. (2005) Once more about glottochronology and the comparative method: the Omotic-Afrasian case. *Orientalia et Classica VI. Aspekty komparatistiki*, 339–408.

Militarev, A. & Starostin, S. (1984) Obščaja afrazijsko-severnokavkazskaja kul'turnaja leksika. In I. F. Vardul' (ed.) *Lingvističeskaja rekonstrukcija i drevnejšaja istorija Vostoka 3: Jazykovaja situacija v Perednej Azii v X-IV tysjačiletijax do n.e.* [Common Afroasiatic-North Caucasian cultural lexicon. In I. F. Vardul' (ed.), *Linguistic reconstruction and earliest history of the East 3: Linguistic situation in the Near East in the 10-4th mill. BCE*], pp. 34–43. Moscow: Nauka.

Pichler, W. (2007) *Origin and Development of the Libyco-Berber Script*. Cologne: Köppe.

Souag, L. (2010) The Western Berber stratum in Kwarandzyey (Tabelbala, Algeria). In H. Stroomer (ed.), *Études berbères V* [*Berber studies* vol. V]. Cologne: Köppe, pp. 177–189.

Starostin, G. (2010) *Glottochronological Classification of Afroasiatic Languages*. Unpublished MS.

Takács, G. (1999) *Etymological Dictionary of Egyptian*, vol. I: *A Phonological Introduction*. Leiden: Brill.

Vycichl, W. (1940) Ägyptische Ortsnamen in der Bibel [Egyptian place-names in Bible]. *Zeitschrift für Ägyptische Sprache 76* [*Journal of the Egyptian language*], 79–93.

Vycichl, W. (1952) Punischer Spracheinfluss im Berberischen [Punic language influence in Berber]. *Journal of Near Eastern Studies 11*, 198–204.

Zaborski, A. (2004) West Cushitic – a genetic reality. *Lingua Posnaniensis 46*, 173–186.

Zima, P. (1990) Songhay and Chadic in the West African context. In H. Mukarovsky (ed.), *Proceedings of the Fifth International Congress*, vol. 1. Vienna: Afro-Pub, pp. 261–274.

16

Levant and North Africa: archaeology

Gregory P. Gilbert

The Holocene prehistory of the Levant and Egypt incorporates both the origins of western Eurasian agriculture and subsequent agriculturalist expansions, as well as one of the world's oldest periods of state formation.

For well over 12,000 years the Levant and North Africa, especially modern Syria, Lebanon, Jordan, Israel, Egypt, Sudan, and Libya, have been at the center of great movements: of ideas, of goods, and of people. The prehistory of the Levant and North Africa was dominated by two core indigenous cultural complexes, the Egyptian and the Levantine. In addition there were many peripheral cultures, including desert, riverine, and seafaring peoples. The core complexes of the Levant and Egypt each acted like powerful magnets attracting or repelling neighboring populations, depending upon time and circumstance (Van den Brink & Levy 2002: 4–6). Although there is material evidence that suggests human migration did occur, the indigenous cultural complexes of the Levant or Egypt were never entirely supplanted. Instead, ideas, goods and people were integrated or absorbed into the core complexes.

The Levant and Egypt were not homogeneous national identities in the modern sense; instead they each possessed significant temporal, physical and cultural gradients, characterized by peer polity interaction. Parts of the Levant, for instance, were influenced by their topographical and geological environment as well as by the geographic proximity of neighbors in Egypt, Mesopotamia, Anatolia and the Mediterranean. Defining what was specifically "Egyptian", as opposed to "Levantine," can sometimes be quite difficult (Kemp 2006: 19–59; Wengrow 2006: 146–148).

The Levant

The spread of agriculture during the Levantine Pre-Pottery Neolithic (c. 9500–6500 BCE) suggests that human migration occurred during this time between the Levant's

The Global Prehistory of Human Migration: The Encyclopedia of Global Human Migration Volume 1,
First Edition. Edited by Peter Bellwood.
© 2013 John Wiley & Sons, Ltd. Published 2015 by John Wiley & Sons, Ltd.

peer polities and away from the Levant lowland and riverine core (which included southeastern Anatolia) into the highlands of Jordan and Syria, northern Iraq, Anatolia, and Cyprus. Archaeological evidence confirms that interregional exchange within the Pre-Pottery Neolithic communities flowed both ways. Obsidian coming from deposits in central Anatolia is found in the Levant, while shells from the Mediterranean coast have been found at inland sites, often at considerable distances from the sea. Evidence for such trade typically occurs in small quantities at any particular site, but it does confirm that at least some itinerant people were engaged in freelance trading. During the Pre-Pottery Neolithic the communication of ideas was relatively fast. Trading networks for supply of prestige goods covered large distances. The Fertile Crescent after the development of agriculture was more of an interaction sphere than a region of migrants displacing indigenous populations (Levy 1998; Ben-Tor 1992: 10–96; Banning 1998).

The Levantine Pottery Neolithic (c.6500–5600 BCE) involved the spread of animal husbandry and agriculture, from the Levant and Anatolia, throughout Europe and into central and southern Asia, in addition to Egypt and North Africa (Bellwood 2005: 65–66). Many Pre-Pottery Neolithic sites in the southern Levant were abandoned before the start of the Pottery Neolithic. As human and domestic animal populations increased, much of the fragile Levant environment was pushed past its sustainable limits, thus precipitating an exodus from the Levantine coastal plains and hinterland. The Pottery Neolithic populations remaining in the Levant adapted to the new conditions with the introduction of a sophisticated ceramic technology, one that originated in Anatolia or northern Syria. The Pottery Neolithic stone technology displays remnants of the Pre-Pottery Neolithic technology, although it had less sophisticated projectile points (presumably due to a lesser reliance on hunting), fewer formalized tools, and relied more upon expedient tools. There is little evidence of interregional exchange at this time, even though Anatolian obsidian has been found in Pottery Neolithic contexts in the Levant. Comparison of the Pottery Neolithic levels in Byblos, Jericho, and the Yarmukian sites in Israel confirms that intraregional exchange within the Levantine core continued to some degree.

The Levantine Chalcolithic cultures (?5800–3500 BCE) developed out of the indigenous Neolithic cultures. Whereas the Late Chalcolithic (4500–3500 BCE) is fairly well defined by its close association with the Ghassulian industry, there is some confusion in the literature relating to the Early and Middle Chalcolithic periods. As the communities in the Levant became more complex during the Chalcolithic period, their trading networks once again expanded. Trade goods included copper from Timna (Wadi Fenan), Anatolia, Iran, or the Caucasian mountains, turquoise from southern Sinai, shells from the Nile and Red Sea, and ivory from North Syria, Egypt, or Africa.

The picture that emerges of the Levantine Pottery Neolithic and Chalcolithic periods is of a cultural complex that was rebuilding itself by gradual adaptation after being devastated by environmental and social upheavals at the end of the Pre-Pottery Neolithic (c. 7000–6500 BCE). There is unlikely to have been any significant level of human migration in such circumstances, other than the movement of people associated with interregional trade. Past interpretations suggesting that Chalcolithic peoples arrived in waves are not supported by the evidence (see Gonen 1992: 78–80). The end of the Chalcolithic is also seen by some scholars as the result of human migrations. Many Chalcolithic sites were abandoned before the Early Bronze Age, but there is no evidence of destruction layers or violence involved. Such changing settlement patterns are more likely the result of increasing social complexity and political factors. Other scholars believe that the southern sites of the Levantine Chalcolithic were destroyed by Egyptians at the time of their unification (c. 3050 BCE). Indeed, interpretations involving large human migrations are not necessary to explain the social transformations that took place at the end of the Chalcolithic and the beginning of the Bronze Age. The Levantine core cultural complex survived for thousands of years by introducing new ideas, by adaptation to environment, and by accepting a level of human migration that could assimilate within, or add to, existing societies without replacing the Levantine cultural traditions.

North Africa

In North Africa, the great Holocene wet phase (c.10,000–6000 BCE) affected the region from Mauretania to the African rift valley and contributed to the rise of African Neolithic societies. It produced a semi-arid environment with summer monsoon rains across the central and southern Sahara, the Sudan, and Ethiopia, associated with some form of plant exploitation (including collecting wild sorghum), Neolithic stone tool technology, simple pottery vessels (often with incised or impressed decoration) and evidence of cattle keeping (see chapters 12 and 13). The sites of Nabta Playa and Bir Kiseiba in the eastern Sahara are most important for understanding these periods (8800–4700 BCE), for although evidence for cattle keeping and ceramics has been uncovered, evidence for agriculture is lacking. For this reason, it has been suggested that the term *Ceramic* should be used in preference to *Neolithic* to describe these Saharan cultures (Shaw 2000: 28). For three thousand years or so they survived as campsites adjacent to lakes that are now permanently dry. With the onset of mid-Holocene desiccation of the eastern Sahara at around 4000 BCE the summer rains failed and the sites were abandoned (Wendorf et al. 2001: 664–675). These desert peoples are assumed to have fled to the Nile where they are depicted, by some scholars, as the originators of Egyptian civilization.

The eastern Saharan people are just one of a number of such groups who lived in Egypt's Western Desert. Every oasis appears to have had some form of occupation in prehistoric times (Kuper 1995). These desert peoples must have influenced the Egyptians, but they could not replace the core cultural traditions of those living in the Nile valley itself. The same would be true for the Neolithic industries of Nubia and the Sudan. The indigenous African Neolithic industries of the upper Nile valley, which may be related to those recorded in the eastern Sahara, were also on the periphery of the Egyptian cultural complex. Although some scholars have suggested that the rise of the Egyptian territorial state was due to Nubian expansion, based largely upon the excavation of the Nubian A-Group cemetery at Qustul (Williams 1986), the archaeological evidence confirms that the political unification of Egypt did not rely upon a Nubian initiative (Wengrow 2006: 171–173).

Excavations at Sodmein cave and the Tree Shelter, near the Red Sea in Egypt's Eastern Desert, have revealed stratified Epipalaeolithic and Neolithic layers, including the remains of domesticated sheep and goats (of Levantine origin) dating to around 5000 BCE (Vermeersch 2008). While it is possible that domesticated sheep and goats formed part of a "Neolithic package" for pastoralists who extended across the Sinai or Arabia and through the Eastern Desert, it is more likely that they arrived via Neolithic communities in the Nile valley. Unfortunately, no Egyptian Neolithic sites dated to approximately 6500–4500 BCE have yet been discovered in Upper Egypt, perhaps because they are either buried under deep alluvium or have been destroyed by erosion during high Nile episodes.

The Nile valley, with its permanent water supply and annually rejuvenated fertile soil, was a natural paradise for Paleolithic Egyptian hunter-gatherers. Epipaleolithic communities located in or on the edge of the Nile valley were able to exploit their natural environments to a greater extent than was ever possible in the rain-dependent, semi-arid Levant. If the Epipalaeolithic Egyptians encountered the early Pre-Pottery "Neolithic package" from the Levant they would have had very little need for adoption. Nevertheless, although there are large gaps in the evidence available for Egypt's terminal Epipaleolithic (c. 8000–?5000 BCE) and Early Neolithic (c. 5300–4500 BCE), the discovery of stone projectile points from Helwan, south of Cairo, suggests that there was some form of interconnection between the Egyptian Epipaleolithic industries and the Levantine Pre-Pottery Neolithic.

It was not until much later, probably during the Levantine Pottery Neolithic (c. 5300 BCE or earlier), that the Egyptians adopted southwest Asian domesticates (Wetterstrom 1993). The evidence for the introduction of agriculture in Egypt comes from a small number of sites in Lower Egypt – the Faiyum, Merimde, and el-Omari (Shaw 2000: 17–88; Wenke 2009; Midant-Reynes 2000: 100–126). All three had a mixed economy, based upon cultivated barley, emmer wheat, flax, and linen, as well as combinations of cattle, sheep, goats, and pigs. There is no evidence for an indigenous domestication of native Egyptian plants or animals (except perhaps cattle); rather, the plants and animals found in these sites were fully domesticated examples of types that originated in the Levant. The major economic difference between Egypt and the Levant was that the Egyptian Neolithic groups, located on the desert fringes, continued to conduct a variety of hunting and gathering activities. A newly discovered Neolithic site at Sais in the western Nile delta may shed more light upon the extent of human migration from the Levant as well as the level of adaptation between Levantine and indigenous Egyptian influences in the Nile valley. Unfortunately, that site has only been partially excavated as it is buried deep beneath the water table (Wilson & Gilbert 2003).

All these Egyptian Early Neolithic sites have specific cultural items which are close, if not identical, to their Levantine Pottery Neolithic counterparts, including bowls with herringbone incised decoration, footed pottery vessels, pear-shaped stone mace heads, and clay figurines. One the other hand, there are significant differences in the use in Egypt of bifacially flaked sickles instead of sickle blades, hollow-based arrowheads of African type, and separate farmsteads constructed of wattle and daub with enclosed courtyards, as opposed to the interconnected mud-brick houses that formed congested villages throughout the contemporary Levant. For example, while the sickles used by Neolithic Egyptians were bifacially flaked from cores (Midant-Reynes 2000: 103, 112; Eiwanger 1993: 48–49, Abb. 15), Neolithic Levantine sickles were produced from regular blades which had been removed from quite sophisticated blade cores (Rosen 1997: 44–60). Such differences in lithic technology are evidence for significant cultural differences. Overall, it is difficult to determine the extent of human migration from the Levant involved at the start of the Egyptian Neolithic, but it is possible to conjecture that sizable Neolithic communities migrated to the Egyptian delta and amalgamated with the indigenous Egyptian Epipalaeolithic population to form a distinctive Nile valley complex (see also chapter 15 for a linguistic perspective on the origin of the Ancient Egyptian language).

By 4500 BCE, the sites of the Middle Egyptian Badarian industry heralded the start of the Late Neolithic in Egypt, although it is possible that earlier Neolithic sites in Upper Egypt have been lost or lie buried deep in the alluvium. The Badarian industry was more complex than its Lower Egyptian predecessors and has many distinctive features, such as polished black-topped pottery, that are considered to be indicative of an indigenous origin. However, Midant-Reynes (2000: 160–164) has identified objects of turquoise, copper, steatite, and marine shell as evidence for contact with or migration from Chalcolithic communities in the Levant.

The Predynastic (or Chalcolithic) period in Egypt (4000–3000 BCE) is characterized as one of rapid progress that transformed Egyptian society and led to the formation of the Egyptian state (Midant-Reynes 2000: 169–230). A century ago, most scholars believed that Egyptian civilization began with an invasion of a "dynastic race" that swept away the indigenous inhabitants and replaced them with another population of Mesopotamian or Syrian origin (see Petrie 1920: 44–50 and critique by Wengrow 2006: 111). Since the 1960s, however, the Egyptian Predynastic period has been interpreted as the creation of an indigenous population, represented by the Naqada complex of burials in Upper Egypt, that gradually increased its power until an Upper Egyptian kingdom was formed, under a Thinite (Abydos) ruler. These Upper Egyptians moved north, conquering or absorbing Middle Egypt and then defeating the less advanced population of the Maadi–Buto complex in Lower Egypt. By about 3200 BCE they achieved the cultural unification of Egypt – Naqada IID in the Predynastic chronology. The subsequent political unification of Egypt as a territorial state required approximately 200 years before the first Egyptian ruler heralded the start of the Early Dynastic period (c. 3000–2686 BCE). Our current understanding of Predynastic Egypt thus involves an expansion of Naqada peoples from south to north within Egypt, as well as the in-migration of peoples from the desert and the southern periphery (Krzyzaniak et al. 1996).

Prior to the expansion of the Naqada people, the Lower Egyptians of the Maadi–Buto complex in the Nile delta had extensive contacts with the Chalcolithic peoples of the Levant. At Maadi, a number of subterranean houses, similar to those found in the Levant (mostly Canaanean), were discovered along with imported pottery vessels, flint blades, copper implements, and lumps of asphalt. This material suggests that there was actually a small Levantine trading community living on the site at about 3200 BCE. By the beginning of the Early Dynastic period, the Egyptians had established a number of permanent posts in the southern Levant, such as En Besor. However, like the settlement at Maadi, these were most likely used for trading rather than being evidence for invasion or colonization at this time.

SEE ALSO: 15 Levant and North Africa: Afroasiatic linguistic history; 17 Anatolia and the Balkans: archaeology

References

Banning, E. B. (1998) The Neolithic period: triumphs of architecture, agriculture, and art. Near Eastern Archaeology 61(4), 188–237.

Bellwood, P. (2005) First Farmers: The Origins of Agricultural Societies. Oxford: Blackwell.

Ben-Tor, A. (ed.) (1992) The Archaeology of Ancient Israel (trans. R. Greenberg). New Haven: Yale University Press.

Eiwanger, J. (1992) Merimde-Benisalame III, Die Funde der jüngereren Merimdekultur [Merimde-Benisalame III, The finds of the early Merimde culture]. Mainz am Rhein: Philipp von Zabern.

Gonen, R. (1992) The Chalcolithic period. In A. Ben-Tor (ed.), The Archaeology of Ancient Israel (trans. R. Greenberg). New Haven: Yale University Press, pp. 40–80.

Kemp, B. J. (2006) Ancient Egypt: Anatomy of a Civilization, 2nd edn. London: Routledge.

Krzyzaniak, L., Kroeper, K., & Kobusiewicz, M. (1996) Interregional Contacts in the Later Prehistory of Northeastern Africa. Poznan: Poznan Archaeological Museum.

Kuper, R. (1995) Prehistoric research in the southern Libyan Desert: a brief account and some conclusions of the B.O.S. Project. Cahier de recherches de l'Institut de Papyrologie et d'Egyptologie de Lille 17, 123–140.

Levy, T. E. (ed.) (1998) The Archaeology of Society in the Holy Land, 2nd edn. London: Leicester University Press.

Midant-Reynes, B. (2000) The Prehistory of Egypt: From the First Egyptians to the First Pharaohs (trans. I. Shaw). Oxford: Blackwell.

Petrie, W. M. F. (1920) Prehistoric Egypt. London: British School of Archaeology in Egypt.

Rosen, S. A. (1997) Lithics After the Stone Age: A Handbook of Stone Tools from the Levant. Walnut Creek: AltaMira.

Shaw, I. (ed.) (2000) The Oxford History of Ancient Egypt. Oxford: Oxford University Press.

Van den Brink, E. C. M. & Levy, T. E. (eds.) (2002) Egypt and the Levant: Interrelations from the 4th through the Early 3rd Millennium BCE. London: Leicester University Press.

Vermeersch, P. (ed.) (2008) A Holocene Prehistoric Sequence in the Egyptian Red Sea Area: The Tree Shelter. Leuven: Leuven University Press.

Wendorf, F., Schild, R. et al. (2001) Holocene Settlement of the Egyptian Sahara I: The Archaeology of Nabta Playa. New York: Kluwer.

Wengrow, D. (2006) The Archaeology of Egypt: Social Transformations in North-East Africa: 10,000 to 2650 BC. Cambridge: Cambridge University Press.

Wenke, R. J. (2009) The Ancient Egyptian State: The Origins of Egyptian Culture (c.8000–2000 BC). Cambridge: Cambridge University Press.

Wetterstrom, W. (1993) Foraging and farming in Egypt: the transition from hunting and gathering to horticulture in the Nile Valley. In T. Shaw, P. Sinclair, B. Andah, & A. Okpoko (eds.), The Archaeology of Africa: Food, Metals and Towns. London: Routledge, pp. 165–226.

Wilson, P. & Gilbert, G. P. (2003) The Prehistoric Period at Sais (Sa el-Hagar). Archeo-Nil 13, 65–72.

Williams, B. B. (1986) The A-Group Royal Cemetery at Qustul, Cemetery L. Chicago: Oriental Institute.

17

Anatolia and the Balkans: archaeology

Mehmet Özdoğan

In recent years, the Anatolian peninsula (Turkey) has become very significant in debates about the homeland of the Indo-European language family and about some fundamental developments in the Near Eastern Neolithic. This chapter discusses some of these archaeological developments, and examines the spread of Neolithic populations after 7000 BCE from Anatolia into southeastern Europe.

The overall picture of Neolithic Anatolia has changed considerably during the last two decades, with the recovery of early Pre-Pottery Neolithic A assemblages (c.9500–8500 BCE) at sites such as Hallan Çemi and Çayönü in southeastern Anatolia, and more recently at Pınarbaşı and Boncuklu in the Konya basin in central Anatolia. Today, not only the southeastern parts of Turkey but also a large section of the Central Anatolian plateau are incorporated into the Near Eastern core area of early agricultural development, on a par with developments further south in the Levant. However, until about two decades ago, the Anatolian peninsula was not considered to be part of the primary zone of neolithization in western Asia. It was assumed that the Neolithic way of life was brought to Anatolia from the southern Levant during the late phases of the Pre-Pottery Neolithic A. Accordingly, during the early 1990s, the earliest Neolithic horizon in Anatolia was regarded as a result of "secondary neolithization" (Cauvin 1988; Bar Yosef & Belfer-Cohen 1992).

However, in spite of the current increase in the number of Neolithic excavations in Anatolia, the question of defining the ultimate origins of the Anatolian Neolithic still remains unanswered. In the southern Levant, the Final Paleolithic cultural sequence from the Kebaran to the end of the Natufian (c.21–11.5 kya) clearly indicates that Pre-Pottery Neolithic cultures developed locally from Paleolithic forebears in that region. However, in the north, and particularly in Anatolia, evidence of occupation during the final phases of the Upper Paleolithic, except along the littoral areas of the Mediterranean, is either absent or extremely sparse. This is true even in the most intensively

The Global Prehistory of Human Migration: The Encyclopedia of Global Human Migration Volume 1,
First Edition. Edited by Peter Bellwood.
© 2013 John Wiley & Sons, Ltd. Published 2015 by John Wiley & Sons, Ltd.

surveyed areas. Pre-Pottery Neolithic settlements appeared in both central and south-eastern Turkey starting about 12 kya, but so far lack forerunners. Thus, for the time being, the origin of the Neolithic in Anatolia remains an open question, until further evidence can be recovered.

In spite of the paucity of data concerning the initial Neolithic phases in Anatolia, there is now ample evidence to develop an insight into how the Neolithic way of life was transmitted westwards into Europe. It is now evident that this process was much more complex than previously envisaged. The development of the Neolithic way of life in Anatolia was not an instantaneous event, but a process of long duration extending through several millennia. Moreover, after the primary phases of diffusion and migration, Neolithic cultures continued evolving to give rise to further migrations, each bearing the marks of successive cultural phases (Figures 17.1 and 17.2; and see Özdoğan 2007; Sagona & Zimansky 2009; Düring 2011).

With Anatolia included, the core or nuclear zone of the Neolithic way of life in western Asia thus extended from the Levant to the Anatolian plateau, and from the upper reaches of the Euphrates and Tigris rivers to Cyprus, embracing a diversity of habitats. This nuclear zone was set apart by its complexity, innovative nature, and high momentum of cultural change, with its component cultures maintaining intensive interaction and sharing knowledge. However, within the core area there were also numerous local cultural variants with distinctive assemblage compositions.

A critical approach to the evidence

At present, discussions about Neolithic expansion westward from Anatolia are based on evidence from three distinct disciplinary fields: archaeology, biogenetics, and linguistics. Even though the main focus in this chapter is on archaeological data, recent advances in genetics are already adding a new dimension to our understanding (chapter 18).

Regarding archaeology, in assessing processes of neolithization in Europe, mainstream debate has focused on data from the Aegean coast and islands and the Balkans, where many Neolithic sites were extensively excavated in the second half of the 20th century. Within this region, there is an overall chronological sequence for the Neolithic from 6000 BCE onwards, commencing with a horizon variously termed Sesklo, Karanovo I, Kremikovci, Starčevo, Criş and Körös (Bailey 2000; Tringham 2000; Perlès 2001). All through the Balkan peninsula, from the Aegean (Sesklo in Thessaly) to southern Hungary (Körös), even in the initial phase, there are hundreds of settlements that share more or less common material elements, such as white-on-red painted pottery, triangular or rectangular pottery cult vessels, steatopygous female pottery figurines, baked clay decorated stamps (so-called *pintaderras*), bone spoons, and large flint blades. What is significant is that, with the exception of sites along the Aegean littoral, all sites begin with this horizon, without any predecessors. It seems evident that a rather rapid and massive population movement took place, seemingly initiated from the Aegean.

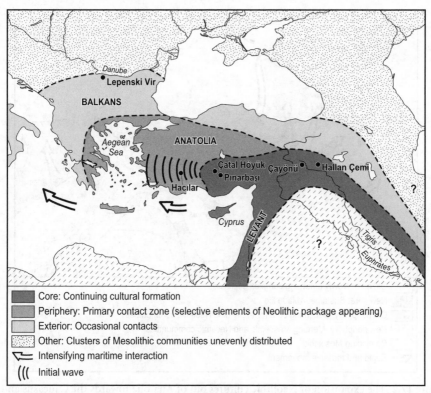

Figure 17.1 The expansion of Neolithic cultures out of Anatolia towards the Caucasus and the Balkans, 7300–5700 BCE. Developments between 10 000 and 7000 BCE (Pre-Pottery Neolithic). Map production by Education and Multimedia Services, College of Asia and the Pacific, The Australian National University.

However, there is still no consensus over what happened prior to the appearance of these settlements, that is when and in what cultural phases the initial migrants arrived. Previous claims for a Pre-Pottery/Aceramic Neolithic phase in the Balkans, mainly at sites in Thessaly and at Lepenski Vir on the Danube, have now been negated (Reingruber 2008). On the other hand, there is growing evidence for the presence of a cultural phase preceding Sesklo, Karanovo I, and Starčevo, termed the Proto-Sesklo in Greece, Proto-Starčevo in the western Balkans and the Monochrome phase in Bulgaria (Perlès 2001; Todorova 2003).

During the last two decades, considerable new data have been recovered on the maritime expansion of the Neolithic way of life. The excavation of Pre-Pottery Neolithic sites in Cyprus dating to the early 9th millennium BCE has provided much needed evidence for the significance of seafaring in the dispersal of early Neolithic populations in the Mediterranean, as well as in the Black Sea basin (Davidson et al. 2006; Manning et al. 2010) (see also chapter 20). Assessment of Neolithic assemblages in both mainland Greece and western Turkey has also confirmed the presence of an active sea route into the Aegean and the northern Mediterranean that did not involve the interior

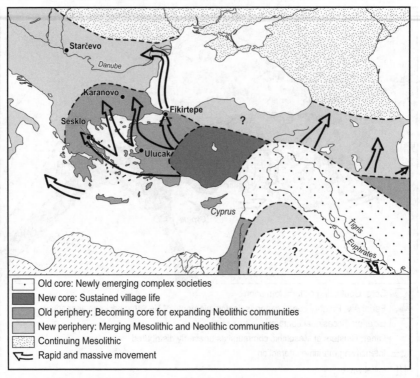

Figure 17.2 The expansion of Neolithic cultures out of Anatolia towards the Caucasus and the Balkans, 7300–5700 BCE. Developments during the 7th millennium BCE, at the start of the Pottery Neolithic phase in Anatolia and the Levant.

Anatolian Plateau. The most distinct marker of this expansion is the so-called "impresso" type of pottery (Özdoğan 2008).

The commencement of a number of Neolithic excavations in western Turkey has not only provided the much needed concrete evidence to understand the neolithization process, but more significantly it has made it possible to consider different models for Neolithic expansion (Özdoğan 2007, 2008; Özdoğan & Başgelen 2007). The diversity in the regions of Neolithic expansion is best reflected in burial customs. Numerous sites have revealed Neolithic burials, either in cemeteries or under house floors, displaying a variety of burial practices even in the same site, ranging from simple inhumation to secondary burial or cremation. The fact that some of these practices were alien to the core area in the east strongly implies that the Neolithic migrants merged with the local population, even sharing the same settlements.

Whether or not Anatolia was the homeland of many present-day European populations is a discussion that has been going on since the early years of the last century. As this subject has been associated with the "identity" of Europe, political or chauvinistic biases occasionally overrun academic concerns (Özdoğan 2007). In this respect, the main issue has been defining the homeland of the Indo-European languages and their early speakers. Because neither written documents nor archaeological evidence could help directly with this quest, other parameters such as farming, deification of bulls, and mother-goddess worship were taken to be the indicators of pre-Indo-European societies, essentially during the Neolithic (Gimbutas 1991). The rediscovery of Çatal Höyük on the Konya Plain then led to an association of Anatolian Neolithic cultures with Indo-European ancestors, at least in the views of some, views soon to be supported by the preliminary results of genetic studies (Renfrew 1987, 2002; Cavalli-Sforza 1996). However, more recent work on Y-chromosomes (Underhill 2002; King et al. 2008) has opened further controversies, and the need for further work has become evident. Along with the work on human DNA, other researchers have undertaken biometric analyses (Pinhasi & Cramon-Taubadel 2009), studies of lactose tolerance (Burger et al. 2007), and DNA analysis of animal domesticates (Bollongino et al. 2006; Evershed et al. 2008). Even if evidence in support of demic movement from Anatolia to Europe is accumulating (chapters 18 and 20), there is still no absolute consensus over its extent or magnitude.

Conclusion

When exactly the westward movement of Neolithic communities into Greece and the Balkans began is still not clear. However, Neolithic communities were established as far west as the Aegean coastal strip of western Turkey by 7000 BCE, as indicated by sites such as Ulucak, Ege Gübre and Keçi Çayırı, reached possibly by following the alluvial valley of the Büyük Menderes stream (Özdoğan and Başgelen 2007). These sites are characterized by mud-slab or mud-brick buildings with red plastered floors, and pressure-flaked lithic tools. Pottery vessels, though present, are rather coarse and extremely rare; the scarcity of pottery at sites such as Hacılar had previously been taken to represent an Aceramic phase, perhaps wrongly. As the timing of this expansion coincided with the so-called "Neolithic collapse" of the Pre-Pottery to Pottery Neolithic transition in southeastern Turkey and the Levant generally, it seems possible to surmise that this initial wave of migration westwards was triggered by ecological problems (Rollefson & Rollefson 1989; Bocquet-Appel & Bar Yosef 2008; chapter 16, this volume). This is further confirmed by the mixed presence of central Anatolian and Levantine elements in the areas of initial expansion in western Turkey. Whether or not this wave extended to the Balkans in its initial phase is not clear; what is evident is that the westward movement of Neolithic communities was not an instantaneous event, but lasted with an increasing pace until about 6400 BCE. The parallels between central Anatolia and western Anatolian sites such as Ulucak and Yeşilova suggests that there was a continuous migration westwards, especially since the pottery sequence from dark-colored fine-burnished wares to red or cream slipped wares in central Anatolia is paralleled in the same chronological order in the newly inhabited areas. By the final phases, migrant farmers seem to have expanded into the Marmara region following the valley of the Sakarya River, and also into the northern Balkans, reaching the Danube, as indicated by sites such as Koprivets. In places where there were local Mesolithic communities, both groups seem to have merged. In this regard, sites of the Fikirtepe culture around Istanbul display a clear mixture of local and introduced elements.

At around 6200 BCE, there seems to have been another more intensive migratory movement that originated in the eastern regions of central Anatolia. Possibly, unstable climatic conditions related to the so-called Labrador/Hudson Bay Climatic Event had a triggering effect in this movement (Berger & Guillaine 2008). The sites of this new wave are rarely in the same locations as before (Özdoğan 2008), yet many maintained their locations over subsequent millennia, in time developing as major archaeological mounds. To this new group belong the Karanovo I, Sesklo, and Starčevo cultures in the Balkans, all associated with new Neolithic elements. The uniform composition of this secondary Neolithic package over a vast territory implies that the expansion was rather rapid. During this era, with the exception of peripheral areas such as the Hungarian plain and western Balkans, there are no further indications of contact with indigenous Mesolithic communities.

Of course, the reality might have been much more complex than the picture of two successive migration phases presented here. Even though new evidence is in strong support of the existence of migration out of Anatolia into Europe during the Neolithic, it is clear that other kinds of knowledge transfer and acculturation were also underway (Sherratt 2004; Özdoğan 2008).

SEE ALSO: 16 Levant and North Africa: archaeology; 18 Europe and western Asia: genetics and human biology; 19 Europe and western Asia: Indo-European linguistic history; 20 Europe: Neolithic colonization

References

Bailey, D. W. (2000) *Balkan Prehistory*. London: Routledge.

Bar-Yosef, O. & Belfer-Cohen, A. (1992) From foraging to farming in the Mediterranean Levant. In A. B. Grebauer & T. D. Price (eds.), *Transitions to Agriculture in Prehistory*. Wisconsin: Prehistory Press, pp. 21–48.

Bellwood, P. & Renfrew, C. (eds.) (2002) *Examining the Farming/Language Dispersal Hypothesis*. Cambridge: McDonald Institute for Archaeological Research.

Berger, J.-F. & Guillaine, J. (2008) The 8200 cal BP abrupt environmental change and the Neolithic transition: a Mediterranean perspective. *Quaternary International* 200, 31–49.

Bocquet-Appel, J. P. & Bar-Yosef, O. (eds.) (2008) *The Neolithic Demographic Transition and its Consequences*. New York: Springer.

Bollongino, R., Edwards, C., Alt, K., et al. (2006) Early history of European domestic cattle as revealed by ancient DNA. *Biology Letters* 2, 155–159.

Burger, J., Kirchner, M., Bramanti, B., et al. (2007) Absence of the lactase-persistence-associated allele in early Neolithic Europeans. *Proceedings of the National Academy of Sciences of the USA* 104, 3736–3741.

Cauvin, J. (1988) La neolithization de la Turquie du Sud-est dans son contexte Proche-Oriental [The Neolithization of south-eastern Turkey in the Middle Eastern context]. *Anatolica* 15, 69–80.

Cavalli-Sforza, L. L. (1996) The spread of agriculture and nomadic pastoralism: insights from genetics, linguistics and archaeology. In D. R. Harris (ed.), *The Origins and Spread of Agriculture and Pastoralism in Eurasia*. London: UCL Press, pp. 51–69.

Davidson, K., Dolukhanov, P., Sarson, G., & Shukurov, A. (2006) The role of waterways in the spread of the Neolitihic. *Journal of Archaeological Science* 33, 641–652.

Düring, B. S. (2011) *The Prehistory of Asia Minor. From Complex Hunter-Gatherers to Early Urban Societies.* Cambridge: Cambridge University Press.

Evershed, R. P., Payne, S., Sherratt, A., et al. (2008) Earliest date for milk use in the Near East and southeastern Europe linked to cattle herding. *Nature* 455, 528–531.

Gimbutas, M. (1991) *Civilization of the Goddess. The World of Old Europe.* San Francisco: Harper.

King, R. J., Özcan, S. S., Carter, T., et al. (2008) Differential Y-chromosome Anatolian influences on the Greek and Cretan Neolithic. *Annals of Human Genetics* 72, 205–214.

Manning, S. W., McCartney, C., Kromer, B., & Stewart, S. T. (2010) The earlier Neolithic in Cyprus: recognition and dating of a Pre-Pottery Neolithic A occupation. *Antiquity* 84, 693–706.

Özdoğan, M. (2007) Amidst Mesopotamia-centric and Euro-centric approaches: the changing role of the Anatolian peninsula between the East and the West. *Anatolian Studies* 57, 17–24.

Özdoğan, M. (2008) An alternative approach in tracing changes in demographic composition: the westward expansion of the Neolithic way of life. In Bocquet-Appel & Bar-Yosef (2008), pp. 139–178.

Özdoğan, M. & Başgelen, N. (eds.) (2007) *Anadolu'da Uygarlığın Doğuşu ve Avrupa'ya Yayılımı. Türkiye'de Neolitik Dönem: Yeni Kazılar, Yeni Bulgular* [Anatolian origins of Neolithic civilization and its dispersal into Europe: the Neolithic in Turkey – new excavations, recent finds] (2 volumes). Istanbul: Arkeoloji ve Sanat Yayınları.

Perlès, C. (2001) *The Early Neolithic in Greece.* Cambridge: Cambridge University Press.

Pinhasi, R. & von Cramon-Taubadel, N. (2009) Craniometric data support demic diffusion model for the spread of agriculture into Europe. *PLoS ONE* 4(8), 1–8.

Reingruber, A. (2008) *Die Argissa-Magula. Das Frühe und das Beginnende Mittlere Neolithikum im Lichte Transägäischer Beziehungen* [The Argissa Magula: the Early Neolithic and early Middle Neolithic in the context of the sphere of Aegean interaction]. Bonn: Dr. Rudolf Habelt.

Renfrew, C. (1987) *Archaeology and Language.* London: Jonathan Cape.

Renfrew, C. (2002) "The emerging synthesis": the archaeogenetics of farming/language dispersals and other spread zones. In P. Bellwood & C. Renfrew (2002), pp. 3–16.

Rollefson, G. & Rollefson, K. (1989) The collapse of early Neolithic settlements in the southern Levant. In I. Hershkovitz (ed.), *People and Culture in Change.* Oxford: BAR 508, pp. 73–89.

Sagona, A. & Zimansky, P. (2009) *Ancient Turkey.* Oxford: Routledge.

Sherratt, A. (2004) Fractal farmers: patterns of Neolithic origin and dispersal. In J. Cherry, C. Scarre, & S. Shennan (eds.), *Explaining Social Change: Studies in Honour of Colin Renfrew.* McDonald Institute Monographs, Cambridge: Cambridge University Press, pp. 53–63.

Todorova, H. (2003) Neue Angaben zur Neolithisierung der Balkanhalbinsel [New approaches to the process of neolithization in the Balkan peninsula]. In E. Jerem & P. Raczky (eds.), *Morgenrot der Kulturen. Frühe Etappen der Menschheitsgeschichte in Mittel-und Südosteuropa. Festschrift für Nandor Kalicz* [Onset of culture. Initial stages of civilization in southeastern and central Europe; Festschrift in honor of Nandor Kalicz]. Budapest: Archaeolingua, pp. 83–88.

Tringham, R. (2000) Southeastern Europe in the transition to agriculture in Europe: bridge, buffer, or mosaic. In T. D. Price (ed.), *Europe's First Farmers*, 2nd edn. Cambridge: Cambridge University Press, pp. 19–56.

Underhill, P. A. (2002) Inference of Neolithic population histories using Y-chromosome haplotypes. In Bellwood & Renfrew (2002), pp. 65–78.

18

Europe and western Asia: genetics and population history

Mark G. Thomas, Toomas Kivisild,
Lounes Chikhi, and Joachim Burger

This chapter examines the genetic history of Europe during the past 20,000 years, looking especially at postglacial recolonization and at the much-debated issue of the origins of the Neolithic populations of the continent. The authors also discuss the different ways geneticists can approach population history, and comment on the importance of natural selection for genes that determine skin pigmentation and enhance the ability to digest the milk sugar lactose.

On a continent-wide scale, genetic data have been used extensively to address three major questions on the demographic history of Europe: (1) What was the relationship between archaic hominins and modern Europeans (discussed in chapter 4); (2) To what extent did the formation and subsequent re-expansion of Ice Age refuge populations shape patterns of genetic variation; and (3) To what extent did Near Eastern farmers replace or interbreed with indigenous hunter-gatherers during the Neolithic transition?

A plentiful supply of samples, well-funded medical studies, and a rich history of archaeological and linguistic research have all contributed to an abundance of both modern and ancient genetic data from various inheritance systems (mitochondrial DNA, Y-chromosome and autosomes) in Europe. What remains more contentious is how such data should be used to infer migration history (Goldstein & Chikhi 2002; Nielsen & Beaumont 2009). While it is beyond the scope of this chapter to discuss genetic inference about population history in detail, we think it is important to outline the three main approaches used, and discuss their strengths and weaknesses. These are (1) phylogeographic analysis, (2) interpretation of summary patterns of genetic data, and (3) population genetic modeling.

Phylogeographic studies (Avise et al. 1987) aim at inferring major demographic events from the geographic distribution of phylogenetically identified clades. This approach is most commonly used with mitochondrial DNA (mtDNA) or Y-chromosome

The Global Prehistory of Human Migration: The Encyclopedia of Global Human Migration Volume 1,
First Edition. Edited by Peter Bellwood.
© 2013 John Wiley & Sons, Ltd. Published 2015 by John Wiley & Sons, Ltd.

data, where the clades are usually defined by some shared but otherwise arbitrarily chosen mutations, and are referred to as haplogroups. In humans, such studies have focused on the estimated ages of haplogroups and their spatial distributions. Inference usually proceeds by relating these ages to the presence of some ancient population in the region where they are most common, then treating their current distribution as the signature of an ancient demographic episode, such as an expansion or migration event (Underhill & Kivisild 2007). While there are issues with estimating the shape of a phylogenetic tree within a species and, more importantly, with defining clades and estimating their ages, the main problem is that mutation and the formation of genealogical trees are very "noisy" processes, and branches of a gene tree may actually be very poor proxies of ancestral populations. As a result, there is a tendency in phylogeographic analysis to attribute patterns in the data to interesting aspects of a population's history, when in fact they may be the result of randomness in the mutation and inheritance processes (Nielsen & Beaumont 2009).

The interpretation of summary patterns is the oldest method of inferring a population's history from genetic data, and includes approaches such as principal components analysis (Cavalli-Sforza et al. 1994) and the distribution of differences between samples of homologous DNA sequences (Rogers & Harpending 1992). Under ideal conditions, certain of these descriptive statistics can act as convenient proxies for processes such as migration, admixture, and changes in population size. However, because of the "noisy" or stochastic nature of inheritance (*drift*) and mutation, the same patterns of genetic data can arise under a range of very different population histories (*equifinality*), and if we were able to "run" a population's history identically, multiple times, then each run would give rise to different patterns in the genetic data (evolutionary variance). Additionally, some seemingly simple demographic processes can give rise to surprising or misleading patterns in genetic data (emergence), such as allele surfing, whereby alleles unaffected by natural selection can "ride" on the advancing wave of an expanding population and reach highest frequencies in locations far removed from their origin (Edmonds et al. 2004). This process can also be mistaken for natural selection (Currat et al. 2006).

The final approach, explicit modeling, is statistically the most secure approach to population history inference (Beaumont et al. 2002; Nielsen & Beaumont 2009). Briefly, different population history scenarios are compared statistically, using either analytical or computer simulation results. One branch of population genetics theory that has been particularly useful here is coalescent theory, which is a retrospective model of gene genealogies for a sample under a defined population history, and allows genetic data to be simulated in an efficient manner (Wakeley 2009). Using the coalescent approach, the probability of getting data identical or similar to the real data can be calculated or estimated. The idea here is that the most likely historical scenarios, including values for migration rates and times of population expansion or contraction, are those under which the data observed are most probable. Using this approach, the problems associated with the "noisy" nature of inheritance and mutation can be accounted for explicitly. However, modeling is often difficult to implement for geneticists and non-geneticists alike. Also, the process usually begins with the simplest models since there are an infinite number of different plausible historical scenarios that could be tested, and use of a complex model when a simple one will do is something of a statistical crime unless there are other prior data that support. However, simple models may appear naive or simplistic to many non-geneticists, and will not reveal the complexities of our demographic past unless the data are very information-rich.

All three approaches have contributed to our understanding of the migration history of Europe. But the first two are somewhat more "interpretative" and are better thought of as means of generating hypotheses from genetic data *post hoc*, rather than independently testing hypotheses that arise from other disciplines such as archaeology and linguistics. The last approach is undoubtedly the best way forward, but challenges remain in developing sufficiently flexible and usable software, and in convincing the wider community of its merits.

Pre-Neolithic contributions to the modern gene pool of Europe and West Asia

Genetic data overwhelmingly indicate that modern European, West Asian, and North African populations are derived from a dispersal of anatomically modern humans (*Homo sapiens*) from sub-Saharan Africa that took place between approximately 50 and 80 kya. However, recent analyses of ancient DNA suggest that Europeans and all other non-African populations can attribute 1–4 percent of their ancestry to early admixture with Neanderthals (Green et al. 2010), as discussed in chapter 4. It is most likely that this occurred before the separation of the East and West Eurasian gene pools because a similar signature is seen in all non-African populations, although Currat & Excoffier (2011) suggest that independent admixture events took place.

A number of phylogeographic studies have attempted to identify the founding mtDNA and Y chromosome lineages of the first *Homo sapiens* populations in Europe and to assess the contribution of these to the present day gene pool (Soares et al. 2010). However, due to genetic drift it is difficult to determine whether more than a handful of such lineages present around 25 kya are likely to have any descendants in Europeans today (Barbujani & Bertorelle 2001). Their current frequencies and diversity distributions have been shaped by random factors such as genetic drift, as well as by allele surfing, admixture, population size fluctuations and migration.

With the benefits of recent and reliable ancient DNA data, some predictions based on phylogeographic criteria (Richards et al. 2000) have found support. For instance, some mtDNA haplogroups, such as U, have been proposed to represent ancestry prior to the Last Glacial Maximum (LGM) in Europe, and haplogroup U2 was recently identified in the 30-kya Kostenki remains in Russia (Krause et al. 2010). Moreover, haplogroups U4 and U5 predominate in a post-LGM hunter-gatherer sample from central Europe (Bramanti et al. 2009) and in a Neolithic hunter-gatherer sample from Sweden (Malmstrom et al. 2009). However, other haplogroups suggested to be pre-Neolithic by Richards and colleagues (2000) are, on the contrary, rare or absent in early Neolithic samples, and some of those found to be common in the latter (e.g. N1a) are equally rare in modern Europeans (Haak et al. 2005; Barbujani & Chikhi 2006).

Attempts to identify Y-chromosome lineages or autosomal variants that might be considered signatures of the first settlers of Europe have met with similar problems, although phylogeographic inferences have been proposed (e.g. Semino et al. 2000). However, due to a lack of corroborating ancient DNA data, claims of Y-chromosome haplotype or autosomal allele signatures for the initial settlement of Europe should be treated with caution. Also, as for mtDNA, genetic drift is likely to make it difficult to make strong inferences without explicit modeling (Chikhi et al. 2002).

Archaeological and palaeoclimatic evidence indicate that the LGM at 24–20 kya led to an almost complete depopulation of northern and central Europe, and humans may have survived only in the glacial refuges of southern Europe and the northern Black Sea (Ramakrishnan & Hadly 2009). The recolonization of central Europe started in a period of post-LGM warming (Banks et al. 2008) that corresponded with the Upper Paleolithic Solutrean culture in France, the Magdalenian in middle Europe and the Epigravettian in south and southeast Europe. But due to the scarcity of ancient DNA evidence from 22–10 kya, it is not known exactly which refuge populations contributed to the overall post-LGM population structure (Street & Terberger 1999).

The distributions of mtDNA and Y variation in extant populations indicate a number of specific haplogroups that may have persisted since this period in a few refuge regions (Richards et al. 2000; Semino et al. 2000). For example, the Y-lineage R-M269, the most common lineage in Western Europe and found in over 110 million men, was initially proposed to have spread from Iberian Paleolithic refuge populations (Semino et al. 2000; Wilson et al. 2001). However, geographic patterns of diversity within this lineage have also been interpreted as indicating a West Asian origin in the Neolithic (Balaresque et al. 2010) – although recent analyses have in turn contested this (Busby et al. 2012). Such views have been debated widely, but ancient DNA studies on human remains of the Holocene period, as discussed below, tend not to favor genetic continuity from Paleolithic/Mesolithic into Neolithic in most parts of Europe.

Demographic events in the Holocene

The major multidisciplinary question concerning the Mesolithic to Neolithic transition in Europe (see chapters 17 and 20) is the extent to which immigrating food producers from the Near East contributed to the ancestry of Europeans after the transition, and until today (Renfrew 1987; Bellwood 2005; Pinhasi & Stock 2011). Unfortunately, and despite many claims to the contrary, genetic analyses have not fully resolved this question. But they have made important contributions and – particularly with recent developments in ancient DNA technology – promise much more in the near future.

One of the first major contributions to the Mesolithic-to-Neolithic debate was made using principal components analysis (PCA) of classical marker frequencies (blood groups and serological variants). In these pioneering and influential studies, spatial clines in major components of genetic variation were quite reasonably assumed to be signatures of past population expansions (Menozzi et al. 1978; Cavalli-Sforza et al. 1993, 1994). The first component of variation in Europe showed a southeast to north-west cline – almost identical to the trajectory of the expansion of Neolithic farming through Europe, and this was interpreted as supporting a major farmer contribution to European ancestry. However, recent simulation studies have revealed some surprising properties of these summary patterns of genetic variation; in particular that under a process of range expansion without admixture with local populations, the first principal component of variation can be perpendicular to the direction of expansion (François et al. 2010). Nonetheless, as we will see later, PCA still has a valuable role to play in understanding genetic history.

MtDNA evidence

Mitochondrial DNA variation in living populations in Europe, western Asia, and northern Africa is characterized by a number of distinct haplogroups (H, I, J, T, U, V, W, X) which all derive from one (N) of the two ancestral clades attributed to the out-of-Africa dispersal of *Homo sapiens* (see chapter 4). Although these haplogroups have pre-Holocene coalescent dates, their presence in North Africa and Europe does not necessarily indicate immigration going back that far. Haplogroups U, H, T, and J, which comprise the majority of European mtDNA lineages, are also found with a substantial degree of variation in western Asia; a likely source of multiple pulses of gene flow into Europe during both the Holocene and the Pleistocene. Although Richards et al. (2000) claimed, on the basis of founder analysis, that less than one-quarter of the mtDNA lineages in Europe had western Asian Neolithic origins, this rather low estimate has not found support from other population geneticists (e.g. Barbujani & Chikhi 2006).

Ancient DNA analysis of human remains from one of the most widespread early Neolithic cultures of Europe, the Linearbandkeramik (LBK, see chapter 20), found that 6 out of 24 samples carried mtDNA haplogroup N1a, which is extremely rare or absent in most modern populations in the region (Haak et al. 2005). The authors concluded that LBK populations were not the direct ancestors of modern Europeans. A later study, which also included mtDNA sequences from late Paleolithic to Neolithic European hunter-gatherer skeletons, as well as modern data, identified large genetic differences between all three groups. A simplified demographic model indicated that such large differences could not be explained by population continuity from Paleolithic times alone (Bramanti et al. 2009). The authors concluded that Neolithic farmers migrated into central Europe around 7,500 years ago.

Mitochondrial DNA sequences identical to those found in the central European LBK sample, as well as in modern Europeans and western Asians, were found in a Neolithic skeletal sample from Hungary. Interestingly, these Neolithic farmers also carried lineages that are present in modern Central and East Asia (Guba et al. 2011). Another ancient DNA study of skeletons of the Pitted Ware culture of southern Scandinavia, late hunter-gatherer people who lived alongside farmers, found a lack of support for population continuity into modern Scandinavians (Malmstrom et al. 2009). In contrast, phylogeographic interpretation of Iberian Late Neolithic ancient DNA data favored continuity between prehistoric and modern inhabitants (Sampietro et al. 2007) although a more recent study including early Neolithic samples favored a major contribution from Near Eastern farmers (Gamba et al. 2012).

As suggested using phylogeographic criteria (Richards et al. 2000), subtypes of haplogroup U have been predominant in all ancient European hunter-gatherer samples analyzed so far (Bramanti et al. 2009; Malmstrom et al. 2009; Krause et al. 2010), despite being relatively rare in Europeans today, except for the Uralic-speaking Sami. Since U4/5-types are present in modern Europeans but absent in Early Neolithic skeletal samples, it now seems likely that modern-day European ancestry has been influenced by regional variation in the extent of admixture between pre-Neolithic hunter-gatherers and Neolithic farmers (Burger 2010). However, spatially explicit modeling of Neolithic admixture that accommodates ancient DNA data is still pending.

Y-chromosome evidence

Similar to mtDNA variation, the Y-chromosome haplogroups in present-day Europe are distinct from those in sub-Saharan Africa and East Asia, but overlap considerably with Middle Eastern and North African populations. Six haplogroups, R1, I, N3, J, G, E3, account for more than 95 percent of the Y-chromosomes in the region (Semino et al. 2000). Notably, while mtDNA haplogroup composition is relatively homogenous across Europe (with the exception of the Uralic-speaking Sami), Y-chromosome variation is considerably more structured geographically, and haplogroup diversity is low in many regions. While attempts have been made to assign haplogroups to European Paleolithic or Near Eastern Neolithic origins (Semino et al. 2000, Soares et al. 2010) – including the widely debated R-M269 lineage (see above) – a lack of well-attested ancient DNA data means that such attempts should be considered speculative.

Despite an inability to confidently assign specific lineages to European Paleolithic or Near Eastern Neolithic origins, it is still possible to use Y-chromosome variation to make estimates of the relative contributions of these groups to modern Europeans. For instance, Semino and her colleagues (2000) considered the Y-chromosome haplogroups with Europe-wide clinal distributions as introduced to Europe by Neolithic farmers, whereas a majority of haplogroups (R1b, R1a, and I, using present-day nomenclature) were interpreted as being derived from pre-Holocene migrations. But instead of focusing on specific haplogroups, Chikhi and his colleagues (2002) used a Bayesian full-likelihood approach that explicitly modeled admixture and genetic drift to infer admixture variation across Europe. They suggested that the contribution of pre-Holocene Y-chromosomes varies enormously across Europe, with a geographic distribution that is best explained by a model of demic diffusion of Neolithic populations through the region (Cavalli-Sforza et al. 1994).

Genome-wide variation and natural selection in European populations

In recent years, the amount of genomic data on Europeans has increased by several orders of magnitude, thanks to improvements in genotyping technology and large-scale medical studies. One way of summarizing variation over many loci is to perform PCA, and when applied to a dataset from living Europeans consisting of around half a million single nucleotide polymorphisms (SNPs), a plot of the first two components showed that geography has been a major factor in shaping patterns of genetic variation, although it should be noted that the first two components account for less than 1 percent of the total variation (Novembre et al. 2008).

Genetic variants that have unusually high frequencies in Europe when compared to other regions may have been influenced by natural selection. Two genes with clear functional significance stand out in this regard: SLC24A5, which is linked to skin colour, and LCT, linked to lactose digestion in adulthood (Sabeti et al. 2006). Variation in the SLC24A5 gene has been shown to explain between 25 and 38 percent of the skin-color differences between individuals of European and African descent (Lamason et al. 2005). The derived allele associated with light skin color is found at near 100 percent in most European populations, but is rare elsewhere, regardless of skin color. It has been suggested that this adaptation favored increased vitamin D synthesis under the lower UVB radiation found at high latitudes (Chaplin & Jablonski 2009). Interestingly, light pigmentation-associated alleles in different genes are common in Asian populations who also have light skin color, indicating that light skin pigmentation has evolved multiple times independently. Both the high haplotype homozygosity and its restricted geographic range suggest that the selective sweep on SLC24A5 occurred recently, perhaps during the Holocene with the shift from a vitamin D-rich (fish) hunter-gatherer diet to a vitamin D-poor farming diet (but see Craig et al. 2011).

Another gene with characteristic signatures of natural selection in Europeans is the lactase gene, LCT. A mutation near LCT (called $-13,910^*T$) is strongly associated with lactase persistence – the ability of some adults to digest the milk sugar lactose. The $-13,910^*T$ variant is common in Europe (Enattah et al. 2002), central Asia (Heyer et al. 2011), India (Gallego Romero et al. 2012), and some African populations (Mulcare et al. 2004). Lactase persistence has itself evolved multiple times and, in some sub-Saharan African and Middle Eastern populations, other genetic variants are responsible for the same phenotype. Interestingly, the $-13,910^*T$ variant is found at frequencies of more than 50 percent in most central and northern European populations today, yet was absent from a sample of early Neolithic individuals from the same region (Burger et al. 2007). This suggests that it rose to high frequency during or after the Neolithic. Itan and colleagues (2009), using spatially explicit computer simulations, estimate that the $-13,910^*T$ allele began to be selectively favored around 7,500 years ago in the Balkans and central Europe, possibly among the progenitors of the LBK culture.

Demographic processes after the Neolithic

In the millennia after the introduction of farming, the population of Europe is thought to have grown dramatically (Bellwood 2005). This would have reduced drift and the likelihood that subsequent demographic events could have had major impacts on the European gene pool. Nevertheless, there were further migrations from both within and outside the continent that are likely to have influenced genetic variation to some degree. One enduring question concerns the influence that highly mobile Late Neolithic groups from the Ukrainian steppes might have had on Europe (Rassamakin 2002; Anthony 2007). Some scholars see here not only the possible origins of Indo-European languages (Gimbutas 1997) but also a major component of European ancestry. This is in contrast to Renfrew's farming-language dispersal hypothesis (Renfrew 1987), which proposes that Indo-European languages spread into Europe with immigrating Neolithic farmers from Anatolia (see chapter 19).

Very little genetic support is available for migrations from the Steppes into Europe, and the evidence is mostly restricted to population dynamics within the Steppes themselves (Lalueza-Fox et al. 2004; Pilipenko et al. 2010). The Hungarians or Magyars are an example of a linguistic isolate in the center of Europe, but genetic analyses consistently place them with their present-day geographic neighbors rather than with their Uralic linguistic relatives (see chapter 21). In such cases, genes and languages do not correlate with each other independently of geography, and therefore genetic data might not be well suited for testing hypotheses of language dispersal.

There is considerable debate on the extent of further migration associated with historically attested cultural transitions. These include Arab expansion, Viking colonization, and the various movements of Germanic peoples during and after the late Roman Empire. Of these, perhaps the most widely debated, in the UK at least, is the extent of migration during the Anglo-Saxon transition in Britain. Two genetic studies using Y-chromosome data and population genetic modeling concluded that the Anglo-Saxon contribution to the English gene pool was greater than 50 percent (Weale et al. 2002; Capelli et al. 2003), an estimate that has proved unpalatable for many archaeologists. Subsequent computer simulations, in combination with historical evidence, indicate that social structure, wealth differentials, and a degree of reproductive isolation between Anglo-Saxons and native Britons could explain this rather high male-line contribution, commencing with a less than 10 percent initial contribution during the migration phase itself (Thomas et al. 2006).

Conclusions

Most genetic variation seen in Europe today derives ultimately, as in other continents, from a Late Pleistocene dispersal of modern humans from Africa. Geography, rather than language, ethnic or cultural identity, appears to be the primary determinant of genetic affinity in Europe. However, ancient DNA studies do indicate genetic discontinuities during and following the Neolithic transition. Most of these changes are likely to have been caused by demographic processes on various scales, including migration, population growth and decline, and admixture, but variation at some loci has been shaped by natural selection. In the near future the application of new genome-wide sequencing technologies, particularly to ancient DNA, as well as the use of more flexible model-based statistical approaches, will hopefully enable us to test questions relating to the peopling of Europe more rigorously.

SEE ALSO: Vol. I: 4 Early Old World migrations of *Homo sapiens*: human biology; 17 Anatolia and the Balkans: archaeology; 19 Europe and western Asia: Indo-European linguistic history; 20 Europe: Neolithic colonization; 21 Northern Europe and Russia: Uralic linguistic migrations; Vol. II: Anglo-Saxon migrations

References

Anthony, D. (2007) *The Horse, the Wheel, and Language: How Bronze-Age Riders from the Eurasian Steppes Shaped the Modern World*. Princeton: Princeton University Press.

Avise, J., Arnold, J., Ball, R., et al. (1987) Intraspecific phylogeography: the mitochondrial DNA bridge between population genetics and systematics. *Annual Review of Ecology and Systematics* 18, 489–522.

Balaresque, P., Bowden, G., Adams, S., et al. (2010) A predominantly Neolithic origin for European paternal lineages. *PLoS Biol* 8, e1000285.

Banks, W., D'errico, F., Peterson, A., et al. (2008) Human ecological niches and ranges during the LGM in Europe derived from an application of eco-cultural niche modeling. *Journal of Archaeological Science* 35, 481–491.

Barbujani, G. & Bertorelle, G. (2001) Genetics and the population history of Europe. *Proceedings of the National Academy of Sciences* 98, 22–25.

Barbujani, G. & Chikhi, L. (2006) Population genetics: DNAs from the European Neolithic. *Heredity* 97, 84–85.

Beaumont, M., Zhang, W., & Balding, D. (2002) Approximate Bayesian computation in population genetics. *Genetics* 162, 2025–2035.

Bellwood, P. S. (2005) *First Farmers: The Origins of Agricultural Societies*. Cambridge, MA: Blackwell.

Bramanti, B., Thomas, M., Haak, W., et al. (2009) Genetic discontinuity between local hunter-gatherers and central Europe's first farmers. *Science* 326, 137–140.

Burger, J. (2010) Population genetics of the European Neolithic and the role of lactase persistence. In G. Grupe, G. Mcglynn, & J. Peters (eds.), *Archaebiodiversity. A European Perspective*. Rahden, Germany: Verlag Marie Leidorf.

Burger, J., Kirchner, M., Bramanti, B., et al. (2007) Absence of the lactase-persistence-associated allele in early Neolithic Europeans. *Proceedings of the National Academy of Sciences* 104, 3736–3741.

Busby, G., Brisighelli, F., Sanchez-Diz, P., et al. (2012) The peopling of Europe and the cautionary tale of Y chromosome lineage R-M269. *Proceedings of the Royal Society B: Biological Sciences* 279, 884–892 Online ref. doi: 10.1098/rspb.2011.1044.

Capelli, C., Redhead, N., Abernethy, J., et al. (2003) A Y chromosome census of the British Isles. *Current Biology* 13, 979–984.

Cavalli-Sforza, L., Menozzi, P., & Piazza, A. (1993) Demic expansions and human evolution. *Science* 259, 639–646.

Cavalli-Sforza, L., Menozzi, P., & Piazza, A. (1994) *The History and Geography of Human Genes*. Princeton: Princeton University Press.

Chaplin, G. & Jablonski, N. G. (2009) Vitamin D and the evolution of human depigmentation. *American J. Physical Anthropology* 139, 451–461.

Chikhi, L., Nichols, R., Barbujani, G. & Beaumont, M. (2002) Y genetic data support the Neolithic demic diffusion model. *Proceedings of the National Academy of Sciences* 99, 11008–11013.

Craig, O., Steele, V., Fischer, A., et al. (2011) Ancient lipids reveal continuity in culinary practices across the transition to agriculture in northern Europe. *Proceedings of the National Academy of Sciences* 108, 17910–17915.

Currat, M. & Excoffier, L. (2011) Strong reproductive isolation between humans and Neanderthals inferred from observed patterns of introgression. *Proceedings of the National Academy of Sciences* 108, 15129–15134.

Currat, M., Excoffier, L., Maddison, W., et al. (2006) Comment on "Ongoing adaptive evolution of Aspm, a brain size determinant in *Homo sapiens*" and "Microcephalin, a gene regulating brain size, continues to evolve adaptively in humans." *Science* 313, 172.

Edmonds, C., Lillie, A., & Cavalli-Sforza, L. (2004) Mutations arising in the wave front of an expanding population. *Proceedings of the National Academy of Sciences* 101, 975–979.

Enattah, N., Sahi, T., Savilahti, E., et al. (2002) Identification of a variant associated with adult-type hypolactasia. *Nature Genetics* 30, 233–237.

François, O., Currat, M., Ray, N., et al. (2010) Principal component analysis under population genetic models of range expansion and admixture. *Molecular Biology and Evolution* 27, 1257–1268.

Gallego Romero, I., Basu Mallick, C., Liebert, A., et al. (2012) Herders of Indian and European cattle share their predominant allele for lactase persistence. *Molecular Biology and Evolution* 29, 249–260.

Gamba, C., Fernández, E., Tirado, M., et al. (2012) Ancient DNA from an early Neolithic Iberian population supports a pioneer colonization by first farmers. *Molecular Ecology* 21, 45–56.

Gimbutas, M. (1997) *The Kurgan Culture and the Indo-Europeanization of Europe*. Washington, DC: Institute for the Study of Man.

Goldstein, D. & Chikhi, L. (2002) Human migrations and population structure: what we know and why it matters. *Annual Review of Genomics and Human Genetics* 3, 129–152.

Green, R., Krause, J., Briggs, A., et al. (2010) A draft sequence of the Neandertal genome. *Science* 328, 710–722.

Guba, Z., Hadadi, E., Major, A., et al. (2011) Hvs-I polymorphism screening of ancient human mitochondrial DNA provides evidence for N9a discontinuity and East Asian haplogroups in Neolithic Hungary. *Journal of Human Genetics*, 56, 784–796.

Haak, W., Forster, P., Bramanti, B., et al. (2005) Ancient DNA from the first European farmers in 7500-year-old Neolithic sites, *Science* 310, 1016–1018.

Heyer, E., Brazier, L., Segurel, L., et al. (2011) Lactase persistence in central Asia: phenotype, genotype, and evolution. *Human Biology* 83, 379–392.

Itan, Y., Powell, A., Beaumont, M., et al. (2009) The origins of lactase persistence in Europe. *PLoS Comput Biol*, 5, e1000491.

Krause, J., Briggs, A., Kircher, M., et al. (2010) A complete mtDNA genome of an early modern human from Kostenki, Russia. *Current Biology* 20, 231–236.

Lalueza-Fox, C., Sampietro, M., Gilbert, M. T., et al. (2004) Unravelling migrations in the steppe: mitochondrial DNA sequences from ancient Central Asians. *Proceedings of the Royal Society B: Biological Sciences* 271, 941–947.

Lamason, R., Mohideen, M., Mest, J., et al. (2005) Slc24a5, a putative cation exchanger, affects pigmentation in zebrafish and humans. *Science* 310, 1782–1786.

Malmstrom, H., Gilbert, M., Thomas, M., et al. (2009) Ancient DNA reveals lack of continuity between Neolithic hunter-gatherers and contemporary Scandinavians. *Current Biology* 19, 1758–1762.

Menozzi, P., Piazza, A., & Cavalli-Sforza, L. (1978) Synthetic maps of human gene frequencies in Europeans. *Science* 201, 786–792.

Mulcare, C. A., Weale, M. E., Jones, A. L., et al. (2004) The T allele of a single-nucleotide polymorphism 13.9 kb upstream of the lactase gene (Lct) (C-13.9kbt) does not predict or cause the lactase-persistence phenotype in Africans. *American Journal of Human Genetics* 74, 1102–1110.

Nielsen, R. & Beaumont, M. (2009) Statistical inferences in phylogeography. *Molecular Ecology* 18, 1034–1047.

Novembre, J., Johnson, T., Bryc, K., et al. (2008) Genes mirror geography within Europe. *Nature* 456, 98–101.

Pilipenko, A., Romaschenko, A., Molodin, V., et al. (2010) Mitochondrial DNA studies of the Pazyryk people (4th to 3rd centuries BC) from northwestern Mongolia. *Archaeological and Anthropological Sciences* 2, 231–236.

Pinhasi, R. & Stock, J. (eds) (2011) *Human Bioarchaeology of the Transition to Agriculture.* Chichester, UK: Wiley.

Ramakrishnan, U. & Hadly, E. (2009) Using phylochronology to reveal cryptic population histories: review and synthesis of 29 ancient DNA studies. *Molecular Ecology* 18, 1310–1330.

Rassamakin, Y. (2002) Aspects of Pontic Steppe development (4550-3000 BC) in the light of the new cultural chronological model. In K. V. Boyle, C. Renfrew, & M. Levine (eds.), *Ancient Interactions: East and West in Eurasia.* Cambridge: McDonald Institute for Archaeological Research.

Renfrew, C. (1987) *Archaeology and Language: The Puzzle of Indo-European Origins.* London: Cape.

Richards, M., Macaulay, V., Hickey, E., et al. (2000) Tracing European founder lineages in the near eastern mtDNA pool. *American Journal of Human Genetics* 67, 1251–1276.

Rogers, A. & Harpending, H. (1992) Population growth makes waves in the distribution of pairwise genetic differences. *Molecular Biology and Evolution* 9, 552–569.

Sabeti, P., Schaffner, S., Fry, B., et al. (2006) Positive natural selection in the human lineage. *Science* 312, 1614–1620.

Sampietro, M., Lao, O., Caramelli, D., et al. (2007) Palaeogenetic evidence supports a dual model of Neolithic spreading into Europe. *Proceedings of the Royal Society B: Biological Sciences* 274, 2161–2167.

Semino, O., Passarino, G., Oefner, P., et al. (2000) The genetic legacy of Paleolithic *Homo sapiens sapiens* in extant Europeans: A Y chromosome perspective. *Science* 290, 1155–1159.

Soares, P., Achilli, A., Semino, O., et al. (2010) The archaeogenetics of Europe. *Current Biology* 20, R174–83.

Street, M. & Terberger, T. (1999) The last Pleniglacial and the human settlement of central Europe: new information from the Rhineland site of Wiesbaden-Igstadt. *Antiquity* 73, 259–272.

Thomas, M., Stumpf, M., & Harke, H. (2006) Evidence for an apartheid-like social structure in early Anglo-Saxon England. *Proceedings of the Royal Society B: Biological Sciences* 273, 2651–2657.

Underhill, P. & Kivisild, T. (2007) Use of Y chromosome and mitochondrial DNA population structure in tracing human migrations. *Annual Review of Genetics* 41, 539–564.

Wakeley, J. (2009) *Coalescent Theory: An Introduction.* Greenwood Village, CO: Roberts.

Weale, M., Weiss, D., Jager, R., et al. (2002) Y chromosome evidence for Anglo-Saxon mass migration. *Molecular Biology and Evolution* 19, 1008–1021.

Wilson, J., Weiss, D., Richards, M., et al. (2001) Genetic evidence for different male and female roles during cultural transitions in the British Isles. *Proceedings of the National Academy of Sciences* 98, 5078–5083.

19

Europe and western Asia: Indo-European linguistic history

Paul Heggarty

Indo-European is, by speaker population, by far the world's greatest language family. This chapter looks especially at the "Steppe" and "Anatolian" hypotheses for Indo-European origins and dispersals, and adds to the discussion begun in chapter 11 about how language families spread in prehistoric times. It also discusses the vexed question of linguistic chronology.

Indo-European: linguistic lessons, and enigmas

The Indo-European family of languages (Figure 19.1), as its very name implies, ranks among the most remarkable of all the tales that our speech tells us of our origins, and our migrations. Or rather, half-tells us: for as well as holding many unexpected lessons on our past, Indo-European poses just as many enigmas; and both are all the greater for the sheer scale of this language family.

The languages of the world represent a couple of hundred independent lineages (plus many more now extinct), of which just one has somehow come to account for the native speech of almost half of humanity (Lewis 2009). Indo-European so outranks all other language families in territory and population that the migrations that carried it must likewise have been uncommonly significant in geographical range, at least cumulatively. Whether they were equally so in demographic terms, however, remains one of the enigmas.

These diverging migrations go back so far into prehistory that Indo-European has long since ceased to be some monolithic language entity; even millennia ago it was already a collection of scores, now hundreds, of different tongues. These are by now so deeply divergent from each other that few speakers of languages from any of

The Global Prehistory of Human Migration: The Encyclopedia of Global Human Migration Volume 1,
First Edition. Edited by Peter Bellwood.
© 2013 John Wiley & Sons, Ltd. Published 2015 by John Wiley & Sons, Ltd.

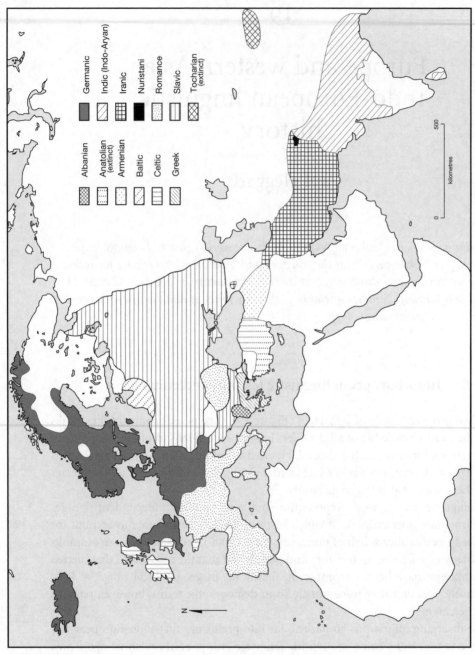

Figure 19.1 The distribution of the major subgroups of the Indo-European languages. After Ruhlen, M. (1987) A Guide to the World's Languages. Volume 1. Stanford: Stanford University Press. Originally published as Figure 10.1 in Bellwood 2005. Map production by Education and Multimedia Services, College of Asia and the Pacific, The Australian National University.

the family's dozen or so main branches (or "subfamilies") are even aware they share the same deep linguistic origin with all the rest. To name but a few, Indo-European languages include French, Russian, Greek, Irish, Persian, Hindi – and English, likewise distantly related to all the others.

Nonetheless, the very definition of any *language family* is that all its member languages ultimately arose out of the same single ancestor language, in this case termed Proto-Indo-European. It entails also that the proto-language was spoken in an original "homeland" far more circumscribed than the family that diverged out of it. A language can only diverge into a family in the first place by spreading into territories distant enough from each other that changes away from its original common form can begin to arise independently, and differently, from one region to the next.

Through this prerequisite of geographical expansion, any language family thus presupposes past migration(s), at least of one form or another. A population itself may migrate, taking its speech with it into ever wider territories, and outnumbering or ousting any population – and their language(s) – established there previously. Alternatively, people may stay put but switch to speaking an outside language, to which some distinct utility attaches through its association with some prestigious cultural complex that is doing the expanding in this case, rather than an actual population. (That said, at least *some* speakers of the expanding language must migrate, in order for the switching population to learn it from them in the first place.) In the first scenario, linguistic ancestries remain in step with genetic ones; in the second, the two no longer match. Whichever it was, Proto-Indo-European evidently enjoyed some great propensity to spread at the expense of other language lineages, thanks to *some* corresponding attributes of the population(s) that spoke it.

Indo-European expansions, modern and ancient

Much of the Indo-European spread dates only to those few recent centuries during which an expansive Europe enjoyed worldwide prominence. Its unequal encounter with the civilizations of the Americas is reflected in how the vast majority of populations there today speak not indigenous languages, but Indo-European ones, principally Portuguese and Spanish (of the Romance branch), and English (of the Germanic branch). Their expansion histories here reflect immigration from Europe: in some areas overwhelming, but in others relatively limited and with massive language shift instead (see Heggarty & Renfrew forthcoming a: §1.3). In Africa, by contrast, for all their use in formal contexts, Indo-European languages are not widely established as *native* tongues, save where European immigration was relatively heavy (e.g. Afrikaans).

The very fact that Europe's diaspora carried with it languages uniquely of Indo-European stock reflects how they had already long dominated that continent (about 97% of Europe's population today). Of the language lineages spoken before it, Indo-European spared just Basque, and on Europe's northeastern fringe Finnish, Estonian, and Sami, all of the Uralic family (chapter 21), as is the early medieval latecomer of Hungarian.

The Romance and Germanic branches now count far more speakers beyond Europe than within it, yet they remain far outnumbered by their greatest sister, Indic (alias Indo-Aryan), which alone counts more than a billion speakers. Extending from half-way across Pakistan as far east as Bangladesh, encompassing three-quarters of India and its people, and northwards up against the Himalayas (e.g. as Nepali), as well as by sea to Sri Lanka, Indic too attests to great migration(s) of some form.

The name Indo-European unhelpfully passes over the span between its eponymous extremes, much of it filled today by Indic's closest sister-branch, Iranic: from Pashto and Baluchi in Afghanistan and Pakistan, back westwards through Persian to Kurdish, and Ossetic in the Caucasus. Armenian too is another separate branch of Indo-European, as was the long-extinct Anatolian that dominated western and central Asia Minor as they emerged into history between three and four millennia ago, first documented in the form of Hittite. Certainly, the migrations that carried Indo-European so far afield are anything but recent. Millennia before the modern age, the family already held sway over most lands from the Atlantic to the Bay of Bengal.

That first spread of (Proto-)Indo-European itself must not be confused with much later movements that repeatedly recast the precise distributions of its various sub-branches and languages. Particularly in Europe, these first favoured Celtic and then Romance (i.e. speaking "in Roman"), until the "great migrations" spread Germanic in the west, then Slavic in the east. Through all of these successive language expansions, however, the constant was that each was drawn from the same wider pool: Indo-European. This was not by chance, but because its own first spread here, long before, had already been so all-encompassing.

There is today near consensus (though see below) that the homeland out of which Proto-Indo-European first emerged lay at neither its Indian nor its (Western) European extreme, but somewhere in between. But beyond that, notwithstanding more than two centuries of hypotheses since the concept of the Indo-European family was first established, the enigma of its origins remains as unresolved as ever. Many a scenario for prehistory has been sketched out to account for it, though recent debate has crystallized around just two.

Rival hypotheses for Indo-European origins and dispersal

The traditional Steppe Hypothesis (e.g. Gimbutas 1970; Mallory 1989; Anthony 2007) associates Proto-Indo-European speech with the builders of the *kurgans* or burial mounds of the Pontic-Caspian steppe, and sets its first divergence to the late 5th or early 4th millennium BCE (the "short chronology" view). The prime motor of its expansion is seen as nomadic pastoralism, based particularly on the domestication of the horse, taken to have conferred great mobility and military superiority on early Indo-European-speaking populations. Their expansion westwards into Europe is linked particularly to the Corded Ware culture in the first half of the third millennium BCE, and to traditional migrationist views of the "coming of the Greeks" relatively late out of the Balkans, and a separate migration into Anatolia. Eastwards, a form of Indo-European would have traversed the steppes into Central Asia, developing (relatively swiftly) into a distinctly Proto-Indo-Iranic form. This is attributed to the Bronze Age "Andronovo"' cultures, and in their southern reaches also the Bactria-Margiana Archaeological Complex, c.2200-1700 BCE. From here, speakers of Proto-Indo-Iranic would have had to cross southwards over the mountain frontier, branching then into Iranic westwards, and Indic eastwards into the Ganges basin. This would have occurred around the first half of the 2nd millennium BCE; that is, either following the decline of the Indus Valley civilization and unconnected with it; or at most contemporary with it, perhaps even an incursion that triggered its fall.

For the Anatolian or Agriculture Hypothesis, meanwhile (Renfrew 1987; Bellwood 2005: ch. 10), Eurasia's greatest language family resulted ultimately from the far-reaching consequences for human societies and demography brought about by the Neolithic "revolution," or at least transition. This sets Proto-Indo-European in the northern arc of the Fertile Crescent, in Anatolia, where its earliest attested descendant, Hittite, was ultimately to be found. From here, Indo-European would be carried by the spread of agriculture, perhaps from as early as 7000 BCE (the "long chronology"'). Westwards it dispersed through the Aegean and Balkans, and ultimately across almost all of Europe. Eastwards, in Renfrew's (1987) original formulation, it traveled by a route far to the south of the Steppes, and in two main stages. First it would have crossed or skirted around the Iranian plateau, relatively swiftly reaching the fringes of the Indus valley. Farming then marked a long pause in its expansion, and so would early Indo-European speech, changing relatively slowly here into its specifically Proto-Indo-Iranic form by the time of the late Indus Valley civilization. The end of the pause would see this language in turn spread and diverge, not least as its Proto-Indic branch moved into the Ganges basin. Farming spread there from as early as 3000 BCE, but with a particularly significant phase just over a millennium later, also within a few centuries of the Steppe Hypothesis scenario (Bellwood 2005: 90–91, 210–217).

The Indus Valley civilization, and its tantalizingly undeciphered inscriptions, lie at the heart of a third school still popular in India itself, namely "indigenous Aryanism" (see Bryant 2001). Its full-blown form would have Proto-Indo-European itself originating in the subcontinent, and somehow migrating westward as far as Europe – but this seems implausible on many levels. The Agriculture Hypothesis, though, does allow for a more limited "indigenist" claim, that at least the *specifically Indo-Iranic* lineage crystallized locally on the Indus, rather than in the steppes of Central Asia (see Heggarty & Renfrew forthcoming b: §3.9).

Both main hypotheses must envisage migrations, then, but ones that could hardly be more different in all key respects: in where they are thought to have emerged from; when; why; and indeed how they were possible at all. The Steppe Hypothesis harks back to traditional long-range "migrationist" explanations of culture history, and to invasions, empowered in this case by horse riding and the wagon (later chariot). "Elite dominance" is taken to have allowed Proto-Indo-European speakers, despite their limited demographic strength, to impose their speech upon conquered indigenous majorities. The Agriculture Hypothesis, meanwhile, need not generally invoke individual movements of more than a few tens of kilometers per generation (as a long-term average, at least). Instead, it privileges "demic diffusion," a gradual spread of the higher population density that farming supports. Earlier, more thinly settled hunter-gatherer inhabitants are outpopulated and absorbed, although cumulatively the genetic signal emerging from the original homeland "dilutes" the further it spreads (see Renfrew 1987: 126–131). This demographic "wave of advance" is a very different form of migration, then, if one even wishes to call it that at all.

The next three sections summarize the great debates on the where, when, and why of Indo-European expansion, focusing on the issue of migration.

Geography

Various approaches have tried to pin down the homeland out of which speakers of Proto-Indo-European first migrated, but none has so far proved conclusive. Early attempts followed an assumption that if linguists can "reconstruct" certain words back to that original language, then its speakers must have known the corresponding *concepts*. Reference is made especially to animal or plant species with particular geographical distributions, or indeed climate and landscapes. While ostensibly a simple and tempting logic, this "linguistic palaeontology" is in fact deeply flawed. Linguistic reconstruction may be reliable and precise on the level of *sound*, where it has largely exceptionless, recurrent sound laws to rely on (such as the famous Grimm's Law and Verner's Law). But there are no parallel *meaning* laws to allow such confidence in exactly what sense or referent a given reconstructed word may have had at particular times deep in prehistory, hence the great scope for speculative and subjective interpretations. Linguistic palaeontologists have put the Indo-European homeland in the most unlikely of places, and argued both for and against each of the two main hypotheses.

Another approach looks for words borrowed between very early stages of Indo-European and other language lineages, taken to suggest that they were then spoken in contiguous territories. At great time-depths, however, the task is fraught with difficulties. Even identifying words as loans at all (rather than chance resemblances) is not clear-cut; chronologies are unproven and inconsistent between families; loans may be indirect though other languages; and so on. Again, competing claims point variously to contact with Uralic, and thus a more northerly, Steppe homeland; or with Semitic, inclining for Anatolia instead.

Alternatively, for many a language family the default candidate region for its homeland is the "center of diversity" where its major sub-branches are most concentrated. In the Indo-European case, however, this rule of thumb helps little, and is effectively discarded: both hypotheses propose homelands where only few branches have ever been attested.

As for where any Indo-European speech is first found, that honor goes to Hittite, in Anatolia. Not until over a millennium later is any presence known on the Central Asian steppe, later still on the Pontic-Caspian. Yet this is as much a function of when writing itself reached these respective regions, and says nothing of how long they might have been established in each. Certainly, though, as central and western Anatolia first emerged into history, all languages known there were of Indo-European stock, as also in the Balkans; not so on the Pontic-Caspian steppe. Eastwards, the deepest branches – Iranic, Nuristani, Indic, and the latter's own earliest sub-branch, Dardic –

all lie *south* of the Caspian and Himalayas, on the route of the Agriculture Hypothesis. On the Steppes, there is no trace of any of them until long after Indic and Iranic had split from each other, and even then, representatives only of Iranic, and indeed of just one already differentiated and specifically "eastern" sub-branch of it. Some such languages, notably Scythian, ultimately did spread by long-distance, horse-born migrations – only not out of the Pontic-Caspian steppe, but *westwards into* it from far to the east, where the earliest known stage of their nascent *eastern* Iranic lineage (i.e. Avestan) clearly originated. As the military prowess of nomadic pastoralism came of age in early historical times, various other language lineages, particularly Mongolic and Turkic, soon emerged from the central and eastern steppes by the same route. And these precedents all headed in the wrong direction across the Steppes for the Kurgan Hypothesis, at least as far as movements to South Asia are concerned.

One other branch of Indo-European is the extinct "Tocharian," stranded in the oases of the Taklamakan Desert – linguistic evidence of the clearest kind of some one-off, long-distance migration along the Silk Route (and associated by some with the Tarim mummies). But it bears no particularly close relationship to any other branch – notably, neither Iranic nor Indic – and thus, frustratingly, cannot decisively illuminate Indo-European origins.

Chronology

As for *when* the expansive migrations of Proto-Indo-European speakers first set the family's divergence in train, linguistic palaeontology has tended to favour the short chronology and nomadic pastoralism. From various reconstructed roots for *horse* it was traditionally claimed that Proto-Indo-European speakers "must have" already domesticated it, when the linguistic data themselves constitute no proof whatsoever of *domestication* (most languages, like English, use irrespectively the same basic word for both wild and domesticated horse). Anthony (2007: 35–36, 78), meanwhile, founds his linguistic case effectively on just "five classic reconstructions" to do with wheeled vehicles – or rather, on his own interpretations and assumptions as to their original meanings. In fact, the reconstructed word forms do not necessarily entail wheeled vehicles at all, as opposed to basic concepts in movement and time that doubtless predated that invention, such as carrying, motion, rotation, and cyclicality. The entire phrase *wheel of the sun*, for example, also reconstructs to Proto-Indo-European as *$sh_2uens\ k^wek^wlos$ (Beekes 1995: 41); just as the same root is used in concepts like the *wheel of fate, life,* and so on. It is no surprise, then, that we can reconstruct word-forms of *wheel, ring,* or *cycle* (Greek κύκλος), whether or not there already existed for speakers of Proto-Indo-European the technological referent to which its "prototypical" meaning would later shift in some languages. The very fields on which linguistic palaeontology most relies for chronological inference are precisely those *least* reliable to that end. For in technology and domestication (correctly understood), referents and concepts typically change and develop incrementally, while pre-existing word roots thus *continue* to be used for them, inheriting and masking their own parallel meaning shifts. Others interpret linguistic palaeontology *against* any association with nomadic pastoralism, and in favor of established farming instead (Krell 1998). For the method's many critics, attempts to "reconstruct Proto-Indo-European culture" (e.g. Dumézil 1958) are a *cause célèbre* of fanciful subjectivity (Bryant 2001: ch.6; Heggarty & Renfrew forthcoming c: §3.3.2, §3.4).

Alternative approaches to "linguistic dating" look to the coarse relationship between the degree of language divergence within a family, and the time span over which it cumulatively arose. They are frustrated, however, by the challenges of pinning mean-ingful numbers on language in the first place, and calibrating any supposed "glotto-clock" against rates of change over time that vary so widely in practice. For many linguists, the traditional approach of "glottochronology" has long been "decisively discredited" (Dixon 1997: 36), so although its results appear to support the Steppe Hypothesis, even its advocates wisely set little store by this (e.g. Mallory 1989: 276). An alternative method, based on more sophisticated Bayesian logic and powerful phy-logenetic analysis algorithms, yields a date range highly consistent with the spread of agriculture instead, repeated for data in the vocabularies of modern Indo-European languages, and the grammar and sound systems of ancient ones (respectively, Gray & Atkinson 2003; Atkinson et al. 2005).

Other commentators fall back on unquantified, impressionistic judgments of how much language change is or is not "conceivable" over a given time span, but such claims are inescapably subjective. Traditional objections that Indo-European languages could not have changed so slowly as the long chronology implies are contradicted by cases like Lithuanian, in which especially "slow" change is precisely what did happen in certain key respects. Much debate surrounds also the dating of the earliest texts of the Rigveda (Indic) and Avesta (Iranic), and their implications in favour of one or other chronology.

Causation

The nature of the relationships between the member branches of Indo-European can hint at the manner in which they diverged. The search for a binary-branching "family tree" for Indo-European, a "perfect phylogeny," effectively fails (Ringe et al. 2002: 86). That there is still, despite two centuries of research, no agreed branching sequence suggests that there may simply never have been one, and that the major sub-lineages emerged instead from an Indo-European dialect continuum, more compatible with a wave-of-advance than sequences of individual migrations (Heggarty et al. 2010: 3830, 3842–3843).

Mounted "Aryans," bursting out of the Steppes to invade, conquer, and thereby impose their languages upon India, Europe, and all points between, certainly make for a stirring migrationist picture long popular among Indo-European linguists, yet it faces strong objections on all levels. The image seems powerful in the light of much later histories, of Turkic-, Mongolic-, and Uralic-speaking peoples, or of "confederations" such as the Huns or Xiōngnú. Their names appeared as sources of dread to the popula-tions of India, China, and Europe, over which Steppe invaders at times succeeded in imposing themselves as a dominant elite. Firstly, however, these precedents date only to historical times; it is an anachronism to assume any necessary analogy with lifeways on the Pontic-Caspian steppe several millennia earlier, long before the key inventions of saddle or stirrup, and at a time for which it remains disputed whether horses were being ridden at all (rather than kept mostly for meat). There is a vast chronological and cultural gap to bridge here, which cannot be glossed over.

Secondly, almost every known precedent is in fact a *counter*-example to the Steppe Hypothesis, linguistically. Dominant elites the invaders may have become, but whenever they subdued already densely settled agricultural regions the one battle they most consistently *lost* was the linguistic one. India and Europe speak no native Turkic or Mongolic tongues today, but continue their own Indo-European. It was precisely the incoming elites who were serial learners of the native languages of the populations they conquered (see also chapter 11 on this theme). The Bulgars from the Steppes may have lent their name to one of the languages of Europe, only it is not their own (which vanished), but that of the Indo-European Slavic-speakers whom they subdued.

Nichols (1992: 20) sees the Eurasian steppe as the prototypical example of a more general concept of language family "spread zone." Yet the steppe ecology that underlies it conspicuously does *not* extend deeply into Europe proper; and nor did any Steppe languages. Hungarian is the one exception which only "proves the rule": for only on the Great Hungarian Plain did nomadic pastoralists of the Steppes (in this case, Magyars) find a rare territory in Central Europe suited to their subsistence regime (chapter 21). For Nichols to extend her spread zone accordion right across Western Europe – but only once, for Proto-Indo-European, to fit a Steppe Hypothesis assumed *a priori* – is no support of any such migration.

There are objections to the spread zone concept both in general (Campbell & Poser 2008: 302–304, 398–399) and specifically in the Indo-European case (Heggarty & Renfrew, forthcoming d: §6.3).

Nomadic migrations did repeatedly sweep certain languages across the thinly populated steppes, but are only known to have done so once they enjoyed military superiority (with saddle and stirrup) from the 1st millennium BCE onwards. And for all their conquests, beyond the steppe itself their linguistic impacts were generally ephemeral. Genghis Khan and the Mongol empire, the Golden Horde, Kublai Khan and the Yuan dynasty, Tamerlane and the Mughals – if even they all failed to spread their languages significantly into the agricultural regions that they conquered, it seems implausible that their nomadic predecessors millennia before could have done so to effect humanity's single greatest language family expansion (Heggarty & Beresford-Jones 2010: 170).

Summing up perspectives: archaeology, genetics and linguistics

Indo-European is an overwhelming linguistic outcome that can have come about only through processes in prehistory of similarly far-reaching import, traces of which might therefore be expected to be visible in the material culture record too. Many Indo-European linguists overlook how the Steppe Hypothesis that they have traditionally preferred seems to most archaeologists rather outdated – out of touch with the move away from such migrationist visions of culture history, and from Gimbutas' (1970) vision of her "Kurgan culture" and any expansive impacts she attributed to it. At the time-depth hypothesized, the predominant direction of cultural influence seems to be *into* the Steppes from the Balkans, rather than the reverse. The unique scale of Indo-European dominance suggests an expansive process of defining significance in prehistory, more powerful than the relatively late rise of warlike nomadic pastoralism. Agriculture seems a rare phenomenon of commensurate impact, yet the general farming/language dispersal hypothesis remains highly controversial in both archaeology and linguistics (even if rather less so in other regions like East and Southeast Asia – see chapters 26, 34, and 36).

In principle, genetic research might help challenge or corroborate one or other of the contrasting visions of Indo-European migrations, only here too the the debate remains very much open. Much is in flux, as powerful new research avenues open up the potential to reshape long-held assumptions. One such avenue is ancient DNA, which Haak et al. (2010) claim supports a demic diffusion cline out of Anatolia with farming. But many scholars prefer to withhold judgment to await whatever picture emerges from the other newly emerging field: full-genome analysis (see chapter 18).

Above all, much remains uncertain in precisely those linguistic analyses that might best help place Indo-European into the real-world context that shaped it. It seems safer to side with those specialists like Clackson (2007: esp. 15–19), who keep an open, agnostic mind as to which of two radically different visions – in time-frame, geography, nature, and causation – most plausibly accounts for humanity's greatest "linguistic migration."

SEE ALSO: 11 Human migrations and the histories of major language families; 17 Anatolia and the Balkans: archaeology; 18 Europe and western Asia: genetics and human biology; 20 Europe: Neolithic colonization; 21 Northern Europe and Russia: Uralic linguistic migrations

References

Anthony, D. W. (2007) *The Horse, the Wheel, and Language: How Bronze-Age Riders from the Eurasian Steppes Shaped the Modern World*. Princeton: Princeton University Press.

Atkinson, Q., Nicholls, G., Welch, D., & Gray, R. (2005) From words to dates: water into wine, mathemagic or phylogenetic inference? *Transactions of the Philological Society* 103, 193–219.

Beekes, R. S. P. (1995) *Comparative Indo-European Linguistics: An Introduction*. Amsterdam: John Benjamins Publishing Company.

Bellwood, P. (2005) *First Farmers: The Origins of Agricultural Societies*. Oxford: Blackwell.

Bryant, E. (2001) *The Quest for the Origins of Vedic Culture: The Indo-Aryan Migration Debate*. Oxford: Oxford University Press.

Campbell, L. & Poser, W. J. (2008) *Language Classification: History and Method*. Cambridge: Cambridge University Press.

Clackson, J. (2007) *Indo-European Linguistics: An Introduction*. Cambridge: Cambridge University Press.

Dixon, R. M. W. (1997) *The Rise and Fall of Languages*. Cambridge: Cambridge University Press.

Dumézil, G. (1958) *L'Idéologie tripartite des Indo-européens*. Latomus series 31, Brussels: Société d'Études Latines de Bruxelles.

Gimbutas, M. (1970) Proto-Indo-European culture: the Kurgan culture during the 5th to the 3rd millennia B.C. In G. Cardona, H. M. Koenigswald, & A. Senn (eds), *Indo-European and Indo-Europeans*. Philadelphia: University of Pennsylvania Press, pp. 155–198.

Gray, R. D. & Atkinson, Q. (2003) Language-tree divergence times support the Anatolian theory of Indo-European origin. *Nature* 426, 435–439.

Haak, W., Balanovsky, O., Sanchez, J. J., et al. (2010) Ancient DNA from European Early Neolithic farmers reveals their Near Eastern affinities. *PLoS Biology* 8(11), e1000536.

Heggarty, P. & Beresford-Jones, D. (2010) Agriculture and language dispersals: limitations, refinements, and an Andean exception? *Current Anthropology* 51, 163–191.

Heggarty, P. & Renfrew, C. (forthcoming a) The Americas: languages. In Renfrew & Bahn (forthcoming).

Heggarty, P. & Renfrew, C. (forthcoming b) South and South-East Asia: languages. In Renfrew & Bahn (forthcoming).

Heggarty, P. and Renfrew, C. (forthcoming c) Introduction: Languages. In Renfrew & Bahn (forthcoming).

Heggarty, P. and Renfrew, C. (forthcoming d) Western and Central Asia: Languages. In Renfrew & Bahn (forthcoming).

Heggarty, P., Maguire, W., & McMahon, A. (2010) Splits or waves? Trees or webs? How divergence measures and network analysis can unravel language histories. *Proceedings of the Royal Society B: Biological Sciences* 365, 3829–3843.

Krell, K. S. (1998) Gimbutas' Kurgan-PIE homeland hypothesis: a linguistic critique. In R. Blench & M. Spriggs (eds.), *Archaeology and Language II: Archaeological Data and Linguistic Hypotheses*. London: Routledge, pp. 267–282.

Lewis, M. P. (ed.) (2009) *Ethnologue: Languages of the World*. 16th edn., Dallas: SIL International.

Mallory, J. P. (1989) *In Search of the Indo-Europeans*. London: Thames & Hudson.

Nichols, J. (1992) *Linguistic Diversity in Space and Time*. Chicago: University of Chicago Press.

Renfrew, C. (1987) *Archaeology and Language: The Puzzle of Indo-European Origins*. London: Jonathan Cape.

Renfrew, C. & Bahn, P. (eds.) (forthcoming) *The Cambridge World Prehistory*. Cambridge: Cambridge University Press.

Ringe, D. A., Warnow, T., & Taylor, A. (2002) Indo-European and computational cladistics. *Transactions of the Philological Society* 100(1), 59–129.

20

Europe: Neolithic colonization

Ron Pinhasi

Chapter 17 examined the spread of Neolithic communities from Anatolia into southeastern Europe, and here the the discussion is continued into Danubian and Mediterranean Europe and the far west. Issues of demic versus cultural diffusion are also raised.

The spread of agriculture into Europe has been a subject of debate for a considerable period of time. The role of archaeology in this debate has largely been focused on the relationship between agricultural dispersals and languages, and the ecological and social processes of interaction between hunter-gatherers and farmers. Radiocarbon-based absolute chronology, which is derived from the dating of key Early Neolithic archaeological phases, attests that the earliest Neolithic settlements in Europe emerged several millennia after those in the Fertile Crescent/Anatolia. The spread of farming in Europe began in the southeastern regions (see chapter 17) and took several millennia to reach the most westerly and northerly regions (Whittle 1996). This chapter provides a brief review of the main theoretical approaches, migration processes, and dispersal routes, together with a summary of key archaeological evidence for farming dispersals across Europe.

Theoretical approaches

Several archaeologists and geneticists have proposed a theoretical stance which contends that the Neolithic transition in Europe did not involve large movements of people and population replacement, but simply the spread of knowledge and technology. This theoretical approach presumes extensive biological and archaeological continuity between Mesolithic hunter-gatherers and Neolithic farmers in Europe. Archaeologists who support this model emphasize the economic, technological, and

The Global Prehistory of Human Migration: The Encyclopedia of Global Human Migration Volume 1,
First Edition. Edited by Peter Bellwood.
© 2013 John Wiley & Sons, Ltd. Published 2015 by John Wiley & Sons, Ltd.

cultural complexity of the Mesolithic cultures, which are then viewed as displaying some pre-agricultural elements that seeded the subsequent development of European Neolithic societies (Whittle 1996).

A competing model argues that the transition to agriculture in Europe was predominantly the outcome of a migration of farming populations from Anatolia and the Near East. The underlying assumption of this approach is that such colonists had only limited interaction with local European Mesolithic hunter-gatherers. These farmers brought with them herds of domesticated cattle, pigs, sheep, and goats, domesticated cereals and legumes, various clay objects and ornaments (e.g. anthropomorphic and zoomorphic clay figurines), and extensive knowledge about farming and related activities. This model was originally proposed by V. Gordon Childe (1925) and was tested archeologically and genetically by Ammerman and Cavalli-Sforza (1984) as an example of a population "wave of advance." The underlying assumption of this model is that continuous population growth amongst the farmers resulted in a "demic diffusion" of colonists across Europe at a relatively steady rate of about 1 km/year.

Pinhasi et al. (2005) reassessed the wave of advance model by analysing 735 radiocarbon dates from sites across Europe, the Near East, and Anatolia, in order to assess the rate of demic or cultural diffusion from a number of probable centers using linear regression analysis. Their results estimated an overall average speed for the spread in the range of 0.6–1.3 km/year, consistent with that predicted by Ammerman and Cavalli-Sforza. However, the Linearbandkeramik culture of central Europe and the Cardial culture of the western Mediterranean (see below) both spread much faster, each across 2,000 km of terrain at rates of 5 km/year, possibly faster (Zilhão 2001).

As indicated by Ammerman (1989), the indigenous transition model entails three propositions:

1   In any given region, there was a settled Mesolithic population ready to accept farming as a way of life;
2   In any given region, Late Mesolithic and subsequent Early Neolithic population densities were similar;
3   There was continuity in settlement locations from Mesolithic to Neolithic.

As will be discussed below, these conditions are not met in most regions of Europe. However, this does not imply that the transition only followed an unvarying wave-of-advance model. As Anthony (1990) has pointed out, different types of dispersal are possible, including streams rather than broad waves, with farmers using a few well-defined routes rather than moving in all directions.

Zilhão (2001) proposes a model for the spread of agriculture in Europe as a punctuated process with two main pulses. The first began in the 7th millennium BCE and involved the spread of farming in two streams, up the Danube valley and along the central and eastern Mediterranean coastline. While the spread of farming up the Danube route was rapid and involved the absorption of local Mesolithic groups, that along the coast was slower due to a stronger presence of hunter-gatherer groups. A second pulse then occurred after 5600 BCE, when agricultural populations reached northern Iberia, western France, the Low Countries, and eventually the British

Isles and Scandinavia. The western Mediterranean route involved maritime colonization from the Gulf of Genoa in northern Italy to the estuary of the Mondego in Portugal in no more than 200 years, implying a colonization speed of 20 km/year. In the more northern regions of Europe, the spread may have entailed greater levels of cultural diffusion and hence adoption of agriculture by indigenous Mesolithic communities.

Zvelebil and Rowley-Conwy (1986) proposed a three-stage model for the adoption of agriculture which took into consideration interaction between farming populations and indigenous hunter-gatherers along established frontiers. During their initial "availability" phase, hunter-gatherers would have adopted a limited number of elements of the farming economy, but otherwise retained their indigenous lifestyle. During the "substitution" phase, hunter-gatherers based a growing percentage of their economy on farming products. During the final "consolidation" phase the former hunter-gatherers emerged as a new farming society.

The above models stress the need to take into consideration the possibility that the introduction of agriculture in Europe involved several dispersal mechanisms:

1   directional movement of a whole population from one region to another, leading to genetic replacement;
2   demic diffusion by means of a wave of advance;
3   leapfrog colonization by small groups targeting optimal areas to form enclaves surrounded by indigenous inhabitants;
4   frontier mobility, or exchange between farmers and foragers at agricultural frontier zones;
5   regional contact, involving trade and exchange of ideas but no demic input; and
6   infiltration of communities by small number of specialists, or a social elite (Zvelebil 2001).

It is important to note that each of these mechanisms would have exerted different impacts on the genetic structures of Neolithic and post-Neolithic European populations, as well as on their biological morphologies.

Craniometric studies

An important source of information about past population movements is provided by statistical analysis of craniometric distances within and between late hunter-gatherer and early farming populations from the Near East, Anatolia, and Europe. For instance, there is a striking homogeneity in the skull morphology of Early Neolithic populations from central Anatolia, Greece, Bulgaria, Romania, Serbia, and Hungary (Pinhasi & Pluciennik 2004; Pinhasi & von Cramon-Taubadel 2009). This homogeneity contrasts with the pronounced cranial heterogeneity of Pre-Pottery Neolithic groups in the Near East beyond Anatolia. The results imply continuous gene flow from central and western Anatolia into southeast and central Europe (see chapters 17 and 18). This can be explained as the outcome of a single large-scale dispersal of central Anatolian farmers, or as the outcome of several consecutive waves (as suggested in chapter 17). However, these analysts emphasize that the contribution of Anatolian farmers to the Neolithic societies of Mediterranean, northern, and northwestern regions of Europe may have been more limited.

Archaeological evidence

Eastern Mediterranean Pre-Pottery Neolithic dispersals

Pre-Pottery Neolithic phases characterize the first three millennia of agricultural origins in the Near East and Anatolia, with spreads to Cyprus, Crete, and Thessaly and the Argolid in mainland Greece (see Figure 20.1). On Cyprus, the site of Akrotiri Aetokremnos on the southern coast has yielded evidence of initial occupation of the island by hunter-gatherers, but these disappeared after the 10th millennium BCE (Simmons 2007; Ammerman et al. 2008). For many years it was assumed by archaeologists that the island was abandoned for three thousand years until its recolonization by northern Levantine seafaring Neolithic farmers during the Pre-Pottery Neolithic B (PPNB) (Manning et al. 2010). But recent excavations at the sites of Shillourokambos, Mylouthkia, Kalavasos-Tenta, and Akanthou indicate that Pre-Pottery Neolithic settlement commenced around 8200 BCE, during the Levantine Early PPNB. More recently, new radiocarbon dates from Ayia Varvara Asprokremnos suggest Neolithic colonization in the early 9th millennium BCE, during the Levantine Pre-Pottery Neolithic A (PPNA) (Manning et al. 2010). The growing archaeological evidence suggests a scenario of several Pre-Pottery Neolithic colonization waves reaching the island.

The only unequivocal evidence for Pre-Pottery Neolithic occupation in Crete comes from level X in Knossos (Cherry 1990). However, the Neolithic expansion of settlement on Crete peaked much later, during the Late Neolithic. The Cyclades were first colonized in the later Neolithic (Cherry 1990), but there are no signs of occupation on the Dodecanese, eastern Aegean, or Ionian Islands until after the Neolithic (Perlès 2001).

Mainland Greece and the Balkans

The archaeological record indicates that Greece was colonized at least twice by Neolithic farmers from the Levant and Anatolia; once by sea during the "Initial Neolithic" pre-pottery phase between 7400 and 6500 BCE, when farmers settled at Franchthi Cave, Argissa, and Sesklo in the Peloponnese. A second colonization occurred between 6400 and 6000 BCE (Perlès 2001; and see chapter 17, this volume). The Mesolithic of Greece is mainly known from four sites only – Franchthi Cave, Sidari, Zaïmis, and Ulbrich – all in northeastern Attica or the Argolid (Perlès 2001). This contrasts with the large number of Early Neolithic sites (more than 250), which cluster mainly in the eastern regions. There are only a few sites from Macedonia and Thrace.

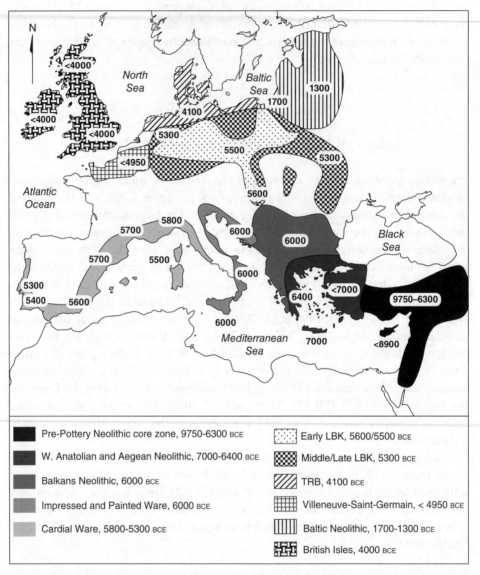

Figure 20.1 Absolute chronology of the spread of the Neolithic from Anatolia and the Levant across Europe in calibrated years before Christ (cal. BCE). Modified from Burger & Thomas (2011), Figure 15.1. Map production by Education and Multimedia Services, College of Asia and the Pacific, The Australian National University.

There is no direct evidence for continuity between Mesolithic and Neolithic in Bulgaria (Todorova 1995), and most Early Neolithic sites are in the east, belonging to the Karanovo I phase at Azmak, Čevdar, and Karanovo itself. Contemporary settlement occurred at Eleshnitsa and Gulubnik in the upper and central Struma valley in western Bulgaria. A progression of Neolithic farmers spread northwards along the Struma and Mesta valleys in western Bulgaria, and northwards along the Ardas valley in Macedonia and southeastern Bulgaria. Most of this settlement occurred between 6500 and 6000 BCE. On the Great Hungarian Plain, evidence for Mesolithic occupation is lacking (Whittle 1996), and Early Neolithic sites date to the first half of the 6th millennium BCE. Between 5500 and 5000 BCE, a relative explosion of settlement numbers occurred in the eastern and northeastern regions of the Carpathian Basin.

The Early Neolithic archaeological records of Greece and the Balkans show a clear contrast in that the Balkan sites reveal a large array of typical Anatolian elements (pottery types, multi-legged pottery vessels, bone spoons), whereas they are absent in Greece (Perlès 2005). Neolithic cultural and stylistic heterogeneity on the Greek Islands is most likely the outcome of various long-distance seaborne movements from the coastlines of Anatolia and the Levant (Perlès 2001, and see chapter 17, this volume). Van Andel and Runnels (1995) propose that the Larissa plain in Thessaly was colonized by relatively small numbers, followed by local demographic growth and subsequent spread as a wave of advance.

Central Europe

The first appearance of the Neolithic in central and western Europe is associated with the Linearbandkeramik Culture (LBK) (Whittle 1996; Bogucki 2003), which originated in western Hungary and eastern Austria c.5600-5500 BCE and then spread rapidly westwards to France and northwards to Poland and Germany (Whittle 1996). The LBK farmers had a preference for loess soils (fine wind-blown dust of glacial origin) for three reasons, according to Bogucki (1996): the loess area was only lightly inhabited by Mesolithic populations, the fertile soil was especially suitable for wheat and barley, and spring flooding helped to replace soil nutrients. Loess fertility could be sustained for years, even under continuous cultivation.

The initial expansion of the LBK was a rapid event which resulted in the occupation of a large geographic area. If the LBK expansion was due to demic diffusion, then the radiocarbon dates from the southeastern LBK zone should be older than those from the north and west. But, at this stage, this is difficult to discern, in accordance with Starling's (1985) settlement pattern observations in central Germany, which show that Neolithic farmers could only colonize certain niches suitable for agriculture, and hence needed to follow specific routes. Consequently, the spread of farming was very rapid, probably both intentional and directional.

During its middle phase, the LBK continued to expand in three distinct movements. One was through the loess lands along the upper Danube into the Neckar Basin and the middle Rhineland. A second was via Moravia and Bohemia into central Germany, eventually reaching the lower Rhine and Meuse. A third occurred along the shoreline of the Baltic Sea (Thomas & Rowlett 1992), where the tempo of expansion was slower. On the western fringe of the LBK distribution and further west towards the Atlantic the archaeological record has yielded Limburg and La Hoguette pottery assemblages that display differences with the LBK proper, possibly involving indigenous hunter-gatherers responding to interaction with incoming farmers (Bogucki & Grygiel 1993; Allard 2007).

The Mediterranean

In southern Europe, Impressed and Painted Ware sites first appear along the western coasts of Greece, Albania, Dalmatia, south Italy, and Sicily at around 6200-6000 BCE (Guilaine 2003; Skeates 2003). In these regions, there is a hiatus between Late Mesolithic and earliest Neolithic dates (Pluciennik 1997). The archaeological record of the western Mediterranean indicates an arrival of Cardial Neolithic farmers in coastal regions between 5800 and 5300 BCE (Zilhão 2003). In Sardinia and Corsica, a period of foraging preceded the introduction of agriculture. There are three excavated pre-Neolithic sites in Corsica, all of which are rock shelters: Strette, in the northern part of the island, and the sites of Arguina-Sennola and Curacchiaghiu in the south. All have yielded dates from the 9th millennium BCE for pre-Neolithic levels (Cherry 1990).

In Corsica, the Cardial Neolithic is dated to 5700-5300 BCE (Tykot 1994). In Sardinia, a human presence is confirmed by 8th millennium BCE radiometric dates for human remains from Grotta Corbeddu. However, Early Neolithic dates from Sardinia fall in the mid-6th millennium BCE and suggest a hiatus of close to a thousand years between the Mesolithic and Neolithic occupations of the island (Pluciennik 1997). The scarcity of dates from central Italy does not allow much discussion regarding the spread of farming in this region, but secure dates fall around the middle of the 6th millennium BCE.

Iberian Late Mesolithic and Early Neolithic sites are located around the periphery of the Peninsula (Zilhão 2003). Along the southwestern coast of Portugal, Late Mesolithic populations survived for as long as 500 years after the first arrival of Neolithic farmers in the estuaries of the Tagus, Sado, and Mira rivers. Contemporary Neolithic populations inhabited the limestone massifs of central Estremadura and the Algarve (Zilhão 2003). The rapid spread of the Cardial culture along the western Mediterranean coastline suggests leapfrog colonization by pioneering maritime Neolithic groups.

The Circum-Baltic region

In southern Scandinavia, the northern European plain, and the eastern Baltic there is a significant body of archaeological evidence indicating that Late Mesolithic hunter-gatherers played an important role in the emergence of farming (Miliskauskas & Kruk 2002). Here, the term "Neolithic" is not always applied to farming societies in the same manner as further south. In the eastern Baltic and parts of western Russia it also encompasses hunter-gatherers with pottery (also often known as "Forest Neolithic" cultures). The Late Mesolithic Ertebølle/Ellerbek cultures of Denmark, southern Sweden, and Schleswig-Holstein and Mecklenburg-Vorpommern in northern Germany represent complex hunter-gatherer societies (Miliskauskas & Kruk 2002) with broad-spectrum modes of subsistence in which the exploitation of both land and sea animals supported continuous year-round occupation (Thorpe 1996).

The appearance of agriculture in this zone coincided with the appearance of the Funnel Beaker Culture (TRB), which first appeared in southern Scandinavia, northern Germany, Czechoslovakia and Poland around 4100-4000 BCE (Miliskauskas 2002a).

The original model for agricultural transition in southern Scandinavia involved immigrant farmers who came from northern Germany (Thorpe 1996), but many researchers now regard the TRB as a local transition with a continuation of foraging and an incorporation of cereal agriculture, domesticated livestock management, and Neolithic technology.

Northwestern Europe

The emergence of Neolithic economies in the Paris basin and on the northwestern Atlantic coast was associated with the Rubané and Villeneuve-Saint-Germain (VSG) cultures respectively (Allard 2007). Rubané material attributes and chronology indicate that it was derived from the western LBK, and the VSG was a later development of the Rubané. Chronological assessment indicates that the Rubané ended around 5000-4800 BCE and was succeeded by the VSG around 4950-4650 BCE (Allard 2007).

In Britain, the emergence of the Neolithic was swift and concordant with a disappearance of the Mesolithic (Thomas 2007). The oldest Neolithic sites, causewayed enclosures and earthen longbarrows, contain domestic livestock and cereal remains and are found in the south at 3900-3700 BCE (Tresset 2004). However, excavations at Balbridie in northeast Scotland also indicate that cereal farming reached this region by 3900-3800 cal. BCE, and the Orkney archipelago by 3600 BCE (Tresset 2004). Farming also reached southern Ireland by 3800-3700 BCE, with evidence for rectangular houses, animal husbandry, and domesticated cereals from sites such as Tankardstown and Cloghers (Tresset 2004).

The extent to which the emergence of Neolithic communities in the British Isles was triggered by incoming continental migrants, or local adoption of farming by Mesolithic bands, or a combination of the two, remains a subject of ongoing debate. The "migrant farmer" hypothesis (Collard et al. 2010) holds that the transition was the result of a rapid colonization by mainland European farmers about 4000 BCE, perhaps by several colonization events (Sheridan 2003), while others argue for adoption of agriculture by indigenous hunter-gatherers (Thomas 2007).

Summary

The archaeological evidence for the appearance of the Neolithic in Europe illuminates a complex process which involved economic, technological, and cultural transformation, as well as migrations by farming and possibly also hunter-gatherer populations. Any current lack of agreement between archaeological, genetic, and linguistic data can perhaps be attributed to a patchiness of data, a need to establish more cross-disciplinary research agendas, and a real complexity of the record. It is likely that the transition involved movements of people, crops, livestock, ideas, and goods across various routes, both by land and sea, as well as local transformations amongst some Mesolithic populations. We are dealing with a series of demographic processes, rather than a single dispersal.

SEE ALSO: 17 Anatolia and the Balkans: archaeology; 18 Europe and western Asia: genetics and human biology

References

Allard, P. (2007) The Mesolithic-Neolithic transition in the Paris Basin: a review. In A. Whittle & V. Cummings (eds.), *Going over the Mesolithic-Neolithic Transition in North West Europe*. Oxford: Oxford University Press, pp. 211–223.

Ammerman, A. J. (1989) On the Neolithic transition in Europe: a comment on Zvelebil and Zvelebil (1988). *Antiquity* 63, 162–165.

Ammerman, A. J. & Biagi, P. (eds.) (2003) *The Widening Harvest: The Neolithic Transition in Europe, Looking Back, Looking Forward*. Boston: Archaeological Institute of America.

Ammerman, A. J. & Cavalli-Sforza L. L. (1984) *The Neolithic Transition and the Genetics of Populations in Europe*. Princeton: Princeton University Press.

Ammerman, A. J., Flourentzos, P., Gabrielli, R., et al. (2008) *Third Report on Early Sites in Cyprus*. Report of the Department of Antiquities, Cyprus. Lefkosia: Department of Antiquities.

Anthony, D. W. (1990) Migration in archeology: the baby and the bathwater. *American Anthropologist* 92, 895–914.

Bogucki, P. (1996) The spread of early farming in Europe. *American Scientist* 84, 242–253.

Bogucki, P. (2003) Neolithic dispersals in riverine interior Central Europe. In A. Ammerman & P. Biagi (eds.) (2003), pp. 249–272.

Bogucki, P. & Grygiel, R. (1993) The first farmers of Central Europe, a survey. *Journal of Field Archaeology* 20, 399–426.

Burger, J. & Thomas, M. G. (2011) The Palaeopopulation genetics of humans, cattle and dairying in Neolithic Europe. In R. Pinhasi & J. T. Stock (eds.), *Human Bioarchaeology of the Transition to Agriculture*. New York: Wiley-Liss, pp. 371–384.

Cherry, J. (1990) The first colonization of the Mediterranean islands: a review of recent research. *Journal of Mediterranean Archaeology* 3, 145–221.

Childe, V. G. (1925) *The Dawn of European Civilization*. London: Kegan Paul.

Collard, M., Edinborough, K., Shennan, S., & Thomas, M. G. (2010) Radiocarbon evidence indicates that migrants introduced farming to Britain. *Journal of Archaeological Science* 37, 866–870.

Guilaine, J. (2003). Aspects de la Néolithisation en Méditerranée et en France [Aspects of Neolithization in the Mediterranean and in France]. In A. J. Ammerman & P. Biagi (eds.) (2003), pp. 189–206.

Manning, S. W., McCartney, C., Kromer, B., & Stewart, S. T. (2010) The earlier Neolithic in Cyprus: recognition and dating of a Pre-Pottery Neolithic A occupation. *Antiquity* 84, 693–706.

Miliskauskas, S. (2002a) Early Neolithic: the first farmers in Europe, 7000-5500/5000 BC. In Miliskauskas (2002b), pp. 143–192.

Miliskauskas, S. (ed.) (2002b), *European Prehistory: A Survey*. New York: Springer.

Miliskauskas, S. & Kruk, J. (2002) Middle Neolithic: continuity, diversity, innovations, and greater complexity. In Miliskauskas (2002b), pp. 193–246.

Perlès, C. (2001) *The Early Neolithic in Greece*. Cambridge: Cambridge University Press.

Perlès, C. (2005) From the Near East to Greece: let's reverse the focus: cultural elements that didn't transfer. In C. Lichter (ed.), *How Did Farming Reach Europe?* Istanbul: BYZAS 2, pp. 275–290.

Pinhasi, R. & Pluciennik, M. (2004) A regional biological approach to the spread of farming in Europe: Anatolia, the Levant, South-Eastern Europe, and the Mediterranean. *Current Anthropology* 45, 59–82.

Pinhasi, R. & von Cramon-Taubadel, N. (2009) Craniometric data supports demic diffusion model for the spread of agriculture into Europe. *PLoS ONE*, 4: e6747. doi:10.1371/journal.pone.0006747.

Pinhasi, R., Fort, J., & Ammerman, A. J. (2005) Tracing the origin and spread of agriculture in Europe. *PLoS Biology* 3, e410 doi:10.1371/journal.pbio.0030410.

Pluciennik, M. (1997) Radiocarbon determinations and the Mesolithic-Neolithic transition in southern Italy. *Journal of Mediterranean Archaeology* 10, 115–150.

Sheridan, A. (2003) French connections I: spreading the marmites thinly. In I. Armit, E. Murphy, E. Nelis, & D. Simpson (eds.), *Neolithic Settlement in Ireland and Western Britain*. Oxford: Oxbow, pp. 3–17.

Simmons, A. H. (2007) *The Neolithic Revolution in the Near East*. Tucson: University of Arizona Press.

Skeates, R. (2003) Radiocarbon dating and interpretations of the Mesolithic-Neolithic transition in Italy. In Ammerman & Biagi (2003), pp. 157–188.

Starling, N. J. (1985) Social change in the later Neolithic of central Europe. *Antiquity* 59, 30–38.

Thomas, H. L. & Rowlett, E. S.-J. (1992) The archaeological chronology of Northern Europe. In R. W. Ehrich (ed.), *Chronologies in Old World Archaeology*, vol. 1. Chicago: University of Chicago Press, pp. 345–355.

Thomas, J. (2007) Mesolithic–Neolithic transitions in Britain: from essence to inhabitation. *Proceedings of the British Academy* 144, 423–439.

Thorpe, I. J. N. (1996) *The Origins of Agriculture in Europe*. London: Routledge.

Todorova, H. (1995) The Neolithic, Eneolithic and transitional period in Bulgarian prehistory. In D. W. Bailey, I. Panayotov, & S. Alexandrov (eds.), *Prehistoric Bulgaria*. Madison: Prehistory Press, pp. 79–98.

Tresset, A. (2004) Beginnings of farming in northwestern Europe. In P. Bogucki & P. J. Crabtree (eds.), *Ancient Europe: An Encyclopedia of the Barbarian World, 8000 BC – AD 1000*, vol. I. New York: Scribners, pp. 273–281.

Tykot, R. H. (1994) Radiocarbon dating and absolute chronology in Sardinia and Corsica. In R. Skeates & R. Whitehouse (eds.), *Radiocarbon Dating and Italian Prehistory*. Archaeological Monographs of the British School at Rome No. 14. London: British School at Rome, pp. 115–145.

Van Andel, T. & Runnels, C. (1995) The earliest farmers in Europe. *Antiquity* 69, 481–500.

Whittle, A. (1996) *Europe in the Neolithic: The Creation of New Worlds*. Cambridge: Cambridge University Press.

Zilhão, J. (2001) Radiocarbon evidence for maritime pioneer colonization at the origins of farming in west Mediterranean Europe. *Proceedings of the National Academy of Sciences of the USA* 98, 14180–14185.

Zilhão, J. (2003) The Neolithic transition in Portugal and the role of demic diffusion in the spread of agriculture across west Mediterranean Europe. In Ammerman & Biagi (eds.) (2003), pp. 207–226.

Zvelebil, M. (2001) The agricultural transition and the origins of Neolithic society in Europe. *Documenta Praehistorica* 28, 1–26.

Zvelebil, M. & Rowley-Conwy, P. (1986) Foragers and farmers in Atlantic Europe. In M. Zvelebil (ed.), *Hunters in Transition: Mesolithic Societies in Temperate Eurasia and their Transition to Farming*. Cambridge: Cambridge University Press, pp. 67–93.

21

Northern Europe and Russia: Uralic linguistic history

Václav Blažek

The author presents the linguistic history of the Uralic language family, comprising mainly hunter-gatherer populations on the northern fringes of Europe and western Siberia. The family also includes Finnish and Hungarian, both national languages today.

The modern distribution of the Uralic languages is shown in Figure 11.1. A number of classifications have been proposed for the subgroups in the family (see Rédei et al. 1974: 38–39; Hajdú 1985: 173–174), but we begin with that presented in 2004–2010, using a so-called "recalibrated" glottochronology. This gives the chronology and family tree in Figure 21.1, with two primary Samoyedic and Fenno-Ugric branches.

There are two methods whose combination allows us to determine the homeland of any given language family. Linguistic paleontology is based on the geographical locations of plants and animals whose designations can be reconstructed in proto-languages (cf. Sebestyén 1941–43/1949–50; Sebestyén 1935 for Uralic tree and fish names). The second method is to examine traces of mutual contact and borrowing between neighboring language families. An absolute chronology can then be estimated if those borrowings can be pinpointed within the subgrouping structures of the donor family or recipient. Another source for chronology may be found in glottochronology.

According to Hajdú (1985: 156–57), Xelimskij (1989[2000]: 15) and Napol'skix (1997: 127–34), the following tree names played a diagnostic role in the Uralic lexicon: *kawse* "spruce, *Picea*"; *ńulkз* "fir, *Abies*"; *jзwз* "pine, *Pinus*"; and *siksз* "Siberian stone pine, *Pinus cembra sibirica*". Napol'skix (1997: 130–34) adds *mura* "blackberry, *Rubus chamaemorus*" and some zoonyms, such as *kunta* "reindeer"; *poča* "(calf of) reindeer"; *śarta* "deer, reindeer"; *tewä* "elk, deer"; *ńuk(з-)śe* "ermine, marten"; *püŋe* "partridge, hazel-grouse"; *küje* "snake"; *kärз* "sterlet, Caspian sturgeon, *Acipenser ruthenus*"; *kewз(-ŋkз)* "salmon, whitefish"; *korз* "*Coregonus lavaretus*/muksun"; *ončз* "*Stenodus nelma, Coregonus njelma*"; *totka* "tench, *Tinca tinca*"; and also Fenno-Ugric

The Global Prehistory of Human Migration: The Encyclopedia of Global Human Migration Volume 1,
First Edition. Edited by Peter Bellwood.
© 2013 John Wiley & Sons, Ltd. Published 2015 by John Wiley & Sons, Ltd.

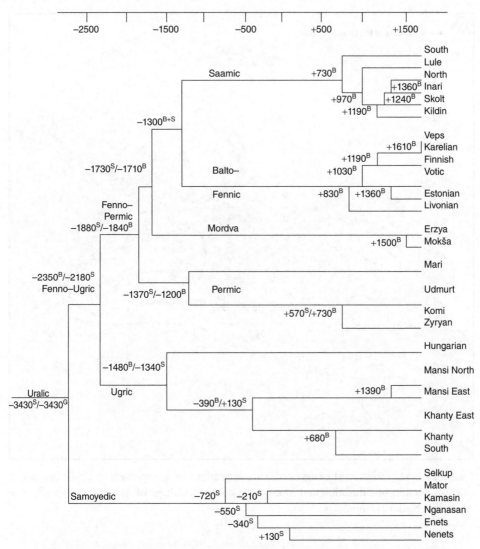

Figure 21.1 A classification and chronology for the Uralic languages.

*śampe "sturgeon, *Acipenser*". The latter has a probable cognate in Samoyedic **su/ümpə̑* *-ŋkə̑* "muksun", where **su/ümpə̑* means "back of a fish", so typical for "sturgeon". These species help us to place the Uralic proto-language somewhere between the Ural mountains in the west and the middle Yenisei River in the east, and from the Polar circle in the north to the southern border of the taiga forest in the foothills of the Sayany and Altai mountains (Figure 21.2). Any location west of the Urals is problematic with regard to the close relationship of Uralic with the small Yukaghir family, located during

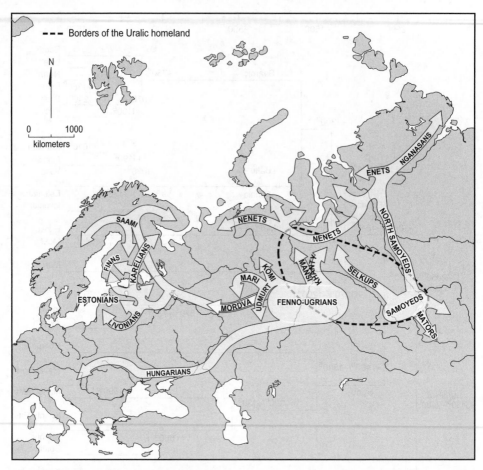

Figure 21.2 Map to show the suggested early migrations of the speakers of Uralic languages. Map production by Education and Multimedia Services, College of Asia and the Pacific, The Australian National University.

the eighteenth century between the lower Lena and Anadyr rivers. The Uralic–Yukaghir divergence is dated to 6600 BC by G. Starostin (2010). The Uralic-Yukaghir divergence is dated to 6600 BC by G. Starostin (2010). The disintegration of Uralic itself has been dated by glottochronology to the 4th millennium BC (Hajdú 1985; Fig. 21.1).

Such Fenno-Ugric tree names as *narkɜ "cedar-nut"; *näŋɜ "larch, *Larix sibirica*"; *śala "elm, *Ulmus*"; plus Fenno-Permic *ńine "bast"; *ńine-puwɜ "linden, *Tilia*"; and the zoonyms *maja "beaver"; *śijele "hedgehog"; *ćorɜ "salmon, whitefish"; and *tokta "diving-duck, *Gavia*" shift the area of the Fenno-Ugric proto-language westwards in comparison with the Uralic homeland (Fig. 12.2). The most likely region would include the central and southern Urals, and the upper basins of the Kama, Pečora and Vyčegda rivers (Napol'skix 1997: 140).

The disintegration of Uralic is traditionally dated to the 4th millennium BCE by Hajdú (1985); more exactly by "recalibrated" glottochronology to 3430 BCE by S. Starostin

(2004); and to 3840 BCE by G. Starostin (2010). In the meantime, before the break-up of Fenno-Permic from Ugric at about 2400 BCE, contacts with the speakers of Indo-European languages had begun. Ancestors of the Indo-European Tocharians influenced Fenno-Ugric during their migration towards Xinjiang in the late 4th millennium BCE. Indo-Iranian speakers and their descendants became southern neighbors of the Fenno-Ugrians perhaps from 3000 BCE onwards, and remained so until their assimilation by Slavs and Turks in the 1st millennium CE (Jacobsohn 1922; Korenchy 1972; Joki 1973; Blažek 1990, 2003, 2005; Katz 2003).

The Kama River was crucial in the westerly spread of the early Fenno-Ugric speakers. This was the biggest tributary of the Volga and led the ancestors of the Permians, Mari, and Mordva (plus the extinct Merya and Muroma) into the middle and upper basin of the Volga. From here, the ancestors of the Fenno-Saamic speakers continued to the basin of the Baltic Sea. During their period of habitation in the Fenno-Scandian region, the ancestors of the Saami assimilated some pre-existing population(s) (cf. Toivonen 1949–50; Xelimskij 1996). In the Mari, Mordva, and Fenno-Saamic subgroups there are influences from the Baltic and in Fenno-Saamic from the Germanic subgroups of Indo-European (Thomsen 1870, 1890; Vaba 1983; Kylstra et al. 1991–96; Ritter 1993; Xelimskij 1995; Blažek 2004). During the past millennium, the influences of Russian and various Turkic languages have grown. In the Volga basin, the Kama river also brought the ancestors of the Hungarians after their separation from the Ob' river Ugric speakers in the 15th and 14th centuries BCE. The Hungarian lexicon indicates significant influence from other languages contacted or assimilated during their passage along the lower Volga, through the Caspian and Pontic steppes and into Pannonia, especially Turkic of the Bulgar-Čuvaš type (Gombocz 1912), Sarmatian-Alanic (Sköld 1925; Abaev 1965) and Pannonian Slavic (Xelimskij 1988[2000]; Richards 2003).

Xelimskij (1989[2000]: 15–17) localized the Samoyedic homeland in the southwest Siberian taiga, within the triangle formed by the cities of Tomsk, Krasnoyarsk and Eniseisk. In the taiga region between the middle Ob' and Yenisei rivers there are attested trees and animals whose names are inherited from Proto-Uralic, including Samoyedic *kåət̂ "spruce, *Picea*", *ńulkå "fir, *Abies*", *je "pine, *Pinus*", and *tit̂eŋ "stone pine, *Pinus cembra sibirica*". Others are attested only in Samoyedic, including *to₁jmå "larch"; *ki(j) "sable"; *munt₁o "ibex"; *pajt₁ʒ "roe"; *pińʒ "ermine"; *pʒnso(j) "flying squirrel"; *tet "otter"; *wiŋkə́nce "wolverine"; *kässʒrä "*Nucifraga caryocatactes*"; *ńuə́nx̌ "diving-duck"; and *seŋkx̌ "grouse". According to Xelimskij (1989) and S. Starostin (2004), the ancestors of the Selkups moved to the north along the Ob' valley in the early 8th century BCE. The North Samoyeds migrated to the north along the Yenisei in the mid-6th century BCE. In the Taymyr Peninsula they assimilated a substratum that is reflected especially in Nganasan. The separations of Kamasin-Koibalsan and Mator-Taigi-Karagas occurred around 200 BCE, possibly a result of Hun (Turkic-speaking) populations attacking the Minussin Hollow. The former moved to the Sayany mountains in the south, and the latter group migrated to the east between the Kan and Mana, right tributaries of the Yenisei. The oldest borrowings in Samoyedic can be identified from Tocharian (3rd millennium BCE?; see Janhunen 1983; Blažek & Schwarz 2008) and proto-Turkic (early 1st millennium BCE; Janhunen 1977). Samoyedic borrowings from Komi, Ob-Ugric, Ket (Xelimskij 1982), Tungusic (Anikin & Xelimskij 2007) and various Turkic languages in Siberia (Joki 1952; Róna-Tas 1988) occurred later.

SEE ALSO: 23 Northern and northeastern Asia: archaeology; 44 North America: North America: Eskimo-Aleut linguistic history

References

Abaev, V. I. (1965) K alano-vengerskim leksičeskim svjazjam [Toward Alano-Hungarian lexical relations]. In G. Ortutay & T. Bodrogi (eds.), *Europa et Hungaria. Congressus Ethnographicus in Hungaria*. Budapest: Akadémiai Kiadó, pp. 515–537.

Anikin, A. E. & Xelimskij, E. A. (2007) *Samodijsko-tungusomančžurskie leksičeskie svjazi* [Samoyedic-Tungusic lexical relations]. Moscow: Jazyki Slavjanskoj Kul'tury.

Blažek, V. (1990) New Fenno-Ugric–Indo-Iranian lexical parallels. In V. V. Ivanov et al. (eds.), *Uralo-Indogermanica* II. *Materials of the 3rd Balto-Slavic Conference*. Moscow: Institut Slavjanovedenija i Balkanistiki, pp. 40–43.

Blažek, V. (2003) Toward the Fenno-Ugric cultural lexicon of Indo-Iranian origin. *Indogermanische Forschungen* 108, 92–99.

Blažek, V. (2004) Balto-Fennic mythological names of Baltic origin. *Baltistica* 39(2), 189–194.

Blažek, V. (2005) Indo-Iranian elements in Fenno-Ugric mythological lexicon. *Indogermanische Forschungen* 110, 160–183.

Blažek, V. (2010) Was there a Volgaic unity within Fenno-Ugric? Paper presented at the conference of Finno-Ugric Studies Association of Canada, Montreal, May.

Blažek, V. & Schwarz, M. (2008) Tocharians: who they were, where they came from and where they lived? *Lingua Posnaniensis* 50, 47–74.

Gombocz, Z. (1912) Die bulgarisch-türkische Lehnwörter in der Ungarischen Sprache [Bulgarian-Turkic loanwords in the Hungarian language] (special issue). *Mémoires de la Société Finno-Ougrienne* 30.

Hajdú, P. (1985) *Uralskie jazyki i narody* [*Uralic languages and populations*] (trans. E. Xelimskij). Moscow: Progress. (Original Hungarian edn. Xajdu 1962)

Jacobsohn, H. (1922) *Arier und Ugrofinnen* [*Aryans and Fenno-Ugrians*]. Göttingen: Vandenhoeck & Ruprecht.

Janhunen, J. (1977) Samoyed-Altaic contacts – present state of research. *Mémoires de la Société Finno-Ougrienne* 158, 123–129.

Janhunen, J. (1983) On early Indo-European-Samoyed contacts. In J. Janhunen (ed.), *Symposium Saeculare Societatis Fenno-Ugricae. Mémoires de la Société Finno-Ougrienne* 185, pp. 115–127.

Joki, A. J. (1952) *Die Lehnwörter der Sajansamojedischen* [Loanwords in the Sayan-Samoyedic]. *Mémoires de la Société Finno-Ougrienne* 103.

Joki, A. J. (1973) *Uralier und Indogermanen* [Uralians and Indo-Europeans]. *Mémoires de la Société Finno-Ougrienne* 151.

Katz, H. (2003) *Studien zu den älteren indoiranischen Lehnwörtern in den uralischen Sprachen* [*Studies in the earliest Indo-Iranian loanwords in the Uralic languages*]. Heidelberg: Winter.

Korenchy, É. (1972) *Iranische Lehnwörter in den obugrischen Sprachen* [Iranian loanwords in the Ob-Ugric languages]. Budapest: Akadémiai Kiadó.

Kylstra, A. D., Hahmo, S.-L., Hofstra, T. & Nikkilä, O. (1991–96) *Lexikon der Älteren Germanischen Lehnwörter in den Ostseefinnischen Sprachen* [*Lexicon of the earliest Germanic loans in the Balto-Fennic languages*], I–II. Amsterdam-Atlanta: Rodopi.

Napol'skix, V. V. (1997) *Vvedenie v istoričeskuju uralistiku* [Introduction to historical Uralic studies]. Iževsk: Udmurtskij Institut istorii, jazyka i literatury.

Rédei, K., Lytkin, V., & Majtinskaja, K. (eds.) (1974) *Osnovy finno-ugorskogo jazykoznanija* I [Elements of Fenno-Ugric linguistics]. Moscow: Nauka.

Richards, R. O. (2003) *The Pannonian Dialect of the Common Slavic Proto-Language*. Los Angeles: University of California.

Ritter, R-P. (1993) *Studium zur den ältesten germanischen Entlehnungen im Ostseefinnischen* [Studies on the earliest Germanic loans in Balto-Fennic]. Frankfurt am Main: Lang.

Róna-Tas, A. (1988) Turkic influence on the Uralic languages. In D. Sinor (ed.), *The Uralic Languages*. Leiden: Brill, pp. 742–780.

Sebestyén, I. (1935) Az uráli nyelvek régi halnevei [Fish-names in the Uralic languages]. *Nyelvtudományi Közlemények* 49, 1–97.

Sebestyén, I. (1941–43, 1949–50) Fák és fás helyek régi nevel az uráli nyelvekben [Tree-names and places connected with trees in the Uralic languages]. *Nyelvtudományi Közlemények* 51, 412–434; 52, 247–261, 307–314.

Sköld, H. (1925) *Die ossetischen Lehnwörter im Ungarischen* [The Ossetic loans in Hungarian]. Lund: Gleerup. Leipzig: Harrassowitz.

Starostin, G. (2010) Glottochronological classification of the language families of northern Eurasia. Unpublished MS.

Starostin, S. (2004) Uralic glottochronological classification. Paper presented at Institute of Santa Fe, NM. Diagram published in Blažek & Schwarz (2008), p. 5.

Thomsen, W. (1870) *Über den Einfluss der germanischen Sprachen auf die Finnisch-Lappischen* [On the influence of the Germanic languages on Fennic and Saamic]. Halle: Waisenhaus.

Thomsen, W. (1890) *Beröringer Mellem de Finske og de Baltiske (Litauisk-Lettiske) Sprog. En Sproghistorisk Undersøgelse* [Contacts between the Fennic and Baltic (Lithuanian-Latvian) languages: historical-linguistic research]. Copenhagen: Blanco Lunos.

Toivonen, Y. H. (1949–50) Zum Problem des Protolappischen [Toward the problem of proto-Saamic]. *Sitzungsberichte der Finnischen Akademie der Wissenschaften* 1949, pp. 161–189.

Vaba, L. (1983) Baltische Lehnwörter der Wolga-Sprachen im Lichte neuerer Forschungsergebnisse [Baltic loans in the Volgaic languages in the light of new research]. *Sovetskoe Finnougrovedenie* 19, 138–145.

Xelimskij, E. (1982) Keto-Uralica. In E. A. Alekseenko (ed.), *Ketskij Sbornik*. Leningrad: Nauka, pp. 238–250.

Xelimskij, E. (1988) Vengerskij jazyk kak istočnik dlja praslavjanskoj rekonstrukcii i rekonstrukcii slavjanskogo jazyka Pannonii [Hungarian language as a source for the proto-Slavic reconstruction]. In Xelimskij (2000), pp. 416–432.

Xelimskij, E. (1989) Samodijskaja lingvističeskaja rekonstrukcija i praistorija samodijcev [Samoyedic linguistic reconstruction and prehistory of the Samoyeds]. In Xelimskij (2000), pp. 13–25.

Xelimskij, E. (1995) Sverxdrevnie germanizmy v pribaltijsko-finskix i drugix finno-ugorskix jazykax [Super-archaic Germanisms in the Balto-Fennic and other Fenno-Ugric languages]. In Xelimskij (2000), pp. 511–535.

Xelimskij, E. (1996) Protosaamskij i samodijskij: korpus ėtimologij v svete sovremennyx dannyx samodistiki [Proto-Saamic and Samoyedic: a corpus of etymologies in the light of the present state-of-the-art of Samoyedic studies]. In Xelimskij (2000), pp. 202–217.

Xelimskij, E. (ed.) (2000), *Komparatistika Uralistika: Lekcii i Stat'i* [Comparative & Uralic studies: courses and articles]. Moscow: Jazyki Russkoj Kul'tury.

22

Central Asia: genetics and archaeology

Ron Pinhasi and Evelyne Heyer

This chapter discusses human migrations in Central Asia, with particular reference to the genetics of the Indo-Iranian- and Turkic-speaking populations and the archaeological record of pastoralism on the Steppes, from the Caspian Sea to the Tian Shan Mountains.

The evolutionary history of modern humans has been characterized by range expansions, colonizations and recurrent migrations over the last 100,000 years (Cavalli-Sforza et al. 1994). Some regions of the world served as natural corridors between landmasses and are of particular importance in the history of human migrations. Central Asia was probably at the crossroads of several such migration routes (Nei & Roychoudhury 1993). It encompasses a vast territory, stretching from the Pamir and Tian Shan mountains in the east to the Caspian Sea in the west; limited to the north by the Russian taiga and to the south by the Iranian deserts and Afghan mountains. The rather uniform low-relief, treeless topography of the Eurasian steppe, mostly unsuitable for rain-based agriculture, facilitated potential contact and movements between human groups. But the archaeological record of this region indicates that the movements and contacts varied in type, intensity, and nature during different prehistoric epochs (Sherratt 2003).

The nature and timing of the emergence and spread of agriculture in Central Asia differed from that in other regions such as the Near East and southeast Europe. This is partly due to the nature of the steppe – a vast open region which is generally not suitable for rain-based agriculture – and partly due to a unique set of socioeconomic, technological, and cultural circumstances. Two of the main processes associated with the emergence of agriculture in Central Asia were the development of pastoralism and the domestication of the horse. In this chapter we review the main genetic and archaeological associations of these processes.

The Global Prehistory of Human Migration: The Encyclopedia of Global Human Migration Volume 1,
First Edition. Edited by Peter Bellwood.
© 2013 John Wiley & Sons, Ltd. Published 2015 by John Wiley & Sons, Ltd.

Genetic diversity in Central Asia

Most previous studies, based on classical markers (Cavalli-Sforza et al. 1994), mito-chondrial DNA (mtDNA) (Comas et al. 1998, 2004; Perez-Lezaun et al. 1999), or the non-recombining portion of the Y-chromosome (NRY) (Hammer et al. 2001; Wells et al. 2001; Zerjal et al. 2002; Chaix et al. 2007), have shown that genetic diversity in Central Asia is among the highest in Eurasia. NRY studies suggest an early settlement of Central Asia by modern humans, followed by subsequent waves of colonization out of this region (Wells et al. 2001). Some mtDNA studies point to an admixed origin from previously differentiated eastern and western Eurasian populations (Comas et al. 2004), and several recent analyses of mtDNA data identify east-to-west expansion waves across Eurasia in the late Pleistocene–Holocene (Derenko et al. 2007; Rootsi et al. 2007; Chaix et al. 2008).

We have conducted an extensive autosomal study of more than 20 populations from this area, in which we have found a high level of autosomal genetic diversity, consistent with previous observations and higher than in Europe, the Middle East, or East Asia (Martinez-Cruz et al. 2011). We propose that the observed genetic diversity is due mainly to the differentiation of one ancestral gene pool into two major population clusters. The first includes Indo-Iranian-speaking populations (Tajiks and three Uzbek populations) who are genetically closer to populations from western Eurasia. The second includes Turkic-speaking populations (Karakalpaks, Kazakhs, Kirgiz, and two other Uzbek populations) who are closer to eastern Asian populations (with the excep-tion of the Turkmen, who are closer to western Eurasian populations). (See Figure 24.1 for the locations of some of these groups.)

This study sheds new light on the putative origins of the Indo-Iranian and Turkic-speaking populations. Most Indo-Iranians belong to two clusters that mostly do not occur in other modern Middle Eastern or European populations. One of these includes populations from Pakistan as well as Central Asia. Altogether, the significant pairwise genetic distance (i.e. F_{ST}) between almost all pairs of Indo-Iranian-speaking popula-tions, their high levels of diversity and the variable level of admixture from putative parental populations seem consistent with the premise that Indo-Iranian speakers were already in the region during the Neolithic.

Brunet's (1998) hypothesis that some of the Neolithic populations of Central Asia have a high antiquity in the region is consistent with our genetic data, which point to an early settlement by ancestral Tajik (Indo-Iranian) people compared to the Turkic groups. However, it is not yet possible to assess the pre-Neolithic ancestry of either of these Asiatic populations. Our results simply indicate a lower genetic differentiation among Turkic speakers, despite their wide geographic distribution, which suggests a more recent common origin for them. Most Turkic-speaking individuals sampled belonged to one Central Asian cluster, only overlapping to a very small extent with the East Asian cluster, thus confirming the results of Li et al. (2009) for the Turkic-speaking Uyghur, Kazakh, and Khanty. This pattern likely reflects the existence of an ancestral group of Turkic speakers, genetically differentiated from East Asian populations, historically and linguistically believed to have originated from the Altai region or

Mongolia (see chapter 23). We see no evidence for a strong Southeast Asian genetic contribution to these Central Asian populations, and an ancient DNA study on skeletal samples from Kazakhstan dated before the 7th century BCE by Lalueza-Fox and his colleagues (2004) revealed a majority of west Eurasian mtDNA haplotypes, in accordance with the affinities of the Indo-Iranian-speaking populations.

The emergence of agriculture

The transition to a fully Neolithic agro-pastoral economy did not occur in the steppe region until several millennia after such a transition occurred in the Fertile Crescent and southeast Europe. Unlike the Near East and Anatolia, where sedentism preceded the development of agricultural societies, the transition to agriculture in the steppe region was a product of contact with, and migration by, Fertile Crescent and southeast European Neolithic communities.

Until the late 1980s, Western researchers had limited information about the Neolithic, Eneolithic, and Bronze Age cultures of eastern Europe and the Soviet regions of Europe and central Asia. Soviet archaeologists assumed that the emergence of Neolithic cultures equated with the first evidence of pottery in the archaeological record, in contrast with Western archaeologists, who viewed the Neolithic more as an economic, technological, and social transition (Telegin & Potekhina 1987; Telegin et al. 2002). Here, we differentiate three "Neolithic" economies in the Eurasian steppe as follows: (1) pottery using hunter-fisher-gatherers; (2) sedentary agro-pastoralists whose subsistence contained only a limited contribution from wild resources; and (3) hunter-fisher-gatherers who incorporated some agro-pastoral elements into their subsistence, either through indigenous development or by trade/exchange with neighboring fully agricultural Neolithic groups. However, the allocation of different archaeological "cultures" into these three categories is not always straightforward. Recent research has highlighted the inadequacy of many chronologies and cultural definitions by typological attributes such as pottery style (Lillie 1998). Emphasis is therefore placed here on well-defined archaeological entities that reveal evidence for a transition to agriculture.

A maritime Early Pre-Pottery Neolithic B dispersal with domesticated crops, sheep, and goats from the Levant/Anatolia to Cyprus (c.8300 BCE, see chapters 17 and 20) is now well documented. This initial dispersal was followed by one or more migrations from northwest Anatolia into Turkish Thrace and further into southeast Europe. It seems plausible that one or more of these westward migrations was also paralleled by the spread of farming eastward to the eastern flanks of the Fertile Crescent and further east into central Asia. In northeastern Iran, western Turkmenistan and central Asia, foundation dates for the Neolithic, which includes pottery, are towards the end of the 7th millennium BCE. Examples are Tepe Sialk and Tepe Chakmak in eastern Iran (c.6300 BCE) and the Jeitun culture in Turkmenistan at c.6000 BCE (Harris 1998, 2010; Fuller 2006). Local Mesolithic sites in these regions do not show evidence of being the progenitors of the Jeitun culture, and it seems most likely that there was a spread of Neolithic agricultural elements from the Fertile Crescent (Harris & Gosden 1996).

In other parts of Central Asia, north of Afghanistan and southeast of Tajikistan, Neolithic cultures began up to half a millennium later, represented for example by the Kelteminar complex of Kazakhstan, the Hissar culture of Tajikistan, the Central Ferghana of Uzbekistan and the Neolithic levels of the Oshkona site in Tadjikistan (Brunet 1998). However, most of these cultures lack archaeological evidence of domesticated plants and animals, and hence may have been associated with pottery-using hunter-fisher-gatherers (Fuller 2006).

In the western zone of the Central Asian steppe, agriculture and animal husbandry were first introduced from Eastern Europe by the Criş culture at about 5800 BCE (Anthony 2004). Further east, in the forest steppe regions of the Dniester and Bug rivers, local Bug-Dniester foragers began to produce pottery in the northwestern Black Sea littoral around 6200–6000 BCE, prior to contact with southern farmers. Around the same period, the Surska-Dnieper culture in the Lower Dnieper area and the Rakushechnyi Yar of the lower Don river provide similar evidence for early pottery making (Telegin et al. 2002). Evidence for hunter–farmer contact is apparent in stylistic elements in Bug-Dniester pottery, and percentages of domesticated cattle and pig bones increase in Bug-Dniester occupational phases a few centuries later (c.5800–5700 BCE; Anthony 2007).

The North Pontic societies east of the Dniester continued to hunt, gather and fish until about 5200 BCE (Anthony 2004, 2007), and the Dniepr Rapids region further east was also populated by hunting-foraging-fishing populations who adopted pottery. Around 5100–4900 BCE, the fully Neolithic Cucuteni-Tripolye and Gumelniţa cultures dispersed eastward into the Dniester and southern Bug valleys.

The origins of pastoralism and horse domestication

As pointed out by Renfrew (2001) and by Khazanov (1984), steppe pastoralism involved a nomadic lifestyle distinct from Near Eastern agro-pastoralism. Nomadic pastoralism entailed periodic mobility in which all the community must move, in contrast to transhumance where only herdsmen moved in and out of permanent settlements. However, identification of pastoralism in the archaeological record is not straightforward because neither the faunal nor the settlement records are sufficiently detailed. For instance, evidence of some wild resources in the diet need not mean that a particular group was not truly pastoralist.

It should be pointed out that pastoral economies in Asia are offshoots of a farming economy (Renfrew 2001), since sheep, goats, and cattle were domesticated by earlier agro-pastoral communities. However, the horse is a special case since it was domesticated in regions of Central Asia where mixed farming developed late and where hunting and gathering remained dominant. The introduction of both cattle and horse breeding are taken to be major developments of the 5th/4th-millennium BCE on the Russian/Ukrainian steppes. Many archaeologists today typically identify the archaeological cultures involved as Indo-European (Lamberg-Karlovsky 2002; Anthony 2007), following Marija Gimbutas (1977), who combined data from linguistic paleontology and archaeology in an attempt to locate the "homeland" of the Proto-Indo-European

(PIE) speakers and to explain their rapid and extensive spread. Gimbutas defined the term "Kurgan culture" to refer to pastoral communities documented from the 5th millennium BCE onwards in the steppe environments of the Volga-Ural-Caspian region. She suggested that these peoples spoke Indo-European languages, maintained a patri-archal society and were militant, mobile horse-riding pastoralists. This was in contrast to the matriarchal, peaceful, and sedentary European (Neolithic, Eneolithic) societies. She also proposed three major incursions or infiltrations of "Kurgan" peoples from the Pontic steppe into Europe, which took place between 4500 and 2500 BCE. However, since the 1990s, Gimbutas' model has lost popularity due to the limited archaeological and genetic evidence for migration from the Steppes into Europe on the required scale at this time (see chapter 18).

The recovery of horse bones from the Eneolithic (Copper Age) settlement of Dereivka on the Lower Dnieper River was once believed to offer the first material evidence for early horse domestication and for the movement of nomads from the east. But Anthony (2007) has shown that the only Dereivka horse teeth displaying evidence of bit wear date to the medieval period. More recently, new evidence has emerged from DNA analysis of modern horses to suggest multiple centers of origin for horse domestication, and not a single center as was previously assumed (Jansen et al. 2002; McGahern et al. 2006). A more recent study by Outram et al. (2009) exam-ines bit wear, metrics of horse limb bones, and organic residues in pottery from several Botai culture sites in Kazakhstan (3500–3000 BCE). Horse bones here often comprise 99 percent of total faunal assemblages, suggesting that the Botai groups were utilizing horses in several different ways, for meat, milk, and perhaps riding.

By 2500 BCE, a different mobile pastoralist strategy dominated the steppes as dependence shifted from horses to domesticated sheep/goats and cattle (Benecke & von Een Driesch 2003). It appears that the emergence of nomadic pastoralism in some regions of Central Asia occurred well after the agro-pastoral economy documented, for instance, in the Jeitun culture at c.6000 BCE. In some regions, such as the Botai culture, nomadic pastoralism developed directly from nomadic hunting-gathering.

Conclusion

Lack of geographic barriers to gene flow within the Central Asian steppe allowed rela-tively easy mobility of human populations, especially during the last 10 kya, following the onset of a milder Holocene climate. Gene flow should perhaps have resulted in a homogenization of genetic diversity, but in fact there is a great degree of heterogeneity which should perhaps be attributed to cultural rather than to geographic barriers. The main divide was between nomadic herders who relied on pastoralism and consump-tion of livestock, and agriculturalists who relied on domesticated crops with variable livestock dependence (mainly sheep and goats, also some cattle). The emergence of nomadic pastoralism was probably associated with the domestication of the horse, although further research is required on whether this lifestyle was initially developed by nomadic hunter-gatherers or introduced by eastern Fertile Crescent agriculturalists. Further research on ancient DNA in Neolithic, Chalcolithic, and Bronze Age skeletons is also required in order to provide a more holistic outlook on the complex interplay between the biological and cultural history of Central Asia.

SEE ALSO: 17 Anatolia and the Balkans: archaeology; 19 Europe and western Asia: Indo-European linguistic history; 20 Europe: Neolithic colonization; 23 Northern and northeastern Asia: archaeology; 24 Northeastern and Central Asia: "Altaic" linguistic history

References

Anthony, D. W. (2004) The farming frontier on the southern Steppes. In P. I. Bogucki & P. J. Crabtree (eds.), *Encyclopedia of the Barbarian World*, vol. 1: *Ancient Europe, 800 BC to AD 1000*. New York: Scribners, pp. 242–247.

Anthony, D. W. (2007) *The Horse, the Wheel, and Language*. Princeton: Princeton University Press.

Benecke, N. & von Een Driesch, A. (2003) Horse exploitation in the Kazakh Steppes during the Eneolithic and Bronze Age. In Levine et al. (2003), pp. 69–82.

Brunet, F. (1998) La néolithisation en Asie centrale: un état de la question [Neolithization in Central Asia: current state of scholarship]. *Paléorient* 24, 27–48.

Cavalli-Sforza, L. L., Menozzi, P., & Piazza, A. (1994) *The History and Geography of Human Genes*. Princeton: Princeton University Press.

Chaix, R., Austerlitz, F., Hegay, T., et al. (2008) Genetic traces of east-to-west human expansion waves in Eurasia. *American Journal of Physical Anthropology* 136, 309–317.

Chaix, R., Quintana-Murci, L., Hegay, T., et al. (2007) From social to genetic structures in central Asia. *Current Biology* 17, 43–48.

Comas, D., Calafell, F., Mateu, E., et al. (1998) Trading genes along the silk road: mtDNA sequences and the origin of central Asian populations. *American Journal of Human Genetics* 63, 1824–1838.

Comas, D., Plaza, S., Wells, R.S., et al. (2004) Admixture, migrations, and dispersals in Central Asia: evidence from maternal DNA lineages. *European Journal of Human Genetics* 12, 495–504.

Derenko, M., Malyarchuk, B., Denisova, G., et al. (2007) Y-chromosome haplogroup N dispersals from south Siberia to Europe. *Journal of Human Genetics* 52, 763–770.

Fuller, D. Q. (2006) Agricultural origins and frontiers in South Asia: a working synthesis. *Journal of World Prehistory* 20, 1–86.

Gimbutas, M. (1977) The first wave of Eurasian steppe pastoralists into Copper Age Europe. *Journal of Indo-European Studies* 5, 277–338.

Hammer, M. F., Karafet, T. M., Redd, A. J., et al. (2001) Hierarchical patterns of global human Y-chromosome diversity. *Molecular Biology and Evolution* 18, 1189–1203.

Harris, D. R. (1998) The origins of agriculture in Southwest Asia. *Review of Archaeology* 19, 5–12.

Harris, D. R. (2010) *Origins of Agriculture in Western Central Asia. An Environmental-Archaeological Study*. Philadelphia: University of Pennsylvania Press.

Harris, D. R. & Gosden, C. (1996) The beginnings of agriculture in Western Central Asia. In D. R. Harris (ed.), *The Origins and Spread of Agriculture and Pastoralism in Eurasia*. London: UCL Press, pp. 370–389.

Jansen, T., Forster, P., Levine, M., et al. (2002) Mitochondrial DNA and the origins of the domestic horse. *Proceedings of the National Academy of Sciences* 99, 10905–10910.

Khazanov, A. M. (1984) *Nomads and the Outside World*. Cambridge: Cambridge University Press.

Lalueza-Fox, C., Sampietro, M. L., Gilbert, M. T. P., et al. (2004) Unravelling migrations in the steppe: mitochondrial DNA sequences from ancient central Asians. *Proceedings of the Royal Society, B* 271, 941–947.

Lamberg-Karlovsky, C. C. (2002) Archaeology and language: the Indo-Iranians. *Current Anthropology* 43, 63–88.

Levine, M. A., Renfrew, A. C., & Boyle, K. (eds.) (2003), *Prehistoric Steppe Adaptation and the Horse*. Cambridge: McDonald Institute for Archaeological Research.

Li, H., Cho, K., Kidd, J. R. et al. (2009) Genetic landscape of Eurasia and "admixture" in Uyghurs. *American Journal of Human Genetics* 85, 934–937.

Lillie, M. C. (1998) The Mesolithic-Neolithic transition in Ukraine: new radiocarbon determinations for the cemeteries of the Dnieper Rapids Region. *Antiquity* 72, 184–188.

Martinez-Cruz, B., Vitalis R., Austerliz F., et al. (2011) In the heartland of Eurasia: the multilocus genetic landscape in Central Asian human populations. *European Journal of Human Genetics* 19, 216–223.

McGahern, A., Bower, M., Edwards, C., et al. (2006) Evidence for biogeographic patterning of mitochondrial DNA sequences in Eastern horse populations. *Animal Genetics* 37, 494–497.

Nei, M. & Roychoudhury, A. K. (1993) Evolutionary relationships of human populations on a global scale. *Molecular Biology and Evolution* 10, 927–943.

Outram, A. K., Stear, N. A., Bendrey, R., et al. (2009) The earliest horse harnessing and milking. *Science* 323, 1332–1335.

Perez-Lezaun, A., Calafell, F., Comas, D., et al. (1999) Sex-specific migration patterns in central Asian populations, revealed by analysis of Y-chromosome short tandem repeats and mtDNA. *American Journal of Human Genetics* 65, 208–219.

Renfrew, A. C. (2001) Pastoralism and interaction, some introductory questions. In K. Boyle, A. C. Renfrew, & M. Levine (eds.), *Ancient Interactions: East and West in Eurasia*. Cambridge: McDonald Institute for Archaeological Research, pp. 1–12.

Rootsi, S., Zhivotovsky, L. A., Baldovic, M., et al. (2007) A counter-clockwise northern route of the Y-chromosome haplogroup N from Southeast Asia towards Europe. *European Journal of Human Genetics* 15, 204–211.

Sherratt, A. (2003) The horse and the wheel: the dialectics of change in the circum-Pontic and adjacent areas, 4500–1500 BC. In Levine et al. (2003) pp. 233–252.

Telegin, D. Y. & Potekhina, I. D. (1987) *Neolithic Cemeteries and Populations in the Dnieper Basin*. British Archaeological Reports International Series 383. Oxford: Archeopress.

Telegin, D. Y., Potekhina, I. D., Lillie, M.C., et al. (2002) The chronology of the Mariupol-type cemeteries of Ukraine re-visited. *Antiquity* 76, 356–363.

Wells, R. S., Yuldasheva, N., Ruzibakiev, R., et al. (2001) The Eurasian heartland: a continental perspective on Y-chromosome diversity. *Proceedings of the National Academy of Sciences* 98, 10244–10249.

Zerjal, T., Wells, R. S., Yuldasheva, N., et al. (2002) A genetic landscape reshaped by recent events: Y-chromosomal insights into Central Asia. *American Journal of Human Genetics* 71, 466–482.

23

Northern and northeastern Asia: archaeology

Yaroslav V. Kuzmin

This chapter introduces the archaeological evidence for migrations in prehistoric Siberia and the adjacent regions of northern Asia. As such, it dovetails with chapters 22 and 24. Most movement can be detected from south to north or along latitudes, rather than from north to south.

Three lines of evidence have been employed to reconstruct prehistoric human movements in northeastern Asia during the Holocene: (1) archaeological data (the main source used here); (2) geochemical sourcing of obsidian and nephrite raw materials to determine their routes of transportation; and (3) physical anthropology and ancient DNA. Most of Siberia, except for the islands in the High Arctic and the Taymyr peninsula, was settled by humans in pre-Holocene times (e.g., Dikov 2004). In this chapter we examine the archaeological evidence for migration during the Holocene.

Mesolithic migrations (c.9500–5000 BCE)

In northern Siberia, a major source of archaeological migration was the pre-pottery Sumnagin cultural complex of Yakutia in eastern Siberia. This originated in the Yenisei River basin at c.10500 BCE (Mochanov & Fedoseeva 1985; see Figure 23.1, arrow 1). The wedge-shaped cores and microblades of this complex are noteworthy. The main tool types were made on blades, such as knives, scrapers, chisels, and pointed tools. Heavy cutting tools are also found. The bearers of the Sumnagin technology then spread rapidly from a secondary Aldan River core region to the north, northeast, and northwest (Pitulko 2003; Slobodin 1999; see Figure 23.1, arrow 2). The Chukotka peninsula was occupied by these groups c.8200 BCE, and by 7400 BCE people had reached Zhokhov Island at 76°N. By 5000 BCE, firm occupation of the Taymyr peninsula was established, as evidenced by the Tagenar 6 site at 71°N (Khlobystin 2005).

The Global Prehistory of Human Migration: The Encyclopedia of Global Human Migration Volume 1, First Edition. Edited by Peter Bellwood.

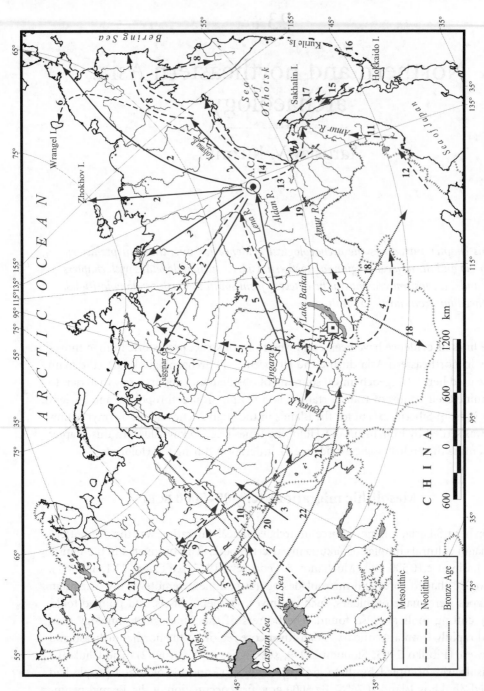

Figure 23.1 Holocene human migrations from the archaeological record in northern and northeastern Asia. The numbers corresponds to those in the text. A.C. – Aldan River core (Sumnagin, Syalakh, Belkachi, and Ymyakhtakh cultures); K. – Kitoi Culture core.

Another important region of early migration was northern Kazakhstan and the Caspian Sea coastline, from where people moved north toward the central Urals, Trans-Urals and southern West Siberia (Koltsov 1989: 140, 147; see Figure 23.1, arrow 3). This movement continued into the Neolithic, after c.6000 BCE (Oshibkina 1996: 261; see Figure 23.1, arrow 10).

Neolithic migrations (c.7000/6000–2500 BCE)

In southern Siberia, the region around Lake Baikal was the source of populations belonging to the Kitoi cultural complex (c.7000–5100 BCE; Weber et al. 2006), which after 5600 BCE moved north into Yakutia and further onwards to the Chukotka peninsula, east to Transbaikal, and west to the Yenisei River (Oshibkina 1996: 291; McKenzie 2009; see Figure 23.1, arrow 4). The same direction of migration continued into the Late Neolithic Ymyakhtakh culture and the Bronze Age Ust-Mil culture, the latter dating after c.2500 BCE (Mochanov & Fedoseeva 1985). Based on data from archaeology and physical anthropology, a movement of the Serovo complex from the Lake Baikal region towards Yakutia and Chukotka in the Late Neolithic/Bronze Age, at c.3000–2000 BCE, resulted in the genesis of the proto-Yukaghir people (chapter 21), believed to be associated with the Ymyakhtakh culture (Kiryak 2010: 96–118). Migrations from the Angara River basin to the north and northeast also occurred at c.3800–2600 BCE (Oshibkina 1996: 300; see Figure 23.1, arrow 5).

In northern Siberia, continuing cultural impulses from Aldan River core region, represented by the Syualakh (c.5200–4000 BCE) and Belkachi (c.4000–2700 BCE) complexes, brought more people northeastwards toward Chukotka (Mochanov & Fedoseeva 1985; Pitulko 2003). The same direction of migration continued into later times, when bearers of the Ymyakhtakh complex mentioned above spread widely in northeast Siberia and the Taymyr peninsula, and at c.1600 BCE reached Wrangel Island (Pitulko 2003; Alekseyev & Dyakonov 2009; Khlobystin 2005; see Figure 23.1, arrow 6). The Taymyr peninsula experienced other migrations at c.2600 BCE from the south (see Figure 23.1, arrow 7).

In northeastern Siberia, people from the upper reaches of the Kolyma River moved into the Kamchatka peninsula between c.6500 and c.2600 BCE (Dikov 2004), and by c.1600 BCE to the Bering Sea coast (Orekhov 1999) (Figure 23.1, arrow 8). The sourcing of nephrite (jade) in central and northern parts of eastern Siberia shows that intensive contact occurred across this region starting in the Early Neolithic, c.7000 BCE, with distances up to 600–1,000 km being traveled from rock source to the site of utilization (Alekseev et al. 2005).

In the Russian Far East, data on obsidian provenances show human contacts between Primorye [Maritime] Province and the Amur River basin, commencing c.12,000 BCE (Kuzmin 2010; see Figure 23.1, arrow 11). Obsidian exchanges between the Neolithic populations of Primorye with the region to the southwest existed since at least c.5000 BC (Figure 23.1, arrow 12). The northern part of the Amur River basin was settled from Yakutia by Belkachi complex bearers at c.3700 BCE (Alekseyev & Dyakonov 2009; see Figure 23.1, arrow 13), and people with pottery moved c.2600–1600 BCE from the

Amur northwards to the Okhotsk Sea coast (Lebedintsev 1999; see Figure 23.1, arrow 14). Intensive contacts occurred between Hokkaido Island and neighboring Sakhalin Island even before the Holocene (Kuzmin 2010; see Figure 23.1, arrow 15, and chapter 27, this volume), and between Hokkaido and the southern Kurile Islands at c.6000 BCE and possibly earlier (Yanshina & Kuzmin 2010; see Figure 23.1, arrow 16). The northern and central regions of Sakhalin were settled by people from the lower Amur after c.3700 BCE (Vasilevsky et al. 2010; see Figure 23.1, arrow 17).

In the Early–Middle Holocene (c.9500–5000 BCE), people were also undertaking secondary migrations to North America from Asia across the Bering Strait (Mochanov & Fedoseeva 1985). Ancient DNA studies have confirmed such long-distance Paleo-eskimo movements from Siberia to Alaska and northern Canada, and eventually by c.3000 BCE to Greenland (Rasmussen et al. 2010; chapter 45, this volume).

In central western Siberia and the Trans-Urals, movements are documented from the west (Cis-Urals) at c.6000 BCE (Oshibkina 1996: 265; Kosarev 1987: 315; see Figure 23.1, arrow 9) and at c.5000 BCE from the south (Kelteminar culture in the Aral-Caspian region) (Oshibkina 1996: 262; see Figure 23.1, arrow 10).

Bronze age migrations (c.2600–1600 BCE)

This time period witnessed intensive movements of people in northern, central, and eastern Asia, especially after the development of horse riding on the central Asian steppes at about 3500 BCE (Outram et al. 2009), together with the use of the wheel and cart (chapter 22). During the Middle–Late Bronze Age, generally corresponding to the 2nd millennium BCE, populations moved out of Transbaikal to the south and east into Mongolia and China (Tsybiktarov 2003; see Figure 23.1, arrows 18). There was also migration from eastern Transbaikal and the Amur River basin to the north, which resulted in the creation of the Ulakhan-Segelennyakh culture of Yakutia (Alekseyev & Dyakonov 2009; see Figure 23.1, arrow 19).

In southern Siberia and adjacent regions of central Asia, two opposite waves of human movement can be detected. From eastern Europe and the southern Urals, the bearers of the Abashevo and Sintashta complexes moved eastwards into western Siberia (e.g. Chernykh 2008; Figure 23.1, arrow 20). At c.2200–1700 BCE the Seima-Turbino complex spread westward from western Siberia, into the Volga River basin and regions to the west (Chernykh 2008; see Figure 23.1, arrow 21). Anthropological data based on cranial measurements reveal a migration of the progenitors of the Late Neolithic Afanasievo culture (c.2900–2400 BCE; Svyatko et al. 2009) from the steppe and forest steppe regions of eastern Europe through Kazakhstan towards the Baikal region of eastern Siberia (Kozintsev 2009; see Figure 23.1, arrow 22). Migration from the Trans-Urals to the north is also documented for the Early and Middle Bronze Age (Kosarev 1987; see Figure 23.1, arrow 23). Some of these movements could have been associated with ancestral Indo-Iranian and Turkic speaking populations discussed in chapter 22, although there can be no certainty of this and a comparison of archaeological and linguistic data in prehistoric central and northeastern Asia has not been undertaken.

SEE ALSO: 21 Northern Europe and Russia: Uralic linguistic migrations; 22 Central Asia: archaeology and genetics; 24 Northeastern and central Asia: "Altaic" linguistic history; 27 Eastern Asia and Japan: human biology; 45 North America: Paleoeskimo and Inuit archaeology

References

Alekseyev, A. N. and Dyakonov, V. M. (2009) Radiocarbon chronology of Neolithic and Bronze Age cultures in Yakutia. *Archaeology, Ethnology & Anthropology of Eurasia* 3(39), 26–40.

Alekseev, A. N., Vetrov, V. M., Dyakonov, V. M., et al. (2005) Vitimsky nefrit v arkheologii vostochnoi Sibiri [The Vitim River nephrite in archaeology of Eastern Siberia]. *Izvestiya Laboratirii Drevnikh Tekhnologyi* 4, 74–79.

Chernykh, E. N. (2008) Formation of the Eurasian "Steppe Belt" of stockbreeding cultures: viewed through the prism of archaeometallurgy and radiocarbon dating. *Archaeology, Ethnology & Anthropology of Eurasia* 3(35), 36–53.

Dikov, N. N. (2004) *Early Cultures of Northeastern Asia*. Anchorage: Beringia Program.

Khlobystin, L. P. (2005) *Taymyr: The Archaeology of Northernmost Eurasia*. Washington, DC: Arctic Studies Center.

Kiryak, M. A. (2010) *The Stone Age of Chukotka, Northeastern Siberia (New Materials)*. British Archaeological Reports, International Series 2099. Oxford: Archaeopress.

Koltsov, L. V. (ed.) (1989) *Mezolit SSSR* [The Mesolithic of the USSR]. Moscow: Nauka.

Kosarev, M. F. (1987). Bronzovy Vek Sibiri i Dalnego Vostoka [Bronze Age of Siberia and the Far East]. In O. N. Bader, D. A. Krainov, & M. F. Kosarev (eds.), *Epokha Bronzy Lesnoi Polosy SSSR* [The Bronze Age in the forest zone of the USSR]. Moscow: Nauka, pp. 248–317.

Kozintsev, A. G. (2009) Craniometric evidence of the early Caucasoid migrations to Siberia and eastern central Asia, with reference to the Indo-European problem. *Archaeology, Ethnology & Anthropology of Eurasia* 4(40), 125–136.

Kuzmin, Y. V. (2010) Crossing mountains, rivers, and straits: a review of the current evidence for prehistoric obsidian exchange in Northeast Asia. In Y. V. Kuzmin & M. D. Glascock (eds.), *Crossing the Straits: Prehistoric Obsidian Source Exploitation in the North Pacific Rim*. British Archaeological Reports, International Series 2152. Oxford: Archaeopress, pp. 137–153.

Lebedintsev, A. I. (1999) *Early Maritime Cultures of Northwestern Priokhot'e*. Anchorage: Beringia Program.

McKenzie, H. G. (2009) Review of early hunter-gatherer pottery in Eastern Siberia. In P. Jordan & M. Zvelebil (eds), *Ceramics before Farming: The Dispersal of Pottery among Prehistoric Eurasian Hunter-Gatherers*. Walnut Creek: Left Coast Press, pp. 167–208.

Mochanov, Y. A. & Fedoseeva, S. A. (1985) Main periods in the ancient history of Northeast Asia. In V. L. Kontrimavichus (ed.), *Beringia in the Cenozoic Era*. Rotterdam: Balkema, pp. 669–693.

Orekhov, A. A. (1999) *An Early Culture of the Northwest Bering Sea*. Anchorage: Beringia Program.

Oshibkina, S. V. (ed.) (1996) *Neolit Severnoi Evrazii* [The Neolithic of Northern Eurasia]. Moscow: Nauka.

Outram, A. K., Stear, N. A., Bendrey, R., et al. (2009) The earliest horse harnessing and milking. *Science* 323, 1332–1335.

Pitulko, V. V. (2003) Golotsenovy Kamenny Vek Severo-Vostochnoi Azii [The Holocene Stone Age in Northeast Asia]. In P. A. Nikolsky & V. V. Pitulko (eds.), *Estestvennaya Istoriya*

Rossiiskoi Vostochnoi Arktiki v Pleistotsene i Golotsene [The natural history of the Russian eastern Arctic in the Pleistocene and Holocene]. Moscow: GEOS , pp. 99–151.

Rasmussen, M., Li, Y., Lindgreen, S., et al. (2010) Ancient human genome sequence of an extinct Palaeo-Eskimo. *Nature* 463, 757–762.

Slobodin, S. (1999) Northeast Asia in the Late Pleistocene and Early Holocene. *World Archaeology* 30, 484–502.

Svyatko, S. V., Mallory, J. P., Murphy, E. M., et al. (2009) New radiocarbon dates and a review of the chronology of prehistoric populations from the Minusinsk Basin, Southern Siberia, Russia. *Radiocarbon* 51, 243–273.

Tsybiktarov, A. D. (2003) Central Asia in the Bronze and Early Iron Ages (problems of ethnocultural history of Mongolia and southern Transbaikal in the middle of the 2nd – first part of the 1st millennia BC). *Archaeology, Ethnology & Anthropology of Eurasia* 1(13), 80–97.

Vasilevsky, A. A., Grischenko, V. A., & Orlova, L. A. (2010) Periods, boundaries, and contact zones in the Far Eastern insular world of the Neolithic. *Archaeology, Ethnology & Anthropology of Eurasia* 1(41), 10–25.

Weber, A. W., Beukens, R. P., Bazaliiski, V. I., et al. (2006) Radiocarbon dates from Neolithic and Bronze Age hunter-gatherer cemeteries in the Cis-Baikal region of Siberia. *Radiocarbon* 48, 127–166.

Yanshina, O. V. and Kuzmin, Y. V. (2010) The earliest evidence of human settlement in the Kurile Islands (Russian Far East): The Yankito Site Cluster, Iturup Island. *Journal of Island & Coastal Archaeology* 5, 179–184.

24

Northeastern and Central Asia: "Altaic" linguistic history

Alexander Vovin

The "Altaic" languages form a major grouping in central and northeastern Asia that includes Turkish, Mongolian, Japanese, Tungusic, and Korean. Their histories of expansion appear mainly to have occurred within the past 2,500 years, but their cultural roots undoubtedly go far deeper in time.

The "Altaic" language family

The debate over whether the so-called "Altaic" languages (Turkic, Mongolic, Tungusic, Korean, and Japonic) represent a valid genetic family, or a contact-based *Sprachbund*, has a long history. The recent major attempt to prove genetic relationship (Starostin et al. 2003) has been critically rejected by specialists in the various member groups of Altaic (Georg 2004a; Stachowski 2005; Vovin 2005a). It seems that the majority nowadays support the *Sprachbund* point of view, with a major exception being the relationship between Japonic and Korean. In the case of these two groups, a debate is still going on between champions of genetic relationship (Unger 2009) and supporters of an area-contact relationship (Vovin 2010). Opinions also differ as to whether "Altaic" should comprise *only* Turkic, Mongolic and Tungusic (micro-Altaic), or these three language groups *plus* Korean and Japonic (macro-Altaic). This chapter adopts a *Sprachbund* framework, but still extends coverage to the macro-Altaic paradigm since both Korean and Japonic share more structural commonalities than differences with the other micro-Altaic languages.

Turkic languages and migrations

The Turkic language family comprises over twenty modern languages and about ten historically attested languages. The homeland of the Turkic language family was perhaps in present-day Mongolia. The detailed classification of the modern Turkic

The Global Prehistory of Human Migration: The Encyclopedia of Global Human Migration Volume 1, First Edition. Edited by Peter Bellwood.
© 2013 John Wiley & Sons, Ltd. Published 2015 by John Wiley & Sons, Ltd.

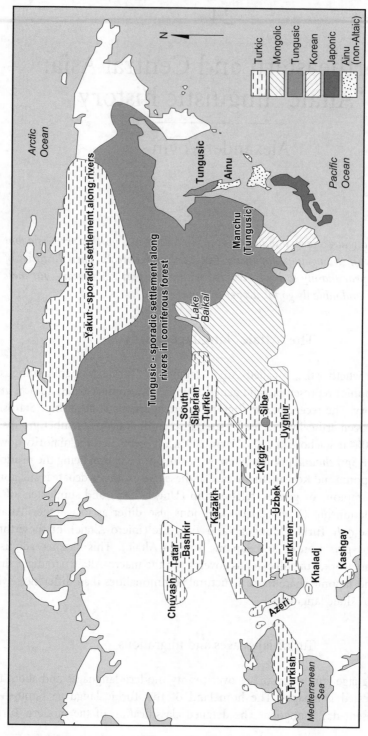

Figure 24.1 Map to show the likely generalized distributions of the Altaic languages prior to the recent expansions of Russian and Chinese. The boundaries are approximate and do not accurately reflect current distributions, especially for the Tungusic, Mongolic, and Turkic languages, many of which are spoken only in small enclaves today. Modified after Ruhlen (1987). Map production by Education and Multimedia Services, College of Asia and the Pacific, The Australian National University.

languages is difficult and somewhat controversial; the most up-to-date attempt is by Schönig (1999). There is a clear binary division between Western Turkic and Eastern Turkic. The former includes only Chuvash among modern languages, and three historically attested languages: Volga Bulgarian, attested only in fragmentary tomb inscriptions, Khazar, and Danube Bulgarian, the last two attested only by personal names, place names and a few glosses. Western Turkic Bulgarian should not be confused with Modern Bulgarian, which is a Slavic Indo-European language. Eastern Turkic includes all remaining modern and ancient Turkic languages.

The speakers of Western Turkic migrated to South Siberia around the beginning of the Christian era, or even slightly earlier, and from there to the Volga region in the 4th century CE (Schönig 1999: 81). The next linguistic split was most likely the separation of Khaladj (an endangered Turkic language in Iran) and Yakut from the main body of Eastern Turkic. This separation likely also occurred in the 4th century CE, with Yakut initially moving to the Baikal region, followed by a late migration into the central Lena River basin which might have occurred as recently as the 16th century. The exact dating of the Khaladj migration is difficult, but since this language has a number of archaic features, such as preservation of initial proto-Turkic *h-, not even found in Old Turkic of the 8th century CE (cf. Khaladj *hadaq* vs. Old Turkic *adaq* "foot"), it should have predated the 6th century CE.

The Oghuz languages probably were next in line, starting to move westward after the collapse of the second Turkic khanate in the 8th century (Schönig 1999: 83), with a subsequent movement of Oghuz Seljuk tribes into Iran in the late 10th or early 11th century, and later into Anatolia. Nothing is known about the initial stage of migration of the Qypchaq Turkic-speaking tribes, but they are found in the Volga region no later than the 11th century. Other Eastern Turkic groups, such as the Sayan Turkic speakers, probably moved to their respective locations comparatively late. The detailed reconstruction of Turkic migrations is further complicated by the fact that various Turkic groups were influencing each other and it is sometimes difficult, if not outright impossible, to disentangle genetic linguistic inheritance from areal influence.

Mongolic languages and migrations

The Mongolic language family comprises 13 modern languages and two historically attested languages. Their dispersal occurred relatively recently, closely connected with Mongol unification in the late 12th to early 13th centuries by Cinngis-khan (Genghis Khan), and the subsequent Mongol conquests in the 13th century (Janhunen 2003a). Thus, for all practical purposes, modern Mongolic languages are probably descendants of the language spoken by members of Cinggis-khan's tribe. Consequently, the homeland of the modern Mongolic languages was the tribal territory of Cinngis-khan in eastern Mongolia, between the Onon and Kerülen rivers. A major exception is the more recent migration of two Oirat tribes, the Torghut and Dörbet, in 1616 CE from Jungaria to the lower Volga region. Some members of these two groups returned to Jungaria in 1771, but those who remained are now the speakers of what is known as the Kalmuck language (Bläsing 2003: 229).

Besides the Mongolic languages proper, there are also para-Mongolic languages that are attested only historically, and less than perfectly. They probably constituted collateral sister branches with the extant Mongolic languages, but we do not and probably will never know how many para-Mongolic languages existed before the Cinggisid unification. Only three para-Mongolic languages are known to us: Xianbei and Tabɣač, both known only from glosses in Chinese sources (for the most recent research see Vovin 2007a); and Kitan, known from imperfectly understood inscriptions of the Liao and Jin empires in North China (Janhunen 2003b; Kane 2009; Wu & Janhunen 2009), as well as from Chinese glosses (Vovin 2003; Shimunek 2007). The phonetic and lexical differences between Kitan and the Mongolic languages are quite significant, as shown by the comparisons of Kitan *ai* versus Middle Mongolian (MM) *ečeg* "father", and Kitan *ńiqo* versus MM *noqai* "dog". Thus, para-Mongolic and Mongolic languages are probably quite distantly related. The homeland of the para-Mongolic languages was likely in southern Manchuria; consequently, the Mongolic languages might have originated ultimately in the same area, or in the Khingan mountain range of western Manchuria, whence they moved westwards to Mongolia, gradually replacing the Turkic languages that were spoken there beforehand.

Tungusic languages and migrations

The Tungusic language family comprises 12 modern languages (most of them moribund or severely endangered), and two historically attested languages, Jurchen and Manchu, that most likely represent two dialects of the same language. The classification of the Tungusic family has a long history of debate and is still controversial. This article follows the recent proposal by Georg (2004b), suggesting a binary split between Northern Tungusic (Ewenki, Ewen, Solon, Neghidal, Kur-Urmi, Oroch, and Udihe) and Southern Tungusic (Nanai, Ulcha, Uilta, Sibe, and modern Manchu). The location of the homeland of the Tungusic language family is also subject to debate: both Menges (1968) and Khelimskii (1985) place it in the Baikal region. Khelimskii's point of view is based on some basic vocabulary parallels between proto-Samoyedic and proto-Tungusic (Khelimskii 1985: 207). However, closer scrutiny reveals that Khelimskii's reconstructions and/or comparisons are either problematic on the Tungusic side, or are limited to Northern Tungusic only, or include unaccounted segments, or have semantic problems.

Much more convincing is the proposal by Janhunen (1996: 169), who places the homeland in the Middle Amur region of Manchuria. This is because both branches of the Tungusic languages are represented there and because all varieties of Northern Tungusic, except Ewen, are still spoken today, whereas in the Baikal region only one northern language – Ewenki – is attested. Janhunen (1996: 171) is probably right to suggest that the northward migration of the Northern Tungusic languages occurred relatively recently, but this only concerns the dispersal of Northern Tungusic speakers over the vast expanses of western, central, and eastern Siberia. The separation of Northern from Southern Tungusic must have happened earlier, as witnessed by proto-Eskimo loanwords found exclusively in Northern but not Southern Tungusic, e.g.

proto-Eskimo *kumaγ became proto-Northern Tungusic *kumgə "louse". The migration of Uilta speakers to Sakhalin must have occurred several hundred years ago, as Uilta loans from Nivx indicate very old Nivx forms prior to the Nivx contractions, e.g. Uilta unigəri was derived from Nivx uńγr "star". The migration of Ewenki speakers to Sakhalin probably was the most recent Tungusic migration, with the exception of a settlement of Manchu speakers in Xinjiang in the 18th century.

Korean languages and migrations

The Korean language family consists of Korean proper and the Ceycwuto Island language, which is frequently mislabeled as a "dialect." The major split within Korean proper is between the main bulk of modern Korean dialects and the Yukcin dialect in the extreme north of Hamkyeng province. The latter should be treated as a distinct language, although it separated from the main bulk of Korean only in the 14th century CE, when part of the population of Kyensang province in the southeastern Korean peninsula was resettled in the newly conquered northeast. There are also two historically attested languages, Old Korean (with only fragmentary attestation) and Middle Korean. The latter can be roughly defined as an ancestor of modern Standard Korean. It is traditionally believed that the homeland of the Korean language family was in the Silla kingdom that was located originally in the southeastern corner of the peninsula (Yi 1987: 27). However, this has been challenged recently on historical and cultural grounds by Unger (2005), and on linguistic grounds by Vovin (2007b). It appears that the migration of Korean speakers to their present location was quite straightforward, from southern Manchuria in the north to the Korean peninsula in the south. The linguistic process of Koreanization took several centuries, and it appears that proto-Korean or pre-Old Korean gradually replaced Japonic languages between the 3rd and 8th centuries CE. The central and southern parts of the Korean peninsula were originally Japonic-speaking. There is, however, solid evidence from different sources that the northern Korean peninsula was predominantly Korean-speaking at least two or three centuries before the 3rd century CE (Vovin 2005b, 2006, 2007c).

Japonic languages and migrations

"Japonic" is a cover term suggested by Leon Serafim to cover both the Japanese and Ryukyuan branches of this language family (Serafim 1999). There are two Japanese and four to five modern Ryukyuan languages, as well as three historically attested Japanese and one Ryukyuan language. In addition, there is fragmentary evidence that Japonic languages were once spoken on the Korean peninsula, attested only as glosses in medieval Korean and Chinese texts. There is almost universal consensus that Japonic languages entered the Japanese islands via the Korean peninsula during the Yayoi period (3rd century BCE to 3rd century CE – see chapter 28), with an initial landfall in northern Kyushu, spreading from here to the rest of the archipelago. Beyond this, the ultimate homeland of the Japonic language family is shrouded in mystery. Proponents of the genetic relationship of the Altaic languages like to see it located in Manchuria, but no evidence supports this. An alternative would be on the eastern seaboard of China, but this is still being researched. The migration of Ryukyuan speakers into the Ryukyuan islands between Kyushu and Taiwan did not start until the 9th century CE, but the linguistic split between Japanese and Ryukyuan clearly preceded this date. There are several hypotheses concerning the homeland of Ryukyuan. Serafim (2003) suggests northeastern Kyushu and the adjacent part of Honshu across the Shimonoseki strait. This seems to be the most viable hypothesis, as it is based on solid linguistic evidence.

SEE ALSO: 22 Central Asia: genetics and archaeology; 23 Northern and northeastern Asia: archaeology; 27 Eastern Asia and Japan: human biology; 28 Japan: archaeology

References

Bläsing, U. (2003) Kalmuck. In Janhunen (2003c), pp. 229–247.

Georg, S. (2004a) Review of Starostin et al. (2003). *Diachronica* XXI(2), 445–450.

Georg, S. (2004b) Unreclassifying Tungusic. In C. Naeher (ed.), *Proceedings of the First International Conference on Manchu-Tungus Studies,* vol. 2: *Trends in Tungusic and Siberian Linguistics.* Wiesbaden: Harrassowitz, pp. 45–57.

Janhunen, J. (1996) *Manchuria: An Ethnic History.* Helsinki: Finno-Ugrian Society.

Janhunen, J. (2003a) Para-Mongolic. In Janhunen (2003c), pp. 391–402.

Janhunen, J. (2003b) Proto-Mongolic. In Janhunen (2003c), pp. 1–29.

Janhunen, J. (ed.) (2003c) *The Mongolic Languages.* London: Routledge.

Kane, D. (2009) *The Kitan Language and Script.* Leiden: Brill.

Khelimskii, E. (1985) Samodiisko-tungusskie leksicheskie sviazi i ikh etno-istoricheskie implikatsii [Samoyedic-Tungusic lexical connections and their ethno-historical implications]. In E. I. Ubriatova (ed.), *Uralo-Altaistika.* Novosibirsk: Nauka, pp. 206–213.

Menges, K. (1968) *Tungusen und Ljao* [Tunguses and Liao]. Wiesbaden: Harrassowitz.

Ruhlen, M. (1987) *A Guide to the World's Languages,* vol. 1. Stanford: Stanford University Press.

Schönig, C. (1999) The internal division of Modern Turkic and its historical implications. *Acta Orientalia Academiae Scientarum Hungaricae* 52(1), 63–95.

Serafim, L. (1999) Reflexes of Proto-Korea-Japonic Mid Vowels in Japonic and Korean. Paper presented at the Workshop on Korean-Japanese Comparative Linguistics, XIVth International Conference on Historical Linguistics, Vancouver, BC.

Serafim, L. (2003) When and from where did the Japonic language enter the Ryukyus? – a critical comparison of language, archeology, and history. In A. Vovin and T. Osada (eds.), *Nihongo keitōron no genzai* [Perspectives on the origins of the Japanese language]. Kyoto: International Research Center for Japanese Studies, pp. 463–476.

Shimunek, A. (2007) Towards a reconstruction of the Kitan Language, with notes on Northern Late Middle Chinese phonology. Unpublished MA thesis, Indiana University.

Stachowski, M. (2005) Turkologische Anmerkungen zum altaischen etymologischen Wörterbuch, (Turcological notes on the Altaic Etymological Dictionary). *Studia Etymologica Cracoviensia* 10, 227–246.

Starostin, S., Dybo, A., & Mudrak. O. (2003) *The Etymological Dictionary of the Altaic Languages,* vols. 1–3. Leiden: Brill.

Unger, J. (2005) When was Korean first spoken in Southeastern Korea? *Journal of Inner and East Asian Studies* 2(2), 87–105.

Unger, J. (2009) *The Role of Contact in the Origins of the Japanese and Korean Languages*. Honolulu: University of Hawaii Press.

Vovin, A. (2003) Once again on Khitan words in Khitan-Chinese mixed verses. *Acta Orientalia Academiae Scientiarum Hungaricae* 56(2–4), 237–244.

Vovin, A. (2005a) The end of the Altaic controversy. *Central Asiatic Journal* 49(1), 71–132.

Vovin, A. (2005b) Are Koguryo and Paekche different languages or dialects of Old Korean? *Journal of Inner and East Asian Studies* 2(2), 107–142.

Vovin, A. (2006) Why Manchu and Jurchen are looking so non-Tungusic? In J. Janhunen, A. Pozzi, & M. Weiers (eds.), *Tumen jalafun jecen akū* [Life for ten thousand years without limit]: *Festschrift for Giovanni Stary's 60th birthday*. Wiesbaden: Harrassowitz, pp. 255–266.

Vovin, A. (2007a) Once again on the Tabɣač language. *Mongolian Studies* XXIX, 191–206.

Vovin, A. (2007b) Cin-Han and Silla words in Chinese transcription. In S-O. Lee, C-Y. Park, & J. H. Yoon (eds.), *Linguistic Promenades: Essays to Honor Professor Chin-woo Kim on the Occasion of his Retirement*. Seoul: Hallim, pp. 603–628.

Vovin, A. (2007c) Korean loanwords in Jurchen and Manchu. *Althai hakpo* 17, 73–84.

Vovin, A. (2010) *Koreo-Japonica: A Re-evaluation of a Common Genetic Origin*. Honolulu: University of Hawaii Press.

Wu, Y. and Janhunen, J. (2009) *New Materials on the Khitan Small Script: A Critical Edition of Xiao Dilu and Yelü Xiangwen*. Folkestone, UK: Global Oriental.

Yi, K. (1987) *Kwuke sa kaysel* [An outline of the history of the Korean language], 2nd revised edn. Seoul: Thap chwulphansa. (Originally pub. 1964.)

25

Eastern Asia: Sino-Tibetan linguistic history

Randy J. LaPolla

The Sino-Tibetan language family enshrines the migratory histories of many East Asian populations, including the Chinese, Tibetans, and Burmese. Its history is intimately associated with Neolithic and Bronze Age developments in China itself, and today it is one of the major world language families in terms of population numbers.

The Sino-Tibetan (ST) languages are spoken throughout China and Myanmar/Burma and in parts of India, Thailand, Laos, and Vietnam (see Figures 25.1 and 33.1). The family includes as its two main branches the Sinitic languages (the Chinese "dialects") and the Tibeto-Burman (TB) languages. This major division is due to different paths of migration, and different types of language contact due to these and other population movements have created great diversity among the daughter languages of the family (see LaPolla 2001 for a more complete discussion).

The archeological and linguistic evidence suggests that the ancestors of the Sino-Tibetan speaking people lived in the central plains of the valley of the Huanghe (Yellow River). By at least 4500 BCE, some members of the original group began moving west, then to the south down through the Tibetan plateau or into the valleys to its east. The group that stayed in the central plains, as well as those who moved south and east in early historical times, eventually became the Sinitic speakers of today, while the group that moved southwest became the Tibeto-Burman speakers.

The movements in both directions were not single ones but consisted of larger or smaller waves, often into the same areas as earlier migrations. Government-encouraged migration was practiced in China as early as the 2nd millennium BCE, and has been practiced by all Chinese governments since then. There have also been massive migrations due to natural disasters, war, and the pull of new economic opportunities. The movement of the Sinitic speakers has almost never been to an area where there were

The Global Prehistory of Human Migration: The Encyclopedia of Global Human Migration Volume 1,
First Edition. Edited by Peter Bellwood.

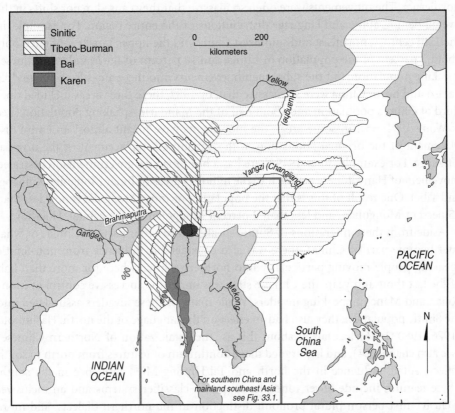

Figure 25.1 The distribution of the major components of the Sino-Tibetan language family, after Ruhlen (1987). For closer details of the situation in southern China and mainland Southeast Asia see Figure 33.1. Map production by Education and Multimedia Services, College of Asia and the Pacific, The Australian National University.

no people; migration almost always involved language contact, either with non-Sinitic languages or other Sinitic varieties, and very often in government-sponsored migrations there was purposeful mixing of peoples. As the Sinitic speakers moved into new areas they often absorbed the peoples already there or, in some cases, were absorbed themselves. From the linguistic evidence, it seems the earliest inhabitants of the southeastern coast of China spoke ancestral Austronesian-related languages, while those in the Yangzi basin and the inland south were speakers of ancestral Hmong-Mien and Tai-related languages. We find influences from these languages in the Sinitic varieties spoken in those areas.

Many of the movements were chain- or domino-like. For example, the migration of over two million non-Sinitic-speaking people from the northern steppes into the central plains in the 2nd and 3rd centuries CE caused at least three million Sinitic speakers to flee south. This not only affected the population of the north, but also of the south, as one out of every six people in the south after the migration was a displaced northerner. The movements were often so massive that they caused major shifts in the overall demographic and language distributions of the entire region. For example, in the 17th century, northeast and southwest China and the upper Yangzi contained only about 5 percent of the population of China, and 10 percent of the Mandarin Chinese-speaking population, but the subsequent movements into these areas from the middle Yangzi and north China were so massive that, by 1982, these three areas included one-third of China's population and about half of the Mandarin-speaking population (Lee & Wong 1991: 55). In some areas, the movements have meant almost an entire displacement of the original population, with concomitant replacement of the original language. For example, since 1949 there has a been massive government-orchestrated movement of Han Chinese people into the minority areas of Inner Mongolia, Xinjiang, and Tibet. One result of this is that the population of Inner Mongolia is now less than 15 percent Mongolian, and less than 2 percent Mongolian in the capital, Huerhot.

Aside from these migrations of Sinitic speakers into other parts of China (or what later became part of China), there was also considerable influence from non-Sinitic speaking people moving particularly into northern China, where for more than half of the last thousand years the Chinese state was under the successive control of Mongolian and Manchu-speaking invaders. While many of these invaders assimilated into the Sinitic population, they also had an effect on the language of the north. Hashimoto (1976, 1980, 1986) has talked about this as "the Altaicization of Northern Chinese" (see also chapter 24), and has argued that a continuum of features from north to south reflects Altaic influence in the north and Tai/Hmong-Mien influence in the south. These features include fewer tones, less complex classifier systems and an inclusive/exclusive first person plural pronoun distinction in the northern dialects, and more tones, more complex classifier systems and other features similar to the Tai and Hmong-Mien languages in the southern dialects. (Tai is the more general term for the large language family that includes Thai, the national language of Thailand.)

Turning to Tibeto-Burman (TB), some of the major migrations took place westwards from China into Tibet and then southwards into Nepal, Bhutan, and northern India. Others moved southwest down the river valleys along the eastern edge of the Tibetan plateau, passing through what has been called the "ethnic corridor" (Fei 1980) into Burma. There were also later minor movements into northern Thailand, Laos, and Vietnam. The two major TB migration paths described above have been responsible for the major split between the Bodish languages (Tibetan and its close relatives) and the rest of Tibeto-Burman. From the closeness of the Tibetan dialects, despite their present wide geographic spread, and from the fact that all dialects show some of the same borrowed features (such as non-TB words for "horse" and "seven"), there must have been contact with northern non-Tibeto-Burman languages before the spread of Tibetan. This spread was relatively rapid throughout Tibet, an area where there were few earlier inhabitants. TB migration into Nepal, Sikkim, and Bhutan was originally almost entirely from Tibet, and many of the TB languages there show a close relation to Tibetan.

Since the failed 1959 uprising against Chinese rule in Tibet a large number of Central Tibetan speakers have moved to Nepal and India. In Nepal, the TB languages are in contact with many non-TB languages, including the national language, Nepali, an Indo-Aryan language which has had a major impact on many of the TB languages. In Bhutan, where there were in the past only Southern Tibetan or Monpa speakers, there is now a large number of Nepali speakers. Many of the TB languages found in northeastern India and Bangladesh came from Burma to the east, but some came down from Tibet. They have been greatly affected by the cultures with which they have come into contact. For example, in Kashmir, Balti and Ladakhi are Western Tibetan dialects, but Balti is spoken in the (Pakistan-controlled) Baltistan area and the speakers of Balti are now Muslims and write their language with the Arabic script. Ladakhi is spoken in the Indian-controlled area of Kashmir, but the speakers are still more culturally Tibetan than Indian. In Manipur, there have been Meithei speakers for at least a thousand years, having moved there from Burma. Meithei is written with a Bengali-based Indic orthography and is heavily influenced by Indo-Aryan contact (Chelliah 1997). Aside from being spoken by about one million people, Meithei has become a lingua franca for many other ethnic groups in Manipur, and this has affected the linguistic form that it takes in each area where it is spoken, a situation we see also in the cases of Mandarin Chinese and Burmese.

The migration of TB speakers southwards into Burma must have started by the 1st century CE. Chinese records dating to the 4th century already talk of a civilized kingdom, known as Pyu, which controlled central and Upper Burma. The Pyu were TB speakers who had come down into Burma along the Irrawaddy valley. They adopted Theravadan Buddhism and a writing system during the 7th century from the Mon (Mon-Khmer speakers), who controlled Lower Burma and the Menam Chao Phraya valley, now part of Thailand. The Chin (Zo), another TB group, also came down into Burma sometime before the 9th century and established a kingdom in the Chindwin valley. In the 8th and 9th centuries, a kingdom called Nanzhao (previously spelt Nan-Chao), located in what is now western Yunnan Province in southwest China, came to dominate Upper and most of Lower Burma. Nanzhao was ruled by Yi (Lolo; TB) speakers, but the population also included Bai (TB), other TB and Tai speakers. Sometime before the 8th century, the migration of the Karen, another TB group, down into Burma weakened the Pyu kingdom, and in 832 Nanzhao destroyed it. People related to the Burmese of today then moved down into Burma, beginning in the middle of the 9th century, from an area of Yunnan that was under the control of the Nanzhao kingdom. They settled from the Northern Shan states to the Kyanksè area south of Mandalay, and about 1000 CE conquered the Mon to the south. As a result, the first Burmese kingdom, the Pagan kingdom, was founded in 1044. However, Mon culture was retained as the official Burmese court culture, and the Mon language (or Pali) was used for inscriptions. The Mon script also became the basis of the Burmese writing system. Much of southern Burma, such as the Irrawaddy delta and the region of Rangoon, was for most of its history part of a Mon kingdom, and the migration of the Burmese south into Mon territory led to a massive language shift of formerly Mon speakers to Burmese. A strong substratum influence of the Mon language on Burmese is still evident (Bradley 1980).

There are a number of Tibeto-Burman speakers in northern Thailand, such as the Akha, Lahu, Gong, Mpi, and Karen. Aside from the Karen, most have moved down from China within the past few hundred years. Northern Thailand was originally populated by Tai speakers, and the recent TB arrivals are now largely bilingual in Thai and their own languages. Their languages show quite a lot of Thai influence and even language shift.

In terms of large-scale areal contact, two large subgroupings can be distinguished within TB: the "Sino-sphere" and the "Indo-sphere" (Matisoff 1990). Features that we frequently find in languages in the Indo-sphere, but not in the Sino-sphere, include the development of retroflex stop consonants and post-head relative clauses of the Indic type (relative clauses are generally pre-head and without relative pronouns in Sino-Tibetan languages). In Sino-spheric languages we often find the development of tones and a movement toward a monosyllabic and isolating structure. Aside from this, there is also a broad tendency to have an iambic stress pattern in the south, most probably due to Mon-Khmer influence, as opposed to a more common trochaic pattern in the north.

SEE ALSO: 24 Northeastern and central Asia: "Altaic" linguistic history; 26 Eastern Asia: archaeology

References

Bradley, D. (1980) Phonological convergence between languages in contact: Mon-Khmer structural borrowing in Burmese. In B. R. Caron (ed.), *Proceedings of the Sixth Annual Meeting of the Berkeley Linguistics Society*. Berkeley: Berkeley Linguistics Society, pp. 259–267.

Chelliah, S. L. (1997) *A Grammar of Meithei*. Berlin: Mouton de Gruyter.

Fei Xiaotong (1980) Guanyu Woguo de minzu shibie wenti [On the problem of distinguishing nationalities in China]. *Zhongguo Shehui Kexue* 1, 158–174.

Hashimoto, M. J. (1976) Language diffusion on the Asian continent. *Computational Analyses of Asian and African Languages* 3, 49–63.

Hashimoto, M. J. (1980) Typography of phonotactics and suprasegmentals in languages of the East Asian continent. *Computational Analysis of Asian and African Languages* 13, 153–164.

Hashimoto, M. J. (1986) The Altaicization of Northern Chinese. In J. McCoy & T. Light (eds.), *Contributions to Sino-Tibetan Studies*. Leiden: Brill, pp. 76–97.

LaPolla, R. J. (2001) The role of migration and language contact in the development of the Sino-Tibetan language family. In R. M. W. Dixon & A. Y. Aikhenvald (eds.), *Areal Diffusion and Genetic Inheritance: Case Studies in Language Change*. Oxford: Oxford University Press, pp. 225–254.

Lee, J. & Wong, B. (1991) Population movements in Qing China and their linguistic legacy. In W. S-Y. Wang (ed.), *Languages and Dialects of China*. JCL Monograph Series, No. 3. Berkeley: Project on Linguistic Analysis, pp. 52–77.

Matisoff, J. A. (1990) On meglocomparison. *Language* 66, 106–120.

Ruhlen, M. (1987) *A Guide to the World's Languages*, vol. 1. Stanford: Stanford University Press.

26

Eastern Asia: archaeology

Zhang Chi and Hung Hsiao-chun

This chapter examines the prehistory of migration in China from the Late Paleolithic onwards, with a focus on the Neolithic and the spreads of early agricultural societies from the Yangzi River and Yellow River basins, and regions in between. Some of these migrations contributed to the origins of many populations in Southeast Asia, to be considered in the following chapters.

The foundations

Chinese paleoanthropologists and geneticists have followed two competing hypotheses regarding the origin of *Homo sapiens* in China (Gao et al. 2010). Some suggest that modern *Homo sapiens* in China evolved partially from indigenous populations of *Homo erectus,* who eventually hybridized with immigrating populations of *Homo sapiens* from Africa. This can be summarized as the continuity with hybridization model (Wu 1990, 1998). However, mtDNA and Y chromosomes studies on modern populations indicate that the ancestors of all modern populations of *Homo sapiens* in China originated in Africa and entered the region via central Asia and/or southeastern Asia. From this perspective, ancestral modern humans completely replaced the earlier populations of *Homo erectus* in East Asia (Jin & Su 2001; Ke 2001). However, both models are under modification today, and the currently most favored one combines out of Africa movement with limited degrees of hybridization with archaic hominins, such as Neanderthals in the west and Denisovans in Siberia (as explained in chapter 4).

In terms of the archaeological record, two lithic tool assemblages existed in China after 25 kya; a microblade tradition in the north and a pebble tool tradition in the south. The northern microblade tradition developed from an earlier central and northern Asian Late Paleolithic blade industry. The subsistence economy of this tradition was focused on the hunting of large or middle-sized mammals (Wang 2005).

The Global Prehistory of Human Migration: The Encyclopedia of Global Human Migration Volume 1,
First Edition. Edited by Peter Bellwood.
© 2013 John Wiley & Sons, Ltd. Published 2015 by John Wiley & Sons, Ltd.

Similar microblade assemblages occur across the whole northeast Asian region, including the Russian Far East, the Korean peninsula, Japan, and further into Alaska and western Canada. In southern China, the pebble tool assemblages are mostly located in caves, and this tradition is related to contemporary so-called "Hoabinhian" assemblages in Southeast Asia (Zhang 2000). Important excavated open sites in northern China include Shizitan in Shanxi province and Nihewan in Hebei province. Most southern Chinese sites are caves, for instance Xianrendong in Jiangxi, Yuchanyan in Hunan, and Bailiandong in Guangxi.

The continuity with hybridization model as currently formulated proposes that these two distinct Late Paleolithic stone tool assemblages developed from indigenous Chinese Early and Middle Paleolithic cultural traditions. In contrast, the replacement model proposes that the microblade assemblages of northern China originated in the Lake Baikal and Altai regions of central Asia, and that the pebble tool tradition was introduced into southern China from Southeast Asia, in both cases by populations of modern *Homo sapiens*. Although these two models remain in opposition, it is still widely agreed that there were two different cultural assemblages in northern and southern China during the Late Palaeolithic, presumably manufactured by distinct human populations.

Early Holocene hunter-gatherer migrations and the emergence of early farmers

During the Last Glacial Maximum, at about 20 kya, and in the following period of glacial retreat, microblade assemblages spread southwards to the Huai River and northern Jiangsu province, between the Yellow and Yangzi rivers. The site of Dagang in Henan province (lower Yellow River valley) is the southernmost find place of microblades, here dated to about 9000 BCE (Zhang & Li 1996). After this time, the microblade assemblages of northern China began to retreat into Inner Mongolia and northeast China, to be replaced gradually to the south by Neolithic assemblages with increasing quantities of pottery and grindstones, often in association with continuing but diminishing numbers of microblades. A representative site of this cultural phase is located at Donghulin in Beijing City (SAMPU 2006). At the same time, populations in the Yangzi basin to the south began to establish the first village settlements. Shangshan in Zhejiang province (c.7000 BCE) is a representative site of this period that contains timber houses raised above the ground on posts, red-slipped pottery, grindstones, and polished axes and adzes (ZPICRA 2007). Subsistence in the Yangzi basin was reliant on tubers and nuts, such as acorns (*Quercus spp.*), walnuts, and foxnuts. Wild rice (ancestral *Oryza sativa*) was also utilized, possibly involving deliberate cultivation (Zheng & Jiang 2007).

After 7000 BCE, during the middle Holocene in southern China, these terminal hunter-gatherer societies on the verge of agriculture began to develop in several different subsistence directions. One group appears to have moved from somewhere near the Yangzi River into the Huai valley at c.7000–6500 BCE, where they started the process of morphological domestication of rice (Zhang 2011). Jiahu phase 1 in the

Huai valley offers an example (e.g. Zhang et al. 1999; Liu et al. 2007; Cucchi et al. 2011), and similar cultural assemblages occur at Baligang in southern Henan (Zhang 2011). So far, the most advanced rate of morphological domestication of rice in China comes from these sites (Deng 2009), where the rice was actually beyond the early Holocene northern boundary of wild rice distribution (Fan et al. 1999). This discovery supports Yan Wenming's theory of peripheral origins for the beginning of rice domestication (Yan 2002).

Another direction of development was adopted by the contemporary hunter-gatherers further south. The Zengpiyan and Dingsishan cultures of the southern Nanling Mountains region of Guangxi became reliant on aquatic animals such as fish and shellfish, commonly heaping their remains into shell middens. These people produced coarse pottery and lived in large settlements with domesticated dogs, but there is no evidence for agriculture or pig domestication. After 6000 BCE, this population started to spread with pottery manufacture from Guangxi into northern Vietnam (Da But, Late Hoabinhian or Bacsonian). Related populations were very widespread at this time in coastal southeast China, northern coastal Vietnam, and along the southern coast of Hainan Island, surviving until the introduction of agricultural economies in the 3rd millennium BCE.

A different development, also involving hunter-gatherers, occurred along rivers in the northern Nanling Mountains, particularly associated with the Gaomiao culture of the Yuanshui valley (c.5800 BCE). These populations appear to have originated amongst contemporary rice-farming populations in the Yangzi basin (see below), dispersing as hunter-gatherers down tributary rivers southwards and westwards into eastern Guangxi and the Zhujiang (Pearl River) delta in Guangdong, where the derived cultural tradition is referred to as Xiantouling, c.5000 BCE. The Gaomiao population seems also to have founded the Keqiutou culture in coastal Fujian, and the early Dabenkeng culture in coastal Taiwan. Other groups moved westwards from the northern Nanling Mountains, along tributaries of the Yangzi River, finally reaching northeastern Guizhou and the Xiajiang region of eastern Sichuan between 5000 and 3000 BCE (Zhang & Hung 2012).

Early migrations of Chinese Neolithic farmers

As mentioned, current evidence suggests that the earliest farming cultures in China developed in the region between the Yellow and Huai Rivers, c.7000-6000 BCE (Zhang 2011; Zhang & Hung in press). Increasing reliance on domesticated forms of rice and millets led to rapid population increase and dispersal, especially in the period from 6000 to 4500 BCE. In the middle and lower Yellow River region of northern China, the Laoguantai culture in Shanxi, the Peiligang culture in Henan, and the Houli culture in Shandong all developed in the ecological zone where rice (*Oryza sativa*), common millet (*Panicum miliaceum*), and foxtail millet (*Setaria italica*) could all coexist. Further north, the Cishan culture in Hebei and the Xinglongwa culture in western Liaoning and eastern Inner Mongolia were both dependent on millet agriculture, rice being unsuited to the cool and dry temperate climate in this region. In the middle and lower Yangzi Valley, the Chengbeixi, early Zaoshi cultures in Hubei and Hunan, and the Kuahuqiao culture in Zhejiang province, were all involved in increasing dependence

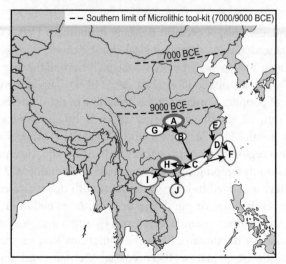

Figure 26.1 Suggested pre-farming cultural and population movements in southern China, 8000–3000 BCE. From the Yangzi basin, it is proposed that (B) Gaomiao, (C) Xiantouling (Lingnan facies of the Daxi culture) and (G) the Xiajiang facies of the Daxi and Yuxiping cultures all developed in connection with (A) the Pengtoushan-Zaoshi complex of the middle Yangzi. Independently to the south, the Da But (I) and Hainan shell middens (J) developed in connection with basal Dingsishan (H). Later, populations from Xiantouling and Kequitou (D), possibly with other influences from Zhejiang (E), moved to (F) Taiwan (Early Dabenkeng, 3500–3000 BCE; Zhang and Hung 2010). Base mapping copyright Australian National University, College of Asia and the Pacific.

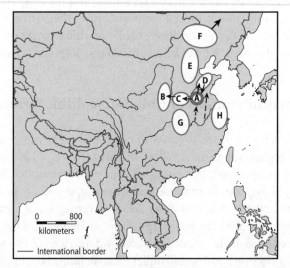

Figure 26.2 Early farming cultures in China, 7000–4500 BCE. (A) Jiahu phase 1, at c.7000–6000 BCE, is considered to be within the oldest region with agriculture. Early Neolithic cultures in the Yellow River Valley include (B) Laoguantai, (C) Peiligang, (D) Houli and (E) Cishan. (F) Xinglongwa is in Inner Mongolia and Liaoning. The Yangzi Valley early Neolithic cultures include (G) Chengbeixi and the lower layer of Zaoshi, and (H) Kuahuqiao (Zhang and Hung in press). Base mapping copyright Australian National University, College of Asia and the Pacific.

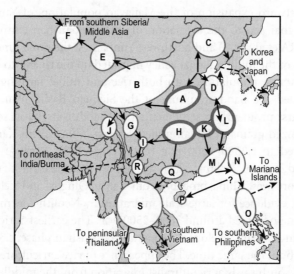

Figure 26.3 The expansion of farming from its Yellow-Yangzi origins c.4500–2500 BCE. Yang-shao and Hougang phase I populations (A) expanded westwards to Xinjiang, with descendants in (B) Hetao of Inner Mongolia, northern Shanxi, Gansu and eastern Qinghai, E) Siba and (F) Xinjiang Neolithic. Expansion with millet agriculture southwards from Hetao gave rise to (G) Yingpanshan, I) Baodun (Sichuan Plain), (R) Yunnan Neolithic and (J) Karuo in Tibet. Neolithic cultures of northeastern China include C) Hongshan and (D) Dawenkou. The Yangzi rice farming cultures include (H) Qujialing-Shijiahe, (K) Fanchengdui and (L) Liangzhu. Movement southwards from the Yangzi gave rise to (M) Tanshishan, (N) late Dabenkeng and middle Neo-lithic of Taiwan, and (O) earliest farming cultures in the northern Philippines. In Guangxi, x(Q) Xiaojin phase 2 and Dingsishan phase 4 were related to (S) the earliest farming cultures in Main-land Southeast Asia (Zhang and Hung 2010). Base mapping copyright Australian National University, College of Asia and the Pacific.

on rice cultivation. By about 5000 BCE the Hemudu culture was well developed in the Qiantangjiang valley in northern Zhejiang, and expanded by boat rapidly offshore into the Zhoushan archipelago in the East China Sea (Wang & Chen 1983).

Between 4500 and 3000 BCE in northern China, the Yangshao and Hougang phase I cultures in central Shanxi, Henan, and Hebei gradually expanded into the Hetao region of Inner Mongolia, northern Shanxi, Gansu, and eastern Qinghai (Han 2003: 76–88). In northeastern China, the Hongshan culture in eastern Inner Mongolia and western Liaoning spread into the lower Liao valley, with a continuing focus on dry-land millet agriculture. Millet and rice agriculture expanded during the 1st millennium BCE from eastern Liaoning into Korea and Japan (Yan 1989; see also chapters 28 and 29, this volume).

Between 3000 and 2100 BCE, the Majiayao and Banshan-Machang populations in Gansu and Qinghai spread into northwestern and southwestern China. After 2000 BCE, one of these groups reached the Hexi Corridor, to form the Siba culture (Yan 1978). Mixed assemblages of central Asian and Siba affinity then spread into Xinjiang (Li 2009), a situation also visible in cranial analyses that reveal a mixed Xinjiang population of southern Siberian and northwest Chinese affinity (K. X. Han 1993). Here, in Xinjiang, early Neolithic farmers from northern China finally encountered the contem-porary agricultural populations of Siberia and central Asia (see chapters 22 and 23).

The southwestward expansion of the Majiayao population, of Yangshao origin in Gansu and Qinghai, led to the formation of the Yingpanshan culture in northwest Sichuan (CCICRA et al. 2002) and northwest Yunnan. At the same time, the Qujialing-Shijiahe farmers of the middle Yangzi Valley migrated up the river into eastern Sichuan. By 2500–2000 BCE, a population with both rice and millet farming from northern Sichuan developed the Baodun culture of the Sichuan Basin (Wang & Sun 1999), leading to the first proto-urban settlements (e.g. Baodun itself) in southwest China. In Tibet, carbonized grains of foxtail millet (*Setaria italica*) from Karuo in Changdu County are dated to c.3500–2500 BCE (CRT 1985: 168). Because millet is so far the only reported crop in Neolithic Tibet, we suppose that the earliest farmers here were migrants from northwest China, probably from Gansu, Qinghai and Sichuan provinces.

The strongest evidence for large scale migration by Neolithic farming populations in southern China occurred around 3000–2500 BCE. The earliest agricultural societies in Guangdong and Fujian developed during the Tanshishan phase, c.3000 BCE, as well as in Taiwan at about the same time. The appearance of rice agriculture in these regions was related with southwards agriculturalist migration from the middle and late phases of the Liangzhu and Fanchengdui cultures of the lower Yangzi Valley. By c.2000 BCE, populations were increasing in numbers rapidly in the coastal regions of southern China and Taiwan, and southwards migration occurred from Middle Neolithic Taiwan into the northern Philippines, and perhaps also to Hainan Island. Archaeological evidence suggests that the earliest Neolithic settlements on Ludao and Lanyu Islands off southeastern Taiwan date to c.2500 BCE. These people migrated from southeastern Taiwan, like those of the Batanes Island between Taiwan and Luzon, where the first human populations arrived c.2500–2000 BCE. This was the beginning of the long journey by ancient Austronesian-speaking populations into island Southeast Asia and Oceania (see chapters 35 and 36).

Finally, in southwestern China, the earliest evidence for rice farming comes from Xiaojin phase 2 in northwestern Guangxi, dated after 2500 BCE. It is believed that the Xiaojin culture developed directly from the Shijiahe culture in the southern middle Yangzi valley. Subsequently, the culture of Dingsishan phase 4 (separate from the earlier Holocene hunter-gatherer phases at Dingsishan discussed above) appeared with rice farming in western Guangxi, c.2000 BCE. Our recent study with Hirofumi Matsumura (Matsumura et al. 2011; see chapter 27, this volume) suggests that these newcomers had different morphometrics from the indigenous hunter-gatherers. In Yunnan, the earliest rice farming did not commence until 2000 BCE and its origin can probably be traced to Sichuan. Some of these agricultural populations, especially from Guangdong and Guangxi, then migrated southwards to establish Neolithic economies in northern Vietnam and other regions of mainland Southeast Asia (Zhang & Hung 2010). Importantly, such archaeological evidence is coincident with studies of human skeletal remains from northern Vietnam (Matsumura et al. 2008, 2011) (chapter 27).

SEE ALSO: 4 Early Old World migrations of *Homo sapiens*: human biology; 25 Eastern Asia: Sino-Tibetan linguistic history; 27 Eastern Asia and Japan: human biology; 35 Southeast Asian islands and Oceania: Austronesian linguistic history

References

CCICRA, CMIAT, & QPAP (2002) Sì chuān mào xiàn yíng pán shān yí zhǐ shì jué bào gào [A preliminary excavation at the Yingpanshan site in Mao county, Sichuan]. In Chengdu City Institute of Cultural Relics (ed.), *Chéng dōu kǎo gu fā xiàn* [*Archaeological discoveries in Chengdu*], pp. 1–77. Chengdu City Institute of Cultural Relics and Archaeology, Cultural Management Institute of Aba Tibetan and Qiang people Autonomous prefecture and Mao County Museum. Beijing: Kē Xué.

CRT (1985) *Chāng Dōu kǎ ruò* [Karuo in Changdu]. Committee of Relics in the Tibet Autonomous Region & Department of History, Sichuan University. Beijing: Wenwu.

Cucchi, T., Hulme-Beaman, A., Yuan, J., et al. (2011) Early Neolithic pig domestication at Jiahu, Henan Province, China: clues from molar shape analyses using geometric morphometric approaches. *Journal of Archaeological Science* 38(1), 11–22.

Deng, Z. H. (2009) Hé nán dēng zhōu bā lǐ gǎng yí zhǐ chū tu zhí wù yí cún fèn xī [Study on the botanical remains excavated from the Baligang Site, Dengzho, Henan]. Unpublished Masters thesis, Peking University.

Fan, S. G., Zhang, Z.J., Liu, L., et al. (1999) Zhōng guó yě shēng dào de zhong lèi dì lǐ fèn bù jí qí shēng wù xué tè zhēng [The species and geographical distribution of wild rice and their biological characteristics in China]. In Biodiversity Committee, the Chinese Academy of Sciences et al. (eds.), *Miàn Xiàng 21 Shì Jì De Zhōng Guó Shēng Wù Duō Yàng Xìng Bǎo Hù* [China's biodiversity conservation toward the 21st century]. Beijing: China Forestry Publishing House, pp. 84–95.

Gao, X., Zhang, X. L., Yang, D. Y., et al. (2010) Xiàn dài zhōng guó rén qǐ yuán yu rén lèi yǎn huà de qū yù xìng duō yàng huà mó shì [Revisiting the origin of modern humans in China and its implications for global human evolution] *Science China Earth Science* 40(9), 1287–1300.

Han, J. Y. (2003) *Zhōng Guó Běi Fāng Dì Qū Xīn Shí Qì Shí Dài Wén Huà Yán Jiū* [A study on the Neolithic cultures of Northern China]. Beijing: Wenwu.

Han, K. X. (1993) *Sī Chóu Zhī Lù Gu Dài Jū Mín Zhong Zú Rén Lèi Xué Yán Jiū* [Collected papers about the racial anthropological study of the ancient Silk Road inhabitants]. Wulumuqi: Xinjiang Renmin Press.

Jin, L. & Su, B. (2001) Reply to John Hawks – the Y chromosome and the replacement hypothesis. *Science* 293, 567.

Ke, Y. (2001) with 22 co-authors. African origin of modern humans in East Asia: a tale of 12,000 Y chromosomes. *Science* 292, 1151–1153.

Li, S. C. (2009) Tiān shān běi lù mù dì yī qī yí cún fèn xī [Study on the cultural remains of the Tianshan Beilu cemetery Phase I]. In School of Archaeology and Museology, Peking University, & National Museum of China (eds.), *Yú Wěi Chāo Xiān Shēng Jì Niàn Wén Jí (Xué Shù Juàn)* [Festschrift in Honor of Professor Wei-chao Yu]. Beijing: Wenwu, pp. 193–202.

Liu, L., Lee, G. A., Jiang, L. P., et al. (2007) Evidence for the early beginning (c.9000 cal. BP) of rice domestication in China: a response. *The Holocene* 17(8), 1059–1068.

Matsumura, H., Oxenham, M. F., Dodo, Y., et al. (2008) Morphometric affinity of the late Neolithic human remains from Man Bac, Ninh Binh Province, Vietnam: key skeletons with which to debate the "two layer" hypothesis. *Anthropological Science* 116(2), 135–148.

Matsumura, H., Oxenham, M. F., Nguyen, K. T., et al. (2011) Population history of mainland Southeast Asia: the Two Layer model in the context of Northern Vietnam. In N. Enfield & J. White (eds.), *The Dynamics of Human Diversity*. Canberra: Pacific Linguistics, pp. 1–23.

SAMPU (2006) Běi jīng shì mén tóu gōu qū dōng hú lín shǐ qián yí zhǐ [Prehistoric Donghulin site in Mentougou district, Beijing city]. School of Archaeology and Museology, Peking

University, Archaeology Research Center of Peking University and Cultural Relics Research Institute of Beijing City. *Kǎo Gu* 7, 3–8.

Wang, H. P. & Chen, J. S. (1983) Zhōu shān qún dǎo fā xiàn xīn shí qì shí dài yí zhǐ [Neolithic sites found in the Zhoushan Archipelagos]. *Kǎo Gu* 1, 4–9.

Wang, Y. & Sun, H. (1999) Bǎo dūn cūn wén huà de chū bù rèn shí [Preliminary study on the Baoduncun Culture], *Kǎo Gu* 8, 60–73.

Wang, Y. P. (2005) *Zhōng Guó Yuǎn Gu Rén Lèi Wén Huà De Yuán Liú* [Roots of Pleistocene hominids and cultures in China]. Beijing: Wenwu.

Wu, X. Z. (1990) Zhōng guó yuǎn gu rén lèi de jìn huà [The evolution of humankind in China]. *Acta Anthropologica Sinica* 4, 312–321.

Wu, X. Z. (1998) Cóng zhōng guó wǎn qī zhì rén lú yá tè zhēng kàn zhōng guó xiàn dài rén qǐ yuán [Origin of modern humans of China viewed from cranio dental characteristics of late *Homo sapiens* in China]. *Acta Anthropologica Sinica* 4, 32–38.

Yan, W. M. (1978) Cóng zhōng guó wǎn qī zhì rén lú yá tè zhēng kàn zhōng guó xiàn dài rén qǐ yuán [Origin of modern humans of China viewed from cranio dental characteristics of late Homo sapiens in China]. *Wén Wù* 10, 62.

Yan, W. M. (1989) Zài lùn zhōng guó dào zuò nóng yè de qǐ yuán [Rethinking the origin of rice agriculture in China]. *Nóng Yè Kǎo Gu* 2, 72–83.

Yan, W. M. (2002) The origins of rice agriculture, pottery and cities. In Y. Yasuda (ed.), *The Origins of Pottery and Agriculture*. New Delhi: Roli Books/Lustre Press, pp. 151–156.

Zhang, C. (2000) Jiǎn lùn nán zhōng guó dì qū de xīn shí qì shí dài zǎo qī wén huà [A brief study of the early Neolithic in southern China]. In Z. P. Zhang & Z. Y. Xu (eds.), *Zhōng Guó Kǎo Gu Xué Kuà Shì Jì De Huí Gù Yu Qián Zhān* [Review and Prospects for the Cross-Century Chinese Archaeology]. Beijing: Kē Xué, pp. 190–198.

Zhang, C. (2011) Lùn jiǎ hú yī qī wén huà yí cún [Cultural remains of the Jiahu phase I]. *Wén Wù* 3, 46–53.

Zhang, C. & Hung, H. C. (2010) The emergence of agriculture in southern China. *Antiquity* 84, 11–25.

Zhang, C. & Hung, H. C. (2012) The final hunter-gatherers in prehistoric southern China, 18000–3000 BC. *Antiquity* 86, 11–29.

Zhang, C. & Hung, H. C. (in press) Jiahu 1: earliest farmers beyond the Yangtze River. *Antiquity*.

Zhang, J. Z. & Li, Z. Y. (1996) Hé nán wu yáng dà gǎng xì shí qì dì diǎn fā jué bào gào [Preliminary report on the excavation of Dagang Microlithic site in Wuyang county, Henan province]. Preliminary report on the excavation of Dagang Microlithic site in Wuyang county, Henan province. *Acta Anthropologica Sinica* 2, 105–113.

Zhang, J. Z., Harbottle, G., Wang, C. S., et al. (1999) Oldest playable musical instruments found at Jiahu, early Neolithic site in China. *Nature* 401, 366–368.

Zheng, Y. F. & Jiang, L. P. (2007) Shàng shān yí zhǐ chū tu de gu dào yí cún jí qí yì yì [Remains of ancient rice unearthed from the Shangshan site and their significance]. *Kǎo Gǔ* 9, 19–25.

ZPICRA (2007) Zhè jiāng pu jiāng xiàn shàng shān yí zhǐ fā jué jiǎn bào [Excavation at the Shangshan site in Pujiang county, Zhejiang]. Zhejiang Provincial Institute of Cultural Relics and Archaeology and Pujiang County Museum. Excavation at the Shangshan site in Pujiang County, Zhejiang. *Kǎo Gu* 9, 7–18.

27

Eastern Asia and Japan: human biology

Hirofumi Matsumura and Marc Oxenham

This chapter focuses on the Holocene population history of Japan and Southeast Asia, as regions strongly influenced by population and cultural developments on the mainland of East Asia. A case is made for significant expansion of agricultural populations in both cases.

Southeast Asia, occupied by anatomically modern humans at least 50 kya, was a corridor through which migrants travelled on their way to Australia and Oceania and beyond (see Figure 37.1(a)). Elucidating the biological relationships between early Southeast Asian *Homo sapiens* and the present-day inhabitants of the region is fundamental to resolving questions surrounding *sapiens* migration history, not least the hypothesis for agriculturally driven demic migration from East Asia into Southeast Asia (see chapter 26). A parallel issue concerns movements of East Asian agriculturalists into the Japanese archipelago (see chapter 28), where recent advances in research methods have demonstrated a rapid population transition and associated large-scale genetic exchange with pre-existing hunter-gatherer populations. An important question is whether the events in Japan were analogous to the situation in Southeast Asia.

Geographic terminology is crucial to the issues discussed in this chapter, as many researchers who support the hypothesis of *in situ* evolution of indigenous Southeast Asians include south China and Taiwan in their definition of prehistoric Southeast Asia. Although such a definition does have certain advantages, in this chapter we designate East and Southeast Asia separately: *East Asia* refers to modern China, Taiwan, North and South Korea, Japan, Mongolia, and the Russian Far East (see Figure 27.1); *Southeast Asia* refers to modern Myanmar (Burma), Thailand, Vietnam, Laos, Cambodia, Malaysia, Singapore, Indonesia, Brunei, the Philippines, and the Andaman and Nicobar Islands.

The Global Prehistory of Human Migration: The Encyclopedia of Global Human Migration Volume 1,
First Edition. Edited by Peter Bellwood.
© 2013 John Wiley & Sons, Ltd. Published 2015 by John Wiley & Sons, Ltd.

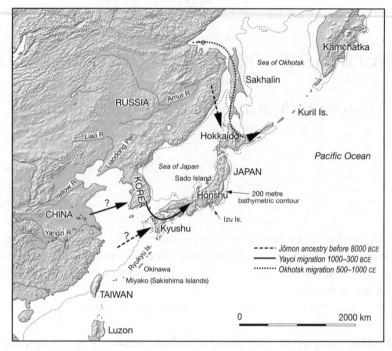

Figure 27.1 Late Pleistocene and Holocene migrations into the Japanese islands. Base mapping by Australian National University, College of Asia and the Pacific.

Migration to the Japanese archipelago

The earliest archaeological evidence for the settlement of the Japanese archipelago dates to the Upper Palaeolithic, at least 30 kya. These early pre-ceramic settlers likely gave rise to the Neolithic (pottery-using) Jōmon who are identified in the archaeological record from around 12 kya. The last several decades have witnessed considerable debate over the origins of the Jōmon peoples. A number of cranial and dental studies suggest that the Jōmon population ultimately derived from Southeast Asia (Turner 1990; Hanihara 1993; Matsumura 2006), while genetic comparisons have suggested a Northeast Asian origin (Omoto & Saitou 1997). On the other hand, ancient mtDNA analysis by Adachi and colleagues (2009) has found considerable interregional haplogroup variation, implying heterogeneity within the Jōmon population. In particular, their analysis using a Jōmon sample from northernmost Japan (Hokkaido), which detected haplogroups specific to Siberian populations, suggests considerable gene flow from Northeast Asia. Hanihara and Ishida (2009), undertaking R-matrix analysis using craniometric data to assess the regional diversity of Jōmon populations, found the Hokkaido region had the highest phenotypic variance among the regional samples examined. This finding led them to conclude that Jōmon ancestors, initially having migrated from the northern part of mainland East Asia, subsequently expanded in a north–south direction through the Japanese archipelago.

Contrary to evidence for a northern origin, Mizoguchi (2011) has demonstrated a close cranio-morphological resemblance between Jōmon and Australian Late Pleistocene cranial series, suggesting a southern origin. Cranial and dental comparisons by Matsumura and Hudson (2005), and Matsumura and colleagues (2011), using samples encompassing a wide geographic area and temporal span, suggest that Late Neolithic and modern Southeast Asians form a population cluster that is intermediate between present-day East Asians on the one hand, and early Holocene Southeast Asians (pre-Neolithic Hoabinhian foragers) on the other, the latter being akin to modern Australians and Melanesians. However, although this study confirmed parallels in cranial and dental morphology between both Jōmon and present-day Southeast Asian populations, it does not prove a single genetic origin for the Jōmon. The reason for this (discussed below) is that present-day Southeast Asia may have a large East Asian (including Chinese) genetic legacy. In fact, the great diversity seen in northern Jōmon crania by Hanihara and Ishida (2009) is also consistent with a multiple-origin scenario. Moreover, the large phenotypic variance seen in Hokkaido might be due to elevated levels of gene flow from Siberia, a scenario consistent with the DNA results.

In summary, the most likely scenario for the Jōmon population, given the varying results from numerous studies, would seem to be that it ultimately derived from the modern human colonizers of Late Pleistocene Southeast Asia and Australia, who subsequently mixed with later migrants from the northern part of East Asia during the early Jōmon period (c.12–7 kya) or before (see Figure 27.1).

In the Japanese archipelago, by far the most significant genetic input occurred with the Yayoi migrations from the East Asian continent, associated with a spread of rice cultivation from about 850 BCE onward. The genes of the Yayoi migrants, who initially occupied western Japan, gradually spread throughout the archipelago and indeed continue to live there even today. In peripheral regions of southernmost and northernmost Japan, where the Yayoi influence was not as intense, populations tend to retain physical characteristics inherited from the indigenous Jōmon people. In particular, the Ainu of the northernmost island of Hokkaido are considered to be the direct descendants of Jōmon indigenes, based on a range of morphological features. This hypothesis, termed the "dual structure" model by Hanihara (1991), is currently widely accepted in discussions of the population history of Japan.

In terms of the Yayoi origin (see also chapter 28), archaeological and linguistic evidence indicates the Korean peninsula as the mostly likely final disembarkation point. Regardless of the actual migratory route, skeletal and mtDNA analyses indicate that the original homeland of the Yayoi colonists was in the Yangzi River region of China (Nakahashi & Li 2002), with close affinities noted between Japanese Yayoi immigrants and populations from the Eastern Zhou and Western Han dynastic periods (c.1000 BCE to 200 CE).

Indigenous communities in Hokkaido, for the most part free of Yayoi influence, seem to have descended from the local Epi-Jōmon and Satsumon cultures, in the process developing their subsequent Ainu identity of ethnographic times. In addition to the Ainu, the immigrant Okhotsk culture flourished in the eastern coastal region of Hokkaido and the outlying archipelago, including Sakhalin and the Kuril islands, between the 5th and 11th centuries CE. The Okhotsk were already well adapted to the subarctic zone and brought technological and behavioral skills to the region that allowed them to pursue the hunting of large marine animals such as whales and sea lions very successfully, and also to exploit a diverse range of other resources. The origins of these relative latecomers has been sought in the lower Amur River region of the Russian Far East, from where the Okhotsk spread to Sakhalin and then Hokkaido. Cranial studies of Okhotsk samples have demonstrated close affinities with groups in their putative homeland along the lower Amur (Komesu et al. 2008). Moreover, mtDNA analyses have demonstrated a close similarity between the Okhotsk and Amur geno-types (Sato et al. 2009a). Such genetic approaches, in addition to cranio-morphological studies (e.g. Hanihara et al. 2008), indicate substantial genetic interaction between Okhotsk and Jōmon-Ainu lineages during and/or prior to Okhotsk colonization of parts of Hokkaido.

New advances in the amplification of nuclear DNA from archaeological specimens also contribute to our understanding of the past population history of this region. Allele frequencies of the *ABCC11* gene for earwax vary by population, with ancient Jōmon and modern Ainu populations sharing a high frequency of the wet-type allele while the majority of Okhotsk samples have the dry-type allele, common also among Siberian populations (Sato et al. 2009b). A study of ABO blood group polymorphisms has also shown differences between Hokkaido Jōmon/Epi-Jōmon samples on the one hand and the Okhotsk on the other hand, with a northern origin for the Okhotsk postulated (Sato et al. 2010).

Migration to Southeast Asia

Tracing the population history of Southeast Asia is rendered difficult by the complexi-ties of the historical migratory processes, both temporal and geographical, as well as the unquantifiable degree of genetic exchange that has occurred for thousands of years. While the skeletal record is poor for the earliest phases of *Homo sapiens* colonization of Southeast Asia, some tentative comments can be made. The earliest *sapiens* popula-tions were pre-ceramic foragers, who expanded throughout mainland and island Southeast Asia during the Late Pleistocene and Early Holocene. Research into the cranial morphology of these early Southeast Asian colonists (e.g. Jacob 1967) initially indicated that they shared a common ancestry with Aboriginal Australians and modern day Melanesians.

Regarding the origins of the phenotypic traits characterizing modern Southeast Asians (such as flat face and light skin coloration, for instance), it was widely believed they arose through a greater or lesser degree of genetic exchange between the original indigenous populations and immigrants from mainland East Asia (Jacob 1967). This model, known as the Two Layer hypothesis, has gained theoretical support from both historical linguistics and archaeology, in which the pre-modern dispersal of the Aus-tronesian, Austroasiatic, Daic (Tai-Kadai), Miao-Yao (Hmong-Mien), and Sino-Tibetan (Tibeto-Burman) language families took place in concert with the expansion of rice-cultivating peoples during the Neolithic and early Bronze and Iron Ages (Higham 2001; Bellwood 2005; Sagart 2008). Linguistic data indicate that southern China and

Taiwan provided the ultimate sources of many of the existing language families of Southeast Asia, while archaeology posits the origins of Neolithic farming societies in the Yangzi basin during the early Holocene, prior to subsequent expansion from southern China into Southeast Asia (Bellwood 2005; Lu 2006; and see chapter 26, this volume).

Current debates over the origins of modern Southeast Asians devolve upon two main issues, the first being whether the earliest occupants of the region had Australo-Melanesian affinities. This question is difficult to resolve due to the dearth of well-preserved skeletal material from the Late Pleistocene/Early Holocene, as well as the relatively poor dating of such material. The second question, and one that has received the most attention in the recent literature, concerns the timing, source, and scale of the population–language–agriculture dispersal package from China/Taiwan and the subsequent degree of genetic exchange with local populations. Resolution of both questions is central to testing the validity of the Two Layer hypothesis as a model for understanding the population history of Southeast Asia.

The only major competing model for Southeast Asian population history is the Regional Continuity model, which argues that modern Southeast Asians are the result of long-standing evolutionary continuity without significant outside genetic input, if any at all (Turner 1990; Hanihara 2006; Pietrusewsky 2010). This model has recently received some support through a series of genetic studies. While a genetic link between Insular Southeast Asian and Formosan (Austronesian) populations has been shown, the common genetic heritage has been argued to derive from the Late Pleistocene colonization of Sundaland, and not from subsequent demographic movement during the Neolithic, as the Two Layer model would hypothesize (eg. Hill et al. 2007; Soares et al. 2008). Further, mtDNA analysis of Austronesian-speaking Cham in central Vietnam has argued that cultural diffusion was a more important factor than genetic exchange (Peng et al. 2010). Moreover, other DNA studies have suggested that Southeast Asia was a major geographic source of East Asian populations, within which the roots of all living populations of Southeast and East Asia were historically united via a single primary wave of entry to the region (e.g. Capelli et al. 2001; HUGO Pan-Asian SNP Consortium 2009).

A wealth of studies do, however, support the Two Layer model and are, importantly, based on the morphological analysis of new skeletal discoveries from Hoabinhian sites, for example Gua Gunung Runtuh from Malaysia, Moh Khiew from Thailand, and Hang Cho from northern Vietnam (Matsumura, 2006; Matsumura et al. 2011). Such work clearly demonstrates that the early colonists of Southeast Asia were descendants of the first occupants of Late Pleistocene Sundaland, who in turn shared immediate ancestry with present-day Australian Aboriginal and Melanesian populations. Equally important is the demonstration of a close dental trait affinity between Hoabinhian and Australo-Melanesian samples on the one hand, and a northern source for contemporary Southeast Asians on the other (Matsumura & Hudson 2005). This supports an immigration rather than regional continuity model for the origins of modern Southeast Asian peoples.

Further recent support for the Two Layer model comes from Man Bac, a 3600- to 4000-year-old cemetery site in northern Vietnam (Matsumura et al. 2011; Oxenham et al. 2011). The Man Bac series is cranio-morphologically heterogeneous, with the majority of crania exhibiting a significant morphological discontinuity with earlier late Pleistocene/early Holocene Hoabinhian and Bac Son series and mid-Holocene Da But cultural assemblages. The close affinity of the majority of Man Bac specimens with later Iron Age Dong Son and Chinese Neolithic samples from the Yangzi River region suggests the initial appearance of immigrants in northern Vietnam with close genetic links to what is now southern China. Man Bac is unique in capturing a sudden change in the cranial morphology of a population, and by proxy its genetic structure, through large-scale migration from eastern Asia. The major population changes evident at Man Bac, potentially symptomatic of northern Vietnam in general at this time, are somewhat analogous to the profound changes in human biology that clearly occurred during the Jōmon/Yayoi transition in Japan.

SEE ALSO: 26 Eastern Asia: archaeology; 28 Japan: archaeology

References

Adachi, N., Shinoda, K., Umetsu, K., et al. (2009) Mitochondrial DNA analysis of Jomon skeletons from the Funadomari site, Hokkaido, and its implication for the origins of native Americans. *American Journal of Physical Anthropology* 138, 255–265.

Bellwood, P. (2005) Examining the farming/language dispersal hypothesis in the East Asian context. In L. Sagart, R. Blench, & A. Sanchez-Mazas (eds.), *The Peopling of East Asia: Putting Together Archaeology, Linguistics and Genetics*. London: Routledge, pp. 17–30.

Capelli, C., Wilson, J. F., Richards, M., et al. (2001) A predominantly indigenous paternal heritage for the Austronesian-speaking peoples of insular Southeast Asia and Oceania. *American Journal of Human Genetics* 68, 432–443.

Hanihara, K. (1991) Dual structure model for the population history of the Japanese. *Japan Review* 2, 1–33.

Hanihara, T. (1993) Craniofacial features of Southeast Asians and Jomonese: a reconsideration of their microevolution since the late Pleistocene. *Anthropological Science* 101, 25–46.

Hanihara, T. (2006) Interpretation of craniofacial variation and diversification of East and Southeast Asia. In M. F. Oxenham and N. Tayles (eds.), *Bioarchaeology of Southeast Asia*. Cambridge: Cambridge University Press, pp. 91–111.

Hanihara, T.& Ishida, H. (2009) Regional differences in craniofacial diversity and the population history of Jomon Japan. *American Journal of Physical Anthropology* 139, 311–322.

Hanihara, T., Yoshida, K., & Ishida, H. (2008) Craniometric variation of the Ainu: an assessment of differential gene flow from Northeast Asia into Northern Japan, Hokkaido. *American Journal of Physical Anthropology* 137, 283–293.

Higham, C. F. W. (2001) Prehistory, language and human biology: is there a consensus in East and Southeast Asia? In L. Jin, M. Seielstad, & C. J. Xiao (eds.), *Genetic, Linguistic and Archaeological Perspectives on Human Diversity in Southeast Asia*. Singapore: World Scientific, pp. 3–16.

Hill, C., Soares, P., Mormina, M., et al. (2007) A mitochondrial stratigraphy for Island Southeast Asia. *American Journal of Human Genetics* 80, 29–43.

HUGO Pan-Asian SNP Consortium (2009) Mapping human genetic diversity in Asia. *Science* 326, 1541–1545.

Jacob, T. (1967) Some problems pertaining to the racial history of the Indonesian region. PhD dissertation, University of Utrecht.

Komesu, A., Hanihara, T., Amano, T., et al. (2008) Nonmetric cranial variation in human skeletal remains associated with Okhotsk culture. *Anthropological Science* 116, 33–47.

Lu, T. L. D. (2006) The occurrence of cereal cultivation in China. *Asian Perspectives* 45, 129–158.

Matsumura, H. (2006) The population history of Southeast Asia viewed from morphometric analyses of human skeletal and dental remains. In M. F. Oxenham & N. Tayles (eds.), *Bioarchaeology of Southeast Asia*. Cambridge: Cambridge University Press, pp. 33–58.

Matsumura, H. & Hudson, M. J. (2005) Dental perspectives on the population history of Southeast Asia. *American Journal of Physical Anthropology* 127, 182–209.

Matsumura, H., Oxenham, M. F., Nguyen, K. T. et al. (2011) The population history of mainland Southeast Asia: two layer model in the context of northern Vietnam. In N. Enfield & J. White (eds.), *Dynamics of Human Diversity: The Case of Mainland Southeast Asia*. Canberra: Pacific Linguistics, pp. 153–178.

Mizoguchi, Y. (2011) Typicality probabilities of Late Pleistocene human fossils from East Asia, Southeast Asia, and Australia: implications for the Jomon population in Japan. *Anthropological Science* 119(2), 99–111.

Nakahashi, T. & Li, M. (eds.) (2002) *Ancient People in the Jiangnan Region, China*. Fukuoka: Kyushu University Press.

Omoto, K. & Saitou, N. (1997) Genetic origins of the Japanese: a partial support for the "dual structure hypothesis." *American Journal of Physical Anthropology* 102, 437–446.

Oxenham, M. F., Matsumura, H. & Nguyen, K. D. (2011) *Man Bac: The Excavation of a Neolithic Site in Northern Vietnam, the Biology*. Terra Australis 33. Canberra: Australian National University E Press (print-on-demand volume). Online at www.epress.anu.edu.au/titles/terra-australis/ta33_citation, accessed Jan. 3, 2012.

Peng, M. S., Quang, H. H., Dang, K. P., et al. (2010) Tracing the Austronesian footprint in mainland Southeast Asia: a perspective from mitochondrial DNA. *Molecular Biology and Evolution* 27, 2417–2430.

Pietrusewsky, M. (2010) A multivariate analysis of measurements recorded in early and more modern crania from East Asia and Southeast Asia. *Quaternary International* 211, 42–54.

Sagart, L. (2008) The expansion of setaria farmers in East Asia: a linguistic and archaeological model. In A. Sanchez-Mazas, R. Blench, M. Ross, et al. (eds.), *Past Human Migrations in East Asia: Matching Archaeology, Linguistics and Genetics*. London: Routledge, pp. 133–157.

Sato, T., Amano, T., Ono, H., et al. (2009a) Mitochondrial DNA haplogrouping of the Okhotsk people based on analysis of ancient DNA: an intermediate of gene flow from the continental Sakhalin people to the Ainu. *Anthropological Science* 117, 171–180.

Sato, T., Amano, T., Ono, H., et al. (2009b) Allele frequencies of the ABCC11 gene for earwax phenotypes among ancient populations of Hokkaido, Japan. *Journal of Human Genetics* 54, 409–413.

Sato, T., Amano, T., Ono, H., et al. (2010) Polymorphisms and allele frequencies of the ABO blood group gene among the Jomon, Epi-Jomon, and Okhotsk people in Hokkaido, northern Japan, revealed by ancient DNA analysis. *Journal of Human Genetics* 55, 691–696.

Soares, P., Trejaut, J. A., Loo, J. H., et al. (2008) Climate change and postglacial human dispersals in Southeast Asia. *Molecular Biology and Evolution* 25, 1209–1218.

Turner, C. G. II (1990) Major features of Sundadonty and Sinodonty, including suggestions about East Asian microevolution, population history and late Pleistocene relationships with Australian Aborigines. *American Journal of Physical Anthropology* 82, 295–317.

28

Japan: archaeology

Mark J. Hudson

This chapter presents archaeological evidence for Jōmon and Yayoi migration within and to Japan. These islands had a remarkable Holocene prehistory that reflected its temperate and maritime location, often developing cultural traditions quite different from those of the East Asian mainland.

The Jōmon was a series of related pottery-using cultures that were found throughout the Japanese archipelago, with the exception of the southern Ryukyu (Okinawa) Islands (for Jōmon biological origins, see chapter 27). The Jōmon period followed the Japanese Upper Paleolithic (which lacked pottery), and dates from around 14 000 to 500 BCE. Hunter-gathering formed the main subsistence base of the Jōmon, but farming was introduced from the Asian mainland in the first millennium before the Common Era, leading to the early agricultural Yayoi period (c. 500 BCE to 300 CE).

Jōmon migrations within Japan and the settlement of the Ryukyu Islands

The people of the Holocene Jōmon cultures of Japan made frequent sea voyages to offshore islands, such as the Izu Islands south of Tokyo and Sado Island in the Sea of Japan. Jōmon people also crossed to Sakhalin and the southern Kuril Islands (see Figure 27.1). In the Late and Final Jōmon (2000–500 BCE) there was frequent interaction between coastal fishing groups in northwest Kyushu and southern Korea, and Jōmon pottery from the Early and Late phases has been found at the Tongsamdong shell midden in South Korea (Sample 1974, 1976; and see chapter 29, this volume).

The most sustained long-distance migration of Jōmon populations was from Kyushu to the Ryukyu Islands. These migrations began around 7000 BCE and appear to have involved several distinct episodes of exploration and then colonization. The Jōmon settlement of Okinawa represents a highly unusual case of the occupation of small island environments by hunter-gatherers (Takamiya 2004, 2006). It is unclear what push/pull factors stimulated this Jōmon migration to Okinawa.

The Jōmon settlement of the Ryukyu Islands only extended as far south as Okinawa Island itself, and the 250 km-wide Kerama Gap between Okinawa and Miyako Island does not seem to have been crossed at this time. South of the Kerama Gap, the Sakishima Islands of the southern Ryukyus were settled around 2300 BCE by groups who had no connection with the Jōmon. Sakishima prehistory can be divided into two stages, an Early Neolithic with pottery (c.2300–1500 BCE) and a Late Neolithic with *Tridacna* adzes but without pottery (c.500 BCE to 1100 CE). Neither of these stages has connections with Japan and both appear to represent migrations from Taiwan or Southeast Asia. Although Taiwan is only just over 100 km from Yonaguni, the closest island in the Sakishima group, the prehistory of Sakishima has no clear links with Taiwan, and the Philippines or Micronesia have been suggested as possible origins.

It is not clear whether the Early and Late Neolithic phases in the Sakishima islands represent two separate cultures with different origins or whether the earlier culture evolved into the latter *in situ* – although on present evidence most experts assume the former. If the prehistoric cultures of the Sakishima Islands did not come from Taiwan, then they must have originated through very long seaborne migrations, yet once they reached the southern Ryukyus they seem to have had almost no further contact with other regions. There is no evidence for agriculture in prehistoric Sakishima and these cultures would appear to represent either migrations of hunter-gatherers, or else agricultural populations who were unable to continue farming once they arrived in the southern Ryukyus. The Sakishima Islands are of great importance in the study of prehistoric migrations in the Pacific since they presumably represent one of the northernmost frontiers of Austronesian expansion.

The arrival of the Yayoi population in Japan

Austronesian expansions to the southern Ryukyus did not bring farming to the Japanese Islands, but migrations from the Korean peninsula to Kyushu played a major role in the spread of agriculture into mainland Japan in the 1st millennium BCE (see Figure 27.1). These migrations were a complex historical process and considerable debate still surrounds aspects of their timing and scale. This debate includes technical questions, such as those relating to radiocarbon dating, as well as broader issues connected to the sociopolitical background of archaeology in Japan. Fujio (2003), for example, notes that with the growing confidence of postwar economic growth from the 1960s, Japanese archaeology has almost invariably emphasized the choice and agency of Jōmon populations in creating the Yayoi, rather than assuming change was brought in from the outside.

In order to understand the role of migration in the formation of agricultural societies in Japan, it is useful to begin by considering three separate types of evidence: from biological anthropology, historical linguistics, and archaeology. Japan has a long and active tradition of research in biological anthropology. Since the late 1980s, it has been widely agreed that there was a large genetic input into Japan in the early agricultural Yayoi period and that the historic Japanese are primarily descended from Yayoi immigrants with a smaller, though regionally variable, heritage from the Jōmon. A detailed review of this evidence can be found in Hudson (1999) (see also chapter 27). Although biological anthropology thus provides crucial evidence supporting migrations into Japan in the Yayoi period, it needs to be noted that no "immigrant type" skeletal remains are known from the very beginning of the Yayoi. This may suggest that the number of migrants was relatively small at first, only increasing in number from the end of the Early Yayoi phase.

Historical linguistics also provides invaluable information for understanding migrations in the Yayoi period. Japanese belongs to the Japonic language family which has two dialect branches: Japanese and Ryukyuan (see chapter 24). Linguists make two conclusions that are important for our consideration of migrations here. First, that Japonic has a relatively short time depth and, second, that it replaced other, now lost, languages in the Japanese Islands within that short time scale. In chapter 24 of this volume, linguist Alexander Vovin states that: "There is almost universal consensus that Japonic languages entered the Japanese islands via the Korean peninsula during the Yayoi period." This conclusion is further supported by a recent phylogenetic analysis of 59 Japonic languages and dialects which concluded that these languages derived from a common ancestor about 2,182 years ago (Lee & Hasegawa 2011).

Compared to biological anthropology and linguistics, there has been less debate in Japan on the archaeology of migration and agriculture. As noted above, many Japanese archaeologists have assumed that farming was adopted by Jōmon populations with little outside migration. In Japanese, a good overview of this material is provided by Fujio (2003). However, a recent study of the Jōmon–Yayoi transition in the Okayama area of the Seto Inland Sea by Kusahara (2010) has shown just how complex and poorly understood this transition was on the ground. More research of a similar nature will be required to understand fully the role of migrations in the formation of Yayoi culture.

A particularly controversial aspect of the archaeology of the Jōmon–Yayoi transition is the presence of new AMS dates that purport to show that the Yayoi period began by 900 BCE, five hundred years earlier than traditional estimates (Fujio 2011). If these dates are correct, they would appear to imply that the spread of farming in the Yayoi was a separate, much earlier phenomenon than the migrations that took place later in the Yayoi period.

Recent archaeological research has also discussed the role of population movements associated with the spread of farming into northeast Japan. Matsumoto (2006) describes archaeological evidence for migrations into the eastern and western sides of northern Honshu between the late 5th and the 11th centuries CE. According to Matsumoto, in the 8th century groups with farming technology and houses with built-in ovens also expanded into parts of southwest Hokkaido.

Later migrations involving Hokkaido and Okinawa

Hokkaido had always been open to migrations from the north, via Sakhalin (see chapter 27). Some biological anthropologists now emphasize the importance of this northern route in the original formation of Jōmon populations (Hanihara & Ishida 2009). The spread of blade arrowheads into Hokkaido in the Early Jōmon may have been associated with another migration from the north (Kikuchi 1986). What appear to have been seasonal migrations were carried out between Hokkaido and the offshore islands of Rishiri and Rebun by the Jōmon people (Keally 1990). The end of the Jōmon period in Hokkaido was marked by an "Epi-Jōmon" phase that saw the abandonment of sedentary settlements and the movement of some Hokkaido populations south into northern Honshu.

The later prehistory of Hokkaido is also marked by several important migrations. The Okhotsk culture moved south from Sakhalin along the eastern coast of Hokkaido in the 6th century CE, later expanding further into the Kuril Islands. After the 9th century, however, this culture experienced growing encroachments as a result of the expansion of Satsumon populations. Satsumon culture developed into that of the historic Ainu by around 1200 CE, and by that time Satsumon/Ainu had already expanded from Hokkaido into Sakhalin and the southern Kurils (Ohyi 1975; Hudson 2004). Satsumon culture included a major agricultural component in southwest Hokkaido, as exemplified by barley, wheat, and millet remains found at the Sakushu-Kotoni River site in Sapporo (Crawford 2011). It is unclear to what extent these plants were cultivated by Satsumon people in other parts of Hokkaido. The Satsumon expansion occurred during the Medieval Warm Period (see Batten 2009), and warmer temperatures in Hokkaido at this time may have contributed to the spread of agriculture to the north.

Although Ainu villages, especially those on Hokkaido, are known to have been very sedentary, some Ainu moved long distances by boat as far as the Amur River and Kamchatka as part of trading activities (Sasaki 1999). After the 16th century, however, Ainu migrations were increasingly limited by Japanese merchants and officials (Hudson, forthcoming a; forthcoming b). After Hokkaido was incorporated into Japanese territory in 1869, there was a large-scale migration of Japanese farmers into the island. The agriculturalization of Hokkaido was associated with numerous forced migrations of Ainu groups, which had devastating effects on Ainu culture and well-being (Aoyama 2012).

In the Okinawa islands in the south, island populations remained in contact with Kyushu and a regular trade in tropical shells developed in the Yayoi period (Kinoshita 2003). In the early centuries of the 2nd millennium CE, there was a population expansion into the Okinawa islands from Kyushu that was associated with the spread of farming and of the Ryukyuan branch of the Japonic language family. This migration continued south into the Sakishima islands of the southern Ryukyus, and the Ryukyu archipelago was brought into one cultural sphere under Okinawan domination by around the 12th century (Hudson 1999).

A long history of research on the origins of the Japanese peoples has examined various routes of migration into prehistoric Japan. Less attention has so far been given to large-scale migrations within the Japanese islands themselves, but there are several major examples from prehistory, including the Jōmon settlement of northern and central Okinawa and Satsumon/Ainu expansions across Hokkaido and into Sakhalin and the Kuril Islands. These latter examples involved substantial migrations by hunter-gatherer populations and require further research to understand their causes and dynamics.

SEE ALSO: 24 Northeastern and central Asia: "Altaic" linguistic history; 27 Eastern Asia and Japan: human biology; 29 Korea: archaeology

References

Aoyama, M. (2012) Indigenous Ainu occupational identities and the natural environment in Hokkaido. In N. Pollard & D. Sakellariou (eds.), *Politics of Occupation-Centred Practice: Reflections on Occupational Engagement Across Cultures*. Oxford: Wiley-Blackwell, pp. 106–127.

Batten, B. L. (2009) *Climate Change in Japanese History and Prehistory: A Comparative Overview*. Cambridge, MA: Edwin O. Reischauer Institute of Japanese Studies, Harvard University.

Crawford, G. W. (2011) Advances in understanding early agriculture in Japan. *Current Anthropology* 52(Supplement 4), 331–345.

Fujio, S. (2003) *Yayoi Henkanki no Kōkogaku* [The archaeology of the Yayoi transition period]. Tokyo: Dōseisha.

Fujio, S. (2011) *"Shin" Yayoi Jidai: 500nen Hayakatta Suiden Inasaku* [The "new" Yayoi period: paddy rice farming began 500 years earlier]. Tokyo: Yoshikawa Kōbunkan.

Hanihara, T. & Ishida, H. (2009) Regional differences in craniofacial diversity and the population history of Jomon Japan. *American Journal of Physical Anthropology* 139, 311–322.

Hudson, M. J. (1999) *Ruins of Identity: Ethnogenesis in the Japanese Islands*. Honolulu: University of Hawaii Press.

Hudson, M. J. (2004) The perverse realities of change: world system incorporation and the Okhotsk culture of Hokkaido. *Journal of Anthropological Archaeology* 23, 290–308.

Hudson, M. J. (forthcoming a) Ainu and hunter-gatherer studies. In M. J. Hudson, A. Lewallen, & M. Watson (eds.), *Beyond Ainu Studies: Changing Academic and Public Perspectives*. Honolulu: University of Hawaii Press.

Hudson, M. J. (forthcoming b) North Japan (Ainu). In V. Cummings & P. Jordan (eds.), *Oxford Handbook of Hunter-Gatherers*. Oxford: Oxford University Press.

Keally, C. T. (1990) The third millennium B.C. Uedomari 3 site, Rebun island, Hokkaido: Life at a far northern outpost of the Ento peoples from Tsugaru. *Sophia International Review* 12, 19–33.

Kikuchi, T. (1986) Continental culture and Hokkaido. In R. J. Pearson (ed.) *Windows on the Japanese Past: Studies in Archaeology and Prehistory*. Ann Arbor: Center for Japanese Studies, University of Michigan, pp. 149–162.

Kinoshita, N. (2003) Shell trade and exchange in the prehistory of the Ryukyu archipelago. *Bulletin of the Indo-Pacific Prehistory Association* 23, 67–72.

Kusahara, T. (2010) Jōmon kara Yayoi e: Okayama heiya no keesu kara [From Jōmon to Yayoi: a case study on the Okayama plain]. *Kōkogaku Kenkyū* 57(3), 82–100.

Lee, S. & Hasegawa, T. (2011) Bayesian phylogenetic analysis supports an agricultural origin of Japonic languages. *Proceedings of the Royal Society B* 278, 3662–3669.

Matsumoto, T. (2006) *Emishi no Kōkogaku* [The archaeology of the Emishi]. Tokyo: Dōseisha.

Ohyi, H. (1975) The Okhotsk culture, a maritime culture of the southern Okhotsk Sea region. In W. Fitzhugh (ed.), *Prehistoric Maritime Adaptations of the Circumpolar Zone*. The Hague: Mouton, pp. 123–158.

Sample, L. L. (1974) Tongsamdong: a contribution to Korean Neolithic culture history. *Arctic Anthropology* 11, 1–125.

Sample, L. L. (1976) Prehistoric cultural relations between western Japan and southeastern Korea. *Asian Perspectives* 19, 172–175.

Sasaki, S. (1999) Trading brokers and partners with China, Russia, and Japan. In W. W. Fitzhugh & C. O. Dubreuil (eds.), *Ainu: Spirit of a Northern People*. Washington, DC: Arctic Studies Center, Smithsonian, pp. 86–91.

Takamiya, H. (2004) Population dynamics in the prehistory of Okinawa. In S. M. Fitzpatrick (ed.), *Voyages of Discovery: The Archaeology of Islands*. Westport CT: Praeger, pp. 111–128.

Takamiya, H. (2006) An unusual case? Hunter-gatherer adaptations to an island environment: a case study from Okinawa, Japan. *Journal of Island and Coastal Archaeology* 1, 49–66.

29

Korea: archaeology

Seonbok Yi

During the Holocene, the Korean peninsula witnessed significant interactions with adjacent parts of eastern Asia, some no doubt involving migration. Korea was also the source region for the Yayoi Japanese during the 1st millennium BCE.

Evidence of Holocene migration is not well documented in the archaeological record in Korea (Korean Archaeological Society 2010). Despite the lack of evidence, however, a two-wave migration model was proposed in the 1970s to explain the origin of modern Koreans (W. Kim 1986), and the influence of this is still felt in the secondary literature (Nelson 1993). The model began with an assumption that there already existed during the Early Holocene a number of fixed and clearly definable population groups throughout Asia. It was suggested that the current modern ethnic groups of East Asia appeared as a result of their relocation. For Korea, the absence of Early Holocene archaeological remains was explained as due to a movement of Paleolithic hunter-gatherers from there northwards at the end of the Pleistocene to follow migrating game animals. Thus, the appearance of the comb-patterned or Chŭlmun (Jeulmun) pottery of the Neolithic period was thought to mark the arrival of a new "Paleoasiatic" or "Paleosiberian" group. Then, some two thousand years later, another wave of migration reached Korea. This time, a "Tungus" group equipped with a Bronze Age culture arrived in Korea, and either replaced or absorbed the earlier Neolithic group to form the modern Korean population.

The two-wave model was based on a number of hypothetical assumptions, none of which was compatible with the archaeological data. It is now clear that the migrations suggested above never happened, and the elusiveness of concepts such as "Paleoasiatics," "Paleosiberians," or "Tungus" in interpreting the archaeological past has been demonstrated (Yi 1991a).

It now appears that the Korean peninsula and neighboring regions were continuously occupied from at least the Late Pleistocene. On the surface, this seems compatible

The Global Prehistory of Human Migration: The Encyclopedia of Global Human Migration Volume 1,
First Edition. Edited by Peter Bellwood.
© 2013 John Wiley & Sons, Ltd. Published 2015 by John Wiley & Sons, Ltd.

with what the North Korean literature has been arguing for Korean origins. However, the North Korean "explanation" of Korean origins claims that ethnic Koreans have formed a "pure-blooded group since at least 500 thousand years ago, without any external admixture." The argument is based upon political aims rather than scientific truth (Yi 1991b, 1992), but prehistoric movements of people into and within the peninsula appear nevertheless to have occurred on a scale insufficiently large to leave visible imprints upon material as well as human palaeontological remains. Sudden appearances of foreign cultural elements, such as the spread of rice cultivation during the Bronze Age, might have involved some degree of population movement, but we lack the evidence that such was the case.

One of the major problems in Korean archaeology is the lack of evidence for post-Pleistocene occupation of the peninsula until around 6000 BCE, which provided room for population replacement arguments such as those described above. The absence of Early Holocene evidence, however, can be explained by invoking a severe degree of erosion and poor preservation. It is also likely that the rising post-Pleistocene sea level submerged many coastal sites. However, a continuous human occupation of Korea may be supported by the discovery at Gosan-ri on Jeju (Cheju) Island, off the south coast, of pottery and chipped projectile points that resemble those of the Russian Maritime Region and northeast Japan, where they are dated to 13–12 kya. The Gosan-ri materials were found below a layer reliably dated to 4300 BCE. Given the location of the site and the distribution of sites with similar remains, we may be assured to find more evidence in the near future.

During the earlier phase of the Neolithic, prior to 3500 BCE, several culture zones are defined in Korea according to patterns in subsistence and pottery styles. Some features of these cultural zones also extended into neighboring regions. For example, the fish hooks and pottery decoration found along the eastern coast of Korea were shared by hunter-gatherers in the Russian Maritime Region, possibly as a result of interaction along the coastlines of the Sea of Japan. Along the south coast of Korea, sites produce obsidian, stone tools, and pottery, such as the Sobata and Todoroki pottery of the Early Jōmon period, that were brought to Korea from Kyushu. Such evidence is usually interpreted as a result of population movement on a limited scale.

Hints of cultural diffusion, exchange and/or population movement are more strongly felt during the later Neolithic period. For example, inland sites often contain marine shells, and evidence for incipient agriculture appeared rather suddenly during the later fourth millennium BCE. As there was no previous presence of crops such as common and foxtail millet in their wild forms, this is usually believed to reflect influence from northeast China. Once present, agriculture spread rather quickly throughout Korea. Thus, the possibility cannot be ruled out that the dispersal of crop cultivation might have been associated with population movement. However, given that it did not replace hunting and gathering but merely helped broaden the subsistence spectrum, such a possibility is unlikely. After all, the number and size of the sites suggests that the total population in Korea during the Neolithic would not have exceeded 10,000 at any time.

While the timing and mode of transition from Neolithic to Bronze Age remains an issue for debate, Neolithic pottery was replaced by new types during the latter half of the second millennium BCE. Termed "Coarse Ware" or "Mumun" pottery, its appearance is usually taken as the beginning of the Bronze Age. Increasingly, evidence suggests that the earliest Mumun pottery appeared between 1500 and 1200 BCE, either as an indigenous development or as a result of cultural diffusion possibly associated with population movement from northeast China. At the same time, several early pottery types found in central Korea are sometimes taken as evidence indicating a southerly movement of groups from the northwestern and northeastern regions of Korea (J. Kim 2008).

It is widely believed that certain kinds of bronze artifact, especially the so-called "*bipa*-shaped" daggers, named after the *bipa* musical instrument, and related items, originated in the Liao basin in northeast China, probably during the late second millennium BCE, and dispersed from there into Korea (Oh 2006). But their southward spread occurred mainly after the 7th century BCE, when they were buried in stone dolmen tombs and stone cists throughout Korea. If an increase in subsistence economic productivity was a prerequisite for the acceptance of metallurgy, the timing is not surprising as cultivation of rice was fully adopted in Korea by this time. Perhaps both rice cultivation and metallurgy were introduced into Korea as a technological package associated with some degree of population influx, a hypothesis yet to be supported by other evidence.

Also by this time, it seems that the Liao River served as a major cultural boundary for the western side of the Korean Bronze Age culture area in a broad sense. In modern geography, this area includes substantial parts of the Liaoning, Jilin, and Heilongjiang provinces of China, as well as the Korean peninsula itself. Throughout this large area, cultural attributes were widely shared in terms of archaeological assemblage composition and mortuary practices. It corresponded to the territories of a number of later polities and state-level societies in Korean history. It is believed that, somewhere between the Liaodong peninsula and the Amnok (Yalu) River, which is the current border between Korea and China, and during the earlier part of the first millennium BCE, the first state-level society of Gojoseon (or Kochosun) was established.

It was at this time, at the dawn of Korean history, that the foundation myths of the ancient kingdoms sometimes hint at the mystical arrival of foreign elites. Later, historical records occasionally suggest an infusion of different ethnic groups into the indigenous society following military and political turmoil. For example, about 1500 years later, the 15th-century records describe how Mongols and other non-ethnic Koreans residing in Korea were acculturated to form the lowermost social caste after the collapse of the Yuan empire in China.

Similar situations would have occurred frequently as ancient Koreans came to encounter the expanding Chinese world. The rise of Gojoseon ultimately led to clashes with Yan, one of the Chinese Warring States. A large section of Gojoseon territory was lost around 300 BCE when the Yan army invaded, led by a general named Qinkai. This should have resulted in the dislocation and relocation of many of the inhabitants who occupied what is currently the Liaodong region of China. Thus, more developed technologies of iron metallurgy and pottery manufacture, which had previously been unknown, appeared widely across both sides of the Amnok. The scale of acceptance perhaps reflected more than purely cultural diffusion alone.

In addition, the tremors from the upheavals in the north were soon transmitted to more southerly locales. Thus, it is believed that the dolmen-building Bronze Age societies of southern Korea, which had yet to become socially stratified, were quickly trans-formed into the hierarchically structured territorial groups of the Early Iron Age, which are symbolized by rich burials containing prestige goods (Lee 2004). The appearance of the new material cultural complex of the period may be attributed to the arrival of refugees from the north, as hinted by fragmentary written records. However, the lack of archaeological investigation for a large part of North Korea makes it difficult to conclude whether such movement actually took place. At the same time, there is little indication of population movement from across the Yellow Sea during the 1st millen-nium BCE, other than rare findings of Chinese-style bronze daggers. Thus, Sino-Korean interaction across the Yellow Sea appears to have been limited to much later periods, as indicated by coastal ceremonial and shipwreck sites.

Two hundred years after the Yan invasion, in 108 BCE, Emperor Wudi of the Western Han dynasty in China destroyed Gojoseon and established Chinese colonies across northwestern Korean and the Liaodong peninsula. The tremendous impact on the indigenous Korean societies is highly visible in mortuary practices and pottery manu-facture. Especially in the southeastern corner of the peninsula, rich burials resembling those of the northwestern region and completely new pottery types suddenly appeared. The occurrence of such a remarkable change might suggest the influx of populations from the north, which could have been a boosting factor for the formation of early states in the southern part of the peninsula. Meanwhile, the Chinese Han Dynasty Lelang colony in northwestern Korea lasted about 400 years, and it is likely that a substantial number of Chinese migrated into Korea at this time. Nevertheless, despite the accumulation of a tremendous amount of information since the 1980s, there is little evi-dence to suggest the arrival of a large number of people, and the Korean peninsula never adopted a Sinitic language.

On the contrary, while evidence is poor for late prehistoric movements of people into the peninsula, it is clear that people moved out of the Korean peninsula in some numbers during the latter part of the first millennium BCE. By this time, agricultural communities carrying out rice cultivation prospered in the southern part of Korea. Large centers with populations of up to several thousand appeared there, and hundreds of thousands of dolmens indicate this rapid population growth vis-à-vis the Neolithic period. With population growth, waves of people began to cross the Korean Strait to reach western Japan, especially Kyushu (chapters 27–28). Artifacts made in Bronze Age Korea are frequently found in sites dating from the late Jōmon to early Yayoi periods in western Japan. Skeletal remains found in Japan also testify to the arrival of immi-grants from Korea at that time. In this newly found environment, Korean settlers established farming villages with all the characteristics of the late Bronze Age culture of southern Korea. The same can be said for Jeju Island off the south coast of Korea.

In sum, the degree and intensity of population movement into the Korean peninsula appear to have increased during prehistory, especially as a result of population growth and military conflict in and against China. While there is little evidence to suggest large-scale movements of people into Korea, a substantial number of immigrants reached Japan from there during the late Bronze Age, contributing much to eventual processes of state formation.

SEE ALSO: 27 Eastern Asia and Japan: human biology; 28 Japan: archaeology

References and further reading

Barnes, G. (1996) *The Rise of Civilization in East Asia: The Archaeology of China, Korea and Japan*. London: Thames & Hudson.

Kim, J. (2008) Mumun togi sidae jogi seoljeongnon jaego [Reconsidering the incipient Mumun model]. *Journal of the Korean Archaeological Society* 68, 94–115.

Kim, W. (1986) *Hanguk Gogohak Gaeron* [Introduction to Korean archaeology], 3rd edn. Seoul: Iljisa.

Korean Archaeological Society (ed.) (2010) *Hanguk Gogohak Gangui* [Lectures in Korean archaeology], rev. edn. Seoul: Sahoe Pyeongnon.

Lee, H. (2004) Chogicheolgi sidae-Wonsamguk sidae jaeron [A reappraisal of the age systems for the period from the 3rd century BC to the 3rd century AD in Korean archaeology]. *Journal of the Korean Archaeological Society* 64, 69–94.

Nelson, S. (1993) *The Archaeology of Korea*. Cambridge: Cambridge University Press.

Oh, K. (2006) *Bipahyeong Cheongdonggi Munhwawa Yonyeong Jibangui Cheongdonggni Munhwa* [Bipa-shaped dagger culture and Bronze Age culture of Liaoning]. Seoul: Cheonggye.

Yi, S. (1991a) Sinseokgi-Cheongdonggi sidae jumin gyocheseolui bipanjeok geomto [A critical examination of the Neolithic-Bronze Age population replacement theory]. *Hanguk Kodaesa Nonchong* 1, 41–65.

Yi, S. (1991b) Minjok danhyeolseongronui geomto [On the so-called theory of ethnic continuity in North Korea]. In Korean Historical Society (ed.), *Bukhaneui Godaesa Yeongu* [Researches on ancient history in North Korea]. Seoul: Iljogak.

Yi, S. (1992) Bukhan gogohaksa siron [History of archaeology in North Korea – a preliminary review]. *Dongbanghakji* 74, 1–74.

Yi, S. (2003) Hangukinui giwon [The origin of Koreans]. In S. Yi, T. Noh, G. Lee, et al., *Hanguk Godaesa Jeilgwon – Hanguk Godaesa Yeongu Baeknyeon* [Lectures on the ancient history of Korea, vol. 1, One hundred years of research on the ancient history of Korea]. Seoul: Garakguk Sajeok Gaebal Yeonguwon.

Yi, S., Han, Y., Noh, H., & Park, S. (1996) *Hangukinui Giwongwa Hyeongseong* [*The origin and formation of Koreans*]. Seoul: Sohua.

30

South Asia: Dravidian linguistic history

Franklin C. Southworth and David W. McAlpin

The ancestral Dravidian languages, related to ancient Elamite of Iran, originated west of the Indus valley and probably spread through there into peninsular India during the 3rd millennium BCE, the period of the Indus Valley civilization. Relationships between the Dravidian and Indo-Aryan languages are also informative about Dravidian prehistory.

The Dravidian languages are spoken mainly in Peninsular India, with several smaller languages in central and northern India (Figure 30.1). The Tamil language is also spoken in Sri Lanka, Malaysia, and South Africa. Primary speakers of Dravidian languages in India are estimated at roughly 200 million (Krishnamurti 2003, 22–27). The four major Dravidian languages, each the official language of an Indian state, have substantial literary traditions, with inscriptions dating from the 1st century BCE for Tamil, 2nd century CE for Telugu, 450 CE for Kannada, and 9th century CE for Malayalam.

Proto-Dravidian or PD, one of the two subfamilies of Proto-Zagrosian (Figure 30.2), branches first into: (1) Proto-North Dravidian (PND), with two members, Kurux and Malto; and (2) Proto-Peninsular Dravidian (PPD), with four subgroups (Tamil-Tulu, Telugu, Gondi-Kui, Kolami-Parji). Here we focus mainly on the three primary groupings, PD, PND, and PPD.

Brahui, formerly believed to be a Dravidian language, has now been shown to be an Elamitic language, thus part of the proposed Zagrosian family which includes Elamitic and Dravidian (McAlpin, in prep.). Brahui was accepted as a Dravidian language for nearly a hundred years following the publication of Bray in 1909 (McAlpin 2003; see Krishnamurti 2003: 91 ff. for the earlier view). The current range of Brahui overlaps with its range in antiquity in southeastern Iran, but there is no evidence for its present location in the Brahui hills of Pakistan before the Baluch migrations around 1000 CE. Thus, it plays no direct role in the following discussion, although vocabulary shared

The Global Prehistory of Human Migration: The Encyclopedia of Global Human Migration Volume 1,
First Edition. Edited by Peter Bellwood.
© 2013 John Wiley & Sons, Ltd. Published 2015 by John Wiley & Sons, Ltd.

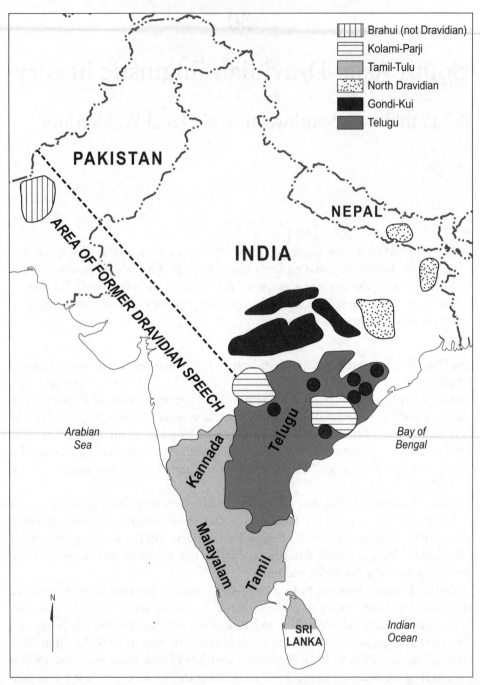

Figure 30.1 Map of the Dravidian languages in modern Pakistan and India. The names of the four literary languages are in bold. Map production by Education and Multimedia Services, College of Asia and the Pacific, The Australian National University.

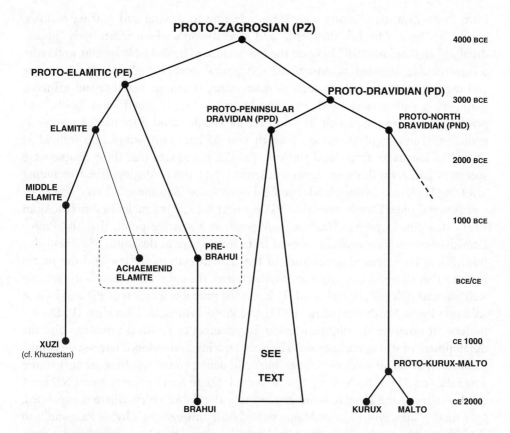

Figure 30.2 A family tree of the Elamite and Dravidian languages. The dating is approximate, and the dashed line around Achaemenid and Pre-Brahui indicates contact. The rightward branch from PND represents the source of Dravidian loanwords in Vedic Indo-Aryan (glossed as Indic in chapter 19).

between Brahui and Dravidian is relevant for reconstructing Proto-Dravidian and Proto-Zagrosian.

While the proposed Elamite–Dravidian connection has been widely known since the publication of McAlpin's 1981 book, it is now on a firmer footing (McAlpin, in prep.). As a result, much earlier work on Dravidian has been based on an erroneous view of the relationships. Even now, statements about Dravidian must include a warning that they may be modified in future, as more Elamo-Dravidian correspondences are identified.

Proto-Dravidian (PD)

The reconstructed vocabulary of PD reflects a society engaged in animal husbandry, with some knowledge of agriculture. Words for sheep, goat and cattle, all inherited from Proto-Zagrosian,[1] along with verbs referring to driving and grazing animals, words for "herd," "flock," "shepherd," and several words which mean both "house/dwelling" and "animal stall," indicate the importance of herding. No specific grains are reconstructible, although reconstructed agricultural terms include words for digging and digging tools, operations such as winnowing, churning, reaping, and grinding grain, along with several words meaning "grain" or "seed," "chaff" and "husk," and possibly a word for the plough. The only reconstructible food plant names are onion/garlic, yam, and eggplant, some of which may be later borrowings into individual Dravidian languages from local sources. Thus, it is unlikely that these people were sedentary farmers at this stage. Several different land types are distinguished, including low lying land, uncultivated land, and field/open space (Southworth 2009).

In general, older Elamite resembles PD, younger Elamite resembles Brahui (McAlpin 1981, McAlpin, in prep.). Thus we may posit, as a starting point, that the Proto-Dravidian community probably moved from somewhere in the south of present-day Iran. Places for extended agriculture in the Iranian plateau are few and the routes between them limited. Coming from southern Iran, the only viable route is the reliably well-watered valley of the Helmand. This was the probable location of PD and its first split into Proto-North Dravidian (PND) and Proto-Peninsular Dravidian (PPD). PD underwent extensive development, including changes to personal pronouns and the development of strong retroflexion. The early Dravidians developed large-scale animal husbandry, living off animals through milk and dairy products, with some agriculture when they could not trade. They spread towards South Asia by two routes. PND went up the valley of the Helmand and crossed into the Kabul valley, where it expanded. One small group, Proto-Kurux-Malto, passed early through the Khyber Pass and into the Indus valley, eventually reaching the Narbada valley. These languages show no signs of early interaction with other South Asian groups, keep a full set of uvulars and a conservative morphology. Malto later moved north to Bihar, and a small group of Kudux speakers were moved to southern Nepal around 1840.

PPD took the direct route through the Bolan Pass into the central Indus valley. As expected, there were massive borrowings for new plants and animals, but more significantly, there was a major phonological shift. All uvulars merged with velars and a new past tense formation in -*t*- was created. After an extended period of expansion and interaction, some continued from the Indus into the South Asian peninsula, probably in a series of movements. The movements in the Indus region involved a migration of pastoralists, perhaps growing grain when they could not trade for it.

Having presumably dispersed throughout the Indus valley, all surviving groups of PPD spread southeast through Gujarat and into the valley of the Tapti. Since the latitude of the Tapti is close to the southern limit for growing wheat, their traditional West Asian winter crops may have failed. Some of them, speaking what became Proto-Kolami-Parji, headed eastward up the Tapti where they encountered new crops. Others continued south through the savannah in the rain shadow east of the Western Ghats, abandoning traditional field agriculture, to become Proto-Tamil-Tulu. A few groups (Tulu and Koraga) may have moved separately down the west coast of India. Steadily expanding, Tamil-Tulu gradually filled up the western and southern parts of the peninsula and the northern part of Sri Lanka. Meanwhile, a second linguistic group, including Proto-Telugu along with Proto-Gondi-Kui, followed the Godavari to interpenetrate the earlier Kolami-Parji.

In the mid-2nd millennium BCE there arose in South India an archaeological complex known as the Southern Neolithic, first attested in several adjoining districts of Karnataka and Andhra Pradesh. From this core region, the complex spread rapidly in all directions until it occupied "a very vast area from the Krishna-Tungabhadra in the north . . . to the Kaveri in the south, and from the Krishna-Godavari mouths in the east to Dharwar in the west" (Sankalia 1974: 521). The area thus described lies entirely within the region now occupied by Dravidian languages. The crop plants identified in Phase II of the Southern Neolithic (2300–1800 BCE) match closely the plant names reconstructed by Southworth (2009) for a period he called "late Proto-Dravidian," which includes the language groups we have classed as subgroups of Proto-Peninsular Dravidian. Many of these crops are still grown in the area today. There is also evidence for the continuation of the activities of specialists in animal husbandry (Allchin 1963). Thus it appears likely that the farmers and herders of the Southern Neolithic were largely Dravidian-speaking, implying that the Dravidian languages were well established in South India by the mid-2nd millennium BCE, though other language groups may still have existed in the area.

In the light of our current understanding of the earlier movements of Dravidian, it is likely that the agricultural development of the Southern Neolithic resulted (in whole or in part) from interactions within PPD-speaking populations. In the authors' opinion, the two groups (ancestral Kolami-Parji and Telugu) of PPD abandoned wheat and barley and adopted new crops, including millets (Southworth 2009; Fuller 2009), creating a locally adapted set that powered population expansion for Telugu (with Gondi?) and for Tamil-Malayalam and Kannada. Thus, it would be a mistake to attribute the entire Southern Neolithic crop inventory to the proto-stage of PPD.

The evidence of Old Indo-Aryan (OIA)

The North Dravidian expansion brought them into contact with Indo-Iranians. Later PPD expansions from the south into the Panjab provided a second point of contact. Possible Dravidian borrowings into OIA, including the Rigvedic ritual language, have been seen by many scholars as evidence of a Dravidian presence in the Panjab during that period. These borrowings increased in frequency during the Rigvedic period, and continued with the eastward movement of the bearers of the Vedic tradition to the Kurukshetra area of Haryana in the late Vedic and post-Vedic periods. As this area contains no evidence of a prior Dravidian-speaking population, such as place names or river names, the sources of these borrowings must have been Dravidian-Indo-Aryan bilingual speakers who were connected to the larger Indo-Aryan-speaking community (Witzel 1999).

The influx of Dravidian, as well as Indo-Aryan-speaking peoples, into the Indus valley may have begun during the 3rd millennium BCE. This is based on archaeological considerations (see e. g. Bellwood 2009: 62–66), as well as the chronology of the polities associated with the Elamite language. Elam was a partner of Sumer in the development of urban civilization and writing. The so-called Proto-Elamite script from sites such as Susa in the lowlands of eastern Mesopotamia, dating from around 3000 BCE, is undeciphered and technically similar to the Harappan script. With a shift to a cuneiform script, Elamite became readable around 2300 BCE. From this time onwards, the two main Elamite centers were Susa itself, occupied in the Old Elamite and Middle Elamite phases between 2600 and 1000 BCE, and Anshan in the mountains near Persepolis (Achaemenid Elamite, 550–330 BCE) (Stolper 2004).

The small but gradually increasing flow of Dravidian loanwords into the Indo-Aryan religious literature and later secular writings must be explained by the slow integration of Dravidian-speaking groups into the wider Indo-Aryan-speaking society over successive generations, during which time Dravidian words passed into colloquial Indo-Aryan and thence gradually into the more conservative ritual and literary contexts.

A few examples of early loanwords must suffice here, as this material has been discussed in detail elsewhere (see Southworth, forthcoming, for an update of earlier work).[2] These and other cases show cognates in the Nuristani languages (situated in the mountains of eastern Afghanistan) and the Dardic languages (in adjoining areas of Pakistan and Jammu-Kashmir), giving these words a distributional profile within Indo-Aryan that is close to that of inherited Indo-European words like OIA *trayaḥ* "three", *bhrātṛ* "brother". Thus these borrowed Dravidian words probably entered the Indus Valley in the mouths of Indo-Aryan speakers who came from west of the Khyber Pass. A number of other words may have entered OIA by the same route, though they are not recorded until later (cf. e.g. Sanskrit *ēḍa* "kind of sheep" ← PD **yāṭu* ← PZ **hēṭu* "sheep, goat"). While Degener (2002) classed the Nuristani languages as an independent subgroup of the Indo-Iranian family, Blažek and Hegedus (2010) estimate that Nuristani and Dardic were both part of the Indo-Aryan branch of Proto-Indo-Iranian, and that they separated from Indo-Aryan at about 1900 and 1600 BCE respectively. Thus, these borrowings are probably earlier than the Vedic hymns.

Apart from Proto-Zagrosian as an ultimate source, Proto-North Dravidian figures as a likely source of the Rigvedic and other OIA borrowings, suggesting that the two main branches of Proto-Dravidian may have already separated from each other before reaching the Indus valley. A possible scenario which would explain these findings is that PND-speaking herders were present for at least several generations in an area near the route later taken by Indo-Iranian speakers moving into South Asia, and that the two groups subsequently had substantial contact, probably involving agricultural techniques. This mixed group, presumably with Indo-Aryan speakers in the majority, may have formed a significant portion of the population of the northern Indus Valley at the time the bearers of the Vedic ritual culture entered the region (for pre-Vedic Indo-Aryan speakers in South Asia see Parpola 1988, 2002).

Other evidence

Most of the Dravidian languages are now located in a monsoonal climatic zone very different from that in which they spent much of their early history. The large areas representing the major literary languages presumably result from expansions of earlier smaller language groups, expansions probably triggered in large part by the "agricultural revolution" which produced the Southern Neolithic. It may not be coincidental that the core area of the Southern Neolithic complex sits astride the boundary of two major PPD subgroups, Tamil-Tulu and Telugu.

Classical Tamil poetic conventions (c.100 CE) keep a recollection of this time. Of the five traditional "landscapes" of *akam* "interior" poetry, three reflect this period: mountainsides (hunter, gatherer, slash-and-burn fields), seashore (fishing), and pastoral (herding). A fourth, river agriculture (rice cultivation) is clearly later (and aesthetically undesirable!). The fifth is drought/desert. The implied context is one of intense economic exchange among the landscapes.

An important part of the background of the Southern Neolithic is the discontinuity in the names of crops, particularly grains, between Proto-Zagrosian and Proto-Peninsular Dravidian. The PPD word for rice (Tamil *(v)ar-i(-ci)*, Kannada *akki*), a widespread and culturally important crop in South India, is derived from a PZ word for "seed", which also retains that meaning in modern Dravidian languages (cf. Tamil *ēlav-arici*, Kannada *ēl-akki* "cardamom seed": DEDR,[3] 907). When Dravidian speakers today refer to wheat, they use a form borrowed from Sanskrit *godhūma*, for example Tamil *kōtume*, *gōtume*. The names of the staple grains of the Southern Neolithic and their modern replacements were borrowed from as yet unknown sources. Thus, it appears that Dravidian-speaking groups lost part of their agricultural knowledge at some period. The Southern Neolithic was a system that combined an older tradition of animal husbandry, including the well-known archaeological cattle pens (ash mounds; Allchin 1963), with a new package of crops, of which the staples were legumes and millets.

There is strong linguistic evidence for a former Dravidian-speaking presence in western India, in the area now occupied by the Indo-Aryan languages Marathi-Konkani, Gujarati, and possibly Sindhi (Southworth 2005: 317–318). This evidence includes lexical and structural borrowings from Dravidian into the Indo-Aryan languages of the area, as well as Dravidian place-name suffixes in Maharashtra and Gujarat. Dravidian-derived river names are also found in Maharashtra (Namboothiry 1987, cited in Witzel 1999: 64). The place-name suffixes and river names can be accounted for as borrowings from PPD at the earliest. Most of the Dravidian borrowings in post-Vedic OIA may well have come from this source, rather than from poorly documented Dravidian speakers in the upper Indus or Gangetic plains. On the other hand, this does not conflict with the suggestion of an earlier movement of Dravidian through this region, as suggested by Bellwood (2009).

In addition to this linguistic evidence, Trautmann (1981) has shown that features of "Dravidian" kinship systems, particularly cross-cousin marriage and compatible terminological categories, are found in the southern part of the present Indo-Aryan-speaking zone. The ancient South Asian historical tradition lists both Maharashtra and Gujarat among the "Dravidian" countries (Thapar 1975). The historian S. B. Joshi (1951) claims that southern Maharashtra was a Dravidian-speaking area as late as the 12th century CE (cited in Deshpande 1979: 102).

A number of archaeological sites in Maharashtra, belonging to the Malwa culture of the first half of the 2nd millennium BCE, were characterized by "pre-Chalcolithic

Neolithic elements" which can be linked to the Southern Neolithic (Allchin & Allchin 1982: 352; see also Bellwood 2009: 60–62). This would imply that the Dravidian presence in this area, which may have extended into the lower Indus valley (Sindh), was in place by the early 2nd millennium BCE at the latest.

The evidence of the Indus Valley writing system (Harappan script)

Over the years, scholars from many countries have attempted to decipher the Indus Valley seal inscriptions, but there is as yet no accepted interpretation of the script. A number of serious attempts to interpret the script as Dravidian have been made, notably by Parpola (1994). The Proto-Elamite script, given its greater age, technical similarity (shapes, number of signs, modifications, etc.), and that it was the closest writing system, was most probably the model for the Indus Valley script. Since we can read neither, this tells us little. Given the significant impact that the Indus region had on PPD and the probable time periods involved, PPD probably played some role in the Indus Valley civilization. But what role? Administrators, priests, or peripheral pastoralists? The hypothesis that the script is Dravidian, while reasonable, remains a hypothesis. Barring major discoveries, this is not likely to change.

Recently, several scholars have questioned whether the script was even a representation of language in any sense, since the brevity of the inscriptions and the frequencies of the signs do not correspond to those of any other known script (Farmer et al. 2005). However, this suggestion has also not been generally accepted (Kenoyer 2009; Parpola 2010).

Apart from the identity of the script, the question whether Dravidian was a dominant language of the Indus Valley civilization has yet to be answered. The paucity of Dravidian loanwords in the earliest Vedic, along with the presence of numerous loanwords from other languages, has been noted by Witzel (1999) as an argument against such domination. However, this may only mean that contact between Dravidian speakers and the bearers of the Vedic tradition was, at least in the early period, mediated by other language groups. Further work on Dravidian borrowings in OIA may possibly throw light on this question (see Southworth forthcoming).

SEE ALSO: 19 Europe and western Asia: Indo-European linguistic history; 31 South Asia: archaeology

Notes

1   PZ *aš "cow"; AE aš "cow, herd", PD *ā(y) "cow" DEDR 334, Br. xar-ās "bull" DEDR 1123 (compounded with xar "male animal?"); PZ *hēṭu "sheep, goat," El. hidu "sheep, goat," Br. hēṭ "she-goat," PD *yāṭu "sheep, goat" DEDR 5152–borrowed into Sanskrit as ēḍa "a kind of sheep"; see Turner (1966), entry 2152.

2   Three examples can be given, as follows.

    (1)   Proto-Zagrosian (PZ) *kōlum "grain" (PE *ǩōlum, El. šulum "standing grain," Br. xōlum "wheat"; PD *kōlum, PPD *kōl-am, Tamil *kūlam "grain" [generic term] DEDR 1906)

is a likely source of Rigvedic *godhūma* "wheat," probably first borrowed into colloquial Indo-Aryan as **kōlum/gōlum* and later Aryanized folk-etymologically; see Witzel (1999: 29) for a different view, and Southworth (forthcoming) for additional detail).

(2) PZ **qal* "field" (PE **xal*, El. *hal* "land," *hal-at* "clay"; PD **qal* "field," PND **qˣal* "field," Kx. *xall* "field", Mt. *qalu* "field on the hills"; PD **kaḷ-am/an* "threshing ground") is the probable source of late Rigvedic *khala* "threshing floor" (but cf. Witzel 1999: 17). Note that PND **qˣal* is the most direct source for OIA *khala*.

(3) PND **qaṭ-q-V* "bitter" DEDR 1135 (Br. *xar-en* "bitter" ← PZ **qaṭ-*) is the probable source of Rigvedic *kaṭuka* "pungent, bitter," while PPD **kaṭu* is probably the source of a later borrowing, Classical Sanskrit *kaṭu* "bitter" (Kuiper 1991: 29).

3   *A Dravidian Etymological Dictionary.* For publication details see Burrow & Emeneau (1984) in the references list.

References

Allchin, B. & Allchin, F. R. (1982) *The Rise of Civilization in India and Pakistan.* Cambridge: Cambridge University Press.

Allchin, F. R. (1963) *Neolithic Cattle-Keepers of South India: A Study of the Deccan Ashmounds.* Cambridge: Cambridge University Press.

Bellwood, P. (2009) Early farmers: issues of spread and migration with respect to the Indian subcontinent. In T. Osada (2009) pp. 55–70.

Blažek, V. & Hegedus. I. (2010) On the position of Nuristani within Indo-Iranian. Paper presented at the Sound of Indo-European 2 Conference in Opava, Czech Republic, Nov. 2010.

Bray, D. (1909) *The Brahui Language. Part I, Introduction and Grammar.* Calcutta: Superintendent of Government Printing.

Burrow, T. & Emeneau, M. B. (1984) *A Dravidian Etymological Dictionary* (DEDR), 2nd edn. Oxford: Clarendon.

Degener, A. (2002) The Nuristani Languages. In N. Sims-Williams (ed.), *Indo-Iranian Languages and Peoples.* London: British Academy.

Deshpande, M. (1979) *Sociolinguistic Attitudes in India: An Historical Reconstruction.* Ann Arbor: Karoma.

Farmer, S., Sproat, R., & Witzel, M. (2005) The collapse of the Indus-Script thesis: the myth of a literate Harappan civilization. *Electronic Journal of Vedic Studies* 11(2) (Dec. 13).

Fuller, D. (2009) Silence before sedentism and the advent of cash crops. In Osada (2009), pp. 147–190.

Joshi, S. B. (1951) Etymology of place-names paṭṭi-haṭṭi, some observations on the history of Maharashtra and Karnataka. *Annals of the Bhandarkar Oriental Research Institute* 32, 41–56.

Kenoyer, J. M. (2009) The origin, context and function of the Indus script: recent insights from Harappa. In Osada (2009), pp. 13–32.

Krishnamurti, B. (2003) *The Dravidian Languages: A Comparative, Historical and Typological Study.* Cambridge: Cambridge University Press.

Kuiper, F. (1991) *Aryans in the Rigveda.* Amsterdam: Rodopi.

McAlpin, D. W. (1981) *Proto-Elamo-Dravidian: The Evidence and its Implications.* Philadelphia: American Philosophical Society.

McAlpin, D. (2003) Velars, uvulars, and the North Dravidian hypothesis. *Journal of the American Oriental Society* 123(3), 521–546.

McAlpin, D. (in prep.) Modern colloquial eastern Elamite. Unpublished MS in preparation.

Namboothiry, M. N. (1987) Indian Toponymy: a critical evaluation of the work done in this field in India with a bibliography. *Puthusseri Ramachandran* 1987, 1–47.

Osada, T. (ed.) (2009) *Linguistics, Archaeology and Human Past in South Asia*. Delhi: Manohar.

Parpola, A. (1988) The coming of the Aryans to Iran and India and the cultural and ethnic identity of the Dāsas. *Studia Orientalia* 64, 195–302.

Parpola, A. (1994) *Deciphering the Indus script*. Cambridge: Cambridge University Press.

Parpola, A. (2002) From the dialects of Old Indo-Aryan to Proto-Indo-Aryan and Proto-Indo-Iranian. In N. Sims-Williams (ed.), *Indo-Iranian Languages and Peoples*. London: British Academy, pp. 43–102.

Parpola, A. (2010) A Dravidian solution to the Indus script problem. *Kalaignar M. Karunanidhi Classical Tamil Research Endowment Lecture, World Classical Tamil Conference, Coimbatore, June 25, 2010*. Chennai: Central Institute of Classical Tamil.

Sankalia, H. D. (1974) *Prehistory and Protohistory of India and Pakistan*. Poona: Deccan College Postgraduate and Research Institute.

Southworth, F. C. (2005) *Linguistic Archaeology of South Asia*. London: Routledge/Curzon.

Southworth, F. C. (2009) Proto-Dravidian Agriculture. In Osada (2009), pp. 101–26.

Southworth, F. C. (forthcoming) Notes on the SARVA CDIAL-DEDR files. To appear on the SARVA (South Asian Residual Vocabulary Assemblage) At www.aa.tufs.ac.jp/sarva/.

Stolper, M. (2004) Elamite. In R. D. Woodward (ed.), *World's Ancient Languages*. Cambridge: Cambridge University Press, pp. 60–94.

Trautmann, T. (1981) *Dravidian Kinship*. Cambridge: Cambridge University Press.

Thapar, R. (1975) Puranic lineages and archaeological cultures. *Puratattva* 8, 86–98. Reprinted in R. Thapar, *Ancient Indian Social History: Some Interpetations*. New Delhi: Orient Longman (1978).

Witzel, M. (1999) Substrate languages in Old Indo-Aryan. *Electronic Journal of Vedic Studies* 5, 1–67.

31

South Asia: archaeology

Dorian Q. Fuller

The archaeology of South Asia indicates a spread of agriculture from the northwest, early in the Holocene, together with internal developments of plant domestication in the Deccan and the Ganges plain. These developments related closely with the spreads of the Indo-European, Dravidian, and Austroasiatic language families in South Asia.

The Indian subcontinent has consistently supported relatively high population densities in comparison to adjacent regions like the Iranian plateau, central Asia, and the Tibetan plateau. This is indicated in part by the persistence in some modern South Asian populations of the oldest non-African haploid genetic lineages in Eurasia (Endicott et al. 2007). The northeastern region of the Indo-Burma borderlands, with its densely forested hills, has posed something of a long-term barrier between South and East Asia, as indicated by the fact that the region boasts one of the major fracture lines in modern human mtDNA haplogroups (Metspalu et al. 2004). During drier glacial climates there was a postulated savannah corridor from here into and through Southeast Asia, but in wetter interglacial periods, such as the current Holocene, this region would act more as a barrier, except to more recent Austroasiatic-speaking groups with shifting agriculture. There was rather more opportunity for migration into and out of South Asia from the northwest, especially in the Early Holocene, when richer vegetation favored the Iranian plateau and Afghanistan, or when groups could take advantage of the drier steppe through pastoral adaptations. Such groups would have included the ancestral Indo-Iranian-speaking peoples, whose languages today dominate northern South Asia, although much crop-, tree-, and place-name vocabulary in the Indo-Aryan languages reveals a large influence of an earlier agricultural substratum attributed to a now extinct series of languages (Southworth 2006; Fuller 2007; and see chapter 30).

Two major sets of factors can be suggested to have constrained and driven demography and population movement within South Asia: variable carrying capacities in different environments, and a shifting of carrying capacity upwards with improving subsistence technologies, most notably agriculture. Thus, a first set of factors in migra-tion from the last years of the Pleistocene through the Early Holocene is likely to have been driven by shifting vegetation zones. In periods such as the Last Glacial Maximum (24–18 kya) and the Younger Dryas (13–11.5 kya), when deserts expanded in north-western South Asia, populations were pushed into tropical India from regions like the Iranian plateau. Wetter eras allowed the reverse. Unfortunately, the archaeology of these pre-Neolithic periods remains poorly resolved.

In recent years, archaeological research combined with better botanical documenta-tion of wild crop progenitors in South Asia has provided a basis for postulating several regional foci of domestication. These were mainly on savannah-woodland ecotones, including the South Deccan, Gujarat, and the western Himalayan foothills, as well as the Ganges basin (see Figure 31.1). Local domestication events were combined with agricultural dispersals in an interconnected mosaic of cultivation, pastoralism, and sedentism (Fuller 2006; 2011). Current evidence is clearest for the emergence of sed-entary village societies which were invariably already dependent on cultivation, and usually had domesticated crops and livestock. In several regions, especially the South Deccan, Gujarat, and the Ganges plains, the beginnings of food production occurred amongst seasonally mobile societies which are hard to identify archaeologically. So perhaps there were two kinds of demographic transition, one from foraging to shifting cultivation, and another to sedentary agriculture (Kingwell-Banham & Fuller 2012). Those with sedentary agricultural economies would have had clear demographic advantages over those practicing less developed economic systems since they would produce more food per unit of land and require less territory.

The introduction of food production in the northwest

The earliest food production in the subcontinent developed in Baluchistan, and prob-ably involved migration from further west. Excavations at the site of Mehrgarh (Jarrige 2008) have uncovered a mud brick village occupied c.7000 BCE by Pre-Pottery Neo-lithic farmers. The domesticated species present (wheats, barley, sheep, goat), the style of architecture, and the baked clay female figurines all point towards an origin across the Iranian plateau, in the "Fertile Crescent." Thus, an Early Holocene migration of agro-pastoralists across the then lightly populated but still relatively lush Iranian plateau is likely (Figure 31.1 (a)). There were, nevertheless, local processes contributing to the diversification and "Indianization" of the Neolithic economy in Pakistan, includ-ing the domestication of local *zebu* cattle (Meadow & Patel 2003; Chen et al 2010), possible additional sheep taming, and domestication of tree cotton (*Gossypium arboreum*). Data from later ceramic Neolithic sites in the Bannu Basin c.4500 BCE (Petrie et al. 2010), and especially from the extensively studied sites of the Harappan civilization (2600–1900 BCE), indicate that agriculture in the Greater Indus region was based on largely on a non-indigenous Near Eastern crop package, including cereals derived from the initial Neolithic migration, and pulses, flax, and safflower that may have arrived later. Genetic evidence suggests that lentils did not come directly from the Fertile Crescent, but underwent successive bottlenecks and adaptations in

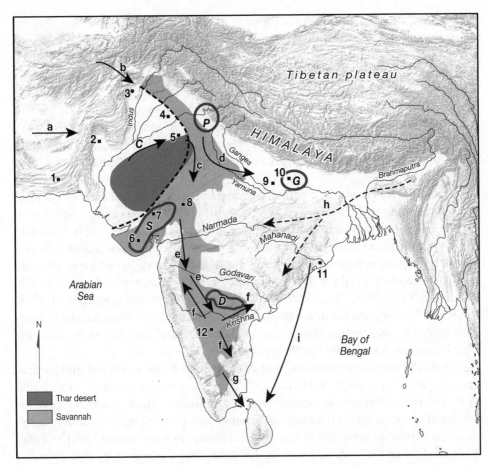

Figure 31.1 Map of South Asia indicating mountain areas, the Thar Desert (stippled) and the savannah area (grey). Important centers of local plant domestications are outlined and designated by letters: greater Saurashtra (S), upper Punjab (P), middle Ganges (G), southern Deccan (D). Major postulated migrational pathways are indicated, including (a) pre-pottery Neolithic migration >7000 BCE, (b) secondary Neolithic migration with lentils 4500-4000 BCE, (c) pre-Harappan migrations through Indus system and east of Thar ca. 3500 BCE, (d) Indus farmer migrations to the Ganges 2500-1500 BCE, (e) savannah pastoralist-forager migrations 3500-2500 BCE [=early Dravidians], (f) Deccan Neolithic agricultural expansions 2500-1200 BCE [=later early Dravidians], (g) Southern millet farmer expansions 1000-1 BCE [=Southern Dravidians], (h) tropical hill cultivators [=Munda groups], (I) rice agriculturalist migration 1000-1 BCE [=pre-Sinhalese]. Selected archaeological sites/site groups are numbered: 1. Miri Qalat, 2. Mehrgarh, 3. Bannu, 4. Harappa, 5. Kalibangan, 6. Rojdi, 7. Loteshwar, 8. Balathal, 9. Damdama, 10. Lahuradewa, 11. Golbai Sassan, 12. Sanganakallu. Map production by Education and Multimedia Services, College of Asia and the Pacific, The Australian National University.

Afghanistan, Pakistan, and India (Erskine et al. 2011). Indeed, all the Near Eastern legumes are so far absent from Mehrgarh, with the earliest being lentils from c.4000 BCE at Miri Qalat (Makran). Other pulses (pea, grasspea, and chickpea) date even later. This evidence for an arrival of additional crops from the Near East, together with a suggested break at c.4500 BCE in the skeletal morphology of populations buried at or around Mehrgarh (Hemphill et al. 1991), is congruent with a second wave of migration from the northwest in the late Neolithic or emergent Bronze Age (Figure 31.1 (b)). Nevertheless, continuity in site locations and material culture suggest integration rather than replacement, and there was an inferred higher birth rate at this time (Wright 2010: 102).

From this period onwards, continuing demographic expansion at Mehrgarh and an increasing number of sites in western Pakistan is evident, indicating migration of agricultural populations into the Indus valley and up its tributaries. Early Harappan sites were widespread through most the Indus system by c.3000 BCE and provide evidence for intensive agriculture using cattle-drawn ards (scratch ploughs without mold boards), secondary products like milk, and probably domesticated water buffalo (Madella & Fuller 2006; Wright 2010: 102). This period saw the expansion of wheat and barley farming into the upper plains of the Sutlej, Ravi, and Ghaggar-Hakra rivers (represented by sites such as Harappa and Kalibangan), and into Rajasthan east of the Thar Desert (represented by Balathal) (Figure 31.1 (c)).

Despite the precocious establishment of agriculture in the northwest and its clear demographic advantages, it was hampered in spreading further east into "inner India" by the change from winter to summer rainfall distribution. The first occurrence of the northwestern crops east of the monsoon frontier took place alongside plausibly indigenous domesticates, especially in the western Himalayan foothills and Gujarat (Fuller 2006; 2011). Further east, in Uttar Pradesh, the Near Eastern crops first appeared alongside rice, which had presumed local Gangetic precursors. Thus, while there may have been some migration from the Indus alluvium into the Ganges, suggested also by material culture in the Harappan era and later (2500–1500 BCE), this would have involved integration with some pre-existing but perhaps more seasonally mobile food producers on the Ganges plains themselves (Figure 31.1 (d)).

Although later migrations from the northwest into South Asia probably occurred, they are unlikely to have been as significant demographically as those of the earlier pre-Harappan/Harappan agricultural populations. While migrations from central Asia in the Late Harappan period after 2000 BCE are often postulated to account for advent of Indo-Aryan languages in South Asia, there are no clear archaeological correlates for such a major migration, nor is there any clear identification of a source culture in central Asia (Lamberg-Karlovsky 2002; Salvatori 2003). Instead, mounting evidence indicates a growing long-distance trade network at this time, a "Middle Asian Interaction Sphere," stretching from Oman to Tajikistan and beyond (Potts 2008). While this was established in the late 3rd millennium BCE, during the Mature Harappan phase, it continued after the decline of the Indus cities, when there is growing evidence for elite material cultural influences flowing into northern and western Pakistan from central Asia. During this era, long-distance movement of crops occurred from central Asia to China, from China to Pakistan and Arabia, and from Africa to India. There is also evidence for the growing importance at this time of revolutionary forms of transport, using horses and Bactrian camels. In this context, migrations that were demographically small but culturally significant might be postulated. Some post-Harappan eastward migration into the Gangetic plains is also implied by the decrease in Indus settlement density and a corresponding increase in smaller villages in the eastern monsoonal zones (Madella & Fuller 2006).

The savanna complexes of western and southern India

The wetter conditions of the Early and Middle Holocene increased the rich tropical deciduous woodlands of peninsular and central India, and promoted the expansion of grassland into the Thar desert. This encouraged increased Mesolithic settlement density in the Thar, as well as movement westwards into Makran from the microlithic traditions of inner India. While those living west of the Thar would have been subsumed into the Neolithic tradition that arrived at Mehrgarh, those living to the east and south became increasingly concentrated as the desert began to re-expand from c.4000 BCE. In this period, Mesolithic sites became frequent in northern Gujarat and Rajasthan, and cultural innovations, including ceramics and the adoption of livestock, occurred by 3500 BCE, for example at Loteshwar (Patel 2009). A savannah corridor now stretched from the grasslands east of the Thar through the center of the peninsula to south India, and livestock may have been adopted here initially to buffer risk and express social wealth. They became increasing important as an adaptation to the grassland and woodland mosaic of mid-Holocene peninsular India. It is most likely in this context that early Dravidian speakers expanded into India (Figure 31.1 (e)) with the adopted innovations of pastoralism and ceramics (Fuller 2007; and see chapter 30). It was along the ecotone between the savannas and deciduous woodlands, perhaps 3500–3000 BCE, that cultivation of indigenous millets and pulses began with suggested foci in Saurashtra (Padri/Anarta cultural tradition) and southern India (Ashmound Neolithic tradition) (Fuller 2006, 2011).

There is no compelling evidence for sedentism associated with the earliest savannah agriculture in India. Instead, sites are few, and those known are plausibly seasonal. In part this was due to transhumance associated with animal herds, but it might also reflect simple shifting forms of cultivation. During this phase these food-producing traditions are likely to have spread within Gujarat and the southern Deccan. As populations increased, sedentism and fixed field agriculture emerged in both regions, certainly by 2500 BCE in Gujarat, when the region entered the Harappan orbit (represented by Rojdi), and from c.2000 BCE in South India, for example at Sanganakallu. In this period, 2000–1500 BCE, there was an emergence and proliferation of Chalcolithic village settlements along the northern rivers of the Deccan peninsula. Subsistence combined native domesticates of Gujarat and South India as well as winter crops from the Indus valley. It is tempting to posit migrations into this area from the northwest as well as the south (Figure 31.1 (f)), and ceramic influences can be found from both directions (Fuller 2005). The period from 1500 BCE saw major demographic growth in the peninsula, including the spread of Neolithic settlement southwards into Karnataka and northern Tamil Nadu. The first agricultural migrations into the wet forests of the Western Ghats took place at this time, as shifting cultivators moved into these more marginal lands (Kingwell-Banham & Fuller 2012).

The end of the 2nd millennium BCE was marked by a major cultural and demographic transition, which saw the abandonment of most agricultural villages and the emergence of a new elite culture represented in the "megalithic" burials of the Iron Age. While a general continuity of population from the Late Neolithic (Chalcolithic) into the Iron Age is posited for the South Deccan (Boivin et al. 2008), this is less clear in the north where abandoned Chalcolithic villages became the norm in western Maharashtra. New megalithic cemeteries and settlements then focused on eastern Maharashtra (Mohanty & Selvakumar 2001). It is clear that "warrior" values were shared by the elites throughout much of the peninsular region, whereas processes of migration are harder to pin down. This period probably saw the expansion of agro-pastoral populations into the far south (Tamil Nadu, Kerala, parts of Sri Lanka), including migration as well as incorporation of hunter-gatherers (Figure 31.1 (g)).

Rice gatherers turned farmers of the Ganges and the east

On the great floodplain system of the Ganges and its tributaries, agriculture developed slowly from an exploitation of "proto-*indica*" rice cultivars or their wild precursors (Fuller & Qin 2009). So far, only one site provides well-dated evidence for such Early Holocene precursors. Lahuradewa in eastern Uttar Pradesh is situated today on an oxbow pond of a former Ganges tributary. The site may have been occupied as early as 9000 BCE, and certainly by the 7th millennium BCE, and it provides evidence for the earliest ceramics recovered so far in South Asia (Tewari et al. 2008). While the excavations suggest domesticated rice agriculture from the lowest levels (thus begging the questions of where and when rice was domesticated), an alternative interpretation of these finds is that they represent wild rice that was managed without being domesticated (Fuller & Qin 2009; Fuller 2011). Living structures at early Lahuradewa are unclear, and seasonal movement seems likely.

Elsewhere in the Ganges plain, aceramic Mesolithic hunter-gatherers persisted throughout the Early and Middle Holocene, similarly focused on oxbow ponds and smaller tributaries such as Damdama, where Mesolithic burials indicate tall and robust populations different from modern people in the region (Stock et al. 2007; Lukacs 2007). This suggests that at least some of the Early Holocene populations of the Ganges were replaced by internal expansion of proto-*indica* rice-cultivator populations from c.2500 BCE onwards, and by external immigrants during subsequent centuries. After the period of rice-cultivator expansion and/or internal demographic growth, sedentary villages appeared and became increasingly common after 2000 BCE. There was cultural continuity into the subsequent Chalcolithic and Iron Age as sites continued to increase in size and number. One of the contributing factors in this was an intensification of rice agriculture as cultivation developed, by 1000 BCE, from simple rain-fed and floodplain cultivation to irrigated paddy fields (Fuller & Qin 2009; Fuller et al. 2010). This demographic expansion and the subsequent archaeological continuity suggest strongly that "inner" Indo-Aryan language speakers were already in place, as this technological revolution occurred from the mid-2nd millennium BCE.

In eastern India, long-lasting settlement mounds and increasing site numbers indicate demographic growth in the plains of coastal Orissa and along eastward-flowing rivers like the Mahanadi. Such established village societies on the coastal plains around Chilka Lake date to the Late Neolithic or Chalcolithic, 1500–1000 BCE, and have provided evidence for agriculture focused on rice, perhaps of Ganges origin, and pulse crops likely introduced from peninsular India (Harvey et al. 2006). Similar assemblages of bone tools reported from Golbai Sassan in Orissa and the lower Ganges site of Chirand could indicate migration between these regions, but limited dating evidence masks any directionality. The subsequent development of more intensive wet rice agriculture at 1000 BCE or thereafter was associated with local population growth, which culminated in early historic urbanism by 300 BCE.

The presence of shouldered stone axes in northeastern India suggests some cultural links with mainland Southeast Asia. Most substantial in the hills, it has been speculated that these eastward links could have reflected the spread of Austroasiatic speakers practicing slash-and-burn cultivation of tubers and upland rice, especially into the Orissa uplands (Figure 31.1 (h)), while lowland sedentary rice farmers colonized the Ganges basin and the central Indian plains. However, the persistence of pockets of North Dravidian- and South-Central Dravidian-speaking tribes in the hills of Jharkhand, western Orissa, and Chattisgarh, as well as shared loan words between the Munda languages (which dominate these same hill zones) and Dravidian, may be indicative of some early migration from the southern peninsula (Fuller 2007).

The intensification of rice production: the last agricultural migrations?

It is only during the Iron Age that rice cultivation became more widely established through South India and was introduced to Sri Lanka. In the latter island (Coningham & Allchin 1995; Deriyanalaga 2007) and Tamil Nadu the first rice cultivation seems to have been associated with the construction of large irrigation tanks and the emergence of hierarchical and sedentary societies. The emergences of interregional trade, social hierarchy, and the availability of rice might all have played roles in any local switch from foraging to agriculture, but a role for migration of rice farmers from more northerly areas also deserves consideration. In these far southern areas the later Iron Age, with its early complex societies, seems to have rapidly become involved in routine long-distance trade in spices that derived from interior rainforests occupied by hunter-gatherers. This provided an unusual trajectory in social evolution, in which some hunter-gatherers or early pastoralists became sedentary farmers and traders, while other foragers became specialist gatherer-traders (see Morrison 2002). In South India, with its indigenous traditions of pastoralism and monsoon millet-pulse cultivation, intensive rice agriculture was probably primarily an adoption linked to subsequent internal migration, perhaps associated with the South Dravidian ancestors of the Old Tamil and Malayalam languages (see chapter 30). On the other hand, in Sri Lanka, where food producers were fewer and foragers more numerous, some migration of northern rice cultivators seems likely to have brought the ancestors of the Indo-Aryan Sinhalese speakers (Figure 31.1 (i)). As available textual evidence indicates, most regional populations of India, with early forms of their regional languages, were in place by the start of the Early Historic period at 300 BCE, and this in turn suggests that the migrations of wet rice farmers in the Iron Age were the last significant agriculturist migrations within South Asia.

SEE ALSO: 30 South Asia: Dravidian linguistic history

References

Boivin, N., Fuller, D. Q., Korisettar, R., et al. (2008) First farmers in South India: the role of internal processes and external influences in the emergence and transformations of south India's earliest settled societies. *Pragdhara* 18, 179–200.

Chen, S., Lin, B-Z., Baig, M., et al. (2010) Zebu are the exclusive legacy of the South Asian Neolithic. *Molecular Biology and Evolution* 27, 1–6.

Coninghan, R. & Allchin, F. R. (1995) The rise of cities in Sri Lanka. In F. R. Allchin (ed.), *The Archaeology of Early Historic South Asia*. Cambridge: Cambridge University Press, pp. 152–183.

Deriyanalaga, S. (2007) The prehistory and protohistory of Sri Lanka. In L. Premathilleke, S. Bandaranayake, S. Deraniyagala, & R. Silva (eds.), *The Art and Archaeology of Sri Lanka I*. Colombo: Central Cultural Fund Publications, pp. 1–96.

Endicott, P., Metspalu, M., & Kivisild, T. (2007) Genetic evidence on modern human dispersals in South Asia. In Petraglia & Allchin (2007), pp. 229–244.

Erskine, W., Sarkar, A., & Ashraf, M. (2011) Reconstructing an ancient bottleneck of the movement of the lentil (*Lens culinaris* ssp. *culinaris*) into South Asia. *Genetic Resources and Crop Evolution* 58(3), 373–381.

Fuller, D. Q. (2005) Ceramics, seeds and culinary change in prehistoric India. *Antiquity* 79, 761–777.

Fuller, D. Q. (2006) Agricultural origins and frontiers in South Asia: a working synthesis. *Journal of World Prehistory* 20(1), 1–86.

Fuller, D. Q. (2007) Non-human genetics, agricultural origins and historical linguistics. In Petraglia & Allchin (2007), pp. 389–439.

Fuller, D. Q. (2011) Finding plant domestication in the Indian subcontinent. *Current Anthropology* 52(S4), S347–S362

Fuller, D. Q, & Qin, L. (2009) Water management and labour in the origins and dispersal of Asian rice. *World Archaeology* 41(1), 88–111.

Fuller, D. Q, Sato, Y., Castillo, C., et al. (2010). Consilience of genetics and archaeobotany in the entangled history of rice. *Archaeological and Anthropological Sciences* 2(2), 115–131.

Harvey, E., Fuller, D. Q., Basa, K. K., et al. (2006) Early agriculture in Orissa: some archaeobotanical results and field observations on the Neolithic. *Man and Environment* 31, 21–32.

Hemphill, B. E., Lukacs, J. R., & Kennedy, K. (1991) Biological adaptations and affinities of Bronze Age Harappans. In R. H. Meadow (ed.), *Harappan Excavation 1986-1990: A Multidisciplinary Approach to Third Millennium Urbanism*. Madison: Prehistory Press, pp. 137–182.

Jarrige, J.-F. (2008). Mehrgarh Neolithic. *Pragdhara* 18, 135–154.

Kingwell-Banham, E. & Fuller, D. Q. (2012) Shifting cultivators in South Asia: expansion, marginilization and specialization over the long-term. *Quaternary International* 249, 84–95.

Lamberg-Karlovsky, C. C. (2002) Archaeology and language. The Indo-Iranians. *Current Anthropology* 43, 63–88.

Lukacs, J. R. (2007) Interpreting biological diversity in South Asian prehistory: Early Holocene population affinities and subsistence adaptations. In Petraglia & Allchin (2007), pp. 271–296.

Madella, M. & Fuller, D. Q (2006) Palaeoecology and the Harappan Civilisation of South Asia: a reconsideration. *Quaternary Science Reviews* 25, 1283–1301.

Meadow, R. & Patel, A. K. (2003) Prehistoric pastoralism in northwestern South Asia from the Neolithic through the Harappan Period. In S. A. Weber & W. R. Belcher (eds.), *Indus Ethnobiology. New Perspectives from the Field*. Lanham: Lexington Books, pp. 65–94.

Metspalu, M., Kivisild, T., Metspalu, E., et al. (2004) Most of the extant mtDNA boundaries in South and Southwest Asia were likely shaped during initial settlements of Eurasia by anatomically modern humans. *BMC Genetics* 5, 26.

Mohanty, R. K. & Selvakumar, V. (2001) The archaeology of the megalithis in India: 1947–1997. In S. Settar & R. Korisettar (eds.), *Indian Archaeology in Retrospect*, vol. 1, *Prehistory*. New Delhi: Manohar, pp. 313–351.

Morrison, K. D. (2002) Pepper in the hills: upland–lowland exchange and the intensification of the spice trade. In K. D. Morrison & L. L. Junker (eds), *Forager-Traders in South and Southeast Asia*. Cambridge: Cambridge University Press, pp. 105–128.

Patel, A. K. (2009) Occupational histories, settlements, and subsistence in Western India: what bones can tell us about the origins and spread of pastoralism. *Anthropozoologica* 44(1), 173–188.

Petraglia, M. & Allchin B. (eds.) (2007), *The Evolution and History of Human Populations in South Asia*. Dordrecht: Springer.

Petrie, C., Knox, R., Khan, F., et al. (2010) Ceramic vessels from Sheri Khan Tarakai. In F. Khan, R. Know, K. Thomas, et al. (eds.), *Sheri Khan Tarakai and Early Village Life in the Borderlands of North-west Pakistan*. Oxford: Oxbow Books, pp. 71–194.

Potts, D. (2008) An Umm an-Nar-type compartmented soft-stone vessel from Gonur Depe, Turkmenistan. *Arabian Archaeology and Epigraphy* 19, 168–181.

Salvatori, S. (2003) Pots and peoples: the "Pandora's jar" of Central Asia archaeological research. *Revista di Archeologia* 27, 5–20.

Southworth, F. (2006) New light on three South Asian language families. *Mother Tongue* XI, 124–159.

Stock, J. T., Lahr, M. M., & Kutatilake, S. (2007) Cranial diversity in South Asia relative to modern human dispersals and global patterns of human variation. In Petraglia & Allchin (2007), pp. 245–268.

Tewari, R., Srivastava, R. K., Saraswat, K. S., et al. (2008) Early farming at Lahuradewa. *Pragdhar* 18: 347–373.

Wright, R. P. (2010) *The Ancient Indus. Urbanism, Economy, and Society*. Cambridge: Cambridge University Press.

32

Trans-Indian Ocean migration

Atholl Anderson

The Indian Ocean played an important role in contacts between Africa and Indonesia, including migration to Madagascar. Evidence for fully prehistoric migration directly across the ocean remains slight, and most such sailings appear to be confined to the past 2000 years.

In the prehistory of the Indian Ocean one of the more debated themes is whether, or to what extent, Southeast Asian seafarers made passages to and from Africa by direct voyaging across the ocean rather than through the long-established monsoonal sailing network that passed along and offshore from the continental rim. In particular, it has been argued that colonization of Madagascar during the 1st millennium CE, by people speaking a Southeast Asian language, represented a direct migration passage.

The Indian Ocean covers about 68 million sq km, but before European exploration in the 16th century only the tropical zone of it (27 million sq km) was readily accessible to voyaging. This forms a huge, approximately equilateral, triangle based on the Tropic of Capricorn, with the implication that transoceanic distances are least toward the north, especially as that area is split by the Indian peninsula and Sri Lanka, and greatest toward the south. The earliest evidence of hominin migration around its shorelines, evidenced by stone artifacts on Flores, dates to around 1 mya (Brumm et al. 2010), and Australia was reached by *Homo sapiens* about 45 kya. The modern populations of Australia, New Guinea, and the Andaman Islands carry mtDNA lineages that probably descend directly from this initial migration.

Maritime travel and migration continued along coasts and amongst nearby islands until about five thousand years ago, when seafarers with planked ships driven by sail began to venture along the northern continental rim of the Indian Ocean. Subsequent incremental extension of passages by Mesopotamian, Harappan, Greek, Roman, Sassanian, and Arab seafarers included offshore passages across the Arabian Sea to India by at least 2300 years ago, and across the Bay of Bengal between India and Southeast

The Global Prehistory of Human Migration: The Encyclopedia of Global Human Migration Volume 1,
First Edition. Edited by Peter Bellwood.
© 2013 John Wiley & Sons, Ltd. Published 2015 by John Wiley & Sons, Ltd.

Asia by 2000 years ago. The Indian Ocean sailing network then became linked with another joining Southeast Asia to China in a vast system delimited largely by the monsoons, to which both sailing technology and seasonal schedules were closely adapted (Pearson 2003; Beaujard 2010). There was frequent transfer of commodities and cultural influences, and some migration, which resulted in trading communities of mixed ethnicity becoming established around the Indian Ocean, notably of South Asians in Southeast Asia and of Southeast Asians, Arabs, and local people along the East African coast, where they developed the distinctive Swahili language and society.

The mercantile emphasis bound this seafaring network largely to the continental perimeter, but it has also been suggested that some migration occurred along a transoceanic route through the zone of easterly trade winds south of the monsoons.

Transoceanic seafaring

There is evidence of biotic and cultural interchange across the prehistoric Indian Ocean (Reade 1996). Asian crops such as coconut, taro, and the greater yam flourished historically and sufficiently widely in equatorial Africa to suggest a prehistoric introduction, while African bananas, most probably of Asian origin, have been dated there to as early as 1000 BCE (Mbida et al. 2001). Whether these translocations were by coastal-insular or transoceanic movement is unknown, but taro occurs in the Maldives (Maloney 1995). Some African crops such as sorghum and pearl millet had reached Southeast Asia by at least the late 1st millennium CE, but as they had been cultivated previously in India 2000–300 BCE, along with rice (Boivin & Fuller 2009; chapter 31, this volume), which eventually reached East Africa, they need not have been transoceanic introductions. Elephantiasis, a disease that originated in Southeast Asia or the West Pacific may have reached Africa before 500 CE, and African malaria (*Plasmodium falciparum*) reached Southeast Asia before the modern period (Blench 2010) but, again, the routes of transmission are uncertain.

Turning to material culture, there is a strong case for the direct introduction of the African xylophone to Indonesia by about the ninth century CE, and an Indonesian form of zither that occurs in East Africa might be a complementary transfer (Blench 2010). The outrigger canoe that occurs in East Africa and Madagascar has clear resemblances in construction and terminology to cognate craft in Southeast Asia (Hornell 1934). However, as outrigger canoes are known from about 300 BCE in Sri Lanka (McGrail 2001: 266), and the same technology found in East Africa also occurred in the Maldives, the immediate origins of the African vessels remain undetermined.

Stronger evidence of transoceanic contact, indeed of migration, is seen in the distribution of the Austronesian language family. It originated in Southeast Asia and spread through the Pacific islands but it occurs also on Madagascar. The Malagasy language originated from the Malayo-Polynesian (Austronesian) languages of the Barito region of southeast Borneo, although it has also components of Old Javanese and Old Malay, possibly introduced during maritime migration (see chapter 35). Linguistic analysis, notably of the Sanskrit loan words within it, suggests that proto-Malagasy can be dated to about the 5th to 7th centuries CE (Adelaar 1996; Blench 1996,

2010). This is the period of the earliest archaeological evidence of settlement on Mada-gascar and the Comoro islands, but most early pottery here has African affinities. Material that might have Austronesian ancestry occurs no earlier than about the 8th century CE (Vérin & Wright 1999). Pre-Austronesian settlement of Madagascar by African groups has been proposed upon evidence of environmental change beginning about 300 BCE (Burney et al. 2003). Nevertheless, the coherence of the Malagasy lan-guage, and the existence of substantial Austronesian religious and social customs in Madagascar, compared to the scarcity of these in South Asia, Sri Lanka, and the Mal-dives, suggest relatively substantial migration and direct transoceanic migration in the mid-to-late 1st millennium CE.[1]

It is also possible that Austronesian migration to Madagascar originated in earlier settlements of Southeast Asians along the coast of East Africa (Dick-Read 2006). The existence of a diverse Austronesian influence in the language, place-names, and culture of the East African coast, together with Arab accounts from the 1st millennium CE of the "Waqwaq" there, suggest that settlement by Southeast Asians in East Africa might have occurred earlier than the colonization of Madagascar (Blench 2010). Some schol-ars suggest that transoceanic Austronesian voyaging to East Africa existed from about 2000 years ago. They interpret classical descriptions of the cinnamon trade, about the 1st century CE, as references to voyages across the Indian Ocean from Southeast Asia. The "rafts" described by Pliny the Elder are interpreted as double or outrigger canoes and the "vast seas" traversed in five-year-long voyages as the Indian Ocean (Dick-Read 2006: Blench 2010). Against this speculation it must be observed that Pliny was clearly referring to cinnamon grown in "Ethiopia" and being transported within the region by local people using watercraft without oars or sails. Similarly, while some authors regard the classical island "Menouthias" as a reference to Madagascar, it was more probably the East African island of Pemba (Alpers 2009).

Whether Austronesian exchange and migration ever had a fully transoceanic character is clearly difficult to determine from the current evidence, and whether such voyages of around 6000 km were technically feasible is equally uncertain. Com-puter simulation of canoe voyages from Southeast Asia indicates that vessels with a modest windward capacity could reach Madagascar in about 150 days, on average (Fitzpatrick & Callaghan 2008), but this is well beyond the sea-keeping ability of an outrigger canoe carrying a colonizing group. Experimental voyaging shows that it could have been done in the larger planked vessels of late 1st millennium CE Southeast Asia (McGrath 1988), but there is no evidence that these were present on the East African coast. In addition, if there was transoceanic voyaging between Southeast Asia and East Africa, then it is curious that this is not reflected in evidence of settlement or sojourn on the central Indian Ocean islands. Whereas there is a 2000-year history of settlement on the Maldives, which formed part of the main mercantile seafaring route, archaeological and palaeoenvironmnetal research on the Christmas, Cocos-Keeling,

---

[1] Since this chapter went to press, two important papers documenting settlement of Madagascar from Indonesia have been published. See Serva et al. 2011; Cox et al. 2012.

Chagos, and Seychelles islands, which lie across the trade route between Asia and Africa (Anderson 2011) has discovered no cultural remains or any other indications of a human history earlier than the period of European exploration. Similarly, no pre-European occupation is recorded for the Mascarenes, not even of contact with Madagascar.

In fact, there is a noticeable difference in the colonization history of the Indian Ocean compared with that of the Pacific. Of the remote tropical islands, only about 2.5 percent of those in the Pacific saw no human occupation prior to the late 2nd millennium BCE, while the comparable figure is around 28 percent for the Indian Ocean islands. The prehistoric Pacific Ocean, with its immense distances, was mainly an ocean of long-distance migration and relatively little subsequent interaction in its far reaches. The relative scarcity of settlement evidence on the Indian Ocean islands suggests that the broad nature of seafaring there was rather different, oriented predominantly to the interests of trade and organized as comparatively short, mainly coastal, passages in systematic trading networks (Anderson 2009).

It was probably through these that most, and perhaps all, people and commodities traveled between East Africa and Southeast Asia. Burma to the Horn of Africa is only half the distance from Java to East Africa, and can be sailed as two passages with a sojourn in South Asia, or entirely along the coast. Transoceanic movement, and possibly migration to Madagascar, cannot be ruled out but it is not supported unequivocally by the current distributional evidence of displaced plants, animals, or material culture traits, nor by the limitations of canoe-based voyaging.

SEE ALSO: 35 Southeast Asian islands and Oceania: Austronesian linguistic history; 41 Polynesia, East and South, including transpacific migration

References and further reading

Adelaar, K. A. (1996) Malagasy culture history: some linguistic evidence. In J. Reade (ed.), *The Indian Ocean in Antiquity*. London: British Museum, pp. 487–500.

Alpers, E. A. (2009) *East Africa and the Indian Ocean*. Princeton: Marcus Wiener.

Anderson, A. J. (2009) Crossing the Green Sea: early maritime mobility in the tropical Indian Ocean. Paper given at the Ancient Indian Ocean Corridors Conference, University of Oxford, Nov. 7–8.

Anderson, A. (2011) Unpublished research results of the Indian Ocean Islands Colonization Project. Dept. Archaeology and Natural History, Australian National University, Canberra.

Beaujard, P. (2010) From three possible Iron-age World-systems to a single Afro-Eurasian World-system. *Journal of World History* 21, 1–43.

Blench, R. M. (1996) The ethnographic evidence for long-distance contacts between Oceania and East Africa. In J. Reade (ed.), *The Indian Ocean in Antiquity*. London: British Museum, pp. 461–470.

Blench, R. M. (2007) New palaeozoogeographical evidence for the settlement of Madagascar. *Azania* 42, 69–82.

Blench, R. M. (2009) Remapping the Austronesian expansion. In B. Evans (ed.), *Discovering History through Language: Papers in Honour of Malcolm Ross*. Canberra: Pacific Linguistics, pp. 35–59.

Blench, R. M. (2010) Evidence for the Austronesian voyages in the Indian Ocean. In A. J. Anderson, J. H. Barrett, & K. V. Boyle (eds.), *The Global Origins and Development of Seafaring.* Cambridge: McDonald Institute Monographs, pp. 239–248.

Boivin, N. L. & Fuller, D. Q. (2009) Shell middens, ships and seeds: exploring coastal subsistence, maritime trade and the dispersal of domesticates in and around the ancient Arabian Peninsula. *Journal of World Prehistory* 22, 113–180.

Brumm, A., Jensen, G. M., Van den Bergh, G. D., et al. (2010) Hominins on Flores, Indonesia, by one million years ago. *Nature* 464, 748–753.

Burney, D. A., Robinson, G. S. and Burney, L. P. (2003) *Sporomiella* and the late Holocene extinctions in Madagascar. *Proceedings of the National Academy of Sciences* 100, 10800–10805.

Cox, M., Nelson, M. et al. (2012) A small cohort of Island Southeast Asian women founded Madagascar. *Proceedings of the Royal Society of London Series B*, doi:10.1098/rspb.2012.0012, 1471–2954.

Dewar, R. E. (1996) The archaeology of the early settlement of Madagascar. In J. Reade (ed.), *The Indian Ocean in Antiquity.* London: British Museum, pp. 471–486.

Dick-Read, R. (2006) Indonesia and Africa: questioning the origins of some of Africa's most famous icons. *Journal of Transdisciplinary Research in Southern Africa* 2, 23–45.

Fitzpatrick, S. M. and Callaghan, R. (2008) Seafaring simulations and the origin of prehistoric settlers to Madagascar. In G. Clark, F. Leach, & S. O'Connor (eds.) *Islands of Inquiry: Colonisation, Seafaring and the Archaeology of Maritime Landscapes.* Canberra: Terra Australis 29, pp. 47–58.

Hornell, J. (1934) Indonesian influence on East African culture. *Journal of the Royal Anthropological Institute* 64, 305–332.

Maloney, C. (1995) Where did the Maldives people come from? *International Institute of Asian Studies Newsletter* 5, 33–34.

Mbida, C. M., Doutrelepont, H., Vrydaghs, L., et al. (2001) First archaeological evidence of banana cultivation in central Africa during the third millennium before present. *Vegetation History and Archaeobotany* 10, 1–6.

McGrail, S. (2001) *Boats of the World.* Oxford: Oxford University Press.

McGrath, W. H. (1988) Some notes on the navigation of 1985 trans-Indian Ocean canoe voyage. *Journal of Navigation* 41, 174–185.

Pearson, R. (2003) *The Indian Ocean.* New York: Routledge.

Reade, J. (ed.) (1996) *The Indian Ocean in Antiquity.* London: British Museum.

Serva, M., Petroni, F. et al. (2011) Malagasy dialects and the peopling of Madagascar. *Journal of the Royal Society Interface* 9, 54–67.

Vérin, P. & Wright, H. (1999) Madagascar and Indonesia: new evidence from archaeology and linguistics. *Bulletin of the Indo-Pacific Prehistory Association* 18, 35–42.

33

Southeast Asian mainland: linguistic history

Paul Sidwell

The major language families of mainland Southeast Asia have reconstructible his-
tories of expansion extending back for at least five thousand years, commencing with
the initial spread of Austroasiatic languages from a homeland region that is still
under debate.

Mainland Southeast Asia (MSEA) displays a mosaic of ethnolinguistic diversity that reflects hundreds of languages belonging to five major families: Austroasiatic, Tai-Kadai (Kra-Dai), Tibeto-Burman, Miao-Yao (Hmong-Mien), and Austronesian (Figure 33.1). The fact that we can readily recognize clearly defined language families means that we can apply the methods of comparative linguistics to reconstruct intermediate and ancestral languages, showing how they likely branched and diversified in prehistory. The lexicons of these now lost ancestral tongues can speak to their level of cultural development, geographical locations, and societal interactions, in ways complementary to the results of other historical disciplines.

The documented history of MSEA is largely restricted to the second millennium CE; prior to that, from around the middle of the 1st millennium CE, there are only modest epigraphic texts and tantalizing references in Chinese chronicles. Some of those texts are the products of societies that remain largely in place, if greatly changed, such as Cambodia. Yet others – for example the Dvaravati Mon of 1st-millennium Thailand, or Champa which flourished for over a thousand years in central Vietnam – are frustratingly fragmented as conquests, migrations, and assimilation variously ended their civilizations, leaving their traces deep within what became foreign territory.

Consequently, comparative linguistics, and where appropriate epigraphy and philology, can offer significant insights into the prehistoric origins, migrations, and interactions of MSEA peoples. The narrative so revealed is of a region dominated early on by Austroasiatic languages, subsequently divided and replaced by great intrusive wedges coming in from the north, and displaced inland from the coasts by expanding trade

The Global Prehistory of Human Migration: The Encyclopedia of Global Human Migration Volume 1,
First Edition. Edited by Peter Bellwood.
© 2013 John Wiley & Sons, Ltd. Published 2015 by John Wiley & Sons, Ltd.

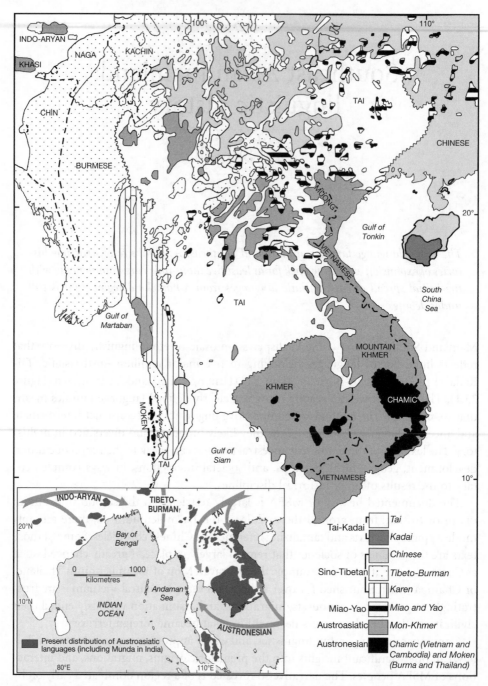

Figure 33.1 Language family distributions on the mainland of Southeast Asia, with an inset showing the likely directions of prehistoric migration of ancestral Indo-Aryan, Tibeto-Burman, Tai and Austronesian speakers, presumably overlying a former Austroasiatic continuum (main map after Lebar et al. 1964). Base mapping by Australian National University, College of Asia and the Pacific.

networks and empires. The movements south out of China have never really stopped: the text that follows works roughly back in time from the more recent to the more ancient periods of human movement and settlement.

Hmong-Mien

The Hmong-Mien languages (also called: Miao-Yao) consist of two subfamilies: Hmongic (about 5 million speakers) and Mienic (about 1.3 million speakers). Speakers are found mainly in the southern Chinese provinces of Guizhou, Guangxi, Yunnan, Hunan, and Guangdong, and in northern Vietnam and Laos (with scattered groups in Thailand and Myanmar/Burma). Remarkably, the Mienic languages are much less diverse than Hmongic, yet are spread over much of the same region. This geographical distribution does not immediately suggest a likely origin point for the family, although it does indicate that similar historical events and processes underlay the dispersal of the family, which must have occurred after the initial separation of proto-Hmong and proto-Mien.

Despite a tradition of folk tales that place Hmong-Mien origins in the distant north (Savina 1924), linguistic evidence firmly places their homeland in central or southern China. Thanks to a series of comparative studies (most recently: Ratliff 2010), the history of the family is now fairly well reconstructed, and the results suggest that the ancestral language had words for both rice-growing and hunting, and terms for animals and plants of the Yangzi River basin (pangolin, river deer, the "painted eyebrow" thrush, cogon grass, *Allium* (onion family), and the medicinal plant *Houttuynia cordata*). Additionally, numerous ancient loans from Old Chinese and Tibeto-Burman are evident. These data suggest that the proto-Hmong-Mien speakers began dispersing southward out of the Yangzi River basin around 2,500 years ago, perhaps connected to the movement of Han Chinese (chapter 25).

A much later phase of Hmong-Mien migration began in the 1840s, and accounts for many of the scattered populations today in Thailand, Vietnam, and Laos. Events such as the Opium Wars and the Taiping Rebellion stimulated substantial movements of peoples, especially from Guizhou, Guangdong, and Guangxi, many of whom traveled via the Yunnan-Guizhou plateau into Indo-China, following a route that Edmondson and Jinfang (1996) call "the language corridor." These migrations are still relatively well remembered, and some communities still maintain contact with their now distant relatives remaining in China.

Austronesian

While there are more than 1,200 Austronesian languages spread across the islands of Southeast Asia and the Pacific, linguists also identify two small groups of "mainland Austronesian" speakers. These are the Moken (also known as Sea Gypsies or Sea Nomads in English, Selung in Myanmar/Burma, Chao Ley in Thailand) who live among the islands off the west coast of the isthmus of Kra; and the speakers of Aceh-Chamic, including the Chamic languages of Indo-China and Hainan, and (somewhat controversially) the Acehnese spoken in northern Sumatra. Austronesian speakers (probably radiating from northwest Borneo, and more closely related to Malayic tribes than other groups) began settling the coasts of Indo-China and the Gulf of Thailand sometime before the 5th century BCE. The sequence of this prehistoric migration, and its specific ethnic makeup, may never be known, but some inferences can be made (see also chapter 35).

The Moken are a small, scattered group of just a few thousand speakers who may represent the remnants of previously more widespread occupation of the Kra isthmus and Malay peninsula, before the area became a much-prized and occasionally contested overland section of the coastal India–China trade route. The thesis by Larish (1999), which includes a reconstruction of proto-Moken, sketches out various structural changes, including innovations in the reflexes of PMP *q, diphthongs, and stress patterns, which demonstrate that proto-Moken must have been somewhat older than Malayo-Aceh-Cham, and therefore likely to reflect the oldest mainland Austronesian group for which evidence survives.

A group of Austronesians (the Aceh-Chams) settled on the Vietnam coast around 500 BCE and eventually built a great Hindu (and later Muslim) civilization – Champa – which today exists only in the form of monumental ruins frequented by tourists. The Acehnese of Sumatra and small Chamic communities of Cambodia, Vietnam, and Hainan are direct descendants of Chamic society, which no longer exists in its historical heartland. Fortunately, the history of these migrations can largely be reconstructed by linguists, for example proto-Chamic (Thurgood 1999) with extensive inferences about Chamic history, and other insightful analyses (Sidwell 2005; Vickery 2005).

During the 1st millennium CE, Champa emerged as a powerful alliance of port cities that came to rival Angkor and Vietnam as a major regional power. Sometime early in this process there was an emigration of northern Chams to Sumatra, establishing what was eventually to become Aceh. It was a strategic move to control an important stretch of coastal route running through the Straits of Malacca, now known as Melaka, as the shorter trans-isthmus route was controlled by others (especially Funan/Cambodia and Dvaravati for much of the 1st millennium CE).

But the dominance of Champa began to give way in the 10th century. The northern capital of Indrapura was sacked by Vietnamese in 982, and many northern Cham left; the U Tsat minority living in Hainan today began with an emigration of Cham from that time. Conflict with Cambodia in the 12th and 13th centuries greatly weakened Champa, leaving the door open for Vietnam to push south and progressively seize more and more territory. By 1471 the Cham polities Amaravati and Vijaya (roughly from Da Nang to Qui Nhon) had fallen. The "Sejarah Melayu" records that after the fall of Vijaya, the two sons of King Pau Kubah fled, with Syah Indera Berman going to Melaka and Syah Pau Ling going to Aceh, where he started the line of Aceh kings (al-Ahmadi, quoted in Thurgood 1999: 22).

The central Cham polity of Kauthara survived until the early 17th century, but the period was marked by substantial emigrations into the central highlands. Strikingly, the present-day area of Chamic-speaking peoples in the central highlands corresponds almost precisely, in terms of northern and southern extents, to the former coastal latitudes of Kauthara. Many Cham also moved up the Mekong river into Cambodia, which by then lacked a central government and had become a neglected backwater. These migrations continued off and on through the 18th century, laying the bases for the substantial western Cham communities who still live there today. The southern Cham state of Panduranga (Vietnamese: Phan Rang) persisted as an entity into the 1830s, when it was finally absorbed into Vietnam.

Kra-Dai

Kra-Dai (also Tai-Kadai, Daic), now representing some of the most important languages in MSEA, is another family that diversified and spread out of southern China over the last 2,500 years, creating one of two great wedges that divided the older Austroasiatic domination of MSEA. It is in southern China that the greatest diversity of Kra-Dai languages still remains. There are three principal sub-branches: Kra – six small languages spoken mainly in Guizhou and the Vietnam-China borderlands; Hlai – about a dozen languages spoken on Hainan Island (glossed as "Kadai" in Figure 33.1); and Kam-Tai. The latter further separates into Kam-Sui and Tai. Kam-Sui consists of about a dozen languages spoken mainly in Guizhou, Guangxi, Yunnan, and pockets of northern Laos. The large Tai group includes more than 60 languages (including Thai and Lao) that are widespread through MSEA and as far west as Assam (India).

The Northern and Central Tai languages – collectively known as Zhuang in China – occupy the original Tai heartland, mainly Guangxi, Hunan, and Vietnam north of the Red River; also historically much of Guangdong, where Tai speakers where probably constituted many of the "Hundred Yueh (barbarians)" mentioned in Chinese annals.

The Southwestern Tai spread rapidly over a vast area, and remain so close that many are still highly mutually intelligible (e.g. Thai and Lao). Tai speakers are thought to have dispersed west and southwest from the China–Vietnam borderlands from around 100 BCE, a period that overlapped with the extension of Chinese rule through the Red River basin. We can date the beginning of this process from the common Tai word for the Vietnamese /kɛːw/ from the name of a Chinese garrison Jiaozhi, established in Vietnam in about 112 BCE. Significantly, southern minorities living under Chinese rule had to take family names around 300 CE, but Tais outside of China had no such practice until recent times.

Tai communities became established through northern Laos and Yunnan, and tradition holds that they settled the Shan hills (eastern Myanmar/Burma) in 569 CE, although the real date was probably somewhat later. Through the 7th to 13th centuries, Tais settled and eventually came to control the previously Mon- and Khmer-dominated territories corresponding largely to contemporary Thailand and much of Laos. The Siamese (Siam, Shan, and Ahom are all variants of the same Tai ethnonym) took Sukhothai from Mon hands in 1239 and by 1257 dominated the entire Upper Chao Phraya valley. In 1262 the rival Siamese kingdom of Lana established its capital at Chiangrai, and by the 1290s had subsumed the northern Mon state of Haripunchai centred at Lamphun. The 1200s also saw Tais migrating westward from the Shan Hills, some reaching Assam, and tradition holds that the Tai Ahom founded their Assamese kingdom in 1228.

Tibeto-Burman

More than 300 Tibeto-Burman (TB) languages are spoken by over 30 million people in a pattern that radiates south and east from the Himalayas and Sichuan along the great river valleys of Asia (Van Driem 2001; see also chapter 25). The history of this family is becoming well understood, thanks to long-term efforts such as the *Sino-Tibetan Etymological Dictionary and Thesaurus* (STEDT) project, and there are now well-developed theories about its origin and spread. TB is the second great wedge that divided Austroasiatic, pushing down through what is today Myanmar/Burma, limiting Austroasiatic speakers to a pocket of Mon in the south and scattered Palaungic communities in the Shan Hills.

The emerging picture places the TB homeland in Sichuan (or perhaps Yunnan), with very ancient westward and eastward migrations into the Himalayas and China respectively. But later movement was also important, and by 1000 BCE the Southern-TB speakers, proto-Karenic and proto-Lolo-Burmese, had separated and begun to migrate deeper into MSEA. The Karens came down the Salween corridor and became established in what is now the Karen State and down into the isthmus of Kra. The Lolo-Burmese (LB) remained and diversified largely in Yunnan and northern Myanmar, spreading south in more gradual and staged migrations.

One LB group, the Pyu, establish a remarkable Buddhist civilization between the 4th and 9th centuries CE in the upper dry zone of the Irrawaddy basin, on an important overland route between India and China. From the 8th century the Nanzhao kingdom of Yunnan (variously claimed to be predominantly Tai or TB) began raiding its neighbors, one result being the movement of the Burmese out of Yunnan and into the territory of the Pyu. Pyu inscriptions strangely ceased for 200 years from the mid-9th century; by the time they resumed the Burmese were well entrenched among the Pyu and completed their conquest of the plains in the early 13th century. Lower Burma remained in the hands of Mon speakers well into historical times, but finally lost out to the Burmese, partly because the British favored the latter. Today, only a small Mon state survives within Myanmar/Burma. These days, many small Burmish and Loloish groups still live in Yunnan, and over the past millennium many have trickled into the Shan Hills, northern Laos, and Thailand. Well-known groups include the Akha, Lahu, Mpi, and others that are viewed as "hill tribes" on contemporary tourist trails.

Austroasiatic

The Austroasiatic languages, with a dozen branches, are spoken by some 100 million people spread in a great arc from Indo-China and the Malay peninsula, through the higher reaches of the Mekong and Salween rivers, to eastern and central India. Aside from the speakers of the Cambodian and Vietnamese national languages, Austroasiatic communities are mostly found in the highlands and/or on the margins of mainstream societies now dominated by Daic, Tibeto-Burman, Austronesian, and Indo-European speaking peoples. This distribution, and the great internal diversity of Austroasiatic, suggest that it is the oldest language family of the region, at least four thousand years old.

Comparative studies of Austroasiatic have been conducted for more than a century, so that there are well-developed historical models for most branches and one extensive preliminary reconstruction for the phylum (Shorto 2006). There is no general scholarly consensus about the homeland or migration paths of the ancient Austroasiatics, but there are three broad scenarios. These include a western origin in northeastern India or in the vicinity of the Bay of Bengal (Van Driem 2001); a northern origin in central or southern China (Scheussler 2007); and a central origin within Southeast Asia (Sidwell 2010).

The main problem, from a comparative perspective, is that there are precious few indications of nested sub-branching within the family. The sound system and lexicon of each Austroasiatic branch can be largely explained by direct development from proto-Austroasiatic, but with few exceptions we lack direct indications that such branches were ever spoken beyond the zones they currently occupy. Consequently, we are left to imagine how the languages could have entered their current locations. Shorto (1979: 278), writing three decades ago, speculated:

> The Northern Mon-Khmers and Khasis are likely to have followed what became a Chinese trade route to India, as the Mundas may well have done before them. But there seems no overriding reason to trace routes for the Mons and Khmers, and other groups who occupied the river-plains, down the rivers from the hinterland rather than up them from the coast.

However, the Nicobarese, Khasi, and Munda speakers are the most isolated from the rest of Austroasiatic, so we can perhaps say something about their geographical histories. Firstly, the Nicobarese languages unquestionably reflect a prehistoric migration from the mainland. Grierson (1906: 15) quotes one Sir Richard Temple: "The Nicobarese have been on the same ground for at least 2000 years, and they have a tradition of a migration from the Pegu-Tenasserim Coast." Linguistically, suggestions have been made that Nicobarese and the Aslian languages of Malaysia share some unique phonetic developments (Diffloth 1977, 1991), but they are difficult to assess because of a lack of comparative work on these groups.

The Khasi inhabit the plateaux around Shillong in Meghalaya State (India) and are surrounded by Tibeto-Burman populations. Scholars have wondered if they represent some kind of link between the Munda of India and Mon-Khmer of Southeast Asia, although recent lexical studies indicate that Khasi is a sister group to the Palaungic languages of the Shan state in Myanmar/Burma. Consequently it is likely that the Khasis represent a migration, as Shorto speculated, possibly sometime in the first millennium BCE.

The Munda problem is much more difficult. Conventional wisdom since Pinnow (1959, 1960) has held that the dozen or so Munda languages of central and eastern India form one of two coordinate branches of Austroasiatic, the other comprising all of the 150 or so Mon-Khmer languages. Pinnow and his followers asserted that the typological complexity of Munda was closest to Proto-Austroasiatic, and by implication they represented the population who stayed more or less in the homeland, while the Mon-Khmers made one or more great migrations eastward in prehistory. More recently, a view has been gaining support that Munda is typologically innovative and Mon-Khmer languages resemble each other typologically because they have retained older features (Donegan & Stampe 2004). From this perspective one need only posit a single pre-Munda migration out of MSEA into India, perhaps four thousand years ago, and perhaps using the same route as that taken later by the Khasis and in the 13th century by the Assamese Tai (Ahom).

The last great movement of Austroasiatic speakers is seen in the success of the Vietnamese, who constitute maybe 80 percent of all Austroasiatic speakers today. During the millennium of Chinese rule until 938 CE, one of the small Muong languages spoken in the Red River valley became greatly influenced by Chinese and rose to become the vernacular of the newly independent civilization. From the 10th century, Vietnamese expanded southwards to displace Chamic, Khmer, and numerous small tribal languages to as far as the Mekong delta. Many southern Khmers (or Khmer Krom) still live in the delta region, but Vietnamese is rapidly advancing. Since 1975 the Vietnam highlands have also been undergoing a linguistic transformation, thanks to a massive organized transmigration from the north, as incoming Vietnamese displace and outnumber the Montagnard populations.

Conclusion

The ethnolinguistic mosaic of MSEA is far from random. Rather, it reveals a great deal about the history of movement of peoples, with complex and conflicting stories of growth and loss, of diversity and homogeneity. Fragmented hill-dwelling communities resulted from various processes. For instance, the Nyahkur of central Thailand are the isolated remnants of the 1st-millennium CE Mon kingdom of Dvaravati, left *in situ* after the mass Mon migrations to Myanmar/Burma. On the contrary, the many pockets of Hmong-Mien speakers in Thailand today are mostly refugees from Qing dynasty China. The largely homogenous lowland populations of Thais and Burmese represent intrusive ethnic groups, relative latecomers who conquered and assimilated earlier societies. Conversely, Cambodian speakers mostly reflect the growth of one local indigenous group who succeeded in building a great civilization at Angkor that absorbed foreign influences without significant immigration.

Historically, the underlying pattern of peoples and languages probably owes most to two factors, the emergence and spread of populations who cultivated rice, and the growth of Chinese political power. The first factor allowed the Austroasiatics to grow and spread over a vast area in prehistory. Later, speakers of other languages, variously moving south to avoid conflict or simply seeking the high-yielding lowlands for themselves, variously displaced and absorbed many of the Austroasiatic speakers, who are now frequently confined to the hills. Other latecomers, such as many Lolo-Burmese speakers, reached the hills of MSEA but were unable to penetrate the lowlands.

SEE ALSO: 25 Eastern Asia: Sino-Tibetan linguistic history; 34 Southeast Asian mainland: archaeology; 35 Southeast Asian islands and Oceania: Austronesian linguistic history

References and further reading

Diffloth, G. (1977) Mon-Khmer initial palatals and "subtratumized" Austro-Thai. *Mon-Khmer Studies Journal* 6, 39–57.

Diffloth, G. (1991) Palaungic vowels in Mon-Khmer perspective. In J. H. C. S. Davidson, *Austroasiatic Languages: Essays in Honor of H. L. Shorto*. London: School of Oriental and African Studies, University of London, pp. 13–28.

Donegan, P. J. & Stampe, D. (2004) Rhythm and the synthetic drift of Muṇḍā. In R. Singh (ed.), *The Yearbook of South Asian Languages and Linguistics 2004*. Thousand Oaks, CA: Sage, pp. 3–36.

Edmondson, J. A. & Jinfang, L. (1996) The language corridor. In *The Fourth International Symposium on Language and Linguistics, Thailand*. Salaya: Institute of Language and Culture for Rural Development, Mahidol University, pp. 983–990.

Grierson, G. A. (1906) *Munda and Dravidian Families*, vol. IV: *Linguistic Survey of India*. Delhi: Banarashidas.

Larish, M. D. (1999) The position of Moken and Moklen in the Austronesian language family. PhD dissertation, University of Hawaii at Manoa.

Lebar, F., Hickey, G., & Musgrave, J. (1964) *Ethnic Groups of Mainland Southeast Asia*. New Haven: HRAF Press.

L-Thongkum, T. (1993) A view on Proto-Mjuenic (Yao). *Mon-Khmer Studies* 22, 163–230.

Pinnow, H.-J. (1959) *Versuch Einer Historischen Lautlehre der Kharia-Sprache* [An attempt at a historical phonology of the Kharia language]. Wiesbaden: Otto Harrassowitz.

Pinnow, H.-J. (1960) Über den Ursprung der voneinander abweichenden Strukturen der Munda und Khmer-Nicobar Sprachen [On the origin of the divergent structures of the Munda and Khmer-Nicobar languages]. *Indo-Iranian Journal* 4(1), 81–103.

Purnell, H. C., Jr. (1970) Toward a reconstruction of Proto-Miao-Yao. PhD dissertation, Cornell University.

Ratliff, M. (2010) *Hmong-Mien Language History*. Canberra: Pacific Linguistics.

Savina, F. M. (1924) *Histoire des Miao* [History of the Miao]. Paris: Société des Missions-Etrangères.

Schuessler, A. (2007) *ABC Etymological Dictionary of Old Chinese*. Honolulu: University of Hawaii Press.

Shorto, H. L. (1979) The linguistic proto-history of mainland South East Asia. In R. B. Smith & W. Watson (eds.), *Early South East Asia*. New York: Oxford University Press, pp. 273–278.

Shorto, H. L. (2006) *A Mon-Khmer Comparative Dictionary*. Canberra: Pacific Linguistics 579.

Sidwell, P. (2005) Acehnese and the Aceh-Chamic language family. In A. Grant & P. Sidwell (eds.), *Chamic and Beyond: Studies in Mainland Austronesian Languages*. Canberra: Pacific Linguistics 569, pp. 211–246.

Sidwell, P. (2010) The Austroasiatic central riverine hypothesis. *Journal of Language Relationship* 4, 117–134.

Sino-Tibetan Etymological Dictionary and Thesaurus (STEDT), University of California Department of Linguistics, online at: http://stedt.berkeley.edu, accessed Jan. 2, 2012.

Thurgood, G. (1999) *From Ancient Cham to Modern Dialects: Two Thousand Years of Language Contact and Change*. Oceanic Linguistics special publications 28. Honolulu: University of Hawaii Press.

Van Driem, G. (2001) *Languages of the Himalayas: An Ethnolinguistic Handbook of the Greater Himalayan Region. Containing an Introduction to the Symbiotic Theory of Language.* Leiden: Brill.

Vickery, M. (2005) *Champa revisited.* Asia Research Institute Working Papers Series 37, 3–89.

Wang, F. (1994) *Miáoyǔ gǔyīn gòunǐ* [Reconstruction of the sound system of proto-Miao]. Tokyo: Institute for the Study of Languages and Cultures of Asia and Africa.

Wang, F. & Zongwu M. (1995) *Miáoyáoyǔ gǔyīn gòunǐ* [Reconstruction of the sound system of proto-Miao-Yao]. Beijing: China Social Sciences Press.

34

Southeast Asian mainland: archaeology

C. F. W. Higham

The Holocene archaeology of mainland Southeast Asia records early retractions of hunter-gatherers in the face of rising postglacial sea levels, followed by the movements of rice cultivators and, later on, traders from India and Chinese armies.

Any review of the patterns of human migration in mainland Southeast Asia must take into account the changing climate since 12 kya and its impact on geography and people. The dramatic global warming that took hold at the end of the last Ice Age caused the sea level to rise by over 100 m within a period of eight thousand years (10,000–2,000 BCE). Nowhere else was more land lost to the rising sea than in Southeast Asia. The Mekong and Chao Phraya rivers, which previously flowed through extensive lowlands before reaching the sea, became truncated, and only elevated areas in the drowned continent of Sundaland, now converted into islands, were open to continued human settlement.

We know that the expansion of *Homo sapiens* saw progressive replacement of earlier hominin species in Southeast Asia. Much of the evidence for the timing and the patterns involved in this migration, however, will have been submerged. The presence of hunter-gatherers by at least 40 kya is documented in caves such as Niah in Borneo and Lang Rongrien in Thailand (Anderson 1990; Barker et al. 2007). But even at that time these sites were some distance from the contemporary coast; and the shore, particularly where estuaries of major rivers reach the sea, is one of the richest hunting and gathering environments known. The archaeological void for the settlement of lowland Sundaland by *Homo sapiens* and the impact of the rising sea on human migration can be filled at present only by two scientific methods. The first is to deduce the genetic origins of those living today, and if possible prehistoric people, through the analysis of DNA and prehistoric skeletons. The second is to infer at least some information from the settlements dating to the period four and five millennia ago on ancient shorelines,

The Global Prehistory of Human Migration: The Encyclopedia of Global Human Migration Volume 1,
First Edition. Edited by Peter Bellwood.
© 2013 John Wiley & Sons, Ltd. Published 2015 by John Wiley & Sons, Ltd.

preserved because at that time the sea rose above its present level and then fell back to leave them slightly inland.

Mutations in mitochondrial DNA and the non-recombining portion of the Y-chromosome are transmitted through all the same-sex descendants of the person in whom the mutation occurred, at least until another mutation occurs. Using data from living people, it is possible to construct a family tree showing where different lines of descent formed. The study of ancient DNA from prehistoric hunter-gatherers has barely begun, although mtDNA from skeletons in Moh Khiew cave in Krabi Province of southern Thailand, dating to at least 11 kya and possibly as early as 25 kya, suggests that they were ancestral to the modern Semang hunters of the same region (Oota et al. 2001). This finding, if substantiated, must be considered in conjunction with the phylogeographic findings of Hill et al. (2007), that Semang mtDNA suggests a local ancestry stretching back about 50,000 years, to the period when anatomically modern humans were first settling in Southeast Asia. The key question in identifying migratory patterns involving Sundaland before 2000 BCE, then, is to define the contribution made from various source populations to the genetic makeup of modern populations. Although the picture is not yet completely clear, there is little doubt that indigenous hunter-gatherers interacted with intrusive rice farmers who moved into mainland Southeast Asia from southern China, and contributed significantly to the gene pool (Mormina & Higham 2010; and see chapter 27, this volume).

The inference to be drawn from the genetic data is that the rising sea led to the migration of those living in both the inland and coastal tracts of Sundaland, and many may have moved into what is now the mainland of Southeast Asia. These coastal communities would have been versed in seafaring, and the warm seas covering Holocene Sundaland must be seen as highways to movement. Resettlement was axiomatic under the extreme environmental changes that took place over a period of at least eight thousand years, until the sea level finally stabilized from about 1000 BCE.

Archaeological explorations along raised mid-Holocene shorelines have identified numerous settlements, and excavations have illuminated the activities of these coastal hunter-gatherers. At Nong Nor in central Thailand, now 22 km from the present shore, a community was settled on a headland overlooking a sheltered marine embayment (Higham & Thosarat 1998). Access to the open sea lay 5 km to the north. These people occupied the site for at least one season of the year, possibly longer, at about 2400 BCE. They made fine ceramic vessels and traded for high-quality stone to fashion their adzes. They collected shellfish from the sandy shore next to the site, but also ventured out to sea to fish for eagle rays and bull sharks, or along the coastline for seals. Only one human burial was found during three seasons of excavation, that of an adult woman found in a seated, crouched position under several pottery vessels. A flexed position is a widespread feature of similar hunter-gatherer groups of this period in Southeast Asia. More information comes from nearby Khok Phanom Di, a large mound that accumulated over a period of at least 500 years from about 2000 BCE. It was positioned amidst mangroves on the estuary of the Bang Pakong River (Higham & Thosarat 2004).

The lowest occupation layers at this site closely track Nong Nor: there are numerous polished stone adzes, and the anvils for shaping ceramic vessels along with potsherds. One child was interred in a flexed position. There followed two phases of burial in

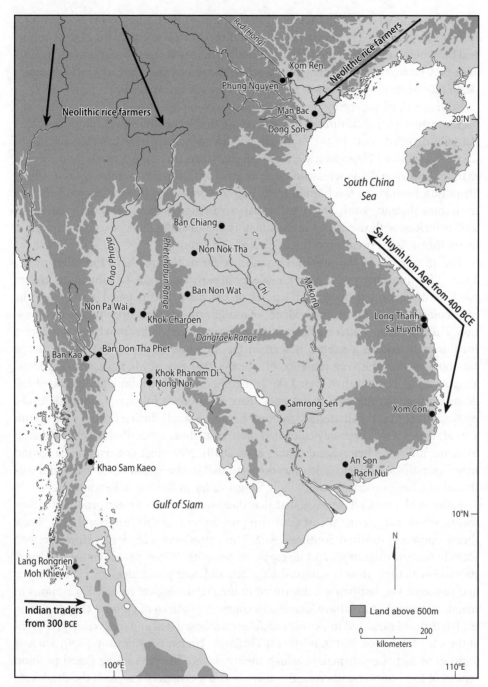

Figure 34.1 Map showing sites mentioned in the text, and directions of the major migrations into mainland Southeast Asia. Base mapping by College of Asia and the Pacific, The Australian National University.

which the dead were interred wrapped in shrouds of sheet asbestos on wooden biers in a supine position. The human bones reveal that the people perhaps carried abnormal haemoglobins in their blood that allowed them to withstand malaria when inheritance was heterozygous, albeit with associated anaemia and thus a very high infant death rate when inheritance was homozygous for the recessive allele (Tayles 1999).

With the third mortuary phase, there were several significant changes. While the basic mortuary ritual continued unchanged, we find large stone hoes and shell sickles. Partially digested food in the stomach cavities in burials contains the remains of domesticated rice (Thompson 1996). At this juncture, there was a marked decrease in marine shellfish and an increase in those adapted to freshwater swamps (Mason 1991). Strontium isotopes in the human teeth indicate that some women came to the site from some distance away. The most logical explanation is that a temporary fall in sea level coincided with the arrival in the site of rice cultivators. This poses a key question in Southeast Asian prehistory: the origins of rice farming.

The answer lies in the prehistoric sequence far to the north, in the valley of the Yangzi River (see chapter 26). Our knowledge of early rice domestication in this region has been transformed by genetic studies of the plant and detailed analyses of the archaeological rice remains for evidence of modifications that reflect sustained cultivation. Thus, the non-shattering habit of domesticated rice results from human selection for this trait, and its presence is seen in the structure of the spikelet base. Initial assumptions that the very presence of rice by 7000 BCE at Shangshan in the lower Yangzi, and at Pengtoushan near Lake Dongting one millennium later, indicated full domestication have now been set aside. Rice received its full set of domestic traits, particularly the loss of shattering, and only became a staple during the 6th millennium BCE. However, it was probably cultivated more casually as a morphologically wild crop for some millennia beforehand (Fuller et al. 2010). Nor must one overlook a second major crop, foxtail millet, which was domesticated in the Yellow River valley and cultivated at Chengtoushan in the Middle Yangzi valley in the 5th millennium BCE.

Fuller et al. (2010) have suggested that there were at least 11 expansionary movements, which they term "thrusts," of rice growers out of this homeland area. Their thrust number 5 involved Southeast Asia. This introduces a key issue. How does one identify human migration, and delineate its patterns? When people move residence, they take with them their language, their genes, and their preferences for material items and customs. The last two are imprinted in the archaeological record. Excavations in mainland Southeast Asia have identified a consistent pattern of cultural change during the late 3rd and early 2nd millennia BCE. These are best dated and most clearly reflected at the site of Ban Non Wat in northeast Thailand (Higham & Kijngam 2009). There is a group of early burials here in which the dead were interred in the flexed position typical of local hunter-gatherers. But there is also a cemetery in which the dead were accompanied by a rich assemblage of mortuary offerings, including ceramic vessels decorated with elaborate incised and impressed designs. They also raised domesticated pigs and cultivated rice. These people settled at the site in the 17th century BCE.

The designs incised impressed on pottery vessels are widely paralleled in other sites in Thailand, Vietnam, and Cambodia. They clearly had some unknown symbolic meaning and it is hard not to suspect a common origin. Rispoli (2008) and Zhang and

Hung (2010) have traced parallels north into the southern provinces of China, and have thereby integrated the archaeological framework with the facts of rice domestication, in terms of the Fuller et al. (2010) thrust 5 (see chapter 26).

We know that this migration brought settled rice farming and domestic pigs, dogs, and cattle to mainland Southeast Asia by about 2000 BCE. The spindle whorl, an artifact associated with weaving, can be traced back in eastern Asia to a Chinese origin. Neolithic communities were involved in long-distance exchange of exotic shell ornaments, they began to clear forest using fire and stone adzes for their fields, and they hunted the prolific game that surrounded their settlements. We know less of the actual nature of the movement south. Was there a flood of newcomers, or a series of regional trickles? And what was their interaction with the long-established indigenous hunter-gatherers? (see chapter 27 for the human biology related to this issue, especially in Vietnam). Again, we can turn to the genetic evidence. There is, in the modern population, a strong presence of deep-seated local genes in addition to intrusive ones associated with the expansive groups of rice farmers. This suggests that there might not have been a major demographic change with the first farmers, and that there was much social interaction with those whom they encountered when they reached Southeast Asia.

These farming communities were involved in an exchange network that stretched back into their northern homeland. By about 1000 BCE this network brought in the technology for smelting copper and tin to cast bronzes. However, there is no evidence for any further inflow of people from the north in late prehistory, prior to the major historical migrations, during the past two millennia, of the Sinitic, Tibeto-Burman, Tai, and Hmong-Mien speaking peoples (see chapters 25 and 33). Rather, the next major evidence for any migration of people into Southeast Asia involved India. The Indian emperor Asoka dispatched Buddhist missionaries to Southeast Asia in the 4th century BCE, and merchant venturers began to visit Southeast Asian port settlements. At the site of Ban Don Ta Phet in central Thailand, Indian exports are found in the cemetery: agate, carnelian, and glass beads, and fine decorated high-tin bronze bowls (Glover 1990). It is possible that this new contact introduced the techniques of iron smelting and forging of a new range of tools and weapons. The clearest evidence for Indian settlement has been found at the recently excavated port city of Khao Sam Kaeo, located on the bank of the Tha Taphao River, which commands the narrowest part of Peninsular Thailand (Bellina-Pryce & Silapanth 2006). Here, the riverine route over the narrow land bridge would have encouraged trade links between the Andaman Sea and the Gulf of Thailand. The monsoon also had a major impact. For half the year, the prevailing wind blows from the southwest, but for the rest of the year it changes to northeast. This would have entailed an enforced wait before return voyages could be contemplated, thereby allowing extended periods of cultural contact. Nor does one need to look far for local resources that would have attracted trade. Peninsular Thailand was once a major source of the world's tin.

Inscribed seals bearing Indian Sanskrit names in the Brahmi script evidence both trade links and exposure to a new language and writing. The form and techniques for manufacturing hard stone and glass beads strongly suggest that Indian craftspeople were involved at Khao Sam Kaeo in establishing the site as a production center. The ceramic remains also suggest that Indian specialists might have set up their workshops there (Bouvet 2006). Similar evidence for Indian presence has long been documented at Oc Eo, on the western edge of the Mekong delta, where the worship of Indian gods and familiarity with the Sanskrit language, Indian Brahmi script and building techniques are recurrent features of such early lowland states in Southeast Asia (Manguin & Vo Si Khai 2000).

Moving up the coast of Vietnam, there are new patterns of migration. Sa Huynh is an Iron Age culture largely represented by cemeteries of lidded jar burials containing cremated human remains. When Indian trade reached this region, these Iron Age communities developed into the civilization of the Chams. The Cham language, and presumably that of their Sa Huynh ancestors, is Austronesian, with its closest parallels in western Borneo. The conclusion is almost inescapable: there was a seaborne settlement of the narrow coastal strip by migratory peoples sailing from island Southeast Asia (see chapters 33 and 35).

The Cham settlement ended in the west with the Truong Son Cordillera, a massif described by the Chinese as the Fortress of the Sky, and in the north against the vigorous and powerful Red River chiefdoms named after the archaeological site of Dong Son, in Thanh Hoa Province. This part of Southeast Asia was exposed to influence from China, and it was under the Western Han, during the late 2nd century BCE and onwards, that the imperial policy of expansion saw the conquest of northern Vietnam and the establishment of a Chinese province. This was followed by an ingress of Chinese settlers who brought with them their improved techniques of agriculture, their iron working and high-temperature-fired ceramic vessels, and their brick tombs. Indeed the Chinese control of northern Vietnam only ended in the 10th century, after leaving an indelible imprint on Vietnamese culture even to the present day. Further details on the contents of this chapter can be found in Higham (2002) and Glover & Bellwood (2004).

SEE ALSO: 25 Eastern Asia: Sino-Tibetan linguistic history; 26 Eastern Asia: archaeology; 27 Eastern Asia and Japan: human biology; 32 Trans-Indian Ocean migration; 33 Southeast Asian mainland: linguistic history; 35 Southeast Asian islands and Oceania: Austronesian linguistic history

References

Anderson, D. D. (1990) *Lang Rongrien Rockshelter: A Pleistocene-Early Holocene Archaeological Site from Krabi, Southwestern Thailand.* University Museum Monograph No. 71. Philadelphia: University Museum, University of Pennsylvania.

Barker, G., Rabett, R., Reynolds, T., et al. (2007) The "human revolution" in lowland tropical Southeast Asia. *Journal of Human Evolution* 52, 243–261.

Bellina-Pryce, B. & Silapanth, P. (2006) Weaving cultural identities on trans-Asiatic networks: Upper Thai-Malay peninsula – an early socio-political landscape. *Bulletin de l'Ecole Française d'Extrême-Orient* 93, 257–293.

Bouvet, P. (2006) Étude préliminaire de céramique Indienne et "Indienisantes" du site de Khao Sam Kaeo IVe-IIe siècles av. J.-C [Preliminary study of the Indian and Indian style ceramics of the 2nd to the 4th centuries BCE from the site of Khao Sam Kaeo]. *Bulletin de l'Ecole Française d'Extrême-Orient* 93, 353–390.

Fuller, D. Q., Sato Y.-I., Castillo, C., et al. (2010) Consilience of genetics and archaeobotany in the entangled history of rice. *Archaeological and Anthropological Sciences* 2, 115–131.

Glover, I. C. (1990) Ban Don Ta Phet: the 1984–5 excavation. In I. C. Glover & E. Glover (eds.), *Southeast Asian Archaeology 1986*. British Archaeological Reports International Series 561. Oxford: BAR, pp. 139–184.

Glover, I. & Bellwood, P. (2004) *Southeast Asia: from Prehistory to History*. London: RoutledgeCurzon.

Higham, C. F. W. (2002) *Early Cultures of Mainland Southeast Asia*. Bangkok: River Books.

Higham, C. F. W. & Kijngam, A. (2009) *The Origins of the Civilization of Angkor*, vol. III: *The Excavation Ban Non Wat, Introduction*. Bangkok: The Fine Arts Department.

Higham, C. F. W. & Thosarat, R. (eds.) (1998) *The Excavation of Nong Nor, a Prehistoric Site in Central Thailand*. Oxford: Oxbow Books.

Higham, C. F. W. & Thosarat, R. (2004) *The Excavation of Khok Phanom Di*, vol. VII: *Summary and Conclusions*. London: Society of Antiquaries.

Hill, C., Soares, P., Mormina, M., et al. (2007) A mitochondrial stratigraphy for island Southeast Asia. *American Journal of Human Genetics* 80, 29–43.

Manguin, P.-Y. & Vo Si Khai (2000) Excavations at the Ba The/Oc Eo complex (Viet Nam). A preliminary report on the 1998 campaign. In W. Lobo & S. Reimann (eds.), *Southeast Asian Archaeology 1998*. Hull: Centre for South-East Asian Studies, University of Hull and Ethnologisches Museum, Staatliche Museum zu Berlin, pp. 107–121.

Mason, G. M. (1991) The molluscan remains. In C. F. W. Higham & R. Bannanurag (eds.), *The Excavation of Khok Phanom Di*, vol. 2 (part 1): *The Biological Remains*. London: Society of Antiquaries, pp. 301–331.

Mormina, M. & Higham, C. F. W. (2010) Climate crises and the population history of Southeast Asia. In A. B. Mainwaring, R. Giegengack, & C. Vita-Finzi (eds.), *Climate Crises in Human History*. Washington: American Philosophical Society, pp. 197–212.

Oota, H., Kurosaki, K., Pookajorn, S., et al. (2001) Genetic study of the Paleolithic and Neolithic Southeast Asians. *Human Biology* 73, 225–231.

Rispoli, F. (2008) The incised and impressed pottery style of mainland Southeast Asia: following the paths of Neolithization. *East and West* 57(1–4), 235–304.

Tayles, N. G. (1999) *The Excavation of Khok Phanom Di. A Prehistoric Site in Central Thailand*, vol. V: *The People*. London: Society of Antiquaries.

Thompson, G. B. (1996) *The Excavation of Khok Phanom Di. A Prehistoric Site in Central Thailand*, vol. IV: *Subsistence and Environment: the Botanical Evidence (The Biological Remains, Part II)*. London: Society of Antiquaries.

Zhang, C. & Hung H.-C. (2010) The emergence of agriculture in southern China. *Antiquity* 84, 11–25.

Southeast Asian islands and Oceania: Austronesian linguistic history

Robert Blust

The Austronesian languages are distributed around more than half of the world's circumference and began their dispersal from Taiwan about 4,500 years ago. This became the greatest oceanic migration episode in history, spanning more than four thousand years until settlers eventually reached the far islands of Polynesia.

Language families differ enormously in the interest they hold for theories of migration. The search for the *Urheimat* or homeland of a language family with a restricted territory such as North Caucasian (34 languages between the Black and Caspian Seas) is relatively unexciting, since it was almost certainly in the Caucasus mountains, a range with a maximum length of 1,110 km and a width of less than 160 km. Where a group of related languages is more widely distributed, however, the homeland question generates far greater interest. This has long been the case for Indo-European, which extended before 1500 CE from Iceland to Bangladesh, and from northern Russia to Sri Lanka. Determining the location of the Austronesian homeland and the patterns of migration from it presents an unparalleled challenge, as the east–west range of the family is more than 2.5 times that of Indo-European. The 1,200-plus Austronesian languages cover an astonishing 206 degrees of longitude (about 23,000 km) from Madagascar at the western end of the Indian Ocean to Rapanui (Easter Island) in the eastern Pacific, and some 72 degrees of latitude (about 10,000 km) from northern Taiwan to southern New Zealand – by far the greatest territorial range of any language family prior to the European colonial expansions of the past 500 years (Blust 2009: 754). How were people with a preindustrial technology able to cross such vast distances? Where did they begin their epic migrations, and when? What was the pattern of territorial expansion, and was it continuous or discontinuous in time?

Since I have the task of addressing these questions through language data a few prefatory remarks about how historical linguists work might assist the general reader. Like all things in nature, languages change over time. If a preliterate language com-

The Global Prehistory of Human Migration: The Encyclopedia of Global Human Migration Volume 1,
First Edition. Edited by Peter Bellwood.
© 2013 John Wiley & Sons, Ltd. Published 2015 by John Wiley & Sons, Ltd.

munity were to persist without dividing for millennia its linguistic history would be lost, since each innovation would "erase"' what it replaced. But population increase gives rise to language split, and because the daughter communities change independently of one another each preserves different features of their common ancestor as they diverge into dialects and eventually distinct languages. The resulting patchwork of linguistic retentions and innovations enables linguists to "reconstruct" many features of the prehistoric parent language, and to propose a phylogenetic model, or family tree.

Traditional language communities were small. Languages with extensive territories, like Latin at the height of the Roman empire or various forms of Chinese throughout the dynastic history of China, were exceptional, and their scope was a consequence of the political, military, and technological ability of their speakers to conquer and administer far-flung territories, as well as the fact that these languages were written, and so capable of wide dissemination. Despite the rise of Indianized states in western Indonesia during the early centuries CE, nothing approaching the scope of the Roman empire or imperial China existed in the traditional Austronesian world.

From these two fundamental considerations (the inevitability of both change and split), it follows that the vast territory occupied by speakers of Austronesian languages is an epiphenomenon of population growth and migration over several millennia; the view that Proto-Austronesian might have been spoken over a significant portion of the territory occupied by its descendants is contrary to everything known about the size of traditional language communities and the dynamics of language split. For a population occupying an area the size of, say, the Philippine archipelago, to maintain a single language of pan-archipelagic scope would have been quite impossible under premodern conditions.

The Austronesian homeland

Historical linguists are concerned with a wide range of problems, one of which is the reconstruction of proto-languages based on a set of procedures called the Comparative Method. The Comparative Method of linguistics is a time-tested tool that has weathered criticism and revision for almost 200 years, and along with the theory of evolution by natural selection stands as one of the great intellectual triumphs of the 19th century. Once reconstruction is sufficiently advanced a language tree can be inferred based on evidence of exclusively shared innovations. Languages that share innovations apart from others in the same family are said to form a subgroup (comparable to a clade in biological phylogenetics). Linguistic subgroups may be nested inside others, or be independent branches within the language family.

The subgrouping of the Austronesian languages reveals a remarkable fact: although only 14 of the more than 1,260 Austronesian languages are found in Taiwan, these languages (together with a dozen others that are extinct) belong to at least nine primary branches of the language family. Stated more fully, the Austronesian family tree appears to have ten primary branches: nine confined to Taiwan and one – Malayo-Polynesian – that includes all other languages. Malayo-Polynesian in turn divides into Western Malayo-Polynesian (possibly not a valid phylogenetic unit) and

Central-Eastern Malayo-Polynesian. The latter contains Central Malayo-Polynesian and Eastern Malayo-Polynesian (EMP), with a subsequent division of EMP into South Halmahera-West New Guinea and Oceanic, a collection of over 460 Austronesian languages in the Pacific that includes the far-flung Polynesian group (Figure 35.1).

A method for determining primary centers of dispersal, or homelands of language families, was proposed by Sapir (1968 [1916]) and formalized by Dyen (1956). These writers and others stress that homelands usually correspond to areas of highest diversity, defined by concentrations of higher-level taxa, not number of languages. The argument is based on parsimony: since any alternative implies multiple in-migrations with no obvious motivation for the preferred destination, a homeland outside the area of greatest diversity is normally rejected. Much the same procedure was developed by Vavilov (1926) to track the dispersal of cultivated plants. The methods used by linguists to infer language-family homelands, then, do not differ fundamentally from those used in the biological sciences to determine centers of origin and paths of dispersal for organic species.

Given its structure, the Austronesian family tree strongly favors a homeland on the island of Taiwan; the great diversity of the Formosan languages is then interpreted as a product of longer divergence *in situ*. Consider dialects of English: the greatest diversity in the United States is found east of the Mississippi River, where English has been spoken longer than in areas further west. For the same reason the English of Great Britain shows far deeper dialect divisions than any part of North America. The earliest radiocarbon (C14) dates for Neolithic cultures in the Philippines postdate 2500 BCE (Bellwood & Dizon 2005). Prior to this, Austronesian languages presumably were found only north of the Philippines. However, we cannot assume that at this early period Austronesian languages were spoken only in Taiwan, which clearly was settled from the mainland of China. Rather, until much later, the early Austronesian world probably included both sides of the Taiwan Strait, and the Penghu (Pescadores) Islands within it (Rolett et al. 2007). A dynamic picture of the Austronesian expansion would thus show a growing territory at the front of the migration wave, but a (not necessarily synchronous) contracting territory at its rear, where the southward movement of the Han Chinese during the past two thousand years has led to the sinicization of many previously non-Han areas, a process that continues today in Taiwan.

Leaving the homeland

The first puzzle in understanding the Austronesian expansion is the long pause between the settlement of Taiwan, by at least 3500 BCE (Tsang 2005), and the settlement of the northern Philippines by related populations over a millennium later. If Taiwan was reached from mainland China, what prevented a similar settlement of the Philippines for so many centuries? We have no definite answer to this question, although Neolithic farmers may have rafted from China to Taiwan, while controlled sailing south to the Philippines had to await the invention of the outrigger canoe (Blust 1999). This idea is supported by the observation that the outrigger canoe complex and key linguistic terminology for it is widespread in the Austronesian world apart from Taiwan (Pawley & Pawley 1994). If the outrigger canoe enabled Austronesian speakers to leave Taiwan,

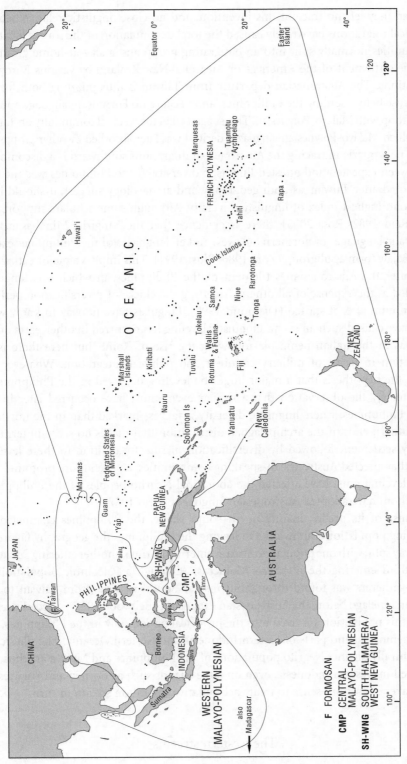

Figure 35.1 The Austronesian languages and their major subgroups. Base mapping by Australian National University, College of Asia and the Pacific.

however, they left no trace of this invention, and no close linguistic relative behind. Historical migrations have rarely caused the total depopulation of the source location; communities normally split into an emigrating group and a stay-at-home group, as with the settlement of the Americas or Australia–New Zealand by various European populations. The Austronesian departure from Taiwan is thus puzzling both for the long pause before settling the Philippines, and because no Formosan language appears to subgroup with Malayo-Polynesian. This suggests that the residual community on Taiwan from which Malayo-Polynesian languages derived was later absorbed by other groups.

The next puzzle in tracing the Austronesian migrations southward is a disconformity between expected and attested linguistic diversity. If the Philippines was the first area settled after Taiwan, as both geography and archaeology suggest, it should have the second highest index of linguistic diversity. Although some scholars support this view (Reid 1982; Ross 2005), there is evidence that the Sangiric, Minahasan, and Gorontalic languages of northern Sulawesi and all languages of the Philippines except Sama-Bajaw form a subgroup (Zorc 1986; Blust 1991). This implies a major extinction event after the Austronesian settlement of the Philippines, in which one language expanded at the expense of all others, "resetting the clock" of diversification perhaps a millennium after it started (Diamond 1992). Linguists have no way to know what could have caused such an event. Linguistic leveling has occurred in other parts of the world, as in the Italian peninsula following the rise of Rome, but here there is an explanation in terms of military conquest and political integration. Whatever the reason, the hypothesis that a major linguistic leveling occurred in the Philippines is supported by the observation that a similar event must have occurred later in the central Philippines, where linguistic diversity is far less marked than in the northern and southern ends of the archipelago, a distribution that makes no sense in terms of primary settlement followed by diversification *in situ*. In addition to these leveling events that affected Austronesian-speaking communities, an even more profound linguistic leveling must have affected the aboriginal Negrito peoples of the Philippines, all of whom have adopted Austronesian languages (Reid 1987).

Because of its predominantly north–south shape, the Philippines channeled an expanding population southward. On leaving the Philippines the geography favored a three-way split, with one population stream entering Borneo, another entering Sulawesi, and a third entering the northern Moluccas. Although a Paleolithic population of hunter-gatherers was found throughout insular Southeast Asia, from Taiwan to the Malay archipelago before the Austronesian expansion (Bellwood 1997), direct descendants of this population survived into the historical period only in the Philippines, the Malay peninsula, and parts of eastern Indonesia and western Oceania. The physically and culturally distinct Negrito populations of the Philippines and Malaya are thus not replicated in western Indonesia, even on large islands such as Borneo and Sulawesi.

It makes expository sense to treat each putative migration stream in turn.

The western streams

Austronesian speakers have been in Borneo for perhaps four thousand years (Bellwood 1997), and it is most likely that they entered the island from the north. Although their sailing capabilities would have enabled them to cover hundreds of miles in leapfrog fashion, the distribution of languages suggests that once landfall was made there was a strong tendency for further migration to proceed on land. A heavy reliance on marine resources led to coastal preferences in the early phases of settlement here and elsewhere in the Austronesian world. Because of its size and shape Borneo conditioned the southward migration of Austronesian speakers differently than the Philippines, leading to a primary linguistic split between populations following the west coast facing the South China Sea and those following the east coast facing the Celebes Sea and Makassar Strait (Blust 2010). There are some indications that the eastern wave in Borneo may have reached Java, Sumatra, and mainland Southeast Asia before the western wave, which is clearly associated with the spread of Malayo-Chamic languages into eastern Sumatra, the Malay peninsula, and coastal Vietnam in the centuries immediately preceding the arrival of massive Indian cultural influence (Blust 1994). Sometime between the 7th and 13th centuries CE, the ancestral Malagasy departed from the Barito River basin in southeast Borneo, apparently in consort with Sriwijayan Malays (Dahl 1951, 1991; Adelaar 1989). The motivation behind this intriguing migration remains unknown, although it may have been initiated by integration into a Malay-based trade network spanning parts of the Indian Ocean, as another migration from the same region evidently gave rise to the Sama-Bajaw peoples of the southern Philippines and scattered parts of Indonesia, who are traditionally known as "sea nomads," but were an integral part of Malay-based trade networks within the Malay archipelago (Blust 2005).

In Sulawesi we must also assume major extinction events, since the initial Austronesian population of the northernmost peninsula was replaced by later movements from the Philippines (Blust 1991). The remaining languages of the island appear to fall into two major groups: Celebic and South Sulawesi (Mead 2003). Beyond this the migration history of this island is unclear.

The eastern streams

On leaving the Philippines the Austronesian speakers who entered the northern Moluccas evidently split very early into two substreams. One of these moved rapidly into the central Moluccas and on to the Lesser Sundas, giving rise to the Central Malayo-Polynesian languages, a division of the Austronesian language family that probably began as an extensive dialect chain (Blust 1993). The other migration stream moved into the Bird's Head peninsula of western New Guinea, where it followed the north coast southeast to the Bismarck archipelago. At some point in this trajectory there must have been a pause that lasted long enough for the several highly distinctive innovations that characterize the Oceanic subgroup to develop. From this point, the evidence of both language and archaeology suggests rapid movement to the Fiji-Tonga-Samoa triangle, where the last long pause in Austronesian migration history occurred, leading to the innovations that clearly define the Polynesian subgroup before the final expansion into central and eastern Polynesia. Both linguistics and archaeology show a long pause in western Polynesia, comparable in length to the first long pause in Taiwan (more than a millennium), and this naturally raises questions of cause. Again, we have no definite answers, but it has been suggested that the permanent settlement of central and eastern Polynesia awaited the invention of the double-hulled canoe, or catamaran, a vessel capable of carrying sufficient population, water, plant propagules, and domesticated animals to successfully colonize small and widely scattered islands (Blust 1999).

The migration history leading to the settlement of Micronesia is more complex. The Mariana islands evidently were settled first, from the central or northern Philippines by at least 1500 BCE (Rainbird 1994; Blust 2000). Palau probably was settled next, possibly from a site in northern Sulawesi before or concurrently with the expansion of Philippine languages into this area, although this remains unclear. Finally, the Nuclear Micronesian languages (Kiribati, Kosrae, Chuuk, Pohnpeian, Marshallese, etc.), which represent a continuation of the "Lapita culture" of western Melanesia, appear to have reached their attested locations from the southeast Solomons sometime before two thousand years ago, with a landfall in the east and a steady expansion westward through the Caroline chain as far as Sonsorol, Tobi, and Mapia, very near the north coast of New Guinea, nearly completing a full circle back to the Proto-Oceanic homeland. The dates and approximate directions for Austronesian migration are indicated in Figure 36.1.

SEE ALSO: 32 Trans-Indian Ocean migration; 33 Southeast Asian mainland: linguistic history; 36 Southeast Asian islands: archaeology; 37 Southeast Asian islands and Oceania: human genetics

References

Adelaar, K. A. (1989) Malay influence on Malagasy: linguistic and culture-historical implications. *Oceanic Linguistics* 28, 1–46.

Bellwood, P. (1997) *Prehistory of the Indo-Malaysian Archipelago*. Honolulu: University of Hawaii Press.

Bellwood, P. & Dizon, E. (2005) The Batanes archaeological project and the "Out of Taiwan" hypothesis for Austronesian dispersal. *Journal of Austronesian Studies* 1, 1–33.

Blust, R. (1991) The Greater Central Philippines hypothesis. *Oceanic Linguistics* 30, 73–129.

Blust, R. (1993) Central and Central-Eastern Malayo-Polynesian. *Oceanic Linguistics* 32, 241–293.

Blust, R. (1994) The Austronesian settlement of mainland Southeast Asia. In K. L. Adams & T. J. Hudak (eds.), *Papers from the Second Annual Meeting of the Southeast Asian Linguistics Society*. Tempe: Program for Southeast Asian Studies, Arizona State University, pp. 25–83.

Blust, R. (1999) Subgrouping, circularity and extinction: some issues in Austronesian comparative linguistics. In E. Zeitoun & P. J. K. Li (eds.), *Selected Papers from the Eighth International Conference on Austronesian Linguistics*. Taipei: Academia Sinica, pp. 31–94.

Blust, R. (2000) Chamorro historical phonology. *Oceanic Linguistics* 39, 83–122.

Blust, R. (2005) The linguistic macrohistory of the Philippines: some speculations. In H. C. Liao & C. R. G. Rubino (eds.), *Current Issues in Philippine Linguistics and Anthropology, Parangal kay Lawrence A. Reid*. Manila: Linguistic Society of the Philippines and SIL Philippines, pp. 31–68.

Blust, R. (2009) *The Austronesian Languages*. Canberra: Pacific Linguistics.

Blust, R. (2010) The Greater North Borneo hypothesis. *Oceanic Linguistics* 49, 44–118.

Dahl, O. C. (1951) *Malgache et Maanjan: une Comparaison Linguistique* [Malgache and Maanjan: a linguistic comparison]. Studies of the Egede Institute, no. 3. Oslo: Egede-Instituttet.

Dahl, O. C. (1991) *Migration from Kalimantan to Madagascar.* Oslo: Norwegian University Press.

Diamond, J. (1992) *The Third Chimpazee: the Evolution and Future of the Human Animal.* New York: HarperCollins.

Dyen, I. (1956) Language distribution and migration theory. *Language* 32, 611–626.

Mead, D. (2003) Evidence for a Celebic supergroup. In J. Lynch (ed.), *Issues in Austronesian Historical Phonology.* Canberra: Pacific Linguistics, pp. 115–141.

Pawley, A. & Pawley, M. (1994) Early Austronesian terms for canoe parts and seafaring. In A. K. Pawley & M. D. Ross (eds.), *Austronesian terminologies: Continuity and Change.* Canberra: Pacific Linguistics, pp. 329–361.

Rainbird, P. (1994) Prehistory in the northwest tropical Pacific: the Caroline, Mariana, and Marshall islands. *Journal of World Prehistory* 8, 293–349.

Reid, L. A. (1982) The demise of Proto-Philippines. In A. Halim, L. Carrington, & S. A. Wurm (eds.), *Papers from the Third International Conference on Austronesian Linguistics,* vol. 2. Canberra: Pacific Linguistics, pp. 201–216.

Reid, L. A. (1987) The early switch hypothesis: linguistic evidence for contact between Negritos and Austronesians. *Man and Culture in Oceania* 3, 41–59.

Rolett, B. V., Guo, Z., & Jiao, T. (2007) Geological sourcing of volcanic stone adzes from Neolithic sites in southeast China. *Asian Perspectives* 46, 275–297.

Ross, M. (2005) The Batanic languages in relation to the early history of the Malayo-Polynesian subgroup of Austronesian. *Journal of Austronesian Studies* 1, 1–24.

Sapir, E. (1968) Time perspective in aboriginal American culture: a study in method. In D. G. Mandelbaum (ed.), *Selected Writings of Edward Sapir in Language, Culture and Personality.* Berkeley: University of California Press, pp. 389–462. (Originally pub. 1916.)

Tsang, C. H. (2005) Recent discoveries at a Tapenkeng culture site in Taiwan: implications for the problem of Austronesian origins. In L. Sagart, R. Blench, & A. Sanchez-Mazas (eds.), *The Peopling of East Asia: Putting Together Archaeology, Linguistics and Genetics.* London and New York: RoutledgeCurzon, pp. 63–73.

Vavilov, N. I. (1926) *Studies on the Origin of Cultivated Plants.* Bulletin of Applied Botany XVI.2.

Zorc, R. D. (1986) The genetic relationships of Philippine languages. In P. A. Geraghty, L. Carrington, and S. A. Wurm (eds.), *FOCAL II: Papers from the Fourth International Conference on Austronesian Linguistics.* Canberra: Pacific Linguistics, pp. 147–173.

36

Southeast Asian islands: archaeology

Peter Bellwood

This chapter complements chapters 35 and 37 by examining the archaeological record related to the early millennia of Malayo-Polynesian sea-borne migration through island Southeast Asia and into western Oceania, between 4500 and 3000 years ago.

Within the Asia-Pacific region, the Holocene inceptions of food production occurred independently in central China and in the New Guinea Highlands. China witnessed the development of cereal (rice, foxtail millet, and common millet) and pig production, and between 6500 and 2000 BCE the populations of many regions, especially in the Yellow and Yangzi basins, underwent unprecedented growth in numbers (some examples of this are given in chapter 10). China has therefore been a potential source of migrant populations into Southeast Asia and elsewhere for much of the Holocene.

The New Guinea highlands belong to a unique high altitude and equatorial cordilleran environment without geomorphic parallel anywhere in the volcanic arcs of island Southeast Asia. Broad highland valleys witnessed the independent Holocene development of fruit and tuber cultivation (bananas, pandanus, yams, and taro), but without cereals or domestic animals (Denham & Barton 2006). New Guinea populations did not expand in numbers to the extent visible in China and Southeast Asia (Gignoux et al. 2011), and are not known to have migrated during the Holocene into Indonesia beyond the eastern islands of Timor and Halmahera.

The original populations of *Homo sapiens* in island Southeast Asia, who eventually replaced *Homo erectus* and *Homo floresiensis*, were related ancestrally to the modern native populations of Melanesia and Australia (see chapter 27). With Neolithic population movement from southern China, through Taiwan into the Philippines and Indonesia, the older Pleistocene population landscape became more and more masked. This landscape is still evident today in the origins of many Pleistocene mitochondrial and Y-chromosome lineages and in the continued existence to the present day of Negrito populations in many Philippine islands. But Indonesia and the Philippines during the

The Global Prehistory of Human Migration: The Encyclopedia of Global Human Migration Volume 1,
First Edition. Edited by Peter Bellwood.
© 2013 John Wiley & Sons, Ltd. Published 2015 by John Wiley & Sons, Ltd.

past four thousand years have become regions of extensive population admixture, revealed by a steep change in the frequencies of many genetic markers in eastern Indonesia (Xu et al. 2012; and see chapter 37, this volume).

The role of China in the prehistory of Southeast Asia has been clarified in a number of the preceding chapters (especially chapter 26). The role of New Guinea and its indigenous Papuan-speaking population has received less attention, partly because the archaeology of the New Guinea highlands reveals no signs of direct and traceable contact with contemporary Neolithic societies in island Southeast Asia. However, Donohue and Denham (2010) suggest that sugar cane, bananas, and taro spread from lowland New Guinea into neighboring eastern Indonesia during the mid-Holocene. While very likely, these movements have not so far been demonstrated archaeologically, and the paleobotanical record from island Southeast Asia is at present too small to resolve the matter. In general, New Guinea populations appear to have restricted their Holocene biological and cultural influences to the western Pacific and the eastern islands of Indonesia, although some degree of agricultural population migration during the mid-Holocene might have occurred within the island itself, in connection with the expansion of the Trans New Guinea (Papuan) language family (Mona et al. 2007; Pawley 2007).

The Austronesian-speaking peoples and their significance

The origin of the Austronesian language family in Taiwan and its dispersal through island Southeast Asia is related in chapter 35. For Proto-Austronesian itself, located in Taiwan, comparative lexical reconstructions reveal an economy focused on rice cultivation, with a large vocabulary for rice in many forms and stages of growth, as well as processing and cultivation vocabulary, with also millets, sugar cane, and possibly aroids (such as taro). Proto-Malayo-Polynesian added many fruits and tubers to this vocabulary, as befitted its probable location in the tropical Philippines (Taiwan is mostly temperate in latitude). Proto-Oceanic (Bismarck archipelago) witnessed the ultimate loss of rice under equatorial climatic and day-length conditions, and possibly also due to competition from indigenous fruit and tuber modes of food production (Bellwood 2011a). Other early Austronesian reconstructions apply to pigs and dogs (but not chickens until Proto-Malayo-Polynesian), pottery, boats and sails, fishing, and a wild placental (not marsupial) mammal fauna. The morphological and semantic integrity of these many reconstructions imply continuous linguistic transmission through time, not late borrowing (Pawley 2002; Ross 2008). Furthermore, the rake-like phylogeny of the main Malayo-Polynesian subgroups implies rapid migrational spread, at least from the Philippines to as far east as western Polynesia (Pawley 1999; Blust 2009; Gray et al. 2009).

Archaeological research on Holocene migration in Taiwan and the Philippines

Understanding of archaeological prehistory in Taiwan and the northern Philippines has recently developed very rapidly (Bellwood 2011b; Bellwood et al. 2011). The main breakthroughs have come with the established presence, by at least 2800 BCE, of an agricultural (rice and foxtail millet) economy for the Dabenkeng Neolithic culture of southwestern coastal Taiwan (Tsang 2005); with the documentation of a six-fold or greater increase in site numbers during the course of the 3rd millennium BCE in eastern Taiwan (Hung 2005: 126); and with the recovery of fine-grained ceramic evidence for the spread, at about 2200 BCE, of Neolithic material culture from Taiwan into the Batanes Islands (previously uninhabited) and northern Luzon (Bellwood & Dizon 2005, 2008; Hung 2005, 2008). This Neolithic spread carried (not necessarily all together) red-slipped pottery with specific rim forms and body shapes, pottery spindle whorls, stone barkcloth beaters, tanged or grooved stone adzes, Fengtian (eastern Taiwan) nephrite, Taiwan slate knives and projectile points, notched pebble net sinkers, domestic pigs (*Sus scrofa*), dogs, and rice (a prehistoric presence of millet still remains uncertain beyond Taiwan). A precise archaeological homeland within the island of Taiwan is not yet identifiable, and it is possible that groups from different regions were involved in many individual movements, with the closest ceramic parallels so far being focused on the southeastern coastline.

In the case of the Batanes, excavations in five caves and rock shelters with plentiful ceramic-period occupation leave no doubt that humans had not previously reached these windswept islands, protected by relatively rough seas and sometimes strong ocean currents, until the Neolithic. There is absolutely no trace in caves or surface finds of prior hunter-gatherer pre-ceramic occupation or flaked lithic tool manufacture. Luzon, to the contrary, had Paleolithic hunters and gatherers in occupation since at least 24 kya and possibly since 67 kya, so the first Neolithic arrivals must have interacted with these groups (Mijares et al. 2010).

The spread of Neolithic pottery from Taiwan into the Philippines and Indonesia

Newly excavated ceramic data establish the development of a tradition of red-slipped plain ware pottery manufacture in southern and eastern Taiwan, emergent by at least 2200 BCE from a prior "Middle Neolithic" tradition with both cord-marking and red slip (Hung 2008; Bellwood & Dizon 2008). By 2000 BCE, this red-slipped plain ware tradition had spread to the previously uninhabited Batanes Islands, as documented in Reranum and Torongan Caves on Itbayat. For northern Luzon (Philippines), current research on the lowest deposits beneath the Late Neolithic shell mound at Nagsabaran (Hung 2008; Hung et al. 2011) suggests that both red-slipped plain ware and incised and stamped pottery appeared together around 2000–1500 BCE. The same tradition of pottery decoration is also reported from Achugao and House of Taga on Saipan and Tinian respectively in the Mariana Islands, western Micronesia, where initial settlement across 2,300 km of open sea occurred from the Philippines at about 1500 BCE (see chapter 40). This appears to have been the first truly long-distance sea voyage in human history, and in a book on global migration it perhaps deserves a round of applause.

Related (but not identical) pottery assemblages appear c.1300 BCE at Bukit Teng-korak in Sabah, northern Borneo (Chia 2003), in association with Talasea (Kutau/

Bao) obsidian from the Bismarck archipelago in western Melanesia. This discovery indicates two-way human movement on a remarkable scale between Borneo and New Britain, over 4,000 km of ocean and intervening islands (Bellwood 1997; and see Figure 36.1).

In other parts of central and eastern Indonesia the incised and stamped pottery appeared much later than the red-slipped plain ware, suggesting that this region, unlike the Mariana Islands, was not a route for the initial spread of pottery decoration into the Lapita complex in western Oceania (see chapter 39). Red-slipped plain ware is dated from c.1500–1000 BCE at Kamassi and Minanga Sipakko in the Karama valley in West Sulawesi (Simanjuntak et al. 2008; Anggraeni 2012), and also occurs at Kendeng Lembu in eastern Java, Uattamdi in Maluku, Leang Tuwo Mane'e in Talaud, Paso in northern Sulawesi, and Madai Cave in Sabah (Bellwood 1997).

The above evidence suggests that a red-slipped plain ware tradition of Taiwan origin was joined, after 2000 BCE, by a very significant tradition of zoned incision with infilling by punctate or circle stamping, the punctate made by a multiple-toothed tool like a tattooing chisel. Some sites have both plain and stamped pottery from the start, others appear to have an earlier horizon of plain ware only, but the picture is still obscure because so many assemblages are very small and come from caves and rock shelters. Perhaps the punctate and circle-stamping tradition was introduced from mainland southern China or Hainan (Rispoli 2008), although it is not possible to rule out Taiwan as the immediate source on present evidence since examples also occur there.

Similar punctate and dentate stamping is a very typical feature of Lapita pottery in western Melanesia (1350 to 750 BCE; chapter 39, this volume), and occurs here with white lime or clay infilling of the designs, as in Luzon and the Marianas, where the greatest similarities occur. It is likely that movement through Luzon and possibly the Marianas into the Bismarck archipelago introduced some of the Lapita decorative repertoire (Hung et al. 2011). But no claim is made that Lapita origins occurred only via the Marianas, since multidirectional movements through Indonesia are also implied by the Bukit Tengkorak obsidian, and could have involved populations speaking relatively undifferentiated languages still very close to Proto-Malayo-Polynesian.

The nature of the food-producing economy that moved with early Malayo-Polynesian-speaking populations into Indonesia is difficult to establish owing to a paucity of data, but it appears that rice cultivation faded in importance in equatorial latitudes, which lack climatic seasonality (Dewar 2003). This crop was never grown by Pacific peoples, except possibly in the Mariana Islands. The domestication of the pig in island Southeast Asia is currently a topic of considerable debate (Larson et al. 2010), rendered complex by the wide distribution of native suids in mainland Asia, western Indonesia (Sundaland), and Sulawesi. Pig bones are widespread in Neolithic sites in Taiwan, and are common in the Neolithic layer at Nagsabaran in the Cagayan valley on Luzon, where teeth of domesticated *Sus scrofa* have been directly AMS-radiocarbon dated to before 2000 BCE (Piper et al. 2009). By 1300 BCE, pigs of the so-called "Pacific clade" had reached Lapita sites in Melanesia, perhaps from northern Mainland Southeast Asia via Indonesia. Pigs were not carried from Luzon to the Marianas in prehistoric times, so did not enter the Lapita zone by this route.

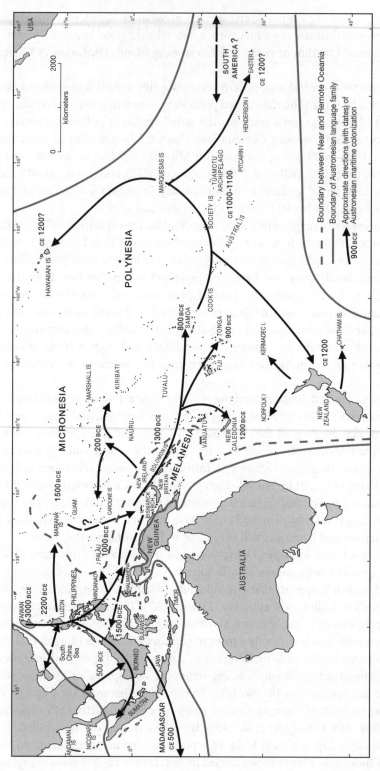

Figure 36.1 Holocene population movements through Island Southeast Asia and across Oceania, as identified from archaeological and comparative linguistic data. Map production by Education and Multimedia Services, College of Asia and the Pacific, The Australian National University.

The nephrite trail

In Taiwan, nephrite (jade) tools and ornaments have been identified from over 100 sites dating between 3000 BCE and 500 CE (Hung et al. 2007). Taiwan nephrite is generally green in color, and was exploited from deposits at Fengtian, located at the northern end of the eastern rift valley of Taiwan. Fengtian nephrite has recently been subjected to a detailed sourcing program (Iizuka & Hung 2005) and can be identified with confidence in terms of the chemistry of its matrix and its zinc chromite inclusion minerals. All green jade artifacts tested from Taiwan and the Philippines are from the Fengtian source, but northern Luzon also had at least one separate white nephrite source that was used in prehistoric times for making adzes.

Jade working was most probably introduced into Taiwan with the Neolithic movement of Pre-Austronesian-speaking populations from southern China, where it was present in the Yangzi basin as early as 5000 BCE. In Taiwan, sawn nephrite adzes appear in the Dabenkeng phase (c.3000 BCE), and the long-lasting tradition of grooving, snapping, drilling and polishing nephrite later developed into the remarkable funerary assemblages of Beinan in southeastern Taiwan (c.1500–500 BCE), with pendants (some anthropomorphic), penannular earrings (some with four circumferential projections), bell-shaped and tubular beads, perforated projectile points, and adzes (Lien 2002). Parts of two Fengtian nephrite bracelets of a type most commonly found in the "Middle Neolithic" phase in Taiwan, dating prior to 2000 BCE, have been recovered from the base of Nagsabaran (c.2000–1500 BCE) in the Cagayan Valley in Luzon. Fengtian nephrite was also imported by at least 1200 BCE into the Batanes Islands.

In conclusion

Four factors render a southwards movement of Neolithic material culture from Taiwan into the northern Philippines, at about 2000 BCE, a virtual certainty. Firstly, there are the strong parallels in material culture between 2200 and 1500 BCE that link southern Taiwan and the northern Philippines, reinforced by the movement of artifacts of Taiwan slate and positively sourced Taiwan nephrite. Secondly, Taiwan has chronological priority of the artifact types concerned, involving an unbroken continuity since at least 3000 BCE, to which can be added the oldest radiocarbon dates for rice and millet in Southeast Asia, domesticated dogs, and probably pigs. Thirdly, there is an absence of closely related Neolithic material culture before 1500 BCE in Indonesia, and there are deep and significant differences in most aspects of Neolithic material culture between Vietnam and the Philippines prior to 1000 BCE (Bellwood et al., forthcoming). Any population movements from the Asian mainland into island Southeast Asia during the Neolithic were likely restricted to the westerly fringes of Indonesia, and might have involved trade rather than migration. Finally, the absence of a prior population in the Batanes Islands implies a movement of people from Taiwan to establish colonization, not an adoption of Neolithic material culture by an indigenous hunter-gatherer population.

From an archaeological perspective, the progression of Neolithic material culture assemblages of ultimate East Asian/Taiwan origin, through the regions settled by ancestral Austronesian speakers, required about four thousand years to unfold from Taiwan to eastern Polynesia (see chapter 41). Populations already resident in island Southeast Asia and Melanesia contributed cultural capital in the form of some shell artifact technologies (especially flaked shell tools), tuber and fruit crops of western Pacific (especially New Guinea) origin, flaked lithic traditions (found commonly mixed with Neolithic assemblages in Indonesian caves), and even translocated species of marsupials in some islands close to New Guinea.

Why did the Austronesian dispersal occur? Within eastern Taiwan, the archaeological record indicates a marked increase in the number of archaeological sites after 2500 BCE (Hung 2008), which suggests population growth and a need for new cultivation land, given that southeastern Taiwan is a rugged area with low agricultural potential. But early Austronesians moved on to settle new islands very rapidly in terms of both archaeology and comparative linguistics (Pawley 1999), traveling the 8000 km from the Batanes Islands to Samoa in less than a thousand years, beyond which a marked slowdown occurred. This rapid movement to western Polynesia surely reflected a reliance on *both* maritime *and* lowland agricultural resources, the latter greatly reduced in extent by the drowning of the most fertile alluvial and coastal soils as the sea attained its maximum mid-Holocene sea level (Bellwood et al. 2008). This would have rendered good coastal and alluvial farmland scarce in the early centuries of Austronesian migration, creating deep estuaries and steep coastlines against rugged island interiors, at least until forest clearance caused soil aggradation to build up fertile lowlands. Advancing maritime technology also fueled the Austronesian spread, with the earliest evidence for canoes and paddles in this region coming from coastal central China during the early Holocene.

After reaching its eventual limits in Madagascar and Polynesia, the Austronesian language family became the most widespread in the world prior to 1500 CE, spanning more than half of the earth's circumference. Madagascar represented an Iron Age migration (see chapters 32 and 35), but the colonization of the open Pacific was purely a Neolithic achievement.

SEE ALSO: Vol. I: 26 Eastern Asia: archaeology; 35 Southeast Asian islands and Oceania: Austronesian linguistic history; 37 Southeast Asian islands and Oceania: human genetics; 39 Oceania: Lapita migration; 40 Micronesian archaeology; 41 Polynesia, East and South, including transpacific migration; Vol. IV: Madagascar and Africa, Austronesian migration

References and further reading

Anggraeni (2012) The Austronesian migration hypothesis as seen from prehistoric settlements on the Karama River, Mamuju, West Sulawesi. Unpublished PhD thesis, Australian National University.

Bellwood, P. (1997) *Prehistory of the Indo-Malaysian Archipelago*, rev edn. Honolulu: University of Hawaii Press.

Bellwood, P. (2011a) The chequered prehistory of rice movement southwards as a domesticated cereal – from the Yangzi to the Equator. *Rice* 4, 93–103.

Bellwood, P. (2011b) Holocene population history in the Pacific region as a model for worldwide food producer dispersals. *Current Anthropology* 52(S4), 363–378.

Bellwood, P. & Dizon, E. (2005) The Batanes Archaeological Project and the Out of Taiwan hypothesis for Austronesian dispersal. *Journal of Austronesian Studies* 1, 1–33.

Bellwood, P. & Dizon, E. (2008) Austronesian cultural origins: out of Taiwan, via the Batanes Islands, and onwards to western Polynesia. In Sanchez-Mazas et al. (2008), pp. 23–39.

Bellwood, P., Chambers, G., Ross, M., et al. (2011) Are cultures inherited? Multidisciplinary perspectives on the origins and migrations of Austronesian speaking peoples prior to 1000 BC. In B. Roberts & M. van der Linden (eds.), *Investigating Archaeological Cultures*. Dordrecht: Springer, pp. 321–54.

Bellwood, P., Stevenson, J., Dizon, E., et al. (2008) Where are the Neolithic landscapes of Ilocos Norte? *Hukay* 15, 25–38.

Bellwood, P., Oxenham, M., Bui, C. H., et al. (forthcoming) An Son and the Neolithic of southern Vietnam. *Asian Perspectives*.

Blust R. (2009) *The Austronesian Languages*. Canberra: Pacific Linguistics.

Chia, S. 2003. *The Prehistory of Bukit Tengkorak*. Sabah Museum Monograph 8. Kota Kinabalu: Sabah Museum.

Denham, T. & Barton, H. (2006) The emergence of agriculture in New Guinea. In D. Kennett & B. Winterhalder (eds.), *Behavioral Ecology and the Transition to Agriculture*. Berkeley: University of California Press, pp. 237–264.

Dewar, R. (2003) Rainfall variability and subsistence systems in Southeast Asia and the western Pacific. *Current Anthropology* 44, 369–388.

Donohue, M. & Denham, T. (2010) Farming and language in island Southeast Asia; reframing Austronesian history. *Current Anthropology* 51, 223–256.

Gignoux, C., Henn, B., & Mountain, J. (2011) Rapid, global demographic expansions after the origins of agriculture. *Proceedings of the National Academy of Sciences* 108, 6044–6049.

Gray, R., Drummond, A., & Greenhill, S. (2009) Language phylogenies reveal expansion pulses and pauses in Pacific settlement. *Science* 323, 479–483.

Hung, H.-C. (2005) Neolithic interaction between Taiwan and northern Luzon: the pottery and jade evidences from the Cagayan Valley. *Journal of Austronesian Studies* 1(1), 109–134.

Hung, H.-C. (2008) Migration and cultural interaction in southern coastal China, Taiwan and the northern Philippines, 3000 BC to 1 CE. Unpublished doctoral thesis, Australian National University, Canberra.

Hung, H.-C., Iizuka, Y., Bellwood, P., et al. (2007) Ancient jades map 3000 years of prehistoric exchange in Southeast Asia. *Proceedings of the National Academy of Sciences* 104, 19745–19750.

Hung, H.-C, Carson, M., Bellwood, P., et al. (2011) The first settlement of Remote Oceania: Luzon to the Marianas. *Antiquity* 85, 909–926.

Iizuka, Y. & Hung, H.-C. (2005) Archaeomineralogy of Taiwan nephrite: sourcing study of nephrite artifacts from the Philippines. *Journal of Austronesian Studies* 1(1), 35–80.

Larson, G., Liu, R., Zhao, X., et al. (2010) Patterns of East Asian pig domestication, migration, and turnover revealed by modern and ancient DNA. *Proceedings of the National Academy of Sciences* 107, 7686–7691.

Lien C.-M. (2002) The jade industry of Neolithic Taiwan. *Bulletin of the Indo-Pacific Prehistory Association* 22, 55–62.

Mijares, A., Détroit, F., Piper, P., et al. (2010) New evidence for a 67,000-year-old human presence at Callao Cave, Luzon, Philippines. *Journal of Human Evolution* 59, 123–132.

Mona, S., Tomasetto-Ponzetta, M., Brauer, S., et al. (2007) Patterns of Y-chromosome diversity intersect with the Trans-New Guinea hypothesis. *Molecular Biology and Evolution* 24, 2546–2555.

Pawley, A. (1999) Chasing rainbows: implications of the rapid dispersal of Austronesian languages for subgrouping and reconstruction. In E. Zeitoun & P. J-K. Li (eds.), *Selected Papers from the Eighth International Conference on Austronesian Linguistics*. Taipei: Institute of Linguistics, Academia Sinica, pp. 95–138.

Pawley, A. (2002) The Austronesian dispersal: languages, technologies and people. In P. Bellwood & C. Renfrew (eds), *Examining the Farming/Language Dispersal Hypothesis*. Cambridge: MacDonald Institute for Archaeological Research, pp. 251–273.

Pawley A. (2007) Recent research on the historical relationships of the Papuan languages. In J. Friedlaender (ed.), *Genes, Language and Culture History in the Southwest Pacific*. Oxford: Oxford University Press, pp. 36–60.

Piper, P., Hung, H.-C., Campos, F., et al. (2009) A 4000 year old introduction of domestic pigs into the Philippine Archipelago. *Antiquity* 83, 687–95.

Rispoli, F. (2008) The incised and impressed pottery of Mainland Southeast Asia: following the paths of Neolithization. *East and West* 57, 235–304.

Ross, M. (2008) The integrity of the Austronesian language family: from Taiwan to Oceania. In Sanchez-Mazas et al. (2008), pp. 161–181.

Sanchez-Mazas, A., Blench, R., Ross, M., et al. (eds.), (2008) *Past Human Migrations in East Asia*. London: Routledge.

Simanjuntak, T., Morwood, M., Intan, F., et al. (2008) Minanga Sipakko and the Neolithic of the Karama River. In T. Simanjuntak (ed.), *Austronesian in Sulawesi*. Depok: Center for Prehistoric and Austronesian Studies, pp. 57–76.

Tsang, C.-H. (2005) Recent discoveries at a Tapenkeng culture site in Taiwan: implications for the problem of Austronesian origins. In L. Sagart, R. Blench, & A. Sanchez-Mazas (eds.), *The Peopling of East Asia*. London: RoutledgeCurzon, pp. 63–73.

Xu, S., Pugach, I., Stoneking, M., et al. (2012) Genetic dating indicates that the Asian-Papuan admixture through Eastern Indonesia corresponds to the Austronesian expansion. *Proceedings of the National Academy of Sciences* 109, 4574–4579.

37

Southeast Asian islands and Oceania: human genetics

Murray P. Cox

This chapter discusses the genetic record of human migration into island Southeast Asia and Oceania, firstly during the Pleistocene, and later during the Neolithic with its associated populations of Malayo-Polynesian speakers. The picture is one of intergradation between Asian and indigenous (western Pacific) population components.

The Neolithic period was a time of great change in island Southeast Asia and Oceania. Many characteristics of the peoples living in this region today have their foundation in the Neolithic, including their languages, modes of subsistence, and many aspects of modern culture. The same is true of their biology. The Neolithic period saw major population movements from mainland Asia, substantially changing the biological makeup of communities in what are today the island nations of Taiwan, the Philippines, Indonesia, Papua New Guinea, and Solomon Islands. Descendants of these Neolithic voyagers ultimately developed the advanced seafaring skills necessary to explore and settle the remote islands of the vast Pacific Ocean.

Genetics as history

History can be reconstructed in many different ways. It can be inferred from the distribution and relationships of languages, an approach first applied in the Pacific during the 1770s by the natural historian Johann Reinhold Forster during Captain James Cook's second voyage. History can be reconstructed from the distribution and relationships of archaeological artifacts. Importantly, however, history is also carried in the DNA of living people, as well as being preserved in the bones of ancient individuals.

Such genetic evidence is often considered to be of recent provenance. In fact, the earliest studies of genetic diversity in the Indo-Pacific region were carried out in the

The Global Prehistory of Human Migration: The Encyclopedia of Global Human Migration Volume 1,
First Edition. Edited by Peter Bellwood.

1920s by Bais and Verhoef (1924) and Heydon and Murphy (1924). These first papers reported ABO blood group frequencies in Java and New Guinea, but new studies were quickly initiated across island Southeast Asia and Oceania. Contrary to popular opinion, geneticists have been helping to reconstruct Pacific prehistory for the last 90 years.

These early studies examined so-called "classical" genetic markers, mainly blood proteins like the well-known ABO blood groups. Markers like this dominated human population genetics for the next sixty years, and proved to be remarkably informative about broad regional trends. One clear pattern was the distinction between populations in Melanesia on the one hand, and island Southeast Asia and Polynesia on the other. Several classical genetic markers exhibit frequency differences between these groups (Cavalli-Sforza et al. 1994; Cox 2008; Mourant et al. 1976). Nevertheless, these early genetic markers lacked resolution over small geographical areas, and reconstructing fine-scaled, directional population movements remained out of reach.

By the mid-1980s, newly developed techniques, particularly the Polymerase Chain Reaction (PCR), were allowing geneticists to study DNA sequences directly for the first time. This was a landmark era for human population genetics and the field has grown rapidly over the past twenty-five years. As with earlier technological developments, these new approaches were quickly applied to questions of Indo-Pacific prehistory. In 1989, Hertzberg and colleagues identified a DNA variant that is largely restricted to Polynesians and connects them firmly, and quite recently, back to the Asian mainland. This study was the first to reconstruct directional movements across the Pacific, a key goal of human population genetics that is still pursued today.

Genetic prehistory of the Indo-Pacific region

Hertzberg and his colleagues studied just one genetic region – mitochondrial DNA (mtDNA), but their work was followed later by studies of the Y chromosome. Mitochondrial DNA is inherited maternally – it is passed down only from a mother to her offspring, while the Y chromosome is inherited paternally – it is passed down only from a father to his sons. These simple modes of transmission provide a tractable model system to study the human past, and most genetic research in the Pacific has revolved around these two important genetic regions (summarized in Hill et al. 2007; Karafet et al. 2010; Tabbada et al. 2010).

However, within the last few years, a third generation of genetic data has appeared on the scene. Multiple ancestry-informative markers drawn from across the human genome (i.e. the autosomal chromosomes) are increasingly becoming the new gold standard in molecular anthropology. Although only a few studies have examined Indo-Pacific populations, they are already providing a broad outline of the region's prehistory, particularly the statistical distribution of Asian-Melanesian ancestry across large swathes of island Southeast Asia and Oceania (Cox et al. 2010). In the west, Taiwanese aboriginals have almost 100 percent Asian ancestry. In island Melanesia, Asian ancestry drops to around 20 percent, but then increases again further east, reaching around 80 percent Asian ancestry in the Polynesian gene pool (Friedlaender et al. 2008; Kayser et al. 2008).

This uneven distribution of Asian-Melanesian ancestry is a direct outcome of a complex history stretching back nearly 50,000 years (O'Connell & Allen 2004). The islands of Southeast Asia and Oceania essentially form a cul-de-sac, characterized by recurrent, unidirectional population incursions from mainland Asia. These movements occurred in at least three phases, broadly aligned with the Pleistocene, Neolithic, and historic eras.

In addition, the genetic history of women appears to have differed slightly from that of men. This disparity is caused by contrasting social histories, particularly marriage practices that affect men and women in different ways. Pulses of immigration during the Neolithic were dominated by matrilineal communities (Jordan et al. 2009), where wealth and status were dispersed through maternal lines. These communities apparently also practiced matrilocal residence, whereby married women remained in their home community, while their husbands moved. This process favored the loss of incursive male diversity (e.g. Asian Y-chromosome lineages) while retaining incursive female diversity (e.g. Asian mtDNA lineages), a process that was recently detected at a genome-wide scale across island Southeast Asia (Cox et al. 2010).

In combination, these processes produced large-scale patterns of genetic diversity that persist in island Southeast Asia and Oceania even today. Broadly speaking, around 60 percent of island Southeast Asian and Oceanic individuals across the region, including both Austronesian and non-Austronesian speakers, carry mtDNA lineages that have existed in the Pacific since the Pleistocene. Conversely, approximately 40 percent of such individuals carry mtDNA lineages that can be traced back to incursive population movements into the Pacific during the Neolithic, often ultimately from China and mainland Southeast Asia. Of course, the exact proportions vary widely across island Southeast Asia and Oceania; for instance, Polynesians largely carry mtDNA lineages that trace back to population movements from mainland Asia during the Neolithic, while New Guinea highlanders predominantly carry mtDNA lineages with local antecedents stretching far back into the Pleistocene. Between these two extremes lies a wide range of regional variation. This is explored in greater detail below.

In the following sections, we will explore how this wealth of mtDNA and Y-chromosome evidence is filling in the regional details of this broad historical outline (also see Kayser 2010).

Pleistocene continuity

Population movements during the Neolithic were inscribed on a palimpsest of genetic diversity laid down during the Pleistocene. Much of the Indo-Pacific region was settled from around 50 kya. These early settlers were part of the first waves of modern humans who left Africa to settle in Eurasia and the Americas, and the descendants of these pioneers continue to dominate parts of the region today.

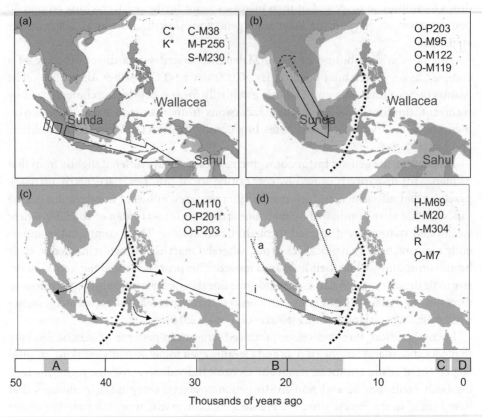

Figure 37.1 A multistage settlement model for island Southeast Asia: (a) Initial wave of colonization 40–50 kya, (b) Paleolithic contribution from mainland Asia, (c) Austronesian expansion, and (d) migration in historic times. Y-chromosome haplogroups and paragroups listed in each panel are postulated to have arrived during each stage. Arrows do not denote precisely defined geographic routes. The dotted arrowhead in panel (b) indicates possible bidirectional gene flow. The dotted line in panels (b), (c), and (d) represents Wallace's biogeographic boundary. Small letters associated with arrows in panel (d) refer to migrations from India (i), Arabia (a) and China (c). Shaded areas with capital letters (A–D) under panels refer to approximate time frames for each stage of colonization. Coastlines in panels (a) and (b) are drawn with sea levels 50 and 120 m below current levels. Figure reproduced unmodified from Karafet et al. (2010) by permission of Oxford University Press.

On the tree of mtDNA diversity (Van Oven & Kayser 2009), these first settlers are represented by the major regional haplogroups P and Q, which today are largely restricted to the Papuan strongholds of eastern Indonesia, New Guinea, and island Melanesia. Populations in this region are also characterized by many unique, low-frequency lineages that branch off early from the mtDNA tree (i.e. shortly after the African diaspora). These lineages reflect the extraordinary isolation and population substructure of this region, a key characteristic of Melanesia to this day.

The same general pattern can be seen on the tree of Y-chromosome diversity (Karafet et al. 2008). Haplogroup C, the first non-African branch, is frequent in eastern Indonesia, New Guinea, and island Melanesia, particularly in its derived form, C-M38*. However, the Out of Africa expansion also caused a rapid radiation of clade K, which includes haplogroups S and M. As with mtDNA lineages P and Q, these Y-chromosome haplogroups are essentially restricted to eastern Indonesia, New Guinea, and island Melanesia, reflecting their long history and relative isolation in this region.

Soon afterwards, movements from the Asian mainland may have introduced the first haplogroup O lineages into western parts of island Southeast Asia.

These genetic patterns dominated the Indo-Pacific for the first four-fifths of its history (from roughly 50 to 10 kya). Indeed, in New Guinea and on neighboring islands, Pleistocene lineages essentially reach a combined frequency of 100 percent even today. However, shortly after 10 kya, the development of agriculture in China, coupled with its rapid spread across island Southeast Asia after four thousand years ago, radically changed the population dynamics in most parts of the Pacific (Bellwood 2005; and see chapters 35, 36, 41). Immigration from mainland Asia, in part flowing through Taiwan and likely associated with the spread of Austronesian languages, substantially altered the genetic constitution of many Indo-Pacific populations. These patterns suggest that related, but slightly different, processes occurred in western island Southeast Asia, eastern island Southeast Asia, and Oceania. These regional variations are discussed in greater detail below.

The Neolithic period

Western island Southeast Asia

The weight of evidence suggests that Neolithic populations followed a two-pronged expansion into island Southeast Asia. One of these movements coursed down into western island Southeast Asia, most likely from Taiwan, particularly affecting the western Indonesian islands of Sumatra, Borneo, Java, and Bali. These Neolithic settlers are represented by a wide range of lineages on the tree of mtDNA diversity. Haplogroup E occurs across island Southeast Asia, and although it may in part have Pleistocene connections, subgroup E1a appears to link island Southeast Asia with indigenous populations on Taiwan. In comparison, the origin of haplogroup F is probably centered on southern China and mainland Southeast Asia; the mainland subgroup F1a1a is today spread widely across both western and eastern parts of island Southeast Asia. Subgroup N9a6 may provide additional evidence of mainland Asian connections, again with southern China and mainland Southeast Asia.

On the Y chromosome, the Neolithic saw a massive influx of haplogroup O lineages into island Southeast Asia, and this haplogroup remains characteristic of western island Southeast Asians today. Subgroup O-P203, which in turn derives from O-M119, probably arrived in western island Southeast Asia from China, possibly via Taiwan, during this time period.

Eastern Island Southeast Asia

A slightly different process seems to have occurred in the east, again likely starting in Taiwan and spreading through parts of the Philippines to the small island groups of eastern Indonesia. A range of mtDNA lineages dominated this expansion, including D5, F1a*, F3b, F4, M7b3, M7c1c, and Y2, all of which show some evidence of connections to indigenous Taiwanese. D5, M7c1c, and Y2 are also common in Sumatra and its offshore islands, Nias and Mentawai, sometimes reaching higher frequencies in western Indonesia than further east. A strong Taiwanese connection is therefore observed across island Southeast Asia, caused either by a geographically broad expansion of individuals with indigenous Taiwanese ancestry, or perhaps by later gene flow from east to west. The absence of eastern haplogroups P and Q in western island Southeast Asia tends to favor the hypothesis of a widespread Taiwanese dispersal.

Undoubtedly the most widely studied lineage in eastern island Southeast Asia is B4a1a1, which incorporates the so-called "Polynesian motif." This is one of the few lineages to link Taiwan and Polynesia, via a relatively low frequency of B4a1a1 in eastern island Southeast Asia (Melton et al. 1995). The full Polynesian motif likely developed in this region, although its antecedents can be traced to Taiwan, as well as further west to the Asian mainland (Trejaut et al. 2005).

On the Y chromosome, this expansion seems to be reflected most clearly in lineages O-M110 and O-P201*. The lineage O-P201*, which in turn derives from O-M122, also connects Taiwan and Polynesia, although O-P201* occurs at lower frequency in Polynesians than mtDNA haplogroup B4a1a1 (Cox et al. 2007).

Today, Pleistocene and Neolithic lineages are found side by side in eastern Indonesia, which partially accounts for the extreme genetic diversity of this region (Karafet et al. 2010). In places, Pleistocene/Neolithic genetic diversity is statistically correlated with Papuan/Austronesian language diversity, even over extremely small geographical areas (Lansing et al. 2007). Indeed the Austronesian expansion appears to be an ongoing process in this region, although the actual cultural underpinnings of these population movements still remain poorly understood (Lansing et al. 2011).

Oceania

Eastern island Southeast Asia provided a staging post for the settlement of the vast Pacific Ocean. Islands as far east as the Solomons were settled by c.40-55 kya, but colonization of the greater Pacific region was only accomplished within the last three to four thousand years. Although their ancestors passed through Melanesia, Polynesians trace relatively little of their biological ancestry to Melanesians (20%), but instead exhibit substantial Asian ancestry (80%). In terms of mtDNA and the Y chromosome, most of the Asian lineages that occur in Polynesians find their immediate antecedents in eastern Indonesia.

For mtDNA, this east–west connection is almost entirely represented by the Polynesian motif. This lineage, which – with the exception of Madagascar – is observed no further west than central Indonesia, reaches frequencies of nearly 100 percent across Polynesia. In some island groups, the Melanesian lineages P and Q also occur, but at frequencies no higher than a few percent. The Y-chromosome story is slightly different. Lineage O-P201* occurs at moderate frequency, illustrating clear connections back to the Asian mainland. However, it is the Melanesian lineage C-P33 that reaches highest frequencies in the Pacific, even attaining a frequency of 100 percent on the most remote Polynesian island, Easter Island/Rapanui (Cox et al. 2007). This lineage stems from C-M208, in turn derived from C-M38, which is characteristic of populations in eastern Indonesia.

The histories of mtDNA and the Y chromosome are therefore similar, but not identical. Both show evidence of founder effects and genetic drift, whereby genetic variants initially present at low frequencies reach high frequencies just by chance. In the case of mtDNA, the lineage that won this battle of chance was of Asian derivation. On the Y chromosome, a Melanesian lineage was instead picked up and carried to high frequency in Polynesians. Of course, when a large number of genomic markers are examined, it quickly becomes clear that Polynesians have predominantly Asian ancestry (about 80%). This provides an important warning that individual genetic markers like mtDNA and the Y chromosome can only tell us so much about our genetic prehistory; a range of markers from across the human genome will be necessary for us to reconstruct a fuller account of the human past.

Transition to the historic period

As the Neolithic period gave way to the historic era, an increasingly large number of cultures began leaving their impact on the Indo-Pacific region. Relatively few traces of these societies are found in the mtDNA (i.e. female) record, mainly lineages – such as I and U7 – that reflect recent European contact. A more cosmopolitan history is recorded on the male Y chromosome, including traces of Chinese (O-M7, O-M134), Arab (J, L) and Indian (H, R, Q) contributions. Importantly, however, none of these lineages reach more than a few percent in frequency today.

Summary

The Neolithic period was a defining era for island Southeast Asia and Oceania. It consolidated genetic patterns that were first laid down during the Pleistocene, but tempered them with new genetic variants emerging from mainland Asia. Following the region's initial settlement, the scale of these processes changed – from relatively local movements within island Southeast Asia during the Late Pleistocene, to regional mobility during the Neolithic, to immigration on a global scale during the historic era (Cox & Hammer 2010). However, on the borders of Melanesia, lineages that trace back to the Pleistocene are still in constant flux with lineages that first appeared in this region during the Neolithic. Many of these population dynamics continue into the present. In a very real sense, the history of Pacific peoples is still being played out.

SEE ALSO: 35 Southeast Asian islands and Oceania: Austronesian linguistic history; 36 Southeast Asian islands: archaeology; 41 Polynesia, East and South, including transpacific migration

References

Bais, W. J. & Verhoef, A. W. (1924) On the biochemical index of various races in the East Indian archipelago. *Journal of Immunology* 9, 383.

Bellwood, P. (2005) *First Farmers: The Origins of Agricultural Societies*. Oxford: Blackwell.

Cavalli-Sforza, L. L., Menozzi, P., & Piazza, A. (1994) *The History and Geography of Human Genes*. Princeton: Princeton University Press.

Cox, M. P. (2008) The genetic environment of Melanesia: clines, clusters and contact. In V. T. Koven, (ed), *Population Genetics Research Progress*. New York: Nova Science, pp 45–83.

Cox, M. P. & Hammer, M. F. (2010) A question of scale: Human migrations writ large and small. *BMC Biology* 8, 98.

Cox, M. P., Karafet, T. M., Lansing, J. S. et al. (2010) Autosomal and X-linked single nucleotide polymorphisms reveal a steep Asian-Melanesian ancestry cline in eastern Indonesia and a sex bias in admixture rates. *Proceedings of the Royal Society B* 277, 1589–1596.

Cox, M. P., Redd, A. J., Karafet, T. M. et al. (2007) A Polynesian motif on the Y chromosome: Population structure in Remote Oceania. *Human Biology* 79, 525–535.

Friedlaender, J. S., Friedlaender, F. R., Reed, F. A., et al. (2008) The genetic structure of Pacific Islanders. *PLoS Genetics* 4, e19.

Hertzberg, M., Mickleson, K. N. P., Serjeantson, S. W., et al. (1989) An Asian specific 9-bp deletion of mitochondrial DNA is frequently found in Polynesians. *American Journal of Human Genetics* 44, 504–510.

Heydon, G. & Murphy, T. (1924) The biochemical index in the natives of the territory of New Guinea. *Medical Journal of Australia*, Sup. 1, 235–237.

Hill, C., Soares, P., Mormina, M. et al. (2007) A mitochondrial stratigraphy for island southeast Asia. *American Journal of Human Genetics* 80, 29–43.

Jordan, F. M., Gray, R. D., Greenhill, S. J., et al. (2009) Matrilocal residence is ancestral in Austronesian societies. *Proceedings of the Royal Society B* 276, 1957–1964.

Karafet, T. M., Mendez, F. L., Meilerman, M. B. et al. (2008) New binary polymorphisms reshape and increase resolution of the human Y chromosomal haplogroup tree. *Genome Research* 18, 830–838.

Karafet, T. M., Hallmark, B., Cox, M. P., et al. (2010) Major east-west division underlies Y chromosome stratification across Indonesia. *Molecular Biology and Evolution* 27, 1833–1844.

Kayser, M. (2010) The human genetic history of Oceania: Near and Remote views of dispersal. *Current Biology* 20, R194–R201.

Kayser, M., Lao, O., Saar, K. et al. (2008) Genome-wide analysis indicates more Asian than Melanesian ancestry of Polynesians. *American Journal of Human Genetics* 82, 194–198.

Lansing, J. S., Cox, M.P., Downey, S. S. et al. (2007) Coevolution of languages and genes on the island of Sumba, eastern Indonesia. *Proceedings of the National Academy of Sciences USA* 104, 16022–16026.

Lansing, J. S., Cox, M. P., de Vet, T. A., et al. (2011) An ongoing Austronesian expansion in Island Southeast Asia. *Anthropological Archaeology* 30, 262–272.

Melton, T., Peterson, R., Redd, A. J., et al. (1995) Polynesian genetic affinities with Southeast Asian populations as identified by mtDNA analysis. *American Journal of Human Genetics* 57, 403–414.

Mourant, A. E., Kopeć, A. C., & Domaniewska-Sobczak, K. (1976) *The Distribution of the Human Blood Groups and Other Polymorphisms*. Oxford: Oxford University Press.

O'Connell, J. F. & Allen, J. (2004) Dating the colonization of Sahul (Pleistocene Australia–New Guinea): A review of recent research. *Journal of Archaeological Science* 31, 835–853.

Tabbada, K. A., Trejaut, J., Loo, J.-H., et al. (2010) Philippine mitochondrial DNA diversity: A populated viaduct between Taiwan and Indonesia? *Molecular Biology and Evolution* 27, 21–31.

Trejaut, J. A., Kivisild, T., Loo, J. H., et al. (2005) Traces of archaic mitochondrial lineages persist in Austronesian-speaking Formosan populations. *PLoS Biology* 3, e247.

Van Oven, M. & Kayser, M. (2009) Updated comprehensive phylogenetic tree of global human mitochondrial DNA variation. *Human Mutation* 30, E386–394.

38

Papua New Guinea: indigenous migrations in the recent past

Bryant Allen

The author discusses a number of recent migrations in Papua New Guinea, recorded in ethnographic and linguistic data. They offer interesting case studies of how groups of different ethnolinguistic background can intermix, and how small numbers of migrants can grow into large numbers of settlers, if and when they reach fertile terrain.

By around 2,500 years ago, the coastline of New Guinea (Figure 38.1) had stabilized largely to its present position and the human population was made up of the same two groups who now occupy the island. These two groups, distinguished mainly by the languages they speak, are known as non-Austronesians or Papuans, who are thought to have arrived as long ago as 50 kya (Summerhayes et al. 2010) and Austronesians, who arrived around 3,300 years ago. By 500 BCE, Austronesians inhabited only relatively small areas on the coast of the New Guinea mainland, with the possible exception of the Markham valley, but occupied much of New Britain, New Ireland, and parts of coastal Bougainville (Foley 1992: 137). Speakers of non-Austronesian languages occupied the greater part of the island of New Guinea.

For the past 2,500 years, until colonization around 1890 CE, the most common form of population movement has been of small groups of people moving small distances, usually as refugees from violent conflict, but also in order to take advantage of better opportunities to trade. In some of these cases, people maintained their languages and their cultures intact. In others, they "disappeared" linguistically and culturally into the groups that were already living at their destination. Typical of this small-scale, short-distance type of migration is the 50 km movement about 200 years ago of people from near Angoram to the Murik Lakes at the mouth of the Sepik River (Swadling 2010). Another is the movement of a small group of Kwanga-speaking refugees into the territory of Urat speakers around 1880. They were given land, now speak Urat, and apart from their oral history there is nothing to record their historic movement across the

---

The Global Prehistory of Human Migration: The Encyclopedia of Global Human Migration Volume 1,
First Edition. Edited by Peter Bellwood.

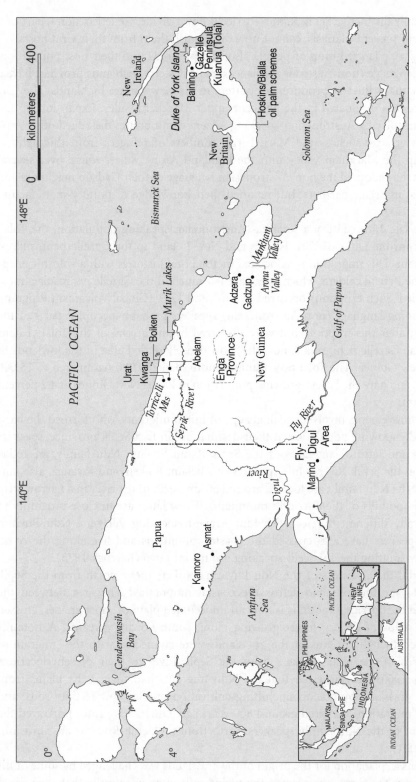

Figure 38.1 The island of New Guinea, showing migrant groups in Papua New Guinea (the eastern half of the island) mentioned in the text. Base mapping by Australian National University, College of Asia and the Pacific.

linguistically distinctive Sepik Ramu-Torricelli Phyla divide. Genetic studies, part of a program to prevent filariasis, cannot now distinguish them from their Urat hosts.

At least one larger group of people also "disappeared" into their host population. Agarabi-language (non-Austronesian) speakers of Eastern Highlands province have a unique status as the sole producers of pottery in the New Guinea highlands. They say their ancestors originated in the adjacent upper Markham valley. Expansion up the Markham valley by Austronesian-speaking Adzera communities dislodged other Austronesian groups, such as the Mari. Large numbers of refugees from this fighting moved up the Markham valley into the highland Arona valley, where over several centuries they adopted the non-Austronesian language of their Gadsup neighbors and occasional marriage partners, but retained their knowledge of pottery manufacture (Ballard 1994).

In the late 18th century a Kuanua-(Austronesian)speaking population, the Tolai, moved from the Duke of York Islands and New Ireland to the Gazelle peninsula of New Britain. This migration is associated in Tolai oral histories with a volcanic eruption of the Rabaul caldera, which may have left much of the Gazelle peninsula almost unoccupied. Such eruptions occurred in 1767 and 1791 (Global Volcanism Program, n.d.). Baining-language (non-Austronesian) speakers probably occupied parts of the peninsula after the eruption, but were displaced by the arrival of the Tolai (Fajans 1985). The Gazelle peninsula is now the most densely settled area in the lowlands of Papua New Guinea. The Tolai now number more than 200,000 (compared to 15,000 Baining), and have the fastest-growing population in Papua New Guinea at 4.2 percent per annum.

Other movements involved small groups of initial migrants, who formed the basis of a rapidly growing population at their destination. In East Sepik province, speakers of Sawos and Iatmul, languages of the Sepik-Ramu Phylum Ndu family, are today located on the Sepik River, while speakers of Abelam, Boiken, and Kwanga, also languages of the Ndu family, are located around 50 km north of the river in a narrow strip along the foothills of the Torricelli mountains. These latter are in close proximity to linguistically different Torricelli Phylum Arapesh-speaking villagers. Ndu Phylum Boiken speakers have also crossed the coastal mountains and live along the coast, effectively splitting the Torricelli-speaking groups into two (Laycock 1973).

How did the ancestors of the Ndu Phylum speakers move north from the Sepik River into the foothills and across the coastal mountains? The area between the Sepik and the Torricelli foothills is now an unoccupied plain of short grasses, crossed by long strips of gallery forest growing along south-flowing streams. A botanist has argued that the origins of the grasslands were connected with the "migration" northwards of the Ndu speakers from the Sepik River to their present locations (Robbins 1960). He suggested that the Ndu migrants had turned the plains from forest to grassland by practicing shifting cultivation on very low fertility soils, and that the "migration" occurred around 800 years ago. Others have since portrayed the movement of the Ndu family speakers north from the Sepik River as an "invasion" (Tuzin 2001).

Robbins' explanation for the origin of the grasslands was challenged by some of his colleagues at the time, who argued the plains soils were so infertile that they could never have supported either forest or agriculture (Haantjens et al. 1965). Another explanation is that, rather than "advancing" across the plains *en masse*, Ndu language speakers, probably in very small numbers, moved away from the Sepik River and up the rivers flowing south from the foothills to settle land to the north of the plains, including the highly fertile floodplains of the Amogu River (Roscoe 1989; Allen 2005). Here, agriculture was intensified and cultural and social innovation allowed population growth and expansion to occur east and west from the river. When this movement occurred is not known, but linguistic evidence suggests between 1,200 and 800 years ago. Today, the Sepik-Ramu languages with the largest number of speakers are those whose ancestral speakers moved from the Sepik River into the foothills, and the Torricelli languages with the largest number of speakers are those whose villages are closest to these "migrants." These Sepik-Ramu and Torricelli villages are larger, occupy land at higher population densities, and practice agriculture at higher levels of land use intensity than other villages in the foothills (Allen 2005: 588).

The most significant movement of people in late Holocene New Guinea occurred from around 1700 CE, when the introduction of sweet potato (*Ipomoea batatas*) increased agricultural productivity significantly and also allowed agriculture to expand on to poorer soils and to land above 2,200 m altitude. Sweet potato, now consumed as their most important staple food by 65 percent of people in Papua New Guinea, reached New Guinea from the Caribbean via Portugal and Portuguese colonies in the Moluccas and Indonesia (Yen 1974). Before sweet potato became available, the staple food in New Guinea at altitudes above 1,500 m was taro (*Colocasia esculenta*), supplemented by banana and yams (*Dioscorea spp*). Taro does not yield a crop above 2,200 m, whereas sweet potato is now grown to 2,800 m. Sweet potato will also yield on poorer soils for longer periods and can be fed to pigs without being cooked. The outcome was a "revolution" in agricultural production and in human populations, numbers of domesticated pigs, social organization, exchange, and trade throughout the highlands (Brookfield & White 1968).

Before the introduction of sweet potato, land above 2,200 m was exploited only for hunting and the production of planted and wild pandanus (*Pandanus julianetti* and *P. brosimos*), which remain important seasonal food sources today. Movements up-slope from lower to upper valleys are well described for Enga province in the highlands of Papua New Guinea, where oral histories record the occupation of the upper valleys and the development of the exchange networks that accompanied the expansion and intensification of agriculture (Weissner et al. 1998; Wohlt 2004). Today, 332,000 people live above 2200 m in Papua New Guinea, the majority of them in Enga Province, where more than one-third of the provincial population of 300,000 lives above this altitude. In the Eastern Highlands, the Fore people transformed their agriculture from taro to sweet potato based systems and expanded away from degraded land in the lower valleys to previously uncultivated land in the upper valleys (Sorenson 1974). However, in Indonesian Papua, major migrations by Dani speakers westward from the Baliem valley appear to have preceded the arrival of sweet potato. They placed pressure on their neighbors, the Lani or Western Dani, who in turn expanded westwards beyond the Baliem watershed and into valleys previously occupied by Moni, Nduga, and Damal speakers (Larson 1987; Ellenberger 1996).

The introduction of sweet potato was also associated within the highlands with the movements by some groups into the territories of their neighbors, with some people being pushed to lower altitudes. A "population-sink" model has been proposed in which groups moving from higher to lower altitudes from the highlands encountered malaria, dysentery, and pneumonia to such an extent that they remained small or disappeared altogether (Baal 1961; Stanhope 1970; Jenkins 1987). In the Southern Highlands however, as a result of conflict generated by population growth consequent upon the adoption of sweet potato, Huli-language speakers expanded to the west around 200 years ago into land previously occupied by Duna speakers, who are now found further to the west. They also moved down-slope to the south into areas then occupied by small and scattered groups known to the Huli as "Tuguba" (Ballard 2002). Today both groups speak Huli and follow Huli customs, but the Tuguba Huli maintain strong oral histories of their original occupation of the land.

Migrations of the kind described so far ceased with colonization. Colonial authorities, determined to stamp out intertribal fighting, prevented the expansion of one group into the territory of another. From around 1890 on the Gazelle peninsula, German colonial police intervened in Tolai attacks on Baining villages. In Indonesian Papua on the Fly-Digul platform, Marind people pushed east across the border into what was then British New Guinea, where colonial police used firearms to stop them. The Asmat expanded to the west, where they eliminated a number of groups, including the Sempan, but when they attacked Kamoro villages near the present-day Freeport in the 1920s, Dutch police killed large numbers of them with rifle fire. At Tari, the expansion of the Huli was stopped in the 1950s by patrol officers and armed police.

The only significant migrations since colonization have consisted of, first, more than 20,000 supporters of the Free Papua Movement (Organisasi Papua Merdeka or OPM), who since 1969 have crossed the border between Indonesia and Papua New Guinea, and second, the occupation of a large-scale resettlement scheme on West New Britain. The refugees have been accommodated in camps administered by the UNHCR, some live in informal settlements along the border in Western and Sandaun provinces, and others have returned. Recently some refugee children have been given PNG citizenship. The West New Britain settlers came from East Sepik, Chimbu, and East New Britain to grow oil palm on 6 ha blocks at Hoskins and Bialla, and now number over 160,000.

SEE ALSO: 35 Southeast Asian islands and Oceania: Austronesian linguistic history; 37 Southeast Asian islands and Oceania: human genetics

References

Allen, B. J. (2005) The place of agricultural intensification in Sepik foothills prehistory. In A. Pawley, R. Attenborough, J. Golson, & R. Hide (eds.), *Papuan Pasts: Cultural, Linguistic and Biological Histories of Papuan-Speaking Peoples.* Canberra: Pacific Linguistics, pp. 585–623.

Attenborough, R. D. & Alpers, M. P. (eds.) (1992) *Human Biology in Papua New Guinea: The Small Cosmos.* Melbourne: Clarendon.

Baal, J. van (1961) Review of "People of the Tor." *Nieuw Guinea Studiën* 5, 339–342.

Ballard, C. (1994) Background archaeology and ethnography. In M. E. Sullivan & P. J. Hughes (eds.), *Archaeological Investigations on the Yonki Terraces*. A report to ELCOM and the National Museum of Papua New Guinea. Boroko: Electricity Commission of Papua New Guinea.

Ballard, C. (2002) A history of Huli society and settlement in the Tari region. *Papua New Guinea Medical Journal* 45(1–2), 8–14.

Brookfield, H. C. & White, J. P. (1968) Revolution or evolution in the prehistory of the New Guinea highlands: a seminar report. *Ethnology* 7(1), 43–52.

Ellenberger, J. D. (1996) The impact of Damal world view on the formation of a local theology in Irian Jaya. PhD thesis, Fuller Theological Seminary, Pasadena.

Fajans, J. (1985) They make themselves: life cycle, domestic cycle and ritual among the Baining. PhD thesis, Stanford University.

Foley, W. A. (1992) Language and identity. In Attenborough & Alpers (1992), pp. 136–149.

Global Volcanism Program (n.d.) Eruptions at Rabaul 1767 and 1791. Smithsonian National Museum of Natural History. At www.volcano.si.edu/world/find_eruptions.cfm, accessed March 26, 2012.

Haantjens, H. A., Mabbutt, J. A., & Pullen, R. (1965) Anthropogenic grasslands in the Sepik Plains, New Guinea. *Pacific Viewpoint* 6(2), 215–219.

Jenkins, C. L. (1987) Medical anthropology in the western Schrader range, Papua New Guinea. *National Geographic Research* 3, 412–430.

Larson, G. F. (1987) The structure and demography of the cycle of warfare among the Ilaga Dani of Irian Jaya. PhD thesis, University of Michigan, Ann Arbor.

Laycock, D. (1973) *Sepik Languages: Checklist and Preliminary Classification*. Pacific Linguistics Series B, No. 25. Department of Linguistics, Research School of Pacific Studies, Australian National University: Canberra.

Robbins, R. G. (1960) The anthropogenic grasslands of Papua and New Guinea. In *Symposium on the impact of man on humid tropics vegetation*. Goroka: UNESCO, pp. 313–329.

Roscoe, P. B. (1989) The flight from the fens: the prehistoric migrations of the Boiken of the East Sepik Province, Papua New Guinea. *Oceania* 60(2), 139–154.

Sorenson, E. R. (1974) The evolving fore: a study of socialization and cultural change in the New Guinea highlands. PhD thesis, Stanford University.

Stanhope, J. M. (1970) Patterns of fertility and mortality in rural New Guinea. *New Guinea Research Bulletin* 34, 24–41.

Summerhayes, G., Leavesley, R., Fairbairn, M., et al. (2010) Human adaptation and plant use in highland New Guinea 49,000 to 44,000 years ago. *Science* 330(6000), 78–81.

Swadling, P. (2010) The impact of a dynamic environmental past on trade routes and language distributions in the lower-middle Sepik. In J. Bowden, N. P. Himmelmann, & M. Ross (eds.), *A Journey through Austronesian and Papuan Linguistic and Cultural Space: Papers in Honour of Andrew K. Pawley*. Canberra: Pacific Linguistics, pp. 151–157.

Tuzin, D. F. (2001), *Social Complexity in the Making: A Case Study among the Arapesh of New Guinea*. New York: Routledge.

Weissner, P., Pupu, N., & Timu, A. (1998) *Historical Vines: Enga Networks of Exchange, Ritual, and Warfare in Papua New Guinea*. Washington, DC: Smithsonian Institution.

Wohlt, P. B. (2004) Descent group composition and population pressure in a fringe Enga clan, Papua New Guinea. *Human Ecology* 32(2), 137–162.

Yen, D. (1974) *The Sweet Potato and Oceania: An Essay in Ethnobotany*. Honolulu: Bishop Museum.

39

Oceania: Lapita migration

Matthew Spriggs

The Lapita cultural complex of island Melanesia and western Polynesia saw the initial human colonization of many Oceanic islands in the centuries around 1000 BCE. Lapita laid the ancestral foundations for many subsequent Austronesian-speaking peoples of Oceania, including Eastern Polynesians and many Micronesians.

The Lapita culture is defined by its distinctive dentate-stamped pottery, instantly recognizable across more than 5,000 km from Aitape in the Sepik River area in New Guinea in the northwest, south and east to Samoa (Kirch 1997; Clark et al. 2001; Bedford et al. 2007; Sheppard et al. 2009). This is the earliest pottery across this entire region. A distinctive set of vessel forms and design elements are found on the pots. An associated cultural "package" includes distinctive shell ornament types, Asian domesticates, and commensals (pig, dog, chicken, and *Rattus exulans*, the Polynesian rat), agricultural crops ultimately of island Southeast Asian and New Guinea origin, fully polished stone adzes, rectangular houses often on stilts in more westerly areas, and a massive extension of earlier obsidian exchange networks in the region.

Lapita is earliest by a few centuries in its Bismarck Archipelago "homeland" to the east of New Guinea, starting around 1350 BCE. In the period from 1150 to 950 BCE it spread west along both north and south coasts of New Guinea, and also southeast through the main Solomons to the Reef-Santa Cruz Islands, Vanuatu, New Caledonia, Fiji, Tonga, Wallis, Futuna, and Samoa, the last four groups being in western Polynesia (Figure 39.1). Its distribution bridges the conventional geographic and ethnic boundaries of Melanesia and Polynesia, and beyond the main Solomon Islands it was the founding culture in a previously unoccupied region. The distance between the main Solomons and the Reef-Santa Cruz Islands is about 380 km and that gap represents a major biogeographic boundary, one perhaps precluding earlier hunter-gatherer settlement and separating Near Oceania from Remote Oceania (Green 1991). The

The Global Prehistory of Human Migration: The Encyclopedia of Global Human Migration Volume 1,
First Edition. Edited by Peter Bellwood.

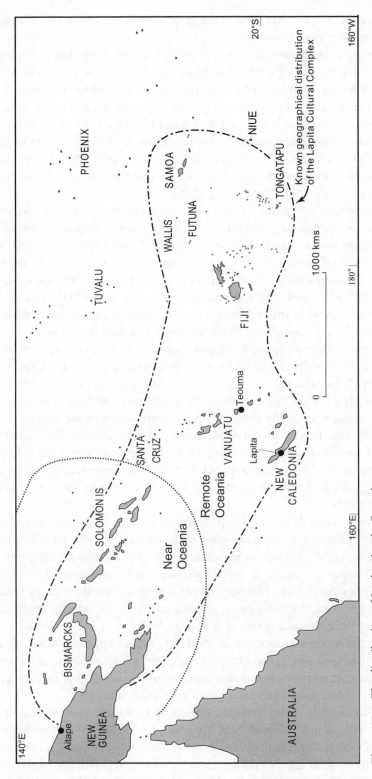

Figure 39.1 The distribution of Lapita sites in Oceania.

technological innovation that allowed the expansion beyond Near Oceania may have been the outrigger sailing canoe.

Lapita must necessarily represent a migration across more than 3,000 km of its distribution beyond the long-settled areas of New Guinea, the Bismarcks, and main Solomons. Whether it represented a migration into Near Oceania from further west is still subject to debate. Some see the origins of Lapita as the eastwards extension by demographic expansion of island Southeast Asian Neolithic cultures (Bellwood 1997). Others see much more local processes of generation at work in the Bismarcks and New Guinea, with the simple addition through diffusion or trade of pottery technology and Asian domesticates such as the pig, dog, chicken, and the commensal Polynesian rat (see, most recently, Torrence & Swadling 2008).

The horticultural system that spread with Lapita out into the Pacific was primarily of New Guinean origin, so something more than a simple migratory spread out of island Southeast Asia is therefore indeed called for. Green (2000) developed what he termed a "Triple-I" model of *intrusion, innovation,* and *integration* to explain the process. He distinguished Southeast Asian elements in Lapita (*intrusion*), those such as certain stone adze forms that appeared to be true *innovations* in the Bismarcks, and elements long present in the region that were adopted as the culture developed and spread – New Guinea crops being the most obvious of such *integrations*.

The ultimate origin in island Southeast Asian of the languages spoken by Lapita communities is, if anything, clearer than the origins of its material culture "package" (ch. 35). This is because only Oceanic Austronesian languages, derived fairly directly from an ancestral Proto-Oceanic believed by linguists to have been spoken in the Bismarcks, are spoken across the Remote Oceanic distribution of the Austronesian language family. The Triple I model should not, therefore, obscure the overwhelming evidence of Southeast Asian origin for much of the material culture and at least some of the people involved in the Lapita spread. Pottery itself, elements of the design system, and the technique of dentate-stamping and the particular vessel forms have Southeast Asian antecedents.

The domestic animals that made up the faunal element of the agricultural systems were all from Southeast Asia, as were many of the shell ornaments and adze forms and, on linguistic grounds, sailing-canoe technology, barkcloth manufacture, rectangular houses, and important aspects of social structure and kin reckoning. Jar burial was a distinctively Southeast Asian Neolithic disposal method, found earlier or contemporaneously in Taiwan, the Philippines, and Borneo, and also attested at the Teouma Lapita cemetery in Vanuatu (Bedford & Spriggs 2007).

Some Lapita technologies existed in pre-Lapita times in parts of New Guinea and/ or Eastern Indonesia and Timor, but are equally part of the Neolithic of Taiwan; fish-hooks are an example. We cannot therefore definitively conclude that their presence in Lapita represents integration rather than a Neolithic intrusion.

The predominantly Asian Neolithic origins of Lapita are being obscured by the nature of sites in island Southeast Asia. We have over 120 Lapita open settlement sites in Remote Oceania alone, dating to a period of only 200–300 years at the most. Less than 10 percent of all Lapita sites are caves or rockshelters. Yet, across the whole of island Southeast Asia outside Taiwan, there are less than 20 dated Early Neolithic open settlement sites, and these cover a period of more than a thousand years. More than 50 percent of island Southeast Asian Early Neolithic sites are caves/rockshelters. We are simply not comparing like with like (Spriggs 2011).

The links between the two regions will become clearer once we have more early Neolithic coastal open sites in island Southeast Asia. As it is, there is a thin but convincing trail of plausibly ancestral dentate-stamped and/or incised pottery of the right period with recognizably Lapita decorative motifs from northern Luzon and Masbate in the Philippines, Bukit Tengkorak in Sabah, the Karama Valley in West Sulawesi, and from the Banda Islands in Maluku, starting from about 1850 BCE (Spriggs 2011).

The Mariana Islands in Micronesia appear to have been settled directly from northern Luzon at about 1450 BCE, just prior to the period of the earliest Lapita sites (Clark et al. 2010; chapter 40, this volume). The early culture there is thus an independent witness to what was available at an early stage of the island Southeast Asian Neolithic, far from any putative direct New Guinea integrative influences on Lapita. The early Marianas sites contain shell fishhooks and shell ornaments very comparable with those in Lapita sites (Butler 1994). Indeed the whole "feel" of the culture is similar, thus bringing into question the degree of Lapita integration as opposed to intrusion in the Bismarcks. Ths suggests Lapita could represent an almost entirely intrusive assemblage in the latter area.

The Lapita design system appears fully formed on the earliest pottery, with the most complex motifs on the earliest pots. This suggests that the full design system was present on some other more perishable media further to the west prior to Lapita: such media could have included woven cloth, bark cloth, wood carving, and/or tattoos. It was transferred to pottery for a few hundred years during Lapita times and then taken off it again, to reappear in the recent past in the ethnographic collections of Polynesian barkcloth and New Guinea arrow-shaft designs, and Southeast Asian house posts and other carvings. Lapita-like designs reappear as well on early Indonesian bronze ceremonial axes and later Neolithic and early Metal Age pottery (Bellwood 1997; Green 1979).

In general, Lapita pots were not widely exchanged; rather it was the designs on them that moved across vast areas. But the few exceptions are very instructive. At Teouma in Vanuatu there are occasional pots from New Caledonia, and from another source, shared with the Reefs–Santa Cruz area Lapita sites, that may have been further west in the Bismarcks. In Tonga a distinctive tan-colored pottery type could have originated from northern Vanuatu or Santa Cruz (Burley & Dickinson 2010).

Through to central Vanuatu, hundreds of flakes of West New Britain obsidian are present in some sites, and this material clearly continued to be imported for some time after initial settlement. In Fiji and New Caledonia, the few New Britain obsidian flakes could potentially have resulted from the initial colonizing voyages. Looking to the west at the same time period, New Britain obsidian has been found as far away as Bukit Tengkorak in Sabah, Borneo (Bellwood & Koon 1989; Chia 2003) and Cebu in the Philippines. Such imports and the homogeneity of language across the Lapita distribution suggest widespread mobility in these early years of Remote Oceanic settlement, with regular voyaging between distant island groups.

What processes of recruitment and social organization allowed such a rapid spread, one that was essentially monolingual while being somewhat more diverse in material culture origins, and extremely diverse genetically? Keegan (2010) has identified matri-lineal descent and particularly matrilocal residence as being typical of colonizing and expanding populations (see also for the Pacific, Hage & Marck 2003; Jordan et al. 2009). To the extent that modern genetic distributions reflect the population history of Lapita times it would seem that it was local Melanesian men who were being preferentially recruited into groups whose core was immigrant women (Kayser et al. 2006). Adult men were often away from their communities, visiting their own natal groups, forging new links or even discovering new islands to settle. Open sea of up to 800 km between Fiji and Vanuatu were clearly no insurmountable barrier to mobility, but the greater sea gaps eastwards of Samoa may well have precluded further extension of settlement in Lapita times (Keegan 2010; Kirch 2010).

While Remote Oceania was impoverished in terms of mammals and edible flora compared to the Solomons in Near Oceania, it did have some novel food sources. These included many species of large flightless ground-nesting birds, giant horned tortoises, land crocodiles, and large lizards. Reefs were pristine too in terms of human exploita-tion. The initial human impact on this native fauna was both rapid and devastating with extinctions occurring within a few hundred years of initial settlement. This may have been one of the factors in the rapid spread of Lapita across Remote Oceania. Even at low population densities, wild resources were clearly finite and rapidly overexploited. But people could expect similar resources on further uninhabited islands or coastlines, and so shift accordingly (Keegan 2010).

These low population densities during expansion also encouraged links back to homelands settled earlier, such as the Bismarcks with their sources of obsidian, to even out demographic imbalances and find suitable marriage partners. This allowed Oceanic Austronesian to develop in step as essentially a single language from the Bismarcks to Samoa, only to split into a series of distinct subgroups once the Lapita network broke down after a century or two.

The evidence nearly everywhere is for cultural continuity from Lapita to post-Lapita cultures. It was the distinctive pottery and the meanings encoded in its designs that seemed to disappear as long-distance exchange declined, populations became more sedentary, and communities turned in on themselves, becoming eventually the island or tribal-centric societies found in much of the region in the recent past (Spriggs 1997).

SEE ALSO: 35 Southeast Asian islands and Oceania: Austronesian linguistic history; 36 Southeast Asian islands: archaeology; 40 Micronesian archaeology; 41 Polynesia, East and South, including transpacific migration

References

Bedford, S. & Spriggs, M. (2007) Birds on the rim: a unique Lapita carinated vessel and its wider context. *Archaeology in Oceania* 42, 12–21.

Bedford, S., Sand, C., & Connaughton, S. (eds.) (2007) *Oceanic Explorations: Lapita and Western Pacific Settlement.* Terra Australis 28. Canberra: Australian National University E Press.

Bellwood, P. (1997) *Prehistory of the Indo-Malaysian Archipelago.* Honolulu: University of Hawaii Press.

Bellwood, P. & Koon, P. (1989) "Lapita colonists leave boats unburned!" The question of Lapita links with Island Southeast Asia. *Antiquity* 63, 613–622.

Burley, D. V. & Dickinson, W. R. (2010) Among Polynesia's first pots. *Journal of Archaeological Science* 37(5), 1020–1026.

Butler, B. M. (1994) Early prehistoric settlement in the Marianas Islands: new evidence from Saipan. *Man and Culture in Oceania* 10, 15–38.

Chia, S. (2003) *The Prehistory of Bukit Tengkorak as a Major Pottery Making Site in Island Southeast Asia*. Kota Kinabalu: Sabah Museum, Monograph 8.

Clark, G. R., Anderson, A. J., & Vunidilo, T. (eds.) (2001) *The Archaeology of Lapita Dispersal in Oceania*. Terra Australis 17. Canberra: Pandanus Press.

Clark, G., Petchey, P., Winter, O., et al. (2010) New radiocarbon dates from the Bapot-1 site in Saipan and Neolithic dispersal by stratified diffusion. *Journal of Pacific Archaeology* 1(1), 21–35.

Green, R. C. (1979) Early Lapita art from Polynesia and Island Melanesia: continuities in ceramic, barkcloth and tattoo decorations. In S. M. Mead (ed.), *Exploring the Visual Art of Oceania*. Honolulu: University of Hawaii Press, pp. 13–31.

Green, R. C. (1991) Near and Remote Oceania: disestablishing "Melanesia" in culture history. In A. Pawley (ed.), *Man and a Half: Essays in Pacific Anthropology and Ethnobiology in Honour of Ralph Bulmer*. Auckland: Polynesian Society, pp. 491–502.

Green, R. C. (2000) Lapita and the cultural model for intrusion, integration and innovation. In A. Anderson & T. Murray (eds.), *Australian Archaeologist: Collected Papers in Honour of Jim Allen*. Canberra: Coombs Academic, pp. 372–392.

Hage, P. & Marck, J. (2003) Matrilinearity and the Melanesian origin of Polynesian Y chromosomes. *Current Anthropology* 44 (supplement): S121–S127.

Jordan, F. M., Gray, R. D., Greenhill, S. J., & Mace, R. (2009) Matrilocal residence is ancestral in Austronesian societies. *Proceedings of the Royal Society* B276, 1957–1964.

Kayser, M., Brauer, S., Cordaux, R., et al. (2006) Melanesian and Asian origins of Polynesian mtDNA and Y chromosome gradients across the Pacific. *Molecular Biology and Evolution* 23, 2234–2344.

Keegan, W. F. (2010) Demographic imperatives for island colonists. In A. Anderson, J. Barrett, & K. Boyle (eds.), *The Global Origins (and Development) of Seafaring*. Cambridge: McDonald Institute, pp. 171–178.

Kirch, P. V. (1997) *The Lapita Peoples: Ancestors of the Oceanic World*. Oxford: Blackwell.

Kirch, P. V. (2010) Peopling of the Pacific: a holistic anthropological perspective. *Annual Review of Anthropology* 39, 131–148.

Sheppard, P. J., Thomas, T., & Summerhayes, G. R. (eds.) (2009) *Lapita: Ancestors and Descendants*. Auckland: New Zealand Archaeological Association, Monograph 28.

Spriggs, M. (1997) *The Island Melanesians*. Oxford: Blackwell.

Spriggs, M. (2011) Archaeology and the Austronesian expansion. *Antiquity* 85, 510–528.

Torrence, R. & Swadling, P. (2008) Social networks and the spread of Lapita. *Antiquity* 82, 600–615.

40

Micronesian archaeology

Mike T. Carson

Micronesia forms a very widespread archipelago, mainly of atolls, in the northern tropical Pacific. Its prehistory witnessed migratory arrivals from at least three major directions: island Southeast Asia, Melanesia, and Polynesia.

The prehistory of human migration in Micronesia involved initial settlement from at least five different sources beginning about 3,500 years ago, plus a network of contact and exchange continuing into the historical (post-European contact) era. This situation was notably more complicated than in other cases in the Pacific islands. Other reviews have provided site-specific details (Rainbird 1994, 2004; Intoh 1997) and only the major patterns are described here.

The Micronesian languages reflect at least two very different groupings and associated histories. Those of the Mariana Islands and of Palau are Western Malayo-Polynesian (WMP), originating in island Southeast Asia and most likely in the Philippines or Indonesia (Zobel 2002). All others are in the Oceanic grouping, originating proximally in Melanesia or Polynesia (Bender et al. 2003a, 2003b). Both WMP and Oceanic groupings share a common Austronesian ancestry, but the individual language communities in Micronesia have since become quite different from one another.

The first episode of human migration in Micronesia was the settlement of the Mariana Islands about 3,500 years ago (Carson 2011), almost certainly from the Philippines, based on a presence of nearly identical red-slipped and finely decorated pottery types in both regions (Hung et al. 2011). Also, the Chamorro language appears to be from a northern Philippines source (Blust 2000; Reid 2002). The first migration episode apparently involved a partial subset rather than a wholesale duplication of the homeland's material culture repertoire. A number of important aspects of material culture common in the Philippines were notably absent in the early Marianas, such as spindle whorls, barkcloth beaters, precious greenstone earrings, and fishing-net sinkers (Hung 2008). Likewise, the earliest red-slipped and finely decorated pottery forms in the

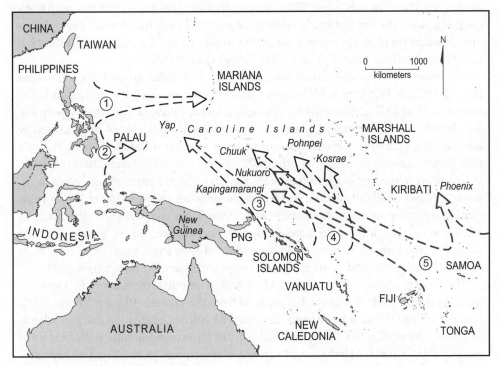

Figure 40.1 Major colonizing migrations in Micronesian prehistory. High islands are shaded.
1 Settlement of the Mariana Islands c.1500 BCE from the Philippines;
2 Settlement of Palau c.1200–1000 BCE from the Philippines or Indonesia;
3 Settlement of Yap c.200 BCE–200 CE or slightly earlier, from island Melanesia;
4 Settlement of Kosrae, Pohnpei, and Chuuk, then various atolls, starting c.200 BCE–200 CE from island Melanesia;
5 Settlement of the Polynesian Outliers starting around 1000 CE.
Map production by Education and Multimedia Services, College of Asia and the Pacific, The Australian National University.

Marianas represented only a subset of the more diverse assemblages found in the Philippines.

Marianas pottery types reveal continued influence from the Philippines, specifically matching types known in the Philippines not only at initial settlement 3,500 years ago but also again around 1000–300 BCE and 200 BCE–200 CE. In addition, horizontal incisions found on the teeth of a number of individuals at one Marianas burial site, dated about 300–200 BCE, match those on inlaid teeth of similar date in the Philippines, again suggesting influence and perhaps an actual movement of people.

A larger and probably more diverse population was flowing through the Marianas region beginning a thousand years ago, likely involving various sources. A new form of megalithic architecture with stone house pillars and capitals, called *latte*, appeared at this time, along with formal village layouts, widespread intensively cultivated landscapes, and the importation of rats and rice, presumably from the Philippines. Concurrently within the Mariana Islands, *latte*-associated populations expanded into the smaller northern islands after 1000 CE, constituting another important migration episode in local culture history. In addition, the scope of external contact expanded to include other parts of Micronesia, according to oral traditions and the hybridization history of breadfruit taxa (Petersen 2006; Zerega et al. 2006).

The second Micronesian settlement migration was to Palau around three thousand years ago (Clark 2005), most likely from a source in the southern Philippines or Indonesia according to linguistic affinity, although a source different from that responsible for Mariana Islands settlement. Later episodes of Palauan archaeology were marked by internal developments of earthwork construction about two thousand years ago and then stonework village complexes after 1000 CE (Wickler 2002; Liston 2009).

The third colonizing migration into Micronesia occurred approximately two thousand years ago, or slightly earlier, and was responsible for the peopling of Yap from an Oceanic-speaking source in Melanesia (Ross 1996). Later contacts with other parts of Micronesia greatly influenced Yapese language and culture. Yapese people quarried aragonite limestone for making their large wheel-shaped stone money in Palau, most frequently after 1500 and continuing into the post-contact era (Fitzpatrick 2002).

The fourth major migration episode involved another movement of Oceanic-speaking people from Melanesia, but separate from the Yapese settlement (Blust 1984), also around two thousand years ago. This migration first targeted the volcanic islands of Kosrae, Pohnpei, and Chuuk, and then spread into the numerous atolls that form most of the Caroline, Marshall, and Kiribati island chains. In the first two centuries CE, a previously dropping sea level stabilized at an elevation that allowed many of the atolls to become emergent and habitable (Dickinson 2003). Another important development was the excavation of pits into the shallow water table in the low-lying atolls, enabling more productive cultivation of swamp taro as a subsistence crop (Weisler 1999).

Beginning about a thousand years ago, monumental stonework ritual complexes were constructed in Pohnpei (Nan Madol) and Kosrae in the Carolines, recorded in local legends as related to people arriving from an unspecified external source. The language histories reveal continued contacts with other Micronesian communities (Rehg 1995), but nothing points to a particular source that can be linked confidently with the stonework monument-building period. In terms of the archaeological evidence, a local development seems just as likely as an immigrant population.

The fifth major migration into Micronesia was part of a larger movement of Polynesians from the southeast into the various "Polynesian Outlier" islands scattered through Micronesia and Melanesia, starting around a thousand years ago (Carson, forthcoming). The Polynesian Outliers in Micronesia include Kapingamarangi and Nukuoro. Also of note are seemingly Polynesian settlements in Kiribati, later abandoned but leaving behind a record of monumental architectural ruins typical of Polynesian contexts of the last thousand years.

These five major colonizing migrations likely occurred some time after the initial island discoveries. Knowledge of an island location could have been retained for some generations, until such time as the necessary preparations could be made involving a sufficient number of colonists and a supply of edible tree and root crops. Without these, only small-scale and short-term habitation could have occurred. A time difference between original discovery and later colonization is nearly impossible to detect for certain, but the concept could explain anomalous early dates in a few cases in Micronesia. Most notorious in this regard is a date of 1200 BCE for one archaeological site in Bikini Atoll of the Marshall Islands (Streck 1990), in contrast to other sites in the Marshalls that all date within the last two thousand years. It could also account for unusually early dates interpreted to reflect human-caused environmental impact in Yap, Palau, and the Marianas prior to the first dates from actual archaeological sites (Athens et al. 2004; Athens & Ward 2002; Dodson & Intoh 1999). In these cases, however, the observed environmental changes were not directly associated with the dated material, and the dating may be interpreted in various ways.

According to computer simulations of drift voyages at the mercy of prevailing winds and currents, accidental "drift" discovery of either Palau or the Marianas was virtually impossible from any source (Callaghan & Fitzpatrick 2007). Therefore, effective settlement almost certainly involved intentional voyaging by skilled sailors and navigators, likely based on some prior knowledge gained from an original discovery. In the case of the Marianas, the initial migratory settlement required an open-ocean crossing exceeding 2,300 km against prevailing winds, by far the longest unbroken voyage in human history at that time.

The most intensive cultural exchange in Micronesia occurred within the geographic range of overnight sailing voyages (approximately 160 km), as reflected in shared similarities of linguistic features over time (Marck 1986). A degree of multilingualism was likely the case for seafaring people traveling long distances between communities. Ethnographically known inter-island exchange systems in Micronesia crossed various social boundaries while creating or strengthening others, also creating opportunities for migration. Yap was central in much of this activity, famously involving the large stone money discs quarried from distant islands of Palau and Guam. Smaller money items were made of specially prized shells. The formalized Yap-focused exchange system known as *sawei* guided movement of tribute among diverse and dispersed clans in the Caroline Islands, reflecting their past relationships via migration (Sudo 1996). The antiquity of the *sawei* potentially dates near the beginning of Yapese settlement about two thousand years ago, yet it became increasingly complex over time as more areas were settled and more relationships entered the system.

SEE ALSO: 39 Oceania: Lapita migration; 41 Polynesia, East and South, including transpacific migration

References

Athens, J. S. & Ward, J. V. (2002) Palaeo-environmental evidence for early human settlement in Palau. In C. M. Stevenson, G. Lee, & F. J. Morin (eds.), *Proceedings of the Fifth International Conference on Easter Island and the Pacific.* Los Osos, CA: Easter Island Foundation, pp. 165–177.

Athens, J. S., Dega, M. F., & Ward, J. V. (2004) Austronesian colonization of the Mariana Islands: The palaeoenvironmental evidence. *Bulletin of the Indo-Pacific Prehistory Association* 24, 21–30.

Bender, B. W., Goodenough, W. H., Jackson, F. H., & Marck, J. (2003a) Proto-Micronesian reconstructions – 1. *Oceanic Linguistics* 42, 1–110.

Bender, B. W., Goodenough, W. H., Jackson, F. H., & Marck, J. (2003b) Proto-Micronesian reconstructions – 2. *Oceanic Linguistics* 42, 271–358.

Blust, R. (1984) Malaita-Micronesian: An eastern Oceanic Subgroup? *Journal of the Polynesian Society* 93, 99–140.

Blust, R. (2000) Chamorro historical phonology. *Oceanic Linguistics* 39, 3–122.

Callaghan, R. & Fitzpatrick, S. M. (2007) On the relative isolation of a Micronesian archipelago: the Palau case study. *International Journal of Nautical Archaeology* 36, 353–364.

Carson, M. T. (2011) Palaeohabitat of first settlement sites 1500–1000 BC in Guam, Mariana Islands, western Pacific. *Journal of Archaeological Science* 38, 2207–2221.

Carson, M. T. (forthcoming) New developments in Polynesian Outlier archaeology. In R. Feinberg & R. Scaglion (eds.), *The Polynesian Outliers: State of the Art.* Pittsburgh: Ethnology Monographs.

Clark, G. R. (2005) A 3000-year culture sequence from Palau, western Micronesia. *Asian Perspectives* 44, 349–380.

Dickinson, W. R. (2003) Impact of mid-Holocene hydro-isostatic highstand in regional sea level on habitability of islands in Pacific Oceania. *Journal of Coastal Research* 19, 489–502.

Dodson, J. & Intoh, M. (1999) Prehistory and palaeoecology of Yap, Federated States of Micronesia. *Quaternary International* 59, 17–26.

Fitzpatrick, S. M. (2002) A radiocarbon chronology of Yapese stone money quarries in Palau. *Micronesica* 34, 227–242.

Hung, H.-C. (2008) Migration and cultural interaction in southern coastal China, Taiwan and the northern Philippines, 3000 BC to AD 100: The early history of the Austronesian-speaking populations. Unpublished PhD dissertation, the Australian National University.

Hung, H.-C., Carson, M., Bellwood, P., et al. (2011) The first settlement of Remote Oceania: Luzon to the Marianas. *Antiquity* 85, 909–926.

Intoh, M. (1997) Human dispersals into Micronesia. *Anthropological Science* 105, 15–28.

Liston, J. (2009) Cultural chronology of earthworks in Palau, western Micronesia. *Archaeology in Oceania* 44, 56–73.

Marck, J. (1986) Micronesian dialects and the overnight voyage. *Journal of the Polynesian Society* 95, 253–258.

Petersen, G. (2006) Micronesia's breadfruit revolution and the evolution of a culture area. *Archaeology in Oceania* 41, 82–92.

Rainbird, P. (1994) Prehistory in the north-west tropical Pacific: the Caroline, Mariana, and Marshall Islands. *Journal of World Prehistory* 8, 293–349.

Rainbird, P. (2004) *The Archaeology of Micronesia.* Cambridge: Cambridge Unviersity Press.

Rehg, K. L. (1995) The significance of linguistic interaction spheres in reconstructing Micronesian prehistory. *Oceanic Linguistics* 34, 305–326.

Reid, L. (2002) Morphosyntactic evidence for the position of Chamorro in the Austronesian language family. In R. S. Bauer (ed.), *Collected Papers on Southeast Asian and Pacific Languages.* Canberra: Pacific Linguistics, pp. 63–94.

Ross, M. D. (1996) Is Yapese Oceanic? In B. Nothofer (ed.), *Reconstruction, Classification, Description: Feschrift in Honor of Isidore Dyen.* Hamburg: Abera, pp. 121–166.

Streck, C. (1990) Prehistoric settlement in eastern Micronesia: archaeology on Bikini Atoll, Republic of the Marshall Islands. In R. L. Hunter-Anderson (ed.), *Recent Advances in Micronesian Archaeology.* Micronesica Supplement 2. Mangilao: University of Guam, pp. 247–260.

Sudo, K. (1996) Rank, hierarchy and routes of migration: chieftainship in the Central Caroline Islands of Micronesia. In J. J. Fox & C. Sather (eds.), *Origins, Ancestry and Alliance: Explora-*

tions in Austronesian Ethnography. Comparative Austronesian Project. Canberra: The Australian National University, pp. 57–72.

Weisler, M. I. (1999) The antiquity of aroid pit agriculture and significance of buried A horizons on Pacific atolls. *Geoarchaeology* 14, 621–654.

Wickler, S. K. (2002) Terraces and villages: transformation of the cultural landscape in Palau. In T. Ladefoged & M. Graves (eds.), *Pacific Landscapes: Archaeological Approaches in Oceania.* Los Osos, California: Bearsville Press, pp. 63–96.

Zerega, N. J. C., Ragone, D., & Motely, T. J. (2006) Breadfruit origins, diversity, and human-facilitated distribution. In T. J. Motely & N. Zerega (eds.), *Darwin's Harvest: Origins, Evolution, and Conservation of Crop Plants.* New York: Columbia University Press, pp. 213–238.

Zobel, E. (2002) The position of Chamorro and Palauan in the Austronesian family tree: Evidence from verb morph syntax. In F. Wouk & M. Ross (eds.), *History and Typology of Western Austronesian Voice Systems.* Canberra: Pacific Linguistics, pp. 405–434.

Polynesia, East and South, including transpacific migration

Atholl Anderson

Polynesia forms the largest archipelago in Oceania in terms of total extent, and its colonization occurred in two separate phases separated by 2,000 years: c.1000 BCE in Tonga and Samoa, but only after 1000 CE in Hawaii, New Zealand, and Easter Island, some of the most isolated habitable landmasses on earth.

Except within New Zealand, migration to and through East Polynesia took place entirely by seafaring. East Polynesia consists of all the islands within the Polynesian triangle except for Tonga, Samoa, and other islands nearby, which are part of West Polynesia, a region colonized about 1000 BCE in the Lapita migration (see chapter 39). When migration to East Polynesia began, how and why it happened, and the identity of the migrants continue to be debated.

In discussing these questions it is useful to divide East Polynesia between tropical East Polynesia (TEP), the islands lying mostly to the north of the Tropic of Capricorn, and temperate South Polynesia (SP), constituting New Zealand and its outlying islands (see Figure 36.1 for locations). In TEP nearly 70 perecent of the habitable islands are atolls and the remainder volcanic; a wide range of tropical food plants can be grown and seafaring conditions are dominated by easterly trade winds, with occasional westerly reversals. All of the SP islands consist mainly of high ground, and they are mostly of continental geology. Prehistoric Polynesian agriculture was restricted to the north of the region and while there are subtropical easterlies in summer, seafaring conditions are dominated by mid-latitude westerlies.

An age of migration

Proposed chronologies of migration from West to East Polynesia have varied by up to two thousand years, largely due to differing preferences amongst scholars between

The Global Prehistory of Human Migration: The Encyclopedia of Global Human Migration Volume 1,
First Edition. Edited by Peter Bellwood.

conflicting radiocarbon dates from archaeological sites and inferred anthropogenic events, such as forest firing, which is marked by charcoal accumulation within sedimentary cores (Anderson 1995). Analysis of East Polynesian radiocarbon dates according to sample type, dating method, and archaeological context can exclude dates of poor quality, a process called "chronometric hygiene." It suggests that migration to East Polynesia began in the late first millennium CE (Spriggs & Anderson 1993). Some scholars still prefer older dates (e.g. Kirch 2007) but continued excavation of sites containing evidence of extinct birds and early types of East Polynesian material culture has provided additional support for a relatively late migration period (Anderson & Sinoto 2002). Previous arguments for human colonization two thousand years ago in SP according to radiocarbon dates on commensal rat bones have been invalidated (Wilmshurst et al. 2008).

Analysis of 1,400 radiocarbon dates from East Polynesia (Wilmshurst et al. 2011) now shows that the central islands of TEP were first colonized between 1000 and 1100 CE, while the other islands were reached between 1200 and 1300. As a few sherds of pottery have been discovered in Cook Islands and Marquesan sites the current dates might be thought a few centuries too late, given the disappearance of pottery in West Polynesia around the mid-first millennium CE, but the loss of pottery is still not dated precisely. In SP, dates for initial colonization in the Kermadec, Norfolk, and subpolar Auckland Islands are indistinguishable from those in New Zealand. Only in the Chatham Islands are they later (1500 CE), but traditions and material culture there suggest that initial migration occurred earlier. The dispersal in SP can be traced by distribution of obsidian from known sources and it shows that the outlying islands were settled from New Zealand. The strikingly contemporaneous radiocarbon chronologies for migratory dispersal in SP are mirrored on the larger scale of East Polynesia as a whole, with initial migration to the apexes of the Polynesian triangle at Hawaii, Easter Island, and New Zealand, all occurring in the 13th century CE. The migratory expansion east and south may have been matched, or perhaps preceded by, a similar movement in the late first millennium CE to the west, in which voyagers from West Polynesia, notably Tuvalu, settled in the "Polynesian outlier" islands (e.g. Tikopia, Anuta, Rennell, Nukuoro) of the Solomons, New Guinea, and Micronesia.

The long pause between settlement of West and East Polynesia, the brevity of confinement to central TEP once migration resumed, and an entire migration period of about 300 years to reach nearly all the islands in an area the size of North America, combine to suggest that the migrating impulse was powerful. It quite probably involved relatively large groups moving within the migratory stream, as indicated by DNA haplotype frequency in New Zealand Maori (Penny et al. 2002). Various propositions have been suggested in explanation of this. One is that population growth in West Polynesia had become unsupportable by the late first millennium CE. The onset of defensive construction about that time might reflect conflict that induced a phase of migration through exile to sea by junior or losing groups, as is commonly asserted in Polynesian traditions (Anderson 2006). Another suggestion is that there was migratory pressure coming from further west, perhaps through the Micronesian island route into Polynesia (Addison & Matisoo-Smith 2010). Linguistic evidence has been employed to propose that the double canoe, with its greater load-bearing capacity and enhanced migratory utility, was a West Polynesian innovation of the post-Lapita era and had, perhaps, come into service immediately prior to the East Polynesian migration period (Blust 1999). Climatic change might also have been important, as in the coincidence of 13th-century dispersal throughout East Polynesia with peak El Niño occurrence during the last millennium. El Niño events increased the frequencies of tropical westerly and subtropical easterly winds, favoring access to the more remote islands, and El Niño frequency might also have been important in producing levels of drought and climatic instability that affected horticultural production (Anderson et al. 2006). Quite possibly a combination of some or all of these factors was involved as the stimulus behind East Polynesian migration.

Polynesian voyaging

The nature of Polynesian voyaging has been debated for nearly 400 years, with accidental, one-way passages an opinion at one extreme, and purposeful, navigated voyaging and long-distance interaction at the other. There is still no consensus amongst scholars, largely because of the scarcity of direct evidence around which it might be built. European explorers described Polynesian sailing vessels but encountered no contemporary Polynesian long-distance voyaging. Polynesian voyaging traditions contain almost no prosaic descriptions of canoes and sailing from the period of migratory expansion. Similarly, navigation methods were not recorded in any detail, except to show that the sun, moon, and stars were used in some way. These probably enabled estimation of latitude, to which dead reckoning and use of land-finding indicators provided some additional aid.

The names and approximate locations of islands between West Polynesia and the Marquesas were known in the 18th-century Society Islands, and credible accounts of voyaging to Tonga were also recorded, but none beyond that region. This is consistent with stone-sourcing studies of basalt adzes from the Marquesas and Samoa, which show movement across the central East Polynesian islands and to, and from, West Polynesia, but the isolation of marginal archipelagos in TEP and between TEP and SP.

There is almost no direct archaeological evidence of ancient voyaging canoes and none of sails, apart from depictions of Polynesian spritsails in rock art, especially in Hawaii. Terms for "mast" and "standing rigging" are not known for early Polynesian languages. Historical observations show that the oceanic lateen sail, derived from Micronesia and probably of Indian Ocean origin, was common in West Polynesia but very rare in East Polynesia. The main East Polynesian type was a triangular sail slung, point down, between two upright spars; the oceanic spritsail. In the 18th century, one spar was often used as, or attached to, a mast, but in New Zealand and possibly in the Marquesas the earliest records suggest that the spars were free-standing or attached to a cross-beam so that they could move backward and forward (Anderson 2000). This is an older type of rig which was possibly used in the initial migrations. It has very little capacity to drive a canoe to windward but it is safe because it can be dropped quickly in rising winds or squalls.

Experimental and simulated voyaging have been used to overcome the scarcity of direct historical evidence. Examples of the former are *Kon-Tiki*, built in the form of a Peruvian sailing raft, and *Hokule'a*, a double canoe which has been sailed from Hawaii to the most distant points of Polynesia (Finney 2006). The core idea of computer simulation is to map the frequency of wind directions across the Pacific then put numerous virtual canoes with defined sailing characteristics to sea from different islands in order to determine which potential routes were more likely used, the relative rates of successful landfall, and the probable sequence of island discovery (Irwin 1992). Experiment and simulation have shown generally that simple drifting would probably not have been sufficient to people the remote Pacific islands, but equally that a sophisticated voyaging ability including windward sailing and astral navigation should have led to more continuous colonization.

There have been different approaches to voyaging evidence. The most prominent since the late 19th century has been "traditionalism," which accepted Polynesian traditions at face value, including the key assumption that the works of the ancestors exceeded those of their descendants. From this, advanced navigation techniques and frequent long-distance voyaging and interaction between remote islands were envisaged. In reaction, Sharp (1956) argued that many traditions were corrupted, Polynesian geographical knowledge was limited, advanced navigation was impossible, and Polynesian canoes suffered problems in sailing, seaworthiness, and seakeeping.

Sharp's critique, however, inspired a renewed "neo-traditionalism" which uses the traditionalist assumptions to argue that Polynesian voyaging technology declined once most of the islands were colonized and therefore that historical evidence does not capture the ability of earlier prehistoric voyaging (Finney 2006). This view has allowed building and sailing techniques from all over the Pacific and beyond to be used for modern voyaging canoes, for example, *Hokule'a*. They do not, however, replicate historical East Polynesian construction or practice. For example, their sails are twice as large as on 18th-century Polynesian double canoes of similar size (Anderson 2008a). Despite that, the experimental data have been used in voyaging simulation studies to argue that such fast, windward-sailing vessels were used in strategic exploration; sailing first toward the prevailing wind, which allowed easier return, and only later, as uninhabited islands became few, in more difficult directions across and before the prevailing wind (Irwin 1992).

Neo-traditionalism remains the preferred model (Finney 2006; Howe 2006), yet historical study shows not a supposed devolution of sailing technology in East Polynesia but rather a late evolution, for example in the introduction of rigging styles associated with the lateen sail to the Society Islands. If earlier sailing rigs were more rudimentary, and confined sailing to directions largely before and across the wind, this might account for the relative difficulty of finding the more remote islands (Anderson 2000, 2008a). Long-distance sailing was still occurring in the 18th century, within the central region of TEP and between TEP and West Polynesia, but there is no evidence of contact with the marginal archipelagos, especially in SP, after the initial colonization phase.

Transoceanic contact

It is agreed that the overwhelming contribution to Polynesian populations and cultures came from the western Pacific and that subsequent East Polynesians were descendants. This is demonstrated clearly by a range of linguistic, artifactual, and biomolecular data (Kirch & Green 2001). The spread by the earliest migrants of "archaic East Polynesian" material culture with its remarkable homology of forms in fishhooks, adzes, and ornaments reflects a shared cultural heritage associated with colonization rather than something developed by later interaction.

Claims for a prehistoric American influence on East Polynesian populations and culture are not generally accepted, but South American origins for the sweet potato and possibly the bottle gourd imply some kind of transoceanic contact. Radiocarbon dating of the sweet potato in East Polynesia to as early as the 13th century suggests that it was transported into Oceania during the East Polynesian migration phase. Its arrival is usually ascribed to Polynesian voyagers sailing to and from the coast of South America. The proposed route is eastward on the mid-latitude westerlies to south or central Chile, then a coasting northward to Peru or Ecuador, and finally departure from there into the tropical easterlies (Green 2005). It has been argued that some aspects of Chilean Mapuche culture – a number of words, canoe construction, and a type of club – have Polynesian antecedents and are consistent with a pre-Columbian introduction of the domestic chicken to south-central Chile (Storey et al. 2007). The evidence is problematic. The clubs have no archaeological provenance and form one end of a range that is otherwise not seen in Polynesia, while the chicken-bone DNA has no Polynesian signature. In fact it is of the type most widely spread globally and the radiocarbon dates upon it have become younger with redating and now reach close to the period of Spanish arrival (Gongora et al. 2008).

Claims that Polynesians reached California from Hawaii are constructed mostly around the existence of the Chumash planked canoe, called *tomol* (Jones & Klar 2005). The argument that this name is a Polynesian term is unconvincing, and both the evidence that Hawaii was not colonized until about 1200–1300 CE and that the *tomol* existed many centuries earlier suggest that this hypothesis does not stand close inspection (Arnold 2007; Anderson 2008b).

The alternative hypothesis is that American food plants and perhaps some close similarities between Easter Island and late prehistoric cultures of Pacific South America, especially in complex aspects of material culture such as megalithic construction using pillow-faced blocks in polygonal masonry, the distinctive bird-man motif, and *tupa* stone tower structures, imply movement from South America to Polynesia, rather than the reverse. As large, capable, sailing rafts with daggerboards that facilitated passages to windward existed in Ecuador at the time of Spanish arrival it is quite possible that they, rather than Polynesian canoes, were the agents of contact (Anderson et al. 2007). It is also possible that Polynesian canoes reached South America occasionally, perhaps accidentally, and that a similar process of infrequent accidental landfalls occurred by South American craft in East Polynesia, in both cases contributing only slight or geographically restricted influences.

Conclusions

Patterns of initial human migration in East Polynesia varied between the tropical (TEP) and temperate (SP) regions. Migration from West Polynesia began 1000–1100 CE and expanded throughout TEP around 1200–1300. Migration to, and through, SP occurred only between 1200 and 1300, with the possible exception of the Chatham Islands. This was also the period when the main migratory impulse reached its greatest extent simultaneously in each of the apexes of the Polynesian triangle (New Zealand, Easter Island, Hawaii). The full movement occurred over about 300 years, which is faster than would be predicted by assuming simple drift passages but slower than expected if migratory voyaging had the sailing and navigational capabilities assigned to it traditionally. Historical evidence suggests that sailing to windward was severely restricted. Population growth, status competition, technical innovation in seafaring, and climatic change may all have played a part in what was nevertheless a relatively sudden and powerful migration burst. The migrants were almost wholly Polynesians but there was some contact with South America, possibly involving both Polynesian and Amerindian voyagers.

SEE ALSO: 39 Oceania: Lapita migration; 40 Micronesian archaeology

References

Addison, D. J. & Matisoo-Smith, E. (2010) Rethinking Polynesian origins: a West-Polynesia Triple-I model. *Archaeology in Oceania* 45, 1–12.

Anderson, A. J. (1995) Current approaches in East Polynesian colonization research. *Journal of the Polynesian Society* 104, 110–132.

Anderson, A. J. (2000) Slow boats from China: issues in the prehistory of Indo-Pacific seafaring. In S. O'Connor & P. Veth (eds.), *East of Wallace's Line: Studies of Past and Present Maritime Cultures of the Indo-Pacific Region*. Rotterdam: Balkema, pp. 13–50.

Anderson, A. J. (2006) Islands of Exile: ideological motivation in maritime migration. *Journal of Island and Coastal Archaeology* 1, 33–48.

Anderson, A. J. (2008a) Forum: traditionalism, interaction and long-distance seafaring in Polynesia. *Journal of Island and Coastal Archaeology* 3, 240–270.

Anderson, A. J. (2008b) Polynesian seafaring and American horizons: a response to Jones and Klar. *American Antiquity* 71, 759–764.

Anderson, A. J. and Sinoto, Y. H. (2002) New radiocarbon ages of colonization sites in East Polynesia. *Asian Perspectives* 41, 242–257.

Anderson, A. J., Chappell, J., Gagan, M., & Grove, R. (2006) Prehistoric maritime migration in the Pacific Islands: an hypothesis of ENSO forcing. *The Holocene* 16, 1–6.

Anderson, A. J., Martinsson-Wallin, H., & Stothert, K. (2007) Ecuadorian sailing rafts and Oceanic landfalls. In A. J. Anderson, K. Green, & B. F. Leach (eds.), *Vastly Ingenious: Essays on Pacific Material Culture in Honour of Janet M. Davidson*. Dunedin: University of Otago Press, pp. 117–133.

Arnold, J. E. (2007) Credit where credit is due: the history of the Chumash oceangoing plank canoe. *American Antiquity* 72, 196–209.

Blust, R. (1999) Subgrouping, circularity and extinction: some issues in Austronesian comparative linguistics. In E. Zeitoun & P. J. K. Li (eds.), *Selected Papers from the Eighth International Conference on Austronesian Linguistics*. Taipei: Academia Sinica, pp. 31–94.

Finney, B. R. (2006) Ocean sailing canoes. In Howe (2006), pp. 100–153.

Gongora, J., Rawlence, N. J., Mobegi, V. A., et al. (2008) Reply to Storey et al.: more DNA dating studies needed for Chilean and pacific chickens revealed by mtDNA. *Proceedings of the National Academy of Sciences* 105, 10308–10313.

Green, R. C. (2005) Sweet potato transfers in Polynesian prehistory. In C. Ballard, P. Brown, R. M. Bourke, & T. Harwood (eds.), *The Sweet Potato in Oceania: A Reappraisal*. Oceania Monographs 56, Sydney: University of Sydney, pp. 43–62.

Howe, K. R. (ed.) (2006) *Vaka Moana: Voyages of the Ancestors. The Discovery and Settlement of the Pacific*. Auckland: David Bateman.

Irwin, G. J. (1992) *The Prehistoric Exploration and Colonization of the Pacific*. Cambridge: Cambridge University Press.

Jones, T. L. & Klar, K. A. (2005) Diffusionism reconsidered: linguistic and archaeological evidence for prehistoric Polynesian contact with southern California. *American Antiquity* 70, 457–484.

Kirch, P. V. (2007) Three islands and an archipelago: reciprocal interactions between humans and island ecosystems in Polynesia. *Earth and Environmental Science (Transactions of the Royal Society of Edinburgh)* 98, 85–99.

Kirch, P. V. (2010) Peopling of the Pacific: a holistic anthropological perspective. *Annual Reviews in Anthropology* 39, 131–148.

Kirch, P. V. & Green, R. C. (2001) *Hawaiki, Ancestral Polynesia. An essay in Historical Anthropology*. Cambridge, Cambridge University Press.

Penny, D., Murray-MacIntosh, R., & Harrison, G. L. (2002) Estimating the number of females in the founding population of New Zealand: analysis of mtDNA variation. *Journal of the Polynesian Society* 111, 207–221.

Sharp, A. (1956) *Ancient Voyagers in the Pacific*. Wellington: Polynesian Society.

Spriggs, M. T. J. & Anderson, A. J. (1993) Late colonization of East Polynesia. *Antiquity* 67, 200–217.

Storey, A., Ramirez, J., Quiroz, D., et al. (2007) Radiocarbon and DNA evidence for a pre-Columbian introduction of Polynesian chickens to Chile. *Proceedings of the National Academy of Sciences* 104, 10335–10339.

Wilmshurst, J. M., Anderson, A. J., Higham, T. F. G., & Worthy, T. H. (2008) Dating the late prehistoric dispersal of Polynesians to New Zealand using the commensal Pacific rat. *Proceedings of the National Academy of Sciences* 104, 7676–7680.

Wilmshurst, J. M., Hunt, T. L., Lipo, C. P., & Anderson A. J. (2011) Recent and rapid initial colonization of East Polynesia shown by high-precision radiocarbon dating. *Proceedings of the National Academy of Sciences* 108, 1815–1820.

42

Australia: linguistic history

Patrick McConvell

The Australian continent has been occupied by humans since 50 kya, but the Holocene seems to have been a dynamic period in terms of human movement, especially within the extensive Pama-Nyungan language family. As in chapters 43 and 44, the record here is one of hunter-gatherer migration.

The early paths of human colonization of Australia are a key part of the story of initial expansion of modern humans and provide early evidence for modern human behavior. The presence of humans in Australia dates back to at least 50 kya. How many groups of people arrived, when, and how they migrated throughout the continent remain matters of controversy and speculation. By 30 kya, most parts of Australia were inhabited by humans (see chapter 7).

Following the Last Glacial Maximum at around 20 kya, some regions of Australia, particularly parts of the arid inland, were largely or wholly abandoned (Hiscock 2008: 60–61). This absence or scarcity of human activity lasted into the Early Holocene in some places, but by the mid-Holocene these regions were once again filling with new populations. In the Early Holocene also, the land bridge between what were to become the separate land masses of New Guinea and Australia was flooded by the sea. Both these changes were associated with human movement, and there are other signatures of human migration throughout the Holocene. Australian archaeology has tended to interpret Holocene cultural change and population growth as resulting not from migration but from *in situ* development. Dixon's (1997, 2002) "punctuated equilibrium" theory, which attributed most similarities between languages to massive linguistic diffusion obscuring very early language family divergence, has also been influential outside linguistics in undermining migration scenarios, although it is supported by few linguists today (McConvell & Bowern 2011).

Comparative historical linguistics offers strong support for the existence of tree-like relationships between languages in Australia, and in combination with data from

The Global Prehistory of Human Migration: The Encyclopedia of Global Human Migration Volume 1,
First Edition. Edited by Peter Bellwood.
© 2013 John Wiley & Sons, Ltd. Published 2015 by John Wiley & Sons, Ltd.

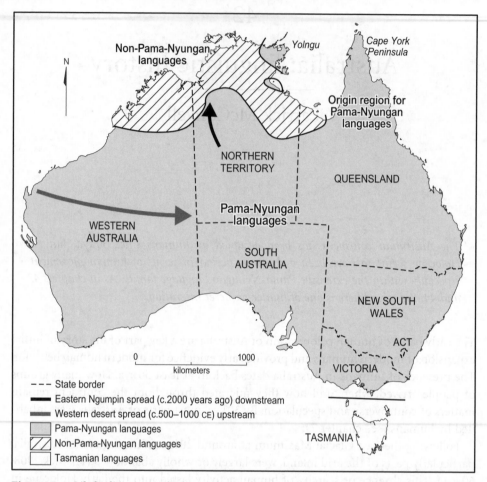

Figure 42.1 Likely directions of Pama-Nyungan language spread in Australia during the past 6,000 years. The northern location of the non-Pama-Nyungan languages is also shown. The linguistic situation in pre-contact Tasmania is not clear. Map production by Education and Multimedia Services, College of Asia and the Pacific, The Australian National University.

human genetics and archaeology this suggests that migrations occurred throughout Holocene prehistory. This is as in other continents where reconstruction of proto-languages provides evidence of prehistoric cultural change (Ehret 2011).

In Australia, there is a language family known as Pama-Nyungan which covers most of the continent. The exceptions are the central tropical north, which is occupied by non-Pama-Nyungan families, Tasmania (where the languages died out with only minimal recording in the 19th century), and eastern Torres Strait, where the islanders speak a Papuan language. Pama-Nyungan is a well-established language family with some hundreds of words and other items reconstructed to the proto-language (Alpher 2004). Quite a number are found only in Pama-Nyungan languages, and not in non-Pama-Nyungan. These shared innovations show that Pama-Nyungan is a valid language family.

Very widespread families such as Pama-Nyungan are known in many parts of the world, and their distributions overwhelmingly result from migration. Pama-Nyungan is different from many of the better known examples of this type in that it is a language exclusively of hunter-gatherers, not of farmers (see chapters 43 and 44 for other examples). The proto-language of Pama-Nyungan is early to mid-Holocene in age. Estimates have generally been in the range of 3000–2000 BCE (Evans & Jones 1997; O'Grady & Hale 2004), but the earliest stages of its spread may have occurred up to two thousand years earlier.

There are indications in human genetics that there was an expansion and spread of certain genetic markers also at around four thousand years ago (Kayser et al. 2001: 185), and this could represent at least part of the migration which spread the Pama-Nyungan language family across most of the continent, There was also an archaeological expansion of backed stone artifacts throughout what is now the Pama-Nyungan speaking area, excluding the central north, matching quite closely the distribution of Pama-Nyungan languages. That spread was most intensive, in terms of numbers of artifacts in archaeological sites, between 2500 and 2000 BCE. However, there was an earlier phase of these backed artifacts around the 5th millenium BCE in the east of the continent (Hiscock 2002, 2008: 148–149). If the tool distribution was linked to the language spread, this suggests that an east to west spread of Pama-Nyungan across Australia occurred in the early to mid Holocene.

This scenario also supports the idea of a homeland for proto-Pama-Nyungan in the northeast, which linguists have proposed on grounds independent of archaeology. A well-known "center of gravity" principle in historical linguistics predicts that the zone of greatest subgrouping differentiation within a language family will be located around the original centre of dispersal, probably close to the original homeland. For Pama-Nyungan, such diversity is greatest along the southern coast of the Gulf of Carpentaria, where at least two small families (Garrwa-Wanyi & Tangkic) appear to be closely related to Pama-Nyungan, and have sometimes been classified as Pama-Nyungan (Evans 2003; Harvey 2009). Close by, in southern Cape York peninsula, following an apparent reduction in the intensity of human occupation through the last glacial maximum and terminal Pleistocene, sites began to be reoccupied at around 5500 BP. Site use further intensified in the period 4500–3500 BP, and this may be a signature of Pama-Nyungan spread into the region at this time (Haberle & David 2004).

The breakup of a linguistic family into subgroups can usually provide a guide to migration paths following the period of proto-language unity. At the present time, the classification of the subgroups of Pama-Nyungan forms a "rake-like" tree with about 20 independent branches, with little internal structure. This suggests a multipronged migration in a number of directions at about the same time, rather than a series of binary or ternary splits in the phylogeny caused by prolonged phases of migrational stability and linguistic innovation. However, several previously proposed subgroups have recently been combined (e.g. McConvell & Laughren 2004), with some specific implications for language dispersal. One large subgroup, termed Nyungic (O'Grady et al. 1966), which covers much of the west of the continent, could have been produced by mid–late Holocene migration and spread of languages from the east. As with expansions of other Pama-Nyungan branches, this would have no doubt replaced earlier languages, except where earlier Holocene abandonment had produced empty areas.

Indications of past population movements are also retrievable from individual vocabulary items. For instance, there is a proto-Pama-Nyungan root *kuya/*kuyu, which means "fish" on the eastern side of the continent and "meat, animal" in the west. The change in meaning results from the migration of Pama-Nyungan speakers through the arid zone southwest of the Gulf of Carpentaria, where there were no rivers (McConvell 1997). Other major economic and demographic changes occurred during the mid-Holocene, discussed by archaeologists as "intensification" (Lourandos 1980; Hiscock 2008: 185 ff.), but these were perhaps not generally related to migration. Such economic changes included the development of seed grinding in the central arid parts of Australia (McConvell & Smith 2003), but in such a case the technology and economic organization might have been diffused by contact alone.

Colonizations by new migrants of regions largely abandoned by former inhabitants, usually in the more arid zones, have been termed "upstream spreads" (McConvell 2010). Some language expansions in the Holocene, however, were achieved by language shift (replacement), which occurs when an indigenous group adopts the language of some new arrivals. This type of language spread has been termed "downstream" because it largely occurs when people from less-well-resourced zones impinge on those in better-resourced zones, which typically lie downstream. Upstream spread is exemplified by the occupation of the vast Western Desert region by the Western Desert language, and downstream spread by the movement of the eastern Ngumpin branch of Ngumpin-Yapa into the Victoria River District of the Northern Territory (McConvell 2010). Confidence in the proposed chronologies of these two spreads is improving with the use of linguistic and interdisciplinary techniques, placing the eastward spread of the Western Desert language, driven by migration, at around 500-1000 CE, and the northern spread of eastern Ngumpin by a combination of migration and language shift at around 2000 years ago. One of the strongest linguistic signatures of downstream migration with language shift is a retention of toponyms (place names) from the languages of previous residents; examples of this are documented in Eastern Ngumpin languages (McConvell 2009) and elsewhere (Baker 2007).

There were many other migration events in the Australian Holocene that still need to be studied using interdisciplinary evidence, both in Pama-Nyungan and in non-Pama-Nyungan languages. One of the most puzzling is the location of a Pama-Nyungan outlier, the Yolngu languages, in northeast Arnhem Land, at least 500 km from the nearest other Pama-Nyungan languages. It has been suggested that the homeland of Yolngu, and possibly of Pama-Nyungan as a whole, was located on the former land bridge between New Guinea and Australia. However, this would place the migration of proto-Yolngu at least 9000 years ago, prior to any plausible date for proto-Pama-Nyungan itself. The Yolngu languages are too closely related to each other to date back this far, with proto-Yolngu having a probable age of around 2,000 years. This group presumably moved from a homeland somewhere on the southern or eastern coast of the Gulf of Carpentaria, close to other ancestral Pama-Nyungan languages, in the area mentioned above as the most likely homeland for Pama-Nyungan as a whole.

SEE ALSO: 7 The human colonization of Australia; 43 North America: Na Dene/ Athapaskan archaeology and linguistics; 44 North America: Eskimo-Aleut linguistic history

References

Alpher, B. (2004) Pama-Nyungan: phonological reconstruction and status as a phylogenetic group. In Bowern & Koch (2004), pp. 93–126.

Baker, B. (2007) "I'm going to where-her-brisket-is": placenames in the Roper. In L. Hercus, F. Hodges, & J. Simpson (eds.), *The Land is a Map: Placenames of Indigenous Origin in Australia.* Canberra: Pandanus Books, pp. 103–130.

Bowern, C. & Koch, H. (eds.) (2004) *Australian Languages: Classification and the Comparative Method.* Amsterdam: John Benjamins.

Dixon, R. M. W. (1997) *The Rise and Fall of Languages.* Cambridge: Cambridge University Press.

Dixon, R. M. W. (2002) *Australian Languages: Their Nature and Development.* Cambridge Language Surveys, Cambridge: Cambridge University Press.

Ehret, C. (2011) *History and the Testimony of Language.* Berkeley: University of California Press.

Evans, N. (ed.) (2003) *The Non-Pama-Nyungan Languages of Northern Australia: Comparative studies of the continent's most linguistically complex region.* Pacific Linguistics 552. Canberra: Pacific Linguistics, Research School of Pacific and Asian Studies, Australian National University.

Evans, N. & Jones, R. (1997) The cradle of the Pama-Nyungans: archaeological and linguistic speculations. In P. McConvell & N. Evans (eds.), *Archaeology and Linguistics: Aboriginal Australia in Global Perspective.* Melbourne: Oxford University Press, pp. 385–417.

Haberle, S. & David, B. (2004) Climates of change: human dimensions of Holocene environmental change in low latitudes of the PEPII transect. *Quaternary International* 118–119, 165–179.

Harvey, M. (2009) The genetic status of Garrwan. *Australian Journal of Linguistics* 29(2), 195–244.

Hiscock, P. (2002) Pattern and context in the Holocene proliferation of backed artifacts in Australia. *Archeological Papers of the American Anthropological Association* 12(1), 163–177.

Hiscock, P. (2008) *The Archaeology of Ancient Australia.* London: Routledge.

Kayser, M., Brauer, S., Weiss, G., et al. (2001) Independent histories of human Y chromosomes from Melanesia and Australia. *American Journal of Human Genetics* 68, 173–190.

Lourandos, H. (1997) *Continent of Hunter-Gatherers.* Cambridge: Cambridge University Press.

McConvell, P. (1997) Semantic shifts between fish and meat and the prehistory of Pama-Nyungan. In D. Tryon & M. Walsh (eds.), *Boundary Rider: Essays in Honour of Geoffrey O'Grady.* Pacific Linguistics C-136, pp. 303–325. Canberra: Pacific Linguistics, Research School of Pacific and Asian Studies, Australian National University.

McConvell, P. (2009) Where the spear sticks up: the variety of locatives in place names in the Victoria River District. In L. Hercus & H. Koch (eds.), *Aboriginal Placenames: Naming and Re-naming the Australian landscape.* Canberra: ANU EPress, pp. 359–402.

McConvell, P. (2010) The archaeolinguistics of migration. In L. Lucassen, J. Lucassen, & P. Manning (eds.), *Migration History in World History: Multidisciplinary Approaches.* Leiden: Brill, pp. 155–190.

McConvell, P. & Bowern, C. (2011) The prehistory and internal relationships of Australian languages. *Language and Linguistics Compass* 5(1), 19–32.

McConvell, P. & Laughren, M. (2004) The Ngumpin-Yapa subgroup. In Bowern & Koch (2004), pp. 151–177.

McConvell, P. & Smith, M. (2003) Millers and mullers: the archaeolinguistic stratigraphy of seed-grinding in Central Australia. In H. Andersen (ed.), *Language Contacts in Prehistory: Studies in Stratigraphy*. Amsterdam: John Benjamins.

O'Grady, G. & Hale, K. (2004) The coherence and distinctiveness of the Pama-Nyungan language family within the Australian linguistic phylum. In Bowern & Koch (2004), pp. 69–92.

O'Grady, G., Wurm, S., & Hale, K. (1966) *Aboriginal Languages of Australia (a Preliminary Classification)*. Victoria, BC: Department of Linguistics, University of Victoria.

43

North America: Na Dene/Athapaskan archaeology and linguistics

R. G. Matson and M. P. R. Magne

The Athapaskan languages, together with their relatives in Siberia, Alaska, and Pacific coastal Canada, record some intriguing episodes of long-distance hunter-gatherer migration during the late Holocene, culminating in the establishment of Apache and Navajo peoples in the southwestern United States.

Speakers of the Athapaskan (also spelled Athabascan) languages are currently spread out across the northern part of North America, in Alaska and western Canada, southwestern Oregon and northwestern California, the southwestern United States, and into northern Mexico. We first review their distribution and then discuss how they spread out over this large area, stressing what is known and what is hypothetical.

The Athapaskan languages proper encompass a single large continuous area across interior Alaska to central Canada (the Northern Athapaskans), and two outlying regions, one of the Pacific Athapaskans in southern Oregon and northern California, and the Apacheans (Apache and Navajo) in the Southwest. A few small, intermediate isolates are not discussed here. In our view, there were five different traditional lifeway adaptations in these three areas. Following Dyen and Aberle (1974), the Northern Athapaskans appear to have had two separate adaptations. Those in the Pacific Drainage had a lifeway that was dependent to various degrees on salmon, although they generally did not have the high population densities and settlement sizes associated with Northwest Coast cultures. Northern Athapaskans further east were more mobile, had less permanent settlements, and were more dependent on winter lake fish and large land mammals. Both adaptations fit the generalizations usually associated with hunters and gatherers.

The Pacific Athapaskans in Oregon and California were salmon fishers, and shellfish and acorn gatherers. They were dependent on stored salmon, lived in relatively permanent winter villages, and had much smaller and more densely populated territories than Northern Athapaskans. They also dropped many cultural traits associated with

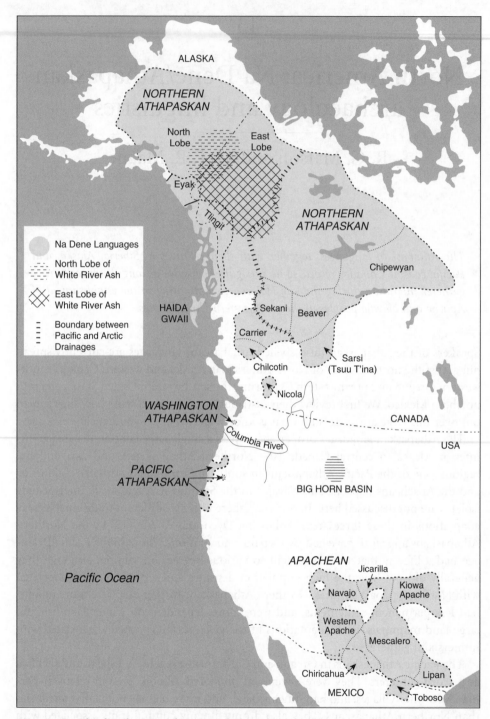

Figure 43.1 The distributions of Na Dene languages and White River volcanic ash.

Northern Athapaskans, even though their languages remain quite similar. The Apacheans of the US Southwest showed two more adaptations, one of maize agriculture (adopted before European contact) with stock raising (adopted from Europeans), and the other a Plains/montane bison-hunting adaptation, using horses in historical times, best illustrated by the Kiowa-Apache. The first maize and stock-raising adaptation, that of the Navajo, was fairly sedentary, but did not include settlements of any significant size. Despite the very different economic adaptations and cosmologies of the Apacheans, their languages are very similar to a number of Northern Athapaskan ones.

In addition to the Athapaskan speakers proper, there is widespread agreement that the Tlingit, the northernmost members of the Northwest Coast Culture Area, speak a language closely related to the Athapaskan family. Next to the Tlingit, the Eyak have a similar relationship to Athapaskan. The Haida, on Haida Gwaii, known until recently as the Queen Charlotte Islands, also members of the Northwest Coast Culture Area, speak a language that may also be related to Athapaskan. The overall linguistic grouping of Athapaskan, Tlingit, Eyak, and Haida languages is often referred to as *Na Dene*, a controversial macrofamily that has waxed and waned in popularity over the last 100 years. There has been a recent surge in its acceptability, although the inclusion of Haida remains contentious.

Migrations

Many archaeologists and linguists believe in the likelihood of a tripartite migration to the Americas, with Paleoindians (Amerindian languages) arriving first (see chapter 8), Na Dene second, and the Inuit-Aleut last (see chapters 44, 45). Since recent research has revealed that Ket, the only remaining member of the Yeniseian language family in central Siberia, is also related to Athapaskan (Kari & Potter 2010), it is possible that the pre-Na Dene language originated in Northeast Asia (but see below).

The origins of language families tend to be located in areas where their primary subgroups are most highly differentiated. In the Athapaskan case proper, such a region is located at the junction of British Columbia, Yukon, and Alaska, and this is also where the Tlingit and Eyak territories touch Athapaskan language territories. If Haida is indeed related to the Tlingit, Eyak, and Athapaskan languages, the location of greatest Na Dene linguistic diversity and the homeland for the Athapaskan languages did not differ significantly.

The situation relating to the Yeneseian Ket language, as reported in Kari and Potter's (2010) work, is difficult to reconcile with existing linguistic and archaeological data and ideas on Athapaskan origins. First, the Ket language appears to be too similar to Athapaskan languages to have been separated from them for the 10,000 year time depth often applied to Na Dene prehistory. Ket may even be more closely related to Tlingit than to Athapaskan, which would indicate that it separated well after the period of early Na Dene migration. If Ket is actually representative of a 10,000-year separation from Na Dene, then much linguistic understanding about language change will be in error, since some languages must have changed at rates remarkably slower than others.

In terms of the archaeological record, microblades, often seen as markers of the Na Dene migration from Asia (Magne & Fedje 2007), arrived in Alaska perhaps as early as 9500 BCE, after the macroblade and bifacial-point progenitors of Clovis. An association of microblade technology with Yeniseian languages in Northeast Asia remains to be systematically investigated. The only other archaeologically documented migration from Asia is the Arctic Small Tool or Paleoeskimo tradition (chapter 45), conventionally seen as evidence of the initial Eskimo-Aleut migration, perhaps four to six thousand years ago.

Archaeological and linguistic solutions to the Dene-Yeniseian dilemma include:

1   Ket actually did separate from Na Dene more than 10 kya and has changed very slowly;
2   Na Dene should instead be identified with the Arctic Small Tool tradition, making it later in time than commonly thought, and microblades should be identified with the Eskimo-Aleut migration;
3   Ket is a "reflux" migration, from the Americas or from easternmost Northeast Asia (eg. the Chukotka Peninsula), approximately four to six thousand years ago.

Option 2 disagrees with current archaeological and genetic evidence, but neither Option 1 nor 3 are supported by positive evidence. Option 3 has the virtue of not having any evidence against it. In these early days of understanding of Ket, its association with Athapaskan and Tlingit appears convincing to most linguists who have examined the issue, but the precise relationships remain to be delimited.

Within Northern Athapaskan languages there is only moderate variability, suggesting that the first linguistic deviations occurred circa 400 BCE according to glottochronology (other linguistic estimates are similar; see Matson & Magne 2007: 133–134). With some exceptions, most of the Athapaskan languages in interior Alaska are very similar, indicating a recent spread. A similar pattern is found to the east. It has been suggested that these two expansions were the result of the North Lobe of the White River volcanic eruption at c.300 CE along the Alaska/Yukon border (Clague et al. 1995), which pushed people both east and west. The linguistic diversity present fits with such an event. The eastern Northern Athapaskan languages, in particular, tend to show continuous variation, rather than being discrete, geographically separate languages, which points towards a recent expansion. This volcanic event may have also caused Northern Athapaskans to move further south into British Columbia, spreading into the interior areas where the salmon storage adaptation existed among Salishan-speaking groups. No technological reason has yet been proposed for this spread, but Northern Athapaskan kinship and social values were preadapted to explore new areas and adopt new technology (Ives 1990; Matson & Magne 2007: 152). A much larger eruption occurred c.800 CE and this has been associated with the migrations to the south, as well as to the east. Although some have questioned that this ash fall would actually have had large and long lasting effects, recent genetic work (Kuhn et al. 2010) shows a decrease in genetic variation at about this time in the caribou herds of this region, one of the most important food resources.

As the Pacific Athapaskan languages appear to be marginally more different from Northern Athapaskan languages than Apachean, this Pacific migration has often been seen as occurring slightly before that to the southwest. The differences between Apachean and Northern Athapaskan languages on the one hand, and between Pacific Athapaskan languages and Northern Athapaskan languages on the other, are in accord with a separation between the Northern Athapaskans and the two southern groups around the time of the second ash fall. The Pacific Athapaskans likely originated in British Columbia, where they had adopted the stored salmon economy, since a remnant group is found in western Washington state. The originating group probably migrated down the Columbia River and up the Willamette River into southern Oregon. The oldest coastal villages there and in northern California are associated with Athapaskan (and Algic) speakers and appear to date about 1500 CE (Fredrickson 1984; Matson & Magne 2007: 148–149), which is in accord with the linguistic diversity among the Pacific Athapaskans. It may be that the Athapaskans introduced the salmon storage economy to this region.

Two additional points should be noted about the Pacific Athapaskans. First, traditional culture-historical archaeology in the area, and thus the archaeological identification of prehistoric Athapaskans, lags considerably behind that in British Columbia and the US Southwest. Second, the slightly greater differences in language from Northern Athapaskan than is exhibited by the Apacheans may be not the result of greater time depth, but of a splitting into small linguistic communities with small territories and more sedentary lifeways.

The Apachean migration to the Southwest

The best-known Athapaskan migration is that of the Apacheans, and this began either at the same time as the Pacific Athapaskan, or slightly later. In contrast with the Pacific Athapaskan migration, a recently abandoned area in the US Southwest was available for the Apacheans. By 1300 CE, two neighboring areas of the Southwest became empty, probably in the wake of climatic changes: the northern Anasazi-occupied zone due to the well-known failure of maize agriculture in the Pueblo III era (Lipe 1995); and the eastern flanks of the central Rocky Mountains after the collapse of the Upper Republican archaeological culture, of which some members also grew maize.

The earliest well-accepted Apachean archaeological culture is the Tierra Blanca complex of the Texas Panhandle region of the southwestern plains (Habicht-Mauche 1992). This culture, dated from 1450 to 1600, is found in the area where the Coronado expedition found people termed "Querechos," usually identified as Apaches, in 1541. The earliest well-accepted Navajo site is in northwest New Mexico and has a tree-ring date of 1541 (Towner 2003; Wilshusen 2010). Thus, we have two well-dated complexes that appear to date the appearance in the Southwest of the Apache and Navajo, both in or near their historical territories. The New Mexico region was part of the area abandoned by the Pueblo III people by 1300.

How did the Apacheans reach the Southwest, and from where did they begin their migration? The simplest hypothesis geographically, that the southernmost Athapaskans east of the Rocky Mountains (the Sarsi or Tsuu T'ina) simply moved down the foothills into the area abandoned by the Upper Republicans and then into the Southwest, is actually unlikely (Magne & Matson 2010). First, Tsuu T'ina is linguistically not as close to Apachean as several other Northern Athapaskan languages. Second, the current position of the Tsuu T'ina was greatly influenced by the early fur trade, and it is quite unlikely they were in their current position prior to European contact (Dyen & Aberle 1974: 250–251). Another Athapaskan group may have been present in that area, but this is a region where there is no archaeological identification of Athapaskans, so this idea is untested.

In contrast, the Carrier, an Athapaskan group in central British Columbia, are closer linguistically to the Apacheans – the second closest according to cognates, although not quite so close as the Chipewyans (Dyen & Aberle 1974: 12). The archaeological presence of Carrier (or a highly similar archaeological culture) is attested in central British Columbia by the time of the second White River ash fall (Matson & Magne 2007). This has led to another idea, that both the Pacific Athapaskan and Apachean migrations left this area at about the same time, with one proceeding southward just inland from the Pacific, and the other moving through Idaho and on to the montane plains, and then southwards. The absence of horses in Athapaskan rock art (the horse being introduced by the Spanish) in the Big Horn Basin in Wyoming supports the presence of Athapaskans (Francis & Loendorf 2002). However, the dating of this occurrence needs to be better defined. It was first thought to date to about 1000 CE, but re-dating suggests c.1500 (Magne & Matson 2010).

The hypothesis of a single southward migration sees the Tierra Blanca complex of the Texas Panhandle region as representing the ancestors of both the Apache and Navajo. One variant hypothesis advocates the Navajo moving directly from the Upper Republican-vacated area of Colorado to northern New Mexico, and would have the Tierra Blanca complex being ancestral only to the Apaches (Towner 2003). Another variant would have two migrations originating in British Columbia, with the Apacheans slightly later than the Pacific Athapaskans. A third hypothesis of an intermountain route west of the Rocky Mountains through the Great Basin, with the Fremont culture representing Athapaskans, can be rejected. Fremont material culture, including ethnically sensitive basketry, has no links to Athapaskan cultures, and the mtDNA conclusively rejects such identification (Matson & Magne 2007: 148).

The Athapaskan identity of both the Apacheans and Pacific Athapaskans has been long noted, with the former first recognized 150 years ago. It has also long been agreed that the Apachean and Pacific Athapaskans migrated from the north. There may well have been some later northerly movements among some groups, most notably the Kiowa Apache. Great distances and the lack of intervening archaeological information may have encouraged ideas based on simplistic map reading and long-distance comparisons of specific material. An example of the latter is the Avonlea point type being seen as an Athapaskan marker, an idea that must now be rejected, as it fits with almost no other information (Walde 2006). As the blank spots on the map become filled in, there is less freedom for such proposals, but much remains to be done and large areas remain to be systematically examined. Understanding of process remains poor. For example, if the second White River ash fall was the initiation of the southward migrations, the conditions and motivations under which a migration might have continued, over such long periods and distances, are still unclear (Magne & Matson 2010).

SEE ALSO: 8 The human colonization of the Americas: archaeology; 44 North America: Eskimo-Aleut linguistic history; 45: North America: Paleoeskimo and Inuit archaeology; 48 Mesoamerica and the southwestern United States: archaeology

References

Clague, J., Evans, S., Rampton, V., et al. (1995) Improved age estimates for the White River and Bridge River tephras, Western Canada. *Canadian Journal of Earth Sciences* 32, 1172–1179.

Dyen, I. & Aberle, D. (1974) *Lexical Reconstruction: The Case of the Proto-Athapaskan Kinship System*. Cambridge: Cambridge University Press.

Francis, J. & Loendorf, L. (2002) *Ancient Visions: Petroglyphs and Pictographs from the Wind River and Bighorn Country, Wyoming and Montana*. Salt Lake City: University of Utah Press.

Fredrickson, D. (1984) The north coastal region. In M. J. Moratto (ed.), *California Archaeology*. Orlando, FL: Academic Press, pp. 471–527.

Habicht-Mauche, J. (1992) Coronado's Querechos and Teyas in the archaeological record of the Texas Panhandle. *Plains Anthropologist* 37, 247–259.

Ives, J. (1990) *A Theory of Northern Athapaskan Prehistory*. Boulder, CO: Westview.

Kari, J. & Potter, B. (eds.) (2010) *The Dene-Yeniseian Connection*. Fairbanks: Anthropological Papers of the University of Alaska, vol. 5 (new series).

Kuhn, T., McFarlane, K., Groves, P., et al. (2010) Modern and ancient DNA reveal recent partial replacement of caribou in the southwest Yukon. *Molecular Ecology* 19, 1312–1323.

Lipe, W. (1995) The depopulation of the northern San Juan: conditions in the turbulent 1200s. *Journal of Anthropological Archaeology* 14, 143–169.

Magne, M. P. R. & Fedje, D. (2007) The spread of microblade technology in northwestern North America. In Y. Kuzmin, S. G. Keates, & C. Shen (eds.), *Origin and Spread of Microblade Technology in Northern Asia and North America*. Burnaby: Archaeology Press, Simon Fraser University, pp. 171–188.

Magne, M. P. R. & Matson, R. G. (2010) Moving on: expanding perspectives on Athapaskan migration. *Canadian Journal of Archaeology* 34, 212–239.

Matson, R. G. & Magne, M. P. R. (2007) *Athapaskan Migrations: The Archaeology of Eagle Lake, British Columbia*. Tucson: University of Arizona Press.

Towner, R. (2003) *Defending the Dinétah: Pueblitos in the Ancestral Navajo Homeland*. Salt Lake City: University of Utah Press.

Walde, D. (2006) Avonlea and Athapaskan migrations: a reconsideration. *Plains Anthropologist* 51(198), 185–197.

Wilshusen, R. (2010) The Diné at the edge of history: Navajo ethnogenesis in the northern Southwest, 1500–1750. In L. L. Scheiber & M. D. Mitchell (eds.), *Across a Great Divide: Continuity and Change in Native North American Societies, 1400–1900*. Tucson: University of Arizona Press, pp. 192–211.

44

North America: Eskimo-Aleut linguistic history

Michael Fortescue

The Aleut and Eskimo migrations have spanned the past five thousand years, cul-
minating in the Thule migration across Arctic Canada to Greenland that started
about 1000 CE. This chapter is complementary to the archaeological record which
follows (chapter 45).

The Eskimo-Aleut language family is particularly well situated for investigating the linguistic reflexes of human migrations. On the one hand, a good deal is known about the prehistoric movements of people in the Arctic, and, on the other hand, there was relatively little contact before modern times with languages outside the family to complicate the linguistic situation (apart from interaction with Chukchi, west of Bering Strait). In fact, the Thule migrations from North Alaska as far as East Greenland about a thousand years ago represent a paradigm case for the rapid expansion of a language into virtually uninhabited regions, with ensuing gradation of innovations and losses away from its original homeland. Contact with the Paleoeskimo people who entered Canada and Greenland many centuries prior to the Thule migration and subsequently died out must have been minimal and apparently left no linguistic trace (nothing is known of their language). The Thule homeland lies by purely linguistic criteria inside Alaska, where the greatest diversity within the Eskimo-Aleut family is found: the major break within the Eskimo branch of the family is between Yupik (actually four distinct extant languages) and the Inuit dialect continuum stretching from North Alaska as far as East Greenland.

Though the Thule migration constitutes the best known and archeologically best attested population movement in the Eskimo-Aleut world (Figure 44.1, no. 2), there have been other less extensive migrations which have also left clear linguistic traces. These include the expansion of Alaskan Yupik speakers to the Pacific Coast of Alaska and the roughly contemporaneous southwestward expansion of Siberian Yupik speakers within Asia (Figure 44.1, nos. 3 and 4); the intrusion of North Alaskan Inupiaq

The Global Prehistory of Human Migration: The Encyclopedia of Global Human Migration Volume 1,
First Edition. Edited by Peter Bellwood.

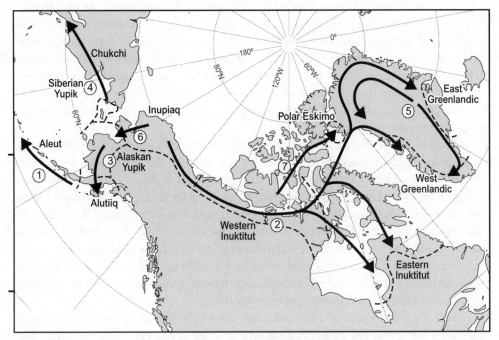

Figure 44.1 The migrations of Eskimos (Inuit and others) and Aleuts since 3000 BCE. Map production by Education and Multimedia Services, College of Asia and the Pacific, The Australian National University.

speakers southwards, breaking an earlier Yupik continuum between Alaska and Chukotka (Figure 44.1, no. 6); the movements of groups of East Greenlanders back via the north of Greenland to the northwest coast of that island and around the southeast coast at least as far as Kap Farvel (Figure 44.1, no. 5); the late appearance of the Polar Eskimos in Greenland from the high Canadian Arctic (Figure 44.1, no. 7); and, in much more ancient times than any of these, the successive movements of Aleuts out along the Aleutian archipelago from the east (Figure 44.1, no. 1).

The Thule migration

The migration of modern Inuit Eskimos eastwards from northern Alaska, that started according to archaeologists somewhat over 1,000 years ago, has left its linguistic traces in a number of ways. Perhaps the most well-known of these concerns the successive simplification of word-medial consonant clusters (through assimilation of the manner and/or place of articulation to the second consonant) the further east one goes. Thus, compared to the maximal array of clusters in North Alaska, the Canadian dialects of Inuktitut first lose alveolar plus other consonant clusters, then labial plus other consonants, and finally velar plus other consonant clusters, tending towards geminates (double consonants).[1]

The greatest simplification is found in Greenland on the one hand and in Labrador on the other, reflecting the splitting of the migratory routes somewhere to the west of Baffin Land. In Greenland, only uvular plus other consonant clusters are found (apart from /ts/), and in Labrador even the latter disappear since uvulars and velars merge. This is discussed in greater detail by Dorais (2010: 127ff.), who suggests a sociolinguistic motivation for the successive simplification; the further eastward the migration reached, the more assimilated forms developed, representing the more relaxed "camp" speech of women and children.

The situation of Polar Eskimo in northern Greenland is interesting in this regard, since in its earliest attested form (in the 1930s) it reflected the same stage of regressive assimilation of clusters as Inuktitut dialects west of Hudson Bay, only reaching the next stage, as on Baffin Land, amongst younger speakers today. This can be attributed to its late arrival in Greenland from somewhere west and north of Hudson Bay. Also, the conservative Rigolet subdialect of southernmost Labrador (as described by Dorais, 2010) displays the same degree of assimilation as the west coast of Hudson Bay, which suggests that the further stages of cluster simplification took place later, following the sedentarization of more easterly groups, with parallel results in more than one place due to a common "drift" towards pure geminates.

Another phonological simplification, this time involving all dialects east of North Alaska, is the loss of the palatalized consonant series of Alaskan Inupiaq. Other phonological developments are more sporadically distributed, but often with (natural) parallel developments in widely separated areas, as for instance the monopthongization of diphthongs in both Malimiut Inupiaq and Greenlandic, or uvular metathesis of */lR/ and */nR/ in Bering Strait Inupiaq and all Canadian and Greenlandic dialects east of Melville Peninsula.[2] In general, East Greenlandic is the most phonologically innovative (with the most reduced inventory of phonemes) and (south)western Inupiaq the most archaic within the Inuit continuum.

There are also morphological and lexical developments that reflect the Thule migrations. The most significant of these is the gradual simplification the further east one goes of the complex system of demonstrative stems inherited by all Eskimo languages. The maximal system, found in central Alaskan Yupik, consists of some 30 individual roots, used in parallel adverbial and pronominal forms, distinguishing extended versus restricted versus obscured forms for each of five directional dimensions (vertical as well as horizontal), some of which are landscape-specific, for example, downslope versus upslope, downriver versus upriver (in coastal Inuit = down coast versus up coast). Of these, North Slope Inupiaq has 25, whereas West Greenlandic has 11, and the Canadian dialects in between have successively fewer from west to east, with eastern Inuktitut maintaining 14. The order in which the distinctions collapse is determined partially by the phonology (compare the cluster simplifications above), and partially by their growing application to purely coastal usage further to the east, especially in Greenland, where *av- "extended over there," for example, has become specialized in the meaning "in the north (up the coast)" (for details cf. Fortescue et al. 2010: 497ff.). Finally, Petersen (1986a) makes an interesting attempt to relate shifts in the reference of animal and plant names between Alaska, Canada, and Greenland to the Thule migrations, as with Alaskan *tuuyuq* "woodpecker" (a species not found in Greenland), but Greenlandic *tuuyuk* "plover."

Another area in which the distribution of a morphological trait seems to reflect the direction of these migrations – but this time with the easternmost dialects maintaining an archaic trait that has become marginalized further west – is the form of the indicative mood. The "original" Inuit indicative in *-vuq* (as opposed to participial *-žuq/tuq*) is best maintained in West Greenlandic, whereas in North Alaska it is only used in restricted "narrative" contexts in conjunction with particle *kiisaimma* "finally." In Canada there is a gradient between narrative usage in the west (like North Alaska) to ordinary indicative usage in the east (like West Greenlandic, but alternating with *-tuq*). Here, it is North Alaska that has innovated, at the same time introducing a new past-versus-present distinction in the indicative. Also, the complexities of verbal inflectional paradigms, which includes dual-versus-plural person subject and object distinctions, largely lost in Greenland, are gradually reduced from west to east (Dorais 2010: 120ff).

Further migrations within Greenland

The routes whereby influence from East Greenlandic reached the fringe dialects (both northwest and southwest) of West Greenlandic remained obscure until recent times, in particular as to how the Upernavik dialect of northwest Greenland could share the same unusual "i-dialect" phenomenon with East Greenlandic, whereby original */u/ becomes /i/ in certain complex environments (see Petersen 1986b and Fortescue 1986 for details). These environments are almost the same in East Greenlandic and in the southernmost west coast dialects. It is now accepted that the most likely explanation is that small groups of mobile East Greenlanders were forced by climatic deterioration to leave northeast Greenland over the north of the island to the west coast during a time when Thule was uninhabited, in the 16th or 17th century. Here they merged with the northernmost group of sedentary West Greenlanders. There were similar movements from east to west around the south of the island, which led to the diffusion of the phenomenon also into the southwest dialects shortly after the disappearance of the Norse settlers in the area. The influence of East Greenlandic is especially strong in the case of the southernmost, Kap Farvel dialect, which displays a number of other East Greenlandic traits such as the reflex of geminate */ll/ as a retroflex alveolar-palatal affricate (reminiscent of the East Greenlandic reflex /tt/). It also shares with East Greenlandic and Upernavik the nasalization of intervocalic */g/ (the latter two dialects also nasalize uvular */R/).

The late arrival of the Polar Eskimos around Thule from the high Canadian Arctic is reflected in certain traits shared with Copper and Netsilik Inuktitut (besides the cluster retention discussed above), in particular the reflex of */s/ as an /h/-like sound. However, isolation from other groups – until the arrival of a small group of refugees from southern Baffin in early historical times – has produced idiosyncrasies not shared with any other dialect. More significant culturally than linguistically, this migration of a few families from Baffin Land in the 19th century has at most left a handful of lexical traces in modern Polar Eskimo.

Traces of other Eskimo-Aleut migrations in the west

On the Asian side of Bering Strait, at approximately the same time as the Thule migration eastward from North Alaska, a westward expansion of Punuk culture whaling people probably speaking Central Siberian Yupik was initiated. This eventually reached as far as the Kamchatkan isthmus in the 15th century, as linguistic evidence suggests, although the Eskimo presence must have been short-lived or absorbed by maritime Koryaks and – especially – Kereks (cf. Fortescue 2004). The evidence includes the collapse of the Chukotian vowel system in these languages, replaced by a simple Eskimo-like one; the effect of Yupik prosody (stress and length) on Kerek; and numerous loan words associated with the sea-mammal hunting way of life. Eskimo-internal data (e.g. prosodic) suggest that the Naukanski Yupik spoken around East Cape, opposite Alaska, has an intermediate position between Central Siberian and Alaskan Yupik, and may in fact constitute a relatively recent intruder from the Alaskan side (cf. Krauss 1985: 4). The now extinct language Sirenikski on the south coast of the Chukotkan Peninsula probably represents, by contrast, a pocket of archaic Eskimo much influenced by Chukchi.

Another general movement on the Alaskan side at about this time – probably more a gradual expansion than a distinct migration – brought Alaskan Yupik speakers into territory previously inhabited by Aleuts and/or unrelated people of the North Pacific coast and adjacent Kodiak Island. This is reflected in the general closeness of Alutiiq (Pacific Coast Yupik) to Central Alaskan Yupik (the generally accepted name Alutiiq reflects the ethnonym *Aleut* – but only because the Russians in the area did not distinguish them from "real" Aleuts); however, it also displays considerably greater lexical influence from Aleut, and there are also idiosyncratic complications in the prosody, perhaps due to contact with Aleut. The Yupik continuum between Alaska and Chukotka that these movements maintained intact was eventually broken by movements southwards on the part of Inupiaq speakers from the north on to the Seward peninsula, less than 500 years ago. This is reflected in the substratum effects on the Seward Peninsula Inuit dialects (involving medial consonant gradation) which stem from the distinctive rhythmic prosody of Yupik (Kaplan 1985).

Finally, a much earlier migration westward from Alaska must be mentioned: that of the Aleuts out on to the Aleutian archipelago. It should be pointed out that the linguistic divergence of Aleut as a whole from Eskimo is very great, owing to lengthy isolation combined with possible substratum effects from some previous population on the Alaskan peninsula. This is of a magnitude quite different from anything found in the more sparsely populated areas further north. It can only be surmised that the movement that separated Aleut from Eskimo occurred soon after the first arrival of the Eskimo-Aleut family in Alaska over Bering Strait, at least four thousand years ago and some two thousand years before the Inuit–Yupik split. The linguistic evidence suggests at least two major phases here – an original spread westwards as far as the outermost Near Islands (reached some 2,500 years ago), overlaid in more recent times (only a few hundred years ago) by a wave bearing specifically Eastern Aleut influence from the Alaskan peninsula. The latter resulted in certain morphological neologisms reaching as far as Attu, the dialect of which in other respects retains a number of archaic features alongside its own phonological innovations (see Bergsland 1994: xxiv ff. for further details). The fact that most morphological and lexical innovations have their origin in the eastern dialect suggests the direction of the movements involved, which has apparently always been from the mainland out towards the remoter islands.

SEE ALSO: 45 North America: Paleoeskimo and Inuit archaeology

Notes

1   Actually the degree of assimilation in North Alaska is somewhat greater in the western Malimiut dialect than in that of the North Slope at Barrow, which has smoothed over cluster plus continuant clusters by regressive manner assimilation.
2   Actually with */lR/ going to /RR/ (a geminate uvular fricative) in the Canadian dialects.

References

Bergsland, K. (1994) *Aleut Dictionary*. Fairbanks: Alaska Native Language Center, University of Alaska Fairbanks.

Dorais, L.-J. (2010) *The Language of the Inuit*. Montreal: McGill-Queen's University Press.

Fortescue, M. (1986) What dialect distribution can tell us of dialect formation in Greenland. *Arctic Anthropology* 23(1–2), 413–422.

Fortescue, M. (2004) How far west into Asia have Eskimo languages been spoken, and which ones? *Etudes/Inuit/Studies* 28(2), 159–183.

Fortescue, M., Kaplan, L., & Jacobson, S. (2010) *Comparative Eskimo Dictionary with Aleut Cognates*, 2nd edn., Fairbanks: Alaska Native Language Center, University of Alaska Fairbanks.

Kaplan, L. (1985) Seward Peninsula Inupiaq consonant gradation and its relationship to prosody. In Krauss (1985), pp. 191–210.

Krauss, M. (ed.) (1985) *Yupik Eskimo Prosodic Systems*. ANLC research papers 7. Fairbanks: University of Alaska Fairbanks.

Petersen, R. (1986a) Nogle dyre- og plantenavne i Alaska og Grønland [Some animal and plant names in Alaska and Greenland]. *Vort Sprog – Vor Kultur* [Our language – our culture] (Papers from Symposium in Nuuk, Greenland, 1981). Nuuk: Ilisimatusarfik and Kalaallit Nunaata Katersugaasivia, pp. 177–187.

Petersen, R. (1986b) Some features common to East and West Greenlandic in the light of dialect relationships and the latest migration theories. *Arctic Anthropology* 23(1–2), 401–411.

45

North America: Paleoeskimo and Inuit archaeology

T. Max Friesen

The Paleoeskimo and Thule migrations represented successive rapid colonizations of vast Arctic regions, in each case moving from west to east, about four thousand years apart. These migrations were made possible by complex technology aiding movement and survival in some of the coldest regions on earth.

The North American Arctic is a vast and variable region, incorporating a range of difficult challenges to human existence linked to extremes of climate and biogeography. Resources are unevenly spread across space and season, and therefore existence in all but a few locations can be precarious. Furthermore, overall population densities have always been relatively low, particularly in much of the central and eastern Arctic, leading to challenges in transportation, communication, and social interaction.

Against this backdrop, migration of various forms and scales was common in Arctic prehistory. This is seen, dramatically, in periodic abandonment and resettlement of a number of regions, with those episodes of resettlement, by default, involving migrations. However, two migration episodes stand out due to their unmistakable archaeological signatures and their epic scale, spanning the entire top of North America.

The Early Paleoeskimo migration

For several thousands of years following terminal Pleistocene deglaciation, only the southern and western fringes of the North American Arctic saw occasional settlement by Paleoindian and other early peoples. However, some time before 2800 BCE, descendants of the Siberian Bel'kachi tradition colonized Alaska (Powers & Jordan 1990). In North America, this new and long-lasting tradition is known as the Arctic Small Tool tradition or Paleoeskimo tradition (the latter term is preferred here), with its earliest

The Global Prehistory of Human Migration: The Encyclopedia of Global Human Migration Volume 1,
First Edition. Edited by Peter Bellwood.
© 2013 John Wiley & Sons, Ltd. Published 2015 by John Wiley & Sons, Ltd.

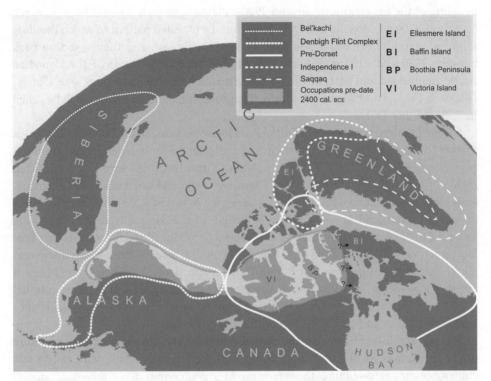

Figure 45.1 Distribution of the Bel'kachi and Early Paleoeskimo cultures. Bold outlines indicate maximum extent of each culture, while the shaded area represents regions occupied by Paleoeskimos before c.2400 BCE.

Alaskan manifestation referred to as the Denbigh Flint Complex (Figure 45.1). The Denbigh Flint Complex is poorly dated, due to a lack of datable organic remains at many sites and generally low archaeological visibility (Odess 2005), but several radiocarbon dates place it in Alaska by around 2500 BCE (Slaughter 2005). However, its origin was almost certainly at least 500 years earlier. Importantly, Denbigh is known from both coastal and interior sites, and is widely regarded as the first society which was fully adapted to life on the northern coasts of eastern Siberia and Alaska, at least during some seasons.

The Paleoeskimo migration to the east of Alaska is highly visible across much of the central Canadian Arctic, due to the Holocene geology of the region. Because of rapid isostatic rebound following the retreat of continental glaciers, land masses are rising relative to sea levels, and many coastlines are made up of flights of beach ridges which become higher in elevation and more ancient as distance from the shoreline increases. Because most prehistoric peoples camped on the coast, elevations can be used as a proxy for age, with older sites located on higher beach ridges. Extensive survey and radiocarbon dating programs by Savelle and Dyke (2009; Dyke et al. 2011) indicate that the earliest Paleoeskimo dwellings in several locations in the central Arctic, from western Victoria Island to Boothia Peninsula, contained organic materials which range in age from 3200 to 2600 BCE. A cautious interpretation of the dates would place initial peopling of the eastern Arctic around 2900–2800 BCE, though it could have occurred as early as 3200 BCE. Savelle and Dyke have found a repeated pattern in which dwelling frequency (and by extension population) was initially low, and then rose to a peak between 2550 and 2100 BCE. Early Paleoeskimo sites across most of the Canadian Arctic archipelago and parts of the northern mainland are referred to as "Pre-Dorset" (Maxwell 1985), and the earliest, pioneering groups predating 2400 BCE will be called here "Initial Pre-Dorset."

Several hundred years after the Initial Pre-Dorset peopling of the Low Arctic, regions further to the east and north saw their first settlement. The Independence I tradition (named after Independence Fiord in northern Greenland) developed in a restricted region of the High Arctic centered on Ellesmere Island and northernmost Greenland, with earliest dates at around 2400 BCE (Grønnow & Jensen 2003). Meanwhile, much of western Greenland saw settlement by people of the Saqqaq tradition, beginning around 2400 BCE (Meldgaard 2004), and coastal Labrador likely also saw its first Pre-Dorset settlement around 2400 BCE (Cox 2003). While there has been much discussion about the relationships between Pre-Dorset, Independence I, and Saqqaq (Maxwell 1985), it now seems likely that they are variants which diverged from a common Initial Pre-Dorset base, with differences resulting from regional variability in available subsistence resources and quality of local lithic raw materials.

Having established its timing and spatial extent, what are we to make of the nature of the migration? Most early Paleoeskimo sites are relatively small, with only a few contemporaneous dwellings, though some larger sites may have served as annual aggregations (Dyke et al. 2011). With notable exceptions, such as several Saqqaq sites in the rich coastal environment of west Greenland, most early sites appear to have been occupied relatively briefly, indicating a high level of mobility and, perhaps, frequently shifting territories based on changing resource distributions. Early Paleoeskimos were capable of acquiring most resources in the Arctic, and in particular both terrestrial and marine mammals, with the probable exception of whales and perhaps walrus, based on a finely tuned technology which included harpoons, spears, and bows and arrows. Other aspects of their technology were equally important to northern life, including tailored skin clothing (inferred from eyed needles), efficient and portable skin tents, and small watercraft which may have resembled kayaks (Meldgaard 2004). Evidence for larger boats and sleds is equivocal, so it is not clear if the migration occurred largely on foot, or with the aid of more complex transportation technologies.

Thus, the migration was probably a relatively continuous process from Siberia through Alaska, reaching the central Arctic by 2800 BCE, or earlier. Here, Initial Pre-Dorset people may have found relatively rich hunting grounds, particularly in terms of terrestrial resources such as caribou and muskoxen, because the migration coincided with the final centuries of the Holocene climatic optimum. In fact, several authors have speculated that muskoxen were a major factor in attracting Initial Pre-Dorset to the region, and in the relative speed of the migration, which may have been due to the ease with which muskoxen were overhunted, resulting in repeated moves to find new herds (Maxwell 1985).

The migration process may have occurred through gradual expansion in which growing populations led to new groups "budding off" and moving to adjacent territories. Perhaps more likely, given the complete lack of other people in this new landscape, Initial Pre-Dorset peoples may have had a lifeway which was not like that of any ethnographically known group; a lifeway which involved extremely high mobility levels and active exploration of previously unknown areas, combined with well-developed mechanisms to keep in contact with other groups in order to maintain an economic "safety net" and provide access to marriage partners. After a few centuries of settlement in the central Arctic, and coinciding with a significant rise in Initial Pre-Dorset population levels, the final phases of the early Paleoeskimo migration occurred in the form of the initial settlement of the High Arctic, Greenland, and Labrador around 2400 BCE.

The factors leading to the Paleoeskimo migration are not clear due to the sparse archaeological record in Siberia and Alaska. Population densities in Alaska were probably low, and there is currently no direct evidence for any local crises which may have forced a migration. Thus, the most likely scenario is that these small-scale, relatively mobile hunter-gatherers moved due to the desirability of the new region in terms of dense and reliable resources.

The Thule Inuit migration

Beginning around 200 CE, and possibly earlier (Mason 2009a), a new group of societies developed in the Bering Strait region of Siberia and Alaska, referred to collectively as the Neoeskimo or Northern Maritime tradition (Figure 45.2). The Old Bering Sea, Punuk, Birnirk, and Thule peoples who made up this tradition represented a fundamentally new way of life, which is ancestral to all modern Inuit, Inuvialuit, and Iñupiat. What is generally recognized as Thule culture was present by around 1000 CE. Thule people lived in large, deep, semi-subterranean houses with effective cold-trap entrances and traveled with the aid of enhanced transportation technology, including *umiaks* (large open skin boats) and, at least during later periods, dog sleds. They hunted with complex technologies which were particularly effective for acquisition of marine mammals including large whales and walrus, as well as allowing continued successful pursuit of seals, land mammals, birds, and fish. In many cases, they lived for much of the year in large winter settlements marked by increasingly complex social structures, widespread trade and interaction, and frequent conflict which included organized warfare (Mason 2009b).

After centuries of continual development and relatively dense occupations in the Bering Strait region, Thule peoples began to move rapidly eastward during the early second millennium CE. Sites relating to the early Thule migration contain several diagnostic artifact types, including "Sicco" and "Natchuk" harpoon heads and a distinctive form of antler arrowhead (Morrison 1999). These artifacts appear at sites across much of the central and eastern Arctic, and wherever they are associated with recently-processed radiocarbon dates on reliable materials, a 13th century date is indicated (McGhee 2000; Friesen & Arnold 2008). Early sites are concentrated in two regions: around Amundsen Gulf in the western Canadian Arctic, and in a more easterly cluster stretching from the northern mainland to northwest Greenland. These sites generally appear in highest frequencies where "highly ranked" resources, particularly bowhead

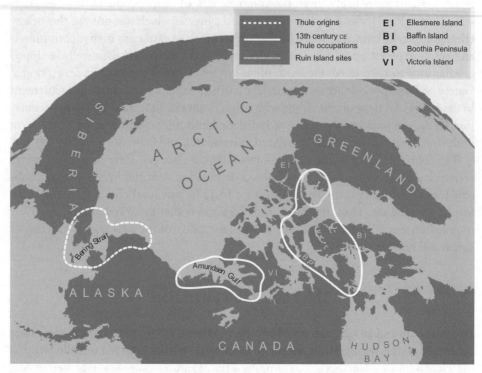

Figure 45.2 Map indicating region of Thule origins, as well as major regions in the central and eastern Arctic settled by Thule peoples during the 13th century CE. The Thule migration proceeded east along the Alaskan north coast to Amundsen Gulf, and then either north or south of Victoria Island to the eastern Arctic.

whales and walrus, were abundant, though early Thule acquired a wide range of resources in each region they settled.

One of the most remarkable aspects of the Thule migration was its speed. Within only a few decades, settlements had appeared from Amundsen Gulf in the western Canadian Arctic to northwest Greenland. The speed of this migration is seen not only in the almost precise contemporaneity of the earliest reliable radiocarbon dates in each region, but also, dramatically, in the fact that a pottery fragment from an early Thule house on western Ellesmere Island, near the northernmost limit of Thule settlement, had a chemical signature suggesting it was manufactured in Alaska (McCullough 1989). Given the fragility of Thule pottery, it is inconceivable that it survived more than a few years of movement. The nature of the migration is difficult to reconstruct, though many early sites are relatively small, with only a few houses – these must represent movement of "compound families," composed of two or more closely related extended families, which were the structural foundation of historic Iñupiat social organization (Burch 2006). Movement likely occurred during the summer, by *umiak*, though sled travel during other seasons was also possible (see Krupnik & Chlenov 2009 for a recent analogous migration). These early Inuit had extensive, heavy tool kits which could only be moved with access to advanced transportation equipment.

Early Thule settlements in the eastern Arctic display some variability in their material culture, which is interpreted as indicating that some groups (particularly those known as "Ruin Island" in the Ellesmere Island/northwest Greenland region) appear to have a closer relationship to Punuk-influenced peoples in the Bering Strait region, while others appear more closely connected to Birnirk-influenced settlements in North Alaska (McCullough 1989). However, the significance of these differences is unclear. Both sets of sites appear at almost precisely the same time, and a majority of their material culture is indistinguishable. Thus, it is likely that all early Thule arrived as part of a closely-linked series of migration episodes.

Much has been written about the motivation for the Thule migration (Friesen & Arnold 2008). An early and still widely held opinion sees them moving in pursuit of bowhead whales, which would have been present in large numbers in the eastern Arctic at the end of the Medieval Warm Period (McGhee 1969/70). A second explanation emphasizes the desire for metal. Meteoritic iron and Norse iron and bronze were available in northwest Greenland, which was settled relatively early in the migration process (Gulløv & McGhee 2006). A third set of motivating factors focuses on the high population densities and widespread conflict in the Bering Strait region, which together may have created social conditions which favored emigration. Debate continues about the relative importance of these factors, but the most reasonable interpretation is that the decision by early migrants to leave Alaska was driven by multiple considerations. Ultimately, the migration represented a search by individuals and families for new territories where they could recreate the economic, social, and ideological structures of their western homeland. Within this context, the speed and direction of the migration would have been impacted by the distribution of subsistence resources, including bowhead whales, and important raw materials, such as metal; as well as the presence of other people such as Dorset Paleoeskimos and Norse settlers.

Conclusion

The North American Arctic is unusual in having very high resolution evidence for two separate large-scale prehistoric migrations. There are several noteworthy similarities between the two cases. In particular, both represent population movements at a huge spatial scale, and at a relatively rapid pace. Paleoeskimos appear to have traversed the entire eastern Arctic in perhaps three to five centuries, while at least some parts of the Thule migration probably occurred within a single generation. In addition, both migrations may have been associated with relatively warm periods.

However, the two instances also offer significant contrasts. The early Paleoeskimo migration occurred across a landscape completely devoid of other people. It is most simply explained as a range expansion of a "pre-adapted" Arctic hunting people entering an environment which rewarded long-distance movement and exploration. The Thule Inuit migration, on the other hand, was made more complex by the fact that the original Thule societies in the west were relatively sedentary and densely populated, with a social organization emphasizing status differences, trade, and warfare, leading to the likelihood that social factors provided an initial "push" to migrating groups. In addition, Thule were entering a region already inhabited by Dorset peoples (the descendants of the early Paleoeskimos who had arrived as part of the first migration). In fact, the nature of interaction between Thule and Dorset peoples remains among the most poorly understood phenomena in eastern Arctic archaeology (Park 1993; Friesen 2004).

SEE ALSO: 44 North America: Eskimo-Aleut linguistic history

References

Burch, E. S. (2006) *Social Life in Northwest Alaska*. Fairbanks: University of Alaska Press.

Cox, S. L. (2003) Paleoeskimo structures in the Okak region of Labrador. *Etudes/Inuit/Studies* 27, 417–434.

Dyke, A. S., Savelle, J. M., & Johnson, D. S. (2011) Paleoeskimo demography and Holocene sea-level history, Gulf of Boothia, Arctic Canada. *Arctic* 64(2), 151–168.

Friesen, T. M. (2004) Contemporaneity of Dorset and Thule cultures in the North American Arctic: new radiocarbon dates from Victoria Island, Nunavut. *Current Anthropology* 45(5), 685–691.

Friesen, T. M. & Arnold, C. D. (2008) The timing of the Thule migration: new dates from the western Canadian Arctic. *American Antiquity* 73(3), 527–538.

Grønnow, B. & Jensen, J. F. (2003) *The Northernmost Ruins of the Globe*. Meddelelser om Grøn-land, Man and Society No. 29. Copenhagen: Danish Polar Center.

Gulløv, H.-C. & McGhee, R. (2006) Did Bering Strait people initiate the Thule migration? *Alaska Journal of Anthropology* 4, 54–63.

Krupnik, I. & Chlenov, M. A.(2009) Distant lands and brave pioneers: original Thule migration revisited. In B. Grønnow (ed.), *On the Track of the Thule Culture from Bering Strait to East Greenland*. Copenhagen: Danish National Museum, pp. 11–24.

Mason, O. K. (2009a) "The multiplication of forms": Bering Strait harpoon heads as a demic and macroevolutionary proxy. In A. Prentiss, I. Kuijt, & J. C. Chatters (eds.), *Macroevolution in Human Prehistory*. Heidelberg: Springer, pp. 73–110.

Mason, O. K. (2009b) Flight from Bering Strait: did Siberian Punuk/Thule military cadres conquer northwest Alaska? In H. Maschner, O. Mason, & R. McGhee (eds.), *The Northern World AD 900–1400*. Salt Lake City: University of Utah Press, pp. 76–128.

Maxwell, M. S. (1985) *Prehistory of the Eastern Arctic*. Orlando, FL: Academic Press.

McCullough, K. M. (1989) *The Ruin Islanders*. Mercury Series No. 141. Ottawa: National Museums of Canada.

McGhee, R. (1969/70) Speculations on climatic change and Thule Culture development. *Folk* 11–12, 173–184.

McGhee, R. (2000) Radiocarbon dating and the timing of the Thule migration. In M. Appelt, J. Berglund, & H.-C. Gulløv (eds.), *Identities and Cultural Contacts in the Arctic*. Copenha-gen: Danish Polar Center, pp. 181–191.

Meldgaard, M. (2004) *Ancient Harp Seal Hunter of Disko Bay*. Meddelelser om Grønland, Man and Society No. 30. Copenhagen: Danish Polar Center.

Morrison, D. (1999) The earliest Thule migration. *Canadian Journal of Archaeology* 22(2), 139–156.

Odess, D. (2005) The Arctic Small Tool tradition fifty years on. *Alaska Journal of Anthropology* 3(2), 5–16.

Park, R. W. (1993) The Dorset–Thule succession in Arctic North America: assessing claims for culture contact. *American Antiquity* 58, 203–234.

Powers, W. R. & Jordan, R. H. (1990) Human biogeography and climate change in Siberia and Arctic North America. *Philosophical Transactions of the Royal Society of London*, A330, 665–670.

Savelle, J. M. & Dyke, A. S. (2009) Paleoeskimo demography on Western Boothia Peninsula, Arctic Canada. *Journal of Field Archaeology* 34, 267–283.

Slaughter, D. C. (2005) Radiocarbon dating the Arctic Small Tool tradition in Alaska. *Alaska Journal of Anthropology* 3(2), 117–134.

46

Eastern North America: archaeology and linguistics

Dean R. Snow

The Eastern Woodlands and Great Plains of North America witnessed the migrations of both agriculturalist and hunter-gatherer populations during the past three thousand years, although correlations with the histories of language families such as Iroquoian and Siouan only came into focus during the past millennium.

The Eastern Woodlands of North America cover the United States from just west of the Mississippi River to the Atlantic, and from the southern portions of the Canadian provinces of Ontario and Quebec to the Gulf of Mexico (Figure 46.1). It is a region of about 7,800,000 sq km. A prairie peninsula covering southern Minnesota, northern Missouri, and most of Iowa and Illinois at the time of European contact indented the eastern forests on the west. Eastern broadleaf woodlands blanketed most of the upland interior. This graded into Atlantic coniferous forests along the southern Atlantic and Gulf coasts. Southern Florida was primarily flooded grasslands. But because the transitions were gradual it is proper to treat this large region as a single entity. The Eastern Woodlands generally lacked natural interior boundaries to foster the evolution of separate cultural adaptations over time.

For now, the first peopling of the Eastern Woodlands appears to have involved the rapid propagation of Paleoindian bands that spread nearly everywhere up to the northern limits imposed by the Pleistocene ice sheet, that persisted in Eastern Canada just north of the Great Lakes. At that time, sea levels were lower along the Atlantic and Gulf coasts of the Eastern Woodlands, but the distribution of Paleoindians along the continental shelf that is now submerged is uncertain (Anderson et al. 2005).

The latter part of the Paleoindian period coincided with the Younger Dryas cold spell, which ended around 9550 BCE. After that date the northern hemisphere moved into the Holocene period and the environment of the Eastern Woodlands began shifting to conditions like those of recent history. Climatic conditions were generally warmer and drier during the Holocene than they had been previously. There were

The Global Prehistory of Human Migration: The Encyclopedia of Global Human Migration Volume 1, First Edition. Edited by Peter Bellwood.
© 2013 John Wiley & Sons, Ltd. Published 2015 by John Wiley & Sons, Ltd.

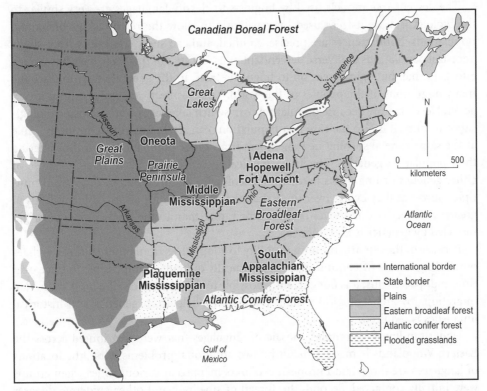

Figure 46.1 Map of the Eastern Woodlands of North America, showing the main ecozones (in italics) and archaeological cultures (in roman). Map production by Education and Multimedia Services, College of Asia and the Pacific, The Australian National University.

several warm peaks, including three very high ones, during the 3,500-year-long period from 7000 to 3500 BCE. Archaeologists have given the general name "Archaic" to the cultures of that long period. Human migration appears to have been largely local in the Eastern Woodlands during those millennia. The archaeological evidence indicates that populations settled into subregional adaptations as environments stabilized. A proliferation of projectile point styles and an absence of long-distance trading indicate that Archaic American Indians were living in bounded if still not yet sedentary communities. These did not interact with others to the degree that had been the case during the Paleoindian period. Local populations were by this time large enough to allow endogamous marriages, and the beginnings of food production based on plants native to the Eastern Woodlands reduced the inclination to follow the sharing strategies that had characterized earlier Paleoindian networks.

   It is likely that the Paleoindians who peopled most of the continent by 9900 BCE derived from a population that spoke dialects of one or at most just a few languages. Once they diversified and made the transition to regional Archaic cultures these cultures evolved on their own, developing varied cultural adaptations and speaking languages that also evolved separately from previously related ones.

The descent-tree models used by linguists to classify languages are very similar to the biological descent-trees used by geneticists to show the relationships of human populations. Both sciences are precise, codified, and can show continuity from single ancestral populations to diverse descendant ones. Because of this there have been many efforts to map biological trees on to linguistic trees, in the general effort to trace the many migrations of the peoples of the world. This has been successful only at a very general level, mainly because populations can switch languages without losing biological continuity. It is also the case that populations can retain linguistic continuity while at the same time absorbing new members from other populations and thus altering their population genetics. The archaeological record is difficult to relate to those of either genetics or linguistics because archaeological cultures tend to draw from multiple sources as they evolve over time, such that the search for ancestral forms leads to greater diversity as one moves back in time rather than to the single points of origin modeled by geneticists and linguists.

Because of the remarkable human ability to adopt ideas from other cultures, archaeological signatures of continuity are also typically difficult or impossible to trace over time and space. Thus, it is not currently possible to detect and describe pre-Columbian migrations by archaeological means alone. Some help from genetics and historical linguistics is required.

Understanding the complex mosaic of languages that were distributed across the Eastern Woodlands is made difficult by two additional problems. First, the locations of languages are those that European explorers mapped at various times when groups were initially contacted. Second, the spread of smallpox and other epidemic diseases ahead of European exploration caused population collapse in some areas and radical relocations before any documentation was possible. Thus, the core of the Eastern Woodlands, an area of about 866,000 sq km or 11 percent of the whole, which contains some of North America's richest archaeological remains, is typically shown as blank *terra incognita* on language and culture maps (Figure 46.2). It covers areas where the largest Eastern Woodlands population densities existed in the early 15th century CE.

By 1492, there were at least 62 language families or single language isolates (families having only single members) in North America. These included perhaps 400 separate languages, of which at least 78 were spoken in the Eastern Woodlands. Linguists have classified 65 of the Eastern Woodlands languages into families of two or more members. There were five language isolates. There were also about eight named but undocumented languages, at least some of which might have belonged to one or another of the documented families (Campbell & Mithun 1979; Goddard 1996).

Linguists have reconstructed varying numbers of lexical terms for proto-languages of the Algic, Iroquoian, Siouan, Muskogean, and Caddoan language families. Smaller families and isolates do not provide the same research opportunities. Archaeologists are sometimes able to work backwards from this fragmentary known mosaic of Eastern Woodland languages, linking historic tribes and chiefdoms that have documented languages to archaeological complexes and their immediate predecessors. However, this technique is convincing for only the last one or two thousand years at the most. Archaeological continuity over time cannot usually be argued with much certainty for greater time depth than that.

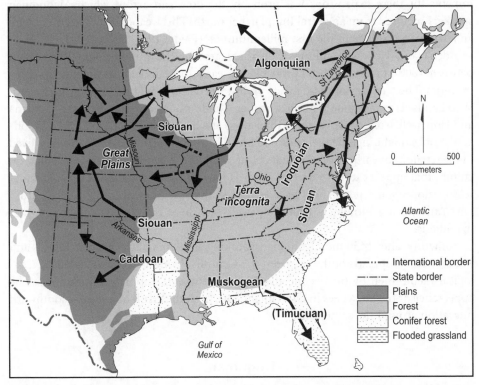

Figure 46.2 Language movements in the Eastern Woodlands, showing language locations in the 16th and 17th centuries and inferred population movements as described in the text (the Timucuan language no longer survives). Algonquian, Siouan, and Caddoan groups all moved on to the Great Plains after the introduction of horses to the Americas during the 16th century. Map production by Education and Multimedia Services, College of Asia and the Pacific, The Australian National University.

Algonquian

Algonquian languages make up the bulk of the languages assigned to the Algic language family. A total of 29 Algonquian languages were spoken historically in the Eastern Woodlands. Cree, Montagnais, and Naskapi speakers were scattered thinly across the eastern Canadian boreal forest north of the Maritime Provinces, New England, and the Great Lakes basin. Based on internal lexical evidence, the homeland of these and other Algonquian languages appears to have been somewhere in the lower Great Lakes region. It is important to note that this was a large region and that Proto-Algonquian was probably spoken in only a small part of it. There may have been other related languages in the same region that have not left any known descendants.

The northern hunters spread into the boreal forest from there. Others spread largely westward south of the upper Great Lakes, where they are known historically as Central Algonquians. Meanwhile Eastern Algonquians spread southward along the Atlantic Coast, through what are now the Middle Atlantic states as far as North Carolina. The impetus for these expansions was probably the bow and arrow, which Algonquian speakers acquired from ancestral Inuit farther north. This weapon provided them with an adaptive advantage in the first millennium CE (Fiedel 1987, 1990, 1994).

Adena and Hopewell cultures flourished around the middle Ohio River basin between 1000 BCE and 400 CE, probably too early to be linked to Algonquian communities. The territory of these major prehistoric cultures is at the core of the Eastern Woodlands *terra incognita* described earlier. We do not know what became of Adena and Hopewell. Nor can we do more than guess at which, if any, modern Eastern Woodlands tribes might include their descendants. The Algonquian-speaking Shawnee lived in the territory of earlier Fort Ancient culture in the 16th century CE, an archaeological culture that appears to have derived from Hopewell roots in the same area. For that reason alone, some researchers have suggested that the Shawnee might derive from Fort Ancient and ultimately from Hopewell, but there is little else to support that hypothesis.

Sometime after 1450 the Algonquian-speaking ancestors of the historic Illinois and Miami nations spread southward from the Central Algonquian region to fill the ecological vacuum left by the decline and departure of Mississippian communities. The appearance of the Shawnees in Ohio might have been the result of a similar southward migration around the same time.

Iroquoian

Based on internal lexical evidence, the homeland of the Iroquoian languages was probably somewhere in the Appalachian uplands that stretch from Pennsylvania to Georgia. Once again, the specific homeland of Proto-Iroquoian was probably in just a small portion of this large mountainous region, and there might have been many related languages at the same time that did not give rise to any known later languages. By 700 CE the ancestors of the Northern Iroquoians were living in what is now central Pennsylvania. One branch of Northern Iroquoians migrated to the piedmont of Virginia and North Carolina around 800 where they can be linked to the archaeological Cashie culture. Ancestral Cherokees remained in the Smokey Mountains to the southwest as the only representatives of Southern Iroquoian. The common ancestor of Southern and Northern Iroquoians has been estimated by some linguists to have been spoken around three thousand years ago (Snow 1994).

The warmer conditions of the Medieval Warm Period made the glaciated soils of New York and southern Ontario attractive to Northern Iroquoian farmers. Clemson's Island culture in Pennsylvania probably identifies them archaeologically. These communities subsequently expanded northward into the lower Great Lakes basin as the climate grew more favorable for upland swidden horticulture based on maize and squash cultivation. Swidden farming required the constant clearing of new farming plots in the upland forest as older fields declined in productivity. This in turn led to the periodic relocations of whole villages so that the women who did the farming could manage the necessary travel to their active fields. Occasionally villages elected (or were forced by warfare) to move much greater distances. The results were clusters of archaeological village sites across the landscape. Such clusters even appeared in the Mohawk and St. Lawrence River basins after 1000 CE. Meanwhile, the older village clusters in Pennsylvania were gradually abandoned (Snow 1995).

Iroquoian villages were comprised of multi-family longhouses that were divided into compartments designed to contain the nuclear families of related females. All of the historic Northern Iroquoian nations were strongly matrilineal. Beans were added to the list of staple crops sometime after the initial expansion northward.

The five nations of the League of the Iroquois became major players in the events of the colonial era. Their confederacy, which probably formed in the 16th century, benefited from Dutch (later English) and French firearms and other trade goods, which enabled them to expel other Northern Iroquoians westward out of the region in the 17th century. Later, in the 18th century, some Iroquois moved southwestward into Ohio and other parts of the vacated core of the Eastern Woodlands. Meanwhile the branch of the Northern Iroquoians that had migrated to North Carolina moved north to rejoin the Iroquois as a sixth nation of the League of the Iroquois.

Mississippian culture and the Siouan languages

Large towns having platform mounds for temples and chiefly residences began to appear along the middle reaches of the Mississippi River valley and the lower Ohio River valley around 800 CE. There were probably speakers in that region of one or more early Siouan languages, and the area was probably at the core of the region in which that language family first evolved from linguistically unknown ancestors. The major site of Cahokia in East St. Louis, Illinois, emerged as the centerpiece of Middle Mississippian culture. Numerous and sometimes very large earthen temple mounds were erected around plazas in Mississippian towns between 1000 and 1450. The culture spread to other parts of the core of the Eastern Woodlands, typically along the rich alluvial soils of major tributaries of the Mississippi where farmers could cultivate permanent fields of maize, beans, squash, and other cultigens (Milner 1998; Neitzel 1999). Thus agriculture and the search for appropriate soils was a major driver of these migratory episodes.

Colonies from the Mississippian heartland moved northward into Wisconsin where descendant Winnebago people still live. Oneota tribal cultures with strong Mississippian ties and Siouan roots emerged in Iowa and portions of six adjoining states. Some Middle Mississippians moved eastward. The latter might account for the presence of Siouan-speaking communities east of the Appalachians, such as the Catawba and Tutelo.

Mississippian culture also spread to the Caddoan, Tunica, Natchez, and other non-Siouan peoples of Louisiana, Mississippi, and southern Arkansas, where it is known as Plaquemine Mississippian culture. Migration occurred within this region when conditions for elaborate chiefdoms deteriorated after 1300 CE.

The seven languages of the Muskogean family probably developed somewhere in the region where they were found historically: Alabama and parts of four surrounded states. The nations of this region adopted Mississippian political and architectural forms, producing a culture known as South Appalachian Mississippian. Along with the Middle and Plaquemine Mississippians they took up the paraphernalia and presumably the practices of what archaeologists refer to as the Southeastern Ceremonial Complex.

Mississippian contraction and dispersal

A series of severe droughts and resulting conflict pushed Mississippian communities into decline after 1350 CE. By 1450, even the largest of them had severely reduced populations and were abandoned. Many remnant communities moved westward to take advantage of bison-hunting opportunities on the prairies and other hedges against crop failures. When horses appeared on the Great Plains in the 17th century the region became even more attractive. The tribes of the Chiwere branch of Siouan, which probably had its origins in Oneota culture, were by then prairie dwellers. Refugees from Cahokia and other Middle Mississippian towns also shifted westward, evolving into the Dhegiha branch of Siouan on the eastern Prairies. The abandonment of Middle Mississippian towns created a vast vacant quarter in this part of the Eastern Woodlands during the years following 1450. The Algonquian-speaking Illinois and Miami nations migrated southward to partially fill it, but the population density of the region did not come back to early 15th-century levels until the arrival of Euro-American settlers (Smith 1992; Milner & Chaplin 2010).

Fifteenth-century decline and dislocation was made worse in the southern part of the Eastern Woodlands after the de Soto *entrada* in the mid-16th century. European diseases led to the earliest severe epidemics in that region, where Muskogean speakers were the best-known bearers of the South Appalachian variant of Mississippian culture. The unrelated Timucua and Calusa cultures of Florida withered quickly in the face of Spanish colonization and missionary efforts. Devastated Muskogean communities came together and reformed in coalescent communities as the new Creek nation. Some Creeks still later took in escaped African slaves and migrated to the vacated drowned grasslands of interior southern Florida, where they came to be known as the Seminoles.

Late movement on to the Great Plains

The introduction of the horse in the Spanish Southwest led to the rapid adoption of mounted nomadism on the Great Plains and elsewhere in the North American West. Some Caddoan and Siouan farming communities, offshoots from the Eastern Woodlands, were already resident in a few river valleys on the Plains, as were a few groups of hunter-gatherers. Shoshonean (Uto-Aztecan) and Athapaskan tribes acquired horses directly from the Spanish in the West. Algonquian, Siouan, and Caddoan groups on the eastern margin of the Plains acquired horses from the western tribes, took up bison hunting, and spread westward across the Plains during the 17th century. Mounted nomadic tribes living in *tepee* villages are a common modern image of American

Indians, but it was a relatively short-lived phenomenon. The nomadic lifeways ended by the late 19th century.

SEE ALSO: 48 Mesoamerica and the southwestern United States: archaeology

References

Anderson, D., Miller, D., Yerka, S. J., et al. (2005) Paleoindian artifact distributions in the Southeast and beyond. At http://pidbac.org/content/fluted.jpg, accessed April 31, 2009. See also http://pidba.utk.edu/maps.htm.

Campbell, L. & Mithun, M. (eds.) (1979) *The Languages of Native America: Historical and Comparative Assessment*. Austin: University of Texas Press.

Fiedel, S. (1987) Algonquian origins: a problem in archaeological linguistic correlation. *Archaeology of Eastern North America* 15, 1–11.

Fiedel, S. (1990) Middle Woodland Algonquian expansion: a refined model. *North American Archaeologist* 11(3), 209–230.

Fiedel, S. (1994) Some inferences concerning Proto-Algonquian economy and society. *Northeast Anthropology* 48, 1–11.

Goddard, I. (1996) Introduction. In I. Goddard (ed.), *Handbook of North American Indians*, vol. 17, *Languages*. Washington: Smithsonian Institution Press, pp. 1–16.

Milner, G. (1998) *The Cahokia Chiefdom: The Archaeology of a Mississippian Society*. Washington: Smithsonian Institution Press.

Milner, G. & Chaplin, G. (2010) Eastern North American population at ca. AD 1500. *American Antiquity* 75(4), 707–726.

Neitzel, J. (ed.) (1999) *Great Towns and Regional Polities in the Prehistoric American Southwest and Southeast*. Albuquerque: University of New Mexico Press.

Smith, K. (1992) *The Middle Cumberland Region: Mississippian Archaeology in North Central Tennessee*. Nashville: Department of Anthropology, Vanderbilt University.

Snow, D. (1994) *The Iroquois*. Cambridge, MA: Blackwell.

Snow, D. (1995) Migration in prehistory: the Northern Iroquoian case. *American Antiquity* 60(1), 59–79.

Snow, D. (2009) The multidisciplinary study of human migration: problems and principles. In P. N. Peregrine, I. Peiros, & M. Feldman (eds.), *Ancient Human Migrations: A Multidisciplinary Approach*. Salt Lake City: University of Utah Press, pp. 6–20.

47

Mesoamerica and the southwestern United States: linguistic history

Jane H. Hill

Mesoamerica witnessed one major linguistic dispersal in the late Holocene, that of the Uto-Aztecans over large areas of Mexico and the western USA. Most other language families associated with maize cultivating farmers were constrained by each other in the narrow isthmian region of Mesoamerica, but the Otomanguean and Mayan populations clearly underwent considerable demographic growth.

Migration is defined here minimally as a one-way relocation of residence into a new region (Cabana & Clark 2011). While the migration accounts of such late prehistoric groups as the Nahua (Uto-Aztec speakers) and K'iche' (Mayan speakers) are now understood as political and symbolic gestures that may not reflect literal history (Fox 1980; Boone 1991), the geographical distribution of Mesoamerican linguistic diversity (Figure 47.1) suggests that migration, both short- and long-range, was an important social process in all periods of Mesoamerican prehistory. Mesoamerican languages include members of the Mayan, Mixe-Zoquean, Otomanguean, Totonacan, Uto-Aztecan, and Xincan families, along with the language isolates Cuitlatec, Huave, Oaxaca Chontal, and Tarascan. Exemplary cases of long-range moves are Huastec, located in northern Veracruz and San Luis Potosí, far from its Mayan relatives in Yucatan and Guatemala, and varieties of Nahua, a Uto-Aztecan language group of central Mexico, spoken in El Salvador and Nicaragua. Proliferation of daughter languages, as in Otomanguean, invites attention to migration, since geographical isolation following upon a split of a speech community is usually involved in such diversification.

Historical linguistic methods have not been shown to be useful in understanding the PaleoIndian Period in the Americas, but for the Archaic Period (8000–2000 BCE), when cultivation first appeared in Mesoamerica, historical linguistic techniques have been applied. Hopkins (1984) and Kaufman (1990) argued on the basis of reconstructed cultivation vocabulary that the language of the "Tehuacan Horizon," mid-Holocene preceramic cultivators of the central Mexican highlands, was probably

The Global Prehistory of Human Migration: The Encyclopedia of Global Human Migration Volume 1,
First Edition. Edited by Peter Bellwood.
© 2013 John Wiley & Sons, Ltd. Published 2015 by John Wiley & Sons, Ltd.

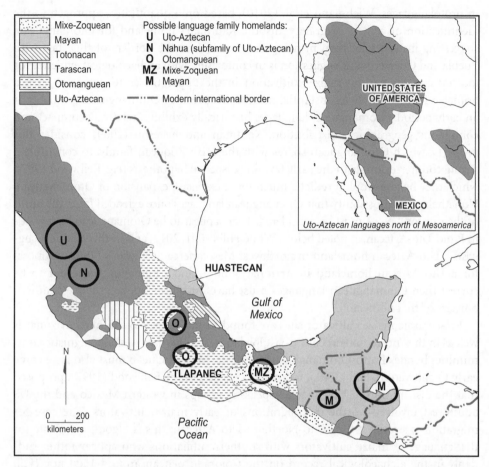

Figure 47.1 The major language families of Mesoamerica and the US Southwest and their likely homelands. Map based on a map by J. Kathryn Josserand and Nicholas A. Hopkins on the website of the Foundation for the Advancement of Mesoamerican Studies, Inc., at www.famsi.org/maps/linguistic.htm. Map production by Education and Multimedia Services, College of Asia and the Pacific, The Australian National University.

Proto-Otomanguean. Kaufman (1990) proposed a split into Eastern and Western Otomanguean by 2500 BCE (dates are glottochronological), and subsequently of each of these into two more subgroups by 2000 to 1500 BCE. This was a period of increasing commitment to cultivation, increasing sedentism, and the earliest appearance of hierarchical societies. Kaufman (1990) also proposed a Proto-Otomanguean homeland in the Basin of Mexico, with moves into surrounding regions leading to the family's diversification.

Locating probable homelands for language families is a crucial first step in work on migration. Methods include the identification of "centers of gravity" (geographic areas encompassing maximal diversity among the languages of a family, that are probable zones of initial radiation), the correlation of reconstructed vocabulary with biogeographical and archaeological data, and the identification of the sources of loanwords in protolanguages. Wichmann et al. (2010), based on a quantitative approach to the identification of centers of gravity, dispute Kaufman's homeland for Otomanguean, suggesting instead a location in northern Oaxaca near the borders of this state with Puebla and Guerrero; this suggestion is in conformity with archaeological evidence for locations of the earliest maize cultivation in the upper Balsas River basin. Such a homeland would imply a substantial northward spread of Otomanguean, probably at an early period. Otomanguean languages historically exhibit a relatively compact and contiguous geographical distribution. Kaufman and Justeson (2009) consider this property, which Otomanguean shares with the Mixe-Zoquean family, to constitute a strong counter-example to the early farming dispersal hypothesis (e.g. Bellwood 1997), which they believe would predict a much more extensive expansion of Otomanguean. Nonetheless, the possibility that Otomanguean languages once extended far to the north of their historic range must be considered. There appear to be Otomanguean loan words in Proto-Uto-Aztecan, as noted below. While Hill (2001, 2012, and in this chapter) suggests a Uto-Aztecan homeland in northwest Mesoamerca, if Fowler's (1983) proposal for a Uto-Aztecan homeland in Arizona, Sonora, and Chihuahua turns out to be correct then Otomanguean languages must have once been spoken on the southern borders of that homeland.

Pre-ceramic maize cultivator sites are found from Chiapas to southern Arizona, as well as in the Yucatecan and Gulf Coast lowlands, so other late Archaic linguistic communities besides Proto-Otomanguean and Proto-Mixe-Zoquean must also have come early to cultivation. Hill (2001), following a suggestion by Bellwood (1997), proposed that the distribution of Uto-Aztecan speaking groups in western Mexico and the US Southwest involved northward migrations of early maize cultivators. The case for migration is strongest for Proto-Northern Uto-Aztecan; this is a good candidate for the language of maize cultivators with southern affiliations who appear rather suddenly in the archaeological record on the Colorado plateau around 1500 BCE (Hill 2002, 2008). Proto-Kiowa-Tanoan, with a probable homeland in this region, may have borrowed some of its maize vocabulary from Proto-Northern Uto-Aztecan (Hill 2008). Hill (forthcoming) argues that Proto-Uto-Aztecan dates to no earlier than 2200 BCE, since reconstructed vocabulary suggests that its cultural repertoire included not only maize cultivation but also acquaintance with pottery. Hints that some vocabulary in those domains was borrowed from Otomanguean languages support the case for an Uto-Aztecan homeland on the northwestern margins of Mesoamerica in Mexico, given the historic location of the northernmost Otomanguean groups. Hill (2009) also argues that Uto-Aztecan speakers were donors into the Mesoamerican linguistic exchange system from a very early date. The ethnographic distribution of the Uto-Aztecan languages to as far north as Idaho can be seen in Figure 47.2.

However, the Mesoamerican-origin hypothesis for Uto-Aztecan remains controversial. Campbell (2002) and Kaufman and Justeson (2009) challenge many of Hill's reconstructions, and reject a Mesoamerican homeland for the group. Merrill and colleagues (2009) reject migration as the process through which maize cultivation spread into the US Southwest, and prefer to see the Uto-Aztecan corridor in western Mexico as the result of a late spread of languages from the north.

The prehistory of Mayan and Mixe-Zoquean peoples remains in dispute. Early movements of Mayan-speaking peoples have been suggested by Kaufman (1976) and

Campbell and Kaufman (1985). They date Proto-Mayan to about 2200 BCE, proposing a homeland in the northwestern Guatemalan highlands, with ancestors of Huastec moving north on the Gulf Coast of Mexico by about 1500 BCE. Kaufman (1976) suggests a probable interaction between Huastecan migrants and Formative Period (2000 BCE–300 CE) expansion of Mixe-Zoquean speakers out of the isthmus of Tehuantepec. Kaufman (1976) dates later major radiations of Mayan languages to between about 1600 and 1000 BCE. Kaufman's dating of the move of Huastecan is disputed by Robertson and Houston (2002), who argue for a Huastecan migration as late as the Post-Classic. Brown (2010) also disputes Kaufman's model, preferring a probable breakup date of Proto-Mayan as late as 400 BCE, and – based on biogeographic data on cultivated plants for which Proto-Mayan terms can be reconstructed – for a lowland homeland for the family. Wichmann et al. (2008) argue that Proto-Mixe-Zoque speakers were already on the Gulf Coast and had begun to split into Mixean and Zoquean, major languages of the Olmec Horizon, by 1800 BCE.

In the Classic period (300–900 CE), the rise of state-level polities and their urban centers, such as Teotihuacan, Monte Alban, and Tikal, attracted groups of diverse origins away from their original homelands, at the same time that these centers maintained complex ties, probably including at least trade and military alliance, with distant regions. The controversy over the role of peoples speaking Nahua languages, a subgroup of Uto-Aztecan, can illustrate here the challenges posed by the intricacies of Classic-Period population movements.

The homeland of the Nahua probably lies no further northwest than the southeastern boundary of their closest linguistic relatives, Huichol and Cora, spoken in Jalisco and Nayarit; Beekman and Christensen (2011) suggest a homeland in western Guanajuato. Kaufman (2001) divides Pochutec from "General Nahua" (all other languages in Nahua besides Pochutec). An episode that Kaufman dates to about 500 CE established an Eastern Nahua dialect chain that eventually extended from Hidalgo to Guerrero, reaching south to the isthmus of Tehuantepec. This group, according to Canger (1988), must have included the so-called "Toltecs" who are credited with influence as far south as Yucatan. In a final episode, this dialect group was replaced in Tlaxcala, Puebla, and the Basin of Mexico, breaking the old Eastern dialect chain, by the "Aztlan migrants" (Canger 1988: 65), who spoke varieties of Western Nahua. The historical Aztecs spoke varieties belonging to this group of dialects.

These episodes probably involved some language shift of local populations to Nahua varieties. Canger and Dakin (1985) note limited evidence that might associate Pochutec with this Western Nahua group. Regardless of its affiliation, Pochutec, a very distinctive variety spoken in Oaxaca, far from the probable Nahua homeland in northwestern central Mexico, must represent the trace of a migration event. But the dating of the various episodes of the Nahua radiation is in dispute. Kaufman (2001) argues that while speakers of Proto-Nahua were in central Mexico, picking up loanwords from Huastecan (Mayan), Mixe-Zoquean and Totonacan, their spread out of central Mexico and subsequent diversification began no earlier than 900 CE. However, Dakin (2004) and Dakin and Wichmann (2000) have suggested that some important Mesoamerican loanwords may have originated in a very early stage of Nahua and date even to the late Formative. While this proposal is challenged by Kaufman and Justeson (2007), recently identified epigraphic evidence supports early dates. Taube (2000) argues that some glyphs at Teotihuacan can be read as Nahua. Macri and Looper (2003) and Macri (2005) suggest Nahua readings for Mayan inscriptions dating as far back as 480 CE at Río Azul in Guatemala. This implies that a southward expansion of Eastern Nahua speakers may have taken place quite early in the Classic period, well before the dates usually assigned to "Toltec" influence on the Maya.

The Post-Classic (900–1521 CE) is understood by most scholars as a period of areal reorganization dominated by militarism. Several long-distance moves dated to the late Classic and to the Post-Classic may represent episodes of expansion that included a military dimension. Speakers of Pipil, a variety of Eastern Nahua (Canger 1988), established colonies in Chiapas, Guatemala, and El Salvador, perhaps in a series of moves continuing between about 800 and 1200 (W. Fowler 1989), although Campbell (1985) rejects the proposal of multiple migrations. Also dating to the Post-Classic is a long-distance move by Subtiaba, an Otomanguean language most closely related to Tlapanec, spoken in Guerrero (Mexico) to Nicaragua, probably around 1200 (Campbell 1997). Finally, an important late move across the Guatemalan highlands by speakers of K'iche', a Mayan language, took place around 1200. Fox (1980) points out that the K'iche' migration accounts include thematic elements that can be traced back to Yucatan and ultimately to central Mexico.

In summary, linguistic evidence, especially multiple examples of languages located at great distance from their closest relatives, make clear that migration was an important process in Mesoamerican prehistory. The intepretation of the linguistic data remains in dispute, and does not permit the isolation of causes. However, since these data suggest migration at so many different periods of history, these causes must have been diverse.

SEE ALSO: 48 Mesoamerica and the southwestern United States: archaeology

References

Beekman, C. & Christensen, A. (2011) Power, agency and identity: migration and aftermath in the Mezquital area of north-central Mexico. In Cabana & Clark (eds.), pp. 147–171.

Bellwood, P. (1997) Prehistoric cultural explanations for widespread linguistic families. In P. McConvell & N. Evans (eds.), *Archaeology and Linguistics: Aboriginal Australia in Global Perspective*. Melbourne: Oxford University Press, pp. 123–134.

Bellwood, P. & Renfrew, C. (eds.) (2002) *Examining the Farming/Language Dispersal Hypothesis*. Cambridge: McDonald Institute for Archaeological Research.

Boone, E. (1991) Migration histories as ritual performance. In D. Carrasco (ed.), *To Change Place: Aztec Ceremonial Landscapes*. Niwot: University Press of Colorado, pp. 121–151.

Brown, C. (2010) Development of agriculture in prehistoric Mesoamerica: the linguistic evidence. In J. E. Staller & M. D. Carrasco (eds.), *Pre-Columbian Foodways: Interdisciplinary Approaches to Food, Culture and Markets in Ancient Mesoamerica*. New York: Springer Science + Business Media, LLC, pp. 71–107.

Cabana, G. & Clark, J. (eds.) (2011) *Rethinking Anthropological Perspectives on Migration*. Gainesville: University Press of Florida.

Campbell, L. (1985) *The Pipil language of El Salvador*. Berlin: Mouton.

Campbell, L. (1997) *American Indian Languages: The Historical Linguistics of Native America.* New York: Oxford University Press.

Campbell, L. (2002) What drives linguistic diversification and language spread? In Bellwood & Renfrew (2002), pp. 49–64.

Campbell, L. & Kaufman, T. (1985) Mayan linguistics: where are we now? *Annual Review of Anthropology* 14, 187–198.

Canger, U. (1988) Nahuatl dialectology: a survey and some suggestions. *International Journal of American Linguistics* 54, 28–72.

Canger, U. & Dakin, K. (1985) An inconspicuous basic split in Nahuatl. *International Journal of American Linguistics* 51, 358–361.

Dakin, K. (2004) Nahuatl -ka words: evidence for a proto-Uto-Aztecan derivational pattern. *STUF-Sprachtypologie und Universalienforschung* 57, 6–22.

Dakin, K. & Wichmann, S. (2000) Cacao and chocolate: a Uto-Aztecan perspective. *Ancient Mesoamerica* 11, 55–75.

Fowler, C. (1983) Lexical clues to Uto-Aztecan prehistory. *International Journal of American Linguistics* 49, 224–257.

Fowler, W. (1989) *The Cultural Evolution of Ancient Nahua Civilizations: The Pipil-Nicarao.* Norman: University of Oklahoma Press.

Fox, J. (1980) Lowland to highland mexicanization processes in southern Mesoamerica. *American Antiquity* 45, 43–54.

Hill, J. (2001) Proto-Uto-Aztecan: A community of cultivators in central Mexico? *American Anthropologist* 103, 913–934.

Hill, J. (2002) Proto-Uto-Aztecan and the northern devolution. In Bellwood & Renfrew (2002), pp. 331–340.

Hill, J. (2008) Northern Uto-Aztecan and Kiowa-Tanoan: evidence for contact between the proto-languages? *International Journal of American Linguistics* 74, 155–188.

Hill, J. (2009) Ancient loan words in the Mesoamerican maize complex. In M. Islas (ed.), *Entre las Lenguas Indígenas, la Sociolingüística y el Español, Estudios en Homenaje a Yolanda Lastra* [Among indigenous languages, sociolinguistics, and Spanish, studies in honor of Yolanda Lastra]. Munich: Lincom Europa, pp. 80–109.

Hill, J. (2012) Proto-Uto-Aztecan as a Mesoamerican language. *Ancient Mesoamerica* 23(2), 57–68.

Hopkins, N. (1984) Linguistic prehistory. In J. K. Josserand, M. Winter, & N. A. Hopkins (eds.), *Essays in Otomanguean Cultural History.* Vanderbilt University Publications in Anthropology, No. 31. Nashville, TN: Vanderbilt University Department of Anthropology, pp. 25–64.

Kaufman, T. (1976) Archaeological and linguistic correlations in Mayaland and associated areas of Meso-America. *World Archaeology* 8, 101–118.

Kaufman, T. (1990) Early Otomanguean homelands and cultures: some premature hypotheses. *University of Pittsburgh Working Papers in Linguistics* 1, 91–136.

Kaufman, T. (2001) The history of the Nawa language group from the earliest times to the sixteenth century: some initial results. At www.albany.edu/pdlma/papers.htm, accessed Nov. 17, 2010.

Kaufman, T. & Justeson, J. (2007) The history of the word for cacao in ancient Mesoamerica. *Ancient Mesoamerica* 18, 193–237.

Kaufman, T. & Justeson, J. (2009) Historical linguistics and pre-Columbian Mesoamerica. *Ancient Mesoamerica* 20, 221–231.

Macri, M. (2005) Nahua loan words from the early Classic Period: words for cacao preparation on a Río Azul ceramic vessel. *Ancient Mesoamerica* 16, 321–326.

Macri, M. & Looper, M. (2003) Nahua in ancient Mesoamerica: evidence from Maya inscriptions. *Ancient Mesoamerica* 14, 285–297.

Merrill, W., Hard, R., Mabry, J., et al. (2009) The diffusion of maize to the southwestern United States. *Proceedings of the National Academy of Sciences* 106, 21019–21026.

Robertson, J. & Houston, S. (2003) El problema del wasteko: una perspectiva lingüística y arqueológica [The problem with Wasteko: a linguistic and archaeological perspective]. In J. P. LaPorte, B. Arroyo, H. Escobedo, & H. Mejía (eds.), *XVI Simposio de Investigaciones Arqueológicas en Guatemala, 2002* [Sixteenth symposium of archaeological investigations in Guatemala]. Guatemala: Museo Nacional de Arqueología y Etnología, pp. 714–724.

Taube, K. (2000) *The Writing System of Ancient Teotihuacan*. Ancient America No. 1. Washington, DC: Center for Ancient American Studies.

Wichmann, S., Beliaev, D., & Davletshin, A. (2008) Posibles correlaciones lingüísticas y arqueológicas vinculadas con los olmecas [Possible correlations associated with linguistic and archaeological Olmecs]. In M. T. Uriarte & R. B. González Lauck (eds.), *Olmeca. Balance y perspectivas. Memoria de la Primera Mesa Redonda* (The Olmec: critical evaluation and perspectives. Memoires of the first Round Table). Mexico City: Universidad Nacional Autónoma de México, pp. 667–683.

Wichmann, S., Müller, A., & Velupillai, V. (2010) Homelands of the world's language families: a quantitative approach. *Diachronica* 27, 247–276.

48

Mesoamerica and the southwestern United States: archaeology

Steven A. LeBlanc

This chapter focuses on the migration of maize farmers and Uto-Aztecan languages from Mesoamerica into the western United States, starting around 2000 BCE. Alternative models are also discussed, but the case for migration is supported by a combination of archaeological and linguistic data.

The spread of maize farming from central Mexico north into the American Southwest, starting around 2000 BCE, has been seen as an important case of diffusion by some and of migration by others. Recently, this proposed migration has been seen as a case of farmer-language dispersal with speakers of Uto-Aztecan spreading north from central Mexico bringing farming and ancestral Uto-Aztecan languages into northwestern Mexico, then into the southern American Southwest and finally into the states of Arizona, New Mexico, Utah, and Colorado. The counter-argument is that corn farming diffused with no appreciable population movement, and Uto-Aztecan originated in the United States and spread south into Mesoamerica.

The northern migration model was first proposed by Bellwood (1997; see Matson 2003 and LeBlanc 2008 for more details). Maize agriculture was initially developed in central or west-central Mesoamerica. It became a viable subsistence strategy sometime around 3000–2500 BCE. At some point prior to 2500 BCE, farmers speaking early forms of Uto-Aztecan began to spread north in either a wave of advance or leapfrogging process, ultimately reaching the desert areas of southern Arizona and New Mexico and northern Sonora/Chihuahua. After a pause of some centuries, the farmers spread farther north into the Four Corners region of northeastern Arizona and southeastern Utah, where they are known archaeologically as Western Basketmaker II. Ultimately, they spread into the Great Basin and desert California where they stopped farming, but continued as Uto-Aztecan-speaking hunter-gatherers.

The Global Prehistory of Human Migration: The Encyclopedia of Global Human Migration Volume 1,
First Edition. Edited by Peter Bellwood.
© 2013 John Wiley & Sons, Ltd. Published 2015 by John Wiley & Sons, Ltd.

Our understanding of these issues is constrained by a surprising paucity of archaeological evidence, except for the last portion of the proposed migration, that from the southern Southwest into the Four Corners area. Overall, it does appear that such a Mesoamerican–American Southwest migration scenario is possible. If farmers advanced between Mesoamerica and southern Arizona at a rate of 2.5–3.7 km per year, which is roughly the rate found for some proposed Old World farmer migrations (LeBlanc 2003), the spread would have taken 500–700 years. Corn farming was certainly 500–700 years older in Mesoamerica than the Southwest, so such a migration is at least plausible. There are three relevant categories of evidence: linguistic (see also chapter 47), archaeological, and genetic.

Archaeological evidence

The relevant archaeological record is understood far better for the US Southwest than for either northwestern or central Mexico. Central Mexico has evidence for a long sequence of the domestication of maize and other crops. Early farming villages are not well known before the use of pottery about 1600–1400 BCE (see Clark & Cheetham 2002 for a regional synthesis). Any Uto-Aztecan-speaking migrants presumably spread out of the core area prior to this time, because the spread of agriculture (either via migration or via diffusion) was not accompanied by pottery, except for some rare non-utilitarian examples from southern Arizona. Whether such pottery was sufficient to account for the apparent ancestral Uto-Aztecan pottery terms as suggested in chapter 47 is not clear, and this apparent anomaly remains unresolved.

Clark and Cheetham (2002: 281) suggest for central Mexico that there was a "noticeable shift in subsistence and land-use patterns and dependency on cultivated crops" combined with indirect evidence of swidden agriculture and significant impact on the environment "all across the lowlands" at about 3000–2500 BCE. This would be evidence of significant population growth and what one would expect to prompt a wave of advance type of spread.

However, our knowledge of the critical time period in the region between the Mesoamerican core area and the Greater Southwest is essentially non-existent. Even in Sonora, the La Playa site has a large number of burials and baking ovens from the relevant time period, but no actual village site has been discovered (Carpenter et al. 2005). Large hilltop habitation sites are known in Chihuahua (Hard & Roney 2005), and the archaeological picture in southern Arizona has recently changed dramatically based on several river-edge habitation sites, with most dates falling between 1200 and 800 BCE. Some sites have hundreds of pithouses, but it is not clear whether they represent large aggregates of people or reuse of the same locality by a small number of people over time. There is ample evidence of maize and large storage facilities, indicating that these people were committed farmers (Huckell 1995; Mabry 1998, 2005; Gregory 2001).

A small portion of the Sonoran La Playa site has produced about 160 burials dating to the first millennium BCE, implying a much larger population at that time than during the prior foraging period (Carpenter et al. 2005). Numerous defensive sites in northern Chihuahua on hilltops adjacent to good farmland, dating to around 1000 BCE, also imply substantial populations. The apparent sudden appearance of farmers has also been proposed for lowland areas around El Paso, but the evidence here is less substantial (O'Laughlin 1980).

The similarity in timing, projectile points, and defensive sites on both sides of the Sierra Madre, and the later documented presence of Uto-Aztecan speakers throughout the region, would seem to support a wave of advance migration along both sides of the mountains. There appears to be no strong evidence for continuity in cultural tradition into the agricultural phase in southern Arizona, Sonora, Chihuahua, or El Paso. The early farmers do not seem to have been the same indigenous Archaic people who just added maize to their diet. In sum, the archaeology from the Mesoamerican core area, northwestern Mexico, and the southern Southwest is compatible with a migration of farmers, but due primarily to the lack of information from the intervening area it is hard to make a very strong case.

It has been proposed that the last stage in this spread of farmers into the American Southwest was associated with what are termed Western Basketmaker II groups, moving north from the low desert such as the Tucson Basin to the Four Corners region of Arizona and Utah. There were two types of Basketmakers (Matson 1991, 2003) and only one group, the Western Basketmakers, were the proposed migrant maize farmers. The Eastern Basketmakers are now considered by some to be an indigenous population of former foragers living in northwestern New Mexico and southwestern Colorado who adopted farming.

The evidence that these two Basketmaker archaeological cultures were distinct is substantial and compelling. Their baskets, sandals, cradle boards, and pithouses are different. They had distinct forms of projectile points and different methods and tools for chipping them. They buried their dead in different orientations. There are some cultural similarities between the Western Basketmakers and the low desert farmers, and the rock art in Chihuahua seems far more similar to the Western Basketmaker rock art than would occur by chance alone (Schaafsma 1997).

Biological evidence

Only mitochondrial DNA is well enough studied for the relevant populations to be relevant for understanding prehistoric migrations. There are four mitochondrial haplogroups (A, B, C, and D) indigenous to the Americas (chapter 9), and the rare haplogroup X is not relevant for this chapter. Overall, high frequencies of A and low D are found in modern central Mesoamerica. Non-Uto-Aztecan speakers in Mesoamerica have between 32 and 93 percent haplogroup A and very low D (0–6%), and modern Nahua (Uto-Aztecan) speakers have 38–63 percent A and a trace (1–2%) of D. A sample of ancient DNA, presumably from Uto-Aztecan speakers, shows a similarly high A (65%), but higher D (17%) (Lorenz & Smith 1996: 310; Kemp 2006: 60). Modern Uto-Aztecan speaking communities between central Mexico and the

Southwest, such as the Tarahumara, Huichol, and Cora, have 18–25 percent A. The Uto-Aztecan Piman of southern Arizona have about 5 percent A and a very low D of 0.5 percent, but it appears there has been significant gene flow between the modern Piman speakers and non-Uto-Aztecan speakers, thus lowering the frequency of A in this population.

The non-Uto-Aztecan-speaking Tanoans, who today occupy the Rio Grande valley, may have been related to the Eastern Basketmakers and have no A or D. The Zuni (also non-Uto-Aztecan) do have 15 percent A, but there is archaeological evidence for a substantial inflow of assumed Uto-Aztecan speakers into the Zuni region in late prehistory that might explain this. The prehistoric Western Basketmakers, at the northern edge of the proposed migration, had about 14 percent A.

Within these haplogroups, there is additional variability in the hyper-variable region. Kemp et al. (2010) see links between the Mexican Cora-Huichol, Tarahumara, and groups in the US Southwest, but not with the Nahua speakers of central Mexico. They see this as not supporting the migration model, but because the Cora-Huichol are considered linguistically and archaeologically to be Mesoamerican, the opposite conclusion seems warranted. There is a burst of mitochondrial DNA variability in the Southwest apparently in the last few thousand years, which probably resulted from rapid population growth. This probably relates to the beginning of farming, but is not necessarily a result of migration.

In summary, there is a clinal decline in the amount of haplogroup A among Uto-Aztecan speakers as one moves north from central Mexico. Haplogroup A goes from 50 percent or more in central Mexico to around 25 percent in far northern Mexico, and even lower in the southern part of the American Southwest. This could be from a dilution in the proportion of haplogroup A as indigenous, non-A-bearing forager women were added to the farmer gene pool. This fits with ethnographic records of interaction among foragers and farmers/herders and with what we know about warfare and conflict on a worldwide basis, although we lack the forager DNA to test this (LeBlanc 2003). It is very hard to explain these data by a diffusion model.

A variant of the albumin gene, Albumin Mexico (AL*Mexico), is present in low frequencies in all major language groups in Mesoamerica and occurs in the Southwest (Smith et al. 2000). It is found at about 5 percent in the Uto-Aztecan speaking Pima, but is very rare among the Numic speakers of the Great Basin (0.5%). It is also rare among the non-Uto-Aztecan Yumans and Apache, and if present at all in Zuni, it is very rare; it is absent among the Tanoan speakers. Thus, Southwestern AL*Mexico seems to be derived from Uto-Aztecan speakers, and was present early enough to enter the Numic gene pool. Given its presence among most of the language families of Mesoamerica, the mutation must have occurred in Mesoamerica and moved north, not the reverse.

There are also discrete dental-trait data from Basketmaker skeletal remains and comparative samples (LeBlanc et al. 2008) that have been interpreted as supporting both a significant biological difference between Eastern versus Western Basketmakers, and the contention that the Western Basketmakers are much more Mesoamerican-like than the Eastern ones. Such data provide some very tentative supportive evidence that the Western Basketmaker population was related to Uto-Aztecan speakers.

Migration into California and the Great Basin

Most of the aboriginal population of present-day southern California spoke a form of Uto-Aztecan, as did the Numic branch throughout the Great Basin and the Comanche of the southern Great Plains. None of these groups were farmers. The abandonment of farming makes ecological sense, and does not imply that the ancestors of these people were not farmers. Based on linguistic evidence the Numic spread was quite late, perhaps in the last thousand years, although it could have occurred more than a thousand years earlier. The previous people of the Great Basin were foragers who seem to have had a long *in situ* history, except for a brief period when Fremont corn farming existed in some regions from around 500 CE into the 13th century, although biologically the Fremont appear indigenous. It seems that the Uto-Aztecan speakers first pushed into California, and later underwent a rapid radiation into the Great Basin, thus replacing the previous foragers.

Alternative models

This discussion of the primary evidence for a linguistic/farmer spread has not focused on alternative models or negative evidence. Many different aspects of the migration model have alternatives. The traditional and alternative models for both the introduction of maize into the Southwest and for the observed differences between Western and Eastern Basketmakers favor *in situ* adoption of maize and local differentiation of indigenous peoples. This traditional model has corn, not people, reaching the Southwest from Mexico (Wills 1988). In this scenario, maize and squash did not allow for a rapid shift from foraging to farming and were incorporated into modified forager lifeways. Over time, these foragers became more dependent on farming, and only well into the past 2000 years did they become committed farmers. However, the strong commitments to farming in the Basketmaker area by at least a few centuries BCE, based on stable isotope data (Coltrain et al. 2007), and likewise in the Tucson area at least several hundred years before, seem to negate this model.

A different version of local development is championed by Mabry (2005; also Merrill et al 2009), who sees less of a sharp break between the earliest maize growers and Archaic populations. Finally, an alternative explanation for the differences between the Eastern and Western Basketmakers is that both could have been ethnically and culturally different forager groups who adopted maize farming. It can also be argued that we happen to have archaeological samples from the eastern and western parts of the Basketmaker range, but few from the people who lived in between, so there may have been more of a gradient than appears.

At present, various lines of evidence provide a fairly good case for a Uto-Aztecan-speaking farmer spread resulting in the wide distribution of the language family. There is supporting evidence from genetics, linguistics, and material culture remains. There is no compelling line of evidence that refutes the migration model. However, the evidence for a substantial difference between the Western and Eastern Basketmakers is still very strong. In addition, there were many later population movements in the Southwest that are documented archaeologically, but these were on much smaller scales than that proposed for the Uto-Aztecan movement.

SEE ALSO: 9 The human colonization of the Americas: population genetics; 47 Meso-america and the southwestern United States: linguistic history

References

Bellwood, P. (1997) Prehistoric cultural explanations for widespread language families. In P. McConvell & N. Evans (eds.), *Archaeology and Linguistics*. Melbourne: Oxford University Press, pp. 123–134.

Bellwood, P. & Renfrew, C. (eds.) (2003) *Examining the Farming/Language Dispersal Hypothesis*. Cambridge: McDonald Institute for Archaeological Research.

Carpenter, J., Sanchez, G., & Villalpando, C. (2005) The late archaic/early agricultural period in Sonora, Mexico. In Vierra (2005), pp. 13–40.

Clark, J. & Cheetham, D. (2002) Mesoamerica's tribal foundations. In W. A. Parkinson (ed.), *The Archaeology of Tribal Societies*. Ann Arbor: International Monographs in Prehistory, pp. 278–339.

Coltrain, J., Janetski, J., & Carlyle, S. (2007) The stable- and radio-isotope chemistry of Western Basketmaker burials: implications for early puebloan diets and origins. *American Antiquity* 72(2), 301–321.

Gregory, D. (ed.) (2001) *Excavations in the Santa Cruz River Floodplain: The Early Agricultural Period Component at Los Pozos*. Center for Desert Archaeology Anthropological Papers No. 21. Tucson: Center for Desert Archaeology.

Hard, R. & Roney, J. (2005) The transition to farming on the Rio Casas Grandes and in the southern Jornada Mogollon region. In Vierra (2005), pp. 141–186.

Huckell, B. B. (1995) *Of Marshes and Maize: Preceramic Agricultural Settlements in the Cienega Valley, Southeastern Arizona*. Anthropology Papers of the University of Arizona No. 59. Tucson: University of Arizona Press.

Kaestle, F. & Smith, D. (2001) Ancient mitochondrial DNA evidence for prehistoric population movement: the Numic expansion. *American Journal of Physical Anthropology* 115, 1–12.

Kemp, B. (2006) Mesoamerica and Southwest prehistory, and the entrance of humans into the Americas: mitochondrial DNA evidence. PhD dissertation, Department of Anthropology, University of California Davis.

Kemp, B., Gonzalez-Oliver, A., Malhi, R., et al. (2010) Evaluating the farming/language dispersal hypothesis with genetic variation exhibited by populations in the Southwest and Meso-america. *Proceedings of the National Academy of Sciences* 107(15), 6759–6764.

LeBlanc, S. (2003) Conflict and language dispersal: issues and a New World example. In Bell-wood & Renfrew (2003), pp. 357–365.

LeBlanc, S. (2008) The case for an early farmer migration into the American Southwest. In L. D. Webster & M. McBrinn (eds.), *Archaeology without Borders: Contact, Commerce, and Change in the U.S. Southwest and Northwestern Mexico*. Boulder: University Press of Colorado, pp. 107–142.

LeBlanc, S., Turner II, C., & Morgan, M. (2008) Genetic relationships based on discrete dental traits: Basketmaker II and Mimbres. *International Journal of Osteoarchaeology* 18, 109–130.

Lorenz, J. & Smith, D. (1996) Distribution of four founding mtDNA haplogroups among Native North Americans. *American Journal of Physical Anthropology* 101, 307–323.

Mabry, J. (1998) *Archaeological Investigations of Early Village Sites in the Middle Santa Cruz Valley: Analyses and Synthesis.* Center for Desert Archaeology Anthropological Papers No. 19. Tucson: Center for Desert Archaeology.

Mabry, J. (2005) Changing knowledge and ideas about the first farmers in Southeastern Arizona. In Vierra (2005), pp. 41–83.

Matson, R. (1991) *The Origins of Southwestern Agriculture.* Tucson: University of Arizona Press.

Matson, R. (2003) The spread of maize agriculture in the U.S. Southwest. In Bellwood & Renfrew (2003), pp. 341–356.

Merrill, W., Hard, R., Mabry, J., et al., (2009) The diffusion of maize to the southwestern United States and its impact. *Proceedings of the National Academy of Sciences* 106(50), 21019–21026.

O'Laughlin, T. (1980) *The Keystone Dam Site and Other Archaic and Formative Sites in Northwest El Paso, Texas.* El Paso Centennial Museum Publications in Anthropology No. 8. El Paso: University of Texas.

Schaafsma, P. (1997) *Rock Art Sites in Chihuahua, Mexico.* Archaeology Notes No. 171. Santa Fe: Museum of New Mexico Office of Archaeological Studies.

Smith, D., Lorenz, J., Rolfs, B., et al. (2000) Implications of the distribution of Albumin Naskapi and Albumin Mexico for New World prehistory. *American Journal of Physical Anthropology* 111, 557–572.

Vierra, B. J. (ed.) (2005) *The Late Archaic Across the Borderlands: From Foraging to Farming.* Austin: University of Texas Press.

Wills, W. (1988) *Early Prehistoric Agriculture in the American Southwest.* Santa Fe: School of American Research Press.

49

Caribbean Islands: archaeology

William Keegan

The Caribbean islands received colonizing populations on many occasions after 5000 BCE, and especially at about 500 BCE, but contacts with adjacent mainland regions always continued. The main linguistic element present at Spanish contact was Arawak-speaking, related to Amazonian Arawak populations.

The Caribbean Islands present themselves as three archipelagos that point to the surrounding mainland (Figure 49.1). If we assume that the mainland was settled first, then we need only draw a line from the mainland to the nearest island and show evidence for cultural affinities. In essence, this is what has been done by archaeologists. The episodic introduction of new technologies has been assumed to represent separate and independent migrations (Rouse 1992). The first involved peoples employing a flaked-stone technology who crossed around 5000 BCE from Central America to Cuba and Hispaniola ("Lithic Age"). The second was by people who used a ground-stone technology and entered the southern Lesser Antilles from Trinidad around 3000 BCE ("Archaic Age"). The third was by the Arawak-speaking peoples who introduced pottery and agriculture around 500 BCE ("Ceramic Age"). Finally, the Island Caribs entered the southern Lesser Antilles just prior to the arrival of Europeans. Although this framework continues to hold sway (Wilson 2007), this chapter will highlight new perspectives on insular Caribbean migrations.

The first Caribbean people

The earliest evidence of humans in the insular Caribbean has been found in Cuba, Hispaniola, and Puerto Rico (Rodríguez Ramos et al. 2010). Called Casimiroid, the oldest sites date to about 5000 BCE. The material culture is composed primarily of large

The Global Prehistory of Human Migration: The Encyclopedia of Global Human Migration Volume 1,
First Edition. Edited by Peter Bellwood.
© 2013 John Wiley & Sons, Ltd. Published 2015 by John Wiley & Sons, Ltd.

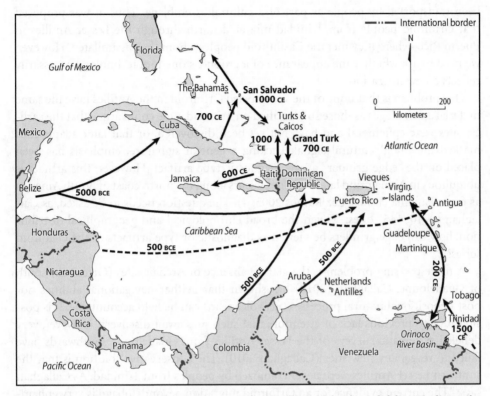

Figure 49.1 Colonization and migrations in the Caribbean islands. Solid lines indicate the primary movement of peoples and goods, dashed lines indicate the movement of goods and ideas, and double arrows reflect evidence for extraction and exchange documented by archaeological evidence. In all cases it is expected that peoples, goods and ideas moved in both directions. The arrows identify general locations and directionality. They should not be viewed as specific source areas. The dates are the earliest available for particular locations. Map created by Joshua M. Torres.

chert blades which are very similar to contemporaneous stone tools from Belize (Wilson 2007). The majority of the sites are quarries, a situation that suggests that they may have been locations at which high-quality chert was collected by seasonal visitors for export to the mainland. We know little else about life in the islands at this time.

The first transition

It has been proposed that the Lithic Age way of life disappeared around 3000 BCE with the introduction of a ground-stone technology by new migrants from Trinidad. Rouse (1992) believed that after the Lithic Age peoples arrived in the islands they severed all ties with their homeland. The arrival of ground-stone tools must have originated somewhere else, and Trinidad, where such tools first appear around 6000 BCE, provided the most likely source. These tools were associated with a way of life that must have been transported by people as part of a cultural assemblage. Thus, it was proposed that Ortoiroid people from Trinidad migrated north through the Lesser Antilles to Puerto Rico, where they met the Casimiroid peoples whom they assimilated. However, we need to ask whether the appearance of a ground-stone tool technology necessarily reflects a new migration.

One problem is that none of the sites labeled Ortoiroid in the Antilles have the same material assemblages as those so identified on Trinidad. One could argue that the earliest sites were ephemeral and have not yet been discovered, or that later adaptations masked the initial cultural signal. Lacking a general signature, emphasis has been placed on the "edge grinder" as the diagnostic type artifact. However, this artifact is ubiquitous in Archaic and later sites and occurs along the north coast of South America as far as Panama (Rodríguez Ramos 2005: 4). The question needs to be asked, as Callaghan (2010: 145) does: "Given the broad chronological and geographical distribution, how can edge grinders be viewed as diagnostic or type artifacts of the Ortoiroid series?"

A more pressing problem is the glaring absence of Archaic sites (Ortoiroid) south of Guadeloupe. Callaghan (2010) has shown that neither navigational abilities nor post-depositional natural processes (i.e. volcanism) can be held accountable. It is possible, due to previous lack of attention, that such sites await discovery. However, very detailed systematic surveys of the Lesser Antilles from Guadeloupe southwards have failed to reveal any new sites (Callaghan 2010). The conservative solution is that the southern Lesser Antilles were never colonized by peoples from Trinidad. As Callaghan says: "The current evidence for an Ortoiroid migration beyond Tobago is very ephemeral. What has been classified as Ortoiroid could at least as easily be Casimiroid" (2010: 146).

In sum, there is little solid evidence for a separate Ortoiroid migration. It is far more likely that the Casimiroids maintained ties with their Central American homeland, and that new practices (including ground-stone tools and a variety of cultigens) arrived in the islands through exchange. Such exchanges certainly included people, goods, and ideas. It is misleading to view mobility and exchange solely as the outcome of population expansion (Hofman et al. 2010; Hofman & Hoogland 2011).

The idea of the Casimiroid migration is justified because the islands previously were unoccupied. If no one was living on an island, then migration is the only way to explain the sudden appearance of people. For the next 2000 years these "pre-Arawak" peoples expanded through the Greater Antilles and as far south as Antigua and perhaps even Martinique (Callaghan 2010), and developed diverse lifeways (Rodríguez Ramos et al. 2010). Pottery became at least a minor component of their cultural inventory by at least 2600 BCE (Rodríguez Ramos et al. 2008), and "the Antillean botanical trinity of manioc, sweet potatoes, and maize . . . has all been documented during Pre-Arawak times in Puerto Rico at least since 1300 BC" (Rodríguez Ramos 2010: 31). Additional cultigens, including yellow sapote and sapodilla, were obtained from Central America. Although these peoples have been characterized as mobile foragers (Rouse 1992), there is evidence for sedentary communities. Finally, there is every reason to assume that pre-Arawak peoples continued to maintain ties to their homeland (e.g. Keegan 2004), especially given subsequent developments that point to exchange relations with the "Intermediate Area" or Isthmo-Colombian region (Rodríguez Ramos 2010).

The second transition

Beginning around 500 BCE there was a dramatic change in the pottery found at sites in Puerto Rico and the northern Lesser Antilles. Called Saladoid, this pottery is associated with the Arawak diaspora that began in the upper Amazon about 1000 BCE and spread along the major rivers of South America (Heckenberger 2005; chapters 50 and 51, this volume). Linguistic evidence proves that the peoples who inhabited the insular Caribbean at the time of Spanish contact spoke Arawak languages (Rouse 1992). Explaining the Arawak migration is complicated by the fact that they colonized islands that were already occupied. Pre-Arawak and Arawak peoples coexisted on Puerto Rico for at least 500 years (Rodríguez Ramos 2010; Rodríguez Ramos et al. 2010). The question is, when and how did peoples colonize the islands, and where on the American mainland did they come from?

Over-water movement was not a significant obstacle. People were able to cross the Caribbean Sea from Central and South America during Archaic times, and it may have been easier to cross this expanse of open water than it would have been to navigate the passages between adjacent islands (Callaghan 2001, 2003, 2010). Establishing a firm initial date for this migration is difficult due to the paucity of "hygienic" radiocarbon dates (Fitzpatrick 2006; see also Fitzpatrick & Ross 2010). Present evidence identifies a Saladoid expression by 500 BCE, but its antecedents may date to as early as 800 BCE.

Explaining this migration is complicated by the distribution of sites and the diversity of pottery styles that comprise the Saladoid expression. The earliest sites are located on Puerto Rico and the northern Lesser Antilles, and the main stepping-stone corridor from eastern South America, the southern Lesser Antilles, remained largely vacant until 200–400 CE (Fitzpatrick et al. 2010). Simple demographic mathematics indicates that a single migrant group could not have left the lower Orinoco of eastern South America around 800 BCE and colonized all of the Lesser Antilles and Puerto Rico by 500 BCE. Even if there were many migrants in the group, they could not have procreated fast enough to establish even one colony on each of the major islands. So multiple migrations are indicated, and at least some islands must have been bypassed. Moreover, recent investigations indicate that Saladoids may have arrived only around 700 CE on the lower Orinoco (Barse 2009), so the initial Saladoid migration into the islands must have originated elsewhere in the Caribbean littoral, and the islands of the southern Lesser Antilles likely were colonized in a southward expansion (Fitzpatrick et al. 2010).

In sum, the second transition began around 1000 BCE, when Arawak-speaking peoples expanded from the northwest Amazon along the major rivers of lowland South America and out to the coast. This expansion is recognized by the distribution of their distinctive Saladoid-Barrancoid pottery, and Heckenberger (2005: 61) suggests that these material remains reflect a fundamental and widely shared "ethos," a macro-Arawak *habitus* predisposed to reproduce: (1) large, fixed populations, fairly intensive subsistence economies, and landscape alteration; (2) institutional social ranking based on bloodline and birth order; and (3) regional integration involving accommodation and acculturation of outsiders. Furthermore, Max Schmidt (see Keegan, in prep.) concluded that this Arawak expansion was not a simple migration of more or less closed masses of peoples who either penetrated uninhabited areas or drove out the former population by force. The intrusion of Arawak cultures into ever-widening areas occurred in continuous repetition. They succeeded in infiltrating previously occupied territories by introducing superior methods of agricultural production in concert with an ideology that distinguished them as superior "others" (cf. Helms 1998).

If we accept that over-water transport from coastal Central and South America was not an issue, that the population could not have grown fast enough to be based on a single propagule, that there was already a well-established Archaic population living in the northern islands, that contacts were maintained throughout the circum-Caribbean region through the exchange of people, material goods, and ideas (Hofman et al. 2010), and that sedentism, hierarchy, and regionality were basic elements of the Arawak colonization of the insular Caribbean, then an entirely new perspective emerges.

The second transition was a gradual process punctuated by the development of a distinctive material culture (Saladoid). The Arawak-speaking colonists practiced matrilineal descent and matrilocal residence (Keegan 2007), which facilitated the movement of entire communities as well as male mobility expressed through the infiltration of Archaic settlements (Keegan, in prep.). Settlement patterns suggest that junior lineages hived off to establish new founding communities that declared their autonomy and "access to origins" (Helms 1998). They arrived from a variety of locations along the Caribbean littoral, which reflects continued contacts with the mainland (Hofman et al. 2010), and is evident in an initial diversity of ceramic styles on Puerto Rico, Vieques, Antigua, St. Martin, Montserrat, and eastern Dominican Republic. What is called the Saladoid became dominant, and its elaborate painted and modeled-incised decorations provide a "veneer" that united disparate communities from Puerto Rico through the Lesser Antilles and into lowland South America (Keegan 2004). We also need to recognize that island colonization was not a one-way street. The exchange of people, materials, and ideas also affected cultural developments on the mainland (Hofman et al. 2010; Hofman & Hoogland 2011).

Unoccupied islands certainly must have been settled through the process of migration, but once colonies were established additional settlements probably reflect social processes, including fissioning, infiltration, and the reshuffling of social groups living on the same or neighboring islands. The earliest Arawak colonists settled first in places that were already occupied by Archaic peoples. The number of identified Saladoid sites increases at an exponential rate; a rate that substantially outpaces the natural population growth rate for humans. It is possible that waves of colonists came to the islands, but the large populations encountered by the Spanish could not have been only the product of a mass migration from the mainland. A more parsimonious explanation is that the Saladoid peoples infiltrated Archaic communities and converted them through the process of "Arawakanization" (see Keegan, in prep.).

The Arawak colonization of the insular Caribbean created a diversity of local expressions that later became consolidated as the Taínos of the Greater Antilles and the Igneri of the Lesser Antilles. These labels mask significant local variation, and fail to recognize the substantial cultural diversity that existed at the time of Spanish contact. The current time-space culture historical framework tends to freeze macro-cultures in time, space, and identity (e.g. Siegel 2010). Recent scholarship has shifted the focus to local developments, mobility, and exchange as significant processes in the creation of insular Caribbean identities (Keegan 2004; Hofman et al. 2010; Rodríguez Ramos 2010).

An excellent example of matrix and network complexity is observed in the Bahamas. Culturally diverse incursions into the Bahama archipelago illustrate the mobility of Caribbean peoples (Berman et al., forthcoming). Around 700 CE people from the north coast of the Dominican Republic established a temporary settlement on Grand Turk where they concentrated on the capture of sea turtles for export. At the same time, Meillacoid peoples from the north coast of Cuba established permanent settlements in the central Bahamas (the oldest known sites are on San Salvador and northern Eleuthera), whence they developed the distinctive Palmetto Ware pottery associated with the proto-historic Lucayans. From the central Bahamas they expanded north and south through the archipelago sometime before 1000 CE. Finally, Meillacoid peoples from the north coast of Haiti established temporary settlements in the Turks & Caicos Islands between 1000 and 1300 CE. These settlements were seasonal, and emphasize the procurement of abundant local resources including fish, salt, and particular shells for beads. There is evidence for interactions among these peoples of diverse origins. The historic labeling of native Bahamians as "Lucayans" fails to capture the cultural complexity of this archipelago.

The final transition

It is impossible to separate the European invasion that began in 1492 from the last stage of precolonial history. The Spanish established a dichotomy of "peaceful Arawaks" (Taínos) and "cannibal Caribs." It is clear that the Spanish did not understand the meaning of the native term "Caribe" (Keegan 1996), and that they defined "Caribs" as fierce people who refused conversion to the Christian faith and could therefore be enslaved. The issue for archaeologists is our inability to identify a unique material signature that would distinguish an island Carib culture. Based solely on one distinctive characteristic reported by the Spanish (warlike cannibals), it is assumed that the island Carib reflect a separate migration into the southern Antilles just prior to the arrival of the Spanish.

The historic island Carib were multilingual. Their root language was the Ignerí dialect of Arawak (Maipuran). In addition, there was a men's creole trading language that incorporated elements from Carib-speaking peoples of eastern South America and reflects their connection to the mainland (cf. Heckenberger 2005). This connection is further emphasized by the migration of Carib-speaking peoples from Guyana (e.g. Galibis) into the vacuum created by the rapid decline of population in the southern Lesser Antilles that began around 1200 (Hofman & Hoogland 2011). The need to embrace the concept of cultural "mosaics" is increasingly evident throughout the Caribbean (Wilson 2007).

Peoples expressing a Saladoid identity colonized the southern Lesser Antilles between 200 and 400 CE (Fitzpatrick et al. 2010). They provided the first strong connection between the peoples of eastern Venezuela and lowland South America and pure Saladoid peoples to the north. About 400 they began to interact more intensively with peoples on the lower Orinoco, from whom they incorporated Barrancoid elements in their ceramic styles. Their South American identity intensified as the Saladoid veneer began to disappear about 600, which is reflected in a greater emphasis on local styles. This new identity is classified as the Troumassoid series, and is reflected in significant changes in vessel form and decoration.

About 1200 the pottery became cruder and there was an unexplained decline in population. Contacts with the Tainos of the Greater Antilles are evident, but there is an increasing association with lowland South America (Hofman & Hoogland 2011). It was recorded after contact that the island Carib claimed that they ate Arawak men and married Arawak women. This comment has been taken as evidence for a separate migration of antagonistic peoples, but it is a common theme among tribal peoples and expresses one element of their relationship with "affinal Others" (Helms 1998). It is more likely that individuals and small groups continuously entered the islands, and that their interactions were not always peaceful. What is explained as a separate Carib migration was more likely an evolving tribal society with continuous exchanges of people and communities from the mainland, but whose identity was historicized through hostile encounters with the Spanish.

Conclusions

The tendency in the past has been to assume that every significant change in material culture reflected a new migration into the insular Caribbean. A more compelling explanation is that changes reflected enduring ties to the mainland. Successive Casimiroid, Arawak, and Carib peoples did colonize the islands. However, the islands were not simply empty isolates that absorbed populations from the mainland. From earliest times, the islands were part of the larger circum-Caribbean region whose porous borders facilitated interaction and local developments. Caribbean peoples developed distinct identities and lifeways, but they did so in relation to their exchange partners on the mainland.

SEE ALSO: 50 Amazonia: linguistic history; 51 Amazonia: archaeology

References

Barse, W. (2009) Early Ronquin: its vessel shapes, chronological sequence, and broader relationships. In M. DaRos & R. Colten (eds.), *Recent Caribbean Archaeological Research at the Peabody Museum of Natural History*. Yale University Publications in Anthropology 50(1). New Haven: Yale University Press, pp. 85–98.

Berman, M. J., Gnivecki, P., & Pateman, M. (forthcoming) The Bahama archipelago. In W. F. Keegan, C. L. Hofman, & R. Rodríguez Ramos (eds.), *Handbook of Caribbean Archaeology*. Oxford: Oxford University Press.

Callaghan, R. (2001) Ceramic age seafaring and interaction potential in the Antilles: a computer simulation. *Current Anthropology* 42, 308–313.

Callaghan, R. (2003) Comments on the mainland origins of the preceramic cultures of the Greater Antilles. *Latin American Antiquity* 14, 323–338.

Callaghan, R. (2010) Crossing the Guadeloupe Passage in the Archaic Age. In Fitzpatrick & Ross (2010), pp. 127–147.

Fitzpatrick, S. (2006) A critical approach to ^{14}C dating in the Caribbean: using chronometric hygiene to evaluate chronological control and prehistoric settlement. *Latin American Antiquity* 17, 389–418.

Fitzpatrick, S. & Ross, A. (eds.) (2010) *Island Shores, Distant Pasts*. Gainesville: University Press of Florida.

Fitzpatrick, S., Kappers, M., & Giovas, C. (2010) The southward route hypothesis: examining Carriacou's chronological position in Antillean prehistory. In Fitzpatrick & Ross (2010), pp. 163–176.

Heckenberger, M. (2005) *The Ecology of Power*. New York: Routledge.

Helms, M. (1998) *Access to Origins*. Austin: University of Texas Press.

Hofman, C. & Hoogland, M. (2011) Unraveling the multi-scale networks of mobility and exchange in the pre-colonial circum-Caribbean. In C. L. Hofman & A. van Duijvenbode (eds.), *Communities in contact. Essays in Archaeology, Ethnohistory and Ethnography in the Amerindian Circum-Caribbean*. Leiden: Sidestone Press.

Hofman, C., Bright, A., & Rodríguez Ramos, R. (2010) Crossing the Caribbean Sea. Towards a holistic view of pre-colonial mobility and exchange. *Journal of Caribbean Archaeology* 10, 1–18.

Keegan, W. (1996) Columbus was a cannibal: myth and the first encounters. In R. L. Paquette & S. L. Engerman (eds.), *The Lesser Antilles in the Age of European Expansion*. Gainesville: University Press of Florida, pp. 17–32.

Keegan, W. (2004) Islands of chaos. In A. Delpuech & C. L. Hofman (eds.), *The Late Ceramic Age in the Eastern Caribbean*. British Archaeological Records International Series. Oxford: BAR, pp. 33–44.

Keegan, W. (2007) *Taino Indian Myth and Practice: The Arrival of the Stranger King*. Gainesville: University Press of Florida.

Keegan, W. (in prep.) Max Schmidt and the Arawakan diaspora: a view from the Antilles. In A. Oyuela-Caycedo & M. Fischer (eds.), *The Arawak Dispersion*.

Rodríguez Ramos, R. (2005) The crab-shell dichotomy revisited: The lithics speak out. In P. E. Siegel (ed.), *Ancient Borinquen: Archaeology and Ethnohistory of Native Puerto Rico*. Tuscaloosa: University of Alabama Press, pp. 1–54.

Rodríguez Ramos, R. (2010) *Rethinking Puerto Rican Precolonial History*. Tuscaloosa: University of Alabama Press.

Rodríguez Ramos, R. & Pagán Jiménez, J. (2007) Las Antillas en el contexto del circun-Caribe: Cincuenta años después [The Antilles in the context of the circum-Caribbean: fifty years later]. In B. Reid, H. Petitjean Roget, & L. A. Curet (eds.), *Proceedings of XXI Congress of the International Association for Caribbean Archaeology*. St. Augustine, Trinidad: University of the West Indies Press, pp. 778–786.

Rodríguez Ramos, R., Torres, J., & Oliver, J. (2010) Rethinking time in Caribbean archaeology: the Puerto Rican case study. In Fitzpatrick & Ross (2010), pp. 21–53.

Rouse, I. (1992) *The Tainos: Rise and Decline of the People who Greeted Columbus*. New Haven: Yale University Press.

Siegel, P. (2010) Continuity and change in the evolution of religion and political organization on pre-Colombian Puerto Rico. *Journal of Anthropological Archaeology* 29, 302–326.

Wilson, S. (2007) *The Archaeology of the Caribbean*. Cambridge: Cambridge University Press.

50

Amazonia: linguistic history

Alexandra Y. Aikhenvald

The language families of Amazonia offer a history of great complexity, albeit with much evidence erased by the spread of Spanish and Portuguese. Homelands for the six major families and some aspects of their migration histories are suggested.

Over 300 languages are currently spoken in the Amazon basin. The six major linguistic families are Arawak, Tupí, Carib, Panoan, Tucanoan, and Macro-Jê (Figure 50.1). There are also many smaller families and isolates. Over 60 percent of indigenous languages are estimated to have become extinct since the European conquest (Loukotka 1968; Dixon & Aikhenvald 1999a; Adelaar 2004; Aikhenvald 2012: 1–19), making the task of revealing the exact linguistic history of Amazonia truly daunting. Various attempts have been made, during the past two centuries, to group different families into macro-groupings or "stocks," but none have a solid backing of consistent proof. Examples are the putative "Amerind," and an "Arawakan" claimed to encompass Arawak proper (or Maipuran), Arawá, Chapacura, Guahiboan, and Uru-Puquina (Aikhenvald 1999).

Linguistic diversity and migrations

The Amazon basin displays a high degree of phylogenetic diversity, that is, a high number of non-demonstrably related linguistic groups. The region also scores highly in terms of diversity of linguistic structures and in the sheer number of languages or linguistic varieties still spoken, or formerly spoken.

The Global Prehistory of Human Migration: The Encyclopedia of Global Human Migration Volume 1,
First Edition. Edited by Peter Bellwood.
© 2013 John Wiley & Sons, Ltd. Published 2015 by John Wiley & Sons, Ltd.

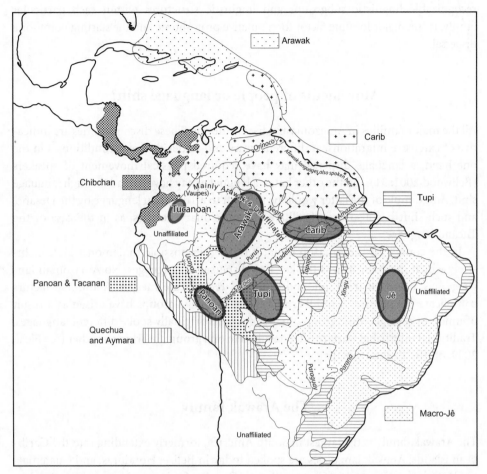

Figure 50.1 The six major language families of Amazonia and their possible homelands. The distributions are approximate and relate to the period before 1500 CE (many regions are Spanish- and Portuguese-speaking today).

For each extant family in Amazonia, we can expect to distinguish: (1) putative reconstructed routes for the dispersal of the family based on linguistic evidence, with an indication of the likely proto-home; (2) migrations of individual groups documented in oral histories; and (3) historically documented migrations (as reconstructed by Nimuendajú 1981).

Most migrations under (3) can be assigned a more or less reliable absolute date. The chronologies of migration types (1) and (2) are essentially relative. Since languages change at different rates, it is next to impossible to provide a reliable absolute dating for the time depth of individual proto-languages and prehistoric dispersals based on purely linguistic evidence (Dixon 1997: 46–49). However, linguistic diversity is typically greater in the homeland than in areas of colonial expansion. The extent of linguistic diversity, understood in terms of the relative genealogical time depths of recognizable linguistic subgroups and linguistic structures within each particular family, is the major locating factor for a putative proto-home and the starting point for a dispersal.

Movements of people or language shift?

All the major families in Amazonia are discontinuous. These discontinuities are indicative of extensive migrations, at different times and under different conditions. On the one hand, a language dispersal may have required physical movement of speakers (Bellwood 2001: 31). On the other hand, a language may have spread through language shift. An example of the latter would be the shift to a Tucanoan language by the Desano, and such shift has also been facilitated by missionary policies, as in the case of the Tucano language.

In the context of the Amazon basin, it is often impossible to demonstrate conclusively which mechanism was the key to a dispersal of languages. No Amazonian language has a written tradition, and historical records are meager. Additional factors complicate the picture. A number of current language groups have arisen as a result of union of several ethnic groups, many of whom originally spoke different languages. Traditional intertribal warfare often resulted in one group absorbing another (see Fleck 2009, on the Panoan groups).

The Arawak family

The Arawak family is the largest in South America, formerly extending into the Caribbean islands. Arawak languages are spoken today in Belize, Honduras, and Guatemala in Central America, and in Guyana, French Guyana, Suriname, Venezuela, Colombia, Peru, Brazil, and Bolivia (formerly extending into Argentina and Paraguay). There are about 40 extant Arawak languages in addition to several dozen that have become extinct since the European conquest.

This family is also known as Maipuran. The family got its name "Arawak" from the language known as Lokono Arawak, Arawak, or Lokono Dian (Guiana). Its second name is based on Maipure, formerly spoken in Venezuela. There is currently no doubt as to the limits of the Arawak family, and up-to-date sources avoid using the discredited term "Arawakan" (Aikhenvald 1999, 2002). The mechanisms of Arawak expansion may have included slave raids, and movements of population in search of further hunting and fishing opportunities, and slash-and-burn farmland.

The suggestion that the Proto-Arawak homeland was on the Upper Orinoco River was argued by Noble (1965) (see criticism in Lathrap 1970: 73). Following Lathrap (1970: 74–77), Oliver (1989: 93–107) argued for Arawak dispersal from the central Amazon floodplains northwards and southwards. His model was based on data from a random selection of individual languages, many not related to Arawak, and also application of lexicostatistical methods which have since been discredited. Alternative homeland suggestions include the Upper Vaupés area, the northern or central areas of Peru, or the headwaters of the Ucayali and Madre de Dios rivers (Urban 1992: 95).

The highest concentration of recorded Arawak languages is found in the region between the Negro and the Orinoco rivers. This is potentially a strong linguistic argument in favor of the Arawak proto-home having been located there (see Figure 50.1). This hypothesis is corroborated by the few mythical traditions of northern origin of Arawak-speaking peoples south of the Amazon. However, the diversity of Arawak languages south of the Amazon in central Peru, around the Rivers Purús and Madeira, must have been greater in the past than it is now. Due to mass extinction of languages this is hard to appreciate.

Migrations of Arawak speakers from the Caribbean coast to the Antilles are estimated archaeologically to have occurred from about 500 BCE (see chapter 49). The settlements of Arawak-speaking peoples south of the Amazon are also believed to be of considerable antiquity. Arawak peoples of the Xingu River basin were the earliest arrivals in that area (the arrival of Carib and Tupí groups there is estimated to be around the 17th century CE: Seki 1999: 219).

The Carib family

Carib languages are spoken in various locations to the north of the Amazon, in Colombian Amazonia, on the Orinoco River in Venezuela, and also in Guyana, French Guyana, Suriname and adjacent areas of Brazil, and in the region of the Upper Xingu and adjacent areas in Mato Grosso. The total number of living and extinct languages is about 43 (Derbyshire 1999; Meira 2009). The linguistic diversity of the three groups spoken south of the Amazon River appears to be greater than that in all the locations north of the Amazon. This has led researchers to suggest that the proto-home of the Carib family was located south of the Amazon (Derbyshire 1999). Villalón (1991) suggested that the centre of Carib dispersal was located in northern Venezuela (also see Urban 1992: 93–94), but her conclusion was based on a count of lexical similarities in a limited sample of languages.

The westernmost Carib-speaking group, the Carihona, probably migrated from the Guianas to the northwestern Amazon prior to the European conquest. Their current location is between the Caquetá and the Upper Vaupés river basins. The language shows linguistic affinities with other languages of the Guianas, which confirms the putative direction of migration (Derbyshire 1999).

The presence of Carib speakers in the Lesser Antilles was documented during the second voyage of Columbus, but there is little historically verifiable evidence in favor of Carib-speaking permanent settlement there in pre-contact times (Allaire 1980; Villalón 1991: 55–56). A mixed language, known as Island Carib, relates to the presence of Caribs on the Lesser Antilles, already settled by speakers of an Arawak language, Iñeri. The male speech employed lexical roots from the language called Carib (also known as Galibi or Karina: Hoff 1994) and grammatical forms from Iñeri. The female speech was fully Iñeri. This linguistic duality is believed to be the result of a military expansion of Caribs to the Antilles (Hoff 1994).

The Tupí family

The Tupí family is one of the largest in Amazonia, with at least 50 known members (Rodrigues 1999a, 2007; Jensen 1999; Gabas 2009). Nine of the ten Tupí branches are spoken in the Amazon basin. Five of these (Arikém, Mondé, Purubora, Ramaráma, and Tuparí) are spoken on the upper reaches of the Madeira River in the Brazilian state of Rondônia. A further four branches extend to the east and northeast: Awetí in the Upper Xingu area, Mawé in the lower reaches of the Tapajós River, Mundurukú on the Upper Tapajós, extending to the east to the middle course of the Xingú River up to Madeira, and Juruna on the lower and middle Xingu. The Tupí-Guaraní branch of the family is the largest in terms of number of languages, but linguistically rather uniform. It has just a few languages outside the Amazon basin.

The routes of Tupí expansion are the matter of some controversy. Early scholars attempting to determine the routes of migration and expansion did not draw a clear distinction between Tupí as a family, and Tupí-Guaraní as a branch of the family (Urban 1992, 1996; Rodrigues 2007; Noelli 2009). The high degree of linguistic diversity of Tupí branches between the Guaporé, the upper Madeira and the upper Aripuanã rivers suggests that this area is likely to have been the dispersal center of the family (Urban 1992; Rodrigues 1999a, 2007). However, a current archaeological model still places the homeland in the region of the confluence of the Madeira and Amazon rivers (Noelli 2009).

The dispersal of Tupí-Guaraní languages could have started in the area between the Madeira and Xingu rivers (Urban 1992: 92). The Tupí-Guaraní languages spoken south of the Guaporé River (e.g. Guarayo and Sirionó) are likely to have reached this region after a long migration down the Juruena and/or the Arinos into the Paraguay and La Plata basins. Some of the migrants eventually reached the Atlantic coast (Jensen 1999: 129–130; Rodrigues 2007).

There are examples of historically documented migrations within the Tupí family. The Cabahyba tribe lived on the Upper Tapajós in the 18th century. In the early 19th century they were attacked and decimated by the Mundurucú. The remainder were chased away and their descendants are the Kawahíb in the upper Rio Madeira. Speakers of Wayampi, the northernmost Tupí-Guaraní language, migrated from the lower course of the Xingú River to the Oiapoque River in the northern Brazilian state of Amapá, and to the Amarakarí River close to the border with French Guiana within the last 350 years, fleeing the Portuguese (Nimuendajú 1924: 204–211; Métraux 1927: 27–35; Nimuendajú 1981).

The spread of Tupinambá-based Tupí-Guaraní languages into northwest Amazonia and central Brazil was facilitated by missionaries. At the time of the European conquest, Tupinambá was the major language spoken on the Atlantic coast of Brazil up to the mouth of the Amazon. Creolized varieties of Tupinambá were adopted as "general" languages of European colonization. Lingua Geral Paulista is now extinct, and Lingua Geral Amazônica (Nhêengatú, meaning "good speech") is still spoken a little in the northeast of Amazonia, and the Upper Rio Negro (Rodrigues 1996).

The Jê branch of the Macro-Jê family

The distribution of Macro-Jê languages covers part of Brazilian Amazonia; most languages are or have been spoken in eastern and northeastern Brazil, with a few branches in central and southwestern Brazil (Rodrigues 1999b). The centre of dispersal of the Jê languages, which form the major branch of the Macro-Jê family, most likely lay outside Amazonia proper, perhaps in the savannas of central Brazil. The Jê peoples who now live in Amazonia entered from the east under pressure of the Portuguese invasion (Rodrigues 1999b; Ribeiro 2009).

The Panoan family

Panoan languages are spoken on the eastern side of the Andes, in Peru and adjacent areas of Brazil (state of Acre) and Bolivia (Loos 1973, 1999; Fleck 2009). The location of the proto-home of the Panoan peoples is believed to be between the headwaters of the Ucayali River and the Madre de Dios (Lathrap 1970: 80; Urban 1992: 97). The Panoans of the Ucayali basin, of the Juruá and the Purús rivers are believed to be relatively recent arrivals from the south. The direction of migration from south to north is supported by distribution of linguistically archaic features (Loos 1973; Erickson 1992: 244).

The Tucanoan family

The Tucanoan language family spans Brazil, Colombia, Ecuador, and northeastern Peru. West Tucanoan languages are spoken in southwestern Colombia along the Putumayo and Caquetá rivers, and along the Putumayo and Napo rivers in Ecuador and northeastern Peru. East Tucanoan languages are spoken in northwestern Brazil and the adjacent areas of Colombia, in the Vaupés river basin. East Tucanoan languages are structurally and lexically similar; their erstwhile genetic relationship may have been obscured by constant contact in the multilingual Vaupés River basin area (Aikhenvald 2002). Most scholars concur that Tucanoan languages are likely to have originated to the west of the Vaupés region, in the hilly regions closer to the Andes than to the main area of concentration of East Tucanoan languages today (Nimuendajú 1982; Urban 1992: 98; Aikhenvald 2002).

Minor language families

Historical-comparative studies of minor families indicate a trend to move towards big river basins. The proto-home of the small Arawá family is believed to have been located in the jungle area between the Purús and Juruá rivers, major southern tributaries of the Amazon. The Paumarí are the only Arawá group located on the banks of a major river, the Purús, and its tributaries the Tapaua and the Ituxí. They must have migrated towards the main river before contact (Dixon 2004). Members of the small Peba-Yagua family in northern Peru (consisting of extinct Peba and Yameo and the extant Yagua) migrated to the banks of the Amazon, as the original Tupí-Guaraní-speaking population there gradually declined (Peña 2009: 11–17, based on oral traditions and explorers' notes). Throughout the post-contact history of the Amazonian peoples, forced migrations into mission settlements have been a frequent practice, but this lies beyond the scope of the chapter.

SEE ALSO: 49 Caribbean islands: archaeology; 51 Amazonia: archaeology

References

Adelaar, W. (2004) *The Languages of the Andes*. Cambridge: Cambridge University Press.

Aikhenvald, A. (1999) The Arawak language family. In Dixon & Aikhenvald (1999b), pp. 65–105.

Aikhenvald, A. (2002) *Language Contact in Amazonia*. Oxford: Oxford University Press.

Aikhenvald, A. (2012) *Languages of the Amazon*. Oxford: Oxford University Press.

Allaire, L. (1980) On the historicity of Carib migrations in the Lesser Antilles. *American Antiquit* 45, 238–245.

Bellwood, P. (2001) Archaeology and language family origins. In A. Aikhenvald & R. Dixon (eds.), *Areal Diffusion and Genetic Inheritance. Problems in Comparative Linguistics*. Oxford: Oxford University Press, pp. 27–43.

Brown, K. & Ogilvie, S. (eds.) (2009) *Concise Encyclopedia of Languages of the World*. Oxford: Elsevier.

Carneiro da Cunha, M. (ed.) (1992) *História dos Índios do Brasil* [History of the Brazilian Indians]. São Paulo: Cia das Letras/FAPESP/SMC.

Derbyshire, D. (1999) Carib. In Dixon & Aikhenvald (1999b), pp. 125–164.

Dixon, R. (1997) *The Rise and Fall of Languages*. Cambridge: Cambridge University Press.

Dixon, R. (2004) Proto-Arawá phonology. *Anthropological Linguistics* 46, 1–83.

Dixon, R. & Aikhenvald, A. (1999a) Introduction. In Dixon & Aikhenvald (1999b), pp. 1–22.

Dixon, R. & Aikhenvald, A. (eds.) (1999b), *The Amazonian Languages*. Cambridge: Cambridge University Press.

Erickson, P. (1992) Uma singular pluralidade: a etno-história pano [A singular plurality: a Panoan ethnohistory]. In Carneiro da Cunha (1992), pp. 239–252.

Fleck, D. (2009) Panoan languages. In Brown & Ogilvie (2009), pp. 833–834.

Gabas, N., Jr. (2009) Tupí. In Brown & Ogilvie (2009), pp. 1105–1109.

Hoff, B. J. (1994) Island Carib, an Arawakan language which incorporated a lexical register of Cariban origin, used to address men. In P. Bakker & M. Mous (eds.) *Mixed languages: 15 case studies in language intertwining*. Amsterdam: IFOTT, pp. 161–168.

Jensen, C. (1999) Tupí-Guaraní. In Dixon & Aikhenvald (1999b), pp. 125–164.

Lathrap, D. (1970) *The Upper Amazon*. London: Thames & Hudson.

Loos, E. (1973) Algunas implicaciones de la reconstruccion de un fragmento de la gramatica del proto-pano [Some implications of the reconstruction of a fragment of the Proto-Pano grammar]. In E. Loos (ed.), *Estudios Panos II* [Pano studies II]. Yarinacocha: Instituto Lingüístico de Verano, pp. 263–282.

Loos, E. (1999) Pano. In Dixon & Aikhenvald (1999b), pp. 227–250.

Loukotka, C. (1968) *Classification of South American languages*. Los Angeles: Latin American Center, UCLA.

Meira, S. (2009) Cariban languages. In Brown & Ogilvie (2009), pp. 183–188.

Métraux, A. (1927) Migrations historiques des Tupí-Guaraní [Historical migrations of the Tupí-Guaraní]. *Journal de la Société des Américanistes* 19(1), 1–45.

Nimuendajú, C. (1924) Os índios Parintintin do Rio Madeira [The Parintintin Indians of the Madeira River]. *Journal de la Société des Américanistes de Paris* (n.s.) 16, 201–278.

Nimuendajú, C. (1981) *Mapa Etno-histórico do Brasil e Regiões Adjacentes* [An ethno-historic map of Brazil and adjacent regions]. Rio de Janeiro: IBGE.

Noble, G. (1965) *Proto-Arawakan and its Descendants*. Indiana University Research Center in Anthropology, Folklore and Linguistics, Publication 38. Bloomington: Indiana University.

Noelli, F. (2009) The Tupí expansion. In H. Silverman & W. Isbell (eds.), *Handbook of South American Archaeology*. New York: Springer, pp. 659–670.

Oliver, J. (1989) The archaeological, linguistic and ethnohistorical evidence for the expansion of Arawakan into Northwestern Venezuela and Northeastern Colombia. PhD thesis, Univeristy of Illinois.

Peña, J. (2009) A historical reconstruction of the Peba-Yaguan linguistic family. MA thesis, Department of Linguistics, University of Oregon.

Ribeiro, E. R. (2009) Macro-Jê. In Brown & Ogilvie (2009), pp. 665–669.

Rodrigues, A. (1996) As línguas gerais sul-americanas [The "general languages" of South America]. *Papia* 4(2), 6–18.

Rodrigues, A. (1999a) Tupí. In Dixon & Aikhenvald (1999b), pp. 107–124.

Rodrigues, A. (1999b) Macro-Jê. In Dixon &. Aikhenvald (1999b), pp. 156–206.

Rodrigues, A. (2007) Tupí languages in Rondônia and in Eastern Bolivia. In W. L. Wetzels (ed.), *Language Endangerment and Endangered Languages. Linguistic and Anthropological Studies with Special Emphasis on the Languages and Cultures of the Andean-Amazonian Border Area*. Leiden: CNWS, pp. 355–364.

Seki, L. (1999) The Upper Xingu as an incipient linguistic area. In Dixon & Aikhenvald (1999b), pp. 417–430.

Spix, J. & von Martius, C. (1831) *Reise in Brasilien in den Jahren 1817–1820* [Travels to Brazil in the years 1817–1820], vol. 3. Munich: Lindauer.

Urban, G. (1992) A história da cultura brasileira segundo as línguas nativas [The history of Brazilian culture according to indigenous languages]. In Carneiro da Cunha (1992), pp. 87–102.

Urban, G. (1996) On the geographical origins and dispersions of Tupian languages. *Revista de Antropologia* 39(2), 61–104.

Villalón, M. (1991) A spatial model of lexical relationshop among fourteen Cariban varieties. In M. Key (ed.), *Language Change in South American Indian Languages*. Philadelphia: University of Pennsylvania Press, pp. 54–94.

51

Amazonia: archaeology

Michael Heckenberger

This chapter complements chapter 50 and discusses the likely migration histories of the Tupí, Carib, Jê, and Arawak language families within the past three thousand years. It also describes the characteristic social features of the ethnolinguistic populations associated with these families.

Migrations were a critical aspect of indigenous history in Amazonia. Immense biocultural and historical diversity across the region indicates complex patterns of population movement and interaction. External influence and actual migrations from the Andean highlands were long thought to explain cultural development in Amazonia, or the lack thereof, spreading early ceramics, agriculture, and complex society during the so-called "Formative Period." Some scholars went so far as to suggest that lowland tropical forests were uninhabitable without agriculture (Bailey 1989), and that later complex societies which immigrated into Amazonia were destined to collapse, creating or reverting to a ubiquitous cultural pattern called the "tropical forest tribe" (Meggers & Evans 1957; Steward & Faron 1959; Meggers 1996). Recent research generally refutes these claims with substantial recent evidence for mid-Holocene settled occupations, some with incipient agriculture of native tuber and tree crops, and semi-intensive farming and political complexity in many areas during the Late Holocene.

Initial colonization of Amazonia occurred during the Late Pleistocene and Early Holocene. Subsequently, regionally distinctive cultural traditions developed during the mid-Holocene. By the onset of the Late Holocene, several broad cultural expansions can be suggested based on ethnolinguistic criteria. Early speakers of languages associated with the Arawak, Tupí-Guarani, Carib, and Jê language families, in particular, were widespread by 500–1 BCE (see chapter 50). Both migration and interaction played important roles in these distributions, particularly within broadly defined riverine (Arawak) and upland settings (Tupí-Guarani, Carib, and Jê) in Amazonia (see Figure 50.1).

The Global Prehistory of Human Migration: The Encyclopedia of Global Human Migration Volume 1, First Edition. Edited by Peter Bellwood.
© 2013 John Wiley & Sons, Ltd. Published 2015 by John Wiley & Sons, Ltd.

Numerous smaller families also form regional enclaves in the Amazon basin, such as Panoan, Tukanoan, Sanuma (Yanomamo), Chapakura, Mura, Yagua, Tikuna, and others. Regional trade languages or *lingua geral* also existed along the Amazon (Nheengatu Tupí-Guarani) and possibly elsewhere (southern Caribbean, Llanos de Mojos) in late pre-Columbian and historic times. The demise of the large agricultural polities along the Amazon and other major rivers during the colonial period created a vacuum into which many groups moved in historic times.

Amazonian ethno-linguistic diaspora

In an important paper in *Science*, Diamond and Bellwood (2003: 597) state that the dispersals of early agricultural populations "constitute collectively the most important process in Holocene human history." Major ethnolinguistic diaspora across the globe have often correlated with agricultural technologies. More specifically, the "farming/language hypothesis" suggests that early agricultural populations expanded rapidly due to adaptive advantages over foragers (see chapter 10). In tropical areas, these diaspora were heralded by innovations in settled life, agriculture, notably root-crop cultivation and arboriculture, regional social integration, and institutional hierarchy.

The Tupí-Carib-Jê macro-family

Rodrigues (1999) has suggested that the macro-Tupí (hereafter Tupí), macro-Jê and Carib language families shared a common origin in southern Amazonian transitional areas, based on shared lexical and other morphological features (Rodrigues 2000). A southern origin for the Carib family is supported by the presence of at least two languages, Bakairi and Upper Xingu, which are distinctive from one another and from the bulk of languages in northern Amazonia. Such a proto-language must lie deep in time, prior to the 3rd millennium BCE, making relations difficult to reconstruct, but the irregular morphological features shared by Tupí, Carib, and Jê suggest shared ancestry rather than later language contact. This broad phylum can be contrasted with the Arawak family, with likely origins in western Amazonia (Epps 2009; Walker & Riberio 2010). This has relevance for the development of two contrasting cultural trajectories: Arawak in riverine settings and Tupí-Carib-Jê in the uplands.

Tupí family

Internal relations within Tupí suggest a homeland in southwestern Amazonia (see Figure 50.1). Three of the eight or more subgroups became widely spread across southern Amazonia, including Juruna, Mundurucu, and Tupí-Guarani. The latter became the most widely distributed family, extending from the Paraguay River to north of the Amazon, and from coastal areas of Brazil to the western Amazon. Reconstructions suggest that an upland horticultural adaptation was typical of Tupian groups, likely based on forest and house gardening of diverse crops, typical of many historically known Tupí speakers. Brochado's (1984) "pincer hypothesis" suggests a two-pronged migration of Guarani to the south along Paraguay River into southern Brazilian coastal areas and a northern expansion of Tupí across the tropical forest uplands of the southern Amazon and then along the forested Atlantic coast. Their distribution forms a wide ring in forested areas on the flanks of the open central Brazilian plateau.

Lathrap (1970), following Rodrigues (1958), concluded that the Polychrome archaeological tradition, like the preceding Amazonian Barrancoid (Arawak) tradition, represented a population expansion of Tupí speakers out of the middle Amazon. This challenged the view of Meggers and Evans (1957) that the Polychrome tradition represented a downriver migration from the Andes. More recent work on existing languages and materials from extinct languages supports the view that Tupí populations were late arrivals along the Amazon River, coincident with the appearance of the Polychrome tradition. Neves (2008) recently suggested a possible late movement from southern Amazonia, marking a major Tupian influence on the central Amazon (Guarita Polychrome). The Kokama language was a late Pre-Columbian Tupian incursion into the Upper Amazon, perhaps related to Tupinamba speakers who arrived in the Middle Amazon in historic times (Rodrigues 1999).

In southern Amazonia and the Atlantic tropical forests, there is an obvious correlation between the distribution of Tupí-Guarani languages and the "Tupí-guaraní" ceramic tradition of southern Amazonia, eastern Brazil, and adjacent areas (Brochado 1984; Noelli 1998). The early evidence for this complex comes from coastal Brazil, near Rio de Janeiro, where it dates to around 2,000 years ago (Scheel et al. 2010), suggesting that the family had expanded by this time far beyond the proposed southern Amazonian homeland (Urban 1992). After this time, some Tupí-Guarani groups along the coasts of Brazil developed large populations in substantial villages, especially in the forested areas of coastal Brazil, the Paraguay River, and southern Amazonia.

It has been suggested that the pre-Columbian polities in the Lower Amazon were the results of mixing speakers of different language families, with distinctive material culture, including Tupí-Guarani (painted pottery), Arawak (modeled and linear incised pottery), and Carib (incised with chevron and other geometric designs) (Neves 2008). In historical times, confederations of diverse multilingual groups, including Tupian enclaves such as Chiriguano (Bolivia) and Mbya (Paraguay River), were present in southern Amazonia, and mixed with Arawak speakers in the linguistic contact zone in southwestern Amazonia. The Juruna and Mundurucu confederacies and the powerful Pacajás confederacy that dominated the lower reaches of the southern tributaries of the Amazon (Tapajós, Xingu, and Tocantins) also represented entrepôts in regional political economies, organized by political rivalry, ritual performance, and exchange of persons, as well as economic goods. Regional trade languages, such as historic period Tupian Nheengatu, were present by late pre-Columbian times.

One of the most remarkable features of Tupian populations, particularly members of the Tupí-Guarani family, is their shared features of cosmology and worldview. Although quite varied in expression, regional political economies were based on the symbolic alterity of individual communities and outsiders based on social relations of predation and incorporation (Viveiros de Castro 1992), including warfare and ritual exo-cannibalism (Whitehead 2009), trophy taking of enemies' bones, for example, Juruna skull flutes or Mundurucu heads (Menget 1993), and rituals of familiarization (Fausto 1998). Southeastern groups, notably Mundurucu, Tapirape, and Kamayura, are still notable for their plaza ritual life, also typical of "macro-Jê" groups of the adjacent central Brazilian plateau (*cerrado*), as well as the Tupinamba in coastal Brazil. The diversity among Tupí-Guarani peoples noted by Viveiros de Castro (1992: 5) was also typical of the "equally metamorphic Carib."

Carib family

There are few extant Carib speakers in southern Amazonia, but those who do survive there (not shown separately in Figure 50.1) are only distantly related to the main group of Carib speakers centered on the Guiana plateau. They include a northern group (Arara-Ikpeng), a southeastern group (Bakairi-Upper Xingu), and a southwestern group (Palmella). Despite the postulated early movement of southern Carib into northern Amazonia, perhaps along the Xingu River corridor, the major dispersal of Carib languages occurred in the general area of the Guiana plateau, where the majority of the historically known Carib languages occur.

Carib occupations in the lower-middle Amazon are suggested by common ceramics in areas dominated by speakers of the family, notably the Konduri tradition along the Trombetas River and Araquin-related ceramics in adjacent areas of the Guianas. These were elaborated into the baroque ceramic styles that reached their apogee in the related Santarém tradition of the Lower Tapajós, although this area and others were clearly composed of diverse groups. A pre-Columbian Carib presence in the Lower Xingu is suggested by incised chevron designs characteristic of these other industries. Lathrap (1970) referred to the "Carib invasion" of the middle to lower Amazon from the Guianas, associated with Konduri and Santarém in late pre-Columbian times, c.1000 CE, but further research suggests more substantial time depth in the southern Amazon, making dispersal areas and the directions of movement less certain (see chapter 50). Of note, the production of Konduri-related ceramics and late chevron-incised designs by Carib-speaking pottery-making groups in the Upper Xingu complicates questions of directionality, but still suggests actual population movements.

In northern areas, Carib expansions have been associated with post-Saladoid (Kayo) ceramics in the Lesser Antilles and the Arauquin and Koriabo ceramic traditions in the Orinoco basin and the Guianas. Boomert (2000) suggests that the Kayo complex represents a population movement of Carib speakers, which spread new patterns of settlement, land use, and technology. In both cases, substantial interaction and pluralism is described between Carib, Arawak, and other groups in historical times (Whitehead 1988).

Carib-speaking peoples of the Guianas were long considered as typical "tropical forest tribes" (e.g. Steward & Faron 1959; Meggers 1996). The assumption that ethnographic groups represented an ancient adaptation to upland forests is still widely accepted within what has been described as a "domestic economy of intimacy" (Viveiros de Castro 1996; Overing & Passes 2000). While sharing certain features (Basso

1977), Carib-speaking groups are noted for their wide sociopolitical diversity, and especially for the several large regional confederations known from early historic times, notably in the southern Caribbean. Recent research documents the great variability in social form and historical process, including major disruptions after 1492. Even in upland areas, regional integration of some groups in the historic period suggests stable political alliances or even small polities, as was true of coastal and upland Carib groups in early colonial times (Whitehead 1988; Duin 2009). In a variety of cases, plural regional social formations, including Carib speakers, were linked in regional political economies. In several cases, cultural and linguistic admixture is preserved in the gender diglossia of extant Caribbean Arawak languages, with distinctive Carib and Arawak features.

Jê family

The languages of the macro-Jê family are distributed largely outside Amazonia, mainly in the central Brazilian uplands and eastern Brazil, principally related to the Jê sub-group, including northern (Mekranoti) and southern (Panara) Kayapo, Suya, Apinaye, Kraho, and other groups (Maybury-Lewis 1978). The earliest circular plaza villages, clearly associated with ancestors of macro-Jê groups, appeared in the western areas of central Brazil (Uru tradition) by 800 CE and in the eastern highland areas (Aratu and Mossamedes traditions) by 1200 CE (Prous 1992). This circular plaza village orientation may reflect proximity to Arawak groups, as also for Carib and Tupí-Guarani groups in southern Amazonia. In some instances, disparate groups formed stable communities and regional alliances, particularly when they spoke related languages. In historic times these included large heterarchical confederacies and, in some cases (northern Kayapo, Karaja, and Bororo), hierarchical systems of sociality and value. The settlement sizes of Jê speakers ranged from small mobile groups to large villages, such as an ancestral northern Kayapo (Pikotati) village with a population estimated to hold several thousand people and 19th-century Apinaye villages with over 1,500 inhabitants (Posey 1994). Such large villages with their plazas and social hierarchies were no doubt in part tied to historical and social relations with other groups, notably the southern Arawak, as well as other members of macro-Jê, such as the Bororo, Erikpatsa, and Karajá, spread across the headwater areas of southern Amazonia.

Arawak family

This was the most widely distributed language family in the Americas in 1492. With the exception of the Intermediate Area (southern Central America and northwest South America), Arawak languages were present across the lowland forests of the neotropics, including four major subdivisions: northern Arawak, including the Caribbean (see chapter 49); central Arawak; southern Arawak; and pre-Andine Arawak. Arawak speakers settled territories in these areas by the 1st millennium BCE, and still occupy them in many cases today, typically focusing on riverine or maritime settings. No genetic relations between Arawak and other language families are generally accepted, although diverse relations with peoples speaking other languages were common. The origin area of proto-Arawak is also disputed, but most agree that it lay in western Amazonia, broadly speaking (Epps 2009; Walker & Ribeiro 2010).

Max Schmidt (1917) wrote the definitive anthropological work on the Arawak-speaking peoples, although it was largely ignored as a model for lowland South American cultural development. His work, an early progenitor of historical ecology, was also clear on the importance of colonialism in shaping the recent history of the Amazon. Schmidt's general observation that Arawak-speaking societies share a variety of features not widely shared by the other major language families is still widely accepted among regional specialists today (Hill & Santos Granero 2002; Heckenberger 2005; Eriksen 2011). Arawak-speaking peoples are distinctive from Tupian, Carib, and Jê groups, notably in their river orientation, settled agricultural lifeways and domesticated landscapes, their tendency to form regional aggregates, and institutional forms of socio-symbolic hierarchy.

Several features of Arawak societies merit emphasis: (1) developed agricultural technology and wetland management; (2) a common tendency to rank by birth order and ancestors, especially founding ancestors; (3) status rivalry, including control over prestige goods and other symbolic capital through control of public space and rituals; (4) regional integration, including formalized trade and ritual. Lathrap (1970) shared Schmidt's view that Amazonia was a major hearth for complex societies, commonly defined by known Arawak historical groups and their immediate pre-Columbian ancestors.

Ceramic assemblages associated with the Amazonian Barrancoid or Incised Rim traditions are widely considered to reflect a presence of early Arawak-speaking groups, particularly during their initial diaspora at c.500 BCE–500 CE. Circular plaza villages and related Saladoid ceramics appeared in the Caribbean islands about 500 BCE (Boomert 2000; chapter 49, this volume). In central Amazonia, occupations with Incised-Rim or Amazonian Barrancoid pottery appeared over two millennia ago. Clear evidence for forest and raised field agriculture and wetland management were important during the past two millennia in areas historically dominated by Arawak speakers, many with demonstrable continuity with later archaeological cultures.

In historical times, cultural pluralism was an important feature of Amazonia, with various Arawak-Carib, Arawak-Tukano, Arawak-Pano, and, in the southern Amazon, Arawak-Tupí-Guarani and multi-ethnic clusters. Along the Amazon itself, relations were no less plural and, indeed, by 1492, most regions were pluri-ethnic. Arawak speakers and culturally related peoples tended to dominate the rivers and coasts, where larger settled population aggregates were concentrated. Hornborg (2005) suggested that language shift, as described from later periods (chapter 50, this volume), and possibly even a trade language may explain the wide distribution of the Arawak family. Extensive interactions between river and maritime focused Arawak and with other groups in regional systems are widely recognized by specialists, but as morphologically complex agglutinating languages, it seems unlikely that the proto-language was formed as a trade language. Furthermore, such an interpretation suggests that diverse languages in riverine and coastal settings and uplands changed quickly across a vast area, including basic changes in the transmission of non-linguistic features of material culture, built environment, and basic bodily disposition.

Conclusion: ecology, movement, and interaction

Contrary to traditional models of pristine nature and culturally uniform tropical forest tribes in Amazonia, recent work documents immense cultural, ecological, and historical variation. Migration, exchange, and pluralism were typical from the earliest times. Late Holocene developments comparable to other tropical forest regions across the globe are notable, especially the ethnolinguistic diasporas of early agriculturalists. The Arawak diaspora, in particular, appears to have reflected developments in settled farming and hierarchical lifeways similar to the Bantu and Austronesian diasporas of Africa and the Pacific respectively (see chapters 12, 13, 35, and 36), and during a similar time span (1500–1 BCE).

The four major ethnolinguistic diaspora in Amazonia differed significantly in terms of the processes of migration, cultural contact, and subsequent cultural development. By the 1st millennium BCE these diaspora were already becoming differentiated, but continued to share common features within language clusters. Two broad ecological adaptations, associated with riverine (Arawak) and upland (Tupí-Carib-Jê) groups, expanded quickly. Overall, there was (and still is) immense cultural variation across the region, including cultural and linguistic mixing between the major language families and numerous small families and "isolates," although seldom developing into broad translocation pidgins (e.g. Nheengatu). Some societies, such as the floodplain groups or those of the northern and southern borderlands, became large and powerful, and others in northwestern Amazonia constructed a regional society that linked Amazonian and Orinoco sociopolitical networks, while others remained relatively small, mobile, and only loosely integrated with other groups.

Ecology, regional geopolitics, sociality and rivalry in and between communities, and historical contingency, all played important roles in the internal developments and regional dynamics of these societies. All groups were engaged in extensive trade and interaction. Patterns of interaction varied greatly from region to region across the Amazon based on local and contingent factors and also varied through time, showing temporally distinctive patterning particularly associated with the major temporal periods from the region and differing in many areas from ethnographically documented groups heavily impacted by colonialism. Recent work emphasizes the diverse way that groups settled into landscapes and, in turn, these were modified by patterned human actions. Nonetheless, well-contextualized studies of cultural and language groups within trajectories of dynamic change in coupled natural-human systems, including rather than excluding people, are generally rare. Comparisons from ethnography, detached from careful historical or archaeological analysis, continue to dominate characterizations of the Amazonian past.

SEE ALSO: 10 Neolithic migrations: food production and population expansion; 49 Caribbean Islands: archaeology; 50 Amazonia: linguistic history; 52 Andes: linguistic history

References

Bailey, R., Head, G., Jenike, M., et al. (1989) Hunting and gathering in tropical rain forest: is it possible? *American Anthropologist* 91, 59–82.

Basso, E. (ed.) (1977) *Carib-Speaking Indians: Culture, Society, and Language*. Tuscon: University of Arizona Press.

Boomert, A. (2000) *Trinidad, Tobago and the Lower Orinoco Interaction Sphere: An Archaeological/ Ethnohistorical Study*. Alkmaar, The Netherlands: Cairi Publications.

Brochado, J. (1984) An ecological model of the spread of pottery and agriculture into Eastern South America. Unpublished PhD dissertation, University of Ilinois, Urbana-Champaign.

Diamond, J. & Bellwood, P. (2003) Farmers and their languages: the first expansions. *Science* 300, 597–603.

Duin, R. (2009) Wayana socio-political landscapes: multi-scalar regionality and temporality in Guiana. Unpublished PhD dissertation, University of Florida, Gainesville.

Epps, P. (2009) Language classification, language contact, and Amazonian prehistory. *Language and Linguistics Compass* 3, 581–606.

Eriksen, L. (2011) *Nature and Culture in Prehistoric Amazonia: Using G.I.S. to Reconstruct Ancient Ethnogenetic Processes from Archaeology, Linguistics, Geography, and Ethnohistory*. Lund Studies in Human Ecology 12. Lund, Sweden: Lund University.

Fausto, C. (1998) Of enemies and pets: warfare and Shamanism in Amazonia. *American Ethnologist* 26, 933–956.

Heckenberger, M. (2005) *The Ecology of Power: Personhood, Place, and Culture in the Southern Amazon, AD 1000–2000*. New York: Routledge.

Hill, J. & Santos Granero, F. (2002).*Comparative Arawakan Histories: Rethinking Culture Area and Language Group in Amazonia*. Champaign-Urbana: University of Illinois Press.

Hornborg, A. (2005) Ethnogenesis, regional integration, and ecology in prehistoric Amazonia: toward a system perspective. *Current Anthropology* 46, 4.

Lathrap, D. (1970) *The Upper Amazon*. London: Praeger.

Maybury-Lewis, D. (ed.) (1978) *The Gê-Bororo of Central Brazil*. Cambridge, MA: Harvard University Press.

Meggers, B. (1996) *Amazonia: Man and Culture in a Counterfeit Paradise*. Washington, DC: Smithsonian.

Meggers, B. & Evans, C. (1957) *Archaeological Investigations at the Mouth of the Amazon*. Washington, DC: Smithsonian.

Menget, P. (1993) Notas sobre as Cabeças Munduruku [Notes on the Mundurucu heads]. In E. Veiveiros de Castro & M. Carneiro da Cunha (eds.), *Amazônia: Etnologia e História Indígena* [Amazonia: ethnology and indigenous history]. São Paulo: Universidade de São, pp. 311–321.

Neves, E. (2008) Ecology, ceramic chronology, and distribution, long-term history, and political change in the Amazonian floodplain. In H. Silverman & I. Isbell (eds.), *Handbook of South American Archaeology*. New York: Springer, pp. 359–379.

Noelli, F. (1998) The Tupí: explaining origin and expansions in terms of archaeology and of historical linguistics. *Antiquity* 72, 648–663.

Overing, J. & Passes, A. (2000) *The Anthropology of Love and Anger: The Aesthetics of Conviviality in Native Amazonia*. London: Routledge.

Posey, D. (1994) Environmental and social consequences of pre- and post-contact situations on Brazilian Indians: the Kayapó and a new Amazonian synthesis. In A. C. Roosevelt (ed.), *Amazonians Indians from Prehistory to the Present*. Tuscon: Arizona, pp. 271–286.

Prous, A. (1992) *Arqueologia Brasileira* [Brazilian archaeology]. Brasília, DF: Universidade de Brasilia.

Rodrigues, A. (1958) Classification of Tupí-Guarani. *International Journal of American Linguistics* 24, 231–234.

Rodrigues, A. (1999) The Tupí. In R. Dixon & A. Aikhenvald (eds.), *The Amazonian Languages.* Cambridge: Cambridge University Press, pp. 107–124.

Rodrigues, A. (2000) "Ge–Pano–Carib" X "Jê–Tupí–Karib": sobre relaciones lingüísticas prehistóricas en Sudamérica ["Ge-Pano-Carib" X "Jê-Tupí-Carib": prehistoric linguistic relations in South America]. *Actas del I Congreso de Lenguas Indígenas de Sudamérica* I, 95–104.

Schmidt, M. (1917) *Die Aruaken* [The Arawaks]. Veit: Leipzig.

Sheel, R., Macario, K., Buarque, A., et al. (2010) A new age to an old site: the earliest Tupí-Guarani settlement in Rio de Janeiro State? *Annais da Academia Brasileira de Ciências* 80, 763–770.

Steward, J. & Faron, L. (1959) *Native Peoples of South America.* New York: McGraw-Hill.

Urban, G. (1992) A História da Cultura Brasileira Segundo as Línguas Nativas [Brazilian cultural history through the lens of native languages]. In M. Carneiro da Cunha (ed.), *História dos Índios no Brasil* [History of the Brazilian Indians]. São Paulo: Companhia das Letras, pp. 87–102.

Viveiros de Castro, E. (1992) *From the Enemy's Point of View: Humanity and Divinity in an Amazonian Tribe.* Chicago: Chicago University Press.

Viveiros de Castro, E. (1996) Images of Nature and Society in Amazonia. *Annual Review of Anthropology* 25, 179–200.

Walker, R. & Ribeiro, L. (2010) Bayeseian phylogeographic of the Arawak expansion in lowland South America. *Proceedings of the Royal Society B* 278, 2562–2567.

Whitehead, N. (1988) *Lords of the Tiger Spirit: A History of the Caribs in Venezuela and Guyana, 1498–1820.* Dordrecht: Foris.

52

Andes: linguistic history

Paul Heggarty and David Beresford-Jones

This chapter focuses on the two major indigenous language families of the central Andes: Quechua and Aymara. The (pre)histories of their origins, expansions, divergence, and convergence are compared with the Andean archaeological record, considered in further detail also in the next chapter.

The indigenous languages of the Andes offer unique insights into migrations long before recorded history. Quechua, for instance – by number of speakers our greatest surviving link to the speech of the New World before European conquest – includes outposts so far-flung as to attest unfailingly to great migrations of some form (Figure 52.1). The exact story that language data tell here, however, turns out to challenge many a long-held assumption about migrations in Andean prehistory. Associating Quechua uniquely with the Incas is but a popular myth and anachronism. Quechua is not a single language, but a broader family of related but mutually unintelligible tongues. *Cuzco-Bolivian* Quechua is quite distinct from the *Ecuadoran* "Quichua" language, for instance; even more so from the Quechua language(s) of Central Peru. These contrasts attest to migrations very different in their time depths and origin points.

Language spreads *may* reflect physical migrations of populations, but by no means necessarily always do (see ch. 11). Major language dispersals are typically a mix of migrations of speakers, and of other populations staying put but switching to a different language, associated with some prestigious cultural complex that is doing the expanding, rather than an actual population.

In the Americas, language decline and extinction themselves have largely tracked the progression of the *net* demographic impact on given regions of incoming migrants from Europe. Native languages have survived well only in two types of context. One is where European immigration remained thin or nil until relatively recently, as in remote parts of the Arctic, sub-Arctic, Amazonia, or the Chaco. The other is where native populations were and remained dense enough not to be swamped by incoming ones,

The Global Prehistory of Human Migration: The Encyclopedia of Global Human Migration Volume 1,
First Edition. Edited by Peter Bellwood.

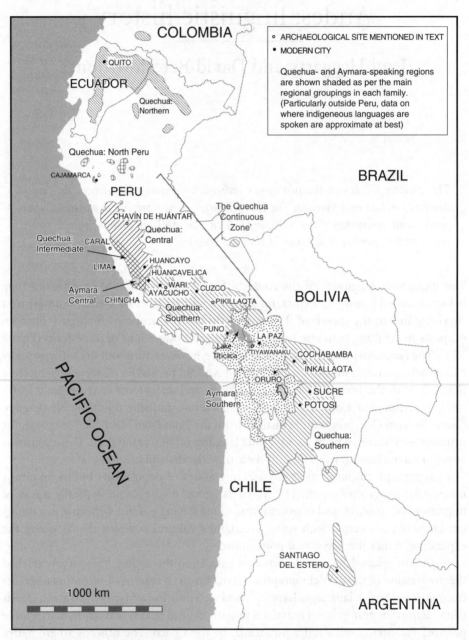

Figure 52.1 Present-day distributions of the Quechua and Aymara language families, and archaeological sites mentioned in the text.

especially in the agricultural heartlands of pre-Columbian civilization: Mesoamerica and the Central Andes.

The central core

Incas – or Spaniards?

The linguist's clearest signs of past migrations are language enclaves that stand isolated at great distances from their nearest linguistic relatives. In good part responsible for these – though in ways far less straightforward than is often assumed – was the final and most widespread of all incarnations of Andean civilization, short-lived though it was: Tawantinsuyu, alias the Inca empire.

Quechua, beyond its original "Continuous Zone" (Figure 52.1), also leapfrogged other native languages to both north and south, so at least *some* population of Quechua-speakers must have traveled to each region. Tellingly, the Quechua spoken in southern Bolivia derives fairly straightforwardly from that spoken around Cuzco in Inca or early colonial times. The Incas certainly fortified lower-lying regions like Cochabamba; garrisons such as those at Inkallaqta likely brought in significant early contingents of Quechua speakers. The Quechua pocket even further south, around Santiago del Estero in northwest Argentina, is also derived essentially from Cuzco. Certain traits, however, hark back to the Quechua of central Peru instead, suggesting an incoming population drawn in part from there too – perhaps expeditionary troops either recruited by the Incas, or accompanying early Spanish forays here (see Adelaar 1995; DeMarrais 2012).

Indeed, it is by no means certain that the Incas played the primary role in these southernmost migrations. It is no accident that within the core Quechua-speaking region in Bolivia lies Potosí, to whose silver mines the early Spanish colonial regime drafted tens of thousands of Indian laborers over many decades. Drawn from the entire archbishopric of Cuzco, most of it far to the north, it is their forced migrations that offer the most convincing explanation for how a Cuzco-like form of Quechua could have established itself so firmly here.

The Spaniards were in fact co-opting here a pre-existing Inca institution: the *mit'a*, a "turn" of duty (i.e. a rotating draft), whether for military service or as labor for public works. A second, separate Inca policy resulted even more directly in forced migrations, of so-called *mitma* populations – literally "outsider" or "newcomer" groups, or in modern parlance effectively "(im)migrant" populations.

The particular circumstances of the later years of Inca rule may well have entailed such migrations of one sort or another, especially to Ecuador, significant enough to account for Quechua's otherwise puzzlingly strong presence there. Tawantinsuyu had become increasingly articulated around not just Cuzco but also a new secondary capital and court in Quito, whose attendant institutions presumably entailed significant movement of people there from elsewhere in the Andes. In 1532, the empire was only just emerging from a civil war and succession struggle between these two centers when the Spaniards captured, and within the year executed, the last Inca emperor, Atawallpa. So abrupt and bewildering was Tawantinsuyu's downfall that it perhaps froze in place further, unplanned "migrations": hosts of troops, and others in the empire's service, left stranded thousands of kilometers from home.

Crucially though, unlike the Quechua of Bolivia or Argentina, that of Ecuador cannot be derived from Cuzco speech. Rather, it is closest to the Quechua language presumed to have been once spoken on the south-central coast of Peru, hence a long-standing alternative hypothesis that looks instead to the regional trading power here in the centuries before the Incas, namely Chincha. Relying heavily on an interpretation of Chincha commerce as seaborne, Torero (1984) proposed that its form of Quechua thus "migrated" as a language of trade, northwards along the Peruvian coast and then somehow high into the Ecuadoran Andes. Hocquenghem (2012), however, dismisses any such trade, given extremely adverse prevailing winds and currents. Overall, the most coherent scenario seems one of *mitma* migration(s) directly into the Ecuadoran highlands during Inca times, but of populations drawn predominantly from the Chincha region, rather than from Cuzco itself.

Quite how substantial such migration(s) may have been remains unclear. For Ecuadoran Quechua also bears telltale traces of language shift, typical of a lingua franca learnt by various existing populations, each originally speaking a different native tongue (see Cerrón-Palomino 2003: 343–344). Strong ethnic identities and ethnonyms duly continue even among Ecuadoran highland populations who today all speak Quechua. Their original linguistic diversity (Adelaar 2004: 166), once unified under powerful Inca control, makes for a scenario of precisely the type in which significant shift towards an immigrant language can occur (see Heggarty & Renfrew, forthcoming a: §5.9). Moreover, here too Quechua seems to have continued consolidating even under the Spaniards, thanks to their preference for it as a single common language of communication with the Indian population (not least for evangelization). Finally, especially in Ecuador but sporadically as far as Bolivia, highlanders migrating down the eastern slopes of the Andes have spread their Quechua (or in the south, also Aymara) into the Amazon lowlands, mostly in historical times.

Elsewhere, other isolated pockets of Quechua are often enthusiastically taken as traces of *mitma* migrations. Of these claims, most plausible are those in regions where the language does not otherwise seem ever to have been widely established, not least the Quechua enclaves of Chachapoyas, Cajamarca and Inkawasi in northern Peru (see Heggarty 2007: 331–332).

Before the Incas

Language migrations in the Andes are far from an Inca story alone, however. Their rule came much too late to have been the major player in the initial rise of the Quechua or Aymara language families, for the core diversity within each dates back a millennium or more before them (Heggarty 2007: 321–324). Peeling back the Inca era expansions leaves Quechua occupying only its Continuous Zone (and not yet quite so far south as Titicaca), plus perhaps the isolated outposts in far northern Peru. This is still a thousand kilometers of tortured mountain topography, however, over which the language had somehow dispersed in relatively short order.

We can also make out a second, underlying layer across much of the same territory: Aymara. This too is a language *family*: the Aymara of the Altiplano today is just one of its members; others survived into early Spanish colonial times in enclaves across southwestern Peru. Aymara place names remain widespread here, and are tentatively identified as far as the central-northern highlands. The little-known "Central Aymara" language (alias Jaqaru/Kawki) is spoken to this day in the highlands immediately southeast of Lima. The Quechua of Cuzco itself is laced with Aymara substrate traces. So despite present-day popular associations, the early distributions of both families in fact point to homelands far to the northwest of Lake Titicaca or even Cuzco. So too does the intense convergence (but not common origin) between them since the earliest stages of their expansion histories.

We thus have two major language-family dispersals to explain, logically through the most significant expansive processes observable in archaeology too – namely, the Andean "horizon" phenomena. The Incas constituted the Late Horizon, whose own significant linguistic impacts we have just seen. Over the preceding one to two millennia, the plausible time span for the initial spreads of Quechua and Aymara, and over broadly corresponding territorial extents, two previous horizons are visible. There are various competing hypotheses as to which polities through Andean prehistory spoke and spread which language lineage(s) (surveyed in Heggarty & Beresford-Jones 2012a). Our own proposal is straightforward: Quechua spread with the Middle Horizon, centered on Wari in the south-central highlands of Peru; in doing so it eclipsed the Aymara left by the Early Horizon, focused on Chavín further to the north (see Figure 52.1). All hypotheses do at least agree that Wari is a prime candidate for propelling *some* major language expansion(s) in the Andes – whether of Quechua, Aymara, or both.

But does any of this prove *migrations*? On first principles and known historical precedents (Heggarty & Renfrew, forthcoming b: §4), the scale and completeness of the main Andean language dispersals incline towards a stronger rather than weaker view of what the Wari and Chavín phenomena really were. They suggest that either powerful and rapid demic diffusion, or significant full-blown migration (forced or otherwise), was a key feature of Andean prehistory long before the Incas (see chapter 53).

The main surviving Aymara language today is spoken in the Altiplano region around and especially south of Lake Titicaca. This superficial match has led to another popular but anachronistic assumption (e.g. Browman 1994), namely that Tiyawanaku was the homeland of the Aymara lineage, and responsible for its expansion over a millennium ago.[1]

Many independent lines of linguistic and (ethno)historical data make this assumption "linguistically speaking, unsustainable" (Cerrón-Palomino 2000: 132), and point to a homeland much further northwest instead. Even as late as the early colonial period, language distributions in the Altiplano were quite different from today's. A better candidate for the language of Tiyawanaku is Puquina (Cerrón-Palomino 2012). What remains unsure is quite when and how Aymara reached the Altiplano from further north, though its minimal dialectal diversity doubtless cannot date to earlier than the Late Intermediate Period, or even (early) Inca times. One obvious candidate for facilitating long-range language "migrations" across highland southern Peru and the Titicaca basin would have been mobile camelid pastoralism (Lane 2011). Migrations, forced or otherwise, as well as language shift, seem to have helped Aymara continue spreading here even through Inca and post-Columbian times.

Distant origins: convergence, agriculture, and intensification

For times before the Early Horizon, linguistics offers no evidence of migrations: no wider relationships in broader, deeper-time families. An old hypothesis that Quechua and Aymara themselves might go back to a common "Quechumara" origin is now widely rejected (see Beresford-Jones & Heggarty 2012: 23–25). Rather, the picture is not of any great family, but of parallels only in broad language structure across an Andean language area (Torero 2002: 518–541). This background bears no marks of migrations and divergence, but a core-and-periphery convergence pattern instead, echoing more network-like and "down-the-line" models of interaction in archaeology (Heggarty & Renfrew, forthcoming b). It seems more compatible with a fairly stable, long-term scenario of groups in relative balance, between whom local-level contact was the rule, along extensive chains articulated by rolling bilingualism and thus language convergence. The "institutions of complementarity" so peculiar to the Andes (see chapter 53) would seem a highly plausible context. The lack of a single great, deep-time language family suggests that no one player had especially dominant reach across the others on any level that might drive an expansive "language migration" of the scale seen in later periods. To link the Pre-Ceramic societies of the Norte Chico on Peru's north-central coast, including the famous Caral, with Quechua *expansion* is another anachronism (Heggarty & Beresford-Jones 2010: 179). There is no linguistic evidence of any significant expansive migrations at this stage.

At first sight this would seem to challenge the general farming/language dispersal hypothesis (Bellwood & Renfrew 2002), for agriculture began here as early as anywhere, but without any contemporary language spread. Farming in the Andes followed a trajectory very different to the Old World, however. Key thresholds of intensification, able to propel major population and language dispersals, were not crossed here until relatively late, at time depths much more in line with the expansions of the main Andean language families. The rise of the Horizon societies might itself be in part associated with step gains in agricultural productivity, perhaps involving maize in particular (see Heggarty and Beresford-Jones, 2010).

Further afield, deeper in time

Outside the core zone of Andean civilization, most significant is Chibchan. While best known through the language encountered by the Spaniards across the central Colombian highlands in Cundinamarca and Boyacá, Chibchan too is actually a broad family. Its member languages lie scattered through northern Colombia, and are at their most diverse in southern Central America, hypothesized therefore as the original homeland out of which at least some migration(s) must have emanated. Quite what might have driven Chibchan expansion, and precisely when (around five thousand years ago?) remain largely matters of speculation, however (e.g. Constenla Umaña 1990). Certainly, there is no evidence that Chibchan ever reached into, let alone connected, the heartlands of Mesoamerican and Andean civilization. Our knowledge of pre-Columbian languages elsewhere in the northern Andes is similarly limited, although various Carib languages do attest to long-range migrations deep into Colombia from that family's presumed homeland in the Guyana Shield (see chapter 50).

In the southern Andes, too, our data are sparse, save for Mapuche (alias Araucanian or Mapudungun). The Mapuche homeland appears to have lain around and south of the Maule River in Chile, where their resistance set the southern bounds to Inca expansion. Mapuche dialectal diversity supports interpretations of migrations eastwards through the Andes, though only a few centuries ago, into enclaves across the Pampas, pressurizing native tongues of Patagonia such as Tehuelche (Heggarty & Renfrew, forthcoming c; Adelaar 2004).

Further afield still, many a grand claim has been staked for language relationships that supposedly attest to migrations of the most spectacular kind, between the Andes and other distant parts of the Americas. In reality, however, the claimed correspondences all too often turn out to be simply "faces in the fire." Two language lineages of the Bolivian Altiplano suffice to illustrate: whether the extinct and little-documented Puquina is really related to Arawak remains in question; much less meaningful still is the claim that Uru has any connection to Mayan (see Campbell 1997). And with Quechua and Aymara generally agreed *not* to have a common origin, far grander constructs that would relate them to the languages of most of the entire Americas in fact come to nothing, along with their putative implications for first settlement (see Heggarty & Renfrew, forthcoming c; Campbell 1997).

Almost all linguistic "evidence" of transpacific contacts likewise unravels (Adelaar 2004: 41) – save for just one arresting case. The words for the sweet potato (*Ipomoea batatas*) in a number of Oceanic languages are strikingly reminiscent of Quechua and Aymara *k'umar(a)* (Adelaar 1998). This could be a mere fluke: occasional one-off resemblances are statistically inevitable (witness English *much* and Spanish *mucho*, not in fact related). But the plot thickens in that the cultivar itself is of South American origin, and a few radiocarbon dates suggest that it may conceivably have reached eastern Polynesia before European contact (see chapter 41). Not that the linguistics confirms any such chronology. Indeed it is crucial to understand the limits of what the *k'umar(a)* data actually mean: a long-distance movement, perhaps, but of a quintessential *loanword*. The only linguistic intimation there may be, then, would be of some sporadic long-distance contact between the Andes and Polynesia, at a date unknown; not of any migration proper that led to permanent settlement, much less of any shared linguistic ancestry across the Pacific.

SEE ALSO: 11 Human migrations and the histories of major language families; 41 Polynesia, East and South, including transpacific migration; 50 Amazonia: linguistic history; 53 Andes: archaeology

Note

1   We prefer this spelling as closer to the original indigenous pronunciation, restoring the second syllable -ya- suggested both by etymology and by the original Hispanicised version *Tiahuanaco*.

References

Adelaar, W. (1995) Raíces lingüísticas del quechua de Santiago del Estero [Linguistic roots of Santiago del Estero Quechua]. In J. Viegas Barros & A. F. Garay (eds.), *Actas de las Segundas Jornadas de Lingüística Aborigen* (Proceedings of the Second Conference on Aboriginal Language). Buenos Aires: Instituto de Lingüística, Universidad de Buenos Aires, pp. 22–51.

Adelaar, W. (1998) The name of the sweet potato: a case of pre-conquest contact between South America and the Pacific. In M. Janse & A. Verlinden (eds.), *Productivity and Creativity: Studies in General and Descriptive Linguistics in Honor of E. M. Uhlenbeck*. Berlin: De Gruyter, pp. 403–412.

Adelaar, W. with Muysken, P. (2004) *Languages of the Andes*. Cambridge: Cambridge University Press.

Bellwood, P. & Renfrew, C. (eds.) (2002) *Examining the Farming/Language Dispersal Hypothesis*. Cambridge: McDonald Institute for Archaeological Research.

Beresford-Jones, D. & Heggarty, P. (2012) Archaeology, linguistics, and the Andean past: a much-needed conversation. In Heggarty & Beresford-Jones (2012b), pp. 1–40.

Browman, D. (1994) Titicaca Basin archaeolinguistics: Uru, Pukina and Aymara AD 750–1450. *World Archaeology* 26(2), 235–251.

Campbell, L. (1997) *American Indian Languages: The Historical Linguistics of Native America*. New York: Oxford University Press.

Cerrón-Palomino, R. (2000) El origen centroandino del aimara [The Central Andean origins of Aymara]. In P. Kaulicke & W. Isbell (eds.), *Huari y Tiwanaku: Modelos vs. Evidencias (primera parte)* [Wari and Tiwanaku: models and evidence (part one)]. *Boletín de Arqueología PUCP* 4. Lima: Fondo Editorial de la PUCP, 131–142.

Cerrón-Palomino, R. (2003) *Lingüística Quechua* [Quechua linguistics]. Cuzco: Centro Bartolomé de las Casas. (Originally pub. 1987.)

Cerrón-Palomino, R. (2012) Unravelling the enigma of the "particular language" of the Incas. In Heggarty & Beresford-Jones (2012b), pp. 265–294.

Constenla Umaña, A. (1990) Una hipótesis sobre la localización del protochibcha y la dispersión de sus descendientes [A hypothesis on the homeland of Proto-Chibcha and the dispersal of its daughter languages]. *Filología y Lingüística* 16(2), 111–123.

DeMarrais, E. (2012) Quechua's southern boundary: the case of Santiago del Estero, Argentina. In Heggarty & Beresford-Jones (2012b), pp. 375–408.

Heggarty, P. (2007) Linguistics for archaeologists: principles, methods and the case of the Incas. *Cambridge Archaeological Journal* 17(03), 311–340.

Heggarty, P. & Beresford-Jones, D. (2010) Agriculture and language dispersals: limitations, refinements, and an Andean exception? *Current Anthropology* 51(2), 163–191.

Heggarty, P. & Beresford-Jones, D. (2012a) A cross-disciplinary prehistory for the Andes? Surveying the state of the art. In Heggarty & Beresford-Jones (2012b), pp. 409–434.

Heggarty, P. & Beresford-Jones, D. (eds.) (2012b) *Archaeology and Language in the Andes*. Proceedings of the British Academy 173. Oxford: Oxford University Press.

Heggarty, P. & Renfrew, C. (forthcoming a) South and South-East Asia: languages. In Renfrew & Bahn (forthcoming).

Heggarty, P. and Renfrew, C. (forthcoming b) Introduction: languages. In Renfrew & Bahn (forthcoming).

Heggarty, P. and Renfrew, C. (forthcoming c) The Americas: languages. In Renfrew & Bahn (forthcoming).

Hocquenghem, A.-M. (2012) How did Quechua reach Ecuador? In Heggarty & Beresford-Jones (2012b), pp. 345–373.

Lane, K. (2011) ¿Hacia dónde se dirigen los pastores? [Where were the herders heading?]. In P. Kaulicke, R. Cerrón-Palomino, P. Heggarty, & D. Beresford-Jones (eds.), Lenguas y sociedades en el antiguo Perú [Languages and societies in ancient Peru]. Boletín de Arqueología PUCP 14, 181–198.

Renfrew, C. & Bahn, P. (eds.) (forthcoming) The Cambridge World Prehistory. Cambridge: Cambridge University Press.

Torero, A. (1984) El Comercio lejano y la difusión del quechua [Long-distance trade and the dispersal of Quechua]. Revista Andina 4, 367–389.

Torero, A. (2002) Idiomas de los Andes: Lingüística e Historia [Languages of the Andes: linguistics and history]. Lima: Editorial Horizonte/Institut Français des Études Andines.

53

Andes: archaeology

David Beresford-Jones and Paul Heggarty

The archaeology of the past five thousand years in the Central Andes bears witness to great mobility – driven, rather than hindered, by extraordinary topography.

The Andean region is one of humanity's rare independent hearths of agriculture and cradles of "pristine" civilization. It also offers a vignette of the tension long at the heart of archaeological thinking, between explanations of change in the past based upon either migrations of human populations, or autochthonous development. For while the Andean archaeological record attests to a great deal of change, precisely how far this was accompanied by permanent, large-scale movements of people remains a moot point.

Recent years have seen a revival of interest in migration in the ancient Andes. Aside from the archaeological record, linguistics and ethnohistory offer powerful evidence for a significant role for migration in the Andean past, and fresh attempts are being made to synthesize data from these different disciplines (as surveyed in Heggarty & Beresford-Jones 2012). New bioarchaeological analyses of human skeletal and dental traits, and stable isotopes, open up further prospects of testing hypotheses about population dynamics by measuring biological relatedness (see reviews by Tung 2008; Sutter 2009). Moreover, many ancient societies in the Andes practiced deliberate skull modification during infancy, an immutable marker of group identity. Studies of modern population genetic variation, too, may eventually offer insights into prehistoric population dynamics, although in the Andean region such studies may be compromised by precisely the sorts of mass migrations that we review here. Nonetheless, by carefully combining these new bioarchaeological data with findings from other disciplines we may now hope to come to a more balanced view: one that neither invokes migration to explain all change in the past, nor abandons it altogether.

Our review here travels backwards in time through the five millennia or so of Andean civilization. At the most recent stages of Andean prehistory, "migration" may

The Global Prehistory of Human Migration: The Encyclopedia of Global Human Migration Volume 1,
First Edition. Edited by Peter Bellwood.
© 2013 John Wiley & Sons, Ltd. Published 2015 by John Wiley & Sons, Ltd.

mean the actual movement of a population, but at remoter periods where evidence is scanty, population dynamics may well be better described as "demic expansion" – the more gradual process whereby one population mixes with or even "drowns out" another.

At first sight, the Andean context may not seem very conducive to any form of major population movement. Topographically, this is one of the most extreme regions on Earth. Several cordilleras run north–south down the spine of South America, rising abruptly from an arid Pacific coast up to altitudes second only to the Himalayas, before descending just as precipitously to the vast, flat basin of the humid Amazon to the east. Uniquely among alpine regions, the Andes also span the tropics. Together, these circumstances entail extreme ecological diversity. The development of civilization was thus played out here through some 6000 m of altitude, with extraordinary tropical environmental diversity across "horizontally condensed" space (Shimada 1985: xi). Far from impeding population mobility, however, the Andean landscape only made it all the more necessary and attractive.

Andean institutions of mobility

Early Spanish colonial texts relate the mytho-histories of the Incas, and of their contemporaries and predecessors, greatly enriching our understanding and stretching it back some way before European impact. These accounts are sometimes contradictory, but despite differing in many details, they nonetheless hold a few core strands in common.

One such strand is that of a complementary relationship between a local, indigenous group and outsiders who arrived in the distant past as conquering invaders. The Incas' own origin myths cast them in precisely this latter role when arriving in the Cuzco region, ultimately from distant Lake Titicaca. The subsequent relationship between locals and outsiders was invariably asymmetric (Urton 1999). Moreover, separate groups were often defined by different subsistence lifestyles, occupying distinct but complementary ecological niches. Historical times attest to invading "llaqwash" camelid pastoralists of the high tundra coexisting in tense yet intimate relationship with autochthonous "wari" agriculturalists in the lower, inter-montane valleys. Indeed many such "institutions of Andean complementarity" (Salomon 1985: 520) unfolded so as to harness the tremendous ecological diversity encountered within relatively short distances across extreme altitude differences.

John Murra, for instance, invoked a "vertical archipelago" concept to explain why, in conspicuous contrast to Mesoamerica, markets seem absent from the ethnohistorical and archaeological records for much of the Andes. Instead, ethnic groups established colonies to control several geographically dispersed ecological tiers, thereby gaining access to a broader range of agricultural products (Murra 1985: 3). The result was that distinct ethnic groups occupied mosaics of territory encompassing diverse, ecologically complementary regions ("discontinuous territoriality" is the term used by Shimada 1985: xix). Rather than hindering migration, then, the fractured topography of the Andean landscape actually drove it, a dynamism writ large into the very institutions and fabric of the Inca empire.

The Inca empire

In 1438 CE the Incas were just one among a mosaic of fractious petty chiefdoms that characterized the southern Andean highlands during the Late Intermediate Period (c.1100–1438). That year, however, marked their final victory over their bitter local rivals, the Chancas, and by the time the Spaniards arrived, less than one hundred years later, the Incas controlled a realm stretching over 4,000 km from Ecuador to Argentina and Chile, comprising over eighty distinct ethnic groups.

The Incas' meteoric first expansion out of their Cuzco homeland was achieved through military force, after which the empire turned to consolidation. A road system covering some 23,000 km was renovated and expanded from a previous age of expansion (see the section on Wari, below), facilitating the movement of both goods and people on a grand scale. Yet of these, by far the more important was the latter, reflecting the apparent Andean ideal of integrating distinct economic zones within a single community, thus circumventing the need for market exchange. Indeed, archaeological evidence suggests that within the Inca empire, interregional exchange of staple products was limited (D'Altroy & Earle 1985).

Rather than as goods, then, taxation was extracted in the form of labor – what Godelier (1977: 188) calls the "Inca mode of production" – whereby ancient traditions of reciprocal labor exchange were elaborated into a system of rotating corvée service (*mit'a*), in exchange for food and drink provided at state-sponsored feasts. Through the *mit'a*, "taxpayers" rendered some forty different kinds of state duties, including farming, herding, major public works, military service, mining, and portage (D'Altroy & Schreiber 2004: 267). Soon this evolved into the permanent relocation of entire communities from their place of ethnic origin (*mitmaqkuna*), either to carry out particular productive activities (*kamayuq*) according to the empire's changing economic needs, or to head off potential revolt by relocating loyal populations amidst recalcitrant ones, and vice versa. It is very difficult to assess from archaeological data the precise numbers of people moved in this way, although clearly they were significant – perhaps as much as a quarter to a third of the empire's entire populace (D'Altroy & Schreiber 2004: 266). Migration was thus a vital instrument of Inca imperial policy.

Nonetheless, there are also indications that scholars may have been misled by the wealth of (semi)historical evidence into overstating some of the Inca empire's impact in this respect. It is all too commonly assumed that the expansion of Quechua, for instance, one of the greatest language families of the New World, can be attributed entirely to its use by the Incas as a lingua franca. But historical linguists have long appreciated that most of Quechua's expansion over the so-called "Continuous Zone" across the Central Andes in fact long predated the Inca "Late Horizon" (see Figure 52.1). Indeed, language dispersals and population resettlements are not the only "Inca" traits whose roots in the Andes go back far earlier.

The Middle Horizon

Max Uhle (1903) was the first to recognize that the Incas had long been preceded by an earlier, underlying "horizon" – a period for which the archaeological record shows some degree of unity or interaction across great expanses of the Central Andes. Between the successive horizons of Andean prehistory were the "intermediate periods" during which that apparent unity broke down into regional fragmentation, especially in the highlands. In principle, then, we should look to the horizons (and perhaps also their immediate aftermaths) for the clearest evidence of migrations and population movement.

The "Middle Horizon" (c.550–1000 CE) was bipolar: a Wari empire with its heartland in Ayacucho, south-central Peru; and a more vaguely perceived sphere of influence of Tiyawanaku, by the shores of Lake Titicaca on the Bolivian Altiplano (Figure 52.1). So similar was their iconography that both were initially conflated, but the two are now recognized as holding mutually exclusive territories and following distinct trajectories in economy and society. Indeed, evidence from their borderlands in the Moquegua Valley suggests that their relationship was often one of military conflict. The precise nature of the influences that Tiyawanaku and Wari exerted, far beyond their respective homelands, has long been a matter of debate, but is now being enriched by new bioarchaeological evidence. Both, it seems, were agents of population movement on significant scales; but whereas Wari's influence was largely expansive, Tiyawanaku's was largely inwards, towards its monumental ceremonial core.

At 3,850 m above sea level on the Altiplano, Tiyawanaku was the highest urban center of the ancient world. The idea that it served as focus for pilgrimage is an old one, and the latest archaeological (Janusek 2004) and osteological (Blom 2005) evidence reaffirms that it was a magnet even for permanent immigration from across the southern Andes, by communities who continued to maintain "ties to their homeland for many generations" (Tung 2008: 675).

The vertical archipelago model, meanwhile, has long been invoked to explain why, far afield on the Tiyawanaku periphery, its material culture is likewise found, but in ecological niches very different to its Altiplano core. Recent bioarchaeological studies (Blom et al. 1998; Knudson 2009) seem to confirm that Tiyawanaku established colonies in Moquegua (Goldstein 2005). Elsewhere however, in the Azapa Valley on the Chilean coast, the eastern valleys of Bolivia, and the San Pedro de Atacama oasis, individuals buried with Tiyawanaku artifacts show none of the cranial-modification (Torres-Rouff 2002), dental (Sutter 2009) or isotope (Knudson 2009) signatures that might suggest migration from the Altiplano. Ultimately, around 1000 CE, the Altiplano core of Tiyawanaku collapsed, which set in train further mass movements as its colonies too dispersed to new locations along the coast and further inland (Owen 2005, Sutter 2009).

Wari, meanwhile, was quite different: an "empire" that expanded from its eponymous urban center to control directly the central and southern coast of Peru between Chancay and Acarí, and the highlands over an even greater extent, from Ancash to Sicuani (Menzel 1967: 147). At its apogee around 800 CE, the city of Wari itself was vast, covering some 15 sq km; today the largest archaeological site in South America. Speculative estimates for its population range between 50,000 and 100,000: by any measure a vast ancient city. Survey data reveal how surrounding populations were gradually drawn into the site (Schreiber 1992: 88), and the Wari archaeological record indicates movements of people across the Andes on a far larger scale than in the intermediate periods before or after.

Material culture suggestive of Wari influence is distributed throughout the high-lands and along the south-central coast of Peru. Sites in the Cuzco region, and Wari itself, have yielded significant quantities of ceramics from Cajamarca, almost 1,000 km to the north. As Menzel (1967: 152) observes, "their abundance [at Wari itself] is such as to suggest that there were colonies of northerners established at the imperial capital." Barracks-like residential facilities are a dominant feature of Wari architecture, commonly interpreted as housing for mobile labor or military personnel (McEwan 1991: 117). The major Wari sites were, it seems, "occupied by large numbers of people, both foreigners from Wari and local peoples" (D'Altroy & Schreiber 2004: 274). And some of these sites were enormous. Pikillaqta, for instance, was but part of the intense Wari occupation of the Cuzco region. Yet this single component site of the Wari periphery covers an area greater than the later Inca imperial capital of Cuzco.

The Wari Middle Horizon was, in large part, based upon the intensification of food production to supply distant urban populations, and undertook great state-sponsored public works to achieve this (Schreiber 1992). Indeed, Isbell (1988: 182) credits Wari with the development of that uniquely Andean form of "state finance": the "Inca mode of production." So fundamental and enduring were the innovations wrought by Wari that they defined the subsequent course of Andean civilization, and certain settlement patterns even to this day (Isbell 1988, Schreiber 1992). The roots of much Inca state-craft turn out to lie in the Middle Horizon: including the road network and the khipu record-keeping device of knotted cords. Moreover, the Wari empire doubtless also drove at least one of the major language expansions in the Andes – again with powerful connotations of population movements. In our view, that language was Quechua, though alternative hypotheses also exist (see chapter 52).

Further back in time

As we move back into remoter periods, our evidence for distinguishing between migration and demic expansion becomes obscured by the passage of time. The nature and extent of the Early Horizon (c.900–100 BCE), for instance, are far less clearly defined. Most would see it as the expression of a proselytizing cult, radiating out from (or in towards) the monumental site of Chavín de Huántar in Ancash, north-central Peru (Burger 1992; see Figure 52.1 for location).

Language, though, again offers a further line of evidence: the earliest plausible time depths for the great language family expansions detectable in the Andes broadly correspond to the Early Horizon, suggesting that considerable population movements may also have been underway (Heggarty & Beresford-Jones 2010: 179–180). Our own view is that it was only at this point that a number of gradual developments finally came together to tip agriculture in the Andes across a crucial threshold of intensification, above all by fully incorporating an ecologically flexible, true cereal – maize. This coalescence of a "mobile food chain" (Jones 2007: 144), that is, a geographically expansive agricultural package, is what we hypothesize may have driven a first major language family expansion in this period – though whether of Aymara or Quechua remains debated (see chapter 52).

At greater time depths, Sutter's (2009) analysis of dental traits in prehistoric Andean mortuary contexts suggests that there were at least two migrations into the Andean region, the first of which presumably occurred following the Palaeolithic settlement of the Americas (see chapter 8). The second, much later wave of demic expansion, perhaps driven by food production, "followed a north-to south route along the Andean highlands and later proceeded from the highlands to the coastal valleys" (Sutter 2009: 21). The timing, driving process, and direction of this second proposed expansion show some correlations with our own proposal. It is of course true that the earliest evidence of Andean complex society is to be found on the Pacific coast (Shady Solís 2008). Nonetheless, just as Julio C. Tello (1923) long since observed, the major *expansions* clearly visible in the archaeological record – Chavín, Wari, Tiyawanaku, and the Incas themselves – all spread out of the Andean highlands, rather than the other way around.

SEE ALSO: 8 The human colonization of the Americas: archaeology; 52 Andes: linguistic history

References

Blom, D. (2005) Embodying borders: human body modification and diversity in Tiwanaku society. *Journal of Anthropological Archaeology* 24, 1–24.

Blom, D., Hallgrímsson, B., Keng, L., & Buikstra, J. (1998) Tiwanaku "colonization": bioarchaeological implications for migration in the Moquegua Valley, Peru. *World Archaeology* 30(2), 238–261.

Burger, R. (1992) *Chavin and the Origins of Andean Civilizations*. London: Thames & Hudson.

D'Altroy, T. & Earle, T. (1985) Staple finance, wealth finance, and storage in the Inka political economy. *Current Anthropology* 26(2), 187–206.

D'Altroy, T. & Schreiber, K. (2004) Andean empires. In H. Silverman (ed.), *Andean Archaeology*. Oxford: Blackwell, pp. 255–279.

Godelier, M. (1977) The concept of "social and economic formation": the Inca example. In M. Godelier, *Perspectives in Marxist Anthropology*. Cambridge: Cambridge University Press.

Goldstein, P. (2005) *Andean Diaspora: The Tiwanaku Colonies and the Origins of South American Empire*. Gainsville: University Press of Florida.

Heggarty, P. & Beresford-Jones, D. (2010) Agriculture and language dispersals: limitations, refinements, and an Andean exception? *Current Anthropology* 51(2), 163–191.

Heggarty, P. & Beresford-Jones, D. (eds.) (2012) *Archaeology and Language in the Andes*. London: British Academy/Oxford University Press.

Isbell, W. (1988) City and state in Middle Horizon Huari. In R. W. Keatinge (ed.), *Peruvian Prehistory: An Overview of Pre-Inca and Inca Society*. Cambridge: Cambridge University Press, pp. 164–189.

Janusek, J. (2004) *Identity and Power in the Ancient Andes: Tiwanaku Cities Through Time*. New York: Routledge.

Jones, M. (2007) *Feast: Why Humans Share Food*. Oxford: Oxford University Press.

Knudson, K. (2009) Tiwanaku influence in the south central Andes: strontium isotope analysis and Middle Horizon migration. *Latin American Antiquity* 19(1), 3–23.

McEwan, G. (1991) Investigations at the Pikillacta site: a provincial Huari center in the Valley of Cuzco. In W. Isbell & G. McEwan (eds.), *Huari Administrative Structure: Prehistoric*

Monumental Architecture and State Government. Washington DC: Dumbarton Oaks, pp. 93–120.

Menzel, D. (1967) Style and time in the Middle Horizon. In J. H. Rowe & D. Menzel (eds.), *Peruvian Archaeology: Selected Readings*. Palo Alto, CA: Peek, pp. 146–164.

Murra, J. (1985) The limits and limitations of the "vertical archipelago" in the Andes. In S. Masuda, I. Shimada, & C. Morris (eds.), *Andean Ecology and Civilization: An Interdisciplinary Perspective on Andean Ecological Complementarity*. Tokyo: University of Tokyo Press, pp. 15–20.

Owen, B. (2005) Distant colonies and explosive collapse: the two stages of the Tiwanaku diaspora in the Osmore Drainage. *Latin American Antiquity* 16(1), 45–80.

Salomon, F. (1985) The dynamic potential of the complementarity concept. In S. Masuda, I. Shimada, & C. Morris (eds.), *Andean Ecology and Civilization: An Interdisciplinary Perspective on Andean Ecological Complementarity*. Tokyo: University of Tokyo Press, pp. 511–531.

Schreiber, K. (1992) *Wari Imperialism in Middle Horizon Peru*. Ann Arbor: Museum of Anthropology, University of Michigan.

Shady Solís, R. (2008) America's first city? The case of Late Archaic Caral. In H. Silverman & W. Isbell (eds.), *Andean Archaeology III: North and South*. New York: Springer, pp. 28–66.

Shimada, I. (1985) Introduction. In S. Masuda, I. Shimada, & C. Morris (eds.), *Andean Ecology and Civilization: An Interdisciplinary Perspective on Andean Ecological Complementarity*. Tokyo: University of Tokyo Press, pp. xi–xxxii.

Sutter, R. (2009) Prehistoric population dynamics in the Andes. In J. Marcus, C. Stanish, & R. Williams (eds.), *The Foundations of South Highland Andean Civilization: Papers in honor of Michael Moseley*. Los Angeles, California: Cotsen Institute of Archaeology, UCLA, pp. 9–38.

Tello, J. C. (1923) Wira-Kocha. *Inca* 1(1), 93–320.

Torres-Rouff, C. (2002) Cranial vault modification and ethnicity in Middle Horizon San Pedro de Atacama, Chile. *Current Anthropology* 43, 163–171.

Tung, T. (2008) Life on the move: bioarchaeological contributions to the study of migration and diaspora communities in the Andes. In H. Silverman & W. Isbell (eds.), *Handbook of South American Archaeology*. New York: Springer, pp. 671–680.

Uhle, M. (1903) *Pachacamac*. Philadelphia: Department of Archaeology, University of Pennsylvania.

Urton, G. (1999) *Inca Myths*. London: British Museum Press.

Index

Compiled by Janey Fisher.

Figures are indicated by *italic* page references.

The Global Prehistory of Human Migration: The Encyclopedia of Global Human Migration Volume 1,
First Edition. Edited by Peter Bellwood.
© 2013 John Wiley & Sons, Ltd. Published 2015 by John Wiley & Sons, Ltd.